Arthur, this one's for you.

— Katherine Cennamo

With thanks to the many teachers I have worked and taught with.

— John Ross

In gratitude to all of the inspirational teachers who have shared their technology integration journeys with me, and to the students who never fail to encourage me to learn more.

— Peggy Ertmer

Technology Integration for Meaningful Classroom Use

A Standards-Based Approach

2ND EDITION

Katherine S. Cennamo
Virginia Polytechnic Institute and State University

John D. Ross
Bethel University

Peggy A. Ertmer
Purdue University

WADSWORTH
CENGAGE Learning

Australia • Brazil • Japan • Korea • Mexico • Singapore • Spain • United Kingdom • United States

WADSWORTH
CENGAGE Learning

Technology Integration for Meaningful Classroom Use: A Standards-Based Approach, Second Edition

Katherine S. Cennamo, John D. Ross, Peggy A. Ertmer

Editor in Chief: Linda Ganster

Executive Editor: Mark Kerr

Managing Developmental Editor: Lisa Mafrici

Developmental Editor: Kassi Radomski

Assistant Editor: Joshua Taylor

Editorial Assistant: Greta Lindquist

Associate Media Editor: Elizabeth Momb

Senior Market Development Manager: Kara Kindstrom

Executive Brand Manager: Melissa Larmon

Art and Cover Direction, Design, Production Management, and Composition: PreMediaGlobal

Manufacturing Planner: Doug Bertke

Rights Acquisitions Specialist: Tom McDonough

Photo Researcher: Jeremy Glover, BSG

Text Researcher: Pablo D'Stair

Cover Image:
  Background: © ziggymaj, Shutterstock
  Students at computers: © Intl St. Clair, Getty Images
  Girl using laptop: © Katrina Wittkamp, Getty Images
  Boys using tablet PC: © kali9, iStock
  Students at laptop, girl with glasses: © Daniel Hurst, photos.com

© 2014, 2010 Wadsworth, Cengage Learning

ALL RIGHTS RESERVED. No part of this work covered by the copyright herein may be reproduced, transmitted, stored, or used in any form or by any means graphic, electronic, or mechanical, including but not limited to photocopying, recording, scanning, digitizing, taping, Web distribution, information networks, or information storage and retrieval systems, except as permitted under Section 107 or 108 of the 1976 United States Copyright Act, without the prior written permission of the publisher.

For product information and technology assistance, contact us at **Cengage Learning Customer & Sales Support, 1-800-354-9706.**

For permission to use material from this text or product, submit all requests online at **www.cengage.com/permissions.**
Further permissions questions can be e-mailed to **permissionrequest@cengage.com.**

Library of Congress Control Number: 2012940277

Student Edition:

ISBN-13: 978-1-133-59420-8

ISBN-10: 1-133-59420-4

Loose-leaf Edition:

ISBN-13: 978-1-285-05565-7

ISBN-10: 1-285-05565-9

Wadsworth
20 Davis Drive
Belmont, CA 94002-3098
USA

Cengage Learning is a leading provider of customized learning solutions with office locations around the globe, including Singapore, the United Kingdom, Australia, Mexico, Brazil, and Japan. Locate your local office at **www.cengage.com/global.**

Cengage Learning products are represented in Canada by Nelson Education, Ltd.

To learn more about Wadsworth, visit **www.cengage.com/wadsworth**

Purchase any of our products at your local college store or at our preferred online store **www.cengagebrain.com.**

Printed in the United States of America
1 2 3 4 5 6 7 16 15 14 13 12

Technology Integration for Meaningful Classroom Use

Brief Contents

CHAPTER 1 Technology Integration: A Standards-Based Approach   1
CHAPTER 2 Self-Directed Lifelong Learning   27
CHAPTER 3 Supporting Student Creativity with Technology   53
CHAPTER 4 Digital Tools That Support Learning   83
CHAPTER 5 Developing Technology-Enriched Learning Environments and Experiences   109
CHAPTER 6 Customizing Student Learning Activities   137
CHAPTER 7 Assessment and Evaluation   163
CHAPTER 8 Demonstrating Fluent Use of Technology   191
CHAPTER 9 Modeling and Facilitating Use of Digital Tools   217
CHAPTER 10 Legal and Ethical Use   243
CHAPTER 11 Diversity and Cultural Understanding   269
CHAPTER 12 Professional Growth and Leadership   293
Supplement Technology Integration and Lesson Planning in the Content Areas   317

Glossary   373
Index   377

Contents

Preface xvii

About the Authors xxi

CHAPTER 1

Technology Integration: A Standards-Based Approach 1

Technologies in Teaching and Learning: An Historical Perspective 2
    Computer Technology in Education 4
    Summary of Technology Integration in Teaching and Learning 10
Defining Technology Proficiency through Standards 10
    The Standards Movement 12
    Technology Standards 14
    The Value of Standards 17
The Technology Integration Continuum 18
    Stages in Technology Integration 19
Chapter Summary 24
Your Portfolio 25
References 25

CHAPTER 2

Self-Directed Lifelong Learning 27

Self-Directed Learning: Definition and Components 28
    The GAME Plan for Self-Directed Learning about Technology: An Example 30
    Summary of GAME Plan 31
The GAME Plan for Learning to Integrate Technology 32
    Set Goals and Take Action 32
Documenting Growth and Competency through Portfolios 39
    Portfolio Development Tools 40
    Steps in Portfolio Development 41
    Summary of Portfolio Development 46
The GAME Plan for Supporting Student Learning 47
    Setting Goals for Student Learning 47
    Taking Action by Providing Learning Experiences 48
    Monitoring Student Progress 49
    Evaluating Instructional Effectiveness 50
Chapter Summary 50
Your Portfolio 51
References 52

CHAPTER 3

Supporting Student Creativity with Technology   53

Developing Creative Thinking through Authentic Instruction   55
    Types of Creative Thinking   55
    Characteristics of Authentic Instruction   57
    Addressing the Challenges of Authentic Instruction   66
    Technology Support for Authentic Instruction   68
    Teacher-Directed Instruction in Support of Authentic Learning   71

Facilitating Creative Thinking While Meeting Content Standards   73
    A Taxonomy for Determining Cognitive Demand   74
    Using Technology to Support Authentic Instruction—An Example   77

Chapter Summary   80
Your Portfolio   80
References   81

CHAPTER 4

Digital Tools That Support Learning   83

Technology as Tutor: Promoting Student Learning Using Technology-Based Tutorials   85

Technology as Mindtool: Promoting Student Learning Using Technology Applications   89
    Databases and Concept-Mapping Tools   89
    Simulations and Animations   93
    Hypertext and Hypermedia   94
    Digital Storytelling   96

Technology as a Conversation Support   98
    Technology as a Collaborative Learning Tool   99
    Technology as a Conferencing Tool   102

Online Resources   105
    Evaluating Information from Online Resources   105

Chapter Summary   107
Your Portfolio   108
References   108

CHAPTER 5

Developing Technology-Enriched Learning Environments and Experiences   109

Technology-Enriched Learning Environments   111
    Technology Support for Whole Group Learning   111
    Technology Support for Small Group Learning   112
    Independent Use of Technology   116
    Summary of Technology-Enriched Learning Environments   118

Supporting Students' Use of Technology Tools and Resources   120
    Before Instruction   121
    During Instruction   128
    After Instruction   129

Planning Learning Experiences and Lessons   131
    Lesson Planning   131
    Technology Support for Lesson Planning   132
Chapter Summary   133
Your Portfolio   133
References   134

CHAPTER 6

Customizing Student Learning Activities   137

with Glenna Gustafson

Using Technology to Differentiate Instructional Content, Processes, and Products   139
Universal Design for Learning   142
    Neural Networks Foundational to UDL   145
    Universal Design in the Classroom   147
Assistive Technologies   151
    Legal Precedents for Assistive Technology   151
    Assistive Technology Continuum   153
    Adapting Hardware and Software   153
    Summary of Assistive Technologies   159
Chapter Summary   160
Your Portfolio   161
References   162

CHAPTER 7

Assessment and Evaluation   163

Assessing Student Learning   164
    Learning Goals Help Determine Assessments   164
    Monitor Learning with Formative Assessments   165
    Summative Assessments Evaluate Learning   167
Assessment Formats and Technologies That Support Them   168
    Forced-Choice Assessment Formats   168
    Open-Ended Response Formats   170
    Authentic Assessments   **170**
    Technologies to Support Authentic Assessment   174
    Summary of Assessment Formats   178
Scoring Expectations and Practices   178
    Scoring Keys   178
    Checklists   179
    Rubrics   180
    Recording and Reporting Student Outcomes   183
Data-Based Decision-Making   186
    Review Performance Data   186
    Use Data to Improve Instruction   188
Chapter Summary   189
Your Portfolio   189
References   190

CHAPTER 8

Demonstrating Fluent Use of Technology 191

Safe and Healthy Use of Technology Systems in Your Classroom 192
- Managing Use of Technology in Your Classroom 194
- Technology-Related Health Practices 196

Maintaining Technology Resources 202
- Solving Routine Problems 202
- Hardware Maintenance 204
- Software Maintenance 207
- Technical Assistance 211

Chapter Summary 215
Your Portfolio 216
References 216

CHAPTER 9

Modeling and Facilitating Use of Digital Tools 217

Professional Communication and Collaboration 218
- Communicating 218
- Volunteering 225
- Extended Learning 227
- Benefits of Enhanced Collaboration 229

Locating and Evaluating Digital Resources 230
- Locating Digital Resources 230
- Evaluating Resources 235
- Read Reviews 236
- Try It Out 238

Chapter Summary 240
Your Portfolio 241
References 242

CHAPTER 10

Legal and Ethical Use 243

Acceptable Use of Digital Resources 244
Copyright and Intellectual Property 246
- Fair Use 248
- Public Domain 249
- Creative Commons Licensing 250

Academic Integrity 251
- Plagiarism 251
- Cheating 253
- Protecting Confidential Data 254
- Password Security 256

Promoting Responsible Use of Technology Resources 257
- Internet Safety 257
- Malicious Software 258

Threatening or Unlawful Online Interactions 261
Using Technology to Support Responsible Internet Use 262
Chapter Summary 267
Your Portfolio 268
References 268

CHAPTER 11

Diversity and Cultural Understanding 269

Learner-Centered Strategies 270
Supporting the Social Needs of Students: Creating a Collaborative Environment 271
Supporting the Cognitive Needs of Students: Promoting Content Learning 272
Supporting the Metacognitive Needs of Students: Promoting Reflection 274

Equitable Access 276
Access to Up-to-Date Hardware, Software, and Connectivity 276
Access to Meaningful, High-Quality, and Culturally Responsive Content 278
Access to Tech-Knowledgeable Teachers 281

Promoting Cultural Understanding and Global Awareness 283
Understanding Your Culture and the Culture of Others 283
Working with Students to Develop Cultural Understanding 286
Respecting Cultural Diversity in the Classroom 288

Chapter Summary 289
Your Portfolio 290
References 291

CHAPTER 12

Professional Growth and Leadership 293

Participating in Local and Global Learning Communities 294
Local Support for Technology Integration 295
Virtual Learning Communities 296
Conferences and Other Formal Learning Opportunities 298
Exhibit Leadership 299

Reflecting on Published Research and Your Own Practice 302
Reflecting on Practice 302
Reflecting on Current Research 304
Teacher as Researcher 308

Chapter Summary 315
Your Portfolio 316
References 316

Supplement Technology Integration and Lesson Planning in the Content Areas 317

Glossary 373

Index 377

List of Tech Tools and Tips

TECH TOOLS & TIPS	Teaching Online 9
TECH TOOLS & TIPS	Video Recording Lessons for Reflection 38
TECH TOOLS & TIPS	Supporting Students' Efforts to Be Self-Directed 48
TECH TOOLS & TIPS	Virtual Field Trips 62
TECH TOOLS & TIPS	Using Educational Games to Support Learning 86
TECH TOOLS & TIPS	Developing a WebQuest 87
TECH TOOLS & TIPS	Creating Multimedia Websites 95
TECH TOOLS & TIPS	Digital Storytelling 96
TECH TOOLS & TIPS	Webconferencing 99
TECH TOOLS & TIPS	Wikis 101
TECH TOOLS & TIPS	Blogs 104
TECH TOOLS & TIPS	Evaluating Web Resources 106
TECH TOOLS & TIPS	Using Interactive Whiteboards 114
TECH TOOLS & TIPS	Facilitating Online Discussions 117
TECH TOOLS & TIPS	Ten Ideas for Using a Teacher Workstation 118
TECH TOOLS & TIPS	Blended Learning 120
TECH TOOLS & TIPS	Built-in Computer Accessibility Features 156
TECH TOOLS & TIPS	Mobile Devices: Support for Students with Special Needs 159
TECH TOOLS & TIPS	Monitoring Student Devices 196
TECH TOOLS & TIPS	Ergonomic Checklist 197
TECH TOOLS & TIPS	Ten Tips for Safe and Healthy Use of Technology in Your Classroom 201
TECH TOOLS & TIPS	Four-Step Troubleshooting Process 205
TECH TOOLS & TIPS	When Storage Isn't There 210
TECH TOOLS & TIPS	Maintenance Schedule 212
TECH TOOLS & TIPS	Learning from BYOD Initiatives 213

TECH TOOLS & TIPS	Top Ten Things to Consider When Creating Websites 223
TECH TOOLS & TIPS	Creating Virtual Field Trips 226
TECH TOOLS & TIPS	Creating Online Presentations 228
TECH TOOLS & TIPS	Using Streaming Media Sites 232
TECH TOOLS & TIPS	Using Podcasts in Your Classroom 233
TECH TOOLS & TIPS	Open-Source Software 234
TECH TOOLS & TIPS	Selecting Apps for Mobile Devices 238
TECH TOOLS & TIPS	Legal Issues Surrounding the Use of Images of Students and Student Work 255
TECH TOOLS & TIPS	Ten Tips for E-mail Use 263
TECH TOOLS & TIPS	Appropriate Use of Technology in Early Childhood Education 282
TECH TOOLS & TIPS	How to Look Your Best on a Webcam 297

Preface

This book is designed to help *all* our future teachers become leaders in teaching and technology integration! That might sound a bit ambitious, but if you think about it, it's a goal that is really not so far out of reach. After interacting with so many exemplary technology-using teachers in our classes and theirs, at workshops and conferences, and through face-to-face and online interactions, we know this much to be true—anyone with a passion for helping students learn *with* technology can succeed. Whether you are old or young, teach first grade or high school, have specialized in art or science, have a variety of previous teaching experiences or are just starting out, or whether you have access to many or just a few technology resources—none of these conditions guarantees or precludes you from joining this special group of master teachers. Rather, what it takes is a keen understanding of how to use technology to support student learning in authentic contexts—which is what this book is about. Believing in the value of technology is a good place to start, but the more critical piece is what you believe about how students learn best. Technology is a tool—a powerful tool—that can connect you and your students to new places and new people, and which allows you to create things you couldn't create otherwise. Technology enables you to transform your student-centered beliefs into meaningful practice.

We know that the majority of you who are using this book are probably very familiar with the many digital technologies that pervade our personal and social lives. You may not even remember a time when you didn't know how to use a computer or cell phone or one of the many other digital devices that we turn to daily. Those of us who did not grow up with these devices have watched in amazement as you and your peers so easily (and constantly) use numerous technology tools simultaneously to communicate with your friends, look up information on the Internet, "like" a new product on Facebook, and follow the latest happenings on Twitter. However, what we have found in our own practice and what has been confirmed by our colleagues in the teacher preparation field, is that although most prospective teachers have these basic, or even advanced, technology skills, they are typically unfamiliar with, or maybe haven't yet considered, how to use these same technologies to support student learning.

Even when students enter our courses with basic computer skills, they face unique challenges to technology integration. Technologies change at lightning speed, making it difficult to keep up to date. In addition, these rapid changes are coupled with evolving teaching and content standards that require you to demonstrate competencies in specific technology skills and to teach in ways that ensure your students master specific learning outcomes. So, we take the stance in this book that it is more important to empower you to be self-directed learners in order to successfully navigate the constantly changing environment of technology integration, than it is to teach a specific body of computer or technology content that will quickly become outdated. For this reason, we have chosen to use a standards-based approach—as opposed to a tool- or content-based approach—as our framework for developing, modeling, and teaching the skills and knowledge necessary for integrating technology in teaching and learning throughout your career. For those of you who may not have grown up surrounded by technology, or who have never had the opportunity to learn the skills your peers have, please note that the textbook's Education CourseMate website provides links to tutorials about common software applications. You will find these tutorials useful whether you are just beginning to learn, or are simply refreshing your technology skills.

Organization

The textbook is divided into twelve chapters, all of which are organized around the 2008 National Educational Technology Standards for Teachers (NETS-T) developed by the International Society for Technology in Education (ISTE). The NETS-T (both the 2000 and 2008 versions) serve as a roadmap for inspired teaching and learning and are credited with creating a target of excellence relating to technology use by teachers. While the earlier set of NETS-T defined what teachers needed to know and be able to do with technology, the 2008 NETS-T are designed to inspire teachers to be creative, innovative digital-age leaders who use technologies to help students learn and thrive in a digital world; as such, this textbook helps you translate those ideals and visions into practical classroom learning experiences and assessments.

Using the principles of self-directed learning as our foundation, the text is designed to help future teachers learn to evaluate and reflect on professional practice to make informed decisions regarding the use of technology in support of student learning. You will learn to self-assess what you currently know about the technology or the learning requirements at hand, determine what you need to know, access resources to help you address specific instructional challenges, evaluate the validity of those resources in terms of what you know and what you need to know, and evaluate the extent to which the resources will meet your learning needs. As you expand your knowledge through the use of additional resources, you will learn to monitor the effectiveness of your learning and problem-solving strategies. In other words, we "teach you how to fish," rather than simply "give you fish."

While one of the main goals of this book is to help you develop content knowledge in the area of technology integration, perhaps more importantly, our goal is to provide you with a number of learning strategies you can use to solve unexpected problems and to build your own understanding of what it means to be an exemplary technology-using teacher. We have included a number of organizational and pedagogical features, some briefly described below, to help you develop these additional forms of knowledge and to build your self-directed learning skills.

New to This Edition

While you'll find this new edition maintains the foundation we established in the first edition, we also recognize that as technology changes, this book must change and improve along with it. As a result, in the second edition you'll find:

- *New* **Tech Tools and Tips** boxes provide brief descriptions or examples of the latest technology tools (e.g., mobile devices), trends (e.g., blended learning), and strategies that are important to consider when planning technology integration. These boxes are listed in a separate Table of Contents making them quick and easy to find.
- *New* **TeachSource Video Cases** boxes direct students to videos on the Education CourseMate website for this book. The videos allow students to see how a certain tool or strategy might be applied in practice. The in-text video introductions also include questions for reflection or in-class discussion.
- *New* **Standards Correlation Chart** on the inside front cover provides an easily accessible listing of the chapters that address specific ISTE Standards.
- *Updated* information throughout with more information about Web 2.0 tools, online and blended learning, gaming, mobile learning, interactive whiteboards, and much more.
- Material previously in Part II of the first edition now appears in a **briefer end-of-book supplement**, which provides current examples of technology integration in practice within specific content areas: English language arts, foreign language, math, science, social studies, health/physical education, visual arts, music, and working with English language learners. For each content area you

will also find two sample lesson plans—for elementary, middle grades, or high school. You can also access these lesson plans on the CourseMate website. This supplement is guided by the national standards that apply to each content domain.
- *New* end-of-chapter **Web Resources**, which can be accessed at the Education CourseMate website for this book.
- *New* **Key Terms** defined in the margins.

Additional Features

In addition to those that are new to this edition, the following organizational and pedagogical features also appear consistently throughout the book:

- *ISTE Standards.* Each chapter begins with a list of the 2008 ISTE NETS-T addressed in that chapter.
- *Outcomes.* Also at the beginning of each chapter is a list of learning outcomes to guide you in your reading.
- *GAME Plan.* Through the use of self-directed learning activities, we model metacognitive strategies that guide the development of your problem-solving skills. This feature incorporates an easy-to-remember acronym called the GAME plan.
- *Stories from Practice.* Case studies, anecdotes, and interviews with practicing teachers are used to place the content within the context of real classrooms. You'll find even more stories in this edition than the last, and you'll also have the opportunity to hear how teachers are using new technologies, especially Web 2.0 tools.
- *Apply to Practice.* Throughout the chapters, activities are embedded that ask you to apply your knowledge to practical problems, investigate the topics in more depth, reflect on your practice, or share your developing knowledge with other members of your learning community.
- *Your Portfolio*: At the end of each chapter, suggestions for portfolio-based artifacts are provided to help you demonstrate and document your progress toward attaining the ISTE standards addressed in the chapter.

In addition to these standard chapter features, several other helpful items are provided to enhance your learning. Each chapter concludes with a summary of the chapter content and a list of references. The back matter includes a glossary of terms and an index.

Online Resources

A variety of online resources provide support materials and references for students and instructors.

- **Education CourseMate**
  For Instructors: Cengage Learning's Education CourseMate brings course concepts to life with interactive learning, study, and exam preparation tools that support the printed textbook. CourseMate includes an integrated eBook, quizzes, flashcards, TeachSource Video Cases, and EngagementTracker, a first-of-its-kind tool that monitors student engagement in the course. The accompanying instructor website offers access to password-protected resources such as an electronic version of the instructor's manual, test bank files, and PowerPoint slides. CourseMate can be bundled with the student text. Contact your Cengage sales representative for information on getting access to CourseMate.

  For Students: Cengage Learning's Education CourseMate brings course concepts to life with interactive learning, study, and exam preparation tools that support the printed textbook. Access an integrated eBook, learning tools

including flashcards, quizzes, TeachSource Video Cases, and more in your Education CourseMate. Go to CengageBrain.com to register or purchase access.
- **WebTutor for Blackboard and Web CT.** Jump-start your course with customizable, rich, text-specific content within your Course Management System. Whether you want to web-enable your class or put an entire course online, WebTutor delivers. WebTutor offers a wide array of resources including access to the eBook, quizzes, videos, web links, exercises, and more.
- **Online Instructor's Manual and Test Bank.** Streamline and maximize the effectiveness of your course preparation. The Instructor's Manual with Test Bank contains a variety of resources for teaching students successful technology integration skills, including information on ISTE standards, chapter outcomes, summaries, portfolio activities, GAME plan activities, application activities, reflection questions, web and video links, and more!
- **Online PowerPoint Slides.** These vibrant Microsoft PowerPoint lecture slides for each chapter assist you with your lectures, covering concepts using images, figures, and tables directly from the textbook.

Acknowledgments

Throughout this journey we have benefited from the support, advice, and encouragement from a number of individuals including Phyllis Newbill and Elza Cruz who provided invaluable assistance in tracking down images, securing permissions, and organizing information; Joni Gardner and Laurene Johnson, who reviewed portions of the manuscript and provided helpful suggestions; Ross Perkins, Jamie Little, and Miriam Larson, who field-tested various versions of the manuscript in their classes; Anita Deck, Desiree Bradley, and Joy Runyan, who helped develop or review lesson plans in some of the content chapters. And for tolerating our absences throughout the many evenings, weekends, and holidays that we spent working on this book, we offer a heartfelt thanks to Arthur, Elliott, and Alice Cennamo; Jeff Mann; and Dave, Mark, Emilie, Laura, and Scott Ertmer.

We would like to thank all the authors who contributed to various portions of this text: John Burton, Sheila Carter-Tod, Gilbert Cuevas, Shelli Fowler, Brian Giza, Glenna Gustafson, David Hicks, Greg Kessler, James Krouscas, Nancy Lampert, Melissa Lisanti, Tammy McGraw, Christine Meloni, Ken Potter, Kerry Redican, Judy Reinhartz, Jill Robbins, and Craig Tacla.

We would also like to gratefully acknowledge our senior editor, Mark Kerr and extend a special thanks to Kassi Radomski, our development editor, who shared our work ethic, responded to many late night emails, and generally supported us throughout this endeavor.

And finally, we would like to express our appreciation to numerous reviewers who provided us with insights and suggestions throughout the development of this edition, including: David Eveland, Johnson Bible College; Amy Williamson, Angelo State University; Susan Gebhard, Salem College; Dawn Moffett, California Lutheran University; Diana Santiago, Central New Mexico Community College; Paulina Kuforiji, Columbus State University; Ruth Ban, Barry University; Sue Anderson, Texas Christian University; Judith Battraw, Indiana University East; Sha Li, Alabama A&M University; John Bouchard, Florida State College at Jacksonville; Margaret Annunziata, Davidson County Community College; Whitney Kilgore, College of South Nevada; Rebekah Nix, The University of Texas at Dallas; and Judith Castleberry, Austin Peay State University.

About the Authors

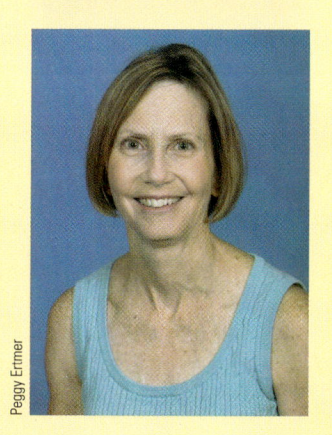

Katherine S. Cennamo is a former elementary school teacher and current Professor of Instructional Design and Technology at Virginia Tech. She has a bachelor's degree in elementary education from Virginia Tech, a master's degree in educational media from the University of Arizona, and a Ph.D. in instructional technology from the University of Texas at Austin. Throughout her career, Dr. Cennamo has focused her work on the application of learning theories to the design of technology-based instructional materials. Through numerous funded projects, publications, presentations, instructional materials, and teaching activities, she has disseminated knowledge of instructional strategies based on established theories of learning. She has also explored the nature of instructional design practice so that scholars and designers alike better understand their work, and she has applied this knowledge in helping to prepare future instructional design professionals. Dr. Cennamo has synthesized much of this work in her textbook, *Real World Instructional Design,* co-authored with Debby Kalk. Currently, her research and service activities focus on developing and sustaining a classroom culture that fosters critical and creative thinking skills in K-12 and higher education environments.

John D. Ross spent the first ten years of his career as a classroom teacher. He taught instrumental music in middle and high school prior to receiving his Ph.D. in instructional design and technology from Virginia Tech in 1999, where his dissertation focused on investigating and promoting self-regulation in a hypermedia environment. He then worked for an educational nonprofit and served as the Director of the Institute for the Advancement of Emerging Technologies in Education and the director of technology for the Appalachia Regional Comprehensive Center, two federally funded programs. Dr. Ross currently works with state departments and districts across the country with issues related to technology planning, professional learning, and curriculum design, and serves as an adjunct faculty member to the Masters of Education program at Bethel University in Tennessee. He is a frequent presenter and workshop leader in areas such as planning for technology, total cost of ownership, online professional development, and creating student-centered learning environments. Dr. Ross is the author of the best-selling book *Online Professional Development: Design, Deliver, Succeed!* from Corwin.

Peggy A. Ertmer is a Professor in the Department of Curriculum and Instruction at Purdue University. Dr. Ertmer completed her Ph.D. at Purdue, specializing in educational technology and instructional design. Prior to becoming a faculty member at Purdue, she was an elementary and special education teacher in the K-12 schools. Dr. Ertmer's research examines the impact that student-centered instructional approaches and technology-enabled strategies have on learning. She actively mentors both students and peers, including pre- and in-service teachers, in the use of case-based and problem-based learning (PBL) pedagogy, technology tools, and self-regulated learning skills. She is particularly interested in studying the impact of case-based instruction on higher-order thinking skills; the effectiveness of student-centered, problem-based learning approaches to technology integration; and strategies for facilitating higher-order thinking and self-regulated learning in online learning environments. Dr. Ertmer has published scholarly works in premier national and international journals, has co-edited three editions of the *ID CaseBook: Case Studies in Instructional Design,* and is the founding editor of an open-access online journal, the *Interdisciplinary Journal of Problem-Based Learning,* published by Purdue University Press.

List of Tech Tools and Tips

TECH TOOLS & TIPS	Teaching Online	9
TECH TOOLS & TIPS	Video Recording Lessons for Reflection	38
TECH TOOLS & TIPS	Supporting Students' Efforts to Be Self-Directed	48
TECH TOOLS & TIPS	Virtual Field Trips	62
TECH TOOLS & TIPS	Using Educational Games to Support Learning	86
TECH TOOLS & TIPS	Developing a WebQuest	87
TECH TOOLS & TIPS	Creating Multimedia Websites	95
TECH TOOLS & TIPS	Digital Storytelling	96
TECH TOOLS & TIPS	Webconferencing	99
TECH TOOLS & TIPS	Wikis	101
TECH TOOLS & TIPS	Blogs	104
TECH TOOLS & TIPS	Evaluating Web Resources	106
TECH TOOLS & TIPS	Using Interactive Whiteboards	114
TECH TOOLS & TIPS	Facilitating Online Discussions	117
TECH TOOLS & TIPS	Ten Ideas for Using a Teacher Workstation	118
TECH TOOLS & TIPS	Blended Learning	120
TECH TOOLS & TIPS	Built-in Computer Accessibility Features	156
TECH TOOLS & TIPS	Mobile Devices: Support for Students with Special Needs	159
TECH TOOLS & TIPS	Monitoring Student Devices	196
TECH TOOLS & TIPS	Ergonomic Checklist	197
TECH TOOLS & TIPS	Ten Tips for Safe and Healthy Use of Technology in Your Classroom	201
TECH TOOLS & TIPS	Four-Step Troubleshooting Process	205
TECH TOOLS & TIPS	When Storage Isn't There	210
TECH TOOLS & TIPS	Maintenance Schedule	212
TECH TOOLS & TIPS	Learning from BYOD Initiatives	213

TECH TOOLS & TIPS	Top Ten Things to Consider When Creating Websites 223
TECH TOOLS & TIPS	Creating Virtual Field Trips 226
TECH TOOLS & TIPS	Creating Online Presentations 228
TECH TOOLS & TIPS	Using Streaming Media Sites 232
TECH TOOLS & TIPS	Using Podcasts in Your Classroom 233
TECH TOOLS & TIPS	Open-Source Software 234
TECH TOOLS & TIPS	Selecting Apps for Mobile Devices 238
TECH TOOLS & TIPS	Legal Issues Surrounding the Use of Images of Students and Student Work 255
TECH TOOLS & TIPS	Ten Tips for E-mail Use 263
TECH TOOLS & TIPS	Appropriate Use of Technology in Early Childhood Education 282
TECH TOOLS & TIPS	How to Look Your Best on a Webcam 297

Technology Integration: A Standards-Based Approach

OUTCOMES

In this chapter, you will learn to

- Reflect on the **history of technology integration** in relation to your teaching practice;
- Identify the **technology standards** that will guide your professional development; and
- Identify your current placement on the **technology integration continuum**.

iste·nets

ISTE Standards Addressed in Chapter 1

This chapter introduces the technology standards of the International Society for Technology in Education (ISTE), on which this book is based. ISTE is an organization whose mission is to provide "leadership and service to improve teaching, learning, and school leadership by advancing the effective use of technology in PK-12 and teacher education" (ISTE, 2008b). We introduce both the National Educational Technology Standards for Teachers (NETS-T) and the National Educational Technology Standards for Students (NETS-S), originally developed by ISTE in 1998 and 2000, respectively, and revised in 2007 and 2008. These standards are placed in the context of the historical uses of technology in education. We address the value of standards for ensuring consistency in the quality of instructional experiences for all students. The chapter concludes with scenarios of how the application of ISTE standards affects the role of the teacher, the role of the student, the resources used, and the instructional activities that occur within the classroom.

I magine yourself teaching a lesson to a classroom of students. Exactly what would you do to engage your students in the relevant content? Would you use technology? If so, what technologies and why? If not, why not? Now consider the technologies you and your students use every day. If you are like many college students, computers, cell phones, and other digital tools are interfaces to your life. You communicate there. You think there. You create there. You take care of the day-to-day events of your life there. You are entertained, informed, stimulated, and soothed. Technology provides a window into your world. But have you thought about how you will integrate technology into your teaching practice?

Our goal in writing this book is to help you build on these familiar technology experiences to learn the skills you need to successfully integrate technology into your teaching and your students' learning. More specifically, this book was written to help you meet the National Educational Technology Standards for Teachers (NETS-T), published by the International Society for Technology in Education (ISTE, 2008a). Four premises provide the foundation for our approach:

1. You are a lifelong learner. This is best summed up by the proverb, "Give a man a fish and you feed him for one day. Teach a man to fish and you feed him for a lifetime." Based on this premise, we have included strategies to support your continued learning, even after this text is completed.
2. Technology provides a *tool* for solving problems—in your case instructional problems—as opposed to *being* a problem as in, "How can I use technology in my class?"
3. It's more important *how* you use technology than *if* you use it. This might sound strange, especially in a technology textbook, but we believe that the decisions you make about integrating technology are based on what you know and believe about good teaching. Although we describe many different uses of technology in this text, we believe that "best practice" is achieved more readily when technology is used to support an authentic learner-centered curriculum.
4. Multiple technologies, including computers, are a natural part of your lives. Most new teachers today have grown up with computer technologies. Some of you have encountered more technologies and some less, but all of you have had access to numerous, and often very powerful, technologies for much of your lives, whether in your schools, homes, jobs, colleges, or other locations. You will be the first generation to naturally use such powerful technologies for teaching and learning, and you are poised to use them in ways we have yet to imagine.

Effective teaching for the 21st century requires that you possess more than content knowledge of math, social studies, Spanish, or whatever your discipline may be; it also requires pedagogical knowledge (i.e., knowledge of how to teach), pedagogical content knowledge (i.e., knowledge of how to teach specific content), and technological knowledge (Pierson, 2001). You will learn specific content and pedagogical knowledge related to your discipline in other courses throughout your college career. In this book, we focus on the intersection of pedagogical knowledge and technological knowledge—in other words, how to teach specific content using appropriate technology tools. As we address this intersection, we'll introduce you to ways to use technology to provide your students with meaningful learning experiences as well as ways that technology can support you in this process.

Technologies in Teaching and Learning: An Historical Perspective

Technologies have been part of teaching and learning for centuries. As the types of technologies have changed over the years, so, too, has their importance to the teaching and learning process. For example, consider two functions of technology—communication and information storage—and how they have evolved from pre-mechanical forms to mechanical to electronic and then to digital forms (see Figure 1.1). By improving existing technologies and developing new technologies, information and communication technologies have become more accessible to the general public while simultaneously

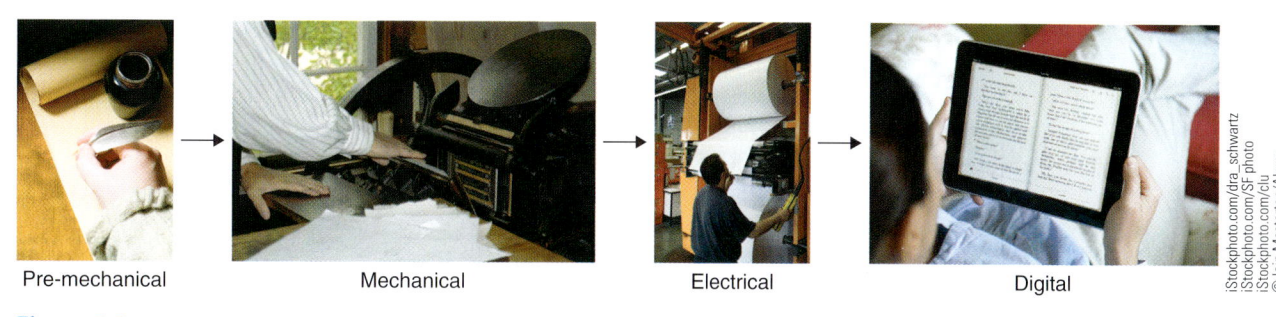

Pre-mechanical   Mechanical   Electrical   Digital

Figure 1.1
Information and communications technologies throughout history.

offering increased speed and greater quality. Can you imagine your life without cell phones, the Internet, and other digital tools that help you communicate with your friends and family?

If you were a teacher when very simple communication and information storage tools were available—in a time we refer to as the pre-mechanical era—you would have had to depend on real objects and face-to-face communication with your students to describe the past, explain the present, and encourage thinking about the future. The accessibility of pre-mechanical forms of information and communications technologies (such as quill, ink, and paper) and their products (such as legal proclamations and religious documents) was quite limited—often reserved for wealthy members of society. Neither the technologies nor their products were used extensively in educational settings.

As technologies moved into the mechanical phase through the creation and use of the printing press, it became possible to produce greater quantities of the products in a form that allowed teachers to retrieve and use information over an extended period of time. Storing and communicating information became much easier—for teachers, students, and the general public. Reliance on face-to-face communication lessened as books were printed and became more plentiful and accessible to wider audiences. Books were the new information technologies!

As information technologies entered the electronic age, accessibility increased even further. The widespread use of the phonograph, radio, and television increased opportunities for communication. You may not believe it, but when these technologies were first introduced all of them were predicted to be valuable teaching tools. The development of audio and video recorders meant that information captured by these tools could be preserved on tape and then made available to the public and, of course, to educators.

As technologies entered the digital phase, additional communication tools were developed. Word processors, digital cameras, e-mail, cellular phones, and a continuing array of information and communication tools have been, and will continue to be, developed. Also, because of the ease with which digital information can be duplicated and transferred to other locations, high-powered storage and retrieval systems and software have become common in places you might not consider—such as your car, television, and refrigerator. These technologies have powerful implications for education. For example, you might already access your textbooks through online databases or websites, or use devices such as your MP3 player, smartphone, or tablet computer to view or listen to your text and associated media files.

The impact of technological improvements and innovations on education obviously goes well beyond the areas of **information and communications technology**, now commonly referred to as **ICT**. Later chapters will present numerous ways in which modern technologies can affect your professional practice including providing lifelong learning opportunities for you and your students, promoting creativity and

information and communications technology
an umbrella term that refers to all technology that supports the manipulation and communication of information

innovation, assessing students' instructional needs and performances, and facilitating your own professional growth. We will discuss the many results you may expect to achieve through the effective use of digital tools and resources in your classroom and increase your awareness of the knowledge, abilities, skills, resources, and environments required for you to use them successfully. Specifically, we'll focus on the use of computers and related digital technologies in support of teaching and learning in educational environments.

Computer Technology in Education

It is customary when discussing computers in education to begin with a history of computers and to break this history into a relatively small number of meaningful phases. This history typically goes back to well-known predecessors of modern computers such as the automated loom, Babbage's Difference Engine, or the abacus. Although accounts of these early predecessors are often quite engaging, they may not seem very relevant to current computer users.

For most of you who will be reading this text, the practical history that counts is largely within your own lifetime. It begins with the first commercially successful "microcomputer," the Apple II introduced in 1977, and gains momentum with the first IBM PC in 1981, followed by the first Macintosh in 1984 (see Figure 1.2). In its relatively short history, the computer has become more powerful, flexible, and easier to use. And yet, educators continue to struggle to understand its role in the classroom (see Table 1.1).

Phase One-Computer as Object of Study (1977–1982)

At first, the computer itself was an object of study because computers were supposed to be the wave of the future—everyone would need to know how to use them. The computer's entry into the mainstream classroom in the 1980s prompted the creation of new curricula and standards in an effort to help students become **"computer literate."** If you had been in school in the 1980s, you might have taken a computer class in which you learned about the history of computers, including the fact that they used to be so big they filled an entire room or series of rooms. You would have learned about now-antiquated punch cards and tape drives. Your studies also may have focused on learning the parts and functions of a computer, rather than how to use it as a tool for learning. The yet-to-be-developed World Wide Web would not have been mentioned as you worked on stand-alone machines, and you probably would have created rudimentary programs using computer languages such as BASIC (see Figure 1.3). Being computer literate meant that you understood computer history, computer architecture and terminology, basic software applications, and programming. Being **technologically literate** is still important today, but the exact meaning of this term (as well as others such as technology proficiency and information literacy) continues to evolve, primarily because technology itself evolves.

Drawing on the earlier lessons of large-scale, mainframe computers, early instructional software was often created by

computer literate
person who has an understanding of computer history, computer architecture and terminology, basic software applications, and programming

technologically literate
having a general, working understanding of current technologies

Figure 1.2
Introduced in 1977, the Apple II was the first commercially successful microcomputer.

Technology Integration: A Standards-Based Approach

Table 1.1 Computers in Education Timeline

First Phase—The computer as an object of study (1997–1982)

1977 Apple II is introduced	First microcomputer brings computing from the scientific, mathematical domain to home, school, and work settings.
1981 IBM releases the first PC	IBM releases DOS-based computers and coins the term PC, or Personal Computer, the new concept in computer technology.
1982	The computer is named *Time* magazine's "Person of the Year," the individual who has had the greatest impact on world events during the year.
Educational software introduced	Drill-and-practice educational software programs predominate.
Educational emphasis	Emphasis on computer literacy: learning *about* technology.

Second Phase—The computer as programming tool (1983–1990)

1983 Logo Programming Language	Logo programming gains acceptance in education in an attempt to address students' higher-order thinking and problem-solving skills.
TCP/IP, SMTP, FTP, HTTP	Standardized communications language, TCP/IP, enables communication between computers via network—the Internet for the "common man" is born.
1984 Macintosh	Apple's Macintosh introduces the terms "desktop" and "icon" into everyday language and ushers in more variety in educational software.
1987 Hypertext	Hypermedia becomes readily accessible with the distribution of HyperCard software on Macintosh computers.
1990 Multimedia boom	Multimedia PCs are developed; simulation software and gaming grow in popularity and complexity; educational databases and other types of digital media are available on CD-ROMs.
Educational emphasis	Emphasis on learning programming languages and using "programmed instruction" such as drill-and-practice software.

Third Phase—The computer as a communication device and resource tool (1991–1996)

1991 WWW is born	Tim Berners-Lee and Robert Cailliau began using hypertext to link different kinds of information as a web of nodes, which learners could access at will.
1993 Mosaic released	The release of Mosaic, a browser with a graphical user interface (GUI), changes the look of Internet communications. "Surfing the web" becomes commonplace.
1993 White House goes online	President Clinton's administration develops www.whitehouse.gov. This heralds a new frontier in website development, with an abundance of educational sites for children.
1995	Microsoft releases the Windows 95 operating system. "Toy Story" is released, the first feature-length movie that is entirely computer generated.
1996 First Ed Tech Plan First national "Net Day"	The first U.S. National Educational Technology Plan is developed. Volunteers help wire local schools for Internet access and local area network (LAN) infrastructure.
Digital explosion	Technology tools grow at an exponential rate and become faster, smaller, and more powerful. Digital music, pictures, audio, video—the applications of this new wave of technology—are virtually limitless.
Educational emphasis	Emphasis on information literacy: learning *with* computers. National education goals emphasize the acquisition of computer hardware and the development of network infrastructure.

Fourth Phase—The computer as learning and social tool (1997–present)

Web 2.0	Teachers and students move from being consumers to becoming creators of online content using wikis, blogs, and other social networking tools.
Anywhere/Anytime learning	Teaching and learning move outside the classroom to include online and hybrid courses, delivered via learning management systems, as well as mobile learning opportunities using smartphones, netbooks, and tablet computers.

(continued)

Table 1.1	Computers in Education Timeline (*continued*)
Educational emphasis	Emphasis on ICT literacy: foundational information, communication, and productivity skills remain consistent while tools will continue to change. Technology as a tool for solving educational problems.
	Emphasis on technology *literacy*: Using technology as a learning tool to enable students to master 21st-century skills such as critical thinking, complex problem solving, collaboration, and multimedia communication.

```
10 INPUT "What is your name?"; N$
20 PRINT "Hello "; N$
30 REM
40 INPUT "Do you use technology? Y/N"; A$
50 IF (A$ = "Y") THEN GOTO 70
60 IF (A$ = "N") THEN GOTO 80
70 PRINT "Good for you!";
80 PRINT "You should!";
90 PRINT "Goodbye";
100 END
```

Figure 1.3
In the 1980s, being technologically literate meant learning to program in computer languages like BASIC.

computer scientists, engineers, and mathematicians. Educators or instructional designers were seldom, if ever, involved even though the goal was to design software that could teach. As you might expect, given that the early machines were not very powerful and the software creators were seldom educators, much of the software from this era was not especially memorable. The idea of designing programs to teach, of course, has survived and matured. Now such programs are usually developed by teams of educators, instructional designers, and graphic designers, as well as programmers, and are tested with real students.

Phase Two—Computer as Programming Tool (1983–1990)

The second phase of computers in education was initiated largely in response to the development of the computer language Logo, which was based on an earlier computer programming language called Lisp (see Figure 1.4). Lisp was

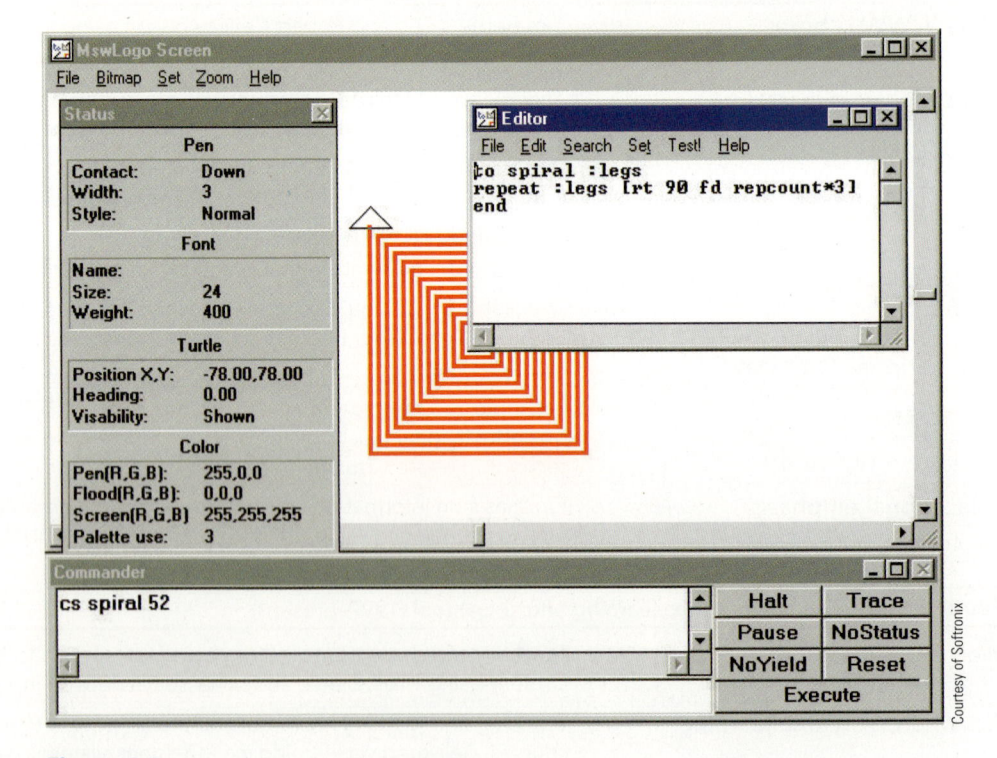

Figure 1.4
The early programming language Logo helped make programming applicable to education.

a complex programming language originally designed to handle mathematical notation and was used in early artificial intelligence programming. In an attempt to make aspects of Lisp more applicable to education, Wally Furzier and Seymour Papert developed Logo (Papert, 1980). Using the Logo programming language, users solved geometric problems by moving a robot-like "turtle" around the floor, and later, by moving a computer-generated "turtle" icon across the computer screen. Also during this period, the notion of "hypertext" was advanced by Ted Nelson. Hypertext allowed users to follow links to related information just like you follow hyperlinks on the web. Hypertext quickly blossomed into "hypermedia," in which buttons, images, and other objects could contain hyperlinks. One of the early multimedia development programs, HyperCard, came bundled with the software that was included on Macintosh computers. With the subsequent release of other multimedia development tools such as SuperCard, also on the Mac, and Toolbook, on the PC, hypermedia flourished. Hypermedia, of course, is still used today, and is most often experienced on websites that contain multiple media and hyperlinks to remote resources.

These two advancements—1) the potential of using programming to teach general problem-solving skills, and 2) hypermedia's potential to "open up" learning software by providing learners with control of their unique paths through the content—heralded the use of the computer as a device to develop higher-level thinking skills. We now know that teaching programming languages to increase general problem-solving skills isn't any more effective than the notion, prevalent at the end of the 19th century, that teaching Greek would "discipline the mind." We also know that open-ended hyperspace that allows students to "find their own paths" through content often leads to no cohesive path at all. Just think about how often you have followed interesting links while using the Internet, only to realize that you had (unfortunately) spent way too much time, lost track of what you were doing, and not completed what you really needed to accomplish—it *is* called "surfing" after all.

Phase Three—Computer as Communication Device and Resource Tool (1991–1996)

It took educators a while to shift their emphasis from learning *about* technology to learning *with* technology (Jonassen, 1996), while simultaneously trying to keep up with the many changes in the technology itself. As computers moved from cumbersome DOS-based systems to easier graphics-based interfaces with the introduction of the Macintosh and then Windows operating systems in the mid-80s, the emphasis gradually shifted from learning programming languages to learning how to use new **productivity applications** that were becoming commonplace in the world of work, such as word processors, spreadsheets, and databases. Both teachers and students began to use presentation software to organize instruction or demonstrate learning in colorful displays. However, materials created with productivity tools, especially presentation software, were also sometimes confusing, especially when they incorporated features such as audio, graphics, and animations at the expense of sound teaching strategies.

The third phase of computer use in education focused on using the computer as a classroom communication device and as a tool to access resources. This movement was further grounded in projects funded by the Advanced Research Project Agency Network (ARPANET). The ARPANET was an early computer network that initially linked scientists and engineers, permitting communication and providing a shared space for collaboration. The size of this early network grew from six connected nodes in the early 1970s to a hodgepodge of several hundred connections by 1983 when a single standard for transmitting digital information across the network, TCP/IP (which stands for Transmission Control Protocol and Internet Protocol), was adopted. TCP/IP (and subsequent standards such as Simple Mail Transfer Protocol, or SMTP) opened up this early "hodgepodge" to almost anyone with a computer. This early network was a critical step toward creating the Internet that has become part of all of our lives.

> **productivity applications** computer programs such as databases, spreadsheets, word-processing and presentation software that allow users to create products more efficiently than is possible without the software, thus, increasing productivity

Figure 1.5
As a result of the first National Educational Technology Plan, schools sought to put computers in every classroom.

The subsequent explosion of networked resources made information *and* misinformation widely available; anyone with a computer could "publish" research, opinion, news, or a wide range of questionable material. The potential for connecting students to each other and to the global community was unleashed.

Initially, there was a widespread belief that placing technology in the schools would make a difference in the way teachers taught and students learned in this new, networked society. Thus, "one computer for every five students" became a U.S. national goal (e.g., President's Panel on Educational Technology, 1997); cash-strapped school systems rushed to get computers and networking infrastructure in place (see Figure 1.5). This ultimately led to the question of how to integrate these technologies effectively into the classroom.

Phase Four—Computer as Learning and Social Tool (1997–current)

Widespread access to the Internet and the growth of web-based information forced a paradigm shift in terms of what technology proficiency looked like and might become. The term **information literacy** became popular and was a focus of the second United States National Educational Technology Plan (U.S. Department of Education, 2000). This shift toward finding, analyzing, creating, and sharing information encouraged educators to consider how technology tools could be used to support learning rather than requiring students to learn basic skills for tools that would soon be outdated.

Given this change in emphasis, it wasn't long before colleges and universities, and even private and commercial organizations, began offering online and blended, or hybrid, courses to enable students from across the country and even around the world to enroll in degree programs. Online learning quickly became one of the fastest growing trends in the educational uses of technology, both at the K–12 and the college levels. In 2007, Picciano and Seaman estimated that nearly one million K–12 students

> **information literacy**
> the ability to recognize when information is needed and to locate, evaluate, and use the needed information effectively

TECH TOOLS & TIPS

Teaching Online

Numerous school districts offer some form of distributed learning classes where one teacher provides instruction for students at a variety of locations. Specialized courses that may not attract enough students at one school to justify hiring a teacher, yet are viable options when students are combined across sites, can be offered through distributed learning. And, of course, virtual schools offer coursework to students who are homeschooled or otherwise unable or unwilling to attend traditional schools. In fact, several states have added online teaching requirements to their teacher certification systems.

The National Education Association (2006) recommends that, at a minimum, training for online teaching for pre-service teachers include:

- evaluating Internet resources for validity of content;
- respecting and enforcing copyright concerns, including Technology, Education, and Copyright Harmonization (TEACH) Act provisions;
- identifying outstanding educational websites for both teacher and student reference;
- issues of accessibility and Section 508 compliance, including adaptive software for the physically, visually, and hearing impaired;
- employing appropriate "etiquette" and observing Acceptable Use Policies; and
- learning to develop lesson plans that foster Internet research skills in students (NEA, n.d., pp. 12–13).

Each of these topics is addressed in this book.

Source: National Education Association Guide to teaching online courses, pp. 12–13 (http://www.nea.org).

---

had taken an online course in the previous school year. At the college level, Allen and Seaman (2010) reported that over 5.6 million students had taken at least one online course during the fall 2010 semester! It is highly likely that you, too, have experienced this increasingly common type of course delivery.

Web-based applications have evolved to the point where it is very easy for web users, including teachers and students, to move from being passive consumers of information to creators of information, in a range of media formats. Social-networking tools, sometimes referred to as Web 2.0 tools, allow you and your students to quickly post text, images, videos, and other media, which other users can then comment on or add content to. You can bookmark information on the web and share those sites with friends and colleagues, a process sometimes called social bookmarking. Examples of this form of socially generated content include the popular networking sites like Facebook and Google+; Wikipedia, the online, user-created encyclopedia; YouTube and education-specific video repositories like TeacherTube; Flickr, an online photo sharing site; and any number of weblogs—or blogs—created by education journalists, teachers, and even students. You no longer need to know how to program for the web in order to post a daily journal or create your own online reference with text, graphics, video, and other media. Like most innovative technologies, these new tools are struggling to establish a firm foothold in educational settings. It is important to consider whether and how these tools can effectively support student learning.

In the first decade of the new millennium, all of this content—whether education-related or not—became increasingly accessible through mobile devices, such as iPods, iPads, and a range of tablets and smartphones. Mobile learning, or mLearning as some people call it, is the latest frontier in terms of leveraging information to support teaching and learning. Students can access and create information, whether in or out of class, with these small, portable devices that may utilize web browsers or education-specific applications, or "apps" for short. This next generation of tools has made its way into the hands—and classrooms—of many students and will undoubtedly continue to grow in popularity as the devices become less expensive and more powerful.

Summary of Technology Integration in Teaching and Learning

So what have we, as educators, learned as we moved through the various phases and stages of technology integration in education? We know that teachers cannot be replaced with technologies. Instead, the role of the teacher has changed over time as teachers have benefited (maybe even just recently) from having powerful tools and ample resources available to support their teaching (see Figure 1.6 and Table 1.1). New technologies make it easier to incorporate new learning theories and pedagogies such as active learning, knowledge construction, cooperative learning, and guided discovery in our classrooms. Notions such as "teachers as facilitators" or "students as active learners" can be implemented with the assistance of new technologies. Technology tools allow access to expanded resources and have the capacity to free students and teachers from mundane tasks so that they can focus on activities that promote greater collaboration, in-depth study, and critical thinking skills. Now, educational software programmers and developers build their products based on well-founded learning theories and pedagogies. Of course, some software may be consistent with your teaching style and classroom goals but others may not be. As you seek to integrate technologies in your future classroom, you must find the digital tools and resources that best support your curriculum, your teaching style, and your students.

Defining Technology Proficiency through Standards

On a national level, several organizations in the United States have attempted to create current definitions of technology literacy or technology proficiency. These definitions reflect the view that many information, communication, and productivity

1977 Apple II is introduced
First microcomputer brings computing from the scientific, mathematical domain to home, school, and work settings.

1981 IBM releases the first PC
IBM releases DOS-based computers and coins the term PC, or Personal Computer, the new concept in computer technology.

1982
The computer is named *Time* magazine's "Person of the Year," the individual who has had the greatest impact on world events during the year.

1983 Logo Programming Language
Logo programming gains acceptance in education in an attempt to address higher-order thinking and problem-solving skills in students.
TCP/IP, SMTP, FTP, HTTP
Standardized communications language, TCP/IP, enables communication between computers via network—the Internet for the "common man" is born.

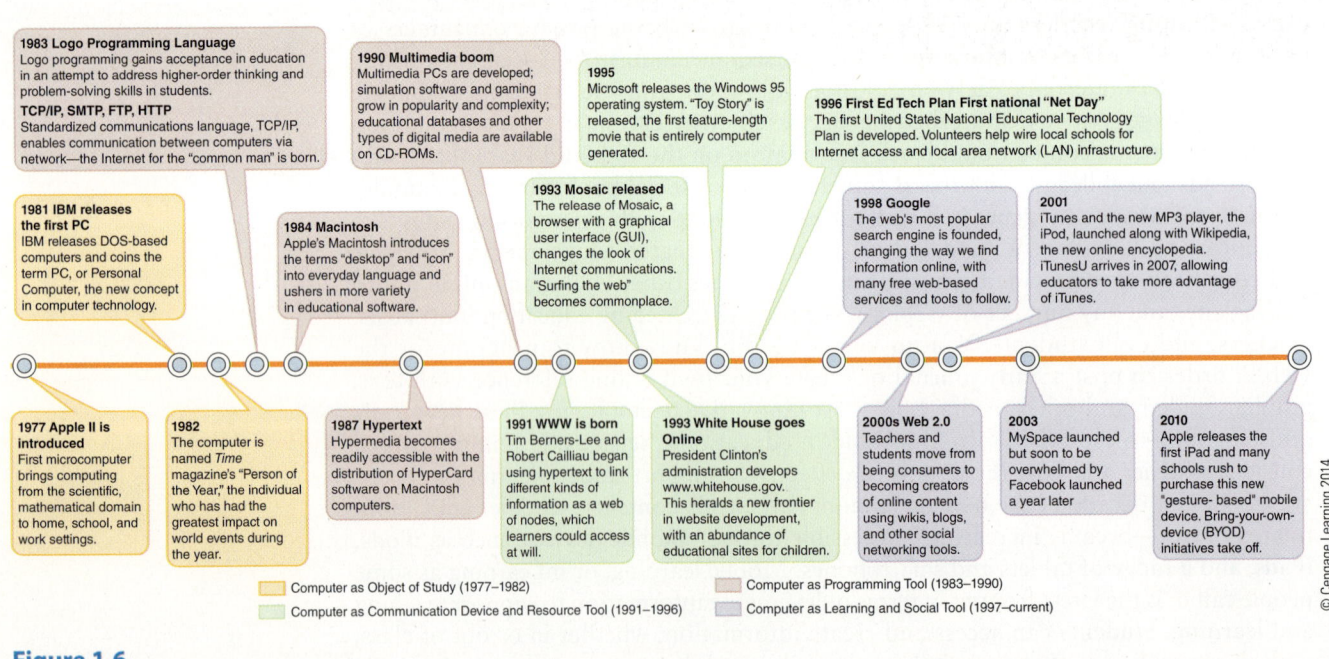

1984 Macintosh
Apple's Macintosh introduces the terms "desktop" and "icon" into everyday language and ushers in more variety in educational software.

1987 Hypertext
Hypermedia becomes readily accessible with the distribution of HyperCard software on Macintosh computers.

1990 Multimedia boom
Multimedia PCs are developed; simulation software and gaming grow in popularity and complexity; educational databases and other types of digital media are available on CD-ROMs.

1991 WWW is born
Tim Berners-Lee and Robert Cailliau began using hypertext to link different kinds of information as a web of nodes, which learners could access at will.

1993 Mosaic released
The release of Mosaic, a browser with a graphical user interface (GUI), changes the look of Internet communications. "Surfing the web" becomes commonplace.

1993 White House goes Online
President Clinton's administration develops www.whitehouse.gov. This heralds a new frontier in website development, with an abundance of educational sites for children.

1995
Microsoft releases the Windows 95 operating system. "Toy Story" is released, the first feature-length movie that is entirely computer generated.

1996 First Ed Tech Plan First national "Net Day"
The first United States National Educational Technology Plan is developed. Volunteers help wire local schools for Internet access and local area network (LAN) infrastructure.

1998 Google
The web's most popular search engine is founded, changing the way we find information online, with many free web-based services and tools to follow.

2000s Web 2.0
Teachers and students move from being consumers to becoming creators of online content using wikis, blogs, and other social networking tools.

2001
iTunes and the new MP3 player, the iPod, launched along with Wikipedia, the new online encyclopedia. iTunesU arrives in 2007, allowing educators to take more advantage of iTunes.

2003
MySpace launched but soon to be overwhelmed by Facebook launched a year later

2010
Apple releases the first iPad and many schools rush to purchase this new "gesture- based" mobile device. Bring-your-own-device (BYOD) initiatives take off.

Computer as Object of Study (1977–1982) | Computer as Programming Tool (1983–1990)
Computer as Communication Device and Resource Tool (1991–1996) | Computer as Learning and Social Tool (1997–current)

Figure 1.6
Timeline illustrating key events in the use of computers use for education.

skills will remain constant while the tools we use to demonstrate them will change. In their description of ICT literacy, the Partnership for 21st Century Skills (2004, 2007) promotes the notion that to be competitive in this new millennium, K-12 students must develop a core of foundational skills (listed in Table 1.2). However, in the 21st century, these skills are often learned with, and facilitated by, the use of ICT tools such as e-mail, the Internet, and productivity software. It is critical that students be prepared not only to use common technologies but also to continually upgrade their technology skills to include new tools that take their place—just as you may have had to adapt from writing letters, to sending e-mail, to text-messaging. According to the Partnership for 21st Century Skills, students demonstrate ICT literacy when they use appropriate 21st-century tools to develop and demonstrate learning skills.

The most recent version of the National Educational Technology Plan (NETP; U.S. DOE, 2010) shifts our focus from an emphasis on technology-for-teaching to that of technology-for-learning and challenges us to leverage technology to create "engaging and empowering learning experiences for all learners" (p. 4). A quick glance at the word cloud in Figure 1.7, created from the executive summary of the NETP, illustrates this new emphasis on students and learning. The goal is to use technology to "enable, motivate, and inspire" all students. As such, this requires that we put students at the center of our curricula and classroom learning experiences and that we allow for flexibility on multiple dimensions. This is in line with our belief that "best practice" is achieved more readily when technology is used to support an authentic learner-centered curriculum. In this view, technological literacy is defined in terms of

> **TEACHSOURCE VIDEO**
>
> Review the video, *An Expanded Definition of Literacy: Meaningful Ways to Use Technology* on the Education CourseMate website. Consider the following questions:
>
> 1. While reading and writing are still important literacies, what other literacies do these teachers describe?
> 2. How do the teachers help students develop new literacies? What strategies and tips do they offer that you could use or adapt?

Table 1.2 21st-Century Skills

Core Subjects	Core subjects: English, reading or language arts, world languages, arts, mathematics, economics, science, geography, history, government and civics
21st-Century Themes	• Global Awareness • Financial, Economic, Business and Entrepreneurial Literacy • Civic Literacy • Environmental Literacy
Learning and Innovation Skills	• Creativity and Innovation Skills • Critical-Thinking and Problem-Solving Skills • Communication and Collaboration Skills
Information, Media, and Technology Skills	• Information Literacy • Media Literacy • ICT (Information and Communications Technology) Literacy
Life and Career Skills	• Flexibility and Adaptability • Initiative and Self-Direction • Social and Cross-Cultural Skills • Productivity and Accountability • Leadership and Responsibility

Source: Partnership for 21st Century Skills. (2007). *Framework for 21st Century Learning.* www.21stcenturyskills.org. Reprinted by permission.

Figure 1.7
Word cloud created from the executive summary of the 2010 National Educational Technology Plan using Wordle.

mastering 21st-century skills such as critical thinking, complex problem solving, collaboration, and multimedia communication.

As you will recall, this focus on technology-for-learning reflects the fourth and most current phase in the movement toward the use of digital technologies (computers, software, the Internet, etc.) as integral parts of the teaching/learning environment. No longer is the goal simply to place technology in the classroom. Rather, the goal is for these tools to become as important to the "work" of teaching and learning as power tools are to the work of building a house. The current goal for technology integration in education is the inclusion of relevant technologies as integral and natural contributors to the entire educational process.

The Standards Movement

The standards movement in education also heavily influences the way in which technology proficiency is defined. Prior to 1983 there was little discussion of standards in education in the United States. In 1983 the report titled A Nation at Risk (National Commission of Excellence in Education, 1983) was published, and in the eyes of many, the modern standards movement began. Among other things, this report included two goals directly related to academic achievement. One goal indicated that students in grades 4, 8, and 12 would demonstrate competency in English, mathematics, science, history, and geography by the year 2000. The other goal stated that U.S. students would be first in the world in science

> ### APPLY to Practice
> #### Defining Technology Literacy
> Over time, many organizations have attempted to define computer literacy, information literacy, and technology literacy.
>
> 1. Find definitions for any of these terms from public and private national organizations, your college or university websites, or other sources. Capture a few of the definitions you find and determine whether you agree with them, and if so, to what degree.
> 2. Log on to a site that covers computer history, proficiency, or literacy. You can find examples of these resources on this book's Education CourseMate website. How do these different sources address computer, information, and technology literacy?
> 3. Discuss your findings with a group of peers. Would you consider yourself to be technologically literate? Based on which definition? What consensus can you reach in your group?

and math achievement by the year 2000. In an effort to determine the criteria for compliance with these goals, minimum standards were needed in many content domains where few, if any, had existed previously. And so, beginning in 1983, and continuing through 1999, efforts were undertaken by the national professional organizations in all the major content areas (English, mathematics, science, etc.) to create a set of curricular standards for their specific disciplines (see Table 1.3).

Over the last 20 years, national professional organizations have developed content standards for their content domains that have influenced the creation of state-specific content standards. Because of the wide diversity in state standards, the National

Table 1.3 National Content Standards Outlined by Professional Organizations

The following content area standards have been developed by national organizations. Links to these standards can be found on the Education CourseMate website.

- Moving into the Future: National Standards for Physical Education by the National Association for Sport and Physical Education
- National Curriculum Standards for Social Studies: A Framework for Teaching, Learning, and Assessment by the National Council for the Social Studies
- National Science Education Standards by the National Academy of Sciences
- National Standards for Civics and Government by the Center for Civic Education
- National Standards for Health Education, by the American Association for Health Education (AAHE)
- National Standards for Music Education by the Music Educators National Conference
- National Visual Arts Standards by the National Art Education Association
- Pre-K-12 English Language Proficiency Standards, by the Teachers of English to Speakers of Other Languages (TESOL)
- Principles and Standards for School Mathematics by the National Council of Teachers of Mathematics
- Standards for the English Language Arts by the National Council of Teachers of English (NCTE) and the International Reading Association (IRA)
- The Standards for Foreign Language Learning, by the American Council on the Teaching of Foreign Languages

> ### APPLY *to Practice*
> #### Locating Content Standards
> 1. Is there a national organization whose content standards you must meet? Locate its website and review its standards.
> 2. Compare your content standards with the standards for two of your fellow students in different fields. How do your standards compare with theirs?

Governors Association Center for Best Practices and the Council of Chief State School Officers are coordinating efforts to develop a common core of academic standards (Common Core State Standards Initiative, 2011). As of January 2012, the Common Core State Standards for English/language arts and mathematics have been adopted by 45 of the 50 states.

In addition, some districts and schools have developed their own content standards to supplement or support state content standards. As a classroom teacher, it is likely that you will focus, primarily, on developing lessons that meet *state* content standards as these are the criteria on which your students will be expected to demonstrate proficiency—usually on high-stakes assessment tests.

Technology Standards

The development of technology standards started a little later. In 1998, ISTE released a set of technology standards for students, the National Educational Technology Standards for Students (NETS-S). Since then, ISTE has developed multiple sets of technology standards, including the National Educational Technology Standards for Teachers (NETS-T) and for Administrators (NETS-A).

The original ISTE NETS were released in a "refreshed" version for students in 2007, teachers in 2008, and administrators the following year. The most recent standards reflect a change in emphasis from computer skills to 21st-century skills. The chapters in this book address the most recent standards for teachers, in other words, the ISTE NETS-T (see Table 1.4); however, you will also learn about the NETS for Students (see Table 1.5) as the NETS-T require that you develop those skills in your students.

Table 1.4 The ISTE National Educational Technology Standards (NETS-T) and Performance Indicators for Teachers (2008)

Effective teachers model and apply the National Educational Technology Standards for Students (NETS-S) as they design, implement, and assess learning experiences to engage students and improve learning; enrich professional practice; and provide positive models for students, colleagues, and the community. All teachers should meet the following standards and performance indicators. Teachers:

1. Facilitate and Inspire Student Learning and Creativity

Teachers use their knowledge of subject matter, teaching and learning, and technology to facilitate experiences that advance student learning, creativity, and innovation in both face-to-face and virtual environments. Teachers:

a. promote, support, and model creative and innovative thinking and inventiveness
b. engage students in exploring real-world issues and solving authentic problems using digital tools and resources
c. promote student reflection using collaborative tools to reveal and clarify students' conceptual understanding and thinking, planning, and creative processes
d. model collaborative knowledge construction by engaging in learning with students, colleagues, and others in face-to-face and virtual environments

(continued)

| Table 1.4 | The ISTE National Educational Technology Standards (NETS-T) and Performance Indicators for Teachers (2008) (*continued*) |

2. Design and Develop Digital-Age Learning Experiences and Assessments

Teachers design, develop, and evaluate authentic learning experiences and assessments incorporating contemporary tools and resources to maximize content learning in context and to develop the knowledge, skills, and attitudes identified in the NETS-S. Teachers:

   a. design or adapt relevant learning experiences that incorporate digital tools and resources to promote student learning and creativity
   b. develop technology-enriched learning environments that enable all students to pursue their individual curiosities and become active participants in setting their own educational goals, managing their own learning, and assessing their own progress
   c. customize and personalize learning activities to address students' diverse learning styles, working strategies, and abilities using digital tools and resources
   d. provide students with multiple and varied formative and summative assessments aligned with content and technology standards and use resulting data to inform learning and teaching

3. Model Digital-Age Work and Learning

Teachers exhibit knowledge, skills, and work processes representative of an innovative professional in a global and digital society. Teachers:

   a. demonstrate fluency in technology systems and the transfer of current knowledge to new technologies and situations
   b. collaborate with students, peers, parents, and community members using digital tools and resources to support student success and innovation
   c. communicate relevant information and ideas effectively to students, parents, and peers using a variety of digital-age media and formats
   d. model and facilitate effective use of current and emerging digital tools to locate, analyze, evaluate, and use information resources to support research and learning

4. Promote and Model Digital Citizenship and Responsibility

Teachers understand local and global societal issues and responsibilities in an evolving digital culture and exhibit legal and ethical behavior in their professional practices. Teachers:

   a. advocate, model, and teach safe, legal, and ethical use of digital information and technology, including respect for copyright, intellectual property, and the appropriate documentation of sources
   b. address the diverse needs of all learners by using learner-centered strategies and providing equitable access to appropriate digital tools and resources
   c. promote and model digital etiquette and responsible social interactions related to the use of technology and information
   d. develop and model cultural understanding and global awareness by engaging with colleagues and students of other cultures using digital-age communication and collaboration tools

5. Engage in Professional Growth and Leadership

Teachers continuously improve their professional practice, model lifelong learning, and exhibit leadership in their school and professional community by promoting and demonstrating the effective use of digital tools and resources. Teachers:

   a. participate in local and global learning communities to explore creative applications of technology to improve student learning
   b. exhibit leadership by demonstrating a vision of technology infusion, participating in shared decision making and community building, and developing the leadership and technology skills of others
   c. evaluate and reflect on current research and professional practice on a regular basis to make effective use of existing and emerging digital tools and resources in support of student learning
   d. contribute to the effectiveness, vitality, and self-renewal of the teaching profession and of their school and community

Source: National Educational Technology Standards for Teachers, 2nd ed. Copyright © 2008, ISTE (International Society for Technology in Education), www.iste.org. All rights reserved. Reprinted by permission.

Table 1.5 National Educational Technology Standards for Students: The Next Generation

"What students should know and be able to do to learn effectively and live productively in an increasingly digital world..."

1. Creativity and Innovation
Students demonstrate creative thinking, construct knowledge, and develop innovative products and processes using technology. Students:
   a. apply existing knowledge to generate new ideas, products, or processes
   b. create original works as a means of personal or group expression
   c. use models and simulations to explore complex systems and issues
   d. identify trends and forecast possibilities

2. Communication and Collaboration
Students use digital media and environments to communicate and work collaboratively, including at a distance, to support individual learning and contribute to the learning of others. Students:
   a. interact, collaborate, and publish with peers, experts or others employing a variety of digital environments and media
   b. communicate information and ideas effectively to multiple audiences using a variety of media and formats
   c. develop cultural understanding and global awareness by engaging with learners of other cultures
   d. contribute to project teams to produce original works or solve problems

3. Research and Information Fluency
Students apply digital tools to gather, evaluate, and use information. Students:
   a. plan strategies to guide inquiry
   b. locate, organize, analyze, evaluate, synthesize, and ethically use information from a variety of sources and media
   c. evaluate and select information sources and digital tools based on the appropriateness to specific tasks
   d. process data and report results

4. Critical Thinking, Problem-Solving, & Decision-Making
Students use critical thinking skills to plan and conduct research, manage projects, solve problems and make informed decisions using appropriate digital tools and resources. Students:
   a. identify and define authentic problems and significant questions for investigation
   b. plan and manage activities to develop a solution or complete a project
   c. collect and analyze data to identify solutions and/or make informed decisions
   d. use multiple processes and diverse perspectives to explore alternative solutions

5. Digital Citizenship
Students understand human, cultural, and societal issues related to technology and practice legal and ethical behavior. Students:
   a. advocate and practice safe, legal, and responsible use of information and technology
   b. exhibit a positive attitude toward using technology that supports collaboration, learning, and productivity
   c. demonstrate personal responsibility for lifelong learning
   d. exhibit leadership for digital citizenship

6. Technology Operations and Concepts
Students demonstrate a sound understanding of technology concepts, systems and operations. Students:
   a. understand and use technology systems
   b. select and use applications effectively and productively
   c. troubleshoot systems and applications

Source: National Educational Technology Standards for Students, 2nd ed. Copyright © 2007, ISTE (International Society for Technology in Education), www.iste.org. All rights reserved. Reprinted by permission.

The Value of Standards

The information presented so far provides a glimpse of the roles of government and professional organizations in the development of standards. However, except for their ability to address legislative and political requirements, not much has been said about the value of standards. Although many reasons can be advanced for the development of standards, the main reasons include (McREL, 2004):

- Standards provide a common set of expectations.
- Standards clarify expectations.
- Standards raise expectations.

So, technology standards, such as those from ISTE, provide a common set of *expectations* across states and localities. Moreover, they *clarify* the level of technology proficiency expected of teachers. Finally, they *raise expectations* by creating an awareness of what can be accomplished. When standards work as intended, they help us achieve first-rate quality—in services, products, and teaching. Throughout this book the ISTE standards are used to provide a common set of expectations, as well as to clarify and raise the expectations regarding the skills you should obtain while developing competency in technology integration within the classroom.

In general, standards refer to a degree or level of requirement, excellence, or attainment expected of an individual or organization. In more simple terms, standards are criteria. Criteria define what is expected, such as the content you are expected to teach. As a teacher, you will be most concerned with meeting standards that relate to how well you address the requirements of your curriculum, how well your students perform, and—specific to this textbook—how well you integrate technology into your teaching. However, it is not enough to look only at criteria when discussing standards.

What makes standards different from other types of quality expectations are the additional factors of compliance and consequences. Compliance refers to who is subject to the standards and on what basis. In most states, you will be expected to demonstrate compliance with a set of technology standards for teachers, and in many cases, those will be the ISTE NETS-T, although a few states and organizations have developed their own sets of technology standards. Demonstration of compliance can occur in a number of ways including being observed by an administrator or other teacher, documenting your proficiency in a portfolio, or perhaps even passing a test.

Standards typically have consequences associated with compliance or noncompliance. These consequences indicate what happens if you do or don't meet the expectations. For example, failure to comply with standards may result in mandatory remedial instruction, delays in pay raises, or in limited employment opportunities. Being compliant may help you get a job or attain benefits such as tenure, monetary rewards associated with reaching higher levels on your career ladder, or the opportunity to teach different courses or work with different students.

So, there are three factors to consider with respect to any standard: criteria, compliance, and consequences. But don't worry—the intent of this book is to help you master ISTE's technology standards for teachers. Each chapter concludes with an opportunity to document effectively what you have learned in a portfolio. You may find other ways to document your skills and knowledge, but this book provides you with suggestions

criteria
with regards to standards, refers to what is expected, such as the content one is expected to teach

compliance
with regard to standards, refers to *who* must meet the standards and what *authority* mandates them

consequences
in the context of standards, refers to the results of meeting or not meeting standards, including remedial instruction and changes in pay schedules

APPLY to Practice

Technology Standards

1. Identify the technology standards that your state expects teachers to meet.
2. How do they align with the ISTE NETS-T used in this book?

for creating and maintaining this common tool. In fact, your school or state may have a portfolio assessment system to which you are required to contribute. If not, in Chapter 2, you will learn about developing your own portfolio using common productivity tools such as word processors, web development software, and so forth.

The Technology Integration Continuum

The overarching goal of the ISTE standards is to enable teachers to create *new learning experiences* that integrate our understanding of how people learn with the relevant technological tools that can support teaching and learning. In order to create new kinds of learning experiences, effective technology integration requires more than simply introducing computers and related technologies into the classroom. To **integrate** means to combine two or more things to make a whole; when we integrate technologies into instruction, we make them an integral part of the teaching and learning process. **Technology integration** requires changes to many instructional components (Dwyer, Ringstaff, & Sandholtz, 1991) including:

- what resources are used;
- what roles the teacher performs;
- what roles students play; as well as
- the nature of the instructional activities.

Based on ISTE's definition, **new learning experiences** are ones in which teachers and students work together to address the requirements of the curriculum while still taking into account individual student needs, interests, and preferences. New information is readily linked to students' prior knowledge. Students are also given some degree of choice in terms of the ways they receive and process information and demonstrate their learning. Instructional activities rely on teaching methods that encourage high levels of thinking and creativity and that allow students to collaborate and communicate—both with other students and teachers—as well as experts outside of the classroom. Students are encouraged to solve authentic problems drawn from real-world situations (e.g., "How can we improve our city so that everyone benefits?" "Why should kids care about the price of gas?"), within the context of one specific content area (social studies, mathematics) or across content areas. This type of authentic problem-based learning requires students to identify and describe the problem, relate it to prior knowledge, develop recommendations to solve the problem, select strategies to pilot those recommendations, and monitor and evaluate how well their strategies worked in solving the problem. Supporting teaching and learning in this type of authentic environment are resources and technologies (Internet resources, databases, spreadsheets, presentation software, and many others) that allow students to work as professionals in an information-based world, support them across varied levels of need, and build and demonstrate both content and technology proficiencies.

The type of learning experiences you create in your classroom will influence the types of technologies that you and your students use (see Figure 1.8). It will also affect *how* you and your students use these technologies. For example, if teachers use presentation software to project to a screen what they formerly wrote on the chalkboard, simply adding computer technology doesn't change their teaching approach to a more powerful one. What is most important is *how* the technology is used. A more learner-centered approach may involve a group of

---

integrate
to combine two or more parts to make a whole

technology integration
making technologies an integral part of the teaching and learning process that impacts resources, teacher and student roles, and instructional activities

new learning experiences
instructional experiences that are created by integrating our understanding of how people learn with the relevant technological tools that can support teaching and learning

Figure 1.8
Technology can help teachers develop new learning environments and experiences.

STORIES from Practice

Using Technology in a Learner-Centered Classroom

Marissa and Tonya both teach 6th grade language arts in a small, rural middle school with a one-to-one laptop initiative. That means that every student and every teacher in the school has access to a wireless laptop computer throughout the school day. When the laptop program began about five years ago, no one knew exactly how to use the technology to support meaningful teaching and learning. Lots of time was spent learning the various tool applications (e.g., word processing, presentation software, etc.) that were now available 24/7. Marissa and Tonya were no different. They would allow their students to type their papers and other assignments, and found many ways to use the tools themselves, but their classrooms still remained fairly teacher-centered. However, about two years into the laptop program, the school district received a large federal grant that enabled them to expand the laptop program to include the entire middle school and high school. Furthermore, the proposed program was not just about the computer; this time the program was situated within the context of a problem-based learning (PBL) pedagogy. That is, the technology was heralded as a tool to enable authentic instruction in the form of problem-based learning. Marissa and Tonya attended special classes offered by the local university and participated in many after-school workshops to learn about PBL and how to implement it in their classrooms.

To get started, Marissa and Tonya attempted one multi-disciplinary unit their first year, converting a previous unit on the rain forest to one that used a more authentic approach. Instead of telling students why we need the rain forest and asking them to remember a list of reasons found in their readings, they allowed the students to explore different reasons on their own by anchoring the unit in the question, "Why should we care about the rain forest?" Students began by individually rank ordering a list of eight "belief" statements and then coming to consensus with fellow group members on their top two beliefs (e.g., "The tropical rain forest is home to many rare animals and plants. Destroying tropical rain forests could make these species extinct." "The tropical rain forest is home to different peoples. No one has the right to destroy these peoples' homes and ways of life."). This initial activity quickly engaged students in a variety of important issues related to rain forest deforestation and gave them reasons to look for additional evidence to support their beliefs. Students searched the Internet, library books, and other available classroom resources (CD-ROMs and videos) to find information that could support their beliefs, converted the information to charts and graphs using spreadsheets, and then, using presentation software, made presentations to their classmates to convince them of the importance of their reasons for saving the rain forest.

According to Marissa and Tonya, students showed more interest and engagement in this unit than in previous years and were very vocal in their enthusiasm for the *way* the unit was run. They liked making choices, working in groups, and using technology to make persuasive presentations. And best of all, they seemed to really engage with the content, becoming quite passionate about what they could do to save the rain forest.

Source: Adapted from Simons, K. D., & Ertmer, P. A. (2005/2006).

students using this same presentation software to create a slide show that includes pictures of artifacts or charts and graphs that summarize research they have completed, manipulating the data and information on the screen itself. While the same technology is being used in both classrooms, the *way* it is being used is quite different.

Stages in Technology Integration

A number of researchers (e.g., Dwyer, Ringstaff, & Sandholtz, 1991) have documented the developmental stages that teachers go through as they move from novice technology users to those capable of using technologies to create meaningful learning experiences. As reflected in our *Stories from Practice—Using Technology in a Learner-Centered Classroom*, teachers initially focus on learning the new technology and using the technology to support traditional instruction. In later stages, teachers begin to develop new approaches to teaching and learning that make the most of the technology available to them. Teachers no longer try to adapt instruction to technology but instead adjust the

TEACHSOURCE VIDEO

Examine one of the following video cases on the CourseMate website: *Math 2.0: Using Social-Networking Tools in the High School Mathematics Classroom*, or *Supporting Problem-Based Learning in the Elementary Classroom*. Describe how technology supports the four common components of instruction identified above. Consider the following questions:

1. Use of resources: How well are they matched to the instruction? What role do technology-based resources play?
2. The teacher's role: What roles do teachers play in these classrooms? Do they lead instruction or do they enable students to engage in higher-order skills through collaborative problem solving? Does technology use replicate traditional seat-based activities or does it support diverse learning styles and preferences in unique settings?
3. Nature of instruction: Do students encounter well-structured problems? Are assessments norm-based or do they allow for reflective responses and accommodate a variety of learning preferences? Is technology central to the instruction?
4. Students' role: On whom is the learning focused? How are the students engaged? How are individual differences supported and nurtured? How does technology support and motivate student activities?

---

fundamental nature of their instruction to enable new learning activities not possible without the technology.

The most recent ISTE standards for teachers are accompanied by a four-stage continuum—beginning, developing, proficient, and transformative—that describes how teachers demonstrate each standard and sub-standard at each stage in their professional development. Following are generalized descriptions of these four stages using the lens of the four essential components identified above (e.g., resources, teacher role, instructional activities, students' role). Notice how the actions of the teacher and students change as we move through the stages, as well as how resources are used and activities are structured. However, be aware that teachers and activities may exhibit characteristics across stages. As you read the descriptions of the four stages, think about where your former teachers and colleagues might fall on the continuum. Where do you think you might be?

Characteristics of the Beginning Stage

- Teachers select and use technologies and other *resources* that support student learning experiences, but classroom instruction may still depend heavily on chalkboards, textbooks, workbooks, and worksheets to support lecture, recitation, and seatwork.
- *Teachers* research and discuss strategies students can use to promote knowledge construction and demonstrate creativity. They monitor safe, ethical, legal, and healthy use of technology and information resources.
- Teachers design *instructional activities* by using or modifying existing learning resources to collect information and create student products. Teachers select and use formative and summative assessments to inform teaching and learning.
- *Students* use technology tools to research and collect information.

Characteristics of the Developing Stage

- Teachers plan, manage, and facilitate student understanding of technologies and other *resources* best suited to support specific learning experiences.
- *Teachers* facilitate and guide students as they employ strategies to construct knowledge and promote creative thought; they model safe, ethical, legal, and healthy use of technology and information resources and help students address threats to security of technologies, data, and information.
- Teachers adapt or create *instructional activities* that allow students to collect and report information through a variety of products and formats. Teachers develop and conduct formative and summative assessments to inform teaching and learning.
- *Students* use technology tools to collect information, synthesize, and create new information in projects guided by their teachers. They explore issues of individual interest related to their learning.

Characteristics of the Proficient Stage

- Teachers demonstrate and model effective use of a variety of existing and emerging technology-based *resources* to encourage students to engage in a range of learning experiences.
- *Teachers* model creativity and knowledge construction and enable students to demonstrative creativity and innovation. Teachers advocate for and effectively instruct students in the safe, ethical, legal, and healthy use of technology and

information resources including emerging policies and practices related to issues such as security, intellectual property, and personal rights.
- Teachers design and customize *instructional activities* in response to students' learning styles, preferences, and abilities, so that students develop questions, propose solutions, and elicit feedback on their learning. Teachers provide students with various opportunities to demonstrate skills and knowledge to adapt future teaching and learning opportunities.
- *Students* use technology in support of collecting and synthesizing information, developing and demonstrating critical thinking, and solving authentic problems through the creation of projects they propose. Students use technology to plan, manage, and reflect on their own learning.

Characteristics of the Transformative Stage
- Teachers engage with students to explore and determine appropriate uses of existing and emerging technology-based *resources* so that students may effectively plan, manage, and evaluate their learning experiences.
- *Teachers* collaborate with and involve students as lead learners to engage in activities to promote creativity and innovation and explore complex issues. They engage students as active participants in the safe, ethical, legal, and healthy use of technology and information resources by encouraging them to establish policies and procedures for its use and determining methods to address its misuse.
- Teachers collaborate with students to identify and develop personalized *instructional activities* that allow students to formulate, evaluate, and test hypotheses to address complex problems that address real-world local and global issues with their teachers, other students, and outside experts and share their information for real-world application. Teachers engage students in the development and analysis of various opportunities to demonstrate skills and knowledge to orient future teaching and learning opportunities toward areas necessary for greatest student success.
- *Students* collaborate and communicate with their teachers, other students, and experts to select and use technology tools that align with learning preferences, styles, and content requirements in order to address real-world, complex problems with multiple answers or solutions. Students routinely monitor, evaluate, and adjust their own learning strategies and thinking.

The scenarios in Tables 1.6 through 1.9 illustrate each of the four aspects of effective integration as implemented by teachers at both early and later stages of proficiency in technology integration. As you read the scenarios, consider how the two teachers profiled in each table differ in their roles, their use of technology resources, the nature of their instruction, and the roles of their students.

If you suspect you're at one of the early stages in technology integration, don't worry! An analysis conducted for the U.S. Office of Technology revealed that it takes time to perfect the skills necessary to integrate technology effectively in the classroom (Mehlinger, 1997). If you are currently using this textbook as part of a typical college course, you may expect to reach one of the higher stages by the end of the course, even if you entered without prior knowledge of how to use computers and other digital technologies in the classroom. If you are taking this course early in your college career and continue to use your skills throughout your education courses, you can expect to be comfortably situated in the "Proficient" stage, as described by ISTE, by the time you graduate. Wouldn't it be wonderful if you were at that stage as you entered the classroom? And with more experience, we're confident that you will be one of those dynamic teachers who functions on a day-to-day basis in the transformative phase.

In order to become and remain a creative, transformative teacher, you will need to continue to learn about new and emerging technologies throughout your career. This book, while organized around the ISTE NETS-T, is, above all, intended to help you

Table 1.6 Use of Technology Resources

The classroom scenarios below demonstrate integration practices of teachers at both early and later stages of technology integration proficiency. As you read them, think about the *resources* available and how the teachers actually used them. How well are they matched to the instruction? What role do technology-based resources play?

Wallace McManus is introducing the scientific method to his fifth grade class. He has used his computer to create a worksheet for his students that identifies steps in the process, including formulating and testing hypotheses. Learning stations are set up around the room where students find containers of water, several dry and wet ingredients, a heating element, and some ice. Wallace plans to have the students propose hypotheses about how the different materials will react to each other and at different temperatures. The students will write down observations in their lab notebooks as they walk around the room and later record their responses on their worksheets. Wallace knows this is a good lab for students to experience, although inevitably some of them tend to be kind of messy while completing the various activities.	Cindy Garcia-Stamos is planning a science lab for her fifth grade students. She and her students have downloaded a map and satellite images from a website of the area surrounding their school. She has asked her students to develop a hypothesis about the potential effects of the proposed four-lane highway on the natural inhabitants of the grass, forest, and wetland areas near their school. She and her students collected soil and water samples during a recent field trip to key areas marked on their maps. They also took digital photos of the animals and plants in the areas they visited. The class will use several different probes to gather data from the samples and will track changes when new elements from the road development are added. Students are working in teams representing various stakeholder groups, including developers and business people in the community, local residents, and administrators at the school. They will use Internet resources to find additional data and then to develop multimedia presentations to share their results with the rest of their class. Students will propose at least one hypothesis about the highway development project and will use the data they collected and analyzed to support or refute that hypothesis. Cindy plans to put copies of the presentations on her class website.

Table 1.7 The Teacher's Role

The scenarios below illustrate the approaches of teachers at both early and later stages of technology integration proficiency. What roles do *teachers* play in these classrooms? Do they deliver instruction or do they use the content to engage students in collaborative problem solving and higher-order thinking? Is technology used to replicate traditional seat-based activities or does it support diverse learning styles and preferences in unique settings?

Principal Novella Mayberry is observing an American history lesson on the economic and political forces that led to The Great Depression. She and the teacher she is observing, Lynette Haines, have been friends and colleagues for a good part of their careers. Lynette's students are always well behaved and quiet as they furiously scribble down notes during her presentation. Novella notes that her friend is using presentation software to support her lectures and is fairly sure that the information is based on the same lecture notes she has used in the past. There's little interaction between Lynette and her students, or among the students themselves. When Lynette asks the students questions, they usually answer by nodding their heads. The class comes to a close as Lynette gives the next reading assignment and distributes a worksheet she has photocopied to the students.	The noise level in Shanika Wallace's fifth grade class is pretty high; students are scattered around the room in small groups while they work on a local history project. "It's the hum of learning," thinks Shanika as students are busy sharing ideas, asking each other questions, and working out solutions. Shanika and her students began this multi-day lesson by developing a rubric that would be used to assess the quality of both the content and the design of the project. This time, Shanika allowed the students to create their own teams of up to four students to work on different aspects of the project. Some students are editing short movies of interviews conducted with their parents and other relatives using the digital video camera, while others are taking digital pictures or scanning artifacts to help document how their community has changed over time. All students are required to respond to prompts that Shanika posts on the class blog every day. This enables Shanika to review their progress and identify any misconceptions, by the class or an individual, that require attention. When they're done with this unit, the movies, pictures, and documents will be housed on her class web page, and both the students and Shanika will assess the work with the rubric, using completed copies posted in each student's online portfolio.

Table 1.8 Nature of Instruction

As you read the two classroom scenarios below, illustrating teachers at both early and later stages of technology integration proficiency, focus on the *nature of the instruction* described in each. What kinds of problems do students encounter: well-structured or ill-structured? What kinds of assessments are used: norm-based or criterion-based? Closed-ended or open-ended? How integral is technology to the instruction?

Steven Tucker is head of the math department at Central High School and is proud of how much he has taught himself about computers and technology. He was one of the first teachers in his school to use presentation software and quickly learned on his own how to use the many animations, sounds, and slide backgrounds to spice up his lectures. He has typed all of his lecture notes, for each of the three different classes he teaches each year, in separate word-processing documents and has organized them in chronological sequence in his folder on the school's file server. He has also typed all of his worksheets and has created folders for the students in each of his classes. He feels that teaching has gotten easier, since he can easily pull up his lecture notes, show the corresponding presentation to his class, and have them access their homework assignments from the file server. They just print them out and turn them in. No more illegible student handwriting to decipher. He has even started using scannable test forms for his tests and that is saving him even more time.	The students in Brenda Williams' geometry class are putting the final touches on a semester-long project that has required them to think about how math is used in daily life. The goal of the project was to design a new park and fitness center for the neighborhood. Students used the Internet to find suitable lots in the area and then used GPS (global positioning system) devices to measure the irregularly shaped lots. Following this, students created scale drawings of the lots and determined the areas of all major sections using geometry software. The students' drawings had to include all of the key features for the proposed facility, including parking, an area for water runoff, and access and features for persons with disabilities. The students estimated building costs using one of the online calculators that Brenda found and linked from her class website. They then created a spreadsheet outlining those costs. Brenda divided her classes into teams of two or three students, and each team presented their ideas to the rest of the class over the last two days of the semester. The class rated each group's solution based on criteria such as cost, feasibility, and creativity.

Table 1.9 The Students' Role

As you read the scenarios below, illustrating practices of teachers at both early and later stages of technology integration, think about how the *students* are engaged in the instruction. On whom is the learning focused? *How* are the students engaged (see Figure 1.9)? How are individual differences supported and nurtured? How does technology support and motivate student activities?

Amy Ferrell's cell phone startles her and she jerks up in her seat. She keeps forgetting to turn off the ringer when she gets to school and it's now ringing deep insider her backpack. She fumbles to find the phone in the darkened class while only her best friend Laurie notices and gives her a smirking grin. Amy and Laurie are in English and are watching a movie version of *West Side Story,* which has taken several class periods. She and her classmates poke fun at the costumes, the funny language, and all the singing and dancing, but at least she understands this language better than when they read *Romeo and Juliet.* She knows she's supposed to understand and respect the works of Shakespeare, but it was hard reading. Some of the students were picked to read some of the scenes in class, like that famous balcony scene that had those lines she didn't realize were from Shakespeare—"wherefore art thou?" and "a rose by any other name"—but she didn't want to read the stilted language in class and didn't volunteer. At least her teacher has let the class choose between watching this movie or a production of the real play. She turns off her phone and settles back down into her seat to continue watching the movie.	Butch Simmons had never really been interested in English and hadn't looked forward to studying *Hamlet,* but his teacher, Mr. Fordham, made it interesting. They still had to read the play, which could be slow going at times, but Mr. Fordham had made it more interesting by explaining the social and political influences surrounding the play and using news websites to demonstrate how some of these same issues exist today. Of course, some of the drama kids wanted to act out scenes from the play, which Mr. Fordham let them do, but he had them record the scenes with their cell phones and then they posted the short videos on a class website in a section called "The Virtual Globe" after the famous theater. Some students had selected famous scenes, like Hamlet's soliloquy and had "translated" it into more modern speech—including a version Butch thought was really interesting that used some current slang. Another group of students had shown the same scene from three different movie versions of the play and had led a discussion about the decisions actors, directors, and other people like costume and set designers make in developing the mood and character of their performances. Butch was surprised to find out that Shakespeare's work had been so influenced by the current events of his time and how some of those same issues were still prevalent in the world. In the past, anything by Shakespeare had just seemed old and hard to understand.

Figure 1.9
Students engaged in technology-integrated learning experience.

identify the learning goals you have for yourself and your future students. Furthermore, it is designed to help you decide which technologies provide the best tools to reach those goals.

In this chapter, we introduced the ISTE standards around which this book is organized. In Chapter 2, we introduce you to our self-directed learning model, the GAME plan, used throughout this book. Remember, one of our primary goals is to help you become a self-directed learner who can successfully navigate the constantly changing environment of technology integration. Chapters 3 through 12 directly address the ISTE standards for technology proficiency for teachers. In these chapters, you will learn to use technology to support effective teaching and learning. Ultimately, the decision regarding how to use technology in the classroom is yours to make.

Chapter Summary

In this chapter we reviewed the history of technology integration within education. You were introduced to the ISTE NETS-T and encouraged to identify the technology standards that you will be expected to meet throughout your professional preparation and practice. You were introduced to stages of technology integration and asked to consider how different classroom practices (use of resources, role of teacher and students, and nature of instruction) change as one moves through the stages.

Throughout this book, you will consider how you will integrate technology into your own teaching. You'll think about how students will interact with technologies, the resources you will provide, the instructional activities you will use, and the role you will assume as a teacher in a technology-rich classroom. As a beginning teacher you may face some challenges—every teacher does. But as part of the first generation of teachers to enter the teaching profession already comfortable with computers and other digital technologies, you are probably more prepared than we were, as beginning teachers. We believe that you are ready to go to the next stage of technology integration within education: using technology as a natural part of the learning process, for both you and your students. Our goal is to help you develop innovative pedagogies in order to reach the goals you have set for yourself and your students.

APPLY to Practice

Technology in Education

1. Reflect on your own experiences using technology for learning. What technologies were used when you were a student? How were they used?
2. How were technology-related skills taught to you as a student? What was emphasized?
3. What skills and knowledge do you already possess to help you meet the challenges of effectively integrating technology into instruction? How did you learn those skills?
4. Discuss your experiences with your peers. Do you have similar experiences? What differences exist?

🖥 Web Resources and Activities

Visit the Education CourseMate website for this book to

- find more information about a wide number of Web 2.0 tools from the "Web 2.0 wiki repository" created by faculty and students at Purdue University;
- find examples of websites related to computer history, proficiency, and literacy;
- review the national standards for your content area(s); and
- visit ISTE's website at www.iste.org for a list of states that have adopted or modeled ISTE's technology standards.

YOUR PORTFOLIO

Identify the technology standards that you are expected to meet throughout your professional preparation and practice.

References

Allen, I. E., & Seaman, J. (2010). *Class differences: Online education in the United States, 2010*. Retrieved August 22, 2011 from http:// www.sloan-c.org/publications/survey/K-12_06.asp

Common Core State Standards Initiative. (2012). Retrieved April 2, 2012, from http://www.corestandards.org/

Dwyer, D. C., Ringstaff, C., & Sandholtz, J. H. (1991). Changes in teachers' beliefs and practices in technology-rich classrooms. *Educational Leadership, 48*(8), 45–52.

International Society for Technology in Education (ISTE). (2007). *National educational technology standards for students*. Eugene, OR: Author.

International Society for Technology in Education (ISTE). (2008a). *National educational technology standards for teachers*. Eugene, OR: Author.

International Society for Technology in Education (ISTE). (2008b). *About ISTE*. Eugene, OR: Author. Retrieved August 28, 2008 from http://www.iste.org/about-iste.aspx

Jonassen, D. H. (1996). *Computers in the classroom: Mindtools for critical thinking*. Columbus, OH: Merrill/Prentice Hall.

Mehlinger, H. D. (1997, June). The next step. *Electronic School*. Alexandria, VA: National School Board Association, A22–A24.

Mid-continent Research for Education and Learning (McREL). (2004). Content knowledge. Retrieved July 28, 2005 from http://www.mcrel.org/standards-benchmarks/docs/purpose.asp

National Commission on Excellence in Education. (1983). *A nation at risk: The imperative for educational reform*. Washington, DC: Government Printing Office.

National Education Association (NEA). (n.d.). *Guide to teaching online courses*. Retrieved April 2, 2012, from http://www.nea.org/assets/docs/onlineteachguide.pdf

Papert, S. (1980). *Mindstorms: Children, computers, and powerful ideas*. New York: Basic Books.

Partnership for 21st Century Skills. (2004). *Learning for the 21st century: A report and MILE guide for the 21st century*. Washington, DC: Author.

Partnership for 21st Century Skills. (2007). *Framework for 21st century learning*. Washington, DC: Author.

Picciano, A. G., & Seaman, J. (2007). *K-12 online learning: A survey of U. S. school district administrators*. Sloan Consortium. Retrieved August 22, 2011 from http://sloanconsortium.org/publications/freedownloads#Surveys

Pierson, M. E. (2001). Technology integration practice as a function of pedagogical expertise. *Journal of Research on Computing in Education, 33*, 413–430.

President's Panel on Educational Technology. (1997). *Report to the President on the use of technology to strengthen K-12 education in the United States*. Washington, DC: Author.

Simons, K. D., & Ertmer, P. A. (2006). Scaffolding disciplined inquiry in problem-based environments. *International Journal of Learning, 12*(6), 297–306.

U.S. Department of Education. (2000). *E-learning: Putting a world-class education at the fingertips of all children*. Washington, DC: Author.

U.S. Department of Education, Office of Educational Technology. (2010). *Transforming American education: Learning powered by technology*. National Educational Technology Plan, 2010. Retrieved March 24, 2010 from http://www.ed.gov/technology/netp-2010

Self-Directed Lifelong Learning

OUTCOMES

In this chapter, you will learn to

- Identify the components of **self-directed learning**;
- Apply the step-by-step actions of the **GAME plan for developing technology skills** including: self-assess technology skills and set goals; develop an action plan; and monitor and evaluate your professional growth;
- **Develop a portfolio** in which you document your developing technology competencies; and
- Design learning experiences and lessons that **support students' learning**.

ISTE Standards Addressed in Chapter 2

The ISTE standards emphasize the need for self-directed learning by both teachers and students. In this chapter, we introduce the GAME plan, a model of self-directed learning that helps you achieve this goal, specifically in terms of the skills required by the NETS-T and NETS-S. Additionally, we describe how your students can benefit from using the GAME plan. Finally, we help you begin the development of a portfolio that will enable you to evaluate your progress in achieving the NETS-T standards.

Think back to the first time you used technology. Undoubtedly, a wide variety of technologies were in use from the very moment you were born. You probably began to watch television and videos at a very young age. You may have played computer games before you even entered school. You probably began to use a word processor many years ago, perhaps even in elementary school. What about the first time you searched the web? Do you remember the first time you communicated with a friend via e-mail or sent a text? It's likely that your initial experiences with technology were somewhat different from your experiences today. And undoubtedly, your experiences today will be quite different from the ones you will have in the future.

This book is based on the premise that learning to teach, in general, and to teach with technology, specifically, are lifelong journeys. As a lifelong learner, much of your learning will be self-directed. That is, you will be responsible for locating learning opportunities and completing tasks to meet your own learning goals. So before we begin discussing the specifics of NETS-T, we introduce you to a self-directed learning model that we'll use throughout this book, a model we call the GAME plan. We describe how the GAME plan can structure both your own learning and that of your students. You will have the opportunity to think about what you already know about integrating technology into the classroom, as well as what you still need to know. We discuss the value of reflection in monitoring your learning and teaching. And finally, we introduce portfolios as a means to document your learning and professional growth.

Self-Directed Learning: Definition and Components

self-directed learning any increase in knowledge, skills, accomplishment, or personal development that an individual selects and brings about by his/her own efforts using any methods in any circumstance at any time; ability to set personal learning goals, take action to meet those goals, and evaluate the effectiveness of the learning processes and learning outcomes

metacognitive learners learners who "think about their thinking" and apply strategies to regulate and oversee their learning

Gibbons (2002) defined **self-directed learning** (SDL) as "'any increase in knowledge, skill, accomplishment, or personal development that an individual selects and brings about by his or her own efforts using any method in any circumstance at any time" (p. 2). You are self-directed anytime you learn a new skill (e.g., how to use a new digital video camera) or pursue more information about an intriguing topic (e.g., the features of a new cell phone that you are considering). As a future teacher you will be directing much of your own learning, so it is important to think about how you learn best. Learners who "think about their thinking" and apply strategies to regulate and oversee their learning are often referred to as **metacognitive learners**. Many of the activities in this book require you to be both metacognitive and self-directed.

Self-directed, metacognitive learners engage in three key processes: planning, monitoring, and evaluating their learning activities (Ertmer & Newby, 1996). During the planning stage, you, as a learner, determine your individual learning goals. You identify what you already know about the task at hand and develop a plan of attack, otherwise known as a learning strategy. You determine what is required by the task, plan your study time and, if possible, arrange for the best learning conditions. During the monitoring stage, you take action to implement your plan, and, as you engage in the task, reflect on whether you are making sufficient progress toward your goals. You determine whether the strategies you have chosen are working to accomplish the learning task effectively and efficiently. During the evaluating stage, you reflect on how well you have met your goals and determine whether you should modify your strategies for future learning tasks.

We have translated the recommendations for self-directed learning into the following four steps, which we call the **GAME** plan:

1. Set Goals.
2. Take Action to meet those goals.
3. Monitor progress toward achieving goals.
4. Evaluate whether the goals were achieved and Extend your learning to new situations.

Throughout this book, we'll use the GAME plan to guide your self-directed learning activities (see Figure 2.1). The GAME plan requires you to think about and take steps to direct your learning process, specifically while learning about technology and how to integrate it within your curriculum. The GAME plan enables you to customize your approach to learning tasks and to develop relevant

STORIES from Practice

Continual Learning

When I first went to college to become a teacher, I rarely saw a computer the entire four years I was there. My high school had only one computer—a TRS-80—which arrived during my senior year, and only the very best math students were allowed to use it, during which times they'd usually write little programs in BASIC that ran their names across the screen or something else equally silly. In college, one of my roommates purchased a Commodore-64 that had an external tape drive, but we used it mostly for playing games. I was never asked to use a computer in my classes, and none of my education courses even covered the topic. It wasn't until working on my master's degree in education that my advisor prompted me to investigate the two computers reserved for graduate students and suggested I use one for writing my thesis. Locked in a former closet were two new computers. One was a DOS-based machine that required a huge manual and a tiring array of key combinations I could barely remember just to apply formatting for different fonts, sizes, bold, italics, and the like. The other was one of the new Macintosh computers. The icons and menus were simple and intuitive. I was hooked.

That little Macintosh computer changed the way I worked and had a big impact on my use of technology in my classroom. I ended up writing my thesis about the growing field of educational software and used that information to help me find and evaluate software, beginning with drill-and-practice software in the early days up until now with the advanced web applications I develop and use to train other educators. Once in my classroom, I quickly learned how to put all my grades in a spreadsheet and I created an inventory program for all the books and materials I was required to keep up with. Most of the time I'd experiment by working through the horribly written print manuals that came with the software, with their frequent mistakes and confusing language. Those manuals were definitely not written by teachers!

As I progressed through my career, the computers and software that I used became more sophisticated. I was excited to move from the rudimentary word-processing program on my computer to page-layout software that I used to create newsletters to send home to parents. I created a monthly calendar that many parents said they kept on their refrigerators. The day I got my first e-mail account, I think my professional life shifted. I had to use a text-based e-mail program, very different from the helpful e-mail programs available now, and I would spend hours sending and receiving very short, text-only messages to other teachers across the country and probably around the globe. That experience prompted me to buy a computer for my home. I participated in some early bulletin boards for teachers where we'd "talk" about techniques we used in class and how we overcame particular problems. I now provide teachers with online learning opportunities that are far more advanced than those of my early bulletin board days. Currently, I get a lot of my information through eZines and some helpful websites, and I try to attend at least one educational technology conference each year. I know technology is going to keep evolving, and I don't want to know or understand it all. Instead, I focus my own professional growth on figuring out what technology is out there to help me do my job faster, smarter, and better.

Source: John Ross.

Goals	Action	Monitor	Evaluate and Extend
• What do I want to know or be able to do? • What do I already know about the topic? • How will I know if I have been successful?	• What information do I need to meet my goal? • How can I find the information I need? • What resources are needed? • What learning strategy will I use?	• Am I finding the information I need? • What patterns are emerging from the information sources? • Do I need to modify my action plan?	• Have I met my learning goals? If not, should I modify my goals or my learning strategies? • What will I do differently in the future?

Figure 2.1
The GAME plan.

skills that are important to you. Furthermore, the GAME plan is designed to prepare you for lifelong learning.

The GAME Plan for Self-Directed Learning about Technology: An Example

We've mentioned how computer technologies are constantly changing, but let's explore those ideas further in order to demonstrate the GAME plan technique. Imagine that your task is to evaluate a new technology to support student learning in your classroom. This actually is something many teachers do on a routine basis. If you were asked to do this, how would you go about tackling this task? For the purpose of this example, let's say you selected a global positioning system (GPS) as a technology that might be beneficial to your students' learning (see Figure 2.2).

Set Goals

The first step in the GAME plan is to *set goals*. At this stage, you'll identify what you need to know as specifically as possible. Imagine that you are a second grade teacher. You've heard that some teachers are exploring the use of global positioning systems to teach content at your grade level. You wonder whether this is something you should think about for your classroom. You'll also recall what you know about a GPS already, based on your experiences with the one in your car. You have some idea of the capabilities and limitations of a GPS but probably have a few questions related to your classroom needs: How have they been used in classrooms? How can they enhance student learning? Would they be appropriate for second graders? These kinds of questions help you focus your goals. You want to learn more about global positioning systems, but your information needs are quite different from those of a high school teacher or an engineer exploring the same topic. So you need to set sub-goals or objectives for your information search. Your sub-goals may be to:

- determine how the capabilities of a GPS can be used for instructional purposes in your classroom;
- determine how a GPS can enhance the learning experiences of second grade students; and
- identify the limitations of using these systems within the classroom.

Take Action

Next, you'll *take action*. You might ask colleagues at your school, at a professional conference, or by e-mail or Twitter, about their uses of a GPS. You might search the web for information on educational uses of this technology, using a variety of search tools, or specifically search websites for teachers. You may use search terms such as "global positioning systems lesson plans second grade." Although the web is a convenient source of information, you might include other approaches such as talking to knowledgeable experts, reading relevant blogs or wikis, or visiting a store with GPS units. The best way to locate relevant information is to use a combination of search methods.

Monitor

As you collect information, you'll *monitor* your learning progress. In all likelihood, you'll find a wide variety of information. You'll probably find information from organizations that are selling this technology as well as from schools and universities, government and professional organizations, and private individuals with an interest in the technology. Often, if you're searching the web, you'll find excerpts from conversations that took place on message boards and in user groups. You're even likely to find a few teacher blogs or lesson plans that describe how other teachers have used GPS

Figure 2.2
Teachers use GPS technologies to help their students collect and plot data from multiple points along a nearby river.

systems. Some of the information may be highly technical, other information may be applicable in vary narrow situations, and some of it is probably of questionable value. Each of these sources has its own particular approach to thinking and talking about the technology.

As you review the information you found, you'll ask yourself, "Am I finding the information I need?" In order to determine whether your action plan is working, you might classify the information you're finding according to each of your sub-goals outlined earlier (e.g., instructional capabilities, learning benefits, limitations). Based on the information you gathered, you'll determine whether you need to modify your action plan.

Evaluate and Extend

As you *evaluate* your learning, you will determine if you have successfully found the answers to your questions about using a GPS with your second graders. In other words, you will evaluate whether or not you have achieved your specific learning goals. If not, consider whether you need to modify your goals or your strategy. If your learning strategy has consisted of searching the web, perhaps you need to broaden your search to include colleagues and regional experts such as your science curriculum coordinator. Or if you have focused on the use of GPS with second-grade students, perhaps you need to expand your focus to encompass multiple grade levels. If your learning strategy has been successful, think about how you can *extend* the results of your learning to some future task. Have you learned something that will help you use a GPS in your classroom? Have you found a good source of information about current and emerging technologies that may be useful to you in the future? How can you share what you've learned?

Summary of GAME Plan

So, during the first phase in the GAME plan, you *set goals* for learning. After you've identified your learning goals, you need to *take action* to meet those goals. As you take action to achieve your goals, you'll need to *monitor* whether you are making sufficient progress and to determine whether the strategies you have chosen are working. Finally, during the *evaluate and extend* stage in self-directed learning, you'll determine whether you met your goals and reflect on whether your approach worked or if you should modify your strategies for the future. As you evaluate your learning progress, the most important question to ask is whether you were successful in meeting your goals.

Because technology is likely to change drastically over the span of your career, becoming a self-directed lifelong learner will enable you to respond in meaningful ways to these rapid and continuous changes. In addition, as a lifelong learner you will be able to keep your skills up to date, and better meet the changing needs of your students. Technology will constantly change, but your knowledge of how you learn won't. In the next section, we turn our attention to using the GAME plan for your own professional development. In particular, we focus on how you will develop the skills, required by the NETS-T, which will allow you to integrate technology into your classroom.

The GAME Plan for Learning to Integrate Technology

Learning, in general, and about technology specifically, is an ongoing process. In Chapter 1, you were asked to reflect on the four stages of technology integration development identified by ISTE. As you recall, the ISTE NETS-T standards are accompanied by a continuum that describes how teachers demonstrate each standard at the beginning, developing, proficient, and transformative stages of development. In Chapter 1, you also began to think about your personal vision for technology integration within your classroom. We all use different technologies in many ways every day, but using them for teaching and learning can be different. You may be able to text or tweet with the best of them, but how can you use those technologies in the classroom? What about social networking or cell phones? All of these technologies, and many that came before them, are now being used by teachers in classrooms across the country, even though they weren't originally designed for teaching and learning. However, someone first had to have a vision of how these tools would work and how to adapt them for classroom use.

In this section, we'll discuss a technique for turning your personal vision into a reality. The first step is to set specific goals for how you wish to achieve and implement your vision. Once your goals are identified, you will then take action, monitor your progress toward obtaining your goals, and evaluate the outcomes. Is your vision closer to being realized? What aspects should be addressed next? Let's consider each of these steps.

Set Goals and Take Action

Think for a while about the technology skills you already have. You can probably conduct information searches using the web, write papers using a word processor, and perform many other tasks using a computer. Think about how you developed these skills. Did you take a class? Did you learn from observation? Did you read a book or complete a tutorial? Did you ask questions of an expert or figure things out on your own? Did you do a combination of these things? A careful consideration of your responses to these questions will tell you a lot about how you, personally, can learn to use and apply technology throughout your career.

One simple approach to self-assessing your technology skills, as well as your skills related to using technology in your teaching, is to create a "technology resumé." Think about how resumés are used. We create them to convince people to hire us! They describe the skills and experiences we have that make us a good match for a position.

> **Jeffrey Ethridge**
>
> Prior to entering the classroom six years ago, my skills and use of technology were very limited. Since then, technology has become an integral part of my classroom as well as in society as a whole. It has changed my approach with how I prepare and deliver lessons for my students.
>
> Skills and Knowledge:
> - Ability to use e-mail to communicate with parents and colleagues for various reasons.
> - Utilize Microsoft Word and related applications such as cut and paste, spell-checkers, dictionaries, and thesauruses.
> - Design visual lecture aids with PowerPoint.
> - Interpret data of students from Study Island and our state assessment portal.
> - Make use of websites for classroom lessons such as virtual fieldtrips and live viewings of areas of study.
> - Explain how to research using the Internet as a source.
> - Maintain my class website and import documents for student use.
> - Construct tests and question banks in game show format.
>
> Experiences:
> - College course that explained and demonstrated the basic use of technology such as Microsoft Office applications.
> - Participated in many professional development sessions that have demonstrated the various technological tools that are available.
> - Small-group instruction to explain the functions of various software applications.
> - Instruction from colleagues who have a firm grasp on technology.
> - Experiment so that I gain a better understanding of the software and applications of the computer.
>
> Skills I want to learn:
> - How to utilize a BlackBerry completely.
> - Drawing and image-editing applications.
> - Incorporating streaming videos in my classroom presentations.
>
> Technology is a vital part of education and its benefits to the classroom teacher are priceless. It is imperative that I continue to grasp a better understanding of all the exciting advantages it allows for me as well as my students. I will continue to work on my skills through tutorials, personal instruction, and hands-on experiences.

© Jeffrey Ethridge. Used with permission.

Figure 2.3
Technology resumé.

Review the example in Figure 2.3 and consider developing a technology resumé yourself. Notice that the resumés go beyond simply listing hardware knowledge and software skills. To be relevant, and to help potential employers understand what you can do, describe the skills you have that are relevant to the job—in this case, teaching—so it's clear how you'll use technology in your classroom. Creating a resumé like this is often an eye-opening experience. Very often we don't give ourselves credit for what we can do. You may know how to use a word processor or search the web, but you may also know how to use these skills to find and create lessons you can use in just about any classroom. Realizing this can be powerful!

Another way to assess your skills is by taking a survey. You're likely to find different technology self-assessment surveys available online, some of which may be based on the NETS-T. Or you may just want to consider how well you already can demonstrate the different skills outlined in the NETS-T. The student standards (NETS-S) also can serve as a starting point for you to assess your own technology skills (see *Apply to Practice—Assessing Your Skills*). Although both the NETS-T and NETS-S are written in fairly general terms, ISTE, fortunately, has developed student technology profiles

APPLY to Practice

Assessing Your Skills

1. Rate yourself on the selected Student Performance Profiles below, using the four-point rating scale provided. Rate how well you can perform the given skill, from not at all to being able to teach it to someone else.
2. How did you do? Identify and discuss gaps between what you currently know and what you should know for each profile.
3. Visit the ISTE website or see Table 1.5 in Chapter 1 to view the NETS-S standards. Consider ways that you can help your students meet these required student standards.
4. View the complete list of 40 Student Performance Profiles on the ISTE website for examples of the types of activities students should be able to do to demonstrate competency of the required standards. Which of these skills do you already have? Which skills do you still need to learn?

Student Performance Profiles

Performance Profiles	I'm not familiar with this	I could do this with help	I can do this on my own	I could teach this to others
Illustrate and communicate original ideas and stories using digital tools and media-rich resources				
Identify, research, and collect data on an environmental issue using digital resources and propose a developmentally appropriate solution				
Engage in learning activities with learners from multiple cultures through e-mail and other electronic means				
In a collaborative work group, use a variety of technologies to produce a digital presentation or product in a curriculum area				
Find and evaluate information related to a current or historical person or event using digital resources				
Use simulations and graphical organizers to explore and depict patterns of growth such as the life cycles of plants and animals				
Demonstrate the safe and cooperative use of technology				
Independently apply digital tools and resources to address a variety of tasks and problems				
Communicate about technology using developmentally appropriate and accurate terminology				
Demonstrate the ability to navigate in virtual environments such as electronic books, simulation software, and websites				

Source: Profiles for Technology (ICT) Literate Students. Copyright © 2007, ISTE (International Society for Technology in Education), www.iste.org. All rights reserved. Reprinted by permission.

that provide specific examples of the types of activities students should be able to do to demonstrate competency in the required standards. ISTE readily admits that these profiles simply represent examples of the types of activities students should learn how to do, rather than a comprehensive curriculum, or even a minimally adequate one (2007, p. 1). Nonetheless, they do provide us with an idea of the types of activities that ISTE members consider appropriate for demonstrating mastery of their most recent set of technology standards for students. Luckily, there is a lot of overlap between NETS-T, around which this book is organized, and NETS-S. After all, you will be responsible for *modeling* the behaviors included in the student standards. Therefore, as you are considering ways that you can meet the required teacher standards, you can simultaneously consider ways to help your students meet the required student standards.

After reflecting on what you already know that will be applicable to integrating technology into your classroom, consider how you will take action to learn more. On one hand, you can attend formal university classes. You're probably enrolled in one right now. On the other hand, you can pursue informal learning opportunities by reading books, completing tutorials, asking others, or searching the web to find answers to your personal questions. As is highlighted in the *GAME plan—Learning New Software* on the next page, in today's Internet-connected world, numerous technology tutorials and examples of tried-and-true teaching strategies are available for you to access online. In other words, you can actually *use* technology to *learn more about* technology. As you well know, the Internet opens up a wide range of opportunities that you may not have locally. You can download lesson plans, or if you develop a lesson that works well, you can post it for others to download. "Teacher stores" and bookstores are at your fingertips. Educational journals and magazines, subscription e-newsletters, and eZines can deliver useful tips and new ideas to your desktop. And of course, you have access to a wealth of background resources and readings. You can find reference materials and others to talk with anytime, anywhere, with the click of a mouse.

If you've never explored the many online resources available for teachers, you may want to begin by with the *Apply to Practice—Exploring Online Resources for Teachers* activity or the resources listed on the textbook's Education CourseMate website. If your learning goals include learning new software applications, you can use the *GAME Plan—Learning New Software* to facilitate your learning or explore the tutorial links on the CourseMate website. As you review the online resources, think about which of these tools could assist you in meeting your learning goals. Now, this is not to suggest that you shouldn't also participate in local professional development opportunities; by all means, we encourage you to take advantage of the various opportunities available to you.

Monitoring and Evaluating Your Professional Growth

Both self-monitoring and self-evaluation are considered essential components of self-directed learning. The ability to monitor and evaluate your personal and professional decisions is enhanced through reflection both "in action" and "on action" (Schon, 1983). In reflecting "in action," you'll continually think about and modify your current behaviors based on the thought processes that occur simultaneously with the action. This relates to the monitor component in the GAME plan. When reflecting "on action" you'll think back over what you did and about what happened, why it happened, how the experience relates to other experiences, and how it should influence future behaviors—the evaluation component. As a reflective learner, you will think about what has been effective in the past, but also continually monitor and evaluate what is effective for you now.

As you develop your skills in using technology for teaching and learning, you can use several techniques to facilitate your own reflective practice. On one hand, the simple act of keeping a journal can support reflection. You may want to consider posting your reflections in a public forum such as a blog, but be careful what you say, especially about your students, school, or administrators. Examining case studies, or

THE GAME PLAN

Learning New Software

You can use the GAME plan to learn about all kinds of new hardware and software. With the many tutorials and resources available online, there's little reason to provide step-by-step how-to information in print. Directions for even the most common applications, like word-processing or spreadsheet software, can quickly become outdated. However, by harnessing your own self-directed learning skills, you can keep up with the changes in your favorite technologies and learn about new ones as they become available.

Set Goals

Identify a piece of software that you would like to learn. Or perhaps your goal is to learn how to use a *familiar* software program to perform tasks that are new to you. For example, you may know how to use presentation software to support your lectures, but you'd like to know how your students can use it to create interactive books.

Take Action

Determine steps you can take to meet your goal within a reasonable timeline. You can explore an online tutorial or read an instructional manual. Perhaps there is someone you know who has advanced skills with the software and can show you how to use it. Your school or library may even sponsor mini-workshops on the software.

Monitor

How well is the action you've selected helping you meet your goals? If you've selected an instructional manual, does it present things clearly and at an appropriate pace? Do workshops or other interactive settings meet your goals? Are you learning useful information or just reviewing skills you already know? Should you take a different approach?

Evaluate and Extend

How effective were your actions in meeting your goals? What did you learn that you can incorporate into your practice? What do you think you still need to learn? Would you take different actions when learning a new software application in the future?

APPLY to Practice

Exploring Online Resources for Teachers

1. Locate and review several teacher sites online. There are some sites listed on the Education CourseMate website and many state departments of education also provide lists for teachers in their states.
2. What do you notice about these sites? What are the common and unique characteristics of each? List your two favorite sites and describe why you selected them.
3. Share your favorites with your classmates. Visit the sites recommended by two of your classmates. How do they differ from yours?

teacher stories, such as those that appear in this text, also provides an opportunity for reflective thinking. Key to effective reflection is the ability to go beyond a simple description of what happened to consider *why* it happened, how it is connected to other events, and what adjustments should be made to subsequent actions based on this understanding.

STORIES *from Practice*

Then and Now

In my first year of teaching (many years ago!), I remember feeling terribly unprepared for the adventure ahead of me. Although I had graduated with honors, my classes had not prepared me for the realities of the classroom. Handling 30 first graders on my own was very different than student teaching. I wasn't sure how to prepare for the first day of class. Other teachers were making posters of classroom rules and nametags for the students. I watched them, and picked up any ideas I could. I tried talking to the other teachers in the building, but they seemed so confident that I was afraid I would seem incompetent if I expressed my insecurities. I desperately wished there was someone I could talk with about my teaching.

But I absolutely loved my job. The kids were fascinating, and my time in the classroom just flew by. So before and after school I'd sit in the library and pour through teacher magazines such as *Instructor*. I spent many afternoons in "teacher stores," selecting resources that would provide me with tips on teaching and classroom management. I spent lots of my hard-earned cash on materials that would help me through the next day in class. I even looked into classes at the local college, simply to give me an opportunity to discuss with peers and professors the day-to-day issues I was facing.

These days, all of these opportunities are available online—anytime, anywhere, with the click of a mouse. I have access to teacher resources, many of which are free. I can talk with peers and more experienced teachers, without worrying about them judging me. I can take college classes or shorter workshops. There are resources that help me learn, and resources that I can use with my students. If I had the online support available to teachers today, those initial classroom experiences would have been very different!

Source: Katherine Cennamo.

If you've never written a reflection on your own work, you may find it takes some time to develop the skill. Some experts (Hatton & Smith, 1995; Moon, 2001) describe different levels of reflection. When you first start writing reflections, you may find that they are more descriptive than reflective. A descriptive account may be a list of events that happened during a class or lesson. For example, a description of a class may include the following statement: "I used a PowerPoint presentation that included short segments from popular movies to help demonstrate different animation techniques."

It's important to be able to describe what has occurred, but reflection should go deeper. Reflection begins when you think about the events you have described and try to determine how you behaved, felt, or thought during those events. A reflective statement on the demonstration of animation techniques might include the following statement: "I thought I was really well prepared, but I discovered that I had way too many slides for my 15-minute presentation. I guess I just had not planned for the time it would take to actually show the movies in addition to making my speech. Because of this, I had to rush through the end. I don't think I made a very good impression!"

Of course, reflections can go even deeper. As you become more comfortable with writing reflections, you may be able to step back a bit and consider others' points of view. You may express your emotions or feelings, as well, and consider how those influenced the situation. In what some call **critical reflection**, you try to understand these different perspectives and use that understanding to set goals for your future behavior or learning. Continuing with the animation example, consider the level of reflection in the following, "I certainly learned something, though! I was probably a little too confident—I didn't actually practice the timing of the program, just ran through it to make sure all the slides loaded correctly and that the content was correct. Since I rushed through the demonstration, the class got a little confused and I had to

critical reflection
trying to understand different perspectives and using that understanding to set goals for future behavior or learning

> **TEACHSOURCE VIDEO**
>
> Go to the Education CourseMate website and watch the video, *Teacher Perspectives: Videotaping your Teaching*, to learn how this teacher uses it to monitor her teaching practices.
>
> 1. What does she learn from videotaping her classes? What are the benefits?
> 2. What additional information do you need in order to incorporate this practice in your own teaching?

spend a lot of time answering questions. Boy, in the future, I'll make sure I practice my presentation—out loud—and time myself. However, I did enjoy the process of developing the presentation. It was a lot of fun to find snippets from popular movies to demonstrate the animation techniques I talked about."

Video recorded lessons can provide valuable data to help you prepare a written reflection on the events portrayed. Even an audio recording can provide insight into your use of common pedagogical practices such as level of language use and questioning techniques. When writing a reflection, begin with a simple description of what happened in the lesson. After describing the events, try to analyze them to determine how and why you behaved as you did. Pay attention to how the actions of your students impacted your actions, and likewise, how your actions influenced the behaviors of your students. It can be a little difficult, at first, to watch yourself on video, but you'll soon appreciate its value once it helps you improve your practice and reach the needs of every student in your class.

You are now aware that a major focus of this book is to help you become a self-directed, lifelong learner. Self-directed learning implies that you take it upon yourself to become your own teacher, that you take the initiative to determine your goals for learning, implement strategies to meet those goals, and monitor your own learning. A key method for monitoring your learning is the process of self-reflection. In Chapter 12, you'll learn a systematic form of reflective practice known as action research, also referred to as teacher research or teacher inquiry. As you will learn, action research is a particularly effective way to monitor and evaluate classroom innovations, such as new technology uses. But for now, let's turn our attention to another common method used to evaluate and reflect on professional practice: the portfolio.

TECH TOOLS & TIPS

Video Recording Lessons for Reflection

Video recorded lessons are a required element for some certification programs, such as National Board Certification from the National Board for Professional Teaching Standards (NBPTS). While National Board certification is something you may consider later in your career, the tips and guidelines they provide are useful when recording lessons for your own self-reflection. (Adapted from http://www.nbpts.org/for_candidates/the_portfolio)

1 You are the focus. A best-case scenario is having someone else record your class. Whether or not this is possible, use a tripod and try to place it on a table or platform. Be sure the camera is at the level of the action. Determine the best angle ahead of time, use as wide an angle on the lens as possible, and keep the camera stationary through recording. All materials and resources integral to the lesson, including text and graphics on a chalkboard, whiteboard, or screen, should be legible on camera. Make a backup copy of every recording immediately!

2 The action has to be visible. Lighting is important both for video recording and digital pictures, so turn on all the lights or open all window blinds or curtains, and do not aim the camera directly into bright light sources, such as a wall containing many windows. If using a projector, try different light settings to capture both information on the screen and interactions in the classroom.

3 Record the best audio possible. Audio is critical, and difficult, to capture in a classroom setting. The built-in microphone on the video camera might work well but the only way to determine what works best is to do a test recording. Often it is better to use an external microphone connected to the camera, perhaps wearing a wireless microphone in a small-group setting, or using a microphone designed for recording in a large room, such as a PZM® microphone. Place the microphone as central to your teaching area as possible. Eliminate extraneous noises, such as fans, air conditioning units, or even pumps in fish tanks.

Source: Adapted from http://www.nbpts.org/for_candidates/the_portfolio

Documenting Growth and Competency Through Portfolios

Portfolios have been used to document student progress for years. Perhaps you or your teachers maintained a portfolio documenting your learning as you progressed through elementary school. You may have attended a school that utilized writing portfolios. Or perhaps you prepared an art portfolio in high school. From these experiences, you know that a portfolio is an organized collection of artifacts that are compiled for a specific purpose. In many cases, portfolios are used to demonstrate your skills and knowledge to others. Teachers, especially, have been using portfolios for many years to document their skills and growth—from their initial teacher preparation programs through their teaching careers. Since portfolios can be used to illustrate progress over time, they provide a means to reflect on, facilitate, and document your individual learning.

Educators describe using portfolios in many different ways. For the purposes of this book, consider the following three categories of portfolio use:

- *demonstrate* compliance with specific requirements so that others can *assess* your skills, as in a portfolio that you would create to document your attainment of course goals or state standards or to obtain teacher certification or licensure (referred to as assessment portfolios);
- *present* and possibly market your skills to others, as in a portfolio that you would use to showcase your skills during your job search process (referred to as employment portfolios); and
- *reflect* on your current skills and future learning needs to guide your individual learning and professional development (referred to as professional development portfolios).

The popularity of **assessment portfolios** is due largely to the belief that they represent an authentic form of assessing learning. Chapter 7 includes information on how you can use portfolios to assess your students; here we focus on how *your* skills might be assessed or evaluated. Assessment portfolios can differ in the amount of control you have over selecting and arranging the artifacts within them. Often, you are required to include specific artifacts in order to demonstrate how you meet particular objectives or standards for assessment. Typically, such portfolios are evaluated using predetermined rubrics. In some cases, you may build your portfolio as you complete specific requirements of a curriculum. Individual artifacts may be evaluated as they are developed as part of regular class work. In other cases, you may have the freedom to select artifacts that you believe represent your best work. In this case, you are responsible for describing how you think a particular artifact demonstrates mastery of a standard or course objective. Combining artifacts of early work with well-polished examples is one way to illustrate growth over time.

Employment portfolios showcase achievement in relation to a desired position or profession. Typically, you have complete control over the look and feel of this type of portfolio as well as the artifacts included. An employment portfolio should represent you well, demonstrating who you are at this particular point in time. The goal is to showcase your skills, perhaps including things like the technology resumé described earlier (see Figure 2.3). As you develop an employment portfolio, think about your audience and try to create a persuasive document that reflects how you are best suited for the position for which you are applying.

Whereas the employment portfolio is developed for future employers and the assessment portfolio is developed for your teachers, the **professional development portfolio** is for you. One of the most rewarding uses of a portfolio is as a tool for individual learning and professional development. Portfolios provide a place for you to collect and reflect on artifacts that document your professional growth over time.

assessment portfolios
a collection of artifacts used to assess student learning; an authentic representation of student learning

employment portfolios
a presentation of artifacts demonstrating competencies in relation to a desired position or profession

professional development portfolio
a personal tool for individual learning that provides a place for collecting and reflecting on artifacts documenting professional growth over time

You may even use them to identify areas for future learning and then to document your progress toward those learning goals. These portfolios provide a place to celebrate your uniqueness while focusing on lifelong, self-directed learning. In all likelihood, the assessment and employment portfolios will represent a subset of your professional development portfolio.

At the end of each chapter in this book, you will notice a *Your portfolio* box, where you will be asked to create artifacts that document your progress toward meeting the standards outlined by the ISTE NETS-T. This assessment portfolio can demonstrate your developing competencies in technology integration and showcase for prospective employers how you meet the NETS-T.

Portfolio Development Tools

Although there are several forms of portfolio development software, no specialized software is needed. Just about any software application that can link pages (or artifacts) can be used. The pages can be as simple as a series of word-processed documents that link to other artifacts. Tools that have been used to develop portfolios include:

- presentation software;
- word-processing or page-layout software;
- multimedia authoring software including audio, video, and podcasting tools;
- WYSIWYG (what you see is what you get) or HTML generators for creating web pages;
- blogs;
- content management systems;
- commercial portfolio development products (e.g., TaskStream);
- proprietary portfolio products, often developed by colleges or universities; and
- open source tools, such as OpenOffice or GoogleDocs.

You should use caution when selecting tools to create artifacts for your portfolio, as well as the actual portfolio development tools, to ensure that you can continue to access and use your portfolio over time. For example, some of us who have been teaching for a while may have old files saved on floppy disks, yet no longer have access to a computer with a floppy drive. This type of problem occurs routinely as software companies discontinue applications or new hardware and software standards are developed. As you select among potential development tools, you may want to consider the following factors:

- *Your skills.* We encourage you to increase your skills but it's important to select a tool that can help you create your portfolio without being so hard you spend all your time learning how to use it.
- *Ease with which you can cross-reference artifacts.* It should be easy to create and edit links among the items in your portfolio and to provide for simple navigation to all areas within your portfolio.
- *Ability to integrate information from a variety of formats.* Make sure all exhibits of your work (e.g., audio, video, images, documents in various formats) can be displayed easily with appropriate fidelity.
- *Access to the tool throughout your career.* Specialized portfolio development software isn't the best tool choice if you won't have access to it after you graduate. If your college or university does use such a system, consider how the artifacts in your portfolio can be presented in an alternative method, whether on a web page or in a series of linked documents.
- *Ability to display portfolio contents in ways that will be useful for multiple purposes and audiences.* Consider the many uses you may have for your portfolio. You may want to post an employment portfolio on the web (and post a link to it on Facebook or LinkedIn) for potential employers to view and also to create a print version to put in a notebook to take to interviews.

- *Ease of updating.* For a portfolio to be useful over time it must be dynamic. Select a tool that permits you to update pages quickly, again focusing on presenting your accomplishments to the intended audience rather than manipulating a complex tool.
- *Need for confidentiality.* If you want to keep any of the materials private, such as your personal reflections or sensitive information about students with whom you work, you may need to use a program that allows password protection of selected content, especially if you choose to post your portfolio on the web.

When preparing an *assessment* portfolio, which you might be doing if you're using this book in a class, you need to assemble a collection of documents and artifacts that demonstrate the achievement of specific standards or objectives. Often, the required items, as well as the format and organization, are mandated by someone else, like your teacher or professor. When preparing an *employment* portfolio, you may be using artifacts from this book, such as the technology resumé mentioned earlier, to showcase your skills. There, too, you may want to demonstrate how the artifacts in your portfolio demonstrate your mastery of standards, such as the ISTE NETS-T. Of course, the artifacts from this course can be used as the beginning of your *professional development* portfolio, where you compile artifacts for your own learning and reflective practice. These types of portfolios are never really completed. By far, the best approach is to create a professional development portfolio as a tool for lifelong learning and then to use a selected subset of that information, as needed, for assessment and employment portfolios. Whatever way you decide to go, this book can get you started.

Steps in Portfolio Development

No matter what type of portfolio you develop, there are several steps in the process (see Figure 2.4). You need to perform the following tasks:

1. Define your purpose, audience, distribution medium, and development tool.
2. Design your portfolio organization and layout.
3. Develop the portfolio.
4. Deliver it to its intended audience.

Define

During the initial phase of portfolio development, you need to define the purpose and audience for your portfolio, as these factors will influence the content and the look of the finished product. The audience for an assessment portfolio consists of the evaluators of the product. When in college, this most likely will be your professors; when in the workplace, it may be a district or school technology coordinator charged with documenting your competency on standards mandated by the state or school district. You may be the only audience for a professional development portfolio, or you may decide to share it with colleagues in order to stimulate conversations around specific professional development issues. Most professional development portfolios don't need a lot of "bells and whistles." And finally, your future employers are the logical audience for your employment portfolio, so you want this type of portfolio to be as polished as possible.

Next, you need to decide on a distribution medium and corresponding development tool. Do you want to distribute your portfolio on CDs, post it on the web, create a notebook, or have the option of sharing any of these formats? Should you create it using a word processor, web development software, a database program, presentation software, or one of the other options mentioned above? In the previous section, we discussed several factors that you may need to consider as you make your decision.

Portfolio Development

Define
- Purpose and audience
- Distribution medium
  - **Analog:** Work samples, written reflections, letters, videotapes, and pictures
  - **Digital:** CD, DVD, web, etc.
- Development tool

Design
- Content
  - Select audience-appropriate documents and artifacts that demonstrate your achievement of specific standards or objectives.
- Arrangement
  - **Use of folders/directories:** To make retrieval and updating easy
  - **Navigation:** Use a table of contents or menus to make location of artifacts easy for users to find
  - **Layout:** To draw attention to important items
- Organization based on your chosen purpose

Develop
- Format artifacts for your distribution medium
  - Convert artifacts (documents, pictures, work samples, etc.) to your selected format.
- Reflections based on three key questions
  - What? So What? Now what?

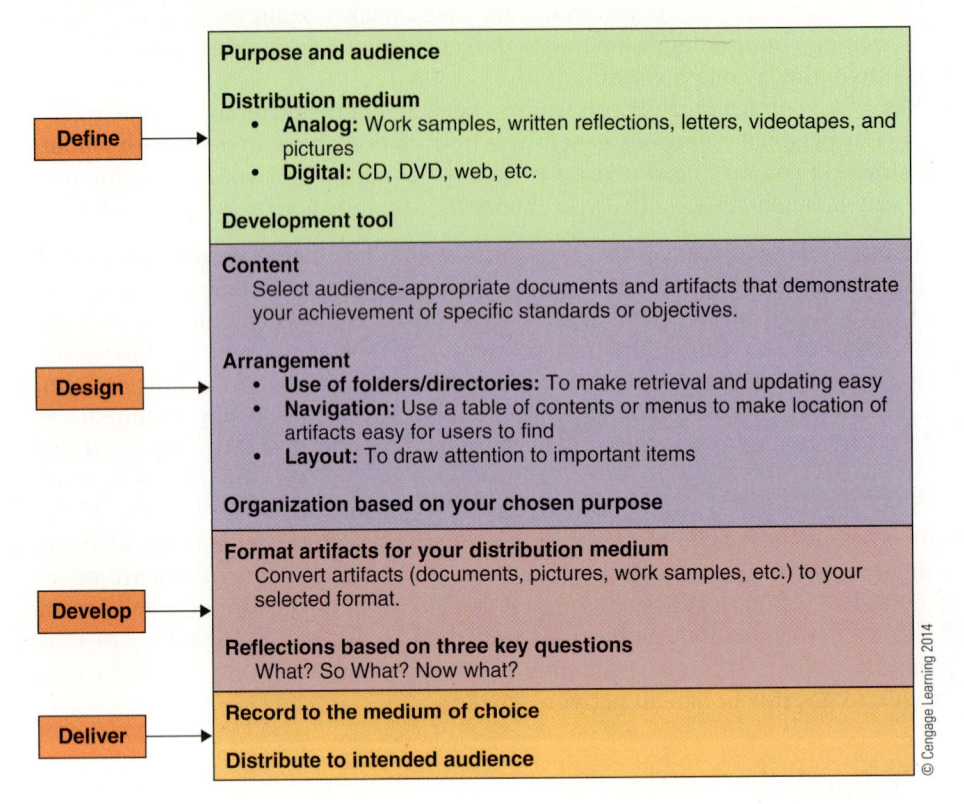

Deliver
- Record to the medium of choice
- Distribute to intended audience

© Cengage Learning 2014

Figure 2.4
Steps in portfolio development.

Design

Once you have determined your audience, purpose, distribution medium, and development tool, you can select audience-appropriate artifacts and design the overall organization of your portfolio. In designing your portfolio, think about what you want to include and why you want to include it. Do you want to include video clips of your teaching? Interviews with your supervising teacher or students? Examples of student work? Lesson plans? As you identify the items you want to include, also consider what you may want to include in the future. This may mean designating space or a placeholder for items yet to be developed. At a minimum, portfolios consist of a collection of work samples. They may include paper items, videos, pictures, and projects.

Once you decide what you want to include in the portfolio, you need to decide on the best way to organize the materials. In terms of grouping and sequencing material, consider your purpose and audience. A chronological order of materials may be best if you're trying to demonstrate growth, or you may be required to organize your artifacts based on a rubric or checklist. If you are trying to demonstrate that you have met certain standards, such as the ISTE NETS-T, you may group artifacts by each major standard, sometimes linking to, or replicating, artifacts that cover more than one standard.

Use common protocols for the medium you have selected to help people understand what is in your portfolio and how they can find it (see Figure 2.5). For example, books use tables of contents and indices to help organize information. In a paper-based notebook, you may want to use dividers or tabs to organize your artifacts into sections that clearly identify the material within. Web pages and multimedia tools use navigation bars, buttons, and links. A consistent series of menus or links on every screen/page of your portfolio can help users understand where they are, what they are seeing, and how to navigate to the next section they'd like to review. Concept-mapping or flowcharting software can prove useful as you plan the organization of your portfolio. Like video and multimedia developers, you may want to create a storyboard of your proposed organization first. Depending on the size and scope of your portfolio, you may just need to create a list or outline. As you develop your organizing plan, consider the following factors:

- *How will you store and find the materials you need to create the portfolio?* Keep in mind that you will have to locate, retrieve, and update many of the items in your portfolio. Consider the use of folders or subdirectories on your computer to help you organize this process, and back up your work often.
- *How will the audience navigate through the artifacts?* The use of one or more menu pages may help someone viewing your portfolio easily locate sections of particular interest. It is better to use multiple pages with fewer topics per page than to confuse your audience by attempting to fit everything into a small number of pages.

Figure 2.5
Examples of different portfolio designs.

Figure 2.5
(Continued)

- *How will you direct the audience's attention to important items within a page?* You want the audience to have a clear picture of what you are attempting to convey. Consistent page layouts will help others locate items within a page, while formatting features can be used to direct attention to specific items on a page.
- *How will you tell your complete story?* A portfolio is often more than just a collection of artifacts. For many, reflections are an essential part of a portfolio that help your audience understand what you selected and why. It is easier to collect your artifacts as they are being made, but if you plan to include reflective pieces, plan for them in your design so they can be added easily.

Develop

When the artifacts have been collected and the layout planned, it's time to develop the actual portfolio. If you're creating a digital portfolio, non-digital artifacts need to be converted to a digital format. This can involve photographing 3-dimensional items with a digital camera or scanning 2-dimensional objects (see Figure 2.6). Audio and video clips may need to be imported into your computer or digitized. Although it may sound like a lot of work to compile a portfolio, it can be rewarding to collect your work in one place.

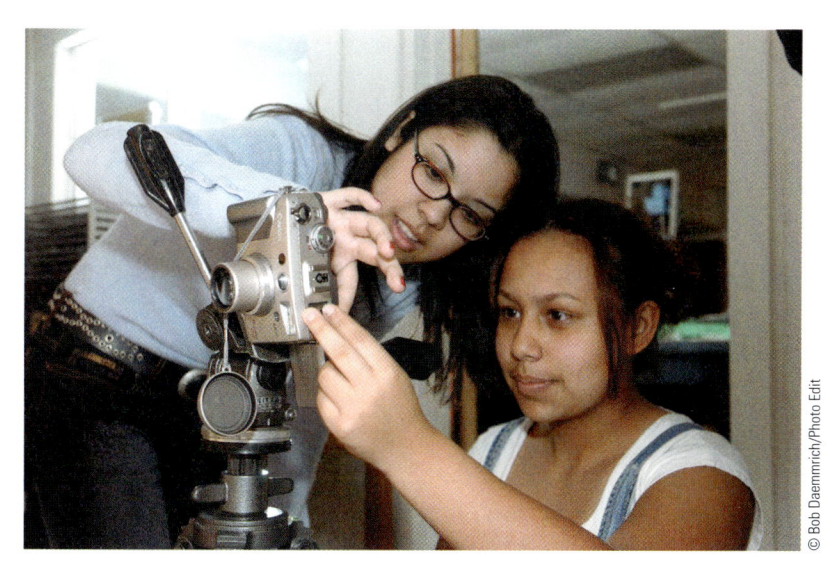

Figure 2.6
3-dimensional items can be photographed for inclusion in a digital portfolio.

You can also simplify the process by collecting artifacts as they are generated and later selecting the most appropriate ones for inclusion in your portfolio. For example, if you receive a positive letter or e-mail from a teacher or colleague, save a copy in a designated portfolio file or directory and later determine how it can be included. The same goes for pictures or videos you may collect that capture you working with students or examples of lesson plans or assignments you complete in your courses. You're not creating a scrapbook of every little detail of your life, so if you can save artifacts in one place as they are created, you can then select the best example to include at a later date.

Typically, portfolios include reflective comments about how each piece fits into the larger framework of your learning progress. Reflections in a portfolio tend to be somewhat formal, compared to the personal reflections we described earlier. As you craft reflections for your portfolio (whether in written, audio, or video format), keep in mind a few pointers:

- Write in first person.
- Read your reflections out loud, to yourself or a friend, to determine whether they are clear and express the level of reflection you desire.
- If the reflection is primarily for someone else, focus on describing the artifact and explaining why it is there.
- If the reflection is primarily for you, focus on crafting a critical reflection that helps further your professional growth.

When reflections are included in professional development portfolios, they typically address three key questions: What? So what? and Now what? (Kottkamp, 1990). "What" refers to the item selected for inclusion in the portfolio. "So what" refers to your rationale for selecting the artifact. In other words, why did you include the artifact? What does it mean to you and your personal growth? "Now what," requires you to look ahead and set new goals for future learning and professional development. You may want to include a more polished version of your reflections and learning goals in your assessment and employment portfolios as well. For example, when preparing an assessment portfolio, consider how each item illustrates your achievement of the necessary standards or objectives. When preparing an employment portfolio, describe how each item illustrates specific skills.

Once the artifacts have been assembled, they can be organized and linked as needed. For example, one artifact may be used to demonstrate several competencies. Also, be sure to link your personal reflections to the relevant artifacts.

Deliver

When you're creating an employment or assessment portfolio, you will need to present it to its intended audience. Digital portfolios can be distributed via the web, CDs, DVDs, or other storage media. Artifacts from the portfolios can even be printed and distributed in a notebook or collected in folders, which can be helpful in job interviews or other settings in which you don't have ready access to a computer.

Summary of Portfolio Development

As you go through this book, we suggest that you develop your own digital portfolio of artifacts to demonstrate your skills in integrating technology for teaching and learning. You can find and download a Portfolio Template on the CourseMate website. You will find that digital portfolios have several advantages over conventional paper-based portfolios. These advantages include:

- easy to control as all artifacts can be conveniently located in one digital space;
- easy to cross-reference and link items;
- easy to repurpose the content to meet an alternative goal, for example to use artifacts collected for professional development for an employment or assessment portfolio;
- easy to store, as they take up less physical storage space than conventional collections; and
- easy to distribute to individuals who want to view your work.

THE GAME PLAN

Portfolio Examples

In this book, you are encouraged to develop a portfolio to demonstrate your mastery of the ISTE NETS-T by completing the "Your Portfolio" activities at the end of each chapter.

Set Goals

Determine the type of portfolio to meet your current goals. Whether you are demonstrating mastery of required competencies, documenting your own personal and professional development, or just entering the teaching field, there are many examples to support your specific purposes.

Take Action

Find examples of employment, assessment, and professional development portfolios. Ask your friends or teachers if they have examples. There are also several excellent portfolio resources on the web.

Monitor

Are you finding examples of each type? Which examples best match your goal? Do you need to locate additional examples before you create a portfolio for your own use?

Evaluate and Extend

Classify the examples that you find as assessment, employment, professional development, or "other" portfolios. What are some distinguishing characteristics of each type? What characteristics or strategies do you think you might adopt or adapt for your own use? Discuss your conclusions with your peers to determine how you might generate a portfolio to meet your goal.

The GAME Plan for Supporting Student Learning

As a teacher, you'll have a variety of responsibilities, but your main duties will undoubtedly be concerned with facilitating student learning. The next several chapters discuss how you can design, deliver, and evaluate your instruction using the structure provided by the GAME plan. In essence, you should have a GAME plan not only for your own self-directed learning, but also for your students' learning. In the following discussion, we provide a brief overview of each step, organized by the questions in Table 2.1.

Setting Goals for Student Learning

As noted earlier, the first stage of the GAME plan is to set goals. This is true for your own self-directed learning as well as your students' learning. Strategic learners begin the goal-setting process by analyzing the task at hand and considering what they already know that can be useful in obtaining their new learning goals. Based on what they know about themselves and the task, they determine the best strategy to achieve those goals. Strategic teachers take a similar approach. When setting goals for your students, begin identifying what they already know and what they need to know about that content in order to determine a strategy to achieve those goals. When you set goals for your student' learning, you answer questions similar to those posed during your own learning process.

- What do my students need to know?
- What do my students already know that can help them meet their learning goals?
- How will I know if they have been successful?

What your students need to know is influenced by a variety of factors, including their individual learning needs. Past performance data can help you clearly identify students' existing knowledge, as well as knowledge deficits. You need to consider their existing

Table 2.1 — GAME Plan for Personal and Student Learning

Steps	Personal Plans to Promote My Learning	Lesson Plans to Promote My Students' Learning
Goals	• What do I want to know or be able to do? • What do I already know about the topic? • How will I know if I have been successful?	• What do my students need to know or be able to do? • What do my students already know that can help them meet the goals of instruction? • How will I know if they have been successful?
Action	• What information do I need to meet my goal? • What learning strategy will I use? • What resources are needed?	• What content information do my students need? • What instructional strategy will I use? • What resources do my students need?
Monitor	• Am I finding the information I need? • What patterns are emerging from the information sources? • Do I need to modify my action plan?	• Are my students understanding the information and mastering the skills they need? • What patterns are emerging from my students' responses? • Should I modify my lesson and unit plans?
Evaluate and Extend	• Have I met my learning goals? • If not, should I modify my goals or my learning strategies? • What will I do differently in the future?	• Did my lesson or unit plan work? • If not, should I modify the goals, the assessment, or my instructional strategies? • What should I do differently in the future?

© Cengage Learning 2014

TECH TOOLS & TIPS

Supporting Students' Efforts to Be Self-Directed

One way to involve students of all ages directly in planning, monitoring, and evaluating their learning activities and sequences is through the use of KWHL charts (see Figure 2.7). A KWHL chart requires students to note information they **K**now about a particular topic, information they **W**ant to learn about that topic, **H**ow they plan to learn the information, and then report what they **L**earned after their efforts are completed.

The creation of a KWHL chart can be supported by a variety of common technologies and is a beneficial activity for both appropriate individuals and groups. Using a KWHL chart, you can engage students in identifying their prior knowledge on the topic (what they Know) and what they need to know (what they Want to learn). Students and teachers can work together to plan "How" they will obtain the knowledge they need. These charts are also useful in monitoring learning, as students can be encouraged to list what they have learned in the L column of the charts. Students should be encouraged to evaluate their learning processes as well. After the lesson is over, ask them to reflect on what they have learned about themselves as learners as well as what they have learned about the content. Although a useful activity on its own, the KWHL chart can also be used to guide student reflections in a portfolio and provide evidence of student growth.

KWHL Chart

What do you KNOW?	What do you WANT to know?	HOW will you learn?	What did you LEARN?

Figure 2.7
KWHL chart.

skills and knowledge, but you also need to take into account what you know about how your students learn best, what motivates them, and the environmental factors that may impact their success. As highlighted in the *Tech Tools and Tips—Supporting Students's Efforts to Be Self-Directed*, a KWHL chart can be a useful way for students to actively participate in goal-setting and can help you identify the gap between what students know and what they need to know.

Your students' learning goals also will be influenced by standards—certainly content standards, and in some states technology standards will influence your instruction. There also will be accountability goals and for most students that means they must perform acceptably on assessments that measure their mastery of those content standards. In Chapter 7, you will learn that by considering your assessments *at the same time* as you set learning goals, you will be in a better position to identify the actions that you need to take to ensure your students develop the skills needed to meet their goals.

Taking Action by Providing Learning Experiences

The actions you take in the GAME plan for your students' learning involve designing and arranging experiences that help them meet their learning goals—in other words, developing instructional activities. The methods you select to facilitate learning will be impacted by the skills and knowledge required by the content you are addressing, the tools and resources you have available, your own teaching style, your students' learning preferences, as well as the types of assessments used to monitor student learning. As you plan the Action you will take to support your students in meeting their learning goals, you will develop lesson plans and associated management strategies. Consider questions such as:

- What content information do my students need?
- What instructional strategy will I use?
- What resources do my students need?

Instructional planning often begins by identifying the content students will need to access in order to achieve the learning goals. After you collect the content information, you'll need to decide how to facilitate your students' understanding of it. As you plan instructional events, this book provides helpful information on strategies that can help you select teaching methods and resources to meet your students' needs. And, of course, you'll need to consider what technology and resources can be used to assist students in understanding the new information.

In Chapter 3, we introduce the principles of authentic instruction as a framework for planning instructional activities that facilitate the development of critical and creative thinking skills. In Chapter 4, we describe how technologies can support the development of creative thinking skills by serving in the roles of tutor, mindtool, or support for conversation, while Chapter 8 focuses on selecting resources in support of student learning. When it comes to actually implementing learning activities, you also need to consider how you will manage your students' instructional experiences. Management considerations, including how you will group learners, are addressed in Chapter 5.

Most of the methods you will explore in this book can be adapted and combined across a variety of content areas and instructional settings. You can also explore content-specific teaching methods and resources for English language learners, language arts, foreign language, math, science, social studies, health/physical education, visual arts, and music in the content area supplement included with this textbook.

Monitoring Student Progress

Just as you must monitor your own learning goals and actions, you must help your students monitor how well they are meeting their learning goals using a variety of formal and informal means. In the rush to "cover" the curriculum, many teachers feel this important step is often overlooked or left out. The rise in popularity of formative assessment strategies re-emphasizes that we need to help students develop skills to monitor their own learning. As you help your students monitor their learning progress, you'll want to consider questions such as:

- Are my students understanding the content and mastering the skills they need?
- What patterns are emerging from my students' responses?
- Should I modify my lesson and unit plans?

Earlier in this chapter, we introduced Schon's (1983) ideas of "reflection-in-action" and "reflection-on-action." The monitoring process involves both forms of reflection. You and your students will reflect "on" their performances in their formal assessments. And you and your students will reflect "in action" as you go about your day-to-day activities in the classroom. Chapter 7 explores in more detail the important role assessments play in monitoring student learning. When they are used to inform instruction or to help students monitor their own learning, they are often referred to as **formative assessments**.

As a teacher, you have access to a wide variety of data on your students' performances, in addition to their scores on formal assessments. You observe their interactions with other students. You hear their responses during group discussions. You see

formative assessments assessment used during instruction to monitor student progress toward mastering learning goals

the strategies they use to solve problems and their reactions to classroom events. Each of these sources of data should contribute to the ongoing monitoring of your students' progress toward meeting their learning goals. You'll make ongoing modifications to your instructional strategies in response to the learning progress of your students. And your students will make ongoing modifications to their learning strategies as they monitor their own progress.

Evaluating Instructional Effectiveness

Evaluating the effectiveness of your instruction is a critical component of the GAME plan for student learning. Just because you have provided instruction, or facilitated learning activities, it doesn't mean that all of your students met the learning goals. Exposure to topics is not enough if your students can't develop new understandings or demonstrate new skills. Evaluation is the key to determining how successful your instruction has been, as well as which resources and methods will most likely be successful in the future. In evaluating the effectiveness of your instruction, you'll consider assessment data of course, but you'll also want to make note of what you have learned about your teaching. Consider questions such as:

- Did my lesson or unit plan work?
- Should I modify the goals, the assessment, or my instructional strategies?
- What should I do differently in the future?

Similar to this stage in your own self-directed learning process, during the Evaluate stage in the instructional cycle, you'll determine whether your instruction was effective in helping your students meet the learning goals. As in monitoring student learning, you will consider a variety of formal and informal data as you evaluate the effectiveness of your instruction. In Chapter 7, you will learn more about assessments and the role data can play in ensuring that your students develop the skills needed to meet their goals. Consider learners' performances and your own subjective reaction to the lesson. The resources you use must match the needs of the curriculum and content standards while also matching the preferences and skill levels of your students. Your assessments, too, must adequately allow students to demonstrate their new skills and understandings. If the activities, resources, and assessments you selected were not effective, you should determine how to modify them in the future. At this stage, you are primarily concerned with the questions of "Did it work?" and "How can it be improved in the future?" Make note of what you have learned about yourself as a teacher as you planned and implemented the lesson. This self-awareness, or reflection-on-action (Schon, 1983) is an important part of a teacher's professional development.

Chapter Summary

In this chapter, we introduced the idea of self-directed learning. We encouraged you to set learning goals, take action to achieve those goals, monitor your learning progress, and evaluate and extend your learning to similar situations in a process we call the GAME plan. You accomplished some of the steps in the GAME plan by exploring the basic technology skills you and your students must have and completing a self-assessment of your current skills and knowledge. We asked you to think about how you learned to use technology in the past in order to discover ways that you might best learn about it in the future. You learned that effective professionals continually reflect on their practice in order to monitor and evaluate their actions. Finally, we introduced the use of portfolios as a means of supporting your personal growth over time and encouraged you to create your own digital portfolio. We also used the structure provided by the GAME plan to illustrate how you can create meaningful lessons that build on and support students' self-directed learning.

In the next chapter, we turn our attention to ways that you can use your knowledge of teaching, learning, and technology to facilitate meaningful experiences for your students. Although you probably have known many excellent teachers, you may have few role models in the area of technology integration. As you lead the way and break new ground in the world of technology integration, self-directed learning will be essential. You and your peers have the opportunity to be the leaders in these efforts!

Web Resources and Activities

Visit the Education CourseMate website for this book to

- view a tutorial on how to search the web;
- see a list of self-assessment tools you can use to determine your current level of technology skills;
- see a list of online tutorials from a number of hardware and software developers;
- review examples of portfolios created with a variety of web development tools and links to step-by-step instructions to develop your own portfolio using a variety of common web development and productivity software tools; and
- download a Portfolio Template.

YOUR PORTFOLIO

1. Investigate whether your school or state has a portfolio system that you are required to contribute to for assessment purposes. If not, create the four key components of your portfolio:
    - *Define* your purpose, audience, and content.
    - *Design* your layout and organization. Don't forget to plan for future additions. You may want to organize your portfolio around the ISTE NETS-T addressed in this book.
    - *Develop* your portfolio template. Add the items that you developed in this chapter. Don't forget about the materials you'll add in the future.
    - Keep in mind the format in which you will ultimately *deliver* your portfolio as you plan and develop your materials.

   You may also want to complete the *GAME plan—Portfolio Examples* presented earlier in the chapter or use the Portfolio Template included on the CourseMate website as a guide.
2. Create a "technology resumé." Refer to the example in Figure 2.3. Use the skills and knowledge addressed in the ISTE performance profiles located on the ISTE website. Include
    - a list of the skills and knowledge you already possess to help you meet the challenges of effectively integrating technology into instruction; and
    - a list of the specific experiences that have contributed to your current knowledge in technology. This may include formal or informal professional development experiences.
3. Reflect on how you have learned about technology in the past and how those prior experiences will influence your learning in the future.
4. Locate a self-assessment instrument and use it to assess your ability to achieve the NETS-T standards or the technology standards required by your state or school district. Include the name of the instrument and the results of the assessment in your portfolio.

References

Ertmer, P. A., & Newby, T. J. (1996). The expert learner: Strategic, self-regulated, and reflective. *Instructional Science, 24*(1), 1–24.

Gibbons, M. (2002). *The self-directed learning handbook.* San Francisco: Jossey-Bass.

Hatton, N., & Smith, D. (1995). Reflection in teacher education—towards definition and implementation. *Teaching and Teacher Education, 11*(1), 33–49.

International Society for Technology in Education (ISTE). (2007). *Profiles for technology (ICT) literate students.* Eugene, OR: Author. Retrieved February 1, 2012 from http://www.iste.org/standards/nets-for-students/nets-for-students-2007-profiles.aspx

Kottkamp, R. (1990). Means for facilitating reflection. *Education and Urban Society, 22*(2), 182–203.

Moon, J. (2001). *Reflection in higher education learning. PDF working paper 4.* Generic centre. Retrieved February 1, 2012 from http://www.heacademy.ac.uk/resources/detail/id72_Reflection_in_Higher_Education_Learning

Schon, D. A. (1983). *The reflective practitioner: How professionals think in action.* London: Temple Smith.

Supporting Student Creativity with Technology

OUTCOMES

In this chapter, you will learn to

- Incorporate aspects of **authentic instruction to promote creative and innovative thinking**, including identifying different types of creative thinking skills, integrating characteristics of authentic instruction into your teaching, identifying technologies that support authentic instruction, and incorporating teacher-directed instruction in response to student needs; and
- **Facilitate creative and innovative thinking** within the context of meeting content standards.

ISTE Standards Addressed in Chapter 3

NETS-T 1. Facilitate and Inspire Student Learning and Creativity

Teachers use their knowledge of subject matter, teaching and learning, and technology to facilitate experiences that advance student learning, creativity, and innovation in both face-to-face and virtual environments. Teachers:
a. promote, support, and model creative and innovative thinking and inventiveness; and
b. engage students in exploring real-world issues and solving authentic problems using digital tools and resources.

Over the last few decades, as technology has become more prevalent in our everyday lives, educators and business and industry leaders have increasingly stressed the importance of developing students' creative and critical thinking skills. To be competitive as a nation, we want our students to be good thinkers, and we want our schools to teach critical and creative thinking skills. One reason for this relatively new emphasis may be that new technologies have allowed computers to do the kinds of work that are readily automated and require little thinking, which then allows people to move into those jobs that computers *cannot* do as readily. These jobs often require people to make subtle decisions and solve complex problems. A second reason is that, due to the rapid pace at which technologies are changing, the workplace is also changing quickly. This puts a premium on teaching students *how* to learn as opposed to teaching specific skills that will be obsolete by the time they enter the workforce.

NETS-T Standard 1 requires that "Teachers use their knowledge of subject matter, teaching and learning, and technology to facilitate experiences that advance student learning, creativity, and innovation in both face-to-face and virtual environments." In doing so, teachers "promote, support, and model creative and innovative thinking and inventiveness," "engage students in exploring real-world issues and solving authentic problems using digital tools and resources," "promote student reflection using collaborative tools to reveal and clarify students' conceptual understanding and thinking, planning, and creative processes," and "model collaborative knowledge construction by engaging in learning with students, colleagues, and others in face-to-face and virtual environments." In this chapter, we'll begin our discussion of Standard 1 by focusing on ways to promote creative thinking through authentic learning experiences. We'll conclude our discussion of Standard 1 in the next chapter.

STORIES *from Practice*

Reflecting on Creative Thinking

I began integrating technology into my classroom my second year of teaching. I started out by using presentations on the interactive whiteboard with my fifth grade students, which allowed them to manipulate items on the board. When I started letting them research the solar system and create their own presentations on the whiteboard, I noticed how they were developing their creative thinking skills. To begin the assignment, we had a short discussion regarding the requirements of the presentation and basic information they had to include. This allowed my students to start at the same point in the assignment and branch out to the topics that interested them—modeling divergent thinking. Students had to use the Internet to find information about the sun, planets, moon, and other aspects of the solar system. While researching, they also had to determine the authenticity of the resources they found. By determining the validity of the information, they were using their critical thinking skills. Once they gathered their information, they were required to produce their own presentations on the interactive whiteboard, reflecting what they had learned. They were required to include pictures, different backgrounds, fonts, and interactive parts in the presentation. When the presentations were finished, we took time in class for them to present them to their peers.

Looking back, I realize that students achieved learner autonomy in my classroom because they were able to research the information they wanted regarding the solar system. When I decided to give my students this assignment, I did not consider the creative thinking skills they would be using. My goal was to enable them to have fun while learning about the solar system. I do wish I had known more about using technology to enhance creative thinking skills. Now that I've learned about different types of creative thinking, I plan on incorporating more of them into future lessons. One of my goals is to prepare my students for life outside of my class, and for me to be truly successful I have to give my students the opportunities to use and improve their creative thinking skills. I know some teachers may feel as though we should only teach what they have to know, but in order to get my students excited about learning, I think giving the kids a little freedom is a great idea. My students enjoyed the experience and wanted to do more things like it; however, I was reluctant because it was such a different approach to teaching and learning. Being able to explain the reasoning behind projects such as this will enable me to justify my decision to allow students to take over what they learn. I also hope it will inspire other teachers to give their students similar opportunities and not be afraid of change.

Source: © Lori Newborn. Used with permission.

Developing Creative Thinking through Authentic Instruction

You may not realize that the standards documents developed by national professional teaching organizations are designed to help teachers achieve "best practice," that is, the kind of instruction that facilitates and inspires student creativity and learning. Based on a large number of national curricular reports from several disciplines, Zemelman, Daniels, and Hyde (2005) culled a list of common recommendations proposed by educational experts and practitioners. These recommendations, captured in Table 3.1, are based on sound learning theory and are backed by many, many years of educational research. At the heart of these approaches, and as the core of Standard 1, is the expectation that teachers will develop students' creative thinking skills by engaging them in authentic real-world problems.

Types of Creative Thinking

If you were asked to define creative thinking, how would you do it? Most of you would probably use the words "original" or "unique." Sometimes people think of creativity as something that only artists (e.g., painters, composers) possess. But

Table 3.1 Common Recommendations from National Curricular Reports

Recommendations of National Curricular Reports

Instruction is *more effective* and *engaging* when there is LESS:	Instruction is *less dull* and *tedious* when there is MORE:
• whole-class, teacher-directed instruction (e.g., lecturing)	• activity, with all the subsequent noise and movement of students
• student passivity: sitting, listening, receiving, and absorbing information	• experiential, inductive, hands-on learning
• presentational, one-way transmission of information from teacher to student	• diversity in teachers' roles, including coaching, demonstrating, and modeling
• valuing and rewarding of silence in the classroom	• emphasis on higher-order thinking; learning a field's key concepts and principles
• classroom time devoted to fill-in-the-blank worksheets, workbooks, and other "seatwork"	• deep study of a smaller number of topics that enable students to internalize the field's way of inquiry
• student time spent reading textbooks and basal readers	• responsibility transferred to students for their work: goal setting, record keeping, monitoring, sharing, exhibiting, and evaluating
• attempts by teachers to thinly cover large amounts of materials in every subject area	• choices for students (e.g., choosing their own books, writing topics, team partners, projects)
• rote memorization of facts and details	• enacting and modeling of the principles of democracy in school
• emphasis on competition and grades in schools	• attention to affective needs and varying cognitive styles of individual students
• tracking or leveling of students into ability groups	• cooperative, collaborative activity
• use of pull-out special programs	• heterogeneous classrooms where unique needs are met through individualized activities
• use of and reliance on standardized tests	• delivery of special help to students in regular classrooms
	• varied and cooperative roles for teachers, parents, and administrators
	• reliance on descriptive evaluations of student growth, including observational/anecdotal records, conference notes, and performance assessment rubrics

Source: Adapted from *Best Practice: Today's Standards for Teaching and Learning in America's Schools,* by Zemelman, S., Daniels, H., & Hyde, A. (2005). Published by Heinemann, Portsmouth, NH. All rights reserved. Reprinted by permission.

according to Sir Ken Robinson (2009a), creativity refers more to the *quality* of things we do, not to specific types of activities. Because creativity refers to the *way* we do things, we can be creative in anything—planning a budget, raising a family, teaching, math, science, engineering, even thinking! According to Robinson, creativity is the "process of having original ideas that have value" (Azzam, 2009, p. 22)

Creative thinking is a form of **higher-order thinking**, which Wegerif (2002) defined as "complex thinking that requires effort and produces valued outcomes" (p. 2). This is consistent with the way we apply creative thinking in real-life situations. Such complex situations are seldom clearly defined and often involve multiple issues and possibilities. When creative thinking is needed, you must be ready to consider multiple possibilities, expect to encounter obstacles, and employ your judgment as you seek the best approach. By involving students in these types of creative thinking tasks, you facilitate and inspire high levels of engagement in the content to be learned and thus promote deep learning.

Creative thinking is not a single process or skill. Rather, it involves many different cognitive skills. Many different types of thinking (e.g., divergent thinking, deductive reasoning) make up creative thinking. For the sake of clarity we describe a few of these specific types of thinking here. However, for simplicity's sake, we will use the term *creative thinking* throughout the rest of this book to encompass all of these variations. Several types of creative thinking are described next. Which of these terms are familiar to you? How are they similar? Different?

> **higher-order thinking**
> creative thinking; "complex thinking that requires effort and produces valued outcomes" (Wegerif, 2002)

- *Divergent thinking.* A type of creative thinking that starts from a common point and moves outward to a variety of perspectives. To foster divergent thinking, teachers ask open-ended questions to prompt diverse or unique thinking among their students. Some examples include: "What predictions can you make about the upcoming hurricane season?" "How might technology in the year 2100 differ from today?" "Based on this rainfall data, what can you infer about the corn production for the upcoming year?"
- *Convergent thinking.* A type of thinking that attempts to bring together thoughts from different perspectives in order to achieve a common understanding or conclusion. Convergent thinking enables students to use sound reasoning and common sense to analyze possible solutions or responses in order to select the one with the most potential, based on a set of criteria. Questions that would elicit convergent thinking include, "How does a sundial work?" "In what ways is a poem like an artistic drawing?" "Which route would provide the quickest way to get from Denver to San Diego?"
- *Innovation.* A type of divergent thinking that aims to produce something that is original and of value. It involves generating and developing ideas, hypothesizing, imagining possibilities, and seeking new solutions. Questions to stimulate innovation include those that prompt students to consider other alternatives, such as "What would happen if . . .?" "How many different ways can you solve this problem?" Alternately, questions may require students to take a different perspective, such as, "How would a politician feel about stem cell research? A priest or minister? A parent of a child with disabilities?"
- *Critical thinking.* A type of convergent thinking that determines the validity or value of something. Sometimes called analytical thinking, it involves precise, persistent, objective analysis. Sample questions include: "How are these ideas similar?" "What is the main claim of the editorial? What evidence supports it? What assumptions underlie it?"
- *Inductive thinking.* A type of reasoning that moves from parts to the whole, from examples to generalizations. Students might be asked to answer the following: "What patterns do you observe?" "Where have we seen this before?" "What might cause this pattern?"

- *Deductive thinking.* A type of reasoning that moves from the whole to its parts, from generalizations to underlying concepts to examples. Sample questions include: "What are the similar components of these two objects?" "What are some examples of this principle?" "Is this an accurate example of this rule?" "How does this example relate to the rule?"

Although there are unique aspects to each of these types of thinking, there are also a number of common features such as complexity, uncertainty, and non-algorithmic reasoning requiring nuanced judgment and interpretation due to the presence of multiple criteria and the potential for multiple solutions to be "correct" (Resnick, 1987).

While "creative thinking" is a phrase that gets thrown around a lot, it's not usually defined, and to make matters even more complicated, it's typically described as either an outcome, or a component, of a variety of different approaches and types of thinking: inquiry learning, interdisciplinary learning, critical thinking, problem solving, informed decision-making, knowledge construction, inductive reasoning, reflective thinking, and innovation, to name just a few. In the next section, you'll notice that many of these labels appear as different variations of, or approaches to, authentic instruction. That's because creativity is often developed through an authentic instructional approach. In other words, the characteristics of authentic instruction (autonomous, active, holistic, complex, and challenging) are often considered critical to the development of creative thinking. In the next section, you will learn how to orchestrate classroom activities in ways that enable your students to apply their creativity to solve authentic problems.

Characteristics of Authentic Instruction

When you examine the list of recommendations in Table 3.1, it probably is easy to see that, while technology is not required to achieve each item, many of them can be more readily achieved when technology is added to the learning environment. For example, adding computers to the classroom can convert the learning environment into one that is very active and student-driven. Students can spend more time exploring topics of interest and creating innovative products that demonstrate their knowledge in ways that go beyond that which would be required to complete a fill-in-the-blank worksheet. Groups of students, with many different abilities and talents, can work together (either virtually or face-to-face) to research and develop solutions to an authentic problem that is facing the school, community, or nation, such as how to improve the physical accessibility of the local community for individuals with

APPLY to Practice

Supporting Creative Thinking with Technology

1. Think about a classroom you have observed lately. Describe one example of students' technology use.
2. To what extent was technology used to develop creative thinking and reasoning skills? Describe the technology and the specific type of thinking skill that was addressed.
3. If the technology was not used to promote creative thinking, can you make suggestions for how to modify the activity to encourage creative thinking? Would a different technology suit the content being addressed more effectively?

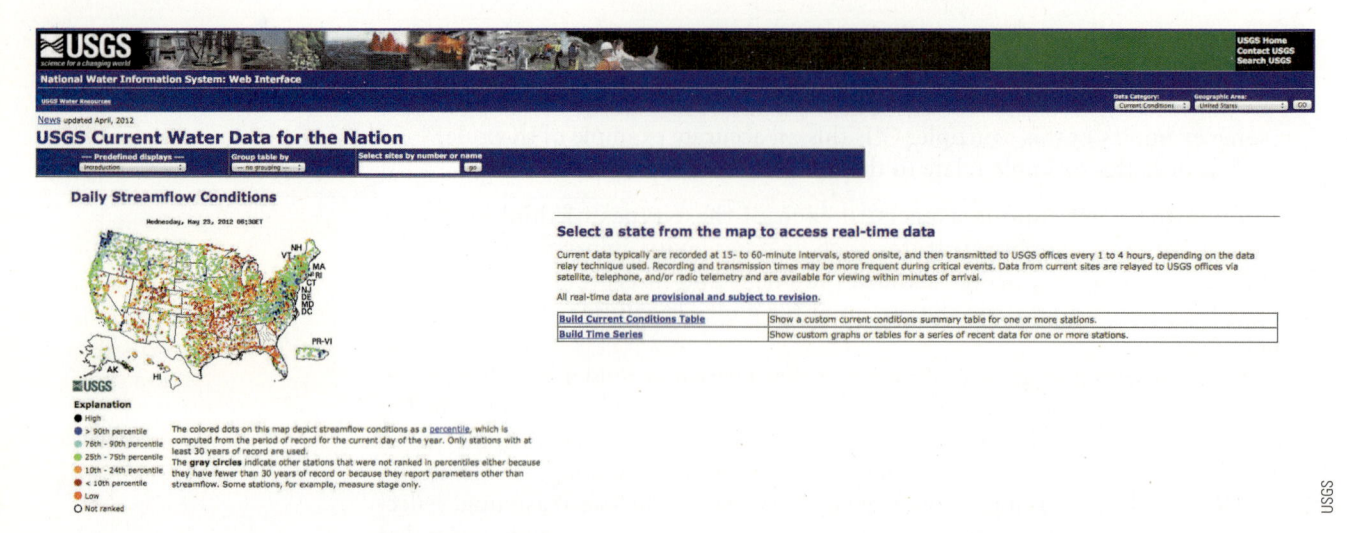

Figure 3.1
Many different Internet resources, such as this interactive map from the United States Geological Survey, provide students access to real-time data.

special needs. Additionally, by using Internet resources, students can access the primary documents of a discipline, as well as a multitude of authentic materials that are typical of those used by experts in the discipline under study (see Figure 3.1). For example, students can access data from NASA spacecraft, view real-time images of approaching weather systems, or watch the video of the birth of a baby panda at the San Diego Zoo.

There are a number of different names for this type of approach to teaching and learning including authentic instruction, engaged learning, learning by design, and learner-centered instruction. But, regardless of the specific label used, these approaches are characterized by a common set of principles and strategies. These include such things as 1) learner autonomy and 2) active learning, and tend to be anchored by 3) holistic, 4) complex, and 5) challenging activities. Because ISTE Standard 1 promotes the use of real-world issues and authentic problems to facilitate and inspire student learning and creativity, we will refer to this approach as **authentic instruction**. We discuss each of the five common characteristics listed above and describe how technology can support your efforts to create these kinds of learning experiences for your students.

> **authentic instruction**
> real-world issues and authentic problems, which facilitate and inspire student learning and creativity

Learner Autonomy

Authentic instruction provides for, and builds on, learner autonomy. We can support the development of learner autonomy in our classrooms in many ways, but one of the basic requirements is that students are able to pursue topics and questions that are interesting and relevant to them. Think about how you felt when you were asked to write about something you were really interested in, compared to having to write about something you had never heard of before, or, worse yet, had heard about, but considered to be a boring topic! You probably weren't very motivated to write about the "boring" topic, were you? But when you were allowed to explore your own interests, and pursue answers to your own questions, then your motivation probably went way up. The level of engagement that results from being able to pursue your own interests is one of the hallmarks of an effective creative task (Egbert, 2009). There are lots of ways to spark student motivation for learning and, fortunately, technology offers some of the most powerful tools available. Yet, technology as a learning tool, in and of itself, will not hold a person's interest indefinitely and is used more effectively when it enables a student to pursue other interests. In other words, technology tools are more likely to grab and hold students' attention when they are used to support the pursuit and attainment of other meaningful goals. For example, in many authentic approaches (such as project- and problem-based learning), the curriculum is anchored by a "driving question," usually presented in the form of a real-world problem or issue that needs to be solved (e.g., How can we use the waste our school produces to reduce our energy costs?). These kinds of approaches engage learners as researchers and problem-solvers; that is, students learn how to 1) ask important questions that are meaningful to them and to the discipline; 2) design and conduct investigations; 3) collect, analyze, and interpret data; and 4) apply what they have learned to new problems or situations. In these types of approaches, technology can be used to support each step of the process: to gather information, to collect and analyze data, to synthesize results, and to present findings to interested stakeholders. Research has shown that students who participate in these types of curricula develop positive attitudes toward learning.

In order for learners to truly function autonomously they must develop self-directed learning (SDL) skills (introduced in Chapter 2), which is another hallmark of creative and innovative thinkers. While the ultimate goal is that students will, over time, assume full responsibility for their learning, teachers need to provide guidance and support while students are in the process of *becoming* self-directed. One effective way that you can do this is through the use of **scaffolds**. Simply stated, scaffolds are external supports for learning or solving problems. The general idea behind a scaffold is that it enables you to accomplish something that you could not accomplish on your own. Think about how a painter is able to reach the upper levels on a building because of the use of a scaffold. Similarly, scaffolds enable students to reach higher levels of understanding that would not be possible without them.

> **scaffolds**
> external supports for learning or solving problems

Typically, scaffolds enable learners to deal with the complexity of difficult tasks by structuring them in ways that reduce, or constrain, that complexity. At the same time, scaffolds help students learn how to accomplish the tasks independently. Scaffolds may assume multiple forms depending on the learning environment, the content, the instructor, and the learners. In addition, they may serve different functions depending on where they are used in the instructional process: at the beginning, to provide entry into the task; in the middle, to support students' inquiry efforts; or at the end, to help students make sense of what they have observed, discussed, or read (Simons & Ertmer, 2006).

While most teachers already use a variety of scaffolds in their classroom instruction, such as project guidelines, templates, and grading rubrics, technology offers another means to support students' efforts (see Figure 3.2). Scaffolds are important instructional tools, especially in authentic learning environments. Fortunately, software applications, specifically designed to help you scaffold student learning, are available. These include tools that allow your students to highlight or organize material and to schedule tasks and receive reminders, as well as tools designed specifically to support various levels of student proficiency. You can even use common productivity tools, such as word-processing software, to scaffold student learning by increasing or decreasing the number of functions students can use in their work (e.g., thesaurus, dictionary, spelling and grammar check). We'll revisit this idea when we discuss the challenges involved in implementing authentic approaches.

Active Learning

Authentic instruction is based on active, experiential learning. There's an old proverb that says, "Tell me, and I will forget. Show me, and I may remember. Involve me, and I will understand." Few people would argue with the idea that we learn best by doing.

Figure 3.2
Scaffolding in this digital book include audio recordings, text-to-speech of any word or passage, translation into Spanish, and suggestions of learning strategies from different characters.

While we can certainly learn many things by reading textbooks and by observing others complete a task, the most natural form of learning involves active, hands-on, concrete experience. Think about how you learned to throw a Frisbee, ride a bike, create a tasty new dish, or sing your favorite song. In most cases, you probably just jumped in and gave each of these things a try: interacting with, and manipulating, the objects/tools at hand and observing what happened. Still, being an active learner doesn't necessarily mean that you have to be *physically* active. What this really means is that you have to be *mentally* active, searching for and manipulating information, synthesizing data, and making interpretations.

Technology supports learning-by-doing in a variety of ways. First of all, technology provides powerful tools (e.g., word processors, databases, image and video editors) that allow you to represent information in a variety of ways (via text, graphics, charts, audio, video) and perhaps, more importantly, to manipulate that information and then observe and interpret the effects of those manipulations. Technology also supports active learning when it is used as a tool to represent and simulate real-world problems, situations, and contexts (see Figure 3.3). For example, through the use of simulation software students can experience what it's like to maneuver *Spirit*, the Mars Land Rover, across the Martian landscape, or to observe, at the cellular level, how cancer cells respond to different types and doses of various drug treatments. Using simulations, learners can engage in activities that would otherwise be too dangerous, expensive, or complex, such as conducting volatile chemistry experiments, navigating a spaceship to the moon, or making risky investment decisions. Simulations can compress time or slow things down so that they are more readily observable, allowing students to repeat the process as many times as needed to understand it.

Technology can also give students access to people, resources, or locations that would be impossible to get to without it. Learners can take virtual field trips to places within their own communities (local museums), across the country (national

Figure 3.3
The ORBITER space flight simulator allows learners to experiment with the physics of space flight without leaving the ground.

parks), or around the world (Great Wall of China). (See *Tech Tools and Tips—Virtual Field Trips*.) Students can rocket into space, participate in critical historical events, or tour the inner workings of the circulatory system. In addition, they can interact with people from other countries and cultures; ask questions of scientists, authors, and other experts; and access real-time data (e.g., census, weather) and primary source documents, all of which allow them to participate in the authentic activities of the discipline.

While mental activity is necessary for meaningful learning, it is not sufficient. Activity needs to be accompanied by both **reflection** and **articulation** (Jonassen, Howland, Moore, & Marra, 2003). That is, learners need to describe what they have done and explain what resulted and why. This is because when we stop to think about *what* we have learned and to reflect on *how* we learned it, we actually achieve a deeper understanding of the knowledge we have constructed, and are more likely to be able to use that new knowledge in different situations (referred to as **transfer**), which is yet another hallmark of creative thinkers. That is, the active (doing) and constructive (creating) processes work hand-in-hand to build understanding. If you don't engage in both processes you are likely to end up with either incomplete knowledge (observations/facts that cannot be interpreted or understood) or inert knowledge (knowledge that is irretrievable when needed).

Holistic Activities

Authentic instruction is holistic. This principle relates to the fact that we gain important skills, including reading, spelling, math, and even technology skills, when we learn them within the context of meaningful activities. This is what businesses sometimes refer to as "just-in-time" training. For example, brief lessons on how to use punctuation will be more meaningful (and therefore more memorable) if they occur within the

---

reflection
learner's ability to think over the process of learning and to describe what she/he has done and what she/he needs to do to achieve meaningful learning

articulation
the ability to describe what one has done, explain what resulted and why

transfer
ability to use knowledge or skills in new situations

TECH TOOLS & TIPS

Virtual Field Trips

Several websites provide access to ready-made virtual field trips you can use in your classroom. The field trips can focus on a variety of topics across a wide range of grade levels, and many websites include teacher resources.

Like any worthwhile instructional activity, arranging and conducting a virtual field trip requires planning. Here are a few basic guidelines that may help you make your virtual field trip a success:

1. Unlike a regular field trip, your worries about students running off in all directions and getting lost are diminished, but not gone. Be sure students know the URL they need to be on and that it is not acceptable to leave the site.

2. Complete your own research before attempting to lead students on the field trip. Spend time at the site or exhibit yourself and get to know it thoroughly. If there are external links (links that go to other sites), follow them to make sure they are appropriate for your students.

3. Build excitement around the virtual field trip. Like a regular field trip, students should look forward to visiting the exhibition. Prepare students with background information about the subject area, including key vocabulary and concepts. Try to come up with a mystery or riddle that students will solve once visiting the online exhibit.

4. Provide goals for students to reach while on the field trip. If computers are limited, divide students into groups and have them complete a treasure hunt. As with all lesson plans, consider how long it will take for students to accomplish the objectives.

5. Provide activities that engage students and extend learning. These activities can include an analysis of data, identification of patterns, or comparing and contrasting information.

6. Create follow-up activities that students must complete after they have left the exhibit.

Source: Used with permission from *Field Trips Go Virtual (Teaching Today)*, www.glencoe.com/sec/teachingtoday/educationupclose.phtml/print/33. © The McGraw Hills Company, Inc.

---

real contexts
learning environments that allow students to solve actual, complex problems

context of writing a letter to a state representative, as opposed to being just one in a series of isolated language arts lessons.

Technology provides the means to situate learning within **real contexts**, and to provide students with the whole picture of an event or process, while still allowing them to focus on the relevant parts. For example, by using videos that allow students to actually view and focus on the red blood cells that carry oxygen from the lungs, learners can more readily understand how these cells work on a molecular level, while still recognizing how they work as part of the circulatory system. By considering the whole system, as opposed to a single part, students are more likely to make far more connections than the teacher would have been able to teach directly (see Figure 3.4).

Another way that technology can facilitate more holistic learning is by enabling learners to make connections across multiple content areas. For example, when working on authentic problems, such as determining why fish are dying in a local river, students must work across multiple content areas to investigate the problem, understand the causes, and pose solutions. As part of the problem-solving process, students must conduct both field (science) and library (language arts, information technology skills) research; analyze data and graph results (science, statistics, math, technology), interview local business owners to understand their perspectives (social sciences) on previous actions taken regarding the disposal of waste materials into the river (history), understand local laws and policy issues (government), and create a persuasive presentation to convince local public officials of a proposed course of action (technology skills, language arts). It's easy to see from just this one example how technology can facilitate many, if not all, of the processes involved in solving these kinds of complex problems while simultaneously allowing students to experience the holistic nature of

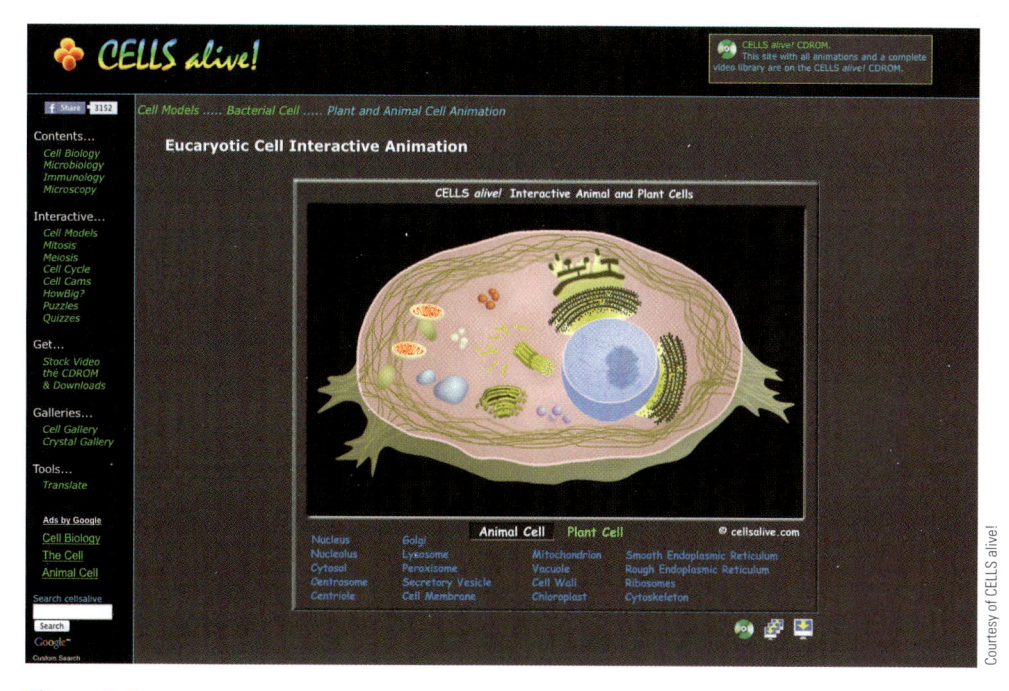

Figure 3.4
Technology, such as this simulation, can help situate learning in real-world contexts that allow students to view an entire process and it's component parts.

analyzing a problem from a variety of different points of view in order to draw reasoned conclusions. Your students could probably complete this type of activity without technology, but can you imagine how much more difficult it would be and how much more time it would take to do so?

Complex Activities

Authentic instruction incorporates real-world and complex problems. Previous methods of schooling placed teachers squarely in the center of the instructional process, serving primarily as knowledge dispensers whose main responsibility was to translate complex information into a form that was more readily transmitted to, and absorbed by, the learners. One way teachers accomplished this was by removing the information from its relevant context and stripping it of any "extraneous" details. What resulted, however, was not meaningful learning, but rather artificial understandings of oversimplified ideas, concepts, and situations. Current research has demonstrated that learning is more successful when it is situated within real-world tasks or simulated in a problem-based learning environment (Jonassen et al., 2003). Such experiences are not only more relevant and engaging, but they also increase the likelihood that students will be able to use what they have learned in new situations; furthermore, they may do so in new and innovative ways.

According to Fred Newmann and his colleagues (Newmann, Bryk, & Nagaoka, 2001), authentic instruction involves more than situating learning within a real context. While an authentic context can illustrate the complexity and richness of a real-world problem, Newmann uses the term **authentic intellectual work** to define, more specifically, how students should work within that context. Authentic intellectual work has three distinct characteristics: 1) construction of knowledge, 2) disciplined inquiry, and 3) value beyond school (see the first two columns of Table 3.2). To the extent that these characteristics are embedded within teachers' expectations for students' work, classroom activities and experiences come closer to modeling best practices.

authentic intellectual work
an approach to teaching in which students work within real-world contexts by engaging in tasks that have value beyond school

Figure 3.5
Using handheld digital technologies students can tackle problems that adults do by collecting and using data in real-world contexts.

Authentic intellectual work starts where the basics end. The real-world aspect implies that students *apply* the basics to tackle projects and problems similar to those that confront adults in their everyday lives (see Figure 3.5). Authentic instruction incorporates assignments that require students to think, develop in-depth understanding, and apply their learning to realistic, important problems. In addition, these assignments are designed to have concrete, practical, aesthetic, or personal value. The goal is to involve students in work that has an impact on others—for example, writing letters, news articles, memos or technical reports; communicating in a foreign language; producing a budget; or creating a painting or composing a piece of music.

Technology can be used in many ways to establish authentic contexts for learning and to engage students in authentic intellectual work including the construction of knowledge, disciplined inquiry, and finding value beyond school. Consider, for example, the last column in Table 3.2 that illustrates some of the ways technology can support each of these components of authentic work.

Challenging Activities

Authentic instruction is challenging. Most of us have experienced the satisfaction and joy that come from completing a difficult task or solving a challenging puzzle. When we see or hear something that we don't understand, we're motivated to figure it out. We might talk to our friends or colleagues, visit the local library or museum, search for information online, or call a related helpline, all with the goal of understanding the phenomenon or solving the mystery. If we can capitalize on these types of natural curiosities in our students, we are more likely to engage them in the topic at hand and to prompt them to take ownership of their learning.

Of course, not every student will find every question or topic equally interesting, or be able to engage in the topic at the same level of sophistication. This is where technology can lend a hand. For example, technology can provide that initial hook that gets students involved in the topic. This might be in the form of a video that captures the faces and voices of real people describing the problems they face in their communities. Or it might be in the form of a game or simulation that challenges them to complete a task in a limited amount of time or to make decisions about how to avoid an impending disaster (see Figure 3.6).

Once students are engaged, technology can be used to promote and support students' understanding of the content. For example, a variety of computer tutorials are available that provide multiple paths through the same content. In some cases, the

Table 3.2 Using Technology to Support the Key Characteristics of Authentic Intellectual Work

Construction of Knowledge	Example: Writing	Technology Support
Assignments require students to manipulate information and ideas by synthesizing, generalizing, explaining, hypothesizing, or arriving at conclusions that produce new meanings and understandings.	The writing assignment asks students to interpret, analyze, synthesize, or evaluate information when writing about a topic, rather than merely to reproduce information.	Students access the *American Memory* collection online from the Library of Congress and evaluate primary documents from the Civil Rights movement, written from different perspectives (e.g., an editorial in the Birmingham Press; Martin Luther King's letter written from the Birmingham jail) prior to writing an opinion piece, stating their own views on the conflict.

Disciplined Inquiry	Example: Writing	Technology Support
1) *Use a prior knowledge base.* Students must acquire the knowledge base of facts, vocabularies, concepts, theories, algorithms, and other conventions necessary for their inquiry (usually the key focus of direct instruction in basic skills). 2) *Strive for in-depth understanding rather than superficial awareness.* Students use information to gain deeper understanding of specific problems. Such understanding develops as one looks for, imagines, proposes, and tests relationships among key concepts in order to clarify a specific problem or issue. 3) *Express their ideas and findings with elaborated communication.* Students use verbal, symbolic and/or visual tools to provide qualifications, nuances, elaborations, details, and analogies woven into extended narratives, explanations, justifications, and dialogue.	The writing assignment asks students to draw conclusions or make generalizations or arguments and support them through extended writing.	1) Students record data and information they have found while exploring online simulations as a way to develop deep understanding of genetic processes (natural selection, crossing over, DNA fingerprinting) prior to participating in a debate about genetic engineering. 2) Students create hypotheses about the proposed evolutionary path of the whale, based on one of three hypotheses. Information is gathered through a web-based lab or WebQuest. Students create an argument, with evidence, to support the specific hypothesis chosen. 3) Students use a combination of technology tools to present their ideas/findings via written essays, photo essays, video essays, presentation software, web-based portfolios, or other means.

Value Beyond School	Example: Writing	Technology Support
Students make connections between substantive knowledge and either public problems or personal experiences. Accomplishments have practical, aesthetic, or personal value.	The writing assignment asks students to connect the topic to their own experiences, observations, feelings, or situations that have played a significant role in their lives.	Students write for real audiences, such as grade or age peers in distant locations, experts, or interested community members, and create a project website that includes their written work, as well as pictures and links to helpful resources.

Source: Adapted from Newmann, F. M., Bryk, A. S., & Nagaoka, J. K. (2001). *Authentic intellectual work and standardized tests: Conflict or coexistence?* (pp. 14–15). Chicago, IL: Consortium on Chicago School Research. Reprinted by permission of the author and Consortium on Chicago School Research.

Note: We have added the ideas in the technology support column to illustrate how technology can be used to achieve the key components of authentic intellectual work, as outlined by Newmann et al.

computer controls when the student moves on to more advanced concepts; in other cases, learners are given control over the amount of information they receive, the number of practice exercises they complete, and the level of success they obtain before moving on.

Technology also affords the opportunity to provide engaging and interesting material to students who read at different grade levels—including English language learners or students who read below grade level. Using the concept of **lexiles**, a scale that matches the difficulty of reading material to student ability, students can engage in

> **lexiles**
> a scale that matches the difficulty of reading material to student ability

Figure 3.6
This simulation from EdHeads allows students to interpret forensic data and make decisions related to a real-world context, providing a challenge that would be impractical to attempt without technology.

relevant authentic materials at a level they can understand. For example, a ninth grade student who reads three levels below his grade may be interested in current events related to baseball, pop music, or the country of his birth. Many newspaper, magazine, and web-based articles are written at a level that the student cannot read or comprehend. Software is available that can match the student's interests with reading materials he can read and understand—sometimes providing real-time articles from news services written at different reading levels. Online databases also provide listings of reading materials in almost any content area organized by lexile. In this way, technology can provide access to interesting and challenging material that is appropriate to the age, interests, and reading level of each student.

Addressing the Challenges of Authentic Instruction

Instructional activities that incorporate all of the components of authentic instruction described here (active, holistic, complex, and so on) are naturally going to be more challenging for your students (and for you!). Giving students choices in their learning, as well as responsibility for managing and assessing their learning processes, may cause confusion and frustration at first. When you have a classroom full of students who are all pursuing different interests, and experiencing a host of different difficulties, you may be tempted to just give up. However, there are lots of strategies and tools you can use to manage the classroom and your students. Many of these strategies are described in Chapter 5. We make note of just two of them here: the use of collaborative work groups and technology-based scaffolds.

Collaborative work groups can ease the challenges of authentic instruction. Although we haven't specifically mentioned that authentic instruction is **collaborative**, this is typically the case. In fact, this is one of the defining characteristics of problem- and

collaborative
a characteristic of authentic instruction; working in groups in which responsibility for learning is shared with others

project-based learning, two prevalent forms of authentic instruction. Johnson and Johnson (1998) and Slavin (1994) have documented student achievement gains when students work in collaborative small groups. This is likely due to a number of different factors including the opportunity to observe more advanced students think through a problem or perform a task, who thus provide models of the knowledge construction process; the ability to divide complex tasks into smaller, more manageable parts; and the opportunity to receive feedback from, as well as to give feedback to, multiple others. Also, working together in pairs or small groups can benefit students both socially and cognitively. Learners depend on each other to reach their goals and, in the process, practice their social interaction skills. When done right, the use of collaborative work groups can ease some of the challenges teachers face when students work independently on a host of different projects. Of course, students need to learn how to work together and their initial efforts need to be supported. Suggestions for managing small groups are provided in Chapter 5.

Although the use of small groups can help teachers address some of the logistical problems they face when implementing authentic learning activities, the primary reason for using them has more to do with what students gain by learning to work with their peers. Both educators and business professionals have increasingly emphasized the importance of developing group interaction and problem-solving skills among our future workers. This suggests that, just as these are important skills for *you* to gain, they are also important skills for your *students* to gain.

At the heart of these collaborative activities is the engagement of students in deep conversations about both the processes and the products of learning. When learners work in teams they must achieve a common understanding of the task at hand and then agree upon the methods they will use to complete it. Through these group conversations learners come to understand and accept that there are multiple ways of approaching tasks as well as multiple methods for solving them. This is what transforms these group activities into meaningful learning. And, of course, technology can support these conversations by providing a platform for participation and by connecting learners across the room or across the globe. Collaboration is one of the key characteristics of Web 2.0 tools, and given that the majority of these tools are free (e.g., Skype, Blogger, Wikispaces), teachers can readily capitalize on their collaborative features. As discussed more thoroughly in Chapter 4, these types of collaborative tools provide a means to illuminate students' thinking, planning, and creative processes.

Scaffolds can ease the challenges of authentic instruction. As noted earlier, another method for addressing the challenging nature of authentic instruction is through the use of scaffolds. While students may feel more motivated to participate in authentic activities due to their holistic and challenging nature, they also may feel more frustrated due to their open-ended nature. Particularly for students who have less experience in inquiry-based methods, scaffolds can help them understand what's involved in the process and what it takes to initiate and complete different inquiry activities. Figure 3.7 provides another example of how a scaffold can help learners get started on a difficult task.

A second approach involves having an expert (the teacher or a more experienced peer) model how to complete a task, investigation, or process. Modeling can prompt students to compare their own approaches with that of the expert, while simultaneously learning the language of the discipline. For example, *Alien Rescue* (Pedersen & Liu, 2002–2003), a multimedia-based problem-based learning (PBL) program, contains a feature in the software that allows students to view video advice from an "expert" at various stages during the process. The expert verbally describes the problem-solving strategies, such as how relevant information is selected and why other information is ignored.

TEACHSOURCE VIDEO

Examine one of the following videos from the Education CourseMate website.

- *Supporting Problem-Based Learning in the Elementary Classroom*, or
- *Integrating Internet Research: High School Social Studies*

How do the activities in the video you watched support the principles of authentic instruction described in this chapter? How do they support:

1. Autonomy through increasing student motivation, providing opportunities for self-directed learning, or scaffold student learning?
2. Active learning with hands-on, interactive experiences by promoting student reflection or requiring students to articulate their learning?
3. Holistic instruction based in real-world contexts in which students observe and interact with the relationships between parts and wholes?
4. Complexity through the use of authentic source documents, data, or experts; outcomes intended to share with a real audience; varied forms of communication?
5. Challenging activities that are personalized for the learner and where learners collaborate with others?

Figure 3.7
Digital technologies can help make challenging authentic problems easier to comprehend and get students started on the task.

Pedersen and Liu noted that students were able to transfer these strategies to a new problem, in a different domain, and speculated that enhancing students' thinking during the problem-solving process enhanced their problem solving in the transfer situation.

In general, scaffolds can be used throughout the instructional process and are especially useful in supporting learners' efforts within problem-centered environments. While teachers, themselves, can provide continuous timely support (referred to as "soft" scaffolds) based on their observations of students' ongoing efforts, technological scaffolds (as one type of "hard" scaffold) can be built into many of the planned activities, based on teachers' knowledge of where students are likely to struggle (Saye & Brush, 2002). Even the automatic features of some productivity tools, such as spelling and grammar tools in word processors, list managers in spreadsheets, and auto-form filling features in web browsers can be considered scaffolds that can support you and your students, depending on how you incorporate them into your classroom activities. If hard scaffolds are put in place to support learners at various stages known to be difficult, the teacher is then free to perform additional soft scaffolding.

Technology Support for Authentic Instruction

Authentic instruction enables you to meet your curricular standards in ways that can engage and support your students' interests, creativity, and motivation. In a problem-centered classroom, your role looks quite different from the way it looks in a traditional, teacher-centered classroom. That is, rather than acting as a knowledge provider you tend to serve more as a resource provider. Furthermore, you engage students' interests by asking thought-provoking questions and providing opportunities for students to construct their own understandings and to be accountable for their own learning.

Table 3.3 summarizes the key components of an authentic approach and lists some of the potential ways in which technology can support teachers' and students'

Table 3.3 How Technology Supports the Components of Authentic Instruction

Components of Authentic Instruction	The Role of Technology
Learner Autonomy	• Supports student interest in a variety of topics; provides the tools needed to pursue the answers to interesting questions • Allows learners to initiate learning on their own via tutorials, simulations, online resources, and discussion groups • Provides tools that support the processes of self-directed learning; setting goals, monitoring progress, reflecting on and articulating learning outcomes
Active Learning	• Engages learners in hands-on, interactive experiences • Provides tools to represent ideas; manipulate information; simulate real-world problems, situations, and contexts • Provides access to people, resources, and places you couldn't access without it • Provides the tools useful for reflection and articulation
Holistic Activities	• Provides the means to situate learning within real contexts • Allows students to observe the relationships between parts and wholes and thus understand how things work together
Complex Activities	• Provides access to authentic documents, real data, and experts that give purpose and meaning to school activities • Allows students to explore information in the context within which it is used • Provides real audiences for students' work • Enables students to communicate ideas in a variety of ways
Challenging Activities	• Increases students' interest in the topic at hand • Promotes and supports students' understanding by providing multiple paths through the information • Provides learners control over their learning processes • Provides access to multiple others, both face-to-face and virtually, for collaborative work • Provides a platform for meaningful conversations with others • Supports development of student independence through the use of scaffolds

© Cengage Learning 2014

APPLY to Practice

Authentic Instructional Strategies and Technologies

1. Identify a learning objective or outcome from your content area and then select one of the methods of authentic instruction from Table 3.3.
2. Describe a lesson activity that incorporates the specific method you have selected. How would you establish appropriate learning experiences to support the activity? What kind of scaffolds or structures would be necessary for different types of learners?
3. Describe specific ways that technologies could be used to support the successful implementation of your strategy. Why did you choose the specific technology? How is it matched to the skills and knowledge required of the learning objective, your skill level and that of your students, and the specific method you have selected?
4. Solicit feedback from your peers and share your ideas on their lesson activities.

efforts within this type of environment. While we recognize that teachers can create and use authentic approaches and strategies *without* the use of technology, we also recognize that with its addition, the task is, hopefully, less difficult, as well as more stimulating.

There are a variety of ways to incorporate authentic experiences and activities into your classroom, including problem-based learning methods, inquiry and discovery methods, inductive methods, role-playing, and simulation, to name a few. Because these strategies often involve exploration, collaboration, and communication, digital technologies can facilitate their implementation. Descriptions of these different methods, and supporting technologies, are presented in Table 3.4. Note that most of the technologies listed with each method can actually be applied across multiple methods.

Table 3.4 Examples of Authentic Instruction and Potential Supporting Technologies

Type of Method	Description	Possible Supporting Technologies
Problem-Based Learning	Students are challenged to learn by working cooperatively to find solutions to real-life problems. Curiosity and interest in the process occurs naturally as students work in virtual and face-to-face teams to solve authentic dilemmas.	• Internet for background information • Data collection tools (probes, etc.) to gather data • Simulation software or online models • Spreadsheets and databases to record and analyze data • Presentation software to present ideas and findings
Inquiry/Discovery Method	Puzzling questions spark students' mental stimulation and quickly get them thinking critically and creatively. Once a situation has been presented, students gather information by formulating their own questions. They research answers in cooperative groups, pairs, or individually.	• Concept-mapping software to map ideas for investigations • Digital cameras or camcorders to gather information • Word-processing software or spreadsheets to create planning charts, timelines, etc. • WebQuests or research using online and other digital resources
Inductive Method	This method begins with a question or series of unknown facts or concepts and moves toward known information. Learners actively search for answers to these "unknowns."	• Internet, CD-ROMs, and databases for reference material • Digital cameras or camcorders to record information • Photo and video hardware and software to create and edit images of findings • Spreadsheet and graphing software to create visual representations of findings
Role-Play	Role-play situations require students to take on the characteristics of someone else. Role-play encourages creativity and high levels of thought. This strategy is most successful when students are given time to research the character they must portray.	• Internet search for information about perspectives of different stakeholders • Audio and video recordings of relevant locations, people, etc. • Discussion boards, blogs, and e-mail to communicate with stakeholders, other experts • Single- and multiplayer gaming software
Simulation	Similar to role-play, simulations involve approximating real-life scenarios in the classroom. Students are involved in the reproduction of possible situations. Simulations often include scripted representations that enable learners to experience world events.	• Simulation software • Virtual environments • Internet resources to support activity in the simulation • Web- or videoconferencing software to support conversations with experts or other stakeholders

Source: Adapted from Musselwhite, T. (2005). *Creating learner-centered middle school classrooms.* New York: Glencoe/McGraw-Hill. Reprinted with permission of Glencoe/McGraw-Hill and the author.

Teacher-Directed Instruction in Support of Authentic Learning

Within the context of authentic activities, **directed instruction** can offer an effective approach under certain circumstances. For example, directed instruction can be preferable when students need just-in-time instruction delivered at the point of need. Students who are working on authentic learning activities may benefit from remediation or practice in prerequisite skills in order to keep up with the pace of the lesson. At other times, students are hindered by their lack of automaticity in the use of certain skills. For example, students who do not know their multiplication tables can be at a disadvantage when performing calculations of the area of a meadow. In these cases, direct instructional methods can provide a useful supplement to authentic learning experiences. Students may find that repeated practice on small chunks of information is the best way to ensure that their skills become automatic. Students who are internally motivated to succeed may also prefer directed instruction as the quickest way to learn new information.

> **directed instruction** comprises instructional methods that present learners with the content to be learned, followed by multiple opportunities to practice or apply the content so as to ensure mastery of the information

Directed Instruction

Directed instruction encompasses a variety of instructional methods that have at their core the introduction of a topic, an interactive presentation of the content to be learned, and extensive practice to ensure mastery of the targeted information (Magliaro, Lockee, & Burton, 2005). Directed instruction is characterized by the following features:

1. Materials and curricula are broken down into small steps and arranged in what is assumed to be prerequisite order.
2. Objectives are stated clearly in terms of learner outcomes or performances. Learners are provided with opportunities to connect their new knowledge with what they already know.
3. Learners practice each step or combination of steps.
4. Learners experience additional opportunities to practice that promote increasing responsibility and independence (guided and/or independent; in groups and/or alone).
5. Feedback is provided after each practice opportunity or set of practice opportunities (Magliaro et al., 2005, p. 44).

Table 3.5 outlines one popular directed instruction method.

Using Technology to Support Directed Instruction

There are a variety of ways that technology can contribute to directed instruction. Drill-and-practice software can provide the repeated practice necessary for basic skills (e.g., math facts, motor skills, spelling) to become automatic. Simulations can model the application of concepts and principles such as the principles of energy and force. Animations can also model procedures (e.g., mitosis, building a bridge) and motor skills, such as with those involved in throwing a bowl on a potter's wheel. Photographs can provide detailed images for analysis.

Tutorials typically include all of the learning events needed for directed instruction (see the discussion of computer tutorials in Chapter 4). Videos can improve student attention and increase motivation, and can provide excellent resources from which to structure an introductory activity—often demonstrating an entire concept or skill prior to breaking it down into prerequisite steps. Many schools are now using video tutorials they find online or create themselves thanks to the popularity of sites like Khan Academy. In fact, because so much instruction is available online that incorporates or models directed instructional strategies, many teachers are finding that these resources can be used by students outside of class so that work during class can focus more on authentic instructional applications.

Table 3.5	Directed Instruction

Madeline Hunter's (1982) model, *Essential Elements of Instruction*, is representative of common approaches to directed instruction. Hunter identifies several events, outlined below, which the teacher should consider in designing a lesson. Although these considerations are often interpreted as a step-by-step series that must be present in each lesson, Hunter emphasized that not all events need to appear in every lesson:

- *Anticipatory Set:* An anticipatory set is a short introductory activity that prepares students to attend to the new content by focusing their attention and bringing prior knowledge of the content into consciousness. These activities can also provide teachers with an opportunity to diagnose students' initial levels of understanding.
- *Purpose:* The teacher simply states the goal, objective, or purpose of the lesson and why it should be of importance to the students. This event further focuses the learners' attention on the relevant content by informing them of what they are expected to learn as a result of the lesson.
- *Input:* The input consists of the factual information and skills students should learn. Hunter suggests that the teacher's role is to determine what information is essential and organize it clearly. Consistent with cognitive approaches to learning, complex information should build on more general information.
- *Modeling:* The input is accompanied by modeling activities where the teacher highlights the critical attributes that distinguish an idea, concept, or procedure from similar things. Using clear examples and non-examples that are relevant to the students' experiences, the teacher demonstrates the application of the new information.
- *Guided Practice:* The next step is to guide students though the process of applying the information to ensure that they will perform the tasks correctly when they are on their own. Guided practice can range from structured activities where the students "follow along," to less structured tasks where the teacher simply circulates around the room to see if students are performing the tasks correctly on their own.
- *Checking for Understanding:* Throughout the lesson, the teacher asks questions to determine how well the students understand the information. Based on the students' answers, the teacher may need to re-teach certain skills or concepts before progressing.
- *Independent Practice:* Guided activities are followed by independent practice where students apply the skill(s) without teacher support. These practice activities enable both students and teachers to determine the extent to which students can perform a task independently. Teachers can assign independent practice activities for homework or in class but they must be sure to provide students with feedback on their performances.
- *Closure:* The lesson concludes with actions or statements that bring the lesson to a logical conclusion. Closure activities review and reinforce the key points to help students assimilate their new knowledge.

© Cengage Learning 2014

APPLY to Practice

Directed Instructional Strategies and Technologies

1. Consider times when directed instruction can and should be incorporated into instruction.
2. What technologies can support directed instruction in your area of study?

A variety of technologies can be used to check your students' understanding. Many computer tutorials or curricular applications include reflection or summary questions at key intervals during the lesson. Students can receive feedback on the questions and may be guided to review material they do not understand well enough. There are interactive technologies, too, that allow for a greater amount of informal formative assessment of student understanding. Whole classes can provide answers to key questions, confidentially or anonymously, to boost student confidence and accuracy of response. Students can use infrared responders and wireless handheld devices to "beam" answers to questions you pose. Computer-generated tests can be used for pretests or posttests on the content and you and your students can track and evaluate data from these tests to determine student growth. Students can also use digital portfolios that include checklists or rubrics to track their mastery of required skills and knowledge.

Facilitating Creative Thinking While Meeting Content Standards

Most educators today would agree that two of the primary goals of education are to help students develop creative thinking skills and to become effective problem solvers. And while many schools and teachers have adopted these goals, they are not commonly addressed in the typical classroom. That may be because teachers don't know where to begin to teach these skills. Creative thinking and problem solving are rather "fuzzy" concepts—hard to teach and even harder to measure. Furthermore, the need to assure that students demonstrate competency on the content standards assessed on state benchmarking tests is one of the major challenges facing teachers today. You might be wondering how you can facilitate creative thinking skills while still addressing content and technology standards.

Let's look at some standards in more detail. You've probably noticed that standards are often written in fairly general terms so they are frequently accompanied by **objectives** that provide greater specificity. For example, look at Table 3.6 and note how each science content standard is translated into more specific language through its related objective.

In a content standard or objective, you will generally find two types of elements: knowledge and skills. The knowledge element identifies the discipline-specific facts, concepts, and procedures one must know in order to demonstrate mastery of the standard. We often do a great job addressing the knowledge components of instruction, especially since they are easy to assess with traditional multiple-choice test formats. Content knowledge is represented by the nouns in the standard or objective. In the examples in Table 3.6, the content knowledge is

- Grade 4: properties of minerals;
- Grade 8: rocks, fossils, ice cores, and Earth's geologic history; and
- Grade 12: the rock cycle; and origin, texture, and mineral composition of rocks.

These curricular elements are the basic content addressed in your lessons. In this science example, the basic content addressed in all three grades is related to rocks and

objectives
statements that describe what the learner will be able to do following the instruction

Table 3.6 Examples of Science Content Standards and Associated Objectives

Grade	Standard	Objective
4	The learner will conduct investigations and use appropriate technology to build an understanding of the composition and uses of rocks and minerals.	Describe and evaluate the properties of several minerals.
8	The learner will conduct investigations and utilize appropriate technologies and information systems to build an understanding of evidence of evolution in organisms and landforms.	Interpret ways in which rocks, fossils, and ice cores record Earth's geologic history and the evolution of life including: Geologic Time Scale, Index Fossils, Law of Superposition.
12	The learner will build an understanding of lithospheric materials, tectonic processes, and the human and environmental impacts of natural and human-induced changes in the lithosphere.	Investigate and analyze the processes responsible for the rock cycle by analyzing the origin, texture, and mineral composition of rocks.

Source: Adapted from Public Schools of North Carolina. (2006). *North Carolina standard course of study*. Retrieved May 9, 2006, from http://www.dpi.state.nc.us/curriculum

THE GAME PLAN

Identifying Content Standards

Set Goals
Learn more about the content standards you will be required to meet when you teach.

Take Action
Find out if there is a national organization whose content standards you must meet. Locate its website and review its standards.

Monitor
Are you locating the standards you need? Do you need to modify your search strategies?

Perhaps you may need to contact a teacher or other expert in your chosen field for help in locating the appropriate professional organization.

Evaluate and Extend
Compare the content standards you found with those located by other students who plan to teach in a similar area. Did you locate the same standards? If not, collaborate with your classmates, or consult with a teacher in the area, to determine which set of standards may be most applicable.

---

minerals, but the facts, concepts, and procedures become more complex as the students mature and progress through the science curriculum.

After identifying the content knowledge, you must determine what your students will do with that content. In other words, what skills must they demonstrate using that knowledge? Do they simply have to recall or define it or will they apply content knowledge in some unique way? Educators often use a familiar taxonomy for determining the level of thinking required by standards. We look at this next.

A Taxonomy for Determining Cognitive Demand

Using what is often referred to as "Bloom's Taxonomy," you can better determine the thinking skill demands of specific content standards and subsequently develop instructional and assessment activities matched to those specific skill demands. In 2001, a revised version of Bloom's Taxonomy was published by Anderson and Krathwohl (see Figure 3.8), with two of the most obvious changes being 1) the use of verbs, rather than nouns, for each of the levels of thinking and 2) a rearrangement of the hierarchy so that the sequence progressed from lower-order to higher-order thinking skills. Notice that creating, or creative thinking, represents the highest level of thinking. However, creative thinkers use all of these types of thinking, especially those in the upper three levels, which are typically referred to as higher-order thinking skills, or HOTS.

It's important to note that content standards at every grade level will include skills from all levels of the hierarchy. Skills of higher cognitive demand are not reserved for higher grades. In reviewing the science standards in Table 3.6, note that the fourth grade standard includes the skill to evaluate—one of the higher categories of skill performance in Bloom's Taxonomy. However, the facts, concepts, and procedures a fourth-grade student is required to evaluate will be different from those of a student in the eighth or twelfth grade.

What level of thinking skill, as outlined by Bloom's Taxonomy, are your students expected to demonstrate? A content standard or objective will indicate

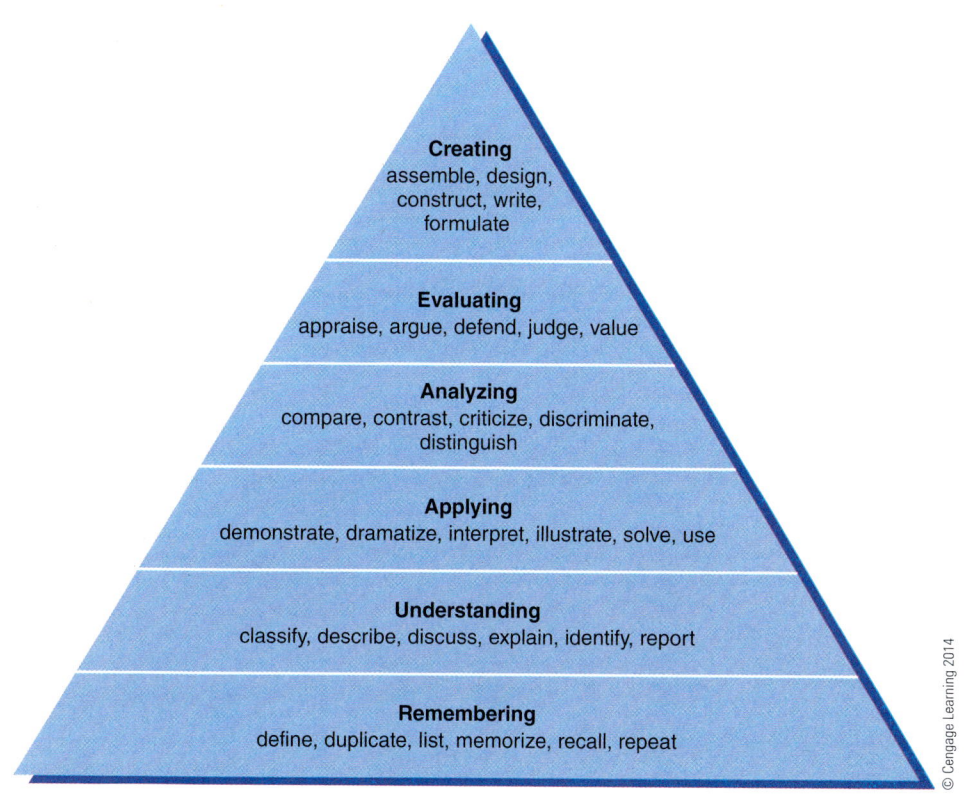

```
                    Creating
                 assemble, design,
                 construct, write,
                    formulate
              ─────────────────────
                   Evaluating
            appraise, argue, defend, judge, value
          ─────────────────────────────
                    Analyzing
         compare, contrast, criticize, discriminate,
                    distinguish
        ─────────────────────────────────
                     Applying
       demonstrate, dramatize, interpret, illustrate, solve, use
      ──────────────────────────────────────
                   Understanding
       classify, describe, discuss, explain, identify, report
     ────────────────────────────────────────
                    Remembering
        define, duplicate, list, memorize, recall, repeat
```

Figure 3.8
Examples of skills in the Cognitive Domain of the revised Bloom's Taxonomy (2001).

the type of skill required by the use of a verb. In the examples in Table 3.6, the skills are

- Grade 4: describe and evaluate;
- Grade 8: interpret; and
- Grade 12: investigate and analyze.

When developing lessons aligned with your content standards, it is critical to know the level of thinking required of your students. When combined with the content knowledge, they help you determine what it is your students should know and be able to do. Based on that information, then, you need to assure that your students have opportunities to both 1) develop those skills during their learning activities and 2) demonstrate those skills during your assessments. One mistake often made by inexperienced teachers is to design activities and assessments at a skill level that is lower than that dictated by the content standard and ultimately assessed on high-stakes assessments. When this happens, students may be aware of content-specific knowledge, but they can't apply it at an appropriate skill level.

In your methods classes, you will learn how to unpack the various content standards and to develop activities that enable your students to master the specific knowledge and skills needed to demonstrate proficiency. However, in this text, our focus is more specifically on how you can use technology-enhanced experiences to support the development of students' understanding and mastery of content standards. While technology skills can be taught in separate classes, and even applied to the development of individual, isolated products, the potential of technology is more fully realized when it is used to support integrated content learning. And while technology can support students' learning of basic skills, it can also enable them to develop advanced writing, research, and

STORIES from Practice

Addressing Content Standards in a Student-Centered Lesson

José Garcia, an eighth grade science teacher, admits he was feeling major trepidation when he first launched challenge-based learning a few years ago. Not only had he never tried this style of pedagogy, but none of his incoming students had experienced a learning environment remotely like the one he was about to introduce. Challenge-based learning focuses on student engagement during the learning process.

"I knew that during the first nine weeks I would be teaching *methods* more than lessons. Before I could expect the kids to take charge of their learning, I had to teach them how to do it." During those early weeks, according to the curriculum guide, he and his students fell further and further behind. "But I had made a commitment to myself and my kids, and my principal supported me every step of the way."

Now, when beginning a new topic, Mr. Garcia begins by consulting the North Carolina Standard Course of Study (NCSCOS), noting his goal, listing all objectives for that goal, and formulating an "essential question" to pose to his eighth grade science students. For example, the NCSCOS science Goal 6 for Grade 8 relates to cell theory and function. Mr. Garcia's essential question is: "What structures, functions, and processes do I have in common with plants, animals, or fungi?"

He then formulates a long list of specific questions he knows his students must be able to answer to demonstrate mastery of the material. For Goal 6, for example, he devised 38 separate questions, ranging in complexity from "What is a cell and what does the Cell Theory state?" to "How does deoxyribonucleic replication occur?"

For each major unit, Mr. Garcia requires the student groups to create a final product. Depending on the levels of technological sophistication his classes have achieved, this may be as simple as a blog or as complicated as a mini-motion picture. If he assigns a movie, he enlarges the groups because of the numerous production jobs—camera operator, audio recorder, actor, director, writer, costume designer, set designer, and so on—that must be done.

He then provides a list of items that must explicitly appear in the final products—for example, certain terms must be defined, a character who portrays a practitioner of a relevant "real-world" profession must appear, etc.— but, he emphasizes, "I let the kids do what they want as much as possible. I promise not to interfere unless they get lewd or present something that might be ethnically or racially offensive."

After an appointed deadline, each group presents its findings and conclusions on each of the individual questions to the class as a whole. Because Mr. Garcia's classroom is essentially "paperless," the students' presentations are generally in the form of sharable blogs that may include photographs, animation, audio/video clips, etc.

Like all other activities in Mr. Garcia's classroom, the presentation phase is completely interactive. "While some students are presenting at the front of the room," he explains, "other students are at the back of the room tracking the information on graphic organizers or Thinking Maps," which are immediately available to everyone in the class electronically. This practice, Mr. Garcia says, frees individual students from taking notes; thus, allowing all students to ask questions, request clarifications, volunteer information, share similar findings, suggest related paths of inquiry, and so forth.

By the end of the presentations, every aspect of every NCSCOS goal and objective has been explored and discussed in depth; every student has shared his/her newfound "expertise;" and every student has access to comprehensive notes, lab reports, and research results covering every aspect of every goal and objective.

Source: Adapted from *Challenge-based learning: José Garcia's innovative approach to student inquiry* by Dan Lewandowski. Reprinted with permission from *José Garcia.* http://www.learnnc.org/lp/pages/6375

---

higher-order thinking skills. For example, technology can help students visualize abstract problems, such as the relationship between population growth and depletion of the world's limited resources, and consider real solutions. When technology handles the underlying, complex computations and intricate data manipulations, students are free to explore relationships, test hypotheses, and construct new knowledge.

Table 3.7 illustrates a few ways that technology can be used to support students' mastery of the sample science standards that were included in Table 3.6. In the supplement to this textbook, we discuss more specifically, how technology can be used to support specific content learning in language arts, social studies, foreign languages, mathematics, science, physical education and health, art, and music.

Table 3.7		How Technology Can Support Student Mastery of Content Standards
Grade	Standard	Technology Possibilities
4	Describe and evaluate the properties of several minerals.	• Use probeware or other tools to analyze mineral samples • Collect videos or digital images of rock samples taken from the surrounding region
8	Interpret ways in which rocks, fossils, and ice cores record Earth's geologic history and the evolution of life including: Geologic Time Scale, Index Fossils, Law of Superposition.	• Create an annotated timeline of Earth's geologic history and the evolution of life • Create a virtual geology exhibit with text, images, video, or other media
12	Investigate and analyze the processes responsible for the rock cycle by analyzing the origin, texture, and mineral composition of rocks.	• Interact with electronic pen pals from schools in other regions to create representative rock samples on Google Earth • Use probeware or other metric devices to analyze mineral composition

© Cengage Learning 2014

Standards and objectives are not a prescription; they do not tell you *how* you must teach in order for your students to achieve them. That is, they do not prescribe the methods you must use nor dictate the materials or resources required to address them. Some content standards specifically mention technology, but as you'll see throughout this book, there are technology tools and resources to help address content standards in all domains regardless of whether they specifically mention technology.

Using Technology to Support Authentic Instruction—An Example

So let's think about how we could use authentic instruction and technology to develop creative thinking skills around the science standards listed above. As an example, let's consider a lesson for fourth graders in which they learn to describe and evaluate the properties of minerals. How can you create a lesson that encourages learner autonomy and provides the opportunity for active learning using holistic, complex, and challenging activities?

In order to establish a realistic context for the lesson, the teacher could introduce the fourth graders to a problem in which a whole box of mineral samples from the geology museum got mixed up and separated from their labels. The museum director needs help from her lab assistants (the students) to straighten out the mess. She asks them for their ideas as to how to accomplish this task. How will they do it? As she facilitates this whole group activity, she records multiple paths to solving the problem and helps the students identify an avenue for investigation.

In the next phase of the lesson, the learners might conduct a web search to learn the basics of mineral identification. The students can be prompted with questions including "What tools will you need?" and "What kind of information do you need about each mineral sample?" The teacher might then refine the problem a bit. She shows the students the labels from the mixed up samples in order to scaffold their learning to make the task more manageable. For the fourth grade level, five or six minerals would be plenty. The next task for the students is to use a spreadsheet to create a data collection table for each of the minerals in order to assist them with their data collection, analysis, and interpretation. The students might search the web for information to fill in their charts. Finally, the teacher reveals the mineral samples. Using information and tools gathered in the prior stages of the lesson, the

STORIES from Practice

If You Build It, They Might Learn!

When state standardized tests are looming, activity can pick up in classrooms as teachers make sure their students are prepared to do their best. Often, teachers turn to drill-and-practice and other types of review to help students get ready, but two middle school teachers in Hall County, Georgia, took a nod from one of their students and chose a more unique way. They built an app.

Math teacher Valerie Lancaster shared the idea with her colleague Shellie Moreland, who teaches language arts. With the state testing season looming, Lancaster asked her students how they wanted to review. A student raised her hand and shared, "Let's make an app." Lancaster looked to Mooreland and asked, "How can we make this happen? What would it look like? What technology do we have to make this work?" Furthermore, the teachers had to determine how they could combine language arts and math on the project, but still keep students in their own classrooms during the 70-minute class time. The teachers went to the drawing board, literally—the interactive white board—and began plotting out a rough design for students to use as boundaries including state standards along with due dates and two presentation dates.

During the two-week App Project, students were most often physically located in their original 4th period classrooms but were required to meet with their combined math and language arts team via web-based resources, such as the learning management system Edmodo, and conversation tools, Today's Meet and Wall Wisher. They did get to meet in combined teams during three class periods over the span of the two-week project. App ideas had to focus on two aspects. First, the design team had to develop the idea for a math study app for students based on seventh grade math standards and second, language arts standards had to be addressed through a marketing campaign for the app.

Students had two presentation days. The first presentation day was strategically placed at the end of week one, during which students practiced presenting their app projects to the class for feedback (see Figure 3.9). The final presentation occurred at the end of week two and included members of the Hall County Board of Education. Besides viewing the app ideas, board members later talked with students about school technology and what they'd need in their classrooms to make projects like this easier to implement. When all was said and done, says Mooreland, "All of my language arts students passed the standardized test and didn't have to rely on the more traditional approach of worksheets and practice tests."

Source: Shellie Mooreland, C. W. Davis Middle School, Flowery Branch, Georgia.

Figure 3.9
A sample of an app project students developed to help study math.

students match the minerals with their labels. At the end of the lesson, the teacher asks each group to share their findings for one of the mineral samples. After all the minerals have been identified, she concludes the lesson by asking her students to describe how they went about solving the problem and what they learned in the process. As a follow-up activity, she might want to give them a few more minerals to identify, using the procedures they determined to be successful in their initial investigations.

By establishing a realistic context for students' learning, the teacher provides a holistic, complex problem in which to ground their learning. In order to encourage learner autonomy, students plan, monitor, and evaluate their own learning—learners are given the freedom to design and conduct their investigations. In this process, they practice self-directed learning skills as they plan, monitor, and evaluate their actions. The teacher models the sort of questions students should ask themselves during the self-directed learning process by asking them how they would accomplish their goals, what tools they might need, and what information they need to solve the mineral identification problem. She scaffolds the challenges of authentic learning by placing her students in collaborative groups where students can pool their knowledge and support each other. Collaborative group work also encourages reflection and articulation as the students explain their reasoning to their team members, and reflect on the reasoning of others. When the teacher presents the mineral labels that the students are to match with the mineral samples, she further reduces the complexity of the problem by constraining their information searches to a manageable number.

Using this approach, the students learn to describe and evaluate the properties of minerals through an authentic learning experience that, as you have learned in this chapter, would help develop their creative thinking skills. Students are given the opportunity to design and conduct an investigation in which they collect, analyze, and interpret data, and then apply what they learned to new problems. By allowing students to decide what information is needed, the instructional time becomes inquiry-driven and the students become active learners. Students have a clear problem to solve, and their understanding of the properties of minerals is rooted in a practical application.

Throughout this book, we provide additional examples of how you can meet content and technology standards while developing students' creative thinking skills. Look for specific examples in our *Stories from Practice* features.

APPLY *to Practice*

Lesson Plans and Content Standards

Find a lesson plan from a website or other lesson planning resource that is relevant to your area of study. Find the standards for your state that are or could be addressed in the lesson you found. If you need some help, some lesson planning sites are listed on the textbook's CourseMate website and most states include a list of standards for all grades and content areas on their websites.

1. List the content standard(s) addressed by the lesson.
2. Briefly describe the activities in the lesson.
3. Determine how well the activities match the required knowledge (nouns) and the skills (verbs) in the content standard(s). Indicate alignment and potential misalignment.
4. Identify the extent to which the activities incorporate the components of authentic instruction. Are there ways in which you could make the lesson more authentic?

Chapter Summary

In this chapter, we described how the components of authentic instruction could be used to facilitate and inspire student creativity and learning. We also described how the principles of authentic instruction could guide your use of technology in the classroom. Specifically, we discussed how different types of authentic instruction (problem-based learning, project-based learning, and others) promote learner autonomy and active learning by anchoring instruction in holistic, complex, and challenging activities. We discussed the occasional need for directed instruction and explored multiple ways in which technology can support this approach as well as each of the components of authentic instruction.

In the last section of this chapter we considered how to reconcile the goal of helping students meet content standards with the goal of promoting creative thinking in your classroom. Using the example of a science lesson on the identification of minerals, we illustrated how you could design learning experiences that provide opportunities for your students to obtain the skills required in the content standards, and at the same time, develop their creative thinking skills.

In the next chapter, we continue our discussion of specific approaches to using technology to encourage the development of creative thinking skills. You will be prompted to think about ways in which common software applications, such as word processing and databases, can be used to support the development of your students' creative thinking skills. We will also consider a variety of ways in which technology can be used to support meaningful conversations and student reflection and collaboration.

Web Resources and Activities

Visit the Education CourseMate website for

- a list of resources about using lexiles; and
- links to the national standards for your content area(s).

YOUR PORTFOLIO

This chapter described how to use technology to facilitate and inspire student learning and creativity through the use of authentic classroom activities. To demonstrate competency in ISTE NETS-T Standards 1 a-b, add the following items to your portfolio:

1. Reflect on how technology can be used to develop students' creative thinking skills. Consider the recommendations from the national curricular reports (see Table 3.1) for creating more effective and engaging instruction that can inspire student creativity and learning. Write a brief reflection of a teaching or learning experience that you think exemplifies a "best practice" lesson. Indicate the role technology played in the lesson and how it supported the tenets of authentic instruction you described above.
    a. What aspects of the lesson worked best?
    b. What aspects would you change if used in the future?

2. Describe a lesson in which you incorporate the principles of authentic instruction. Locate a set of national or state standards that your future students may be required to meet. Select one standard around which to design a lesson.
    a. Identify how you will address each of the five components of authentic instruction: 1) learner autonomy, 2) active learners, 3) holistic, 4) complex, and 5) challenging activities.
    b. Describe specific ways that technologies could be used to support the successful implementation of your strategy.

References

Anderson, L.W., & Krathwohl, D. (Eds.). (2001). *A taxonomy for learning, teaching and assessing: A revision of Bloom's taxonomy of educational objectives.* New York: Longman.

Azzam, A. M. (2009). Why creativity now? A conversation with Sir Ken Robinson. *Educational Leadership, 67*(1), 22–26.

Egbert, J. (2009). *Supporting learning with technology: Essentials of classroom practice.* Upper Saddle River, NJ: Pearson.

Hunter, M. (1982). *Mastery teaching.* El Segundo, CA: Instructional Dynamics.

Johnson, D., & Johnson, R. (1998). *Learning together and alone: Cooperative, competitive, and individualistic learning* (5th ed.). New York: Allyn and Bacon.

Jonassen, D. J., Howland, J., Moore, J., & Marra, R. M. (2003). *Learning to solve problems with technology: A constructivist perspective* (2nd ed.). Upper Saddle River, NJ: Merrill/Prentice Hall.

Magliaro, S. G., Lockee, B. B., & Burton, J. K. (2005). Direct instruction revisited: A key model for instructional technology. *Educational Technology Research and Development, 53*(4), 41–55.

Musselwhite, T. (2005). Creating learner-centered middle school classrooms. New York: Glencoe/McGraw Hill. Retrieved June 4, 2012, from http://www.glencoe.com/sec/teachingtoday/subject/creating_learn_centered.phtml

Newmann, F. M., Bryk, A. S., & Nagaoka, J. K. (2001). *Authentic intellectual work and standardized tests: Conflict or coexistence?* Chicago, IL: Consortium on Chicago School Research.

Pedersen, S., & Liu, M. (2002–2003). The transfer of problem-solving skills from a problem-based learning environment: The effect of modeling an expert's cognitive processes. *Journal of Research on Technology in Education, 35*(2), 303–320.

Public Schools of North Carolina. (2006). North Carolina standard course of study. Retrieved June 4, 2012, from http://www.dpi.state.nc.us/curriculum

Resnick, L. B. (1987). *Education and learning to think.* Washington, DC: National Academy Press.

Robinson, K. (2009a). TED and Reddit ask Ken Robinson anything. Retrieved September 6, 2011, from http://blog.ted.com/2009/08/12/ted_and_reddit_1/

Saye, J. W., & Brush, T. (2002). Scaffolding critical reasoning about history and social issues in multimedia-supported learning environments. *Educational Technology Research and Development, 50*(3), 77–96.

Simons, K. D., & Ertmer, P. A. (2006). Scaffolding disciplined inquiry in problem-based learning environments. *International Journal of Learning, 12*(6), 297–306.

Slavin, R. (1994). *Cooperative learning: Theory, research, and practice.* New York: Allyn and Bacon.

Wegerif, R. (2002). *Literature review in thinking skills, technology, and learning.* Future Lab Series, No. 2. Retrieved December 16, 2011, from http://archive.futurelab.org.uk/resources/publications-reports-articles/literature-reviews/Literature-Review394/

Zemelman, S., Daniels, H., & Hyde, A. (2005). *Best practice: Today's standards for teaching and learning in America's schools.* Portsmouth, NH: Heinemann.

4

Digital Tools That Support Learning

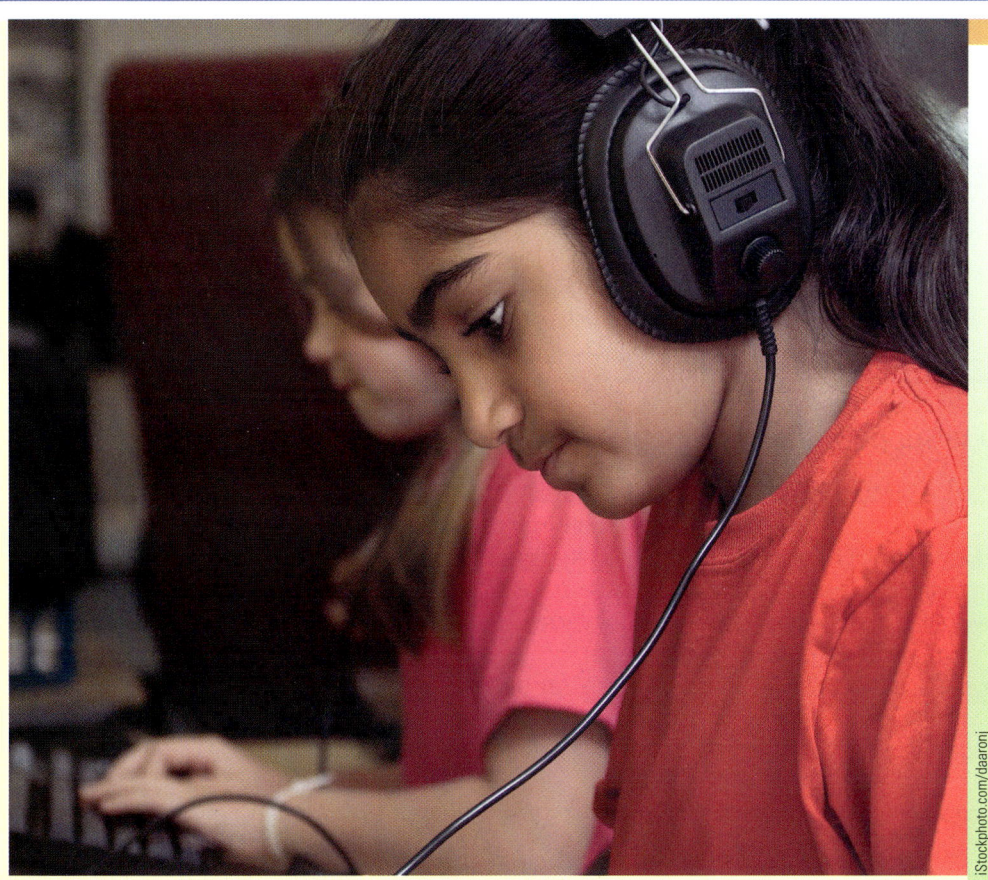

OUTCOMES

In this chapter, you will learn to

- Promote student learning by employing **technology-based tutorials** or developing online tutorials in the form of WebQuests;
- Help students represent, manipulate, and reflect on what they know through the use of **technology mindtools** including: databases, concept maps, computer-based simulations, or visualization tools, as well as hypermedia activities, such as digital storytelling;
- Use **technology as collaborative learning tools to support conversation**; and
- **Locate** and evaluate relevant **digital tools and resources found online** in support of instruction in face-to-face and virtual environments.

It's amazing how much a learning environment can change when technology is added to the mix! While technology is not essential to creating authentic, learner-centered instruction, it offers a powerful resource for engaging students in authentic experiences, typically increasing both their motivation and their learning. In the last chapter, you learned about the importance of developing students' creative thinking skills. You learned that creative thinkers are self-directed, confident in their knowledge, motivated, and flexible in their thinking. You also learned how authentic instructional methods can support the development of creative thinking skills by providing opportunities for students to engage in holistic, complex, and challenging activities that promote learner autonomy and active learning; how content standards can be taught through authentic learning experiences; and how technologies could support both authentic learning and directed instruction.

iste.nets

ISTE Standards Addressed in Chapter 4

NETS-T 1. Facilitate and Inspire Student Learning and Creativity

Teachers use their knowledge of subject matter, teaching and learning, and technology to facilitate experiences that advance student learning, creativity, and innovation in both face-to-face and virtual environments. Teachers:
c. promote student reflection using collaborative tools to reveal and clarify;

(continued on page 84)

students' conceptual understanding and thinking, planning, and creative processes; and

d. model collaborative knowledge construction by engaging in learning with students, colleagues, and others in face-to-face and virtual environments.

NETS-T 2. Design and Develop Digital-Age Learning Experiences and Assessments

Teachers design, develop, and evaluate authentic learning experiences and assessments incorporating contemporary tools and resources to maximize content learning in context and to develop the knowledge, skills, and attitudes. identified in the NETS-S. Teachers:

a. design or adapt relevant learning experiences to incorporate digital tools and resources to promote student learning and creativity.

In this chapter you will learn how to design learning experiences that incorporate digital tools and resources to promote student learning and creativity. Wegerif (2002) described three primary roles that the computer can serve: computer as tutor, computer as mindtool, and computer as a support for reflection and conversation. This categorization provides us with a starting point for thinking about different ways we can use technology to engage our students in creative thinking. Remember, the distinction being made here among the different computer/technology roles has more to do with *how* the tools are used, not with the tools themselves. And, although Wegerif used the general term, *computer*, we've expanded this label to encompass a wider range of digital technologies, from laptops, to calculators, to smartphones, to tablets. And since we often use the web to locate instructional resources, we'll also discuss strategies to assist you in locating reputable resources and tools that can be used as tutorials, mindtools, and supports for conversations.

STORIES from Practice

Using Technology to Support Creative Thinking

I teach high school biology in a unique setting. While my students are probably no different from most freshmen and sophomore students you might know, I teach this course with two other biology teachers using a method we devised a number of years ago, called Team-Taught Biology. Technology is a key component to our approach, enabling us to engage students in the biology content in very interesting ways. Learning happens when people are *active* and technology simply allows us to provide more of those opportunities, because we don't have to lecture. Although I teach biology, my primary goal for my students is not that they learn biology, but that they become independent learners and critical thinkers. And the independent learning happens only if you give them control. Technology puts them in control. As long as I was telling them what to do and when to do it, there was no chance that they would ever become independent learners. As soon as you give students control over their own education, it's terribly empowering. We want students to be self-directed learners; we want them to be critical thinkers. And I think in the information age that's especially important. Because there is so much junk disseminated by technology—especially on the Internet.

Technology allows for another learning alternative, another option, another way of providing information. Right now, we already have two or three primary options for using technology in the classroom. One is the Internet—we have an activity every single unit, where students can go to the Internet and interact in that environment, demonstrate understanding, come back and report it. We also have computer tutorials, which have eliminated the need for a lecture. That frees us up to be mentoring instead of spouting knowledge. The third way that technology is used is to do labs that can be done in no other way. Computers enable us to present data that are outside the realm of a biology classroom, such as ozone data, or to examine the dotted wings of a butterfly. As far as I am concerned that is the best use of technology—when it is used in ways where you couldn't teach any other way.

Arranging our classroom in this way, and using technology to support alternative approaches, provides students with the opportunity to pick those types of learning activities that they enjoy the most. It is not total freedom. There are some things that they have to do. But for every individual there is enough of a selection, enough of a choice. They can't do everything. They can't do all the learning activities, so they get to ignore some of them. And they can ignore those things that they dislike.

The best thing about this approach is that it has taken me off center stage. In the traditional classroom, the teacher is the center, the teacher is the active individual. But in Team-Taught Biology, we have set up a situation where everybody is active. And I think that, while that doesn't guarantee learning, it certainly increases the chances that it's going to happen.

Source: Based on Ertmer, P. A. (2003). VisionQuest: Envisioning and achieving integrated technology use. Retrieved June 24, 2006, from http://www.edci.purdue.edu/vquest

Technology as Tutor: Promoting Student Learning using Technology-Based Tutorials

When technology is used as a **tutor**, it is typically used as a teaching machine, that is, to teach new content to students. Now that more and more students have access to a wide range of digital technologies, 24/7, the use of technology-based tutorials is becoming more common. Students generally know, or quickly learn, how to access the tutorials embedded within a software program, video game, or phone "app" in order to learn how to complete specific tasks using the program. For example, when first learning to use iMovie or MovieMaker, students are encouraged to work through a series of embedded tutorials that take them, step-by-step, through the basic tasks involved in creating and sharing their own movies.

Technology-based tutorials typically provide a complete lesson on a specific topic including 1) presenting new information, 2) providing practice, and 3) evaluating student performance (see Figure 4.1). For example, Study Island, Education City, Carnegie Learning, and Discover Education all offer activities designed to help students learn content related to specific state standards using a tutorial approach. (Some even provide tutorials about how to use their tutorials!) Students engage in web-based lessons, practice what they've learned through tailored exercises, and then complete interactive games or traditional assessments to determine their current knowledge needs.

Some tutorials go a step further and provide each student with detailed, personalized support, and are often referred to as **intelligent tutoring systems** (ITS). These tutoring systems are a type of educational program that tracks student responses; makes inferences about each student's strengths and weaknesses; and then tailors feedback, provides additional exercises, or offers hints to improve performance. So, after the student completes a series of practice exercises, immediate feedback is provided. If questions are answered incorrectly, students are shown

> **tutor**
> the use of software to explicitly teach or provide practice with a specific body of content

> **technology-based tutorial**
> a complete lesson on a specific topic offered via technology, including presentation of information, practice exercises, and feedback

> **intelligent tutoring system**
> a type of educational software that tracks student responses, makes inferences about strengths and weaknesses and then tailors feedback and subsequent instruction to improve performance

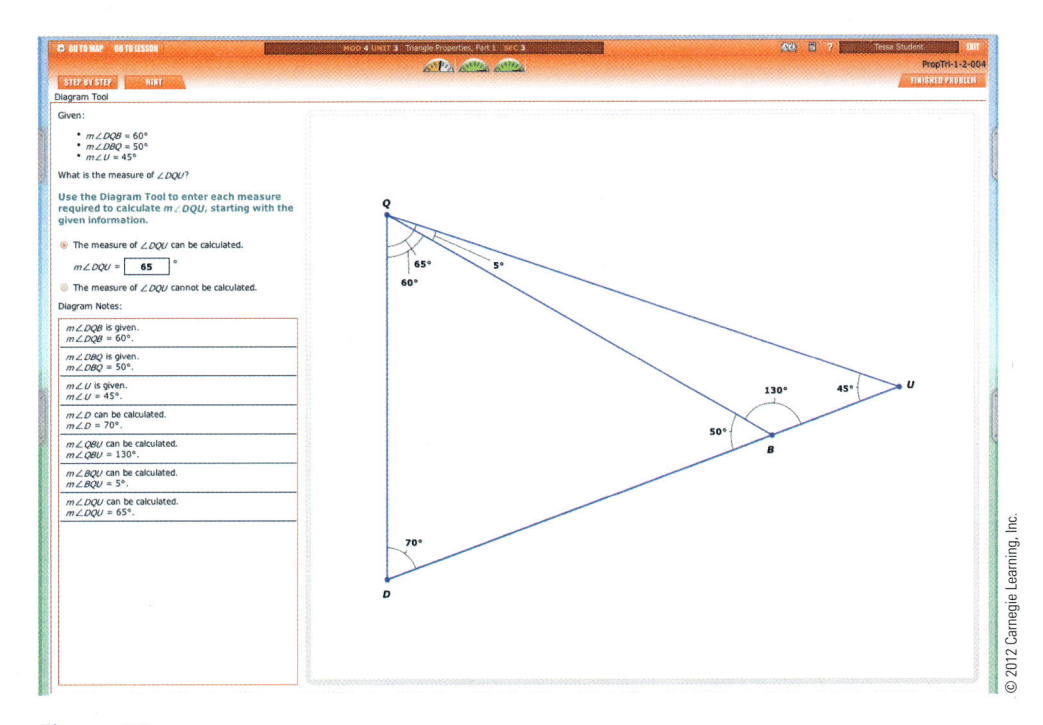

Figure 4.1
Computer tutorials cover many topics, such as this math tutorial from Carnegie Learning that adapts to student responses.

TECH TOOLS & TIPS

Using Educational Games to Support Learning

Gaming proponents Gee and Schaffer (2010) list the following ways educational games can support learning. Replace the word "player" with "student," and you can see the great potential games have for promoting learning.

1. Games are built around problems and require players to use facts, information, strategies, and skills to solve the problems.
2. Games incorporate a range of valuable skills necessary in the real world, such as collaborating with others and generating creative or innovative solutions.
3. Games assess ability and differentiate based on how well the player performs, often determining whether the player is ready to go to the next level or not.
4. Games collect a variety of different types of information about players over time.
5. Games incorporate both learning and assessment in such a way that it's hard to tell them apart. The actions of a player have consequences and provide some kind of feedback that helps the player determine what to do next, or possibly to repeat.
6. Games provide hints, data, information, and even sensory information that help players get better at the game.
7. Games are designed to appeal to a wide range of people or they won't be successful.

© Cengage Learning 2014

the correct answer, along with a detailed explanation. If extra help is needed, the program automatically prompts the students to work on remedial material for that topic. Other names for this type of software include integrated learning software (ILS) and computer-adapted instruction (CAI).

Educational games are another category of technology that you might not think of as being tutorials, but even games designed for entertainment present new information, allow you to practice, and give you feedback, often in real time. On one end are drill-and-practice games that allow students to build or test foundational knowledge they need in a content domain. You can find many of these games online for younger or even older students who may be novices in a new area of content. But the educational gaming movement is pushing to incorporate some of the more sophisticated components of games usually found in complex video games. These games allow students to practice more complex skills, skills that may cross subject areas, and receive feedback on their performances in settings that are highly engaging.

The web can provide access to numerous tutorials, but as you know, it can teach new content in other ways as well. You can locate information on a variety of topics such as how to calibrate a whiteboard, prepare balanced meals, or use video in your classroom. In order to scaffold, or support, your students' use of the web, you might want to create a WebQuest that *acts* as a tutor. A **WebQuest** is an organized format for presenting lessons that utilize web-based resources (see example in Figure 4.2). A typical WebQuest contains elements that most educators agree comprise sound instructional components:

- an introduction that motivates and prepares students for the activity;
- a clear statement of the intended outcomes of the lesson;
- the steps that students should follow;
- criteria on which they will be evaluated; and
- concluding activities where students reflect on and extend their learning.

You may want to create your own WebQuest (see *Tech Tools and Tips—Developing WebQuests*) using simple web-development software, or access one of the many

WebQuest
an organized format for presenting lessons that utilize web-based resources

Developing a WebQuest

Dr. Bernie Dodge and Tom March at San Diego State University are credited with creating the WebQuest structure. As outlined on Dr. Dodge's website (Dodge, 2006), a WebQuest consists of five student components and a teacher page. The following descriptions are from the WebQuest website.

Component	Purpose	Task
Introduction	The purpose of this section is to both prepare and grab the students' attention.	Write a short paragraph to introduce the activity or lesson to the students. If there is a role or scenario involved (e.g., "You are a detective trying to identify the mysterious poet.") then here is where you'll set the stage. Also, in this section you'll communicate the Big Question (Essential Question, Guiding Question) on which the WebQuest is centered.
Task	The task focuses learners on what they are going to do—specifically, the culminating performance or product that drives all of the learning activities.	Clearly describe what the result of the learners' activities will be. Don't list the steps that students will go through to get to the end point. That belongs in the Process section.
Process	This section outlines how the learners will accomplish the task. Scaffolding includes clear steps, resources, and tools for organizing information.	To accomplish the task, what steps should the learners go through? Learners will access the online resources that you've identified as they go through the Process. In this section, you might also provide some guidance on how to organize the information gathered.
Evaluation	This section describes the criteria needed to meet performance and content standards.	Describe to the learners how their performances will be evaluated. The assessment rubric(s) should align with the culminating project or performance, as outlined in the task section of the WebQuest. Specify whether there will be a common grade for group work vs. individual grades.
Conclusion	The conclusion brings closure and encourages reflection.	Summarize what the learners will have accomplished or learned by completing this activity or lesson. You might also include some rhetorical questions or additional links to encourage them to extend their thinking into other content beyond this lesson.
Teacher Page		The teacher page includes information that helps other teachers implement the WebQuest including descriptions of target learners, standards, notes for teaching the unit, and, in some cases, examples of student work.

Source: Dodge, B. (2006). http://webquest.sdsu.edu

WebQuests available online. Like any lesson plan you find on the web, you may need to modify WebQuests to meet the needs of your class but be sure to credit the original source.

With the right teacher input and program design, a technology-based tutorial can be an effective way to infuse activities into the curriculum that require and develop creative thinking. In this way, they begin to blur the line between a strict tutorial and a mindtool (described next). Proponents believe that WebQuests are great resources for promoting higher-level thinking, so again, it's *how* you use the technology that is important. For example, the teacher can ask students to work in groups around a portable or desktop device (whether a desktop, laptop, or tablet computer) and then when the tutorial prompts them with a challenge or a question, they can discuss their

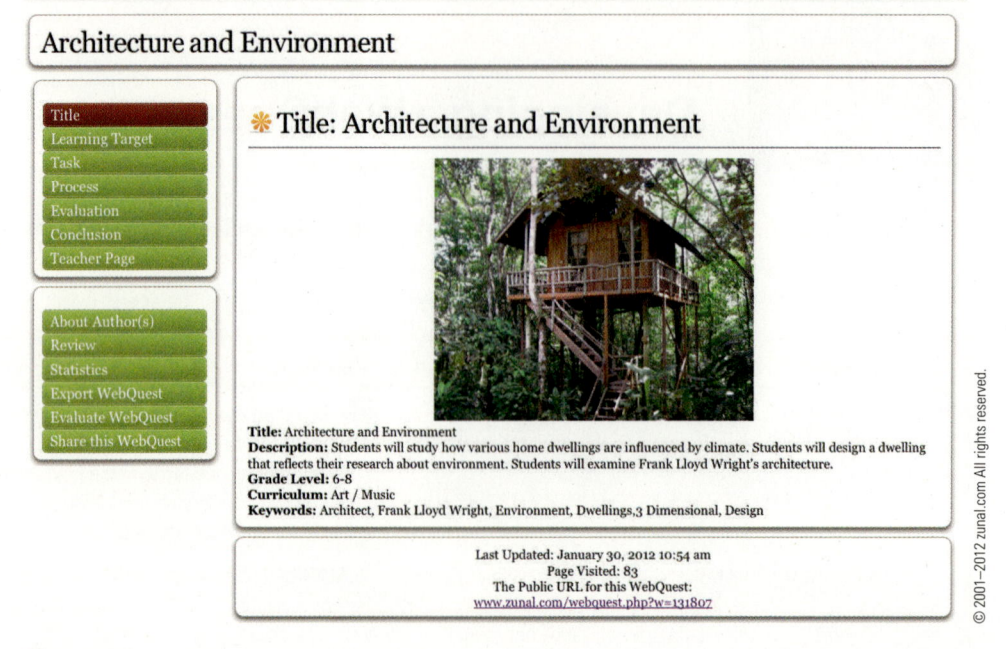

Figure 4.2
WebQuests direct learners to relevant websites to complete the required learning tasks.

ideas before reaching consensus on what the group response should be. In Table 4.1 we include a list of specific characteristics that Wegerif (2002) demonstrated to be effective in establishing and sustaining effective discussion among students when they were working around a digital device. Think about how you could use these characteristics as guidelines to help you select effective software for your classroom. In addition, think about how you could incorporate these characteristics into other approaches and strategies you use in your classroom, with or without the use of technology-based tutorials.

Just like a teacher, technology-based tutorials can initiate or frame a meaningful discussion. Unlike a teacher, however, the software will never be intolerant or pass judgment on students' responses. When used as intended, tutorials provide opportunities for students to learn new knowledge or skills. When used in more open-ended ways, they can provide additional opportunities for students to engage in activities that support creative thinking through reflection, meaningful conversations, and self-assessment.

Table 4.1 Characteristics of Effective Technology-based Tutorials

- Challenges and problems have meaning for students and provide a range of alternative choices worth discussing.
- Challenges engage learners with the content of the software, not its interface.
- A clear purpose or task is evident to the group and is kept in focus throughout.
- On-screen prompts ask group members to talk together, to reach agreement, and to provide opinions and reasons.
- Resources for discussion, including information on which decisions can be based, are provided. Opportunities are included to review decisions in light of new information.
- Students are not prompted to take turns, beat the clock, or establish competitive ways of working.
- For younger students, audio input or multi-choice answers minimize typing unless the learners have keyboarding skills (reported in Wegerif, 2002).

> ## THE GAME PLAN
> ### Using Technology-based Tutorials to Support Creative and Higher-Order Thinking
>
> **Set Goals**
>
> Learn more about technology-based tutorials and how you might use them to develop critical and creative thinking skills among your students.
>
> **Take Action**
>
> Locate a technology-based tutorial that is designed for your grade level or content area. You may be able to find them in your media center, lab school, or at a cooperating school in your district. As another possibility, consider the programs you have on your computer (iMovie, Powerpoint, etc.) or that you access regularly online (Skype, Dropbox) and explore the tutorials that are provided to help you learn how to use the programs.
>
> **Monitor**
>
> Review the tutorial and determine the extent to which the characteristics listed in Table 4.1 are incorporated. You may want to create a table, rubric, or checklist to guide your work.
>
> **Evaluate and Extend**
>
> Suggest ways to use the tutorial to increase opportunities for students to engage in creative and higher-order thinking. Identify the types of thinking your activities best address.

Technology as Mindtool: Promoting Student Learning Using Technology Applications

Mindtools are technology applications that enable learners to represent, manipulate, or reflect on what they know, rather than to reproduce what someone else knows (Jonassen, 2006). By requiring students to think about what they know in different, meaningful ways, mindtools engage students in critical thinking about the content they are studying. By functioning as intellectual partners with students, mindtools enable them to act smarter than they would without the tools. For instance, in order for students to create databases, they must engage in analytical reasoning; in order to create a web page, they must actively construct representations of their thinking. In some cases, the *products* created when using technology-based tutorials can function as mindtools because they are used to demonstrate what students are thinking and what they have learned. Students cannot use technology mindtools without thinking deeply about what they are doing.

Jonassen (2006) described a number of different types of mindtools including databases and concept-mapping tools (also referred to as semantic-organization tools); simulations and visualization tools; and hypertext and hypermedia (referred to as knowledge-building tools). Although other technology applications may also be used as mindtools (e.g., media-authoring software, expert systems, modeling tools), our goal is not to present an exhaustive description of all the possibilities, but to introduce you to the idea of how you can use common software applications as mindtools to promote creative thinking among your students.

> **mindtool**
> the use of technology as an organizational tool, simulation and visualization tool, or knowledge-building tool

Databases and Concept-Mapping Tools

Database and concept-mapping software are applications that help students think about, and then communicate, the underlying structure of a content area. Since structure underlies all knowledge, tools that require students to identify that structure can help increase their understanding of the content.

Have you ever made a grocery list and then organized it by aisles in the store so that you could find the items you needed more readily? On a relatively simple level, you structured your list based on your understanding of two things: 1) how the store (content) was organized (e.g., by food types) and 2) how to classify the items on your list into the different categories. Now, if there were many different ways to classify the items on your list (by quality, supplier, brand names, etc.), and all of them were relevant to your shopping needs, then you would have to think more carefully about how to organize your list.

Databases

database
a type of software that organizes information

Databases are a type of software that organizes information. When we use a computer database we can search for information in a variety of ways and receive the results almost instantaneously. Although databases are most often used for the purposes of organization and retrieval of information, they can also function as mindtools, especially when students are asked to create them. In order to build a database, you must first understand which relationships facilitate its use and then search for, and locate, the information needed to fill it. This requires the integration and organization of a content domain, which requires creative thinking skills. For example, if you were asked to create a database of different lesson plans used by teachers in your school, what are some of the categories you would use to classify each? Of course, you'd want to be able to locate a lesson by its title and subject area, and also by grade level and standard. But would it also be important to know what materials and resources are required for the lesson? Would you need to know what accommodations were made for students with special needs or those who need enrichment? And what about being able to relate the information in the lesson plan database to information in a teacher database that would allow you to find out if another teacher had used it or made some kind of modifications to it? As you can see, the planning stage of designing a database is one of the most crucial parts of the process, and it is this aspect that requires students to use the creative and critical thinking skills of analysis and evaluation.

Databases have been used to help students understand the organization of a range of content areas and can be used to teach thinking skills. Young students will probably need help actually developing a database, but you can guide them through the planning process during a group activity. For example, students in a second- or third-grade class can help you classify different types of clip art images you typically use that are then stored in a database. Students from upper elementary grades, and higher, can access, and sometimes add to, a range of databases online.

collaborative database
a special type of database that supports a shared process of knowledge building

Collaborative databases are a special type of database that supports a shared process of knowledge building. The goal is to engage students as scientists in the problem-solving process. That is, students generate hypotheses about a given problem situation; gather information through research and observation in order to confirm, modify, or refute their hypotheses; and then seek feedback from others who either collaborate in the investigation or review their published work. Examples of this type of collaborative database are the Knowledge Forum and Wikipedia.

To help you understand why this is called a collaborative database, picture an environment that consists of text and graphical notes, all produced by students, and accessible through typical database search procedures. Students are given a question, search for and find information, and then record it via notes in the database. Other students then comment on the notes and add new notes. Before students can send a message, however, they must label the message using a limited set of categories (e.g., claim, evidence, counterargument). So, for example, if students post an opinion, they are prompted to support that opinion with evidence, an example, or reasoning. Teachers have used Knowledge Forum effectively in many different areas of the curriculum.

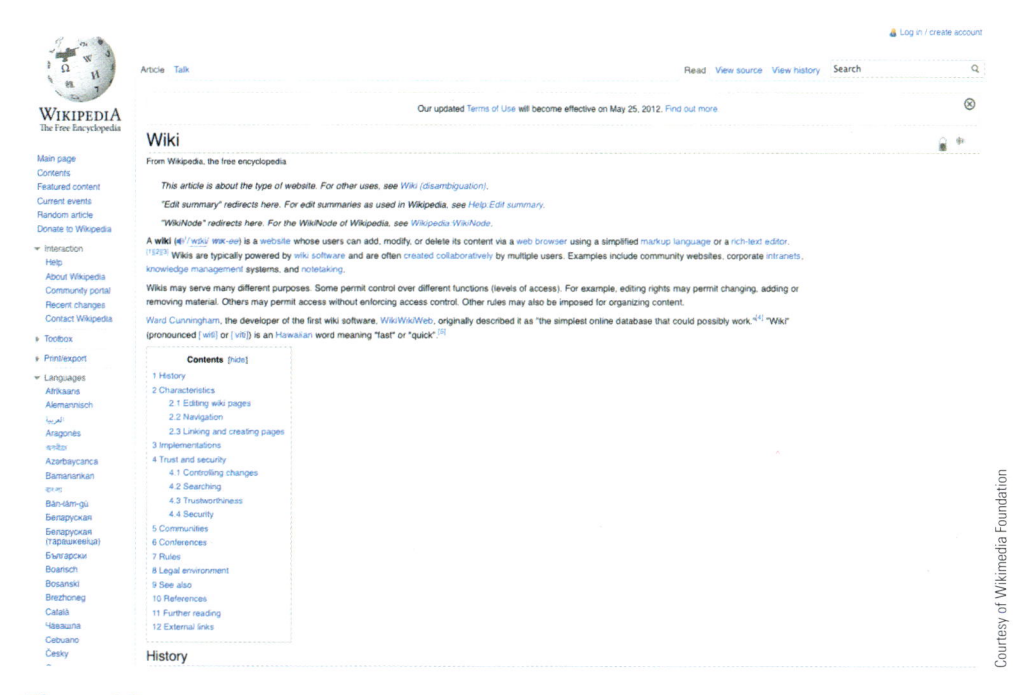

Figure 4.3
Wikipedia, a popular example of a collaborative database.

An example of a more public collaborative database is the popular online encyclopedia, Wikipedia (see Figure 4.3). This website utilizes a database that can be accessed through web pages by multiple users who create and store information that is then reviewed, revised, added to, and linked to other information. Although somewhat controversial, and even banned in some schools, having students create and post an article to Wikipedia that contains sufficient research and is ultimately approved can be a challenging and worthwhile activity for students. Although we use Wikipedia as an example of a collaborative database here, wikis are one of several tools that can also be used to support communication, depending on how they are used. So you see, it all comes back to *how* the technology is used to support teaching and learning.

Visualization Tools and Concept Maps

Visualization tools allow learners to picture, or represent, how various phenomena operate within different domains. These tools can be used to help students visualize scientific phenomena, the predominance of certain data, or even the structure of an argument. **Word clouds**, for example, can be used to analyze text passages by changing the size of each word in the cloud based on the number of times it appears in the passage—the more often a word is used, the larger it appears. Students can use word clouds for pre-reading activities by projecting what the main ideas of a passage might be, or they can be used to summarize text-based information after it's been read. For example, see the Wordle created by a first-grade teacher in the *Stories from Practice—The Power of Collaboration*.

Visualization tools are also available that can illustrate more complex relationships, such as enabling students to manipulate complex data sets to increase their understanding of statistical arguments. There are even some search engines that present results in graphic form to show connections among key information. Many people prefer these visual representations over a long block of text.

Graphic organizers are a type of visualization tool that can help learners sort or record information. There are many different types of graphic organizers, including data

---

visualization tools
tools that allow learners to picture, or represent, how various phenomena operate within different domains

word cloud
a visualization tool that can be used to analyze text by changing the size of each word in the cloud based on the number of times it appears in a given passage

grids, tables, diagrams, flowcharts, storyboards, and Venn diagrams. While most of these organizers have been used since long before computers were invented, today we have software that can simplify the creation of many of them. For example, the International Reading Association makes a tool available on its website ReadWriteThink that allows users to create Venn diagrams, and the popular Inspiration concept-mapping software includes numerous templates for most content areas. Spreadsheet applications also often have graphing capabilities that allow you or your students to display numeric data in various formats. Some tools, like Inspiration's InspireData, allow you to interact with the data you're viewing so you can see the impact of changes to the data set. Students can drag and drop information to test predictions or hypotheses.

concept map
a graphical tool for organizing and representing knowledge

Concept maps are "graphical tools for organizing and representing knowledge" (Novak & Canas, 2006, p. 1) and may be some of the most popular types of visualization tools used in classrooms. For example, Figure 4.4 presents a sample concept map about the seasons. Concepts (e.g., seasons, amount of sunlight) are included inside circles or boxes, relationships between the concepts are represented by lines or arrows, and labels are used to describe the relationships (e.g., causes, is determined by). The concepts may also be referred to as nodes and the relationships as links.

There are many ways to use concept maps. Students can use them to organize and represent what they already know about a topic and add to the map as they explore and learn new information. Creating a concept map involves 1) identifying the important concepts in a domain of knowledge, 2) arranging those concepts spatially, 3) identifying relationships among the concepts, and 4) labeling the nature of the relationships among those concepts. Because students have to manipulate information, and think about the

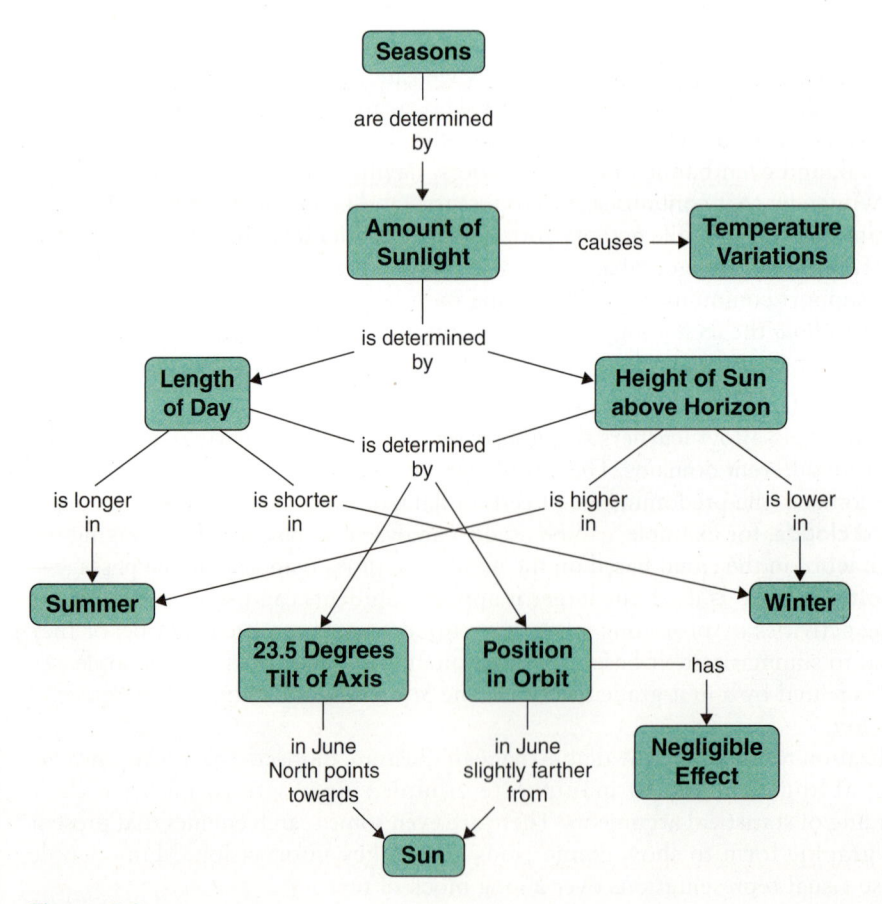

Figure 4.4
Example of a concept map.
Source: Novak & Canas, 2006.

relationships among different concepts, creating a concept map encourages convergent thinking. Students are forced to think about how concepts in a domain fit together and to identify additional ideas or concepts that need to be included. There are a variety of software tools that facilitate concept-mapping including bubbl.us, WiseMapping, and the popular Inspiration and Kidspiration applications. Interestingly, even though Inspiration was developed for K-12 teachers and students, some scientists, engineers, and other professionals have adopted it as a powerful way to visualize their thinking.

Simulations and Animations

Simulations provide simplified versions of phenomena, environments, or processes that allow students to interact with, or manipulate, variables and observe the effects of those manipulations (see Figure 4.5). If you remember using Oregon Trail, Sim City, or dissecting a digital frog as you were going through school, then you have an idea of what a computer simulation is like. And now there are many more. You can visit the Sistine Chapel without leaving your chair, explore the inner workings of animal and plant cells, or build an amusement park to explore physics and motion. However, not all simulations promote creative thinking (at least not automatically). While simulations have the potential to promote creative thinking, their usefulness will depend on why and how you and your students use them.

Although often less complex than simulations, animations can also help students explore phenomena to build deeper understanding. Even though animations often have set consequences and don't allow users to change what happens, they are still helpful, especially for understanding complex processes, with the idea of complexity being relative to a student's age, experience, and ability. Animations can often be stopped and started, reversed, or slowed down, so students can see the relationship of elements in the animation better, whether it's a short animation of a storm system moving through the region or an animation showing the relationships among the sun, moon, and tilt of the earth's axis. Students of all ages can create their own animations to demonstrate understanding using a variety of software, including presentation software such as PowerPoint or Keynote, video- or image-editing software, or applications specifically designed for 2D or 3D animations.

One type of simulation software that can be especially powerful is a **microworld,** which allows learners to manipulate, explore, and experiment with specific phenomena in an

simulation
a simplified version of phenomena, environments, or processes that allow students to interact with, or manipulate, variables and observe the effects of those manipulations

microworld
a type of simulation software that allows learners to manipulate, explore, and experiment with specific phenomena in an exploratory learning environment

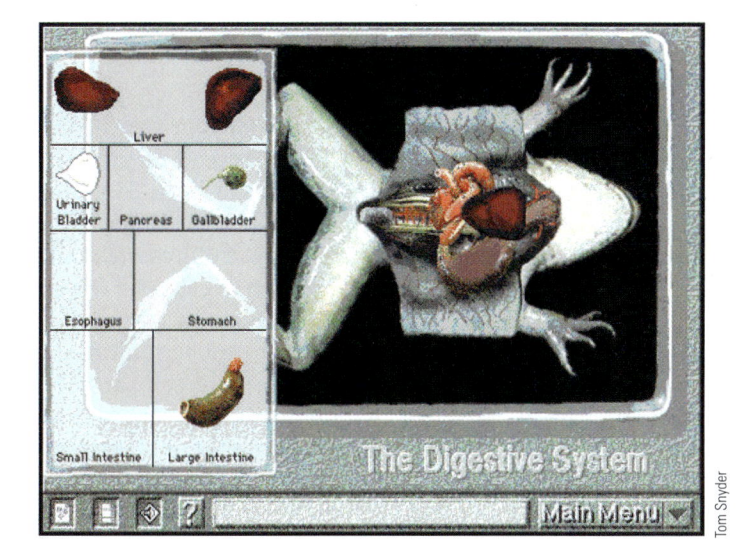

Figure 4.5
Operation Frog is a simulation that allows students to dissect a frog without the frog or the smell.

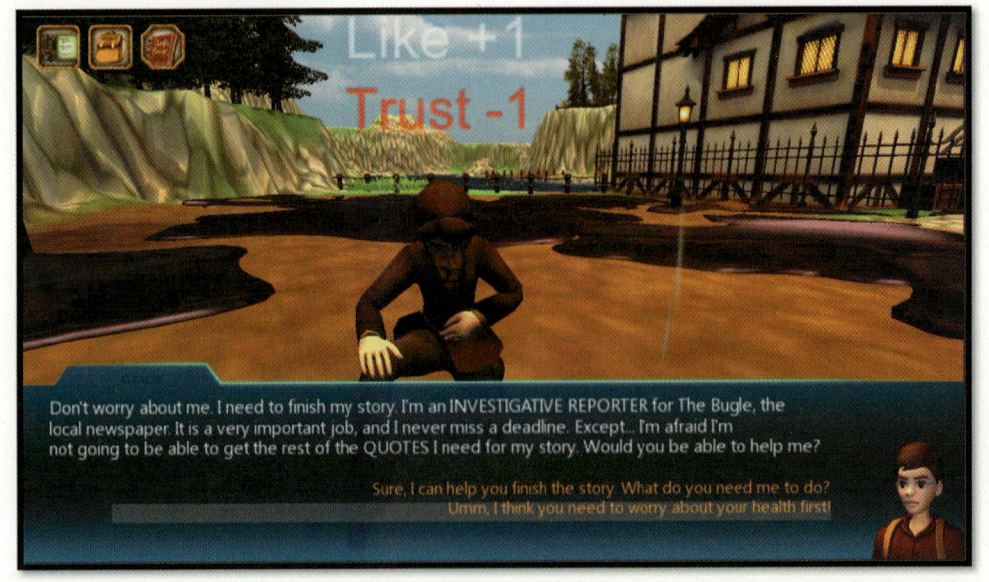

Figure 4.6
Some Microworlds, such as this one from Atlantis Remixed, incorporate familiar gaming features within a complex, real-world problem.

exploratory learning environment. Think about some of the video games you or your friends have played. Typically, you must master earlier levels of the game in order to move on to more complex, advanced levels. These adventures occur in a microworld, a lifelike context in which you manipulate objects and observe the effects of your actions on other objects in the environment (see Figure 4.6). As a more academic example, consider that of Interactive Physics, which enables learners to build and test mechanical design models. Through the use of demonstrations, car crashes, and falling objects, students explore such topics as momentum, force, and acceleration. Students can change any aspect of the environment (friction, incline of the surface, etc.) and observe what happens to the other aspects of the environment. This, then, enables them to generate and test hypotheses about relationships among the objects in the microworld. According to Jonassen et al. (2003), microworlds can foster the development of problem-solving strategies, critical thinking skills, and creativity.

Hypertext and Hypermedia

You are probably very familiar with hypertext and hypermedia from your experiences with websites. **Hypertext** refers to a nonsequential, or nonlinear, method for organizing and displaying text. **Hypermedia** is basically hypertext with media elements (e.g., images, sounds, videos, animations, or others). While reading hypertext is not likely to lead to noticeable learning benefits, *creating* or *constructing* effective hypertext and hypermedia tends to require creative thinking skills. That is, when developing hypertext documents students need to think about the conceptual structure of a content area and then reflect on the nature of the links between the content. Designing multimedia products, such as websites, is clearly a complex skill requiring the ability to analyze, evaluate, and synthesize information. Wegerif (2002) lists a number of different kinds of creative thinking skills needed in order to design effective multimedia presentations, including research, organization, and reflective thinking skills. Can you think of different ways that you could help your students master each of these important skills?

Websites are the most common form of hypermedia in use today. If you've never created a website before, the process is quite similar to that used for creating a portfolio (see Chapter 2), and there are many different ways you can create them, such as by starting a blog, creating a wiki for a class project, or using templates from Google Sites or

---

hypertext
a nonsequential, or nonlinear, method for organizing and displaying text

hypermedia
hypertext with media elements (e.g., images, sounds, videos, animations, or others)

Digital Tools That Support Learning   95

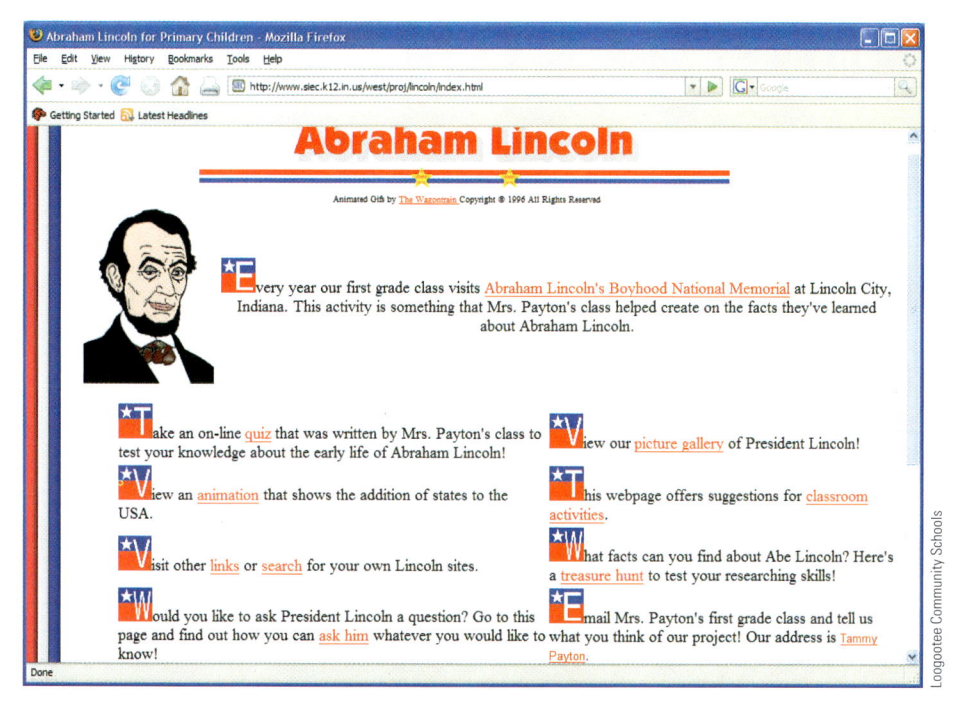

Figure 4.7
Even very young students can create hypermedia, such as this web page created by first-grade students at Loogootee Elementary West in Indiana.

other organizations. Many of these templates allow you to drag-and-drop components, like calendars, images, videos, announcements, and polls. It's really not necessary any more to know much HTML to develop a website, but you still need to take some steps to ensure your site is effective. By following the four steps of define, design, develop, and deliver, you and your students can benefit from the creative processes involved in analyzing, evaluating, and synthesizing information to create multiple effective paths through a relevant content area (see Figure 4.7).

TECH TOOLS & TIPS: Creating Multimedia Websites

As with your portfolio, it's useful to begin by defining your audience: Who is the primary audience of the site? The secondary audiences? Next, define your goals: What is the purpose of the site? Third, define your content. What information do you want to include? How should the information be linked within and across web pages? And finally, identify your web-development tools. Investigate whether your school or school system has a specific content management system or web-development software that you are required to use.

After you identify your audience, goals, and content, you can begin to plan the structure of your site, determining the most effective way to display and link the content. One useful way to organize your content is to create a storyboard of your web pages. You can physically represent individual web pages with pieces of paper, index cards, or self-stick notes, or digitally by using presentation software, concept-mapping software, or even the drawing tools in most word-processing programs (see Figure 4.8). On each storyboard "page," sketch where you will place your text and graphic elements. After you have some sense of what will be on each page, you should also plan the navigation. Traditionally, this has been done with flowcharts that indicate the hierarchal organization or branching structure of the site. Again, you can use software, such as concept-mapping software, or draw the flowchart by hand. But storyboards and flowcharts don't have to be fancy—their primary goal is to serve as planning aids.

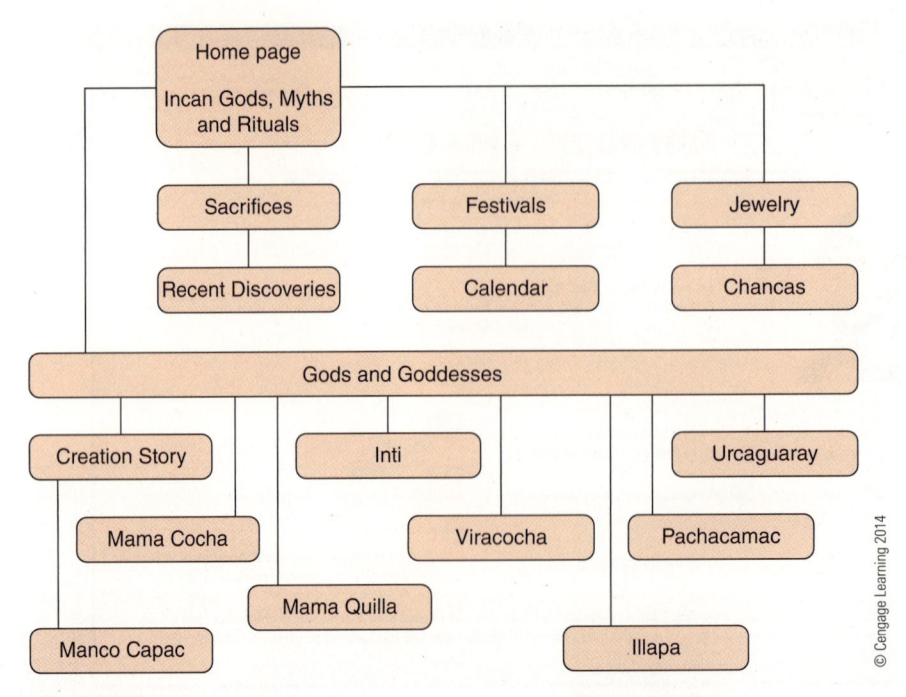

Figure 4.8
This flowchart, developed with common word-processing software, shows the organization of an educational website about Incan gods, myths, and rituals.

Digital Storytelling

Another popular use of computers as mindtools is through the creation of digital stories. As with other mindtools, digital stories enable learners to reflect, represent, and communicate what they know. Based on the premise of oral storytelling, digital storytelling involves students' creation of a short movie or presentation that presents a compelling personal perspective. It may be a story from their own experiences, such as describing their experiences with asthma or how they overcame adversity—or from their research as when they "become" settlers in the new world. Typically, stories are told from a personal perspective to allow the viewer to see an event, moment, or place from another's

render
process of constructing a single, complete movie file from a collection of clips, stills, transitions, and/or audio input

TECH TOOLS & TIPS

Digital Storytelling

Each step in creating a digital story is elaborated upon below.

1 Write a Script. Solid writing is at the core of digital storytelling. Students need to clearly identify the purpose of their stories and the messages they are trying to convey. They may need help in the development of "hooks" by examining other digital stories available online or even written works to determine what makes an effective story lead. It's also important for students to learn how to write an effective "wrap-up." You may want to provide a set of questions to guide them in their writing and storytelling, ask them to draw or otherwise create a visual image of the main point of the story, or have them create concept maps in order to clarify and focus their writing.

Typically, digital movies are 2 to 3 minutes in length so it's a good idea for students to read their stories aloud at this point and time them to make sure they are within the recommended time limit (Jakes & Brennan, n.d.). As they read aloud, students may become aware of things they want to change. This revision process is a natural part of self-monitoring.

2 Develop a Storyboard. After students are comfortable with their scripts, they should create their storyboards. Storyboards should contain the narration, a description or sketch of the associated images, any text that may appear on the screen, and a note about any music or sound effects required. At this stage, students begin to visualize what their narratives should look and sound like. For each chunk of the script, students write or draw a brief description of an image they want to use to illustrate the idea. Students will not yet have *collected* the images; instead, the storyboard ensures that their image searches will be productive and effective by focusing their efforts. Typically, 20 to 25 images are needed to illustrate a 2- to 3-minute story (Jakes & Brennan, n.d.).

If your students are not familiar with storyboarding, you might want to engage them in "backwards storyboarding" by watching a commercial and creating the matching storyboard. Or have them use comic strips as an example of a storyboard, and then create a video movie of the comic strip. Through storyboarding, students learn to think in new ways as they visualize written work.

3 Locate Images. After they have identified the images they want to locate, students can begin researching, finding, or creating images. Students may film full-motion video or they may use still images to illustrate their stories. They may use digital images from their own collections, scan images or graphics that are not in digital form, or download images from the web. When selecting images and video clips, make sure students pay strict attention to copyright rules and regulations (see Chapter 10). Fortunately, there are a variety of websites such as Pics4Learning, SURWEB, and the American Memory Project from the Library of Congress that provide images and video segments that can be used for such projects legally. Digital storytelling projects provide a wonderful opportunity to teach your students about copyright regulations. Remember, students should not begin researching images until their scripts and storyboards are well developed.

4 Create the Digital Story. After the script and the storyboard are written and the images are located, students need to record their narrations, load the audio files and images into a moviemaking program, and output the finished products as movie files.

Recording the narration can be the most challenging part of the story creation process in terms of classroom management. Students must record their narrations individually in a quiet place—something that can be difficult in a room full of students. One option is to have a parent volunteer, older student, or another student go to a quiet place and record each student's narration on video, with the lens cap on (Banaszewski, 2002). The video can then be loaded into the moviemaking program and the audio extracted. Another option is to use microphones that eliminate background noise (Jakes & Brennan, n.d.). Experienced teachers recommend that students record their narration in two- to three-sentence chunks so that if they make a mistake, they don't have to go back and record the entire script.

Following this, students will use moviemaking programs to synchronize their sound files with the appropriate images and then output the results as a movie file. Several of these programs are available for free (such as iMovie for the Mac or MovieMaker for the PC), while others are commercially available. Most of these programs are easy to use and require a minimum of prior instruction. Still, some authors suggest that students work together on a group project prior to producing individual projects so that they become acquainted with the software and production process.

After students are satisfied with their sequence of images and accompanying sound files, they **render** their projects into movie files. Rendering can take a while, so students might first render their movies at a low quality so that they can determine if they are satisfactory to them before taking the time to render as a higher-quality file.

5 Share with Others. The final step is for students to share their stories with others. As students view the stories created by their peers, they develop a deeper understanding of the perspectives of others. One way to structure the class viewing is by following the steps used in "writers' workshops" (Banaszewski, 2002). Following the viewing of a digital story, the audience first comments on the things they appreciate about the movie, and then offer suggestions for improvement. The movie's creator simply accepts these appreciations and suggestions without comment. Following the audience's response, the movie's creator can ask the audience questions about things that they wonder about relative to the movie. There are also a variety of websites where students can post their movies to share them with a global audience.

If you have limited access to technology, steps 1, 2, and 5 can occur in the classroom using traditional materials, but if you have more frequent access to technology, a variety of software can enhance the process (Jakes & Brennan, n.d.). Prior to script writing, students can create a timeline of the event (Buckingham, 2003). They can then select one or more moments in time to elaborate on in the digital story. They can create concept maps of the ideas they want to develop, adding details through nodes and links. As they develop their scripts and storyboards, they can use word-processing software to write the scripts, then cut and paste from the scripts into storyboards—which can be as simple as using a table in a word processed document. And with the right equipment, movies can be output to video or DVDs to be shown in the classroom using commonly available VCR or DVD players.

TEACHSOURCE VIDEO

Go to the Education CourseMate website for this text and watch any of the following videos: *Data Collection and Visualization in the Elementary Classroom*, *Integrating Technology to Improve Student Learning: A High School Science Simulation*, or *Using Blogs to Enhance Student Learning: An Interdisciplinary High School Unit*.

1. Identify examples from the classroom videos where students were engaged in a technology-supported activity in which the technology performs as a
   - Tutor
   - Mindtool
   - Simulation or visualization tool
2. Describe effective uses of technology and suggest ways technologies might be used more effectively in these examples.

TEACHSOURCE VIDEO

Go to the Education CourseMate website and watch the video, *Digital Storytelling in the High School Classroom*, and then answer the following questions:

1. Describe how the teacher uses digital storytelling to engage the students in the creative thinking process.
2. How do students use project management skills, research skills, organizational and representational skills, presentation skills, and reflective skills in the creation of their digital stories?

support for conversation when technology is used in such a way that it contributes to conversations among learners, and thus facilitates group and community learning

point of view; yet, effective digital stories also have a theme to which viewers can relate. For example, a student in one teacher's classroom created a digital story about adopting a "shelter" pet, then used his experience to create a public service announcement urging others to adopt abused animals. As illustrated by this example, a digital story is grounded by a strong personal narrative that uses a "hook" or "lead" to draw others in. Stories typically highlight specific events or moments in time and conclude with a wrap-up that spur others to action or provide "lessons learned."

Throughout the years, digital storytelling has evolved into a recommended series of steps and procedures. Students begin by developing a personal narrative, then select the most powerful point in their written work to develop into a script. Based on the storyboard, students select images to supplement their scripts. Although students may create their own images through digital photography, videotaping, or scanning images, they often select images from those available on the web or from royalty-free clip-art collections. The next step involves recording the narration—often the most challenging step. Using readily available software such as iMovie or GarageBand on the Mac or MovieMaker on the PC, students arrange their images, synchronize them with their recorded narration, and output the file as a movie. Some teachers may use more widely available presentation software, such as Microsoft PowerPoint or Apple's Keynote software, for supporting digital storytelling activities, especially with younger students. Presentation software allows even very young students to insert pictures and text, and record audio in support of digital storytelling. As with the development of other types of multimedia, students are required to apply project management skills, research skills, organizational and representational skills, presentation skills, and reflective skills.

As a mindtool, digital storytelling helps students learn to write more effectively through the visualization of their stories (Jakes & Brennan, n.d.). As such, it provides authentic, personal learning experiences for your students. Additionally, throughout the process, students learn skills that are important to a variety of content areas such as writing for an audience, researching and organizing information, and communicating effectively, as well as technology and information literacy skills. While the idea of telling stories digitally seems to resonate best with language arts, the concepts and skills your students learn in the process can be adapted to other areas, such as for a lab or field trip report in science, presenting arguments or viewpoints about famous historians or events in social studies, or even exploring the application of geometry and algebra in real-world settings in a math class.

The opportunity to develop a personal story is extremely motivating for students, and the tangible outcome of the process contributes to confidence-building necessary for creative thinking. Students need to be self-directed in their efforts to plan their actions, monitor their progress toward achieving the goals of their projects, and evaluate their efforts. You can help students in the evaluation process by providing them with rubrics in advance that allow them to self-assess their projects.

Technology as a Conversation Support

While the previous two sections focused primarily on how technology can be used to increase *individual* learning outcomes, in this section we discuss how technology, as an interactive tool, can serve as a **support for conversations** among learners, and thus contribute to *group and community* learning outcomes. In the next two sections, we talk more specifically about how technology can be used to promote collaborative learning outcomes among learners who are both near and far.

Technology as a Collaborative Learning Tool

Imagine if you will, two students working at the computer to complete a WebQuest their teacher created about key events that led to the secession of South Carolina from the Union and whether the Civil War could have been prevented. As the pair work together, they engage in a heated debate about the pros and cons of different decisions. They may continue this conversation outside of class by sharing new resources they find by texting, e-mailing, or working on a shared document online. They make predictions about potential outcomes and then, after

TECH TOOLS & TIPS: Webconferencing

Webconferencing tools are becoming more affordable and can be found in many classrooms. Multifunction webconferencing tools, such as WebEx or Adobe Connect, put a multitude of functions at your fingertips. Depending on your needs, you may also be able to use the limited functionality of low-cost or free software such as iChat from Apple that supports the sharing of documents. Some webconferencing tools also support live video through the use of inexpensive web cameras, or webcams. Common webconferencing features and their educational applications are listed below.

1. **Presentation Slides.** Share your class lecture with students at a distance. The most universally accepted presentation software is Microsoft PowerPoint.

2. **Desktop Sharing/Shared Control.** With sharing, you or your students can reach out and touch someone's desktop—virtually. This is helpful for guiding students through a complex process or when students are presenting to you or the rest of the class.

3. **Document Sharing.** Document sharing allows real-time collaboration on word-processed, spreadsheet, or other documents in support of peer-to-peer or small-group work.

4. **Web Tour.** So many instructional resources are available on the web that it is important to be able to visit and show websites to your students who are located at a distance.

5. **Shared Whiteboard.** Just like a chalkboard or whiteboard in the classroom, you and your students can write, draw, or annotate images displayed on a whiteboard space. You may need to practice your mouse skills, however, to take advantage of the palette of tools available with most whiteboards.

6. **Lecture Mode.** You can't always control the quality of phone connections, and some users cannot mute their phones. The background noise from poor connections increases in volume with the number of students connected. Lecture mode can allow you to mute all lines while you're presenting as well as designate individual lines as the primary speaker for questioning or student presentations.

7. **Chat.** A chat feature can be helpful for allowing participants to ask questions or otherwise interact without interrupting the audio connection. You may want to establish policies for using chat, however, so students continue to focus on learning outcomes and don't get too distracted with side conversations.

8. **Webcam Support.** Having a webcam can increase visual cues for participants that are sometimes missing in text- or audio-based distance learning. Some options for webcams include showing multiple webcams, facial tracking if participants move, and webcam shifting that displays the stream of the participant who is currently speaking.

9. **Polling, Quizzes, and Surveys.** Take a quick pulse of the opinions in the room or collect formative assessment data to measure student understanding through these features that usually include common forced-choice response types.

10. **Recording and Replay.** Did one of your students miss class due to illness or travel? Or maybe one of them would like to review a complex discussion or check the accuracy of his or her notes. Webconferencing services can offer both audio as well as screen recordings.

STORIES from Practice

The Power of Collaboration

Kathy, a first grade teacher in Moose Jaw, Canada, recently began changing her classroom practices in order to take advantage of the collaboration opportunities provided by a variety of Web 2.0 tools. She explained:

One of the objectives in first-grade social studies is that you understand that people in different places eat different things and that you see different cultures . . . so we talked about that in our classroom. Our classroom is a little bit multicultural, and so we began by talking about what all of them had for breakfast. And then, we decided we wanted to know what other people around the world would have for breakfast. I set up a Google Doc, and each of my students typed in what they had for breakfast and where they lived. And then I just put a little link to the Google Doc on my blog, and I put a link on Twitter and I said, "Can you help some grade 1 students? Tell us what you have for breakfast." People responded from all over. A lot of people responded from Australia to tell us what they had, and people from all over the U.S. and some from Canada as well. And so then we looked at all those responses. We actually had several hundred people who responded so that was a lot of information for my first graders. So, I copied that information and put it into Wordle and then the largest things that came up were the things that were most often mentioned, so we could see which ones were the most common. From there, that lead us to wonder what vegemite is and what vegemite tastes like, so we tasted vegemite and then we made a word cloud of all my students' responses to what vegemite tasted like, whether it was good or not. See the pictures I've included (Figure 4.9).

I think this project was successful because the kids were learning the value of collaboration, learning from other people. I also think it was successful because the students learned from each other. And then they were able to learn from other people and they were able to learn something that they didn't expect to learn, like about the vegemite. When I began the project, I just thought we would poll the students in my class, but technology enabled me to take the learning beyond what I originally intended. I could have just said to my students, "Australian kids have vegemite for breakfast. Kids in China have rice for breakfast." But, instead, my students learned these things from other people and that's so much more powerful than me just telling them.

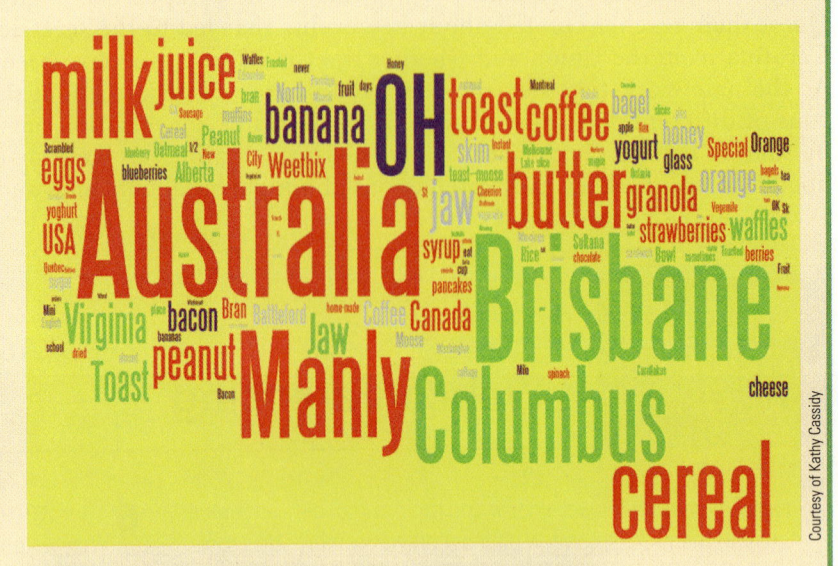

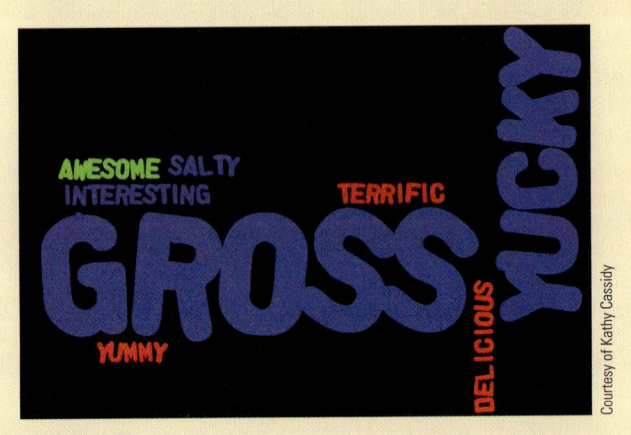

Figure 4.9
Word clouds created with Wordle from responses to the questions, "Where do you live?" and "What did you have for breakfast?"

Source: © Kathy Cassidy. Reprinted by permission.

TECH TOOLS & TIPS

Wikis

A **wiki** is a piece of server software that allows users to create, edit, and link web pages quickly, which is what wiki means in the Hawaiian language—"quick" or "fast." Wikis are a great tool when students need to complete a task together—whether doing research, writing a paper, or planning a presentation. If they aren't all in the same class or if work needs to get done in the evening or on the weekend, wikis allow them to coordinate their efforts much more efficiently than sending a bunch of e-mails back and forth. And they don't have to know web-authoring languages or other complicated tools to do so.

Most wikis work in a similar way. With the click of a button, each student can make changes to a web page. Because changes are attributed to specific users, the community can verify the accuracy of the information or ask for additional details. So, for example, after Emilie creates a wiki page, she simply saves it. Then when her classmate, Scott, accesses it, he clicks an "edit" button, makes some changes, clicks "save" and it's a web page again, ready for the next student to access and modify. Edit—Write—Save! Following this simple process, it's easy for the students to coordinate their writing efforts. Specific websites—including some wikis—are available to help teachers create and use wikis in the classroom.

Consider the following tips when incorporating a wiki in your instruction.

1 Collaborate. Wikis work best in support of collaborative projects, so begin by determining a project that addresses your content standards and is suited to student collaboration.

2 Access. Determine who will have access to your wiki. For class projects, you may have a private wiki that only students in your class can post to; however, ultimately you may want to share wiki content with other students, parents, the community, or others.

3 Format. Determine appropriate formatting of text and other elements to help students understand effective visual communication strategies.

4 Post. Set expectations for posting. Let students know how often and how much they should post and what *not* to post, such as contact information.

5 Notify. Make sure your wiki is configured to notify the wiki monitor or administrator (probably you) when changes are made.

6 Nurture. Just as when using any new tool, wikis need a little nurturing. Use the wiki in class during instruction, model appropriate use, and guide students to the wiki for appropriate activities.

some discussion, come to agreement about which steps to take next in order to present their findings to the rest of the class. In this scenario, technology acts merely as a prompt or resource for students' conversations, and therefore, as a means to illuminate their thinking. It is this use of technology, as a mediator of conversation, we discuss here.

In traditional classrooms, teachers may have discouraged students from talking to each other during individual seatwork, but here we recognize some of the positive outcomes that can result from the conversations that occur among students as they work through complex problem-solving situations. For example, in a study conducted in the early 1990s, Teasley and Roschelle (described in Wegerif, 2002), observed pairs of students using a simulation, called the Envisioning Machine, that was designed to teach Newtonian physics. The authors described how the computer program provided a shared focus, the means to uncover the true meaning of the language used to represent the physics concepts being addressed (velocity, acceleration), as well as the means to resolve conflicts by testing out alternative views. In interpreting the results, the authors claimed that it was the *conversation* between the learners, as prompted by the computer simulation, which led to the observed learning gains.

When used as a collaborative learning tool, technology is used not only for stimulating effective language use but also for focusing children's learning activities on specific curricular tasks. What seems to be important here is not the computer software, per se, but the quality of the conversation that occurs around it. This, then, prompts us to think about the teacher's role in an "engaged" classroom and how she or he is responsible for supporting high levels of meaningful conversation.

As noted earlier in our discussions about supporting student collaborations (see Chapter 3), it is important that you prepare your students to work together effectively, whether around a technology device or not. Through these activities students learn not only to work together, but also to use language as a tool for collaborative reasoning, problem-solving, and knowledge construction. Research suggests that, *in combination with the right instructional strategies,* technology can support the development of transferable creative thinking skills (Wegerif, 2002).

Technology as a Conferencing Tool

Communication in an online forum is different from face-to-face (F2F) communication; in some ways worse, and in some ways better. While we lose important information (facial expressions, body language, tone of voice, etc.) online, we also eliminate information that can cause bias or prejudice (knowledge of age, gender, disabilities, etc.). Video- or web-based conferencing can open up many new possibilities for participation. There are many claims that conferencing can be an effective support for the development of creative thinking skills. The reasons for this tend to relate to 1) the ease with which everyone can participate, and 2) the ability to be able to think through your responses before responding. In addition, having several conversations occurring simultaneously can prompt more metacognitive reflection. Think about the relative ease with which you participate in multiple conversations with your friends when texting or chatting on Facebook. Now, put that into a context where you are all focused on making a decision, or solving a problem, and you can see the potential for developing good thinking (as well as communication and management) skills.

There are a variety of ways in which you can use technology as a conferencing tool with your students (see *Tech Tools and Tips—Webconferencing*). Popular tools like Skype, ooVoo, and iChat are one way. **Blogs** and **wikis**, featured in *Tech Tools and Tips* on pages 101 and 104, are others. E-mail, listservs, newsgroups, and forums all offer additional possibilities. For example, ePals can connect your students with students in other countries through written exchanges on topics of mutual interest. In a similar fashion, but on a classroom level, Kidlink offers a network run by 500 volunteers in over 50 countries who provide free educational programs related to helping children understand themselves, identify and define goals for life, and collaborate with peers around the globe, individually or through school. Interaction among participants takes place through hundreds of discussion rooms, mailing lists, chat channels, and Kidlink's website (see Figure 4.10). The Global Schoolnet is another example of using technology to connect students from around the world to explore community, cultural, and scientific issues that prepare them for the workforce and help them to become responsible and literate global citizens.

Additional conferencing activities that can support collaboration among students include those that focus on the joint collection, analysis, organization, and presentation of information. Typically, students at geographically dispersed sites collect local data and then compare and contrast patterns (e.g., related to health, climate, plant and animal species) across locations. This, then, allows students to look for overarching patterns in the data, requiring creative thinking. For example, Journey North engages students in a global study of wildlife migration and seasonal change. Students share their own field observations with classmates across North America. As one example, students followed the migration of the monarch butterfly as it journeyed north from Angangueo, Mexico, to Washington, DC (see Figure 4.11). Other seasonal changes that students have helped track include the first frog heard singing and the first maple syrup sap run.

Web-based conferencing allows students to engage directly in knowledge creation with others who are not physically present. By providing access to multiple perspectives, students are challenged to think more deeply about the topic at hand. And while it is not intrinsically superior to work collaboratively with those outside the classroom, than with those within, it can be more motivating (Wegerif, 2002).

---

blog
online journaling and threaded discussion tool for use on the web; abbreviation for weblog

wiki
a page or collection of web pages designed to allow users to create, edit, and link web content quickly

Digital Tools That Support Learning 103

Figure 4.10
Kidlink connects kids from all over the world using a variety of conferencing tools.

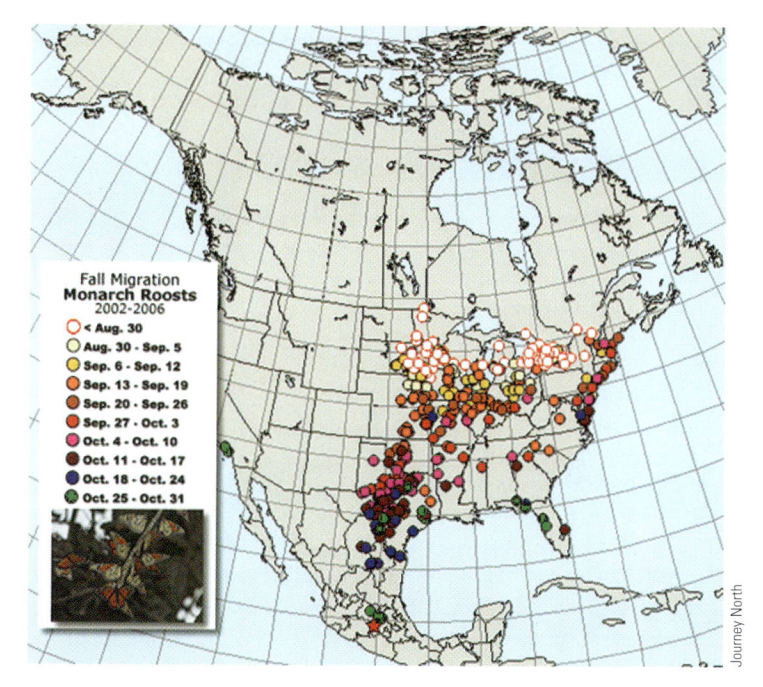

Figure 4.11
Students across the globe can use Journey North to collect and share information about the migration of monarch butterflies.

TECH TOOLS & TIPS

Blogs

Weblogs, or **blogs** as they are more commonly referred to, belong to the realm of journaling and threaded discussion tools. The following tips are designed to help you decide whether and/or how to incorporate blogs into your classroom.

1 **Use blogs to achieve an instructional goal.** Blogs can help students practice and demonstrate different styles of communication, especially through writing. In a writing-intensive class, students can post entries using different forms, such as writing a persuasive paragraph or posting an interview with a friend. In terms of communication, you can emphasize design elements to guide the organization of entire blogs, postings by your students, and the incorporation of media. You can also support collaboration and help students develop critical communication skills by guiding their responses to classmates' postings.

2 **Students will need guidance on what and how to post.** The blog you use in your classroom may be different from a personal blog as it will have to meet instructional purposes. Help your students understand the form of language that is appropriate, which may require avoiding the use of common Internet acronyms and shortcuts. Set a reasonable goal for posting, perhaps once a week, and use clearly stated writing prompts to guide your students' posts. And by all means, create your own blog as a model for students (see Figure 4.12). The best way to determine the match of a technology to your instruction is to do it yourself.

3 **Just as with any other resource, teach your students to use multiple sources and cite them appropriately.** Learning to cite sources is a foundational skill for all students and writing a blog should be no exception, even if the source is a friend, a TV show, or another blog. Using multiple sources can help students not only support the positions in their postings but actually help them formulate their own opinions and ideas more clearly. Determine an appropriate format for citations and require it for postings. Common academic citation styles such as APA or MLA may not be standard for blogging but may be appropriate for young scholars developing their citation skills, especially if you require them in other forms of student work.

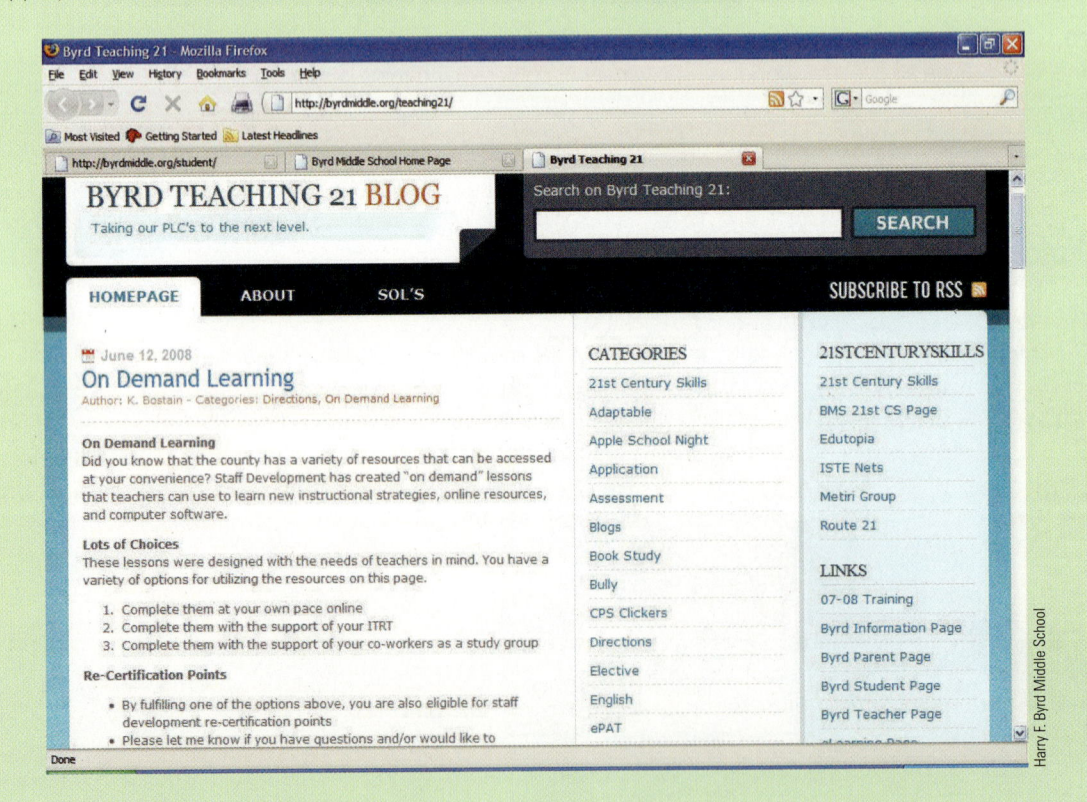

Figure 4.12
Teachers and students use blogs to communicate with other teachers and students, parents, and the world.

Harry F. Byrd Middle School

> **4. Help your students understand how to make their blogs personal without revealing personal information.** The nature of a blog is to share personal reflections, opinions, and feelings. At the same time, blogs and shared discussion spaces have sparked controversy because students tend to share personal information, such as pictures and contact information.
>
> **5. Find exemplary blogs, review trusted resources.** Review how other teachers are using the technology by attending conferences, reading journal and magazine articles, or searching the web. In the case of blogs, there are online and print publications that review educational blogs and guide you toward exemplars. There are even some awards available for exemplary blogs. Find and read other blogs and determine what characteristics best suit your teaching style and the requirements of your curriculum.

Online Resources

As you noticed in the previous discussion, the web provides access to a variety of sites where the computer is used as a tutor, mindtool, or support for conversation. Fortunately, or unfortunately, anyone can publish on the web through personal or organizational websites, postings on message boards, blogs, wikis, and more. In contrast, printed information often has to undergo strict reviews prior to publication. Academic journal articles are subject to peer review by other professionals in the field. At a minimum, the content found in books, magazines, and newspapers is reviewed by the publication's editor. Even opinion pieces, like "letters to the editor," are reviewed prior to publication. But this isn't true of information published on the Internet. The ease with which individuals can post and access information creates a critical need to strategically search for and carefully evaluate the information you find on the web.

Evaluating Information from Online Resources

Students should learn how to verify the legitimacy of content on the Internet. You should also be especially careful to review websites in their entirety before using them with your students.

There are numerous examples of web pages that appear to be valid resources but that provide incorrect and sometimes extremely inflammatory information. Some hate groups have been known to post information about historical events and figures, such as civil rights leader Martin Luther King, Jr., that appears to be authentic, at least on the surface. Students who do not take the time to review all of the material closely, who are naïve or do not realize the information is incorrect, or who unknowingly copy and paste information from these websites can turn in projects with information that is not only biased but full of hate speech and prejudice.

Web developers who develop sites with URLs that are just slightly different from a legitimate source are using the practice of **typosquatting**. In this case, an ".org" or a ".net" or other domain suffix may be used instead of the appropriate ".edu" or ".gov" in an attempt to trick unwary students (or others) looking for legitimate information. The White House is one famous object of typosquatters. The inappropriate material found on the alternate site can simply be fictitious, or sometimes highly offensive. Typosquatting also involves the use of common misspellings of words to prey on people with poor keyboarding and spelling skills.

A simple web search will reveal many sites that discuss information evaluation techniques. Numerous checklists and rubrics are available that provide useful tools for you. You may already have your own techniques to evaluate the validity and reliability of web information sources. In evaluating web resources, it's useful to answer the standard questions of who, what, when, why, and how.

Who created the website? Is the source credible? What credentials or background does the author have that qualifies him or her to write about this topic? Does the author provide credentials such as occupation, affiliation, years of experience, position, and education?

Search the web for additional information about the author or look for information through other reputable sources. Can you find a personal home page or campus

> **typosquatting**
> the practice of creating a website with a URL just slightly different from a legitimate source

listing for this author? Can you find other publications through a source such as the Educational Resources Information Clearinghouse (ERIC), sponsored by the U.S. Department of Education? Information about the background of the author of a web page is sometimes found on the bottom of a page or through a separate link. Is there a mail-to link or an e-mail address included? It may be a cause for suspicion if the site author is not clearly stated or contact information is not provided.

If the source is a website, look at the URL to learn about the sponsor and location of the site. What does the ending of the URL tell you? Is the page sponsored by a professional organization, school, school district, university, company, government office, or commercial company? What can you find out about the organization? Does the organization have an inherent bias? Does it seem logical that information such as this would reside on this site? It's a good idea to examine the credentials and reputation of the organization or organizations affiliated with a website, just as you examined the credentials of the author.

Many educators originally excluded use of the popular site Wikipedia, because of the ease with which the information was added. The idea was people could—and did—post just about anything! But that's not the case any longer, as Wikipedia has developed guidelines to ensure posted information meets quality requirements, often through the use of documentation for its contents. So, in effect, they too are asking their contributors to evaluate the information they post online. Some teachers have developed activities that require students to post information to Wikipedia that meets the criteria for acceptance. At the very least, Wikipedia and some sources like it can provide a good starting point for student research, as students can see what resources are included and often access them to get more information.

What is the value of the information? How thorough is it? Does the information appear accurate based on your prior knowledge? Does the information appear to be well researched? Is the information well documented? Are assumptions and conclusions well documented? How current or relevant are the references? Are primary sources of information indicated? Are there references or links to supporting information? If the information resides on a web page, does the page reference only information on the same server? If so, be especially aware of potential biases. Most importantly, does the

TECH TOOLS & TIPS

Evaluating Web Resources

Who is responsible for the information resource?
- The name of the author(s) is evident.
- The author's authority, credentials, background, and/or expertise are clearly stated.
- The site includes background information for the author(s), such as previous works, publications, affiliations, etc.
- The name of any sponsoring institution or organization is included, along with a current link to that organization.
- The relation between the author(s) and the sponsoring organization is specified.

What about the content?
- The resource provides thorough information that adequately meets the information need.
- The title of the resource clearly conveys its content.
- The source for information is documented; links to the source are included.
- The content is free from spelling and grammatical errors.

When was the information published?
- The information is current, including original date of the document and latest update.
- Linked information is up to date; links are active.

Why is the resource published?
- The purpose of the resource is clear and its content reflects that purpose, whether it is to inform, persuade, entertain, or sell.
- Informative or entertaining resources are free from bias. Persuasive or sales sites are easily identifiable.

How useful is the resource?
- Information is presented clearly at the level appropriate to the target audience.
- The resource is logically organized and easy to navigate, including a search box and/or site map if the resource is large.

information agree with other information you have found? It's always a good idea to cross-check information using print and non-print sources, as well as websites.

When was the information created? What was the date of the original document? When was it last updated? Information such as this helps you determine if the content is up to date and timely. If using a website as the source of your information, check to see if the links work properly and lead to related materials. Lots of outdated links often indicate that the site has not been updated in a while.

Why was the website created? What is the purpose of the information? Was it created to sell a product, make a political point, or have fun? Is it to inform, persuade, explain, or entertain? Was it designed to summarize existing research, advocate a position, or stimulate discussion? Who is the intended audience? Does the intended audience impact the content or slant of the information? For what level is the information written? An examination of the purpose of the information can illuminate biases that may be present in the content.

How is the information presented? Does the information appear to be fact or opinion? Does it make sense? Can you detect any bias? Is the information presented in a thoughtful, orderly, well-reasoned manner? Do the words used tend to evoke strong emotions? Is the information free from errors in writing and grammar?

Chapter Summary

In this chapter, we described how technology could serve as a tutor, mindtool, and as a support for conversation, depending on how it is used (Wegerif, 2002). When technology is used as a tutor, the software explicitly teaches or provides practice with a specific body of content. When technology is used as a mindtool, it serves as an organizational tool, simulation and visualization tool, or knowledge-building tool. As a support for conversation, the computer software contributes to conversations among learners, and thus facilitates *group and community* learning. Since the web is a popular way to access technology-based tutorials, mindtools, and conversation supports, we also discussed techniques for evaluating web-based resources.

Although there are many ways that technology can be used to promote creative thinking skills among students in your classroom, it should be fairly clear from our discussion that simply using technology will not accomplish this goal. Rather, technology needs to be used purposefully in the ways discussed in this chapter and in an environment that explicitly supports students' efforts to be good thinkers. For example, technology-based tutorials, by themselves, will rarely have enough depth to develop students' creative thinking skills, but when used as the basis for a discussion, students can achieve these higher levels more readily. The same is true for technology tools such as concept maps and simulations: effectiveness as a thinking tool depends on *how* the tools are used.

There are many technologies you can use to "reveal and clarify students' conceptual understanding and thinking, planning, and creative processes" (ISTE, NETS-T 1.c). As you may realize, the effectiveness of a technology-supported lesson will depend, to a large degree, on you as the instructional leader in the classroom. In the next chapter, we will turn our attention to ways that you can support your students in their collaborative and independent learning efforts through questioning strategies, scaffolds such as project guidelines, modeling technology use, and other techniques that encourage your students to become autonomous, self-directed thinkers.

Web Resources and Activities

Visit the Education CourseMate website to

- explore the WebQuest website at San Diego State and other WebQuest resources;
- find a list of sites that support teachers' creation and use of wikis;
- access links to concept-mapping software as well as some websites that give examples of concept maps;

- link to Interactive Physics and other microworld resources;
- access a list of resources related to visualization tools;
- access a list of common tools and services that schools and teachers can use to create websites, including a few free resources;
- examine links to useful sites that support digital storytelling;
- learn more about the projects that use computers as conferencing tools; and
- access information and websites for evaluating web-based resources.

YOUR PORTFOLIO

This chapter described how to use technology to facilitate and inspire student learning and creativity through the use of authentic classroom activities. To demonstrate competency in ISTE NETS-T Standard 1.c and d and Standard 2.a, add the following items to your portfolio:

1. Reflect on the lesson description you developed in Chapter 3. Identify how technology is used as a 1) tutor, 2) mindtool, or 3) conversation support. Can you generate activities that demonstrate at least one of each type of use?
2. Describe activities for your lesson in which your students use technology as a collaborative and/or reflective tool to illuminate their thinking.
3. Describe one instance where you engaged in technology-supported learning, either face-to-face or virtually. Did the technology serve as a tutor, mindtool, or support for conversation? Explain why you classified your use of technology as you did.

References

Banaszewski, T. (2002). Digital storytelling finds its place in the classroom. Retrieved June 5, 2012, from http://www.infotoday.com/mmschools/jan02/banaszewski.htm

Bitter, G. G., & Legacy, J. M. (2008). *Using technology in the classroom* (7th ed). New York: Allyn & Bacon.

Buckingham, D. (2003). *Media education: Literacy, learning, and contemporary culture.* Cambridge: Polity Press.

Carnegie Learning. (2006). Secondary solutions to help all students achieve proficiency in math. Retrieved June 5, 2012, from http://www.carnegielearning.com/secondary-solutions/

Dodge, B. (2006). The WebQuest page. Retrieved May 5, 2012 from http://webquest.org/index.php

Ertmer, P. A. (2003). VisionQuest: Envisioning, and achieving integrated technology use. Retrieved June 12, 2012 from http://www.edci.purdue.edu/ertmer/projects.htm

Forcier, R. C, & Descy, D. E. (2005) *The computer as an educational tool* (4th ed.). Upper Saddle River, NJ: Merrill/Prentice Hall.

Gee, J. P., & Schaffer, D. W. (2010). Looking where the light is bad: Video games and the future of assessment. *Phi Delta Kappa International EDge,* 6(1), 3–19.

Jakes, D. S., & Brennan, J. (n.d.) *Capturing stories, capturing lives: An introduction to digital storytelling.* Retrieved June 6, 2012 from http://www.jakesonline.org/dst_techforum.pdf

Jonassen, D. J. (2006). *Modeling with technology: Mindtools for conceptual change* (3rd ed.). Upper Saddle River, NJ: Merrill/ Prentice Hall.

Jonassen, D. J., Howland, J., Moore, J., & Marra, R. M. (2003). *Learning to solve problems with technology: A constructivist perspective* (2nd ed.). Upper Saddle River, NJ: Merrill/Prentice Hall.

Novak, J. D., & Canas, A. J. (2006). *The theory underlying concept maps and how to construct them* (Technical Report IHMC Cmap Tools, 2006-1). Florida Institute for Human and Machine Cognition. Retrieved June 5, 2012, from http://cmap.ihmc.us/Publications/ResearchPapers/TheoryUnderlyingConceptMaps.pdf

Wegerif, R. (2002). *Literature review in thinking skills, technology, and learning.* Future Lab Series, No. 2. Retrieved June 5, 2012, from http://archive.futurelab.org.uk/resources/publications-reports-articles/literature-reviews/Literature-Review394/

Wikipedia. (2007). *Wiki.* Retrieved June 5, 2012, from http://en.wikipedia.org/wiki/Wiki

5

Developing Technology-Enriched Learning Environments and Experiences

OUTCOMES

In this chapter, you will learn to

- Establish **technology-enriched learning environments** for independent learning, small-group learning, and whole-class instruction;
- Support **students' use of technology tools and resources** through the actions you take for planning the lesson, during the lesson, and after the lesson; and
- Plan **learning experiences and lessons** for technology-enriched learning environments.

ISTE Standards Addressed in Chapter 5

NETS-T 2. Design and Develop Digital-Age Learning Experiences and Assessments

Teachers design, develop, and evaluate authentic learning experiences and assessments incorporating contemporary tools and resources to maximize content learning in context and to develop the knowledge, skills, and attitudes identified in the NETS-S. Teachers:

b. develop technology-enriched learning environments that enable all students to pursue their individual curiosities and become active participants in setting their own educational goals, managing their own learning, and assessing their own progress.

ISTE NETS-T Standard 2.b requires that you "develop technology-enriched learning environments that enable all students to pursue their individual curiosities and become active participants in setting their own educational goals, managing their own learning, and assessing their own progress." But what would a "technology-enriched learning environment" look like to you? How would you set up and manage such an environment? What equipment would it have and what sort of pedagogical activities would it support?

It's likely that, like Janice in the *Stories from Practice—Creating Technology-Rich Learning Experiences*, you also aspire to be the best technology-using teacher possible. Janice finds a way to use whatever technology is available to her in a way that enhances meaningful student learning. She bases her selection of digital technologies on her goals for student learning, and she develops techniques that help her students manage their uses of those technologies. At the end of each lesson, she and her students reflect on what went well and what needs to be improved in the future. In this chapter, you will learn to plan for and manage technology-enriched learning environments—where students work in groups as well as individually—in order to help your students achieve their educational goals, manage their own learning, and assess their own progress.

STORIES from Practice

Creating Technology-Rich Learning Experiences

I'm Janice, and I teach second grade at a large elementary school. While there is a computer lab available in the school, I just tend to use the four computers we have in the classroom. I think it's a matter of being really organized. I never wanted to be one of those teachers who had a computer just sitting in the back of the room. If the community's going to pay for things, then I wanted to use them, and I wanted to use them for the right reasons. And so I learned, by researching articles, how to find the appropriate curriculum goals and how to utilize the computer as a tool to reach those goals.

For example, I have curriculum objectives that I have selected for students to master each day. From these objectives, I design a computer-assisted lesson that lasts a minimum of fifteen minutes. I begin by presenting this first as a whole-group activity using a computer and projector. After the concept of the objective has been presented, the students are divided into cooperative groups to complete an activity using the computer as a tool. The project is designed to help the students practice and master the curriculum objectives.

I don't spend a lot of time trying to group my students in specific ways. Rather, cooperative groups are randomly determined using UNO cards. The color of the card determines which group the student will join. Then, the number of each card determines the specific job that each student has to complete. Number one is the reader, number two is the typer, number three is the timer who keeps the group on task, and number four manipulates the mouse at the computer station. Each person is responsible for his/her individual job, but the other group members are available to help and problem solve. The entire group is responsible for successfully completing the day's activity. The groups work together to solve problems while I circulate among them, observing and offering encouragement. Randomly assigning students to groups seems to avoid a lot of problems within the groups; students don't complain about whom they are working with or what job they got. They just get right down to business.

It's pretty interesting to watch my students work, all huddled around a computer terminal, especially when the project is authentic and meaningful to them. For example, last year we exchanged e-mail letters with students in a high school English class who were interested in writing children's books. My students worked in groups to respond to letters sent by the high school students. The second graders thought of the stories and offered suggestions as the stories developed. The final draft was typed by the high school class and illustrated by the second grade.

My students are young, but they work well when they have the opportunity to fulfill important roles in their groups. At the end of each work period, I provide them with the opportunity to discuss what went well and what didn't go so well in their groups. Students share ideas about how to work together as well as how to solve simple computer problems that they encountered. If they didn't complete their work, others offer suggestions for what they can do the next time to improve their work habits.

Not too long ago, I realized my ultimate goal was to be the best technology-using teacher possible. So I thought, if I sit around and wait to purchase the latest and greatest technology system, I'm not going to get anything accomplished. And I just realized that I need to use everything I have, so that I can prove to the administration that I need a better system. If I use everything to its fullest extent and say I need to look further, then I have a reason to go to them.

My emphasis with my students is on developing their problem-solving skills. I figured that the best way for me to help them develop these was by giving them the opportunity to practice, and reflect on, problem situations that they can attack and solve on their own. Managing my room in ways that allows students to take charge of these situations gives them the kind of practice they need.

Source: Ertmer, Gopalakrishnan, & Ross, (2001).

Technology-Enriched Learning Environments

Some classrooms have one or two computers, some have clusters of four or five computers and still others have access to a computer lab (see Figure 5.1). Some schools have carts full of laptops, tablet computers, or mobile devices such as iPods that can be checked out for classroom use. Other schools have "mini-labs" distributed throughout the school that are shared by several classes. It's also quite possible that you will be required to teach online at some point in your career. No matter what technology resources you have available, you will have the option for your students to work as a whole group, in small groups, or independently. This section focuses on instructional methods for those common arrangements with specific attention to computer use in a classroom setting, although you will have similar considerations for other types of technology such as scanners, probeware, calculators, digital cameras, and so on. As you read this chapter, think about what it means to work as a whole group, small group, or independently in an online, blended, or face-to-face setting.

Technology Support for Whole-Group Learning

When computers are used for whole-group work, they are typically used as presentation devices. If you only have one or two computers in your classroom, this is one of the most effective uses of a single computer. With this type of display, your single computer can be used to run simulations, model exemplary or completed projects, support a discussion through the use of concept-mapping software or notes created with a word-processing application, guide students on WebQuests or virtual field trips, and connect your classroom to the outside world through e-mail and web resources. Short streaming media clips can help you gain and focus student attention, orient students to an activity or task, or bring in the viewpoint of outside experts. You can use online quizzes or surveys as a group activity to review content or, with wireless responders, students can actually take quizzes and tests or otherwise provide formative feedback through an interactive whiteboard (see *Tech Tools and Tips—Using Interactive*

Figure 5.1
You will encounter a variety of computer configurations in the schools—some ideal, and some less so.

Whiteboards) or an other response system that interfaces with your single computer. The ideas are limitless.

To be used as a presentation device, additional equipment will be needed to make the computer screen visible to the whole class. Most popular—and most common—is a **data projector**, which connects to the computer and projects a computer desktop image onto a blank wall, screen, or whiteboard. Data projectors offer excellent resolution, the ability to zoom in, and easy control of projection size. When coupled with an interactive whiteboard, you have an excellent option for whole-class presentation and interaction. In fact, a description of a current teacher "workstation" might consist of an Internet-connected laptop or tablet computer, whiteboard, projector, and printer (see the *Tech Tools and Tips—Ten Ideas for Using a Teacher Workstation* later in this chapter).

Even in online learning environments, the entire class might want to engage in the same task simultaneously. In those cases, technologies that support synchronous learning activities should be explored. Web and video conferencing applications (discussed in Chapter 4) allow presentations to be made to the entire class at the same time, while providing opportunities for the class members to interact with the instructor and other class members through text, audio, or video. There are also online sites that support collaboration between a few or many students (Figure 5.2). Students can create and edit documents together, interact on a wiki, or even share interactive whiteboards.

Of course, when a computer is used for presentations, whether in the classroom or online, you need to prepare your materials carefully in advance. Presentation slides need to be developed, websites need to be located and bookmarked, and demonstrations need to be practiced.

> **data projector**
> connects to the computer and projects a computer desktop image onto a blank wall, screen, or whiteboard

Technology Support for Small Group Learning

Many times, the activities that you have planned will benefit from the collaboration that occurs when students work in small groups. Johnson and Johnson (1991)

Figure 5.2
E-Pals is one of the many sites that support collaboration between students.

Developing Technology-Enriched Learning Environments and Experiences   113

established guidelines for effective cooperative learning groups back in the 1970s. These guidelines include the need for positive interdependence, individual accountability and responsibility, and a consideration of the group process. For group work to be effective, it's critical to establish classroom norms that support a culture of collaboration.

When students have to work together around a single computer, it can be difficult for more than four students to work productively. And with cameras or mobile devices, two may be the limit. Students may be tempted to let the most technologically savvy students dominate the work, but it's important to establish an atmosphere where dominance by a few individuals is not tolerated. Group work provides an excellent opportunity for the more proficient students to support less proficient students in developing their technological competencies, yet take care to ensure that each student gets an equal chance to work with the technology.

Group work is most equitable and productive when specific roles are assigned and the principles of cooperative learning are followed. Depending on the age and abilities of your students, you may want to assign roles to individual students or have the group divide tasks among the members and cycle through them in turn—allowing each student to be the recorder, reporter, and so forth. In order to assign roles, think through the various tasks that are required by the group activity and divide them among the students (see Figure 5.3). For example, if students are conducting research on the web, one student could lead the discussions, one could take notes, one could enter search terms in the computer, and another could track the results of the searches.

Figure 5.3
Students work together at the computer; each student is responsible for a role such as researcher, recorder, or reporter.

Sometimes the biggest decision a teacher has to make is *how* to assign students to groups. While some teachers like to group students who have similar qualities together, others like to mix the students up. Sometimes teachers allow students to work with friends; other times, they prefer that their students work with those they don't know as well. Using a model he refers to as cooperative workgroups, teacher Scott Mandel (2003) develops groups in his classrooms based on a learning profile inventory he administers to his students at the beginning of the year. Mandel uses an instrument based on Gardner's theory of multiple intelligences (see Figure 6.1 in Chapter 6) to determine student strengths and preferences and then assigns groups by ensuring there is a mix of students with different preferences in each group. This way,

APPLY *to Practice*

Student Roles

1. Work with your peers to brainstorm a list of all the possible roles that students can play in collaborative work using technology.
2. Determine the skills and knowledge students must have to participate in each role as well as commonly available technologies that can support them. For example, a "recorder" may capture notes from the group using audio, word-processing, or concept-mapping software.
    - What group behaviors are essential for the group to be successful?
    - What individual behaviors are important to each role?
    - How will you monitor how successful students are in their roles?
3. Compare the list your group created with the lists created by other groups in your class. Merge the lists to create a comprehensive list for your class. Consider adding the master list to your portfolio with a description of how it was developed.

TECH TOOLS & TIPS

Using Interactive Whiteboards

Interactive whiteboards have become a common sight in many classrooms (see Figure 5.4), but not all teachers who have whiteboards take advantage of their many potential benefits. Although little empirical research is available that ties the use of a whiteboard directly to student learning, the whiteboard certainly supports proven pedagogical methods and tools. As you review these ten tips for using a whiteboard in your classroom, keep in mind that the most important consideration is *how* you use the whiteboard to support your instruction.

1 Project Clear Visuals. The clarity of visuals is a hallmark of the whiteboard. A bonus is the ease with which text, images, and video can be presented and manipulated (e.g., quickly changing fonts, colors, sizes, etc.). This can be helpful for supporting students with a wide range of learning needs and preferences, especially English language learners, some students with special needs, and those with visual learning preferences. Most boards also include handwriting recognition and can insert handwritten notes as legible text into spreadsheets, word processing, and other documents.

2 Use Any Software. Whiteboards can be used with any software installed on the computer to which they are connected, making them ideal for one-computer classrooms. You can access CDs, DVDs, and other videos, as well as a range of animations and simulations found on the Internet and through stand-alone software. You can even scan in images or hand-drawn student work for use with your entire class. Some interactive whiteboards can also be shared from a distance in support of virtual learning.

3 Save and Review Work. Important documents, diagrams, or other files created during class can be saved as media files that students can access after class or be printed out and distributed immediately. Documents, websites, and images you use in your instruction on the board can be exported to a class website to support absent students, student review, or to keep parents informed of lessons covered in your class.

4 Interact with Your Instructional Materials. The interactive whiteboard allows you to display and interact with documents, images, video, and animations. You can pause video and circle pertinent features. Still images, such as a diagram of a cell, can be labeled onscreen. Documents can be created and manipulated through highlighting, commenting, or showing changes. One unique feature is the reveal tool that

Figure 5.4
A single computer connected to a projector and interactive whiteboard can be a valuable resource for you and your students.

(continued)

allows you to select portions of the screen to display, or not, thus allowing you to highlight or hide information on the board as easily as opening a shade or pointing your finger.

5 Use or Create Templates. Use the built-in templates (e.g., maps, grids, number lines, diagrams, musical staves) and the built-in tools (e.g., timers, rulers, protractors, calculators, probability tools, notepads, cameras) in many different classroom activities. Or, if you wish, scan in your own images or backgrounds.

6 Involve Your Students. Students can manipulate items directly on the board, adding their own ideas (either typed from the keyboard or handwritten on the board), can underline or highlight text to identify main ideas and keywords, can annotate images, or even move items around, as when creating a concept map or diagram. Using the whiteboard can be motivational and mastered by students of all ages.

7 Support Student Presentations. Present student projects using a variety of software, web resources, and document formats—controlling the presentation (opening and closing files, windows, menus, etc.) entirely from the whiteboard. Teachers use whiteboards with students in most grades, even students in primary grades. In fact, students with less-developed fine-motor skills can often operate the board easily.

8 Interact with Your Students. Whiteboards support interactive learning environments that promote discussion and opportunities for participation in small group or whole-class settings. Several boards support classroom response systems through which students can anonymously or confidentially respond to polls or other formative assessments and from which data can be captured, reviewed (immediately, if preferred), or recorded in a grade book.

9 Manage Resources Flexibly and Efficiently. You can easily move back and forth between open documents or applications to provide multiple examples, enrichment, or instructional interventions for those students who need them. Less time is spent on resource management than when using a chalkboard or even a computer with a projector. Many users report that using their fingers or stylus is easier and faster than using a mouse. Wireless slates, available with some boards, allow you and your students to interact with the board from anywhere in the classroom.

10 Share with the Greater Teaching Community. Many whiteboard companies offer online communities where you can download lesson plans, presentations, and templates to use in your classroom. You can post to these communities, too, and may find teachers with similar interests with whom you can communicate and collaborate.

Sources: Bell, M. A. (2002); Smith, H. J., Higgins, S., Wall, K., & Miller, J. (2005).

students who may have strong interpersonal skills are tapped to be leaders, and those with linguistic preferences can serve as writers or recorders. These groups do not change often, either, so that students build up group routines and processes.

Whether students are collaborating online using their individual computers or in class around a single workstation, effective collaborative work is characterized by a balance between group responsibility and individual accountability. It's important to clarify whether the tasks can be divided or whether all students must know how to do each task. Often, group members are responsible for both their own individual learning and the learning of other group members. Stress that each individual has something to offer the group and that no one set of skills is more important than another in the functioning of the group. Create an atmosphere of collaboration instead of competition. Stress that each group member has a responsibility to educate the other members on the skills for which he or she has expertise.

Students should be evaluated on their group process skills (see Figure 5.5) as well as their products. When working in small groups, teachers often conclude the group work with reflection on the group process, as illustrated by Janice in the *Stories from Practice—Creating Technology-Rich Learning Experiences*. In Chapter 2, you learned that reflection is an important part of becoming a self-directed learner. Students should evaluate themselves and each other on the extent to which they took turns, listened to one another, accepted responsibility for the group, and completed their assigned tasks. Even young students are capable of reflecting on their work and making positive suggestions to improve.

You may also want to involve students in establishing a list of rules that can help them monitor and manage their learning during group work. Morrison and Lowther (2002) suggest that group rules include items such as:

- Every team member is important.
- We work as a team and as individuals to accomplish our goals.

	1 None of the Time	**2** Some of the Time	**3** Most of the Time	**4** All of the Time
Helping: The students offered assistance to each other.	1	2	3	4
Listening: Group members listened respectfully to each other's ideas.	1	2	3	4
Participating: Group members participated in each step of the process.	1	2	3	4
Persuading: Students exchanged, defended, and rethought ideas.	1	2	3	4
Questioning: Students interacted, discussed, and posed questions to all members of the team.	1	2	3	4
Respecting: Group members encouraged and supported the ideas and efforts of others.	1	2	3	4
Sharing: Students offered ideas and reported their findings to each other.	1	2	3	4

Figure 5.5
Group process rubric.
Source: Hall, A. Group Participation Rubric—WebQuest. Phoenix, AZ: Arizona State University at the West campus. Retrieved September 13, 2008 from http://coe.west.asu.edu/students/ahall/webquest/grouprubric.htm. Reprinted by permission.

- Diversity in opinions is important. We respect the right to be different but work toward consensus.
- We seek solutions to our problems, instead of blaming or criticizing.
- We structure our work according to individual needs.
- We help those who require assistance.

Independent Use of Technology

Students can use technology independently in a variety of settings. Your entire class may be engaged in individual use of a device, as when each student has a tablet computer or accesses the course content at home, or students may use a single classroom computer one at a time. When computers are used independently, coordinating technology-supported work with other instructional activities deserves special consideration.

At times, the entire class needs to work on the same task at the same time. For example, you may want all of your students to complete a learning game on fractions. Although the whole class may be involved in the same activity, the technology itself, a desktop, laptop, or tablet, for example, would be used individually. Unless you expect your students to complete this activity outside of class time, you will need access to a mobile cart of computers, tablets, or whatever device is appropriate, or a computer lab in order for each student to work on an individual device. Typically, access to a lab or mobile cart of devices is available at an assigned time each week or must be reserved as needed. For example, each class might use a lab for one class period each week. When access to technology is available only during specific time periods, you'll need to carefully plan the activities that occur before and after use. If students are to complete a lesson on fractions in the computer lab on Tuesday, you might want them to explore fractions using hands-on manipulatives during class on Monday and follow

Facilitating Online Discussions

Facilitating online discussions takes skill. You want to keep the group conversation going and establish a human presence—without access to the nonverbal cues available in face-to-face classroom situations. Matthews-DeNatale and Doubler (2000) outline a range of actions you might want to take to move the discussion forward.

1 Summarize. Sometimes participant messages contain so many different kinds of information that it becomes difficult for the group to see developing patterns, common threads, or areas of disagreement. In these cases, it can be helpful to summarize things for them. For example, you may want to point out discrepancies in data, asking the group why they think this happened. Often this question will prompt group members to redo an investigation, or to develop an investigation variant that will help explain the differences in data. If you present the group with a summary, make sure that you end your message with a question for the group so that your collation doesn't come across as the "final word." As the course progresses, encourage group members to try their hand at summarizing; this communicates to them that you aren't the only one who can play the "summarizer" role.

2 Moderate. If a discussion develops into many simultaneous threads, it may be useful to refocus the group by writing something like, "We have several areas of discussion developing here. Perhaps it would be useful to take them one at a time beginning with (name of topic)." Then end with a question about that topic that will help them explore the topic in more depth.

3 Guide. If one topic is being discussed at great length while another is being ignored, consider posting a message that says something like, "We seem to have given a good deal of attention to (name of topic). What about (name of new topic)?" Some groups have difficulty keeping their theoretical discussions rooted in their first-hand experiential data. They may need your guidance in exploring the topic's relevance to their investigation data (or teaching plans). Ask, "What does your data tell you?"

4 Prompt. Consider gently prodding if the discussion seems to diminish prematurely or if you think that an important topic has been overlooked. You might want to ask an open-ended question to rekindle the conversation—a question designed to encourage substantive discussion. Or you might want to simply write a message saying, "It has been more quiet than usual in this discussion. What's on your mind?"

5 Troubleshoot. Are people posting attachments that don't show up (or are too large)? Does one person's investigation data indicate he or she put too much dye in the water? Would group members benefit from a timeline or deadline reminder? In each course, minor technical glitches can affect the group discussion. Be on the lookout for these kinds of things, and help participants resolve these problems. If the problem is not something you know how to resolve, ask the designated technical support staff member to help with technical assistance.

6 Mediate. Each group has a unique set of challenges and personalities. This is true of group work in both online and face-to-face settings. If you mediate the conflict quickly and with a light touch, the group will probably return its focus to the topic.

7 Problem Solve. There are some situations that require immediate attention on the part of the facilitator:

- A string of off-topic "social" messages in the content discussion areas, often a problem at the beginning of the course. Suggest that they move the conversation thread to another forum.
- A group member whose posts are excessively authoritative (a.k.a. someone who is stuck in "teacher" mode). Contact the person via phone and discuss ways to re-cast messages in a more collegial tone.
- The person who has gone AWOL. Check participation and send an e-mail message to any participant who has not posted that week.

It is essential that these problems are addressed expeditiously and in a way that saves face for all group members. While an e-mail message may be sufficient, sometimes it really pays to pick up the phone and talk with the person individually. If personalities continue to clash and the group discussion erupts into a "flame war," you may also want to write a message to the whole group. Remind them of their signed agreement to the established acceptable use policy and advocate a return to civility. In the unlikely event that one message is particularly abusive or offensive, you do have the option to delete that message, but use this power only as a last resort.

Source: Extracted with permission from Matthews-DeNatalie, G. & Doubler, S. (2000). *Facilitating Online Learning: Tips and Suggestions.* TERC (Cambridge, Ma) and Lesley University (Cambrige, MA). Available at http://scienceonline.terc.edu/facilitating_online_learning.html

their computer lesson with an assignment on Wednesday where they apply the skills they practiced in the lesson.

Other times, students will need to work independently on a single classroom computer or device. For example, students may need to contribute their own research report to a class book or post data related to a science experiment. You can still use technology individually even if you have access to only a few devices (or even just one), but scheduling technology time requires special attention. Take a look at your classroom schedule and lesson plans to determine when students would be able to work with necessary technology without missing other critical activities. After you have determined the available blocks of time for use, either assign students to time blocks or post the schedule of open time blocks so students can schedule their own technology time. However, you'll need to take measures to ensure equitable access. The main thing to avoid is using technology as "a reward." Rather, it should be incorporated as a learning tool for all students to meet both teacher- and student-selected learning goals.

Summary of Technology-Enriched Learning Environments

Any of these instructional groupings can occur with almost any physical arrangement of technology. Although the national numbers suggest that Internet-capable computers and other technologies are widely available in the nation's schools, you may have little

TECH TOOLS & TIPS

Ten Ideas for Using a Teacher Workstation

These days, the ideal teacher workstation often consists of an Internet-connected laptop or tablet computer, interactive whiteboard, projector, and printer. This equipment is considered by many to be the basic teaching equipment in a classroom. And while it would be great for every child to have access to his or her own device, there are still plenty of things you can do with the teacher workstation. Here are ten ideas.

1. Use online maps or Google Earth to teach geography and history. You can start by using places the students know or would like to know to increase interest and engagement.

2. Write a book collaboratively, about any subject of interest, integrating texts, pictures, and narration.

3. Perform an experiment. You can perform a dissection, make crystals, or mix chemicals. Have different students conduct different parts, get someone to take pictures and upload them to the interactive board environment, or you can use a document camera to do it in real time.

4. Focus on grammar. You can have grammar rules and examples on the board, listen to grammar podcasts, and get students to match rules and examples or create their own examples.

5. Take a virtual field trip. After reading a book, go online and find out about the places mentioned. Visit museums from across the world. Foreign language students can explore countries or regions where their language is spoken.

6. Sponsor a virtual career day and have parents or community members—near or far—interact with your students through webconferencing software or a webcam.

7. Collect student feedback or monitor student learning through wireless responders. Some mobile devices can be used to interact with polling software, such as texting with a phone.

8. Create interest in learning basic facts, like the elements in the periodic table, geography, or multiplication tables. Find or create an interactive presentation, such as the Periodic Table of Videos or a Jeopardy-based game that the students can interact with on the board or through wireless responders.

9. Connect to another classroom, either in your district or across the globe through a program like ePals, and share and learn about culture, language, and what it's like to be a kid somewhere else.

10. Capture lessons, such as solving math problems, as short videos or screen captures, and post them online so students can use them to review content, or catch up if they're absent.

© Cengage Learning 2014

> ### APPLY to Practice
> #### Computer/Technology Arrangements
> 1. Create a description of an instructional activity appropriate for various technology settings. Include a description of how the technology tools will be used within each setting.
>   - A one-computer classroom
>   - A classroom with five computers or devices
>   - A lab or portable lab setting
> 2. Share your descriptions with your peers. Create a comprehensive list of all the ideas proposed by your class. Consider adding the master list to your portfolio with a description of how it was developed.

choice in determining what technologies are in your school or classroom. Certainly, school administrators should work to provide equitable access to resources for teachers, staff, and students, but what happens if your class has limited technology? What if there is just a single computer?

As noted earlier, a single computer connected to a display, either a projector or large monitor, can be a valuable resource for supporting your instruction. You can present information slides or websites, students can present their projects, you can demonstrate software and procedures before students go to the lab, and so forth. A single computer as a learning station can support the differentiation of instruction and flexible grouping strategies. Students can use software on the computer for initial practice, remediation, or enrichment. A computer-centric learning center can easily support student inquiry at most grade levels when connected to the Internet or networked databases supported by the school's library or media center. A variety of peripherals can also be connected to the computer to support a wide range of content areas. For example, your one-computer learning station can be connected to a classroom weather station, a digital microscope, a drawing tablet and pen stylus, a variety of scientific measurement devices including probeware, a piano keyboard, or digital cameras and video cameras. When connected to a printer, either directly or via the school's network, you can also print examples of student work that can be stored in portfolios or sent home to parents.

When there are a few devices in the classroom, several students can work on individual projects simultaneously while the rest of the class does some other task, or each device can be assigned to a group of students for small group work. One of the computers or tablets could be connected to a projector or large monitor for whole-class instruction. When you have access to enough devices for your whole class in a lab, library media center, or using a mobile cart, it might seem easier, or preferable, to have students use them for individual work. But as you learned in Chapter 4, research suggests that collaborative learning can improve the effectiveness of most activities (Wegerif, 2002), and the same is true for technology-based activities. Asking students to work together, especially around digital devices, increases the level of conversation in which students engage, which can result in greater learning. You don't want to rule out this type of technology use, just because you have enough devices for students to work individually. Be sure to consider the specific learning goals that students are trying to achieve, and then select your technology-to-student arrangement and instructional groupings to help them best achieve those goals. When planning for online teaching, you may find it easiest to first plan the lesson as if you were to teach it face-to-face, and then think about how you can provide similar learning experiences online—targeting the same learning outcomes.

Supporting Students' Use of Technology Tools and Resources

The effectiveness of any instructional resource, whether a website, software, video, or textbook, lies partially in the content and design of the resources, but the main impact comes from the way you use it. Whether students are working at home, in a computer lab, with laptop computers in the classroom, with a classroom set of calculators or handheld computers, or on a limited number of classroom computer workstations, both you and your students are responsible for preparing for meaningful interactions with the technology. If you are designing a blended learning course, you'll need to consider which aspects of the course can best be served online, which aspects are best served face-to-face, and how to schedule and organize the two parts so they are integrated as seamlessly as possible (see *Tech Tools and Tips: Blended Learning*).

> **blended learning**
> learning activities in which part of the instruction is provided online and other aspects are provided in the classroom

TECH TOOLS & TIPS

Blended Learning

As mentioned in Chapter 1, blended learning is a fast-growing trend in K–12 schools. **Blended learning** refers to any situation in which part of the instruction is provided online and other aspects are provided in the classroom.

Blended learning environments range from those in which the curriculum is completely online but supplemented by face-to-face interactions, to those in which classroom instruction is simply enhanced through interactions with online content or resources. Staker (2011, pp. 7–8) provides the following descriptions of six blended learning models, identified through a study of 40 schools:

1. **Model 1: Face-to-Face Driver.** The programs that fit in the face-to-face-driver category all retain face-to-face teachers to deliver most of their curricula. The physical teacher deploys online learning on a case-by-case basis to supplement or remediate, often in the back of the classroom or in a technology lab.

2. **Model 2: Rotation.** The common feature in the rotation model is that, within a given course, students rotate on a fixed schedule between learning online in a one-to-one, self-paced environment and sitting in a classroom with a traditional face-to-face teacher. It is the model most in between the traditional face-to-face classroom and online learning because it involves a split between the two and, in some cases, between remote and on site. The face-to-face teacher usually oversees the online work.

3. **Model 3: Flex.** Programs with a flex model feature an online platform that delivers most of the curricula. Teachers provide on-site support on a flexible and adaptive as-needed basis through in-person tutoring sessions and small group sessions. Many dropout-recovery and credit-recovery blended programs fit into this model.

4. **Model 4: Online Lab.** The online-lab model characterizes programs that rely on an online platform to deliver the entire course but in a brick-and-mortar lab environment. Usually these programs provide online teachers. Paraprofessionals supervise but offer little content expertise. Often students that participate in an online-lab program also take traditional courses and have typical block schedules.

5. **Model 5: Self-Blend.** The nearly ubiquitous version of blended learning among American high school students is the self-blend model, which encompasses any time students choose to take one or more courses online to supplement their traditional school's catalog. The online learning is always remote, which distinguishes it from the online-lab model, but the traditional learning is in a brick-and-mortar school. All supplemental online schools that offer à la carte courses to individual students facilitate self-blending.

6. **Model 6: Online Driver.** The online-driver model involves an online platform and teacher that deliver all curricula. Students work remotely for the most part. Face-to-face check-ins are sometimes optional and other times required. Some of these programs offer brick-and-mortar components as well, such as extracurricular activities.

Planning and managing blended learning experiences is not that different from planning and managing any other lesson that incorporates digital technologies, even if much of the primary content is presented online. The considerations discussed in this chapter hold true whether you simply enhance a lesson by showing an online video clip to the entire class or your students obtain the majority of the course content through participation in an online class. As you read this chapter, think about what it means to be a teacher in a blended learning environment.

In many ways, teaching online or blended learning classes is similar to face-to-face teaching, but in other ways it's very different. You still need to plan instructional activities and respond to the needs of your students. You still need to communicate with them and provide feedback in a timely manner. On the other hand, course materials must be prepared far in advance, and communication with your online students will occur primarily through writing and interacting one-on-one instead of in a group, although alternate forms of communication and grouping can take place. Whether the technology resources are to be used individually, in small groups, or in large groups, to supplement classroom instruction as part of a blended learning approach, or in a fully online course, it is important to consider what you have to do before, during, and after the lesson to support students in their self-directed learning efforts.

Before Instruction

As a teacher, you know, or will soon know, that preparation is essential! When you use a textbook resource, you read the book carefully and direct your students to the sections that need special attention. You may have them answer certain questions or do particular assignments. Preparing for the use of digital resources requires the same care. Consider how you will scaffold students' learning activities so that they are able to complete their tasks as autonomously as possible, given their current ability levels.

Plan

Begin by examining, in detail, the resources you plan to use with your students. You may want to perform a trial run of the same tasks that you will ask your students to do and make note of the problems you encounter. As you review digital resources, determine what components or sections align with your students' learning goals; students may not need to complete the entire program, view the entire video, or explore the entire website.

Also determine the time required to complete the activities. Some activities are easier to stop and start than others. Check whether a game or activity can be saved at any time or only at the end of a level, and plan accordingly. You may want to estimate a little extra time if students need to become familiar with the program before they use it for academic tasks.

After you have become familiar with the resources you plan to use with your students, analyze your learners in relation to the skills you want them to acquire. Determine the prerequisite skills your students need in order to participate successfully in the technology-based activities and to learn the content. For example, young students may need help with typing activities. Older students might need a review of math concepts in order to select the best formula to be entered in a spreadsheet. Consider also the attention span of your students. How long can they stay focused and interested in one task? Make sure the learning experience is appropriate for your students and their learning goals.

As you plan your instruction, think about the tasks that students should perform before, during, and after the technology-based activity. Should students collect data for a spreadsheet or create a rough outline of their papers before they log onto their computers? Should they practice the skills they learned in a tutorial after they return to their desks? How will students move from task to task? What procedures will help them manage their own learning? Carefully think through a class activity and determine which parts of the lesson lend themselves to technology use and which ones do not. A checklist of things to do prior to and after working on the computers can be helpful for many students. You may want to work with them to develop their own checklists to help them think through the tasks that should be done. Above all, make sure the link between what they are learning in the classroom and their computer work is very clear! Students should see the technology as essential to their classroom work rather than as an "add on."

Table 5.1 lists activities that typically need to be performed when using a few common software programs. Use the guidance provided in this table to develop your own list of teacher preparation activities for other types of technology-enriched learning experiences.

As you plan your lessons, ALWAYS have a backup plan in case of unexpected technical problems. Some teachers find it useful to set up learning centers or stations where students can work through specific activities at one station, with some activities requiring the use of digital technologies and others not. Supplemental activities can

Table 5.1 Teacher Preparation Required for Software Programs

Software Type	Preparation
Tutor	
Tutorial	Select sections of program that match your objectives. Identify necessary prerequisite skills.
Drill and Practice	Identify prerequisite skills and sections to be completed by students.
Mindtools	
Simulation or Problem solving	Identify prerequisite skills and sections of the program that correspond to objectives. Assign students to small groups for collaborative problem solving. Consider appropriate whole-group problem-solving activities.
Database	Develop a sample of what students should generate. Decide what fields are needed, collect data, generate sample report. Create a print or electronic worksheet for students to complete with information that will be entered into the database or let students create their own. When manipulating data, use small groups to make predictions and organize and interpret data.
Word processing	Create a sample student project. Assure that directions are clear, planned resources are suitable, and time allocated adequate.
Spreadsheet	Plan for the data collection process, if applicable. Plan specific data manipulations. Create sample spreadsheets with data. Determine how data will be presented, as a chart or graph. Prepare a template or provide directions for students to create their own. When manipulating data, use small groups to make predictions and organize and interpret data.
Support for communication	
Face-to-face collaborative learning	Choose digital resources that promote conversations and support your learning goals. Assign students to pairs or small groups, depending on the nature of the assignment. Establish ground rules for collaboration. Develop a worksheet or handout for assessment.
Discussion lists, blogs, wikis	Set up a list, blog, or wiki site and assign appropriate permissions. Establish ground rules for postings. Determine if students will work individually, in pairs, or in teams to post or respond to postings. Ensure student safety, especially if using a public space.
Chat, instant messaging	Assign students accounts. Determine who will be chatting with whom, and for what purpose. Prepare a handout or presentation about appropriate language and safe use of instant messaging. If messages are part of your assessment, determine how you will retain the messages. Ensure student safety, especially if using a public chat room.
Video and webconferencing	Determine equipment needed for video and audio transmission such as webcams, microphones, headsets, and adequate bandwidth. Decide on which functions of the resource to employ (such as chat, polls, and document sharing). If the conference is essentially a classroom presentation, arrange the room so that all can see and hear the presentation, using projection equipment if necessary. If the conference is interactive, work individually or in pairs at individual computers. Prepare handout or presentation with instructions for participation.

Source: Adapted from Morrison, G. & Lowther, D. (2002). Integrating computer technology into the classroom, 2nd ed.

be on different but related topics. You may want to assign readings or have students participate in experiments or learning games to reinforce or broaden their understanding. Of course, you need a backup plan in case you encounter nontechnical problems, too, like when you plan to go outside to collect soil samples and it rains. Make sure that all activities clearly relate to specific learning outcomes and are not perceived as unnecessary "busy work."

One challenge you will face is *how much instruction* to provide when using a new application or visiting a new website. Do you need to teach students to use the software or do they already know how? You may be tempted to provide detailed, step-by-step instructions or, conversely, to simply let them discover how to operate the program on their own. The ideal amount of instruction to provide will vary, depending on the abilities of your students. Unless the goal of the lesson is to learn the new application, you may want to minimize the amount of time devoted to learning functionality, yet provide enough support so that your students do not struggle unnecessarily. And if you want them to learn technology skills within the context of the lesson, don't forget to make these skills part of your lesson goals.

If possible, teach students skills that generalize across applications as well as skills they need to figure out new digital resources on their own. For example, students should learn to explore the menu structure of a resource to determine what options are available within a computer program or website. One good option is to provide students with simple directions to get them started, and then let them have time to discover specific features of the resource on their own while you monitor the success of their chosen strategies. If you choose this option, don't forget to allocate additional time within your schedule for students to explore the capabilities of the resource.

Develop Student Guidelines

When working in technology-enriched learning environments, students will benefit from having guidelines that indicate what they should accomplish during the lesson (their goals for learning), what they are expected to have ready beforehand, and what they should do after they finish using the technology, including self-assessment activities. Table 5.2 lists typical preparation and follow-up activities for several types of common software applications, from the student's perspective. Use these examples to develop your own list of preparation and follow-up activities for other types of technology-enriched learning experiences.

Your guidelines should provide enough detail to clearly convey your expectations as to how your students should manage their time, before, during, and after technology use. Prepare any handouts and assignment sheets needed—either digital handouts that students access from a file server or web page or paper-based copies. Assignment sheets might contain a description of the assigned task, the problem statement, guiding questions, URLs, tips for using technology, and reflection questions. Sometimes you need a series of assignment sheets such as general instructions, technical guidelines, resource guides, rubrics, and example projects.

When a technology task is new, it might be helpful to provide your students with step-by-step **technical guidelines**. When preparing step-by-step guides, try to anticipate and minimize the confusion that could occur if students worked from unclear instructions. It's a good practice to 1) perform the task that you are asking the students to do and write down each step you take, 2) prepare your instruction guide following the steps that you recorded, then 3) try to perform the task again, using the instructions you developed, 4) make notes of any steps that were left out or unclear and finally, 5) correct the instruction sheet as needed. Make sure you work through the instructions exactly as you wrote them in order to test their accuracy. Develop step-by-step guides only for those tasks students will need. Typically, these would be procedures,

technical guidelines
step-by-step instructions for using technology

Table 5.2 Student Preparation and Follow-up Activities

Software Type	Before Technology Use	After Technology Use
Tutor		
Tutorial	Complete activities that build prerequisite skills.	Apply skills learned to different but related tasks to solidify knowledge gains.
Drill and Practice	Complete activities that introduce the skills practiced in the lesson.	Continue to practice skills in other ways.
Mindtools		
Simulation or Problem solving	Review rules and procedures for skills that are to be applied.	Synthesize what was learned through discussions or individual reflections.
Database	Determine data fields needed, if not assigned. If sharing data across groups, then all groups should have the same database fields. Determine when to collect data, create data fields, and enter data. Review prior learning and gain the new skills necessary for the activity through readings, research, assignments, tutorials, practice problems. Generate predictions about what will be found.	Discuss findings in whole-class or small-group settings, referencing the databases during discussions. This may lead to the development of new questions, further analysis, or additional research. Reflect on learning that occurred. Generate a group report that includes reports from the data. Build on the lesson by making connections to other lessons and making additional predictions.
Word processing	Brainstorm and conduct discussions to clarify goals of the task. Identify where to find resources. Review prior learning and skills associated with the task.	Conduct group presentations of products created. Reflect on the process through group debriefing or journal writing.
Spreadsheet	Collect and organize data prior to entering it. Review prior learning on topic and ensure that students have skills necessary to complete the task. Read materials, complete tutorials, work practice problems as necessary.	Interpret and make predictions from the data. Explore activities that further enhance learning or develop critical thinking skills.
Support for Communication		
Face-to-face collaborative learning	Review ground rules for effective collaboration. Set expectations for participation.	Reflect on what worked and what did not work in the collaborative effort.
Discussion lists, blogs, wikis	Review ground rules and instructional goals. Draft postings. Establish goals for reading and responding to others' postings.	Use the information from the products. Reflect on postings and/or responses.
Chat, instant messaging	Review ground rules and instructional goals.	Use the information learned in the chat. Reflect on the chat experience.
Video and Webconferencing	Check all equipment, connections, and setup. Review ground rules and instructional goals.	Use the information from the conference. Reflect on the experience.

Source: Adapted from Morrison, G. & Lowther, D. (2002). Integrating computer technology into the classroom (2nd ed.). Reprinted by permission of Pearson Education, Upper Saddle River, NJ.

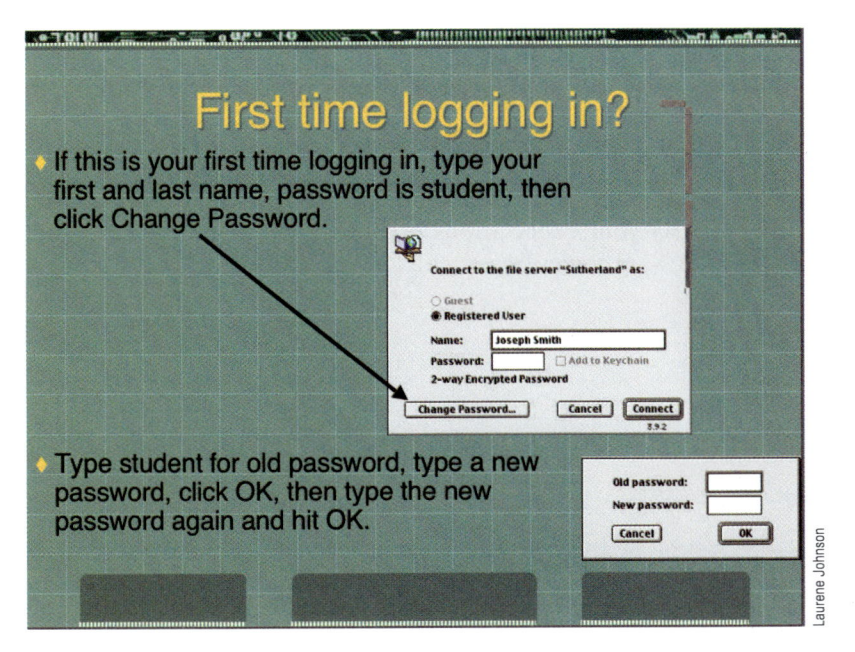

Figure 5.6
Technical guidelines can help learners with the steps involved in a new technology task, such as logging into a school network.

activities, and software that are very different from those used in the past. Students often need instructions on how to get started and how to get help when they encounter difficulties (see Figure 5.6).

You can use technology to create your step-by-step guides. You can create a document and insert graphics using word-processing software or develop a series of tutorial web pages linked from your class website. Screen-capturing software that takes a picture of your screen is available with most operating systems, such as Apple's Grab or the Snipping Tool on Windows. You can also capture action on your screen and narrate it using screen-recording software, such as TechSmith's Camtasia, QuickTime, or the free website, Jing. Screen recordings can play back sequences of actions and are helpful for illustrating processes, such as using menu commands in a video-editing program or how to access resources like a class file server.

When a lesson requires multiple resources, a **resource guide** can assist students in using their time wisely. A resource guide lists the materials and digital resources that are applicable to the lesson. The use of web resources deserves special mention. Some teachers create and organize bookmarks (or "favorites") in web browsers to help guide students' activity on the Internet. Another way to ensure that students use their time wisely when searching for information on the web is to create a list of URLs that contains information relevant to your lesson. As you locate sites for use in your lesson, you can simply copy and paste the links into a word-processed document. If this document is loaded on a computer with Internet access, students can open the web pages by clicking on the links in the word-processed document. Another option is to create a web page—one that can be linked from a school or class website—or use a social bookmarking site, such as Diigo or Symbaloo, that includes those links. Then, all you have to do is to provide the URL of that page to your students. The advantage of a web-based version is that you and your students would have the page available from any device with Internet access. You may also want to embed your resources into an instructional activity, such as a WebQuest as described in Chapter 4.

As you prepare materials for your students, it's important to make your expectations of quality clear through rubrics, checklists, or models of exemplary student work (for

resource guide
lists of the materials and digital resources that are applicable to the lesson

> **rubrics**
> help students understand what is expected in a final product, usually describing varied levels of performance

more information on rubrics, checklists, and assessing quality, see Chapter 7). Let students know the manner in which their finished products should be delivered to you, the expected length, any formatting requirements, and whether they can work with other students or not. **Rubrics** help students determine the critical components that need to be reflected in the final products. This, then, enables them to set daily goals for completion and to monitor their progress toward realization of the final product. **Exemplars** can further clarify your expectations by providing models of acceptable performance. You may even want to develop a template for students to use as they go

STORIES from Practice

Powerful Learning with Simple Technologies

Sometimes some simple technologies can support a variety of learning opportunities. I experienced this myself in one of my graduate classes working with teachers. In my class I try to introduce teachers to different resources each week. I try to use most of the resources before I introduce them, but there are so many different resources becoming available that I hear about at conferences, from newsletters, or just from other teachers that I don't always get a chance to use them thoroughly. That was the case with Wordle, an online site for creating word clouds.

During the first week of class I ask my students to read the executive summary of the National Educational Technology Plan (U. S. DOE, 2010) which we then discuss. The first time I did this, I created a word cloud of the text of the entire executive summary (see Figure 1.7). That's 16 pages of text! I did it just as an experiment and posted a link to the Wordle for my students as another way to consider the content of the plan.

There are many different word cloud sites available that have different features. They usually allow you to add your own words, change colors, and some let you make clouds in different shapes. The basic idea, however, is that words that are mentioned most often are the largest, so they're more prominent in the resulting image. You can copy and paste text in, like I did, or enter and manipulate select words. When you take a look at the Wordle of the executive summary, you'll notice that the largest word is "learning," followed by "students" and "education." The word "technology" is in there but smaller than these. I was hoping that they'd pick up that while this is a technology plan, learning and students were the focus. I thought it was an interesting experiment and left it at that.

That's when my students took over. While the activity focused on the National Educational Technology Plan, several times students have latched on to the word cloud idea and used it in their own instruction. One was an English teacher whose students were reading Harper Lee's *To Kill a Mockingbird*. They were in the midst of reading this famous novel when she introduced the idea of a word cloud to her students. She created an example and demonstrated the Wordle site to her students and told them their assignment was to summarize the novel through a word cloud and justify their decisions for fonts, colors, and word choice. She said the students couldn't wait to share their word clouds the next week. Many used the site, but some drew theirs by hand (which was a good demonstration of allowing choice and flexibility). The students were highly engaged and had many great ideas from the activity. Some even related that they created other word clouds, such as descriptions of their friends and even one for the school's marching band. Ultimately, the students' word clouds were posted outside of the teacher's class room for all to see, which generated even more interest in using this simple online tool, and several teachers approached her for help in implementing word clouds in their own instruction.

Instead of summarizing, another student—also an English teacher—saw my original word cloud and took the initiative to incorporate it into his classroom as a prewriting activity. He suggested that the graphic representation of the words really got his students thinking, and he felt the creative output of their writing was better than more routine writing assignments. Perhaps the format made it easier for students to visualize their writing, or maybe it was just more engaging. Either way, he found it a simple and effective way to introduce content-based skills to his students.

I love when my students take an idea from my class and run with it—especially when they teach me something new about it. Word clouds are one example, but there are many others that have happened over the years. There are now so many simple tools out there for teachers and students to create posters, comics, graphics, videos, and many other types of resources that you can incorporate in a variety of settings, that the only limitation is your own creativity.

Source: John Ross.

through the lesson. A template can illustrate proper formatting, scaffold students as they learn to perform the task on their own, save time, and help avoid frustration. For example, you may want to set up a template for a student web page so that students can focus on adding the content rather than on learning the web authoring program. If students are working with an application that requires detailed setup and formatting, a template can be especially useful.

exemplars
models of acceptable performance

Prepare Technology

Before you begin your lesson, you'll need to prepare the technology—often computers. If you're using a computer lab, make sure you know how the computers are configured and are comfortable with any lab management software before you bring your class to the lab. When you're in a computer lab or rotating students through computer stations in your classroom, computer time is often limited so it's important for students to make the most of the time they have available. If you are using mobile devices, calculators, wireless laptops from a cart, or other portable technologies, determine how the materials will get to the learning area and how the students will access them. Regardless of the setting, the tasks discussed next deserve consideration.

In a lab, turn on computers and open applications. Some computers and software take a while to boot or load, so this simple step can save precious computer time. If students will circulate through computer stations, make sure you direct them to leave the applications open for students who follow. When accessing a file server, you may notice reduced network speed if all of your students log on or download files from a file server at the same time. Some teachers combat this slowdown in service by allowing students to sign in before class starts or staggering access to the file server.

Make sure the correct resources are loaded and working properly. You may even incorporate student technology helpers, lab assistants, or parent volunteers to do this with you. Test the software and procedures on the computer that your students will be using. Just because a series of steps works on your home computer, that doesn't mean they will work in the lab! Load any other resources your students may need, such as a list of relevant URLs, a worksheet that students should fill in, or templates.

You'll also need to develop a system for your students to store their work. You may want to create a folder system where students are instructed to store their files in a specific location. Some learning management systems also support file storage. Files can be stored by student name or by subject. It's also useful to establish a file naming system to make it easy for you and your students to locate their work. For example, high school teachers may want to set up a separate folder for each of their classes and direct students to save their work there, using their last names and the date as the file name. Provide explicit instructions and remind students how to save their files.

It's a good idea to have students save their files in more than one location: for example, on the computer's hard drive and on a remote server or removable USB drive. Different schools will have different options available. There may be a server where your students have file space. If not, use removable media such as portable hard drives or USB drives (sometimes called thumb, flash, or jump drives among other things) or even cloud-based drives or services (such as DropBox or WindowsLive) to back up students' work. Some online services, such as Google Docs, automatically save work. As we've said before, things can go wrong! This is especially true when several people use the same computer, so encourage students to back up work routinely and save often.

For various reasons, you'll also have to establish procedures for students to move their files from one device to another. Students also may need to exchange files with other students, such as when they are working on a group project. Files can be shared through a school's computer network or remote servers as well as through removable media devices such as USB drives or portable hard drives. Some tablets and mobile devices don't have USB or other connections but are entirely wireless. In these cases, schools may have to provide student e-mail accounts or incorporate apps for cloud-based sharing or learning management systems. Keep in mind that students may need extra space to save large files such as videos or graphics.

During Instruction

Once your instructional time begins, you'll need to clearly communicate your expectations of what students should do before, during, and after they use the technology—before they actually start using it.

If the entire class will eventually perform the task, it's often useful to demonstrate it to the whole class using a projection system, even performing the task using a document camera. A demonstration can familiarize students with an interface and reassure them that the procedure is not excessively difficult. If you choose to do a classroom demonstration, make sure you only demonstrate enough of the program for them to get started successfully and do not overwhelm them with more information than they can remember. Online tutorials and screen captures (described earlier in this section) can provide a scaffold to those students who need more guidance on software operations.

Set up your classroom to make it easy for students to work independently by developing consistent rules and procedures that students should follow when they work with digital technologies. You don't want progress to come to a screeching halt when printers jam, computers freeze, or the Internet is down. When using technology, unexpected things can happen, and both preparation and flexibility are essential. When students are working independently, walk through the work areas to ensure that they are on task, understand the assignment, and are not having technical difficulties (see Figure 5.7).

Many teachers have found it useful to initiate procedures for students to signal that they need help other than the commonly raised hand. As you probably know, many times, a problem can be solved if you just keep at it. Some teachers have signs that are used to signal the need for assistance; others use something as simple as a colorful paper cup set on top of the computer monitor to signal that help is needed. Lab management software often includes helpful applications such as chat or instant messaging that allows students to ask questions without interrupting class.

Figure 5.7
Let your students know you are available to help during computer time.

But even with job aids and a signaling system, it's hard for one teacher to get around to a whole class of students who need help. You may want to initiate procedures where students routinely ask their peers on either side of them for assistance before asking you. Some teachers use "elbow partners" or encourage students to "ask three before me." Or you may identify several technology-savvy students in your class who can serve as peer helpers. You may even want to strategically place "technology leaders" around the classroom. Don't underestimate the ability of your students to provide support to each other!

Parents, older students, and other volunteers can supervise students' use of technology; just make sure they have clear guidelines as to how to do so. Ideally, volunteers should supervise through coaching, and modeling when necessary, rather than completing the task for your students. Teach your volunteers to ask guiding questions to help the students figure out the answers on their own. If it becomes clear that a student is having great difficulty in performing a task, the volunteer can model the desired behavior. Use your volunteers as a means for students to get individualized attention on tasks that are challenging for them. If your students are very young, you may want parents or older students to help with some of the tasks that may be too difficult, such as typing text into a word processor.

Once the students are working independently, try not to interrupt them to make announcements. If you find that several students have the same problem or you are answering the same question repeatedly, a general announcement may be in order; but, to the best of your ability, try to cluster your announcements and keep your interruptions to a minimum. When a whole-class demonstration would be particularly helpful, lab management software can allow you to block students' access to their computers, and display your own computer or that of one of your students as an example. Lab management software also helps you identify individuals struggling with or going off task so that you can guide them from the teacher workstation or provide individual help at their computers.

You may want to involve your students in establishing specific rules for technology use. Rules should include respect for each other's work and modeling positive digital citizenship. Students should learn never to alter or delete any files other than their own. Students should know to use the technology only for the assigned lesson unless they have permission to do otherwise. You can enforce this rule through routinely viewing the "history" of sites accessed by a web browser. Use the establishment and enforcement of classroom rules as an opportunity to teach students about the safe and ethical use of digital resources (see Chapters 8 and 10). Overall, keep the rules as clear and unambiguous as possible. And don't establish too many rules so they are reasonably enforceable.

After Instruction

As with any other kind of instruction, you should critically evaluate lessons that incorporate digital technologies in order to make them more effective in the future. You may keep a reflective journal, make notes on your lesson plans, or create a series of documents using word-processing software. Keep records of successful activities and procedures, plans for the next time you teach the topic, and other comments that can help you improve on your instruction in the future. Will you use the lesson again? Why or why not? Was the software a good investment of time and money? Are modifications needed in the way the digital resources were used in the classroom? What sort of modifications? Were there technical difficulties? Conceptual difficulties? Overall, how well did it work?

Before you begin your reflections, it's a good idea to set up a consistent system to manage your notes. You can create your own database of the software, websites, or other digital resources you have used, complete with teaching suggestions, number of copies, handouts for students, and helpful hints. It's worth the time to set up an organizational system for

> **TEACHSOURCE VIDEO**
>
> Go to the Education CourseMate website and view the video *From the Classroom to the Field: Portable Technologies in the High School Classroom* and then respond to the following questions.
>
> 1. What are the effective uses of technology employed by individual students, small groups of students, or whole-groups for instruction?
> 2. Identify the steps the teachers went through to prepare for as well as to follow up from the lesson presented in the classroom video.

Table 5.3 — Technology Integration—Steps to Take Before, During, and After Instruction

Before instruction

Plan for technology integration:
- Explore the resources to determine what features align with your instructional goals
- Estimate time needed for tasks
- Analyze learners and identify prerequisite skills
- Decide what should be done before, during, and after the instruction
- Plan backup activities in case of technical problems

Develop student guidelines, including instructions, handouts, and rubrics
- Create instructional demonstrations, handouts, and posters
- Develop evaluation rubrics, checklists, and templates
- Create or identify example projects
- Identify resources and create resource guide or WebQuest

Prepare learning environment
- Gather and arrange materials for students' access
- Turn on computers and open applications
- Make sure resources are loaded and working properly
- Develop file storage system
- Model legal software use

During instruction

- Group students
- Let students know what they should do before, during, and after computer time
- Demonstrate tasks that everyone will do
- Provide handouts or tutorials for complicated instructions
- Let students know what they should bring to the computer station
- Make links between class goals and computer time explicit
- Walk through instructional area while students are working
- Guide students through activities or use trained volunteers to facilitate the instruction
- Enforce classroom management procedures
- Keep interruptions to a minimum
- Use prompts to keep the timing of the lesson on track
- Announce stop time in advance
- Monitor or assess student understanding; engage students in self-assessment

After instruction

- Take notes on what happened
- Reflect on what went well and what did not
- Decide how to change the lesson for the next time you teach it
- Set up system to manage suggestions, handouts, reflections, and other materials
- Analyze assessment data
- Plan for re-teaching, follow-up, or enrichment
- Put materials away or organize computer files
- Record student progress

© Cengage Learning 2014

your computer files, just as you would set up an organizational system for your actual classroom. In many schools, grade level or content level teams meet to discuss instruction, the resources used, and the effectiveness of them. "Best practice" ideas and lesson plans are generated by these teams and can be stored electronically for use by all the teachers on the team from year to year.

THE GAME PLAN

Technology-Enriched Learning Environments

Set Goals
Learn more about how teachers support student learning in a technology-enriched learning environment.

Take Action
Volunteer to assist a local school with technology integration efforts. If possible, try to assist with a lesson at the grade level in which you are interested in teaching.

Monitor
Reflect on the teacher's classroom management strategies. How did he or she support students' self-directed learning? What was done to provide technical training and assistance? What rules and procedures were enforced?

Evaluate and Extend
Make note of things that worked well and things that you would consider changing if you were in charge of the class. What did you learn by working in the classroom? Make a short presentation of the best classroom management techniques you observed and share them with your colleagues. Your peers may have observed different techniques that could be useful.

Planning Learning Experiences and Lessons

All of these elements and more come together in teachers' lesson plans. As a teacher, you'll have to plan what you will do with your students for almost every minute of the school day. In planning your life, you probably have a monthly calendar that you use to keep track of the "big picture." But you probably also have a daily schedule where you plot out exactly what you will do when. And you may have "to do" lists that remind you of what you need to accomplish in any given day. As a teacher, you will engage in similar levels of planning.

Curriculum plans, sometimes called curriculum maps, provide an overview of the year. Unit plans span several days. Daily lesson plans provide a "road map" for your day-to-day activities in the classroom. They provide a checklist of items that you must remember to collect for the class, a reminder of what you want to say to the students, and a record of what works (and what doesn't) from year to year. You need to see both the "big picture" of what you are trying to accomplish and the details that must be attended to on a day-to-day basis. All of these levels of planning—curriculum plans, unit plans, and daily plans fall under the broad umbrella of "lesson planning."

Lesson Planning

At the most global level, you will probably look at the entire school year to plot out what topics will be addressed at what point throughout the year. All the teachers in your school who teach similar subjects or grade levels may engage in this planning together, or you may need to do it on your own. Many times, the topics that you teach are mandated by state or district curriculums or content standards that must be met at a particular grade level. The textbooks and other resources adopted by your school district also may be used for guidance. This annual plan may be driven by a district- or state-developed curriculum plan, scope-and-sequence chart, or pacing guide.

The annual curriculum plan is further divided into unit plans. As you may know, a unit plan covers several days, weeks, or however long it takes to teach a particular topic. Unit plans may focus on one content standard or may address multiple standards, such as a strand of related content standards. An interdisciplinary unit addresses a set of standards from several content areas. For example, consider the standards covered in a project in which your students investigate the proposed building of a new school. This project may require them to research the social and legal implications of the site selection (social studies), research and determine the impact on indigenous plants and animals (science), measure land forms and design possible layouts (math), and write a persuasive document that is presented orally with video or other media (language arts).

Unit plans are further divided into daily lesson plans. Often, teachers develop draft lesson plans when they develop their unit plans and modify them on a daily or weekly basis, depending on how well students mastered previous lessons. As you think about your daily lesson plans, identify tasks that you need to do before class, during class, and after class.

Technology Support for Lesson Planning

Planning lessons, especially for a new teacher, can take some time. However, the digital technologies available to support the lesson planning process will not only make it easier for you to develop lessons, but by supporting collaboration with other teachers across your school or district and linking to real-time student performance data, these tools support the development of more effective lessons with greater efficiency.

There is no standard lesson plan format, but many lesson plans have similar features. Undoubtedly, your school or district will have lesson plan templates you can use. In fact, you may be required to use a specific form. There are a variety of tools, too, that can support this valuable step in the cycle of instruction. Paper-based lesson planning books have given way to stand-alone lesson plan software which has evolved into networked content management systems that allow teachers to collaborate and tie their lessons to student information systems. When used as part of a suite of tools, networked lesson plan software can be used to post objectives and assignments to a website for both students and parents and may be linked to an electronic gradebook where the student outcomes for those assignments can be viewed in a secure environment. Lesson plan software may include several templates or may be customized to meet the needs of your school or district. Teachers in every school are familiar with a process of developing lesson plans to guide their work, although they may follow different methods to create them.

Since you will develop lesson plans as a result of using this book, we have provided templates for you. In keeping with the spirit of this textbook, the lesson and unit plan templates are organized around the GAME plan process. You can use the unit and daily lesson plan templates (see the end of this chapter and the Education CourseMate website) or one of your own to complete activities in this book and for your portfolio. These templates are flexible enough to use or adapt in your practice and will also help you to demonstrate your understanding of the lesson planning process to prospective employers.

APPLY to Practice

Lesson Plans

1. Find out if you are required to use a particular lesson plan format.
2. Search the web and other sources of lesson plans to locate several plans that you might like to use in your classroom.
3. Investigate several of the many sources of lesson plans on the web (for example, http://free.ed.gov/ from the U.S. Department of Education).
4. Select at least one plan that you might like to use in your classroom. Would you classify it as a unit plan or individual lesson plan?
5. Modify the plan to meet your needs and preferred lesson plan format.

Chapter Summary

This chapter focused on planning for technology-enriched learning experiences that support students in setting their own educational goals, managing their own learning, and assessing their own progress. You learned techniques to use digital technologies individually, in small groups, and in whole-group settings. We stressed the importance of preparing materials for students, preparing the technology, and preparing the students for technology use. All of these elements and more come together in teachers' daily lesson plans.

In the next chapter, you will learn how the principles and practices of differentiated instruction, Universal Design for Learning, and assistive technologies can help you better address the diverse learning styles, working strategies, and abilities of the needs of all learners.

Web Resources and Activities

Visit the Education CourseMate website for

- observation forms for use when making field visits, especially those focused on technology use;
- links to lesson plan sites for teachers; and
- a daily lesson GAME plan template and unit plan template.

YOUR PORTFOLIO

To further demonstrate competency in ISTE NETS-T Standard 2b, add the following items to your portfolio:

1. Return to the lesson description that you developed in Chapters 3 and 4. Develop a plan to support students' self-directed learning within your lessons.
   a. Using the lesson plan template at the end of this chapter or another lesson plan format of your choice, outline the activities that you and your students will engage in before, during, and after the lesson. If your lesson will span several days, you may want to use the unit plan template as well as the daily lesson plan template provided in this chapter and on the CourseMate website. Consider the following:
      - How much time is required to complete the technology-based activity?
      - What prerequisite skills do your students need?
      - What should your students do *before* they engage in the technology-based activity?
      - How will students use the technology? How will you work with the students while they are engaged in technology-based activities? Will they have additional support available?
      - What should they do *after* they complete the technology-based activity?
   b. Develop student guidelines such as instruction sheets, technical instructions, resource guides, and rubrics.
   c. Create a checklist of things that you will do to prepare the computers and other technologies.

References

Bell, M. A. (2002). Why use an interactive whiteboard? A baker's dozen reasons! *Teachers.net Gazette*, 3(1). Retrieved January 25, 2012 from http://teachers.net/gazette/JAN02/mabell.html

Ertmer, P. A., Gopalakrishnan, S., & Ross, E. M. (2001). Technology-using teachers: Comparing perceptions of exemplary technology use to best practice. Journal of Research on Technology in Education, 33(5). Retrieved June 14, 2012 from http://www.iste.org/Content/NavigationMenu/Publications/JRTE/Issues/Volume_331/Number_5_Summer_2001/jrce-33-5-ertmer.pdf

Hall, A. (n.d.) Group participation rubric for WebQuests. Phoenix, AZ: Arizona State University at the West campus. Retrieved September 13, 2008 from http://coe.west.asu.edu/students/ahall/webquest/grouprubric.htm

Johnson, D. W., & Johnson, R. T. (1991). *Learning together and alone* (3rd ed.). Englewood Cliffs, NJ: Prentice Hall.

Matthews-DeNatale, G. & Doubler, S. (2000) Facilitating Online Learning: Tip and Suggestions. TERC (Cambridge, MA) and Lesley University (Cambridge, MA). Retrieved June 15, 2012 from http://scienceonline.terc.edu/facilitating_online_learning.html

Mandel, S. M. (2003). *Cooperative work groups: Preparing students for the real world*. Thousand Oaks, CA: Corwin.

Morrison, G., & Lowther, D. (2002). *Integrating computer technology into the classroom* (2nd ed.). Upper Saddle River, NJ: Merrill/Prentice Hall.

Schon, D. (1983). *The reflective practitioner: How professionals think in action*. London: Temple Smith.

Smith, H. J., Higgins, S., Wall, K., & Miller, J. (2005). Interactive whiteboards: Boon or bandwagon? A critical review of the literature. *Journal of Computer Assisted Learning*, 21(2), 91–101.

Staker, H. (2011). *The rise of K-12 blended learning: Profiles of emerging models*. Mountain View, CA: Innosight Institute. Retrieved February 12, 2012 from http://www.innosightinstitute.org/blended_learning_models/

Wegerif, R. (2002). *Literature review in thinking skills, technology, and learning*. Futurelab Series, No. 2. Berkshire, U.K.: Futurelab. Retrieved June 14, 2012 from http://archive.futurelab.org.uk/resources/documents/lit_reviews/Thinking_Skills_Review.pdf

TECHNOLOGY INTEGRATION FOR MEANINGFUL CLASSROOM USE

Daily Lesson GAME Plan

Lesson Title:	**Related Lessons:**
Grade Level:	**Unit:**

GOALS

Content Standards:

ISTE NETS-S

- ☐ Creativity and innovation
- ☐ Communication and collaboration
- ☐ Research and information fluency
- ☐ Critical thinking, problem solving, & decision-making
- ☐ Digital citizenship
- ☐ Technology operations and concepts

Instructional Objective(s):

ACTION

Before-Class Preparation:

During Class

Time	Instructional Activities	Materials and Resources

Notes:

MONITOR

Ongoing Assessment(s):

Accommodations and Extensions:

Back-up Plan:

EVALUATE AND EXTEND

Lesson Reflections and Notes:

TECHNOLOGY INTEGRATION FOR MEANINGFUL CLASSROOM USE

Unit GAME Plan

Unit Title:

Related Lessons:

Grade:

Subject(s):

GOALS

Content Standards:

ISTE NETS-S

- [ ] Creativity and innovation
- [ ] Communication and collaboration
- [ ] Research and information fluency
- [ ] Critical thinking, problem solving, and decision-making
- [ ] Digital citizenship
- [ ] Technology operations and concepts

Instructional Objective(s):

ACTION

Date	Schedule of Lessons	Materials and Resources

MONITOR

Assessment(s):

Accommodations and Extensions:

EVALUATE AND EXTEND

Unit Reflections and Notes:

6

Customizing Student Learning Activities

OUTCOMES

In this chapter, you will learn to

- Select and use a broad range of technology resources to **differentiate content, processes, and products** to customize and personalize student learning;
- Explore the principles of **universal design for learning** and how they help teachers design learning experiences that address diverse learning styles and abilities; and
- Explore **assistive technologies** as well as **ways to adapt common technologies** that can help individualize learning.

ISTE Standards Addressed in Chapter 6

NETS-T 2. Design Digital-Age Learning Experiences and Assessments

Teachers design, develop, and evaluate authentic learning experiences and assessments, incorporating contemporary tools and resources to maximize content learning in context and to develop the knowledge, skills, and attitudes identified in the NETS-S. Teachers:

c. customize and personalize learning activities to address students' diverse learning styles, working strategies, and abilities using digital tools and resources.

Addressing the learning needs of every student in a class of 20, 30, or more students might sound formidable, as most classes include students with various learning preferences and backgrounds. In any one classroom, there are students of various abilities, from those designated as gifted and talented to those with identified learning disabilities. Some classes may also include students who require physical, mental, or emotional support in order to overcome barriers to learning. In other cases, the obstacles to learning are cultural or related to limited English proficiency, yet these students are often the same age, of comparable maturity, and with similar interests as their classmates. Consider the *Stories from Practice—Just Your Typical Classroom* that opens this chapter. It's not a real classroom, but a scenario based on our experiences

STORIES from Practice

Just Your Typical Classroom

Fifth-grade teacher, Brigit Tartaruga, is writing her lesson plans for the upcoming week, to address science standards related to the rock cycle. Her students have to identify the three types of rocks and explain how they are generated through the cycle. Among her class of 27 students, she knows that three of them—Bill, Walter, and Naomi—are in the gifted-and-talented program and will need enrichment activities to stay engaged in the lessons. She also knows that Walter has a history of missing deadlines, not turning in assignments, and being unable to keep his desk or class notebook organized. In addition, she knows that Marina, as an emergent English speaker, will have difficulty with some of the academic language since her family speaks no English at home. Marina and her family place a lot of emphasis on succeeding in school, and she often gets frustrated, sometimes to the point of tears, during long or challenging assignments. Three of Brigit's students, Wendy, Jeffrey, and Mason, have learning disabilities that must be taken into consideration. Wendy has a learning disability that makes it difficult for her to decode unfamiliar words, and Brigit knows that—particularly in science—Wendy can become discouraged with the language in the textbook. Jeffrey has limited visual capacity and Mason is accustomed to using an augmentative communication device, a technology to support his limited speaking capacity, but has recently received a tablet computer with several apps to support his communication. At this point in the year, Brigit is familiar with Mason's Individualized Education Program (IEP) and has worked with his occupational therapist and a co-teacher to understand his abilities and how he can demonstrate them through the technologies he uses every day. Of course, scattered throughout the class are those who do or don't like collaborative work, do or don't enjoy using computers, do or don't have strong problem-solving skills, and so on. In other words, it's a pretty typical class.

---

differentiation
providing flexibility during teaching in terms of content, process, and product, based on the needs of your students

differentiated instruction (DI)
purposefully designing instruction to accommodate the known needs of one's students and providing them with different content, strategies, and means of demonstrating the desired learning goals

universal design for learning (UDL)
an approach to instruction in which teachers remove barriers to learning by providing flexibility in materials, methods, and assessments

working with hundreds (if not thousands) of teachers across the country. The scenario was developed to begin the discussion about the various needs students bring to the classroom and how teachers can differentiate their instruction to meet those needs. This chapter encourages you to have that same discussion.

Digital technologies can help you "customize and personalize learning activities to address students' diverse learning styles, working strategies, and abilities using digital tools and resources." The ISTE standard for this chapter, more than any other, truly emphasizes the unique needs, abilities, and preferences of individual students and requires you to use strategies and resources in your classroom that support all of your students and their uses of educational technology—a process many refer to as **differentiation**. While federal law guides how you must accommodate needs for some of these students, other differentiation strategies are based on respect for all individuals and their backgrounds, interests, and abilities. Technology can be a tremendous asset that helps teachers differentiate their instruction to support the diverse learning needs of children. Whether used to capture and report student data, make materials accessible to students with special needs, or provide access to resources beyond the school walls, technologies can do a great job of "leveling the playing field" for students with different abilities, needs, or preferences.

This chapter explores customizing and personalizing learning through the lens of two constructs that have similar intents, that of 1) **differentiated instruction**, sometimes referred to as DI, and 2) **universal design for learning** (UDL). Differentiated instruction is an older concept that builds on the tenets of constructivist learning theory, leverages recent understandings from brain research, and relies on the growing interest in learning styles (Anderson, 2007). It has become more popular due to the growing diversity of the student population in the general education classroom. The more recent concept of UDL has its origins in special education policy and practices supporting students with learning disabilities (Basham et al., 2010; Edyburn, 2010). When looked at holistically, both constructs have at their core the concept of purposefully designing and delivering personalized and customized instruction to meet the learning needs of diverse students. In addition, both constructs rely on the use of data to determine student needs, how instruction should be customized to meet those needs, how effective it is, and how well students perform. And since they're both about designing and delivering instruction, the GAME plan process we've already introduced for designing instruction is right in line with these ideas.

Using Technology to Differentiate Instructional Content, Processes, and Products

Differentiated instruction *is* personalized and customized learning. Spend any time in a classroom, and it quickly becomes apparent that students have different experiences, interests, and abilities. People learn differently and have different preferences as to what and how they like to learn (Gardner, 1995; Bransford, Brown, & Cocking, 1999). It might be said that there's a need to differentiate instruction simply because all students *are* different! Think about your current classmates. There are some who are outstanding athletes while others are not, have interests in different kinds of music and art, like to work in groups or alone, enjoy reading . . . or not, excel with technology . . . or not. Knowing we're all different may be obvious, so why would any teacher try to teach such diverse people the same content, using the same strategies, with the same materials, and expect the same outcomes?

Because of student differences, teachers often provide some variation during their instruction, such as reacting to student questions and confusion by rewording statements or using different examples. But the concept of differentiated instruction goes further than these common, minor adjustments most teachers make on a daily basis. Differentiated instruction refers to designing instruction specifically to accommodate the known needs of your students and to provide them with different content, strategies, and means of demonstrating the desired learning goals. Differentiated instruction is proactive, not reactive. It's purposeful and begins before instruction occurs, just as we've been emphasizing with the GAME plan. It's still about content and mastering learning goals, but the ways students get there and how they express their learning can vary.

Unfortunately, differentiated instruction is one of those concepts in education that many people hear about but do not understand clearly. One way to think about differentiated instruction is to determine what it is *not*. Differentiated instruction is not a collection of teaching strategies. You don't just decide to use the DI strategy in this lesson and not in that one. There's also not just one way to differentiate instruction. Instead, successful differentiation is grounded in strong content knowledge, effective pedagogy, and knowledge about the individual differences of your students. And since students will continue to be different class after class, year after year, you may find yourself using different strategies for different classes—even for the same learning goals. Finally, differentiated instruction does not refer to making some students do more or less than others. It doesn't mean that students who need enrichment just write longer sentences, or do more problems, or teach other students. It doesn't mean that students with special needs always get two answer choices instead of four; and it certainly doesn't mean they cover fewer standards. Instead, differentiated instruction means you purposely design and deliver instruction that helps every student master the required learning goals—usually based on a set of standards—depending on their readiness, interests, and other factors that make up their learning profiles (Tomlinson, 1999).

The key to differentiation is providing flexibility and choice in terms of the *content* and *processes* you use in your classroom and the *products* that students create to demonstrate their learning. You still have to address the same curriculum with your students, but the content you use doesn't always have to be the same. Students can develop fluency and vocabulary whether reading from basal readers, newspapers or magazines, websites, or popular novels. They can learn about geometry by graphing problems from a book, building 2- or 3-D models, watching video demonstrations, using an online manipulative, or practicing games like pool or croquet. The key is finding the right content that students can use to reach those learning goals required by your curriculum, and the ever-growing number of high-quality digital learning resources makes it easier to differentiate the content you incorporate into your instruction.

These examples also suggest that the instructional strategies and learning activities that provide student practice don't have to be the same for all students. The strategies and activities are the processes you use in your classroom and relate to the Take Action step in the GAME plan. Advocates of differentiated instruction (Anderson, 2007; Levy, 2008; Tomlinson, 1999; Tomlinson & Imbeau, 2010) emphasize that while there are many different processes you can use to differentiate your instruction, a critical strategy is the use of flexible grouping. Groups often change in the differentiated classroom and are rarely based on random assignment. Rather, they are based on ability, interest, or even learning preferences.

Finally, teachers can differentiate instruction by allowing students to demonstrate new skills and knowledge in varied ways. Some students may create a graphic organizer of key concepts and terminology, others may create a short presentation that includes information synthesized from Internet research and interviews with experts, while others may feel comfortable playing a game, composing a paper, or completing a more traditional assessment. Some teachers confuse differentiating products simply with varied activities. For example, after reading a story, some students may be asked to color a picture of their favorite character, others to build a diorama, and others to create a story map that identifies the major characters and their relationship. If your standards are not related to coloring or crafting, the picture and diorama are not appropriate products to demonstrate the required skills and knowledge. Instead, if your standards are related to dissecting and understanding characters, a story map may be right in line. Make sure each product matches your standards. Truly differentiated products depend on what is appropriate for demonstrating the content standards, the resources that are available, and what is relevant to the student.

Some teachers have concerns about providing customized instruction to students. This is based on the idea that in order to be "fair" they have to offer the same instruction with the same materials using the same assessments for every child. There's a difference between "fair" and "equitable," however, and proponents of differentiated instruction (Tomlinson & Imbeau, 2010) note that even students recognize we're all different. What's fair is to address the same standards for every student. It's not fair to ignore a student's abilities, experiences, interests, and learning preferences.

Knowing what, how, and why to differentiate requires teachers to know and understand their students' abilities, interests, and learning preferences, what is referred to as the student **learning profile** (Tomlinson, 1999). Gender and culture can influence each student's learning profile, as can his/her preferred learning style. In order to better accommodate individual student learning profiles, some teachers may determine student learning preferences or learning styles through inventories related to Gardner's theory of multiple intelligences (see Figure 6.1), Myers-Briggs Type Indicators, Dunn and Dunn learning styles model or others (Levy, 2008). Teachers also use inventories, surveys, pre-assessments, and other means to learn about their students' backgrounds and interests and what they know or can do as it relates to the content and even technology use. In addition, teachers continually monitor student learning to know

learning profile
a description of a student's abilities, interests, learning preferences, and other relevant information that can impact learning

Gardner's Multiple Intelligences

In his 1983 book, *Frames of Mind,* Howard Gardner proposed the theory that individuals possess multiple intelligences. The seven original intelligences and an eighth intelligence added later suggest that people learn and express themselves in different ways. According to Gardner (1993), each of us has varying degrees of the culturally and biologically influenced intelligences.

Bodily-Kinesthetic Intelligence is manifested through physical actions with the body, manipulating objects, touching and feeling objects to better connect and internalize feedback from the environment.

Interpersonal Intelligence refers to the capacity to be highly empathetic and to connect with others and to understand their desires, motivations, and needs.

Intrapersonal Intelligence enables one to be introspective and to have a deep understanding of one's abilities, fears, and motivations.

Linguistic Intelligence is a capacity to understand and/or communicate effectively through written and spoken languages.

Logical-Mathematical Intelligence refers to the ability to use strategies for analysis that include detecting patterns, carrying out mathematical processes such as calculations, and testing hypotheses through reason.

Musical Intelligence includes a preference for processing and expressing one's self in all things musical, such as a strong affinity for pitch, rhythm, and timbre.

Naturalist Intelligence, the most recently added intelligence, suggests a capacity to relate well to natural environments, and to understand natural laws and processes as well as evolving cultural patterns.

Spatial Intelligence includes the ability to mentally and physically divide and order space, to use imagery to understand a space and imagine how it might be transformed.

Gardner does not suggest that the theory is prescriptive and will result in a single instructional approach. In fact, he admits that his theory has often been misinterpreted and that inappropriate applications have resulted in a negative perception of the theory by some educators (Gardner, 1995). He does, however, suggest that schools cover too much content in too little depth. Instead, he recommends that teachers take the time to cover material in greater detail through a variety of methods and materials. Gardner says that schools that have most effectively applied multiple intelligences take human differences seriously. Any uniform approach to education—including a uniform approach to assessment—is bound to appeal to a minority of students and alienate or frustrate the rest.

Figure 6.1
Gardner's multiple intelligences.

where they are along their learning paths and when they've mastered required content. This ongoing use of data corresponds to the monitoring and evaluation stages of the GAME plan.

As you can imagine, there are many different digital technologies and resources available to support differentiating content, processes, and products, as well as to collect and manage the ongoing data necessary to understand individual student learning profiles. Table 6.1 presents several ideas for using technology to differentiate content,

Table 6.1 Ideas for Differentiating Instruction with Technology

Differentiate Content

Access primary documents including images and audio files from museums or the Library of Congress.
Create or find WebQuests on different topics of study.
Review Today's Front Pages from the Newseum.
Incorporate an academic search engine or one designed for children.
Use short video clips from an education video-sharing site.
Use data from government agencies such as NASA, NOAA, or travel sites from other countries.
Incorporate text readers for digital books or web pages.
Use a social bookmarking site, such as Diigo, or a web curation site, such as LiveBinders to identify and organize information used in a lesson.

Differentiate Process

Use a comic book creator or app Incorporate a virtual field trip with a local business, museum, or point of interest.
Explore consequences and manipulate outcomes through a simulation or digital model.
Write a storyboard for a video or presentation.
Play or create a learning game on an educational website or using an app.
Create a digital story using presentation software that incorporates text, images, and/or video.
Assign groups based on learning profiles or interests.
Connect with other classrooms through e-mail or videoconferencing.

Differentiate Product

Create a concept map before and after instruction.
Create a public service announcement about an environmental or social issue.
Demonstrate a process through a narrated screen capture video.
Generate an oral history using digital audio and images.
Publish to a blog.
Create an infographic using clip art and text.
Research and create an entry for a popular wiki site, such as Wikipedia.
Post a video to an educational video-sharing site.
Create a digital portfolio matched to standards.

© Cengage Learning 2014

processes, and products in your classroom. In fact, this entire book may be considered a presentation of technologies to support differentiation, but the DI movement began before digital technologies were so prevalent in classrooms. Building on the capacity of digital technologies to customize and personalize learning environments, the Universal Design for Learning framework was developed with these digital technologies squarely at its core.

Universal Design for Learning

Growing out of the reauthorization of the Individuals with Disabilities Education Act (IDEA) of 1997 (Edyburn, 2010), the principles of universal design for learning (UDL) suggest that teachers can remove barriers to learning by providing flexibility in materials, methods, and assessments (Rose & Meyer, 2002). Note how similar that sounds to differentiating instruction through content, process, and product. Although originally conceived for students with special needs, the more flexible you are with the teaching strategies, materials, and assessments in your classroom, the greater the chance they will be accessible to the diverse needs and preferences of *all* the students with whom you work.

But how is technology critical to universal design for learning? While universal design may incorporate some methods and materials that may be fairly low-tech, digital media and applications provide the greatest flexibility in terms of planning, implementing, and assessing learning activities. In fact, some propose that technology is *essential* for implementing UDL successfully (Edyburn, 2010). Unlike the preponderance of print-based and analog audio and video materials that once dominated in classrooms, digital media can be created, stored, cataloged, searched, adapted, and even linked together much more easily. Using common software and hardware, teachers and students can find information in a variety of formats, transform it so it is easy to see or hear or understand, repurpose or modify it, or generate new information and media that can be used to demonstrate new understandings or skills (Figure 6.2). By adhering to the universal design guidelines, you can develop instruction and assessments that better meet the diverse needs of students.

Undeniably, the one organization that has led the effort to promote universal design for learning is the Center for Applied Special Technologies (CAST). The education researchers at CAST have conducted or used brain research that relies on sophisticated brain-imaging technologies to better understand how and why people learn, and then used this knowledge to develop the UDL principles (see Figure 6.3) and some learning tools built on those principles. They have promoted the concept of universal design for learning through publications and professional development. They have informed the development of the National Instructional Materials Accessibility Standards

Figure 6.2
Using common software and hardware, digital media can be created, stored, cataloged, searched, and adapted relatively easily.

I. Provide multiple means of representation.

1. *Provide options for perception.*	2. *Provide options for language, mathematical expressions, and symbols.*	3. *Provide options for comprehension.*
1.1 Offer ways of customizing the display of information. 1.2 Offer alternatives for auditory information. 1.3 Offer alternatives for visual information.	2.1 Clarify vocabulary and symbols. 2.2 Clarify syntax and structure. 2.3 Support decoding of text, and mathematical notation, and symbols. 2.4 Promote understanding across language. 2.5 Illustrate through multiple media.	3.1 Activate or supply background knowledge. 3.2 Highlight patterns, critical features, big ideas, and relationships. 3.3 Guide information processing, visualization, and manipulation. 3.4 Maximize transfer and generalization.

II. Provide multiple means for action and expression.

4. *Provide options for physical action.*	5. *Provide options for expression and communication.*	6. *Provide options for executive functions.*
4.1 Vary the methods for response and navigation. 4.2 Optimize access to tools and assistive technologies.	5.1 Use multiple media for communication. 5.2 Use multiple tools for construction and composition. 5.3 Build fluencies with graduated labels of support for practice and performance.	6.1 Guide appropriate goal setting. 6.2 Support planning and strategy development. 6.3 Facilitate managing information and resources. 6.4 Enhance capacity for monitoring progress.

III. Provide multiple means for engagement.

7. *Provide options for recruiting interest.*	8. *Provide options for sustaining effort and persistence.*	9. *Provide options for self-regulation.*
7.1 Optimize individual choice and autonomy. 7.2 Optimize relevance, value, and authenticity. 7.3 Minimize threats and distractions.	8.1 Heighten salience of goals and objectives. 8.2 Vary demands and resources to optimize challenges. 8.3 Foster collaboration and community. 8.4 Increase mastery-oriented feedback.	9.1 Promote expectations and beliefs that optimize motivation. 9.2 Facilitate personal coping skills and strategies. 9.3 Develop self-assessment and reflection.

Figure 6.3
UDL principles, guidelines, and checkpoints.
Source: CAST (2011). *Universal Design for Learning Guidelines version 2.0.* Wakefield, MA: Author. Retrieved from www.udlcenter.org/aboutudl/udlguidelines/downloads. Used with permission.

(NIMAS) signed into law as part of the reauthorization of IDEA in 2004 that requires that instructional materials be accessible to all students, which often means digitally. They have also developed UDL guidelines for educators (CAST, 2011) based on three primary principles that correspond to three neural networks that influence learning. The guidelines also contain checkpoints for teachers to use as a reference for designing and delivering instruction.

Neural Networks Foundational to UDL

The UDL guidelines are based on the multifaceted nature of the brain, specifically the recognition, strategic, and affective networks. While research identifies these three primary networks that influence learning, the way that each network reacts to stimuli, prompts responses, and promotes engagement, along with the degree of influence each has over the other can be as unique across individuals as fingerprints and personalities. These networks are not to be confused with the popular idea of learning preferences or styles, such as being verbal, auditory, or kinesthetic learners. Instead, all learners, regardless of preferences, are influenced by these three networks. The growing body of knowledge about these three networks is important for understanding how you can incorporate aspects of the UDL framework into your instruction in order to provide your students with greater access to learning. To us, the identification and description of the neural networks helps to explain why people have different learning preferences, styles, and needs. The following sections explore each network.

Recognition Networks

In order to recognize something, such as a letter, word, picture, person, sound, smell, or other sensory input, you rely on the **recognition networks** of your brain. The recognition networks help you to identify patterns, such as the use of symbols for language or music, the organization of features to tell the difference between people's faces, as well as more subtle patterns such as the use of irony or comedy in a poem or performance. In terms of learning, the recognition networks process the "what" that should be learned.

> **recognition networks**
> neural networks in the brain that help to identify sensory data, such as objects, facts, and patterns

Similar to the other two networks, recognition networks reside in a similar general area of the brain of each individual, but even the simple task of identifying a word on a page involves a number of different systems and subsystems within this area—in this case, recognition systems that process information related to vision that help you recognize color, shape, orientation, context, meaning, and other attributes. Hearing the word at the same time calls into play additional systems related to processing sound—all of which operate in parallel.

Not everyone has the same capacity for recognizing sensory data. With the many systems that operate simultaneously within these networks and the varying capacities that individuals have for recognizing sensory data, it is easy to understand that the dominance of, or damage to, one of these systems can result in a preference or even a disability for a particular type of activity or medium. For this reason, proponents of UDL suggest that digital media provide the flexibility needed to reach the widest number of students, students who rely on different strengths and preferences due to the working of their recognition networks.

You can follow the first principle of the UDL guidelines and implement teaching strategies that support recognition networks by *providing multiple means of representation,* such as presenting information and content in different ways with different media. Examples of these strategies include providing multiple examples that tap into different senses and highlighting critical features whether through the use of labels and arrows on charts and diagrams, physically highlighting passages, or using different font colors, sizes, and treatments within text. You can support recognition networks further by allowing students to use multiple media and formats to access information, practice skills, and demonstrate mastery (see Figure 6.4), as well as providing background context for new information or skills (Rose & Meyer, 2002).

Consider the challenge faced by Brigit, the teacher in the *Stories from Practice— Just Your Typical Classroom*. As you recall, she was preparing lesson plans to address science standards related to the rock cycle. Based on what Brigit knows about the students in her class, some of them have strengths in auditory processing, others learn best through visuals, while some may not have sufficient background experiences to make sense of the information. In order to support the variety of recognition network strengths present in her class, Brigit could provide her students with several examples of the rock cycle using a variety of media. That is, some students could read text, while others could view an animated movie with or without captions. A detailed graphic representation of the cycle with key ideas and processes highlighted or otherwise indicated might help some, while still others may need pictures or actual rock samples to better understand the different types of rocks. Students who are overwhelmed by the technical terms may benefit from a website with hyperlinks that allows them to click on each rock type to learn more, or they might need to relate this new topic to prior learning, perhaps the water cycle—another cyclical process.

Strategic Networks

The processes you follow to plan, execute, and monitor your actions are related to the **strategic networks**. The actions you take are highly dependent on the outcomes you expect to achieve. For example, if your students are expected to learn the scientific names for the three types of rocks for a test on Friday, they would most likely take different actions than if they were preparing for the state science fair. The resulting actions can be either mental or physical. In terms of learning, strategic networks operate on "how" things can be learned.

Like the recognition networks, strategic networks rely on systems and subsystems that operate in parallel. As you become more familiar with a process, your routines become more automatic until you might be considered an expert. Experts perform differently from novices in many of the processes related to learning, such as identifying problems; proposing hypotheses; planning, organizing, and selecting strategies; monitoring their own performances; and seeking assistance (Bransford, Brown, & Cocking, 1999).

Think of an activity in which you consider yourself to be an expert, such as riding a bicycle, playing a musical instrument, or even walking and talking. You looked and behaved much differently when you first started any of these activities. Now consider the many types of processes your students may employ to accomplish a single learning goal. A lesson that results in a product such as a paper, web page, or presentation can require both fine and gross motor skills (such as moving about the room, operating a keyboard or mouse, or retrieving and opening a book), speech (such as communicating with lab partners or asking a question), general learning strategies (such as creating a task schedule, monitoring how well you are meeting objectives, or choosing a different strategy if the first one did not work well), and expression (creatively responding to the lesson requirements or incorporating personally relevant information). All of these processes are carried out in the brain by the strategic networks.

The second UDL principle, *providing multiple means for action and expression*, suggests you can support the brain's strategic networks by providing opportunities to

Figure 6.4
You can support recognition networks by allowing students to use multiple media and formats.

> **strategic networks**
> neural networks that control processes for planning, executing, and monitoring your actions

practice skills with various levels of support and supplying ongoing, relevant feedback. Demonstrating concepts and skills through the use of varied models of performance can allow students with different abilities to identify with a preferred mode and degree of performance for mastery. Flexibility is the key, and strategic networks, like recognition networks, can be supported by incorporating multiple media and formats to demonstrate mastery (Rose & Meyer, 2002).

Affective Networks

The **affective networks** can influence one's motivation for and engagement with a particular goal, method, medium, or assessment and can be impacted by feelings, emotions, prior experiences, cultural backgrounds, and more. The affective networks process "the why" of learning. Because the affective networks are influenced by prior knowledge and past experiences, each student has the potential to react differently to any one instructional event. For example, during the rock cycle lesson, students who have lived in Hawaii might bring in pictures or samples of volcanic rock and tell stories about Pelé, the goddess of fire and volcanoes, and how local legends influence the culture of people from these islands. Students from other areas could share tales from their families that illustrate the influence of geology on human existence, such as living in a coal mining community, visiting Native American tribes in the deserts of the Southwest, or handling the topographical challenges of living in some parts of the Atlantic or Pacific coastlines. In addition, feelings and emotions can be influenced from one day to the next, such as when you are feeling ill, tired, or upset over an argument with a relative or friend. You or your students may be highly engaged in an activity one day but may be less so the next.

> **affective networks** neural networks that relate to feelings and emotions, and which influence motivation for and engagement with a particular goal, method, medium, or assessment

By offering choices of media and tools within the scope of your required content, you are supporting students' affective networks (see Figure 6.5). This corresponds to the third principle from the UDL guidelines, *provide multiple means of engagement*. Choice can increase initial motivation and engagement and can sustain interest throughout a project. Choice can also be offered in terms of student rewards as well as the context in which the learning will take place. Motivation and engagement can also be heightened by specifically teaching self-regulation strategies and promoting self-reflection so that students can monitor their own actions and determine their progress towards learning goals. Incorporating strategies like the GAME plan can actually impact your affective network, once you have developed familiarity with them. Ultimately, digital technologies allow you to more easily provide activities at varied levels of difficulty or challenge students at all levels of ability through a variety of engaging materials (Rose & Meyer, 2002).

Universal Design in the Classroom

How can you use your knowledge about these three networks in your classroom? Perhaps of greater concern is the question, "How does technology play a role in all of this?" As you may recall, digital media provide greater flexibility than static linear media, such as print-based materials and analog audio and video, for adapting materials to students' needs. We are also in a time when the quality of digital resources for education is much better than when computers first entered our classrooms. Combined with the growing number of mobile devices at lower price points, access to digital technologies for learning has increased in all grades and for all students. In the UDL framework, digital technologies are key elements for providing flexibility in the development and implementation of three fundamental aspects of the teaching/learning cycle: 1) setting learning goals, 2) taking action by providing learning activities, and 3) assessing student progress to monitor and evaluate student growth.

Figure 6.5
By offering choices of media and materials, you can support students' affective needs.

Setting Goals

As a teacher, you develop learning goals for your students that allow them to obtain the skills and knowledge required by curricula and standards. When incorporating the UDL guidelines, learning goals should

- allow students to clearly understand the outcomes (recognize "what" should be learned);
- be achievable through a variety of media (provide multiple opportunities for "how" the lesson can be learned); and
- communicate the importance of the goal to students (emphasize "why" the learning is important).

With any true differentiation, rather than "dumbing down" the curriculum or providing only a portion of the curriculum to some students, an approach based on the UDL guidelines should allow all students to meet all required learning goals through flexible means.

In order to create learning goals that meet these criteria, you should focus on the outcomes—what is it you really want your students to know and be able to do? Once decided, UDL emphasizes that achieving outcomes should not be contingent upon the media or methods used to achieve them. Relying simply on any one medium, such as a printed textbook, immediately imposes barriers on some students, but UDL focuses on *removing* barriers to learning. Of course, if students are required to learn a specific skill that is directly tied to a specific medium, such as operating a table saw, dribbling a basketball, or playing the C-minor scale on the clarinet, the medium of instruction becomes less flexible. But for many academic goals, especially those in core curricular areas, there may be a great deal of flexibility to choose which media are used to help students build the knowledge and skills needed to achieve content standards.

Individualizing Learning

Once clear learning goals have been set, the UDL framework suggests that teachers utilize instructional strategies that allow individual students greatest access to *active learning*—not just receiving information passively. (Refer to chapter 3 for more information about active learning as a component of authentic instruction.) Teaching methods that promote active learning include:

- Provide students with choices in the media, tools, and context in which the learning will take place.
- Provide multiple examples that tap into different senses.
- Provide opportunities to practice skills with various levels of support and ongoing relevant feedback.
- Include activities with varied levels of difficulty to challenge students at all levels of ability with a variety of engaging materials.

Central to these strategies is the use of digital technologies to provide students with flexibility as they meet the demands of learning goals. These ideas, especially the emphasis on flexibility and choice, are also consistent with the concept of differentiating process and product and Howard Gardner's idea of multiple intelligences, as described in Figure 6.1 on p. 141.

A common science objective for a fifth-grade class related to the rock cycle is to describe and explain how different topographical formations, such as canyons, valleys, meanders, and tributaries are formed and worn away by the movement of rocks and soil. On one end of the spectrum, a learning activity may require that all students do library research and write a short paper about the topic. Although some students may do well with this task, others may do better with some other options. For example, students who are struggling readers or English language learners will benefit from the use of visuals and may better understand the natural process by viewing videos or simulations they can manipulate and review more than once. Notes they take can be organized using concept-mapping software that can generate an outline from which they work on a larger report. Some students may use online communication tools to collaborate, such as creating a wiki with their classmates that identifies important topographical landmarks in the region or state with each student contributing information about how they were formed. The wiki can support images, text, and hyperlinks to relevant resources and can track which students have created and edited the content.

Monitoring and Evaluating Student Learning

Knowing that universal design discourages reliance on a single medium for achieving goals and providing learning activities, you will probably not be surprised to know the same is true for assessing student progress. Student assessments that are limited to a single medium, such as taking a quiz or test with pencil and paper, immediately impose barriers that prevent some students from accurately demonstrating their skills and knowledge. Any medium used for assessment will have inherent properties that either support or conflict with students' abilities, preferences, and interests. The challenge is to match assessments with instructional goals and activities such that students can truly demonstrate their knowledge and skills. As discussed in Chapter 7, the method and media used for assessment should also be matched to those used for instruction.

Although as a teacher, you will have little control over the format by which standardized "high-stakes" tests are administered, you will have control over the types of assessments that you offer in your classroom. Universal design for learning suggests following similar practices for assessment as for providing learning activities: that is, incorporate a variety of media to allow students some flexibility in demonstrating mastery of the instructional goals. Unlike high-stakes summative tests, universal design encourages the use of assessments that are closely related to the instruction, both in time and in format.

Digital tools offer several opportunities for embedding assessment strategies within the learning process. Many learning games are not only highly engaging but also include embedded assessments that require students to apply skills or knowledge as they try to solve the game or get a good score. Simulations, animations, and manipulatives can allow students to test theories or potential solutions. Students with access to online curriculum tools may have their progress checked and reported automatically and then, depending on their performance, be assigned more complex content or required to repeat instruction and practice.

Managing Choice and Flexibility

Both differentiated instruction and universal design for learning suggest that instruction can be designed and implemented for students with diverse learning styles, preferences, abilities, and motivation. All this choice and flexibility can seem overwhelming. It brings up visions of students scattered about the classroom all doing something different, learning something different, using something different... in other words, mayhem. But it's not really a free-for-all. Your curriculum and standards still suggest learning goals that are used to organize your instruction. You may have some students using different types or levels of content or working with different resources, but they're all still focused on the same curriculum and learning goals.

One way to think about how much flexibility is necessary is to consider the **Response-to-Intervention** (RTI) framework for grouping students and delivering instruction based on student ability and achievement measures. More common in lower grades but gaining ground in higher grades, RTI models are commonly represented by a triangle or pyramid divided into three levels, what some models call tiers (see Figure 6.6). The levels represent the focus of your instruction, with all students receiving primary instruction, some students needing some supplemental instruction, and a few requiring intensive instruction, often at the individual level. From the RTI movement, it is commonly suggested that your primary instruction (and the methods and resources it incorporates) should be effective for approximately 80 percent of your students; an additional 10–15 percent may need some supplemental instruction or activities, and only 5–10 percent will require individual instruction (Basham et al., 2010).

This three-level approach to delivering instruction is helpful for understanding how any differentiated process can be administered effectively. For example, as you consider levels of choice in differentiating instruction, RTI suggests that your primary instruction should routinely support a majority of your students. There may be some students who need alternate approaches or choices and a few with specific needs. While DI and UDL both emphasize flexibility and choice, instruction also has to be manageable. With limited resources, time, and personnel (often just you), having every student doing something different during every lesson isn't manageable. Often, however, that's not necessary, and the leveled approach that is common in RTI models can easily be adopted within other approaches to differentiation.

Digital technologies can be incorporated into all levels of instruction, but play a significant supporting role for students who need supplemental or individualized instruction. These may include technologies that allow students to build prerequisite skills and knowledge through

---

response-to-intervention (RTI)
framework that uses diagnostic and progress-monitoring assessments to help group students for instructional interventions of varied intensity and types

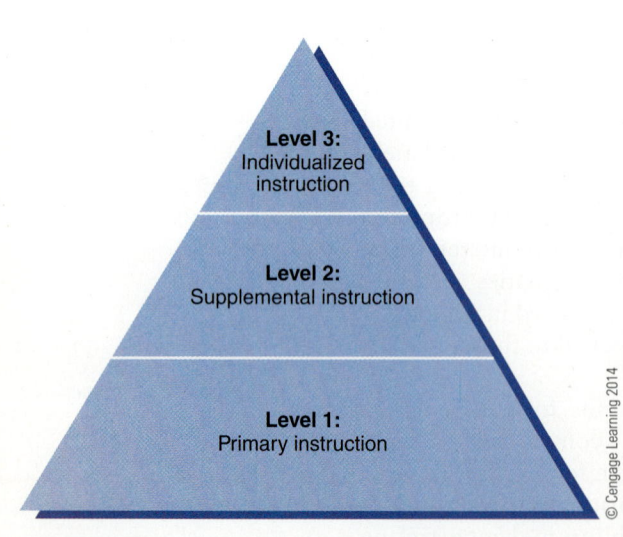

Figure 6.6
Common levels of instruction based on an RTI approach.

- Level 3: Individualized instruction
- Level 2: Supplemental instruction
- Level 1: Primary instruction

varied media formats or those that can provide additional practice and feedback for students struggling with critical learning goals. Many digital technologies are also available to provide customized and personalized instruction by helping students manage the physical, social, and academic requirements of participation. Students can use adaptive digital curricula that present information, provide opportunities for practice at a developmentally appropriate level, and supply feedback on performance. These adaptive learning resources can also help to determine when students are ready to progress to the next level and provide supplemental instruction based on curricular goals.

> **TEACHSOURCE VIDEO**
> Examine the video, *Managing Flexibility*, on the Education CourseMate website and then answer the following questions.
> 1. What advice do these teachers give for differentiating instruction?
> 2. What strategies can students use? Teachers?

Assistive Technologies

Some students may be required to use specific technologies for a significant portion of their learning—and you may be required to understand how to use them in order to help these students achieve their learning goals. Used in this way, these technologies are specifically designated as assistive technologies. Many of you may be asking, "Why do I need to know about assistive technologies? I'm not going to be teaching special education." While that may be true, consider that according to the most recent data available, 95 percent of students between the ages of 6 and 21 with disabilities served under IDEA spent time in general education classrooms, with the majority spending 80 percent or more of the day in a general education classroom. That's more than 6 million students, representing 9.1% of the general population in that age group. (U.S. Department of Education, 2008). In the past, these students would have been assigned to classrooms separate from their same-aged peers who do not have identified disabilities. However, recent legislation, such as the reauthorization of the Elementary and Secondary Education Act (Pub. L. No. 107-110), has mandated that students with disabilities be assessed alongside their peers without disabilities. Since these students are likely to be in every classroom, this next section provides an overview of how and why assistive technologies can make the difference between successful and unsuccessful educational and social experiences in your classroom.

Legal Precedents for Assistive Technology

Assistive technology, or AT, was first defined in the *Technology-Related Assistance of Individuals with Disabilities Act of 1988* (Pub. L. No. 100-407), sometimes referred to as the "Tech Act." This definition has been used in several laws since then, such as the *Individuals with Disabilities Education Act (IDEA)* which was reauthorized

assistive technology any item, piece of equipment, or product system used to increase, maintain, or improve functional capabilities of individuals with disability

APPLY to Practice

Meeting the Needs of Diverse Learners

1. Select a lesson plan that you have developed or one that is available from a print or online resource. Describe activities and assessments in the lesson plan that would allow you to meet the needs of students with differing abilities, interests, and experiences. Consider students with the following needs:
   - students who do not have the same background experiences
   - students who prefer to learn by doing or through experiential learning
   - students who have difficulties focusing on and deriving meaning from print
   - students with high ability and interest in the subject who require enrichment
2. How does a differentiated approach to instruction help you plan your instruction? What resources are available to help you meet these challenges? What roles does technology play?

in 2004 (Pub. L. No. 108-446). Specifically, assistive technology refers to "any item, piece of equipment, or product system, whether acquired commercially or off the shelf, modified, or customized, that is used to increase, maintain, or improve functional capabilities of individuals with disabilities" (Pub. L. No. 108-446). It's important to understand that it is not the device itself that makes it assistive technology, but how it is used to support individuals. Some technologies may be considered assistive technology for some students, but not for others.

IDEA requires that states "ensure that all children with disabilities have available to them a free appropriate public education that emphasizes special education and related services designed to meet their unique needs and prepare them for employment and independent living" (Pub. L. No. 108-446). In order to qualify for special education and related services, it is not sufficient for a student to demonstrate or be diagnosed with a definable sensory, physical, mental, or cognitive impairment, but that the special education or related services support that student in participating in educational activities (Mendelsohn & Fox, 2002).

IDEA requires the development of a written **Individual Education Program (IEP)** for all students who qualify for special education. The IEP is developed through significant parental involvement, and in cooperation with classroom teachers and other school officials, such as guidance counselors, special education teachers, school psychologists, or occupational therapists. Once written, and as the child's teacher, you are required to follow procedures described in the IEP, which may include the use of assistive technology. If assistive technology is prescribed in a student's IEP, find out how you and your colleagues will receive professional development in order to appropriately incorporate the assistive technology in your teaching.

Some students with disabilities may not qualify for special education but are still covered by Section 504 of the *Rehabilitation Act of 1973* (Pub. L. No. 93-112). Section 504 states: "No otherwise qualified individual with a disability shall, solely by reason of his or her disability, be excluded from the participation in, be denied the benefits of, or be subjected to discrimination under any program or activity receiving Federal financial assistance." Most schools receive federal financial assistance and therefore are required to adhere to the tenets of the Rehabilitation Act.

Section 508 of the Rehabilitation Act also requires that electronic and information technology resources be accessible by individuals with disabilities. This is a major concern for publishers and developers of educational resources as the amount of digital media and online services that are used by schools continues to increase—with some states allowing for the adoption of digital materials in addition to or in lieu of textbooks. You and your fellow teachers should be cognizant of how digital media, including software and online resources—even school-generated web pages—are compliant with Section 508.

The importance of assistive technology as a valuable resource for helping people with disabilities was reaffirmed with the passage of the *Assistive Technology Act of 1998* (Pub. L. No. 105-394), sometimes referred to as the "AT Act," and its reauthorization in 2004 (Pub. L. No. 108-364). The AT Act builds upon its predecessor, the Tech Act, by extending funding for assistive technology to states and six U.S. territories. Its reauthorization mandates differentiating instruction through UDL principles for students, especially students with disabilities. (Caverly & Fitzgibbons, 2007).

Many individuals may find it difficult to distinguish assistive technology from technologies that simply assist learning. Upon examination, all technologies are tools that make some part of our lives simpler by capitalizing on our strengths and removing barriers. Think about the tools that you may have used today, whether they are word processors, Internet browsers, or other devices. Maybe you enlarged fonts for easier viewing or organized tasks in a digital calendar so you could meet immediate deadlines. You used these tools to assist you, but for some students access to these types of tools can be required to support their learning, classifying them as assistive technology.

> **Individualized Education Program (IEP)**
> an individualized plan for a student with disabilities that describes the measures teachers must take to accommodate the learning needs of the student

By definition, an AT device can include a wide range of tools, such as an item, a piece of equipment, or a product system. For example, one solution for a student having difficulty holding a pencil might be a simple plastic pencil grip (item). For another student who is unable to use a pencil, a portable word processor (piece of equipment) might be the tool used to assist with the task. Touchscreen computers are other pieces of equipment making great inroads for even very young students who have this difficulty (see *Tech Tools and Tips—Mobile Devices: Support for Students with Special Needs*). And for yet another student, a computer with voice-recognition software (product system) might be chosen to assist with writing. There are numerous classifications of AT devices based on their function (Bryant & Bryant, 2003). Keep in mind that individuals may use one or more devices for a variety of functions.

Assistive Technology Continuum

Assistive technology tools can be classified along a continuum that moves from devices that are considered to be "low tech," to tools and devices that are more complex or "high tech" (see Figure 6.7). Generally, "low-tech" devices are inexpensive tools often lacking moving parts and having limited functionality. Additionally, they require little or no training to use. Often low-tech tools can be found in your desk or kitchen junk drawer and include clothespins, shelf liner, paper clips, sticky notes, and hook-and-loop tape. More complex examples of low-tech tools include calculators, talking picture frames, spell checkers, timers, and battery-adapted toys.

"Mid-tech" assistive technologies use some form of power source, are moderately priced, and may require initial training for use. Mid-tech tools include tape recorders, CD players, portable word processors, leveled augmentative communication devices, and talking dictionaries.

"High-tech" assistive technologies, found at the highest level of the continuum are more complex and expensive. High-tech multifunctional tools often can be customized to meet individual needs and may require extensive training in order to use. Computers, computerized voice-output devices, environmental controls, and software programs are forms of high-tech tools.

Unfortunately, assistive technologies are not well understood by all teachers, guidance counselors, and others who work with students with IEPs. Many do not know or realize what AT devices, or assistive uses of common technologies, can be used by students who could benefit from them. It is unclear how many students who qualify for AT use actually are able to take advantage of it in schools, with one survey noting that use is especially low for students with high-incidence disabilities in general education classes (Quinn, Behrmann, Mastriopieri, & Chung, 2009). These are the students with disabilities most teachers are likely to work with in general education classes, as high-incidence disabilities refer to communication disorders, learning disabilities including attention deficit hyperactive disorder (ADHD), mild to moderate mental retardation, and emotional or behavioral disorders (Jackson, 2011).

How do you use this information to improve your instruction and provide greater opportunities for all students to succeed in your classroom? Although selecting assistive technology for students who qualify for special education or related services should be a team decision that will undoubtedly involve all members of the IEP team, you should be aware of some common **accessibility features** provided by familiar software and hardware (see *Tech Tools and Tips—Built-in Computer Accessibility Features*), and there are several simple adaptations that you can make to the computer hardware and software used in your classroom to provide access to all students.

accessibility features features built into hardware and software that provide greater access to the technology, especially for people with disabilities

Adapting Hardware and Software

Computer hardware and software can be used by many students who experience physical, cognitive, visual, organizational, or auditory disabilities. The computer and its software

High-tech
- environmental controls
- augmentative or alternative communication devices
- speech synthesizers
- voice-recognition systems
- FM amplification systems
- text-to-speech software
- word-prediction software
- trackball, mouse stick, and switches
- touch-sensitive pads
- eye-tracking technology
- abbreviation-expansion software

Mid-tech
- word-processing software
- prewriting, organization, concept-mapping software
- portable word processors
- large-print word processors
- ergonomic, alternative, programmable, or virtual keyboards
- hyperlinked multimedia
- electronic organizers
- scanning reading pens
- leveled voice output devices
- Telecommunication Devices for the Deaf (TDDs)
- captioning
- text messaging
- American Sign Language software
- Descriptive Video Services (DVS®)
- Closed-Circuit Television Magnification (CCTV)
- Braille notetakers, embossers, and refreshable Braille displays
- talking dictionaries
- audio/video recorders
- CD/MP3/other media players

Low-tech
- scanning print using an optical character recognition (OCR) scanner
- enlarging print and visuals onscreen
- talking picture frames
- calculators
- timers
- switch toys
- spell checkers

© Cengage Learning 2014

Figure 6.7
The AT Continuum: Examples of assistive technology.

can provide students who have diverse learning needs with a means for accessing and interacting with the curriculum. However, some students will need to have adaptations made to the computer software, hardware, and position to provide more effective access.

Commonly Available Software

Many software applications include methods for easily adapting the presentation of information to benefit students with various needs, while others have accessibility features built right in. Many people have less than perfect eyesight, and digital tools such as web browsers, word-processing applications, and document readers like Adobe Reader allow you or your students to quickly change the size of documents or fonts on a screen. Some may require a menu command or a keyboard shortcut to quickly change font sizes (try pressing the Command and + keys on a Mac or the Control and + keys on a PC at the same time in a web browser or PDF document). Some web pages also include buttons for changing font sizes right on the page.

Many productivity applications, especially those related to word processing, can support students with a variety of learning styles and abilities (Hasselbring, 2000). **Word-processing applications** are almost universal on computers found in schools and provide a variety of supports to help your students. The ability to quickly create, edit, and revise manuscripts that look professional can benefit everyone. Features built into many word-processing and specialized composition programs can also support a wide range of student learning activities such as highlighting errors in spelling or grammar and creating keyboard shortcuts for common tasks, as well as creating toggle keys paired with sounds for aural identification of keys and shortcuts. Some have built-in accessibility features such as text-to-speech or the ability to embed or read alternate tags (descriptions) for images and tables for those using screen reading software.

Word-prediction software is used primarily by students with learning disabilities and helps students identify words quickly based on common usage patterns, arrangement of letters, or suggestions based on grammar (see Figure 6.8). This is a more advanced version of what some smartphones and other mobile devices do when trying to autocorrect our spelling. This software supports communication tasks and helps students to overcome limited language skills. Other writing aids and comprehension software, such as concept-mapping software, can support brainstorming, concept organization, outlining, and generating schematics important to clearly formulating and communicating ideas.

Networked **communication tools** offer great flexibility in the methods and settings in which students can communicate with one another as well as with teachers and outside experts. Collaboration and communication are important skills for all students to develop, but these skills are especially important for students with disabilities and those with limited language skills (Hasselbring, 2000). Tools that allow students to communicate asynchronously provide the opportunity for students to develop and communicate their ideas at their own pace, as opposed to class discussions that may discourage participation for those students who need extra time to formulate, refine, and express ideas. Many customized communication tools, often referred to as

> **word-processing applications**
> software that allows users to create, edit, and revise written documents

> **word-prediction software**
> software that suggests words based on common usage patterns, arrangement of letters, or rules of grammar

> **communication tools**
> numerous technologies used to communicate synchronously or asynchronously, such as phones, e-mail, texting, and others

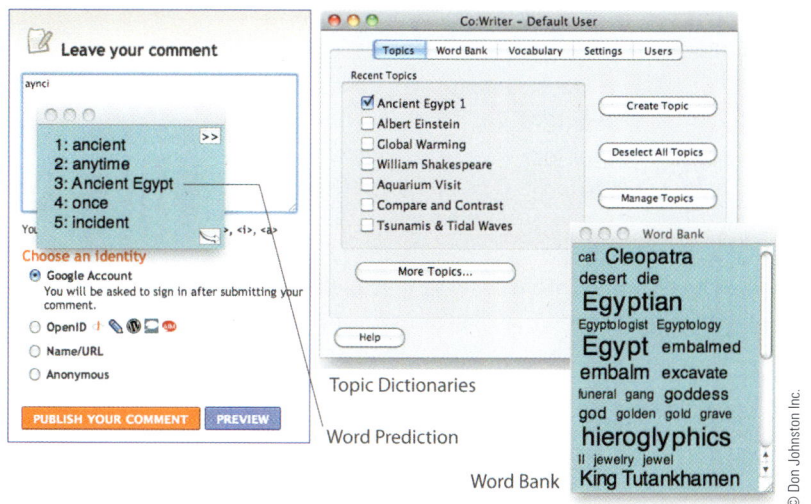

Figure 6.8
Word-prediction software is especially helpful for students with learning disabilities such as dyslexia.

augmentative and alternative communication (AAC) devices
hardware and software that allow students with disabilities to communicate through pictures, words, and symbols

multimedia tools
instructional tools that contain information in multiple formats, including text, sounds, images, animation, or movies

augmentative and alternative communication (AAC) devices, also exist that allow students with disabilities to communicate through pictures, words, and symbols. AAC apps are available for some mobile devices, as well.

Students who need additional information such as definitions, examples, images, and other explanations of words and concepts, can benefit from the flexibility of **multimedia tools** with embedded hyperlinks. The linked material may incorporate text, audio, or visual information that helps students with diverse learning preferences find support in a mode that they prefer. Some of these extended features are also now accessible in word-processing applications and web browsers. Some caution should be used in hyperlinked environments, however, as students can quickly become overwhelmed or highly engaged in material that is unrelated to the instructional goals. Strategies for combating these problems include creating a list of approved websites that are either bookmarked on student computers or linked from a general class launch page, as well as previewing multimedia materials and providing job-aids, such as templates or checklists, to clearly structure student participation. Some software applications may allow you to turn off certain features in order to allow students to focus on specific curricular skills.

Positioning

Appropriate positioning of a computer for some students may be as simple as moving the user, the keyboard, or the monitor. Students who are provided with the necessary physical supports and clear visual access when working with computers will be able to concentrate on their work better. A variety of commercially designed chairs, desks,

TECH TOOLS & TIPS

Built-in Computer Accessibility Features

As mentioned earlier, additional accessibility features for making the mouse and keyboard more accessible can be found in the Control Panel for Windows and System Preferences in the Mac operating systems. Several of the most commonly listed features are listed below.

Tutorials and additional information are available from the Microsoft and Apple websites.

Accessibility Features in Computer Operating Systems

Feature	Purpose
StickyKeys	Provides a way for one-handed or single-finger typists to press two keys at once, for example, pressing SHIFT, lifting your finger, and then pressing the D key to make a capital "D."
MouseKeys	This feature on the keys on the numeric keypad is used to control all of the mouse functions for users who have difficulty controlling a traditional mouse.
RepeatKeys	Allows the user to adjust how fast the auto-repeat works. This helps to eliminate a string of unwanted characters when a key is depressed.
SlowKeys	Provides a way to adjust the length of time a key must be held down before the computer interprets a press as input.

Feature	Purpose
Zoom (MAC) Magnifier (WIN)	This display option makes the computer screen more readable by creating a separate window that displays a magnified portion of the screen.
Display Adjustment	These settings offer the user the ability to select their preferred settings for color, size, and text for the computer display.
VoiceOver (MAC) Narrator (WIN)	This text-to-speech utility reads what is displayed on the screen—the contents of the active window, menu options, or text that has been typed.

© Cengage Learning 2014

> ## APPLY *to Practice*
> ### Built-in Accessibility Features
> 1. Choose either the Windows or Mac operating system and explore the accessibility features found in each. If you need more help, visit the Microsoft and Apple Accessibility websites that have tutorials, videos, and other information. Links to these sites can be found on the companion website of this textbook.
> 2. A detailed description and list of the accessibility features for each operating system can be found at each of these sites. Print and add to your class notes or portfolio.

and tables are available that can make positioning of the student and computer easier; however, many adaptations can be made at no or low cost. Remember, also, that when working on positioning issues with a student who has a disability, an occupational therapist may be available to assist you. Additional information about how to arrange your classroom computer workstations in ways that promote students' ergonomic health is included in Chapter 8.

Keyboard Adaptations

Access to the computer can often be improved by adapting or modifying the traditional keyboard, mouse, and monitor. For young students or those with physical or visual difficulties, the traditional keyboard may be difficult to use because of the size of the keys. However a few inexpensive alterations can provide access for some students. Several ways that the traditional keyboard can be modified are listed below:

- Place large, colored alphabet stickers on the keys for easier visual access.
- Use stickers, stick-on felt or rubber pads, or small buttons to mark keys that students might use the most frequently. These changes add visual distinction and texture to the keys.
- Create a key guard from a piece of heavy-duty cardboard. Cut out only the sections for the keys that the student might need to access. Commercially made key guards are also available.

Commercially adapted keyboards are designed or configured to meet a variety of physical or sensory needs (see Figure 6.9). "Small form factor" or one-handed keyboards, like InfoKeys BAT Keyboard, are designed to provide physical access. Large key or "tactile feedback" keyboards, such as BigKeys, provide access to the visually impaired. Some keyboards utilize a variety of keyboard overlays that match functional uses like the Intellikeys. There are also onscreen keyboards, like My-T-Soft, which are software programs that allow text input with a mouse, a touch screen, or a single external button called a switch. Additional adaptations can be made to the keyboard from within the operating systems for both Windows and Mac. For more information on these adaptations, see the Tools for Use box about built-in accessibility features.

Mouse Adaptations

Mouse adaptations can be made in a similar way to keyboard adaptations (see Figure 6.10). By adding a button, pom-pom, or colored sticker to the left mouse button, students will have a visual or sensory reminder of the different buttons. By turning the mouse upside down, students can use the mouse more like a trackball. Use the settings within your operating system's control panel or system preferences to deactivate the right-mouse button if needed. Settings can also be found here to select a larger mouse arrow, change the functionality of the right- and left-mouse buttons, and slow down the mouse speed.

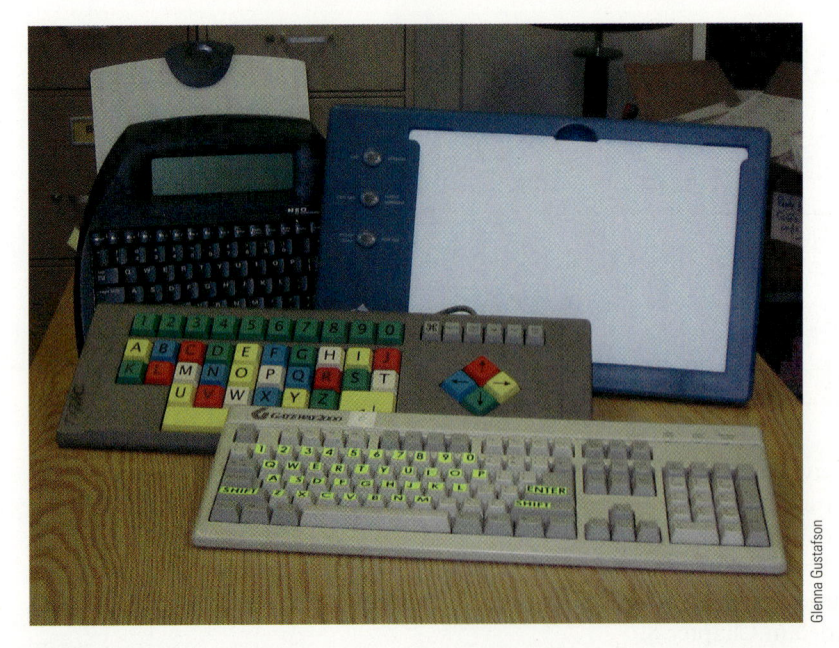

158 CHAPTER 6

Figure 6.9
Keyboard adaptations. From left to right: Alphasmart, a portable word-processing keyboard; Intellikeys, a membrane keyboard; BigKeys with colorful and enlarged key targets; and a traditional keyboard that has been adapted using colored alphabet stickers.

Figure 6.10
Mouse adaptations. From left to right: a traditional mouse adapted with a pom-pom glued to indicate the left mouse button; a single pillow switch when combined with a switch interface can be used as a mouse alternative; a Biggy trackball provides the user with bright colors; the handle of a joystick can also be adapted to meet a variety of needs.

Numerous commercial mouse alternatives are also available. These include trackballs, track pads, joy sticks, and game controllers. Each of these alternatives provides a different means of physical access.

Summary of Assistive Technologies

The use of the term *assistive technology* has legal ramifications as well as impact on how you deliver instruction in your classroom. When students have assistive technologies identified in their IEPs, you are required to use those devices in your instruction with those students. Luckily, more common technologies now provide accessibility features that you can quickly learn and incorporate, perhaps for all of your students. For any student who is required to use a specific assistive technology with which you're unfamiliar, request professional development so you use it appropriately and meet the goals of the student's IEP.

Digital technologies are a tremendous benefit to all students, especially those with special needs, as they provide multiple ways to access content, practice new skills and apply new knowledge, receive feedback, and demonstrate learning. Whether your students use assistive technologies or technologies to assist their learning, spending time learning the functions and benefits of these technologies could ultimately benefit all of your students.

TECH TOOLS & TIPS: Mobile Devices: Support for Students with Special Needs

Small, powerful, touch-screen computing devices, such as smartphones, the iPod touch, and especially the iPad, have made a great splash in the educational technology press as tools to support students with special needs. These lightweight, portable, wireless technologies place numerous resources and tools into the hands of students when and where they need them. Since their launch in 2010, iPads, more than any other mobile device, are thought to hold the greatest potential when it comes to supporting students with special needs, whether this potential has clearly been documented or not (Newton & Dell, 2011).

Some of the reported benefits include the obvious portability and the fact that a keyboard isn't required to interact with many of the apps (applications). These devices are often light, and even very young students have shown that they can manipulate the touch screen, including opening and closing apps, with little to no training. Students can use these devices to access content once contained in numerous heavy books and can also access digital class information on websites and from learning management systems, from school, home, or just about anywhere. These devices can also access organizational tools, like calendars, that can send reminders or notifications of homework due, as well as many common tools used in classrooms today such as word-processing and presentation apps, references tools, calculators, cameras, videocameras, and a variety of apps for creating and editing different media. There are also educational games, videos, podcasts, and more that students can access.

Unfortunately, because they are so new, and not originally designed for education, there is little empirical evidence to show that these devices enable students to make significant achievement gains. In this early stage of their development, the information is mostly anecdotal or based on opinion, but that certainly hasn't stopped schools and districts from purchasing them and educational technology experts from writing, blogging, and touting ways they can support special education.

It's important to remember that a technology in itself, especially a piece of hardware, is not likely to impact student achievement on its own. As with all technologies, it's how you use it that matters. Determine student needs first. Students with IEPs may have clearly defined needs that you may be able to match to existing apps and potential uses. Even then, be sure to use the device—and teach the students how to use the device—so that it best matches the needs they are intended to address. These devices do have the potential to support students with special needs, especially when considering the many apps that are being developed for them. But you should select apps with care. See *Tech Tools and Tips—Selecting Apps for Mobile Devices* in Chapter 9 for more information about finding the right app for your students.

THE GAME PLAN

Learn More about Assistive Technologies

Everyone's special! And while we can all benefit from technologies that assist learning, students with Individual Education Programs (IEPs) are perhaps the group that has most benefitted from the many digital technologies now available to support learning. One of the best resources for learning about assistive technology is the TechMatrix (www.techmatrix.org), launched with funds from the U.S. Department of Education. The TechMatrix keeps track of many different technologies, especially those specifically intended as assistive technology. It also includes short information briefs about using technology in many different educational settings, including differentiating instruction with technology.

Set Goals

Learn more about specific assistive technologies that can help customize and personalize learning experiences.

Take Action

Visit the TechMatrix website and find technologies that support a learning need or are in an area of interest to you. Using the TechMatrix reviews, compare and contrast the technologies you find, including the primary use and some pros and cons. Determine which one(s) may best meet the need or area of interest you identified.

Monitor

The TechMatrix continues to grow as new technologies are developed, identified, and reviewed. You may want to limit your search to specific areas of instruction (e.g., reading, math, or technology integration) or specific disabilities (e.g., autism, hearing or visual impairments, or ADHD).

Evaluate and Extend

You are encouraged to review the research or evidence presented for each technology provided in the review on the TechMatrix to support your selection. Share your findings with others or tackle this as a small-group project.

Chapter Summary

As a classroom teacher you face the challenging task of trying to meet the needs of an increasingly diverse student population. This chapter has used two common constructs—differentiated instruction and universal design for learning—as frameworks by which you can incorporate technologies to personalize and customize learning. Hopefully, you see how these processes complement each other and the role digital technologies can play to help make them more effective and manageable.

As you learned in this chapter, these frameworks are tools to help you make instructional decisions to support students with diverse needs, including students with learning disabilities, who can be supported via technology. This information should encourage you to proactively develop lessons that are inclusive of all students in the learning environment, and identify, use, and evaluate appropriate technology resources that clearly support all students, regardless of special needs.

Assistive technologies also offer the promise of supplementing and enhancing abilities and compensating for barriers that diverse learners might experience. Greater access to and participation in the educational environment for all learners is the ultimate goal for using assistive technology. In order to meet this mandate, general and special educators need to know how to locate and select the appropriate assistive technologies for a diverse student population. You may need to use these technologies to customize learning for some of your students.

By using the techniques introduced in this chapter, you should be able to incorporate strategies for equitable use of technology resources in your school and classroom regardless of inherent student characteristics or ability levels. In the next chapter, you will learn techniques for collecting and reporting assessment data that can provide you with the information you need to customize and personalize your students' learning.

Web Resources and Activities

This chapter is paired with an extensive list of web resources. Visit the Education CourseMate website for information about

- models and frameworks to customize and personalize instruction, including the websites from national organizations such as CAST and the National Center on Response to Intervention;
- some of the learning disabilities or special needs your students may exhibit as well as examples of assistive technologies available to support them;
- alternate keyboards and keyboard adaptations, alternate input devices, and many other assistive technologies; and
- built-in accessibility features in common operating systems found on the Microsoft and Apple Accessibility websites.

YOUR PORTFOLIO

To demonstrate competency in ISTE NETS-T Standards 2.c, review the lesson plan you have been developing throughout Chapters 3, 4, and 5 and modify it to provide evidence of customizing and personalizing learning activities to address students' diverse learning styles, working strategies, and abilities using digital tools and resources.

1. Create a narrative description of how you can proactively support all students by applying the principles of differentiated instruction or universal design for learning. If necessary, modify your lesson plan to incorporate these principles.
   a. If using differentiated instruction, consider how you can differentiate content, process, and product to accommodate diverse learners. Explicitly mention the role of technology in your description.
   b. Consider downloading the *UDL Guidelines—Educator Checklist* from CAST. Describe how you can proactively design your instruction in order to adhere to the principles and guidelines given in the checklist. Explicitly mention the role technology plays in setting goals, individualizing instruction, and monitoring and evaluating student learning.

2. Identify any assistive technologies, or simply technologies, necessary to assist with learning in your lesson and describe how they support students' needs.
   a. Include commonly available technologies, such as word processors and web browsers that allow you to change font sizes for readability, calendar programs that help keep students organized, or concept-mapping software that allows students to organize ideas.
   b. Also explore specialized tools that may require additional training or support, such as modified keyboards or alternate input devices.
   c. Consider the benefits all students may have when using technology tools in a way that may be considered assistive, regardless of whether they have an IEP or not.

References

Anderson, K. M. (2007). Differentiating instruction to include all students. *Preventing School Failure, 51*(3), 49–54.

Basham, J. D., Israel, M., Garden, J., Poth, R., & Winston, M. (2010). A comprehensive approach to RTI: Embedding universal design for learning and technology. *Learning Disability Quarterly, 33*(4), 243–255.

Bransford, J. D., Brown, A. L., & Cocking, R. R. (Eds.). (1999). *How people learn: Brain, mind, experience and school.* Washington, DC: National Academy Press.

Bryant, D. P., & Bryant, B. R. (2003). *Assistive technology for people with disabilities.* Boston: Pearson.

CAST (2011). *Universal design for learning guidelines version 2.0.* Wakefield, MA: Author. Retrieved June 14, 2012 from http:// www.udlcenter.org/aboutudl/udlguidelines/downloads

Caverly, D. C., & Fitzgibbons, D. (2007). Techtalk: Assistive technology. *Journal of Developmental Education, 31*(1), 38–39.

Edyburn, D. L. (2010). Would you recognize universal design for learning if you saw it? Ten propositions for new directions for the second decade of UDL. *Learning Disability Quarterly, 33*(1), 33–41.

Gardner, H. (1983). *Frames of mind: The theory of multiple intelligences.* New York: Basic Books.

Gardner, H. (1993). Education for understanding. *The American School Board Journal, 180*(7), 20–24.

Gardner, H. (1995). Reflections on multiple intelligences: Myths and messages. *Phi Delta Kappan, 77*, 200–209.

Hasselbring, T. (2000). Use of computer technology to help students with special needs. *The Future of Children, 10*(2), 102.

Jackson, R. M. (2011). *Curriculum access for students with low-incidence disabilities: The promise of UDL.* National Center on Accessible Instructional Materials at CAST, Inc. Retrieved June 14, 2012 from http://aim.cast.org/learn/historyarchive/backgroundpapers/promise_of_udl

Levy, H. M. (2008). Meeting the needs of all students through Differentiated Instruction: Helping every child reach and exceed standards. *The Clearing House, 81*(4), 161–164.

Mendelsohn, S., & Fox, H. R. (2002). Evolving legislation and public policy related to disability and assistive technology. In M. J. Sherer (Ed.), *Assistive technology: Matching device and consumer for successful rehabilitation* (pp. 17–28). Washington, DC: American Psychological Association.

National Center on Response to Intervention. (2010). *Essential components of RTI—A closer look at response to intervention.* Washington, DC: U.S. Department of Education, Office of Special Education Programs, National Center on Response to Intervention.

Newton, D. A., & Dell, A. G. (2011). Assistive technology. *Journal of Special Education Technology, 26*(3), 47–49.

Pub. L. No. 93-112. (Rehabilitation Act of 1973).

Pub. L. No. 100-407. (Technology-Related Assistance for Individuals with Disabilities Act of 1988).

Pub. L. No. 101-336, 104 Stat. 327. (Americans with Disabilities Act of 1990).

Pub. L. No. 101-476. (Individuals with Disabilities Education Act of 1990—IDEA).

Pub. L. No. 105-394. S.2432 (Assistive Technology Act of 1998).

Pub. L. No. 107-110. (No Child Left Behind Act of 2001).

Pub. L. No. 108-364. (Assistive Technology Act of 2004).

Pub. L. No. 108-446. (Individuals with Disabilities Education Improvement Act of 2004).

Rose, D. H., & Meyer, A. (2002). *Teaching every student in the digital age. Universal design for learning.* Alexandria, VA: Association for Supervision and Curriculum Development.

Tomlinson, C. A. (1999). *The differentiated classroom: Responding to the needs of all learners.* Alexandria, VA: Association for Supervision and Curriculum Development.

Tomlinson, C. A., & Imbeau, M. B. (2010). *Leading and managing a differentiated classroom.* Alexandria, VA: Association for Supervision and Curriculum Development.

U.S. Department of Education. (2011). *30th Annual Report to Congress on the Implementation of the Individuals with Disabilities Education Act, 2008.* Washington, D.C.: Office of Special Education and Rehabilitative Services, Office of Special Education Programs.

7

Assessment and Evaluation

OUTCOMES

In this chapter, you will learn to

- Identify appropriate technology-based resources for **assessing learning** and your instruction;
- Select **assessment formats and the technologies that can support them**;
- Develop **scoring expectations and practices** for technology-based projects and technologies to facilitate them; and
- Collect, analyze, and report student performance data and use that information for **data-based decision making**.

ISTE Standards Addressed in Chapter 7

NETS-T 2. Design and Develop Digital-Age Learning Experiences and Assessments

Teachers design, develop, and evaluate authentic learning experiences and assessments incorporating contemporary tools and resources to maximize content learning in context and to develop the knowledge, skills, and attitudes identified in the NETS-S. Teachers:

d. provide students with multiple and varied formative and summative assessments aligned with content and technology standards and use resulting data to inform learning and teaching.

When you think about your assessment experiences as a student, what feelings come to mind? How have different teachers in your school career used assessments? What were their purposes? What were the benefits of those assessments for your teachers? What were the benefits to you as a student?

Maybe you didn't think about assessments as being beneficial when you were a student. But well-designed assessments are a critical part of the teaching-learning cycle and do more than just help determine grades. Assessments can provide valuable information to students, teachers, and the larger community—information that can be used to inform teaching and improve learning. Assessments have a wide range of uses including, but not limited to:

- providing feedback to students on their progress toward achieving learning goals;
- motivating students and providing opportunities to build confidence;
- monitoring the progress teachers are making in their curricula;
- evaluating the effectiveness of instruction;
- determining participation in supplemental or enrichment programs;
- providing information to parents, communities, and others in the public about school performance;
- comparing students and schools to others or to established criteria; and
- measuring progress of students or schools over time.

ISTE NETS-T Standard 2 requires you to "design, develop, and evaluate authentic learning experiences and assessments incorporating contemporary tools and resources to maximize content learning in context." Standard 2.d further requires you to "provide students with multiple and varied formative and summative assessments aligned with content and technology standards and use resulting data to inform learning and teaching." This chapter will focus on using technology to support formative and summative assessments and monitoring and reflecting on student data.

Assessing Student Learning

Assessment data can be used to set goals for student learning, monitor learning through formative assessments, evaluate learning through summative assessments, and help to determine the effectiveness of your instruction and the technologies you selected to support it. Assessments, therefore, are an important part of the learning process. How does assessment support learning? Classroom assessments that promote learning (Assessment Reform Group, 1999, p. 7):

- involve sharing learning goals with students;
- aim to help students know and recognize the standards for which they are aiming;
- involve students in self-assessment;
- provide feedback that leads to students recognizing their next steps and how to take them;
- are based on the belief that every student can improve; and
- involve both teachers and pupils reflecting on assessment data.

Previously, we noted that the GAME plan involves determining learning goals for your students and planning the actions you will take to help your students master them. The actions you take are your instruction *and* your assessments. Assessments can give you ongoing feedback so you can monitor your instruction and ultimately evaluate whether students have achieved the learning goals you set. In this chapter, we focus on how technology can support the assessments that help you complete the GAME plan instructional cycle, mentioned earlier.

Learning Goals Help Determine Assessments

When you develop or select assessments you need to consider three components related to the learning goals: 1) the behavior, skill, knowledge, or attitude to be demonstrated, 2) the conditions under which they will be demonstrated, and 3) the criteria that specify the required level of performance. As you know, the behavior, skills, knowledge, or attitudes your students are required to master are outlined in your content standards (see Chapters 1 and 3). Performance conditions identify equipment, supplies, or other resources—including technologies—that are allowed or even required during the assessment of student skills. They also include any time limits or other constraints imposed upon students as they are demonstrating what they've learned.

Criteria clearly describe what acceptable performance looks like. Criteria can be conveyed through models, samples, rubrics, checklists, or a simple list of what an acceptable answer should include (e.g., "Your report should include five sources and no grammatical or factual errors."). When scoring criteria are shared with students before embarking on an activity, students can use the criteria to set goals for their own performances and can continue to monitor their performances throughout their learning, whether creating a web page, writing an essay, or preparing a presentation for the class. Students can also use grading criteria to determine the essential elements of complex projects, making the project seem more approachable by breaking it down into milestones or component parts. Technology can be used to help students manage these projects. Some teachers have students create learning contracts, timelines, or management plans to keep them on track, especially when implementing large projects (McCain, 2005).

Whether an intended consequence or not, the assessment activities you select will indicate to your students which skills and knowledge you feel are most important or worthwhile. If you test factual knowledge, students will believe that facts are most important; if you test critical and creative thinking skills, students will pay more attention to developing these skills. So, if your goal is to create a learning environment that, according to NETS-T 2, "maximizes content learning in context," what type of assessments would you choose? How can your assessments communicate the interest and excitement you have for your content area, or even your interest in lifelong learning? Think about the messages you send to your students when you select and use various assessment methods. Do these messages include a focus on meaningful understanding, or are they focused on how to pass a test at the end of the year?

There is no magic formula to determine the right assessment task or the appropriate technology for every performance goal or assessment task. In fact, a variety of technologies and formats may fit any number of assessment tasks and can be used equally well across different content areas. In practice, you should incorporate a variety of assessment formats and tools that are matched to your students' learning goals, are relevant to the content being studied, and that provide an adequate picture of student understanding.

Monitor Learning with Formative Assessments

Formative assessments are used during your day-to-day instruction and provide feedback so you can make adjustments, if necessary, based on your students' needs. In this view, they're more of a process than an event. Formative assessment strategies, according to Heritage (2010), are "aligned to the short-term sub-goals, which are the focus of the lesson, and data from them provide teachers with a steady stream of information to keep learning moving forward" (p. 28). Formative assessments provide feedback to your students on how they're doing, what they're learning, and where they're going. They can use the data to monitor their progress towards their learning goals and determine where they may need extra help or a change in strategies.

Formative assessments can include both formal and informal measures, sometimes using numeric scores, and at other times using percentages, check marks, or even short narrative responses that provide information to your students. As mentioned above, formative assessment often occurs through the daily dialog teachers have with students and students have with each other or in self-reflection. Still, there are different ways to collect this data, many supported by technology. The collection and analysis of these different types of data also do more than help you determine student needs. All of these pieces add up to the opportunity to determine the effectiveness of your instructional methods and materials—including the technologies you've selected.

You can collect informal data from your students through questioning, checklists, graphic organizers, journals, and other methods. Survey-type questions can be used to collect information about how well students are mastering content as well

> **formative assessments** assessment used during instruction to monitor student progress toward mastering learning goals

as information related to their interests, motivation, and learning preferences. Exit polls or exit cards—using paper note cards—are another quick method teachers use to gather informal data from students that is easily supported by a variety of technologies. On exit cards, students quickly note what they have learned during a class and list any difficulties they still have. Some teachers replicate this process digitally by having students send a short e-mail with their progress at the end of class. The anonymity many of these technologies provide may encourage some students to give you feedback when they might otherwise be reluctant to voice their opinions in front of their peers.

Another example of formative assessment involves the use of wireless responders or personal response systems (see Figure 7.1). Wireless responders look similar to remote controls and allow individual students to "beam" responses anonymously, or at least confidentially, to questions posed to an entire class. This type of live polling is ideal for monitoring learning and can help you and your students quickly determine content areas that require further instruction or where there are obvious gaps in understanding.

There are a variety of wireless tools, including applications for mobile devices, that can be used to support this type of interaction. Simple versions allow for students to select from one of four to six buttons (e.g., A, B, C, or D depending on the corresponding answer choice) with more complex versions available that allow students to enter text or work out problems or enter calculated responses, such as the solution to a math problem. The students' responses are beamed using infrared or radio frequency to a central source that is connected to a computer at the front of the room. These systems may also be connected to or built into some type of display hardware such as an interactive whiteboard (see *Tech Tools and Tips—Using Interactive Whiteboards* in Chapter 5). Software is also available that allows students to complete these assessments online if the entire class has access to computers, laptops, or other devices that support web browsers. Detailed data collection, analysis, and reporting can occur instantaneously. Student data can also be stored and tracked over time to give you a picture of individual student growth and the need for supplemental instruction.

Figure 7.1
Wireless responders allow students to "beam" responses to questions posed to the entire class.

As suggested above, feedback is critical to formative assessment. Your students will benefit most when they receive feedback about the *quality* of their work and suggestions for improvement—not just whether their responses were right or wrong. To improve learning, they must also receive feedback about their progress *during* instruction. **Outcome feedback**, knowing whether a response is correct or not, is the simplest and most common type of feedback, but it provides little guidance to students (Butler & Winne, 1995). Early drill-and-practice software often provided this type of feedback, in which student responses were boldly acknowledged as "CORRECT" or "INCORRECT," but rarely with an explanation why. For formative assessment to achieve maximum benefit, feedback must provide an explanation of why an answer is correct or incorrect. It should support students when they are using appropriate strategies and content knowledge, and guide them when they are not. **Cognitive feedback** refers to this type of feedback that helps students develop a better understanding of what is expected for performance, how their current understanding or skill levels compare to those expectations, and how they might improve their performances (Butler & Winne, 1995). Providing this level of feedback during instruction is the central purpose of formative assessment.

Summative Assessments Evaluate Learning

Your students will be required to complete some summative assessments that you have developed as well as some developed by external agents, such as the state, college entrance boards, the military, and others. **Summative assessments** are used to determine how well students have mastered learning goals or standards and occur at the end of instruction. Student mastery of content standards is usually ultimately assessed through externally developed large-scale assessments offered at the end of a grade level (sometimes called EOG assessments) or the end of a course (also known as EOC assessments).

Of course, summative assessments to evaluate learning can also be developed by teachers, such as unit tests or final exams. Regardless of who develops or administers them, summative assessments are usually a final step in the presentation of a lesson, unit, or course rather than part of the instruction. Grades or scores associated with summative assessments can carry from low to very high stakes. (Of course, some students may feel *all* grades are high stakes!) Generally, the data from these tests are used to measure the performance of individual students, groups of students, instructional programs, and even the effectiveness of your own instruction. Summative assessments are well established in the culture of schooling. We're sure that you've taken many of these yourself.

When selecting technologies to support summative assessments, go back to the three components mentioned earlier when discussing learning goals: 1) the behavior, skill, knowledge, or attitude to be demonstrated, 2) the conditions under which they will be demonstrated, and 3) the criteria that specify the required level of performance. The technologies you select should be appropriate for the behavior or skill you are addressing and should mirror the conditions under which students should perform them. Students should have adequate instruction, practice, and feedback using the technologies they'll be required to use during assessment, so the technologies don't prevent them from demonstrating what they've learned. Some teachers design the assessments first—before the instruction—so they're sure to design instruction that provides adequate practice with the resources used during assessment. You don't want any surprises at the assessment stage.

It's important not to isolate the assessment strategies and tools you use in the Monitor and Evaluate stages of your instruction and just "tack them on" at the end. The cycle of instruction is iterative, and the stages overlap. As you will learn in the next section, you plan your assessments as you set goals for student learning. In addition, some of the assessments you develop may be part of your instructional actions.

---

outcome feedback
whether or not a response is correct

cognitive feedback
provides an explanation of why an answer is correct or incorrect to help students develop a better understanding of the goals for performance, how their current understanding or skill levels compare to those goals, and how they might improve their performances

summative assessments
assessments used to evaluate learning after presenting a lesson, unit, or course

Assessment Formats and Technologies That Support Them

There is little agreement regarding the classifications of assessment formats. In fact, some assessments can blur the lines between different formats and include elements of several. So we can better address the types of technologies that support assessment, we group assessment formats into three broadly defined groups: 1) forced-choice assessments, 2) open-ended response assessments, and 3) authentic assessments, which we further break down into project- or performance-based assessments. The first two types generally require answers that can be considered correct or incorrect, but authentic assessments are more complex. They might be considered ill-structured, meaning that they are complex and may have more than one right answer. In some cases, they may not have a truly correct answer, but some answers that are better than others. Next, we explore the characteristics of each of these four broad categories and the technologies that support them.

Forced-Choice Assessment Formats

Review the stages in technology integration, presented at the end of Chapter 1, through which most teachers progress. Remember that one of the first ways that teachers build their skills with new technologies is to replicate familiar strategies. This is true for both instruction and assessment, and in terms of assessment, most people are familiar with forced-choice question formats. These are the customary multiple-choice, true/false, matching, and fill-in-the-blank question formats that are popular on large-scale exams and that have influenced the assessment practices of many teachers.

A benefit of this assessment format is that it can be quick to administer and score. Also, items can be readily developed or obtained in these formats, especially for constructs with lower levels of cognitive demand. It is possible, but difficult, to develop forced-choice questions that accurately assess skills and knowledge at a higher level of cognitive skill, for example when students are required to analyze, evaluate, or create information. Depending on your level of technology proficiency, and that of your students, there are a variety of technologies that support the inclusion of forced-choice formats in your assessment toolkit.

You will probably have access to digital test-item banks, including ones that you and your colleagues develop. Item banks may be available from publishers of state-adopted resources, such as textbooks, or may be available for purchase from assessment vendors. Some states and districts offer online access to item banks that may include items from previously administered large-scale assessments. Test-item banks may provide good formative and summative assessment items for your own classroom.

Items for summative assessments must be kept secure; however, some states and districts are tackling the development of online formative assessment opportunities that are available for teachers, students, and parents at all times on an on-demand basis. These assessments capitalize on the growing number of online assessment systems—both state-based as well as vendor-provided systems—that have been developed since the late 1990s. Beginning with familiar formats, many online assessment systems began by replicating common paper-and-pencil formats, the most popular of which was the forced-choice response (Bennett, 1998).

Of course there is a variety of testing software that supports forced-choice question formats. Scannable test forms, available in several formats, are used in many classrooms. As you probably know, students use a question booklet (or sheet) to read the questions and indicate their answers by filling in the appropriate "bubbles" on a form that can be read by a test scanner. Open-response questions (e.g., essay or short answer questions) can also be included on some forms, but you'll probably still have to grade these responses yourself.

Online testing software is available in many schools and ranges from highly secure summative tests that are matched to state content standards to online assessments you create yourself. Even if your school or district does not have access to a commercial online quiz generator, several free services are available online (see Figure 7.2).

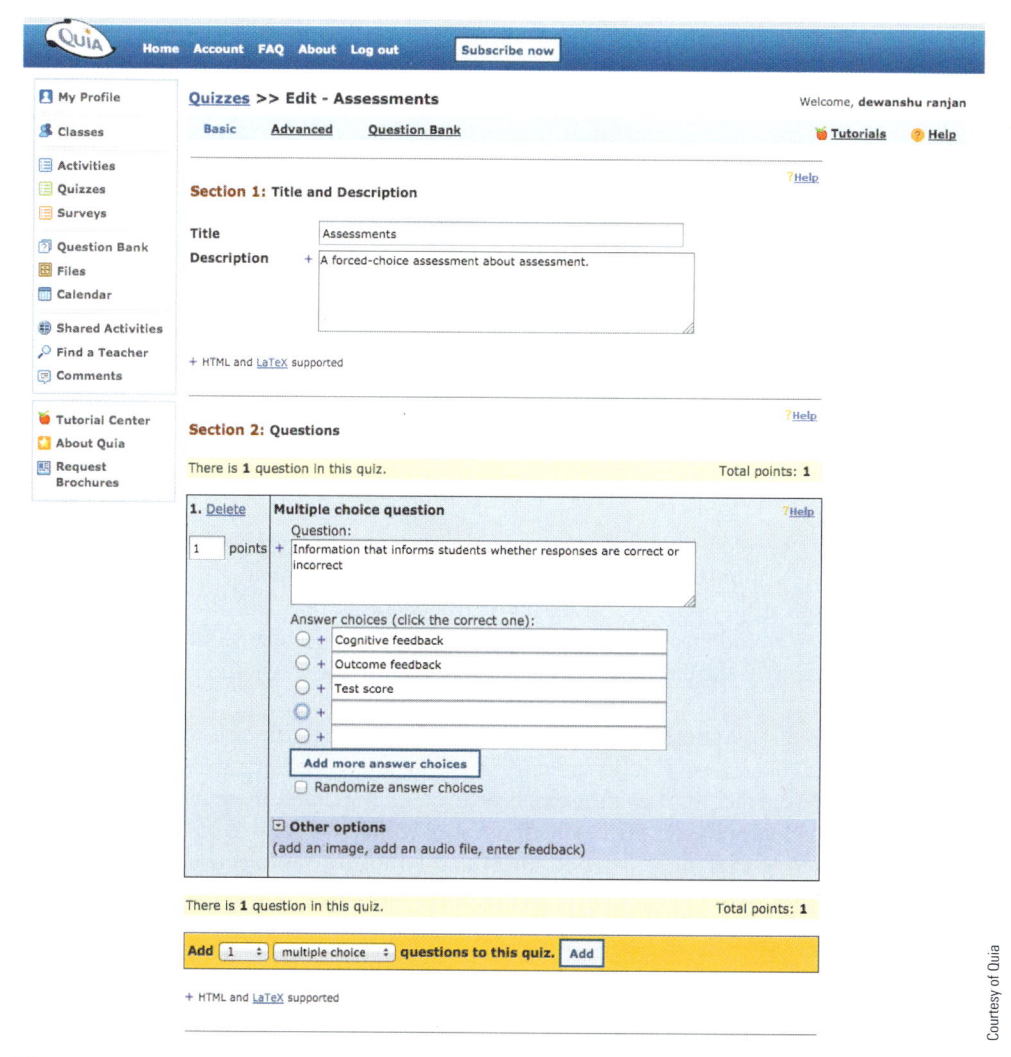

Assessment and Evaluation 169

Figure 7.2
There are many quiz-generating programs and services available online, like this one from Quia.com.

THE GAME PLAN

Forced-Choice Assessments

Set Goals
Learn more about one of the technologies used to support forced-choice assessments. Choose one of the technologies presented in this chapter such as item banks, online assessments, or wireless responders.

Take Action
Review at least one example of these tools by investigating it online, finding a video about it, visiting a school that uses it, reading about it in journals or magazines, or attending an educational conference with a vendor display area.

Monitor
Determine how the assessment matches the demands of your content areas. Talk with other students in your class or with practicing teachers to determine how the tools can be used in your own teaching.

Evaluate and Extend
Discuss the strengths and weaknesses of the technology with others and determine strategies for incorporating the technology in your classroom.

Many of these require you to register your students, often using a student identifier, so that results can be e-mailed to you or accessed later. Check with your school first before using any service in which student information is recorded. Many learning management systems also incorporate testing software so that instruction, assessments, and grades are all kept secure within the same online environment. Another popular technology that supports the use of forced-choice items is the wireless responder or personal response system, discussed earlier in this chapter.

Open-Ended Response Formats

Because it is difficult to write high-quality, forced-choice questions that truly tap into higher-order thinking skills, open-ended questions are often employed when students have to demonstrate higher levels of cognitive skill, such as the application or synthesis of rules, procedures, or concepts or to demonstrate creative and original thoughts and ideas.

What does the following bring to mind? "Explain in your own words what is meant by . . ." How about, "Compare and contrast the following . . ."? These are examples of prompts for open-ended questions in the form commonly known as short-answer or essay questions. Responses may be restricted ("in 100 words or less . . .") or extended for more in-depth responses. You've undoubtedly encountered many of these questions in your career as a student and may have a few yet to experience. Although these formats are familiar, you should consider why and when to use open-ended responses and their implications for your assessment practices.

On the plus side, open-ended questions often take little time to develop. On the scoring end, however, they usually take longer than forced-choice responses in which there is only one correct answer that can be scored by machine. In general, open-ended questions can be less reliable, primarily due to the subjective nature of scoring them.

Any technology that supports text entry can be used to incorporate responses to open-ended questions. This extends beyond word-processing software, as a variety of communication and collaboration tools exist that allow students to respond to your queries. For example, students can demonstrate and extend their learning through participation in threaded discussions, e-mail, or even chat. Digital tools such as blogs or threaded discussions allow for an added layer of reflection and revision as you, other students, and even the original author can return to a posting and provide a critique, clarification, or demonstration of further understanding or skill. Both stand-alone and web-based tools allow students to support their text-based entries with video, graphics, and other media.

Several online tools are also available that are dedicated specifically to collaborative work, many of which can support peer review as a type of formative assessment. Even word-processing applications include commenting, annotation, and tracking features that allow you and your students to incorporate suggestions, options, and revisions within a single document. They also include tools, such as grammar and spell checkers, that can support students who experience difficulties in these areas when critical thought outweighs the need for mechanics.

Authentic Assessments

In Chapter 3 we introduced you to the concept of authentic intellectual work and described how authentic instruction uses real-world contexts to engage students in the actual work of a discipline. In an **authentic assessment**, students are required to demonstrate understanding of concepts and perform skills within the context of that authentic activity, that is, by replicating real-world performances as closely as possible (Svinicki, 2004). In these cases, the assessments may be intricately embedded or linked to the instruction so that it may not be apparent to students that there is a formal assessment. Students in science classes can perform experiments using probes and other measurement devices that scientists use and record their findings in a laboratory notebook—digital or paper; students can demonstrate writing proficiency by using word processing and layout software to create brochures or newspapers; students in

authentic assessment
assessment in which students are required to demonstrate understanding of concepts and perform skills within real-world contexts

math classes can use real-world data sets they graph and analyze to make projections related to changes in economic factors or wildlife populations.

Wiggins (1998) lists six characteristics of an authentic assessment:

1. The assessment is realistic; it reflects the way the information or skills would be used in the "real world."
2. The assessment requires judgment and innovation; it is based on solving unstructured problems that could easily have more than one answer and, as such, requires the learner to make informed choices.
3. The assessment asks the student to "do" the subject, that is, to go through the procedures that are typical to the discipline under study.
4. The assessment is done in situations as similar as possible to the context in which the related skills are performed.
5. The assessment requires the student to demonstrate a wide range of skills that are related to the complex problem, including some that involve judgment.
6. The assessment allows for practice, feedback, and second chances to solve the problem being addressed.

In the popular instructional design model Understanding by Design (Wiggins & McTighe, 2006), teachers use a "backwards design" approach that incorporates performance tasks as culminating assessments to lessons or units of study. Using standards as the basis for learning goals, teachers then develop assessments that require students to "do" the subject, as described above. Students may assume the role of a professional who would use the skills and knowledge described by the learning standards, and are required to focus their performance towards some realistic audience and context. And just as in the real world, the assessment problem is often complex and may not have one clear, correct answer. In this model, the pursuit of the problem is more important than getting the "right" answer. There are, however, better answers than others, and students are often required to describe how they came to their solutions and justify their choices. For example, students in geometry or algebra may design new buildings or cities and create and present 2- or 3-dimensional models for the most effective, cost-efficient, or aesthetically pleasing solution to a planning board. Students in social studies may propose alternate endings to historical conflicts or participate in forums similar to a Model United Nations to suggest solutions to complex social problems, such as affordable housing and health care, sustainable sources for clean air and water, or new sources of energy.

Think of the typical science fair project. This is a project that is often built around a specific problem, whether determined by the student or the sponsoring organization. The problems often meet the requirements for authentic assessment as students are required to perform like scientists in terms of the research they complete and the tools they use. They also usually complete some type of performance in terms of explaining their projects and their new understandings, and demonstrating skills that have been developed. So in this case, you may have an authentic, problem-based project that is assessed via performance and a product! These distinctions are not as critical as developing assessments that appropriately meet the demands of your curriculum and the needs of your students—it usually doesn't matter if you can explicitly state whether you are engaging in project- or performance-based activities, or both. But because these are common forms of assessment that you are likely to employ, let's look at what we mean by these forms of authentic assessment.

Project-Based Assessments

Many assessments require students to create some type of product, from a simple diagram, document, or model to complex products with multiple components, and often do this as the result of some type of project. Although project-based assessments can be used for formative purposes, they are often employed in summative settings, such as the generation of capstone projects at the end of a year or course of study. There are a variety of methods for incorporating project-based assessments in a classroom, as well as many different tools to support them.

STORIES from Practice

Performance Tasks

While forced-choice assessments address factual recall, comprehension, and application of basic skills, district leaders at Henrico County Public Schools outside of Richmond, Virginia, were interested in developing assessments that measured more complex skills. I worked with district staff and four teachers from Henrico County to develop and pilot a performance assessment that was designed to address "21st Century Skills" such as information fluency, collaboration and communication, critical thinking, and creativity. Using the framework for a performance task from *Understanding by Design* (Wiggins & McTighe, 2006) and informed by modifications suggested by CLA in the Classroom (Chun, 2010), the following task was developed and piloted in eighth-grade classrooms and subsequently used as a model for performance tasks in additional content areas. In the description below, the categories of goal, role, situation and the like are taken from the Understanding by Design framework.

The Cell Phone Debate

Goal: The students were asked to decide whether cell phones should or shouldn't be allowed for use during school. The task was presented to students in the form of a news bulletin video from the central office (see Figure 7.3).

Role and Audience: Students assumed the role of a student representative to the school board.

Situation: In this hypothetical situation, one school board member was reported as championing cell phone use because of the many ways that educators are now incorporating cell phones during instruction. A second board member was reported to be highly opposed to the use of cell phones and suggested they were a threat to students and could lead to cheating and other inappropriate uses.

Product: A library of documents related to cell phone use and performance data from the school district was provided. The documents provided information on both sides of the issue. And true to real life decisions, the documents contained some extraneous information as well as information from various levels of authority—including an e-mail, white papers, a podcast from a call-in radio show, and select data from the county's school report cards (see Figure 7.4).

On day 1 (90-minute class periods), students had to make a decision either for or against cell phone use and use information from the documents

Cell Phone News Challenge
by Tom Woodward PLUS 1 year ago
Part of a performance based assessment where students argue a side for cell phone use in school.

Figure 7.3
The performance task was presented to students in the form of a news bulletin video from the central office.

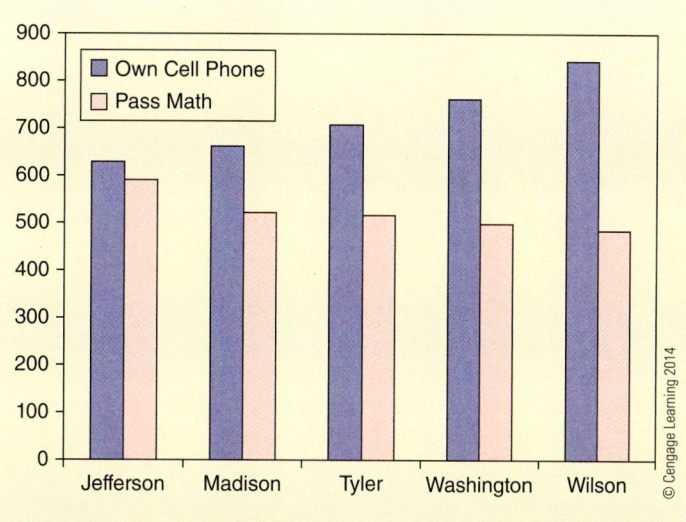

Figure 7.4
Documents included real data from the county school report cards, but with fictitious school names.

to support their decision. On day 2, students had to create a "product," but could only use materials they could access from their laptops, which included an Internet browser. Student products varied from short papers and letters to the school board, to presentations using different online and stand-alone applications, as well as some short movies.

Criteria for Success: The county staff developed a rubric for classroom observation that addressed 21st Century skills. The components of the rubric were used to evaluate student products.

Source: John Ross.

Project-based assessments can be administered at varying degrees of difficulty and cognitive complexity. At the lower end are projects with well-defined parameters. They may be prescriptive and provide students with some, but limited choices. Often, there are components that are correct or not, and so are able to be graded using checklists or are compared to some specifications. At this end, students may be developing foundational skills that they can then apply in more creative and innovative ways later. For example, students learning to use desktop publishing or video-editing software may create simple or short projects that illustrate their ability to complete common tasks in the application. In desktop-publishing software this may include using a template to learn how to insert and edit images or changing the size, color, and orientation of text. In video-editing software, students may create short projects that incorporate transitions, titles, and other effects before moving on to longer, more open-ended projects.

But project-based assessments can also be complex and evolve over a period of time, in which the projects require solutions to complex problems that may have no one right answer. A project or series of projects may serve as the culminating assessment in problem-based learning, as described in Chapter 3. Problem-based learning can help students meet standards and learning goals that require higher-order thinking skills, such as those related to identifying a problem, selecting and monitoring strategies for solving the problem, applying knowledge, and evaluating the success of one's efforts. At these higher levels, problem-based learning encourages students to use the information and tools that professionals use to solve problems they are likely to face in a professional setting. Problem-based learning can also be assessed with performance-based assessments, discussed next, as a well-designed problem can easily require students to demonstrate new knowledge and skills through performance with the only limitations being the appropriate fit to the content being explored.

Which technologies are right for project-based assessments? The same you choose for your instruction. Language arts teachers may use word-processing, desktop-publishing, or blogging software. Math teachers may incorporate 2- and 3-D modeling software or manipulatives. Science teachers may incorporate simulations or real-world data sets. Whatever you use for your instruction is a good candidate for assessment, and vice versa. In fact, we really encourage you to align your technology choices this way.

Performance-Based Assessments

There are a variety of ways students can demonstrate mastery through performance. Performance-based assessments are possible in all content areas but may be most easily exemplified by domains that require communication skills or the development of psychomotor skills in conjunction with other content knowledge, such as sports, the fine arts, and many lab sciences. In these cases, it's easy to see that students are required to "do" the subject in obvious ways. But performances can very quickly extend beyond the demonstration of basic and foundational skills and require students to demonstrate complex behaviors based on their understanding of foundational knowledge and the application of creative and innovative thinking. A unique type of performance-based assessment, called a **performance task** (see *Stories from Practice—Performance Tasks*), is a central focus of the popular Understanding by Design model (Wiggins & McTigh, 2006), and is an assessment well suited to authentic intellectual work, as described in Chapter 3.

Oral communication is a ubiquitous teaching and assessment tool. Teachers ask their students questions to determine prior knowledge, levels of understanding or misunderstanding, or simply to clarify a point. This type of questioning and dialog can be informal or can be used in formal settings, such as in the case of an oral exam or interview. And although this is a book about the use of technology, it's important to emphasize that technology should be used only when it facilitates learning, and not simply as a novelty. Sometimes you'll just want to ask a question—no technology required. But there are some ways that technology can support assessment through dialog. Obviously, there are many technology resources that support written communication, including journals, blogs, and word-processing applications, but digital recording is so easy and available that more complex types of communication can be stored and reviewed to monitor and evaluate student learning.

The ease with which digital audio and video can be captured and edited allows it to serve as a tool for demonstrating student skills and knowledge. As demonstrated by the hundreds, if not thousands, of live early morning news shows at elementary schools across the nation, even young students can master basic video capture and editing. Class or small group discussions can be captured and stored in portfolios. Student presentations can be recorded and kept as an account of content understanding. Music teachers often employ recordings of students—as individuals and in group settings—to assess their performances. Physical education teachers use digital cameras and video cameras to record students dribbling and kicking balls, diving, or performing other sports to evaluate them for form and process. And although this section focuses on technology that supports *student* assessment, the value of using video to record your own teaching as a means of evaluating and developing skills (see *Tech Tools and Tips—Video Recording Lessons for Reflection* in Chapter 2) cannot be overstated.

Technologies to Support Authentic Assessment

Projects and performances can incorporate a wide variety of technologies, from research papers composed using word-processing software to multimedia projects that include graphics, video, and audio. Students may conduct research on the web, use a digital camera to take pictures to support their presentations, create graphics using drawing programs, and demonstrate their knowledge using presentation software. They may research their own business, start a philanthropic movement, or create products or performances that can be posted online and shared across the world. Any of the same tools you can use to support authentic instruction can be used for assessment. In the following discussion, we'll focus on just a few of the many technologies that can help you assess student learning when using authentic assessments: 1) concept maps, 2) simulations and games, and 3) portfolios and work samples.

> **performance task**
> a type of performance-based assessment that requires students to "do" the subject in question, often through open-ended problems in an authentic context

Concept Maps

As you recall from Chapter 4, concept mapping—sometimes referred to as mind mapping—is a graphic technique for representing understanding. Concept maps traditionally consist of **nodes** representing concepts and **links** that show the connection between nodes (see Figure 7.5 for an example of one type of a concept map). Concept-mapping software is available for use by young students; however, the concepts that can be addressed and the resulting maps can become extremely complex and thus are suitable for use with older students, as well. Concept mapping is not dependent upon technology, but concept-mapping software is widely available for facilitating the process. A variety of map templates are readily available, including Venn diagrams (see Figure 7.6), plot analysis, timelines, lab reports, and many others.

The nodes and links in a concept map help reveal student thinking and can illuminate misconceptions. Your students can compare their maps to those created by experts—including yourself—and this comparison can provide specific cognitive feedback essential to good formative assessment. You can also compare the modifications students make to a concept map they create at the beginning of a lesson and revise at the end, in order to assess growth in understanding. Although paper-and-pencil concept maps may also be analyzed for student misconceptions and understanding, the widespread availability of concept-mapping software increases its utility. As such, it has become a popular technology in classrooms at all grade levels.

One concern regarding using concept maps for assessment is how to implement concept mapping consistently across classrooms to generate valid and reliable results. Although technology supports concept mapping, it cannot resolve the human-dependent implementation issue. Concept maps do rate high in terms of utility, however, and can be integrated into many different content areas.

nodes
concepts, as represented in a concept map

links
in a concept map, the connections or relationships between concepts

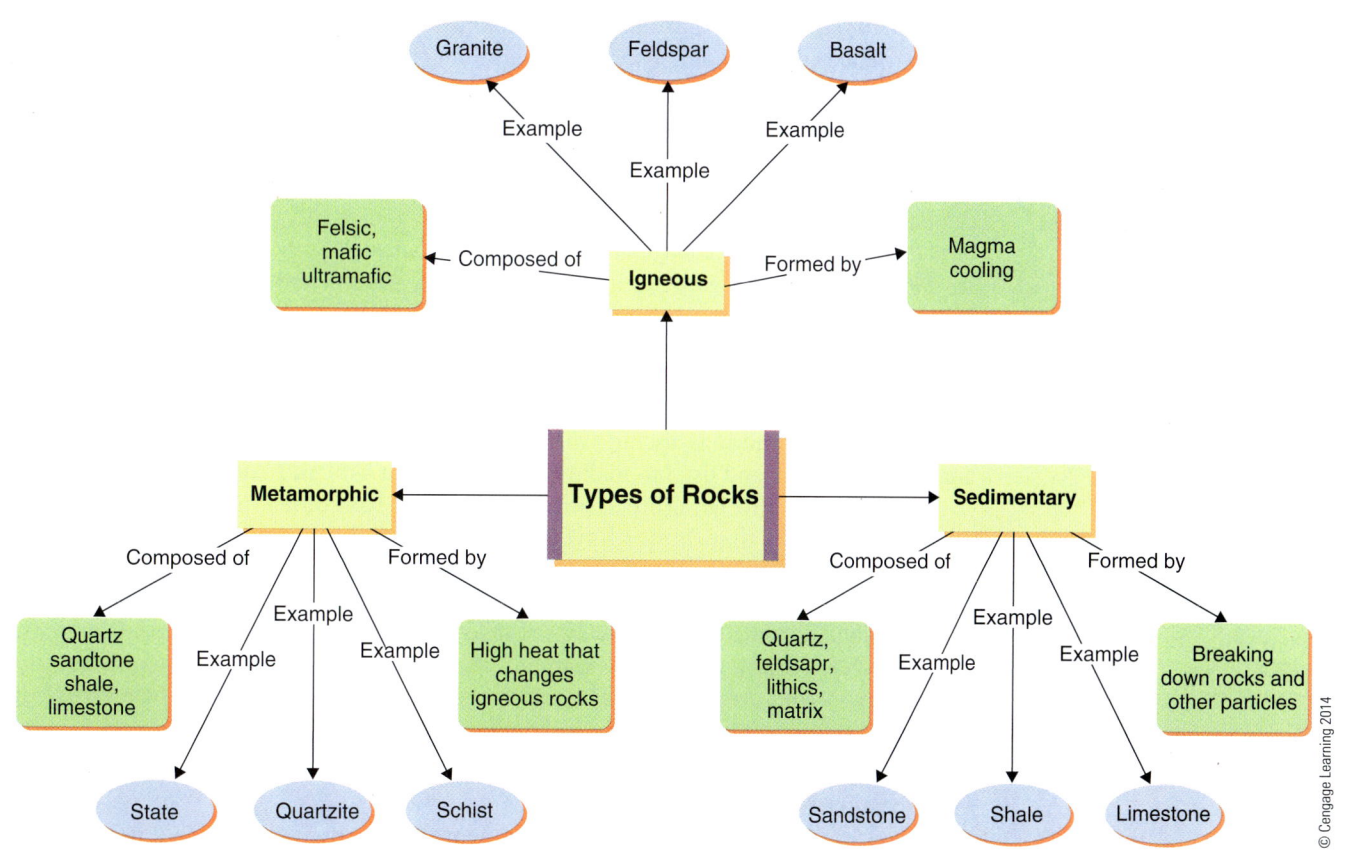

Figure 7.5
Example of a concept map.

Venn Diagram

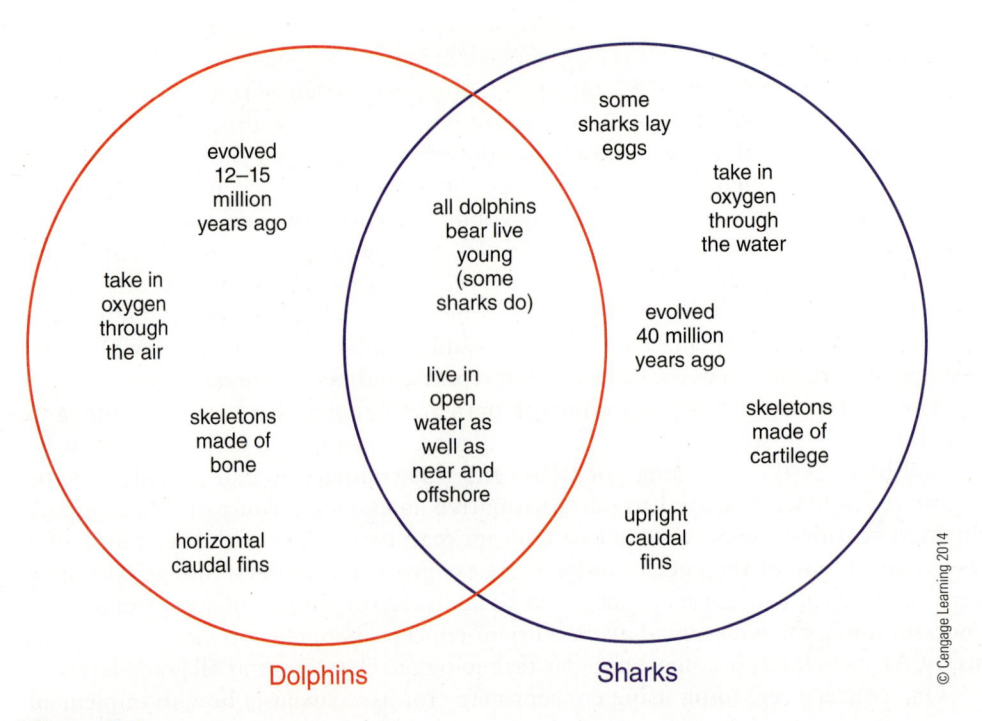

Dolphins (left circle):
- evolved 12–15 million years ago
- take in oxygen through the air
- skeletons made of bone
- horizontal caudal fins

Overlap:
- all dolphins bear live young (some sharks do)
- live in open water as well as near and offshore

Sharks (right circle):
- some sharks lay eggs
- take in oxygen through the water
- evolved 40 million years ago
- skeletons made of cartilege
- upright caudal fins

© Cengage Learning 2014

Figure 7.6
Example of a Venn diagram.

Simulations and Games

Simulation and gaming software can provide access to learning activities that might otherwise be difficult or impossible to create in a classroom. The simulations and games available for use in your classroom range in sophistication from simple free animations that can be found online to complex virtual environments. You can access online simulations of weather-related events or space missions and collect student performance data using a digital journal or laboratory notebook. Students can access historical simulations and work in small groups to create presentations to give to the rest of the class, complete structured worksheets, or write reflective essays guided by questions you pose. Students can participate in a range of games, from short drill-and-practice types to more complex ones that mimic popular multi-player games found outside of school.

These types of software are unique in that they not only provide opportunities for learning but can support assessment, as well (see Figure 7.7). Simulation software can capture different elements of student performance data, such as the paths they follow through the software and the choices they make. Games usually include some type of score but can also report different types of performance data, such as time spent, items mastered or not, and may include different levels of difficulty. That data can then be analyzed, reported, and used to make judgments about skill and knowledge proficiency.

You may have to generate scoring procedures for some simple simulations or educational games that do not have data analysis and reporting features built into them. You can combine the use of these software applications with other assessment methods, such as journals or short quizzes, in order to check for students' progress on their learning goals. However, the selection and use of simulations, games, or virtual environments for assessment should meet the same standards as any technology in your classroom and should be appropriate for the content being studied, the needs of your students, and the learning goals they are trying to meet.

Portfolios and Work Samples

As you already know through the development of your own professional portfolio in conjunction with this textbook, portfolios contain examples of work that can be compared to competencies or standards—often through the use of some type of checklist or

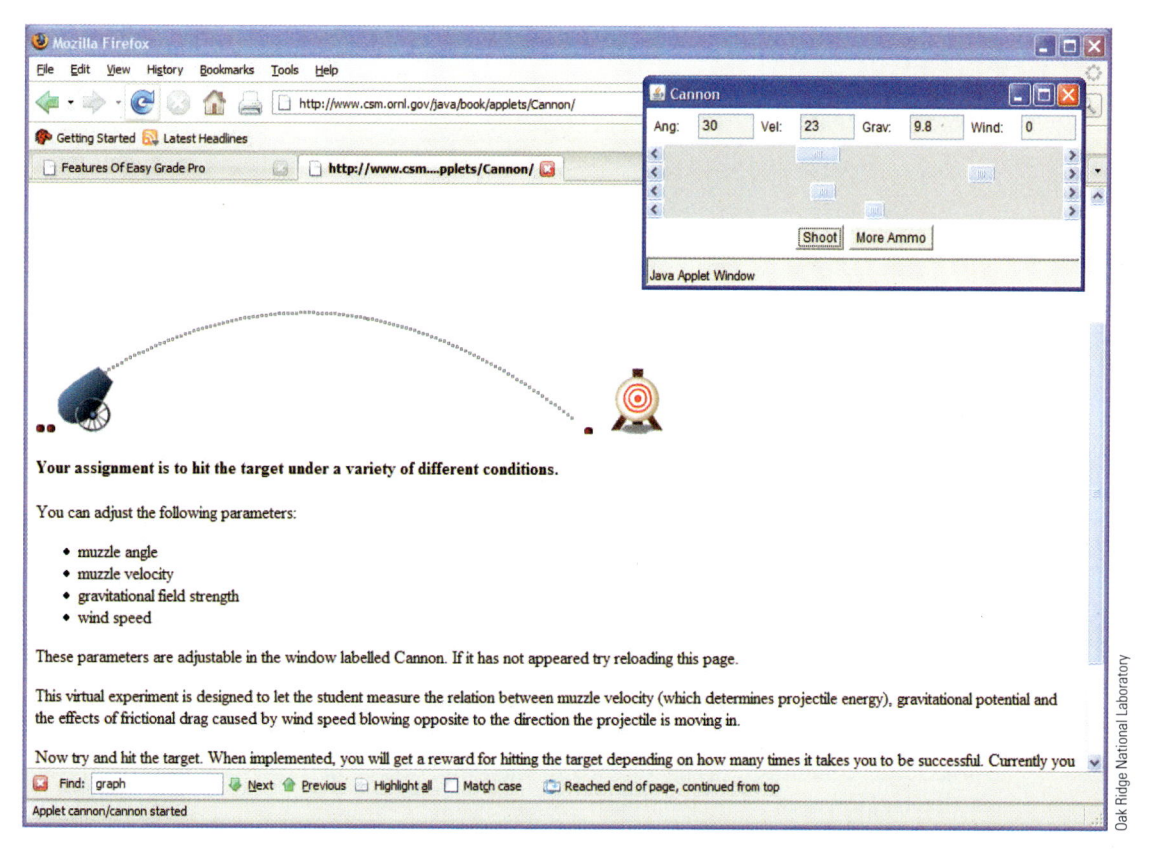

Figure 7.7
This ballistics simulation has a simple form of self-assessment. Once the student correctly manipulates the cannonball to hit the target, the target bursts into flames.

rubric. When incorporating portfolios in your instruction and assessment, it is important to determine an organizing structure in advance and make it apparent to your students. For example, your own portfolio for this class is probably organized around the ISTE NETS-T. To facilitate learning and student growth, your students themselves should determine what artifacts to include. However, the guidelines and criteria for the selection of materials contained in the portfolio should be explained and made clear to your students. And sometimes you may want all students to include a specific artifact or work sample as a means of evaluating their mastery of expected standards.

As you know, portfolios also serve as a means for self-assessment and self-reflection, as it is common that students write or explain why they have selected the artifacts in their portfolios, what those artifacts demonstrate in terms of their learning or understanding, and why they feel they are exemplars. In digital portfolios, this reflection may be an audio or video recording. Your students will likely need guidance and practice in creating reflections. (See information about creating self-reflections in Chapter 2.) Reflection provides a natural opportunity for providing cognitive feedback to your students as you review and discuss the portfolio artifacts with them.

Both the process of artifact selection and the subsequent assessment of portfolios rely on some subjective judgment. Also, portfolio use is usually not standard across classrooms. Your students' portfolios will be highly dependent on your classroom practices, and not all teachers will place the same emphasis on portfolio development, allot the same amount of class time for their development, provide the same access to outside resources

> **TEACHSOURCE VIDEO**
>
> Go to the Education CourseMate website for this book and view one or more of the teacher interview videos, such as *Teacher Interview: Digital Storytelling in the High School Classroom*, *Teacher Interview: Data Collection and Visualization in the Elementary Classroom*, *Teacher Interview: Supporting Problem-Based Learning in the Elementary Classroom*, or *Teacher Interview: Math 2.0: Using Social Networking in the High School Mathematics Classroom*.
>
> 1. Describe the different methods and resources the teachers will use to assess student learning.
> 2. What role does technology play in their assessments? Consider how the teachers match their selected technology to the demands of their content.

> ## THE GAME PLAN
> ### Authentic Assessments
>
> **Set Goals**
> Just as you did with forced-choice assessments, learn more about one of the technologies used to support project- or performance-based assessments. Choose one of the technologies presented in this chapter such as concept maps, simulations, or portfolios.
>
> **Take Action**
> Find an example and consider how it can support assessment for learning. Determine the types of data it provides and what settings it seems best suited for. Find a copy to download and explore.
>
> **Monitor**
> Determine how the assessment matches the demands of your content area. Can you find examples of its use in your content area? What additional information might you need in order to apply it in your classroom practice?
>
> **Evaluate and Extend**
> Discuss the strengths and weaknesses of the technology with others and determine strategies for incorporating the technology in your classroom.

or help, or collaborate with students to the same degree in terms of selecting relevant artifacts. However, while portfolios may pose challenges when compared *across* classrooms, one of the primary benefits of portfolio use is that they can help teachers and students *within* a classroom become more systematic in analyzing and learning from student work samples than would normally occur during instruction (Shepard, 2000).

Summary of Assessment Formats

Formative and summative assessments can be classified as forced-choice, open-ended, project-based, or performance-based. While you've probably been assessed using all of these formats, this section introduced you to a variety of technologies that can support them. But assessments are useless unless you score them to evaluate students' progress and determine whether your students learned what they set out to learn. Common scoring procedures are the focus of the next section.

Scoring Expectations and Practices

Once you've selected an assessment or assessment format, you must determine a method for obtaining an appropriate score for each student's performance. Scores, or grades, receive a great deal of attention in education, and you want to be sure that not only are your assessments adequate to allow students to demonstrate their proficiencies, but also that the judgments you make based on those assessments are fair and accurate. Some scoring practices and guidelines are provided below.

Scoring Keys

When an assessment allows you to make an objective judgment as to whether a response is right or wrong, grading is rather straightforward. Your student either got it right or not. When students are required to choose between a limited set of possible answers, as with multiple-choice, matching, and true-false questions, grading guidelines consist of a list of correct responses. These forced-choice assessment formats easily lend themselves to computerized test administration and scoring.

A popular technology for scoring forced-choice responses is a test scanner, as mentioned earlier. There is also software available that will allow actual document scanners to read and score the famous "bubble sheets" that scanners rely on and with which you are undoubtedly familiar. You can create multiple test forms to increase security, and a test scanner can score all forms within a few minutes. Test scanners may also support item analysis of an assessment to determine whether any items were too easy or too hard, which can help you improve the match among your standards, instruction, and assessment.

Some open-ended test formats require constructed responses that also can be judged right or wrong. Some can be scored by computer, but in these cases spelling really counts! Short-answer questions and even some essay tests can be scored using keys that consist of a list of acceptable answers. Scoring keys for these open-ended formats should include common variations in wording for each acceptable response. Although this type of test can also be administered and scored by computer, developing a program to score constructed responses is more difficult than developing one to score forced-choice responses.

You may have already taken essay tests that have been scored by a computer without realizing it. In several state and national tests, essays are now scored strictly by technology. At one time, these student responses were scored by multiple human raters who had to undergo intensive training and were reviewed frequently for the consistency and reliability of their grading. Vantage Learning is one company that has developed software, which it calls IntelliMetric, that uses artificial intelligence (AI) and examples of student writing to review and score student writing assessments. The computer scoring has been compared to, and often surpasses, the reliability of human scoring. One problem is that the scoring engine requires hundreds, if not thousands, of student samples to provide the best results, so it is still impractical for use in most classrooms. However, some states that have shifted to the assessment of student writing online also provide websites that teachers and students can use to practice and receive feedback.

Checklists

This chapter has introduced a variety of assessments that cannot be scored neatly by a completely objective format. Class discussions, observations, responses to open-ended questions and essays, problem-based learning projects, performance tasks, and portfolios offer unique challenges to scoring. Usually, teachers rely on checklists or rubrics to score these types of assessments and to reduce the subjective quality of their judgments.

Checklists are a simple way to score the observation or demonstration of a skill. These can be factual recall skills or more complex skills involving analysis and evaluation. For example, the Think-Aloud Checklist in Figure 7.8 can be used to determine students' use of comprehension strategies in a reading assignment. You can create a simple checklist in which you decide if the parameter or skill you are looking for is present or not. The simple oral presentation checklist in Figure 7.9 was generated online using the free PBL Checklist maker from ALTEC at the University of Kansas—the group that has created the popular 4Teachers website.

Did the student...	Check for each instance	Comment
Make predictions		
Use imagery by describing pictures		
Link new information to prior knowledge		
Talk through confusing points		
Use comprehension strategies		

Figure 7.8
Collecting data using a think-aloud checklist.

PBL Project Based Learning
Oral Presentation Checklist: Grades 9–12

Teacher Name: Mr. Ross

Student Name: _____ Reviewer Name: _____

Date: _____

Project: Oral Report

Category	Responsibilities
Delivery	☐ I maintained eye-contact most of the time. ☐ I spoke to the entire audience, not just one or two people. ☐ My pronunciation was clear and easy to understand. ☐ My rate of speech was not too fast or too slow. ☐ My voice varied in pitch; it was not monotone. ☐ I did not use filler words (e.g., "uhm," "uh," "ah," "mm," "like," etc.) ☐ My body language was not too tense or too relaxed. ☐ I used meaningful gestures.

Figure 7.9
Checklists can be used to score projects or performances.

As illustrated in Figure 7.9, checklists can also be used to score projects or performances. Care should be taken to determine whether a check mark on the checklist actually corresponds to student understanding and skill. Are you grading the student or the project? Multiple measures of assessment may be necessary to help you develop a clear picture of student understanding.

Checklists can be developed and implemented using a variety of technologies, and since their purpose is to collect data quickly and easily, the use of technologies to capture, store, and report that data makes them even more powerful. Some checklist and grading apps are available for use on handheld or tablet computers that allow you to enter data onscreen. And although not every helpful checklist or inventory is currently available for handheld devices, common productivity software, such as word-processing and spreadsheet software, is supported by many of these devices and can allow you to quickly develop those checklists you use regularly for assessment. Storing the results of checklist data in spreadsheets and databases provides powerful analysis and reporting features, and you can create these documents online, such as through a Google form, to access them anywhere you have an Internet connection. Simple summaries and graphs that give you individual and group profiles can be created quickly; they also can help you determine the need to modify your instruction for reteaching or enrichment.

Rubrics

Generally, checklists are one-dimensional. Usually, either the students did the tasks or they didn't. Rubrics, however, provide an added dimension that allows both you and your students to determine gradations in quality. Rubrics are common methods for assessing project- and performance-based projects, especially those supported by technology. Rubrics are malleable and can be created for any content area and assessment mode, such as the scoring of projects, essays, portfolios, or live or recorded student performances.

Multimedia Project Rubric

Assignment: Interview a friend or relative to create a biographical web page/site. You must collect the following information:

- Date and place of birth
- Your reason(s) for interviewing this person
- Most memorable event in his/her life
- An accomplishment for which he/she is most proud

Your web page/site must contain at least five paragraphs of text, one image, and one hyperlink to a supporting resource. Any quotations must be correctly formatted and appropriately cited.

Score	0	1	2	3
Content features	Several of the required content elements are not included or are inaccurate.	Some of the content elements are not included or are inaccurate.	All of the content elements are included.	All content elements are included and are explained with significant detail and supporting data.
Grammar and punctuation	There are many errors in grammar and punctuation.	There are a few errors in grammar and punctuation.	There are one or two errors in grammar and punctuation.	There are no errors in grammar and punctuation.
Writing style	The writing is very difficult to read throughout with little or no variation in sentence structure and vocabulary is below grade level.	The writing is somewhat difficult to read in some points with little variation in sentence structure and vocabulary is below grade level.	The writing is easy to read with some variation of sentence structures and appropriate grade-level vocabulary.	The writing is both interesting and easy to read with a variety of sentence structures and appropriate and challenging vocabulary.
General design features	The information is difficult to view and text is difficult to read. The use of images, colors, and other media consistently detract from the presentation of the information.	Some of the information is difficult to view and/or text may be difficult to read. The use of images, colors, and other media may detract from the presentation of the information in some instances.	The information is presented clearly with text that is easy to read. The use of images, colors, and other media does not detract from the presentation of the information.	The information is presented in a creative manner with text that is easy to read. The use of images, colors, and other media is imaginative and adds to the presentation of the information.

Figure 7.10
Analytic rubric for multimedia project.

Rubrics are framed by some type of scale, but the degrees of the scale are clearly described or defined to demonstrate different levels of quality. Generally, a three-, four-, or five-point scale is manageable, depending on the complexity of the task, project, or performance to be scored. Too many "quality" levels for a simple skill or too few for complex skills erode the effectiveness of the rubric. Another consideration is whether to begin your rubric scale at no points (0) or 1. Your rubric should relate to the standards or learning goals for the activity, lesson, or project, and the descriptions should clearly describe the levels of performance rather than be subjective judgments (Brookhart, 1999). For example, a descriptor for an exemplary writing sample that notes that all sentences and proper nouns begin with a capital letter is a clear description of the expected level of performance; whereas, use of the terms "good" or "weak" are subjective and provide little concrete feedback or a justifiable position.

Rubrics can be analytic or holistic (Brookhart, 1999). An **analytic rubric** breaks the assessment down into component categories (see Figure 7.10). For example, an analytic

analytic rubric
a type of assessment rubric in which component categories are broken down

Multimedia Project Rubric

Assignment: Interview a friend or relative to create a biographical web page/site. You must collect the following information:

- Date and place of birth
- Your reason(s) for interviewing this person
- Most memorable event in his/her life
- An accomplishment for which he/she is most proud

Your web page/site must contain at least five paragraphs of text, one image, and one hyperlink to a supporting resource. Any quotations must be correctly formatted and appropriately cited.

---

3 Points—All content elements are included and are explained with significant detail and supporting data. There are no errors in grammar and punctuation. The writing is both interesting and easy to read with a variety of sentence structures and appropriate and challenging vocabulary. The information is presented in a creative manner with text that is easy to read. The use of images, color, and other media is imaginative and adds to the presentation of the information.

---

2 Points—All of the content elements are included. There are one or two errors in grammar and punctuation. The writing is easy to read with some variation of sentence structures and appropriate grade-level vocabulary. The information is presented clearly with text that is easy to read. The use of images, colors, and other media do not detract from the presentation of the information.

---

1 Point—Some of the content elements are not included or are inaccurate. There are several errors in grammar and punctuation. The writing is difficult to read in some parts with little variation in sentence structure and vocabulary is below grade level. Some of the information is difficult to view and/or text may be difficult to read. The use of images, colors, and other media may detract from the presentation of the information in some instances.

---

0 Points—Several of the required content elements are not included or are inaccurate. There are many errors in grammar and punctuation. The writing is very difficult to read throughout with little or no variation in sentence structure and below grade-level vocabulary. The information is difficult to view and text is difficult to read. The use of images, colors, and other media consistently detract from the presentation of the information.

Figure 7.11
Holistic rubric for multimedia project.

holistic rubric
a type of assessment rubric in which descriptors touch on each area of instruction/learning without breaking the areas down into separate rating scales per category

rubric for a student history presentation may include categories about accuracy of information, proper grammar and spelling, and writing style, as well as elements of design. A **holistic rubric** may have descriptors that touch on each of these elements, but it does not break them down into separate rating scales per category (see Figure 7.11).

Rubrics have become popular due to their valuable pedagogical aspects. Rubrics can help you determine the activities and resources needed in your instruction. Since rubrics define different degrees of quality of products and performances, they are likely to delineate the critical skills and knowledge necessary for mastery. For example, a rubric that defines excellence regarding the appropriate citation of Internet resources requires your students to 1) find and evaluate appropriate web-based resources and then to 2) cite them according to an accepted standard. If they've never done this before, your rubric reminds you to provide them with this knowledge before they can successfully meet the required criteria, but not all students are familiar with rubrics and some may need guidance on how to use them at first.

Another benefit of rubrics can be achieved when they are jointly developed with students. Although this does take some time and you may not choose this approach each time you create a rubric, the process helps students develop skills in determining what constitutes best performance. Providing students with examples of differences in quality of performance or products can help them grasp the differences between various degrees of acceptable performance—for example, a 3-point and a 4-point performance. Students can then apply this understanding when creating their own products or performances.

Rubrics also provide a mechanism for providing detailed feedback to students (Andrade, 2005). Underlining or circling critical elements in the descriptors in a rubric can be much quicker than generating detailed feedback for every student. In addition, they set expectations at the beginning of your lesson so students can better set their own goals for performance. They can support formative self-assessment and peer assessment when students use them to determine how well they're doing by comparing their work to the descriptors in the rubric. A descriptor for exemplary performance that notes that "there are no spelling errors" when compared to a descriptor that states "there are two or three misspelled words" gives the students a real measure for determining excellence. However, Shepard (2000) also cautions that simply providing explicit criteria may not truly promote student learning if students manage to mechanically address the criteria without actually developing the relevant skills or knowledge. She suggests that students be allowed to use rubrics for self-assessment as a way to understand what the criteria mean, not just to apply them mechanically.

Rubrics can be created using commonly available software applications. There are also websites that not only allow you to enter your descriptors to automatically generate a rubric, but also provide rubric examples and templates you can use for guidance. The popular Rubistar website by ALTEC at the University of Kansas allows you to quickly create, customize, and save a rubric. If you are just learning to create rubrics, the Rubistar engine can even suggest descriptors for each level of your rubric for a range of common teaching models, such as the 6+1 Trait Writing Model, or even for specific skills, such as the use of manipulatives or the explanation of mathematical concepts. In addition to using this and similar web-based rubric generators, you may want to collaborate with other teachers in your school or district to develop rubrics based on your state's content standards. Joint development and use can help to improve the validity and reliability of your assessments and rubrics. Rubric templates, examples, and actual rubrics matched to lesson and unit plans can be stored digitally on shared directories or within lesson-planning software.

Recording and Reporting Student Outcomes

Once you have scored your assessments, you typically need to report the results to a variety of other stakeholders, not only the students but also to parents and school administrators. Maybe you still own a few handwritten report cards, perhaps from your earliest years of school. These are artifacts of a bygone era, as illustrated by *Stories from Practice—Using a Digital Gradebook*. Digital gradebooks and student information systems (SIS) not only save teachers hours of time from having to provide handwritten summative reports at the end of a grading period, but also make it easier to generate early reports to inform parents of student success as well as poor performances. Standalone gradebook software may allow you to print progress reports for an entire class in a few minutes, whereas online gradebooks can provide reports on demand—even for parents and students. Many learning management systems also include an online gradebook, which can support frequent and consistent communication between home and school, often through secure e-mail or other messaging tools. The greatest boon is the early identification and reporting of student difficulties that can lead to identifying helpful interventions before the problems become insurmountable.

Digital gradebooks can provide confirmation of trends in student performance early in the instructional process (see Figure 7.12). Although you will undoubtedly have some indication that certain students are having difficulties based on their daily performances and participation, some digital gradebooks provide visual cues and organizational features to quickly and easily identify low-performing students with the simple click of a button. Graphing features are common in many digital gradebooks, and student performances can often be visually represented in easy-to-read, colorful line or bar graphs. You can use these features to check the performances of individuals or groups of students over time, or to compare performances across groups. You

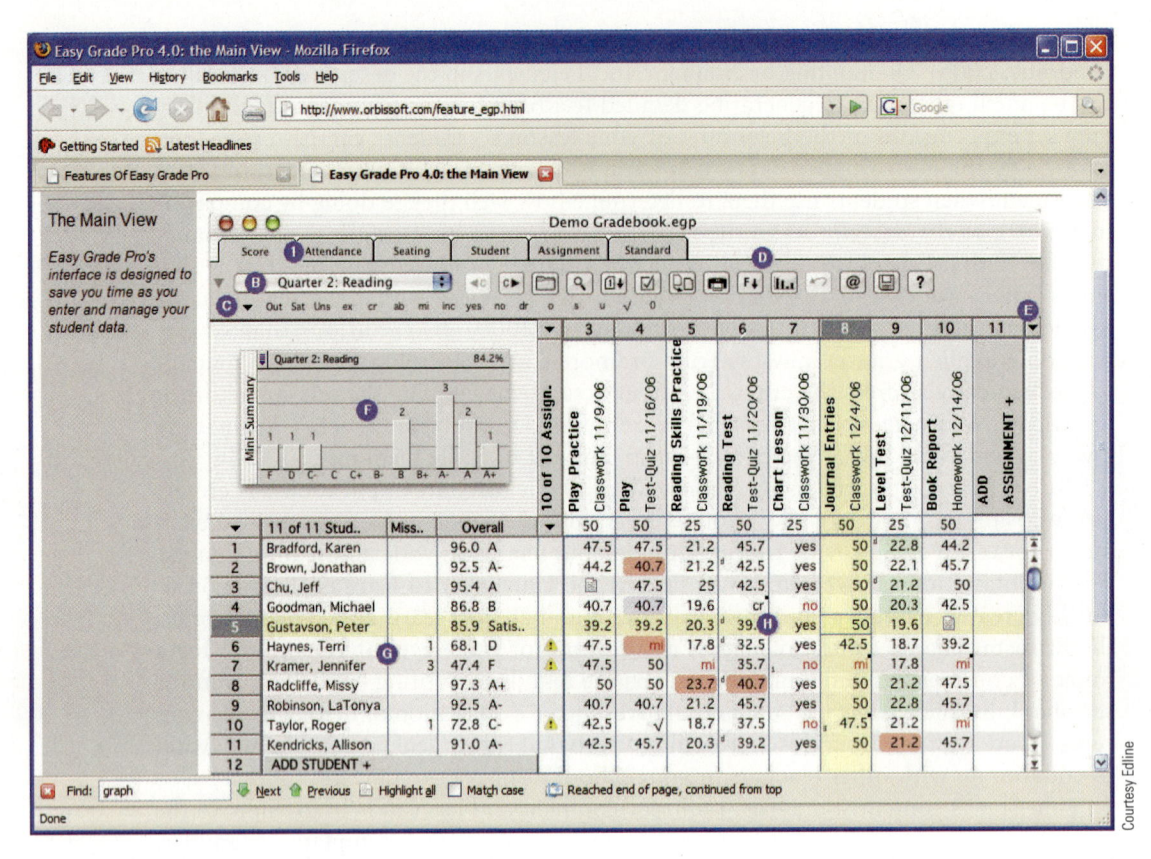

Figure 7.12
Electronic gradebooks typically include graphical analysis tools that can illustrate trends in student performance.

may want to track select groups of students, such as students formally designated as "at-risk." Networked gradebooks may allow you and your colleagues, such as a grade-level team, to track the progress of an individual student or groups of students across multiple classes using real-time data. Try doing *that* with paper gradebooks!

Ongoing and final grade averages are easily calculated using digital gradebooks and are often available to students and parents throughout the grading period. Different types of grades, such as weighted grades or grades for multipart assessments, are easily included and assigned appropriate percentages without the need for a calculator. Using predetermined formulas, student grades in a class will always be calculated the same way, reducing the possibility of error. As long as you set up the weights and averaging criteria correctly, you have little chance of incorrectly reporting student grades.

Digital gradebooks and online SIS can often store and report more than grades. They can help record student attendance. They can tie into learning management systems that present content online and present longitudinal data about student performance as well as identify specific student needs. They can link to cafeteria and health records. They can indicate class and transportation schedules, such as the appropriate buses students should ride. Teachers and staff throughout the building can access some SIS, sometimes through wireless devices. Some may even allow you to include a picture of each student. All of these data are important for understanding more clearly how and why your students perform the way they do.

If your school or district has not adopted a networked digital gradebook or SIS, you can still use digital technologies to record a great deal of data. Digital collections of student performance, attendance, and related data can be as simple as keeping records in a directory (folder) on a file server. Even

TEACHSOURCE VIDEO

Go to the Education CourseMate website and view the video, *Teacher Perspectives: Reporting Student Information Digitally*. Consider the benefits of using digital gradebooks and web-based student information systems to report student information to students and parents.

1. Do you have concerns about using digital reporting?
2. What benefits do these technologies provide? For the teacher? For students? For parents?

STORIES from Practice

Using a Digital Gradebook

I had the pleasure of visiting a local middle school to interview teachers and the principal. This middle school—a National Blue Ribbon School as designated by the U.S. Department of Education—is known for its innovative and exceptional use of technology. The school incorporates a web-based gradebook and reporting software that allows teachers to post student assignments and grades as well as communicate with parents online. When asked how this technology had affected her practice, one veteran teacher half-jokingly replied that she had been brought into the technology world "kicking and screaming" and that she would only give up her paper-based gradebook "over my dead body." However, she then went on to elaborate that despite her original reluctance to use the online gradebook, she couldn't imagine teaching without it now. It had helped to break down communication barriers between her and the parents, many of whom did not have the opportunity to visit the classroom as often as parents did when she began her career. To her, it had "brought the parents into the classroom." Now she routinely uses the system not only to post final grades but also to inform parents of upcoming assignments and to prompt greater home involvement when students need extra help or encouragement with an assignment. The only negative feedback, joked the principal, had come from the students who groaned that their parents now knew "what they did in school" every day and were able to ensure schoolwork was completed and supported at home.

The gradebook program allows teachers to analyze and chart student performance individually, by group, or by class, and to send confidential messages to parents with real-time grade data via e-mail. These data reports allow teachers to quickly determine whether they need to reteach content to the entire class, a group, or an individual. Some of the teachers in the school described how they post helpful web resources and even their class lecture notes or presentations on the website so that both parents and students can use it to support or supplement instruction outside of class. The veteran teacher reported that the parent of one of her students routinely downloaded her classroom presentations at work and that her whole office would look forward to reviewing them. Not only does she think that this practice provides great public relations for the school, but "it's like that parent's in the classroom getting the same lesson her child did that day."

Source: John Ross.

APPLY to Practice

Reporting to Stakeholders

1. Investigate common features of digital gradebooks or student information systems (SIS). You can do this by investigating product websites, reviewing product descriptions in journals and magazines, visiting a local school that utilizes one, or attending an educational conference and viewing vendor demonstrations. You may even consider asking for a demonstration for you and others in your class from a product representative. It may be best to divide and conquer by having teams or groups of students investigate different products and share their information.
2. As you review various systems, consider the following questions:
   - What technology skills, required to operate the system, are you confident with and which ones would require practice or training?
   - What kinds of data are collected? Can you include standards or learning goals and student progress toward those standards?
   - What kind of progress reports can be created for sharing with students in class or with parents, such as in a parent conference?
   - How is two-way communication supported between you and stakeholder groups? Does it provide options for families with limited Internet access or for exporting data in different formats?
3. Compare and discuss your findings with other members of your class.

stand-alone (as opposed to networked) digital gradebooks often include the opportunity to record student attendance and to create anecdotal notes. Records such as these can be compared to other compilations of student data that may be stored in different offices throughout the school. A variety of data are sometimes required to fully understand student performance; new digital technologies often provide a means for you to develop a better understanding of your students and their learning needs.

Data-Based Decision-Making

Educators have become highly focused on the use of data to make decisions about the effectiveness of resources, instructional methods, programs, and even schools and those who work in them. This increasing reliance on data for accountability blossomed through the standards movement at the end of the last century and took a giant leap forward with the passage of the *No Child Left Behind Act* (Pub. L. No. 107-110). This influential legislation initiated the development of high-stakes assessments in additional grades (grades 3-8) and tied funding and accreditation to student performance on those assessments. The legal and financial implications of requiring continued improvement of *all* students highlighted the need for educators to better understand, and have access to, data to support instructional decisions.

A few years ago, data collection and analysis in the classroom were limited to tracking attendance and grading students' progress. Although teachers have always collected data through formal and informal assessments, you are entering the teaching profession when there is a greater call for more data collection and more sophisticated analyses of that data. One of the tremendous benefits that networked technologies have brought to the classroom teacher is having easy and immediate access to the many types of student data that once were found only in paper-based records stored in disparate locations across the school and district. Digital technologies provide powerful tools that simplify analyzing and reporting that data. Digital tools also allow you to make connections among state-mandated performance standards, lesson plans, and your actual instruction. Greater access to a wide variety of student data provides more opportunities for you to make better-informed decisions about your instruction than was possible for generations of teachers before you.

Review Performance Data

All teachers should familiarize themselves with the past performance data of their incoming students. Except for very young students, you will have access to student data from external assessments such as end-of-course exams, as well as classroom grades, attendance records, behavior and discipline reports, and a variety of diagnostic data for a range of skill and knowledge assessments that may have been created by the school, district, or other entities.

It is easiest to use past performance data if they are available digitally, as more and more student records are, but they should be used even if available only on paper. Several districts and states are developing online access to student performance data from state-administered assessments. These websites often allow teachers access to all state-administered performance data. These data can be displayed for individuals or groups of students. Longitudinal reports can show student performance trends over time. Comparisons across content areas may identify weaknesses in one area that are impacting performances in another, such as when limited language proficiencies compound students' efforts to understand science or social studies texts that are above their reading levels. These same data, stripped of student identifiers, can also be reported to parents, community members, and policy makers at the local and national levels through the generation of school report cards (see Figure 7.13).

Assessment and Evaluation 187

NCLB Data for School Year 2011-2012

MOUNTAIN VIEW HIGH SCHOOL - Need Improvement
MONONGAHELA COUNTY

Group	Number Enrolled for FAY	Number Enrolled on Test Week	Number Tested	Participation Rate	Percent Proficient	Met Part. Rate Standard	Met Assessment Standard	Met Subgroup Standard
Mathematics								
All	305	326	313	96.01	71.09	Yes	Yes	✓
White	268	283	274	96.81	69.81	Yes	Yes	✓
Black	17	21	20	95.23	58.82	NA	NA	NA
Hispanic	*	*	*	*	*	*	*	*
Asian	10	10	9	90.00	100.00	NA	NA	NA
Indian	*	*	*	*	*	*	*	*
Multi-Racial	*	*	*	*	*	*	*	*
Pacific Islander	*	*	*	*	*	*	*	*
Spec. Ed.	27	30	27	90.00	18.51	NA	NA	NA
Low SES	63	72	68	94.44	50.00	By Average	Yes	✓
LEP	7	10	9	90.00	66.66	NA	NA	NA
Reading/Language Arts								
All	305	326	314	96.31	59.60	Yes	Yes	✓
White	268	283	276	97.52	58.80	Yes	Yes	✓
Black	17	21	20	95.23	35.29	NA	NA	NA
Hispanic	*	*	*	*	*	*	*	*
Asian	10	10	8	80.00	100.00	NA	NA	NA
Indian	*	*	*	*	*	*	*	*
Multi-Racial	*	*	*	*	*	*	*	*
Pacific Islander	*	*	*	*	*	*	*	*
Spec. Ed.	27	30	27	90.00	3.70	NA	NA	NA
Low SES	63	72	69	95.83	39.68	Yes	Confidence Interval	✓
LEP	7	10	9	90.00	50.00	NA	NA	NA

Needs to Improve
Graduation Rate = 69.7

West Virginia Department of Education

Figure 7.13
Online school report cards are a common method for communicating school data to educators, parents, and the general community.

Use Data to Improve Instruction

Systematic reflection on student data can help you set and revise goals for student learning, monitor the effectiveness of learning activities, and then select and revise instructional strategies. It can also help you determine the effectiveness of your technology choices. If students performed poorly on an assessment, is it because they did not understand the concept? Or maybe they couldn't operate the technology? How did the learning activities you selected impact the performance of your students on your assessments? What changes might you make in the future? Over time, the data you collect from a variety of assessments can help you monitor the effectiveness of a lesson and help you both hone your teaching skills and improve the activities you use in your classroom. Digital technologies have become invaluable for collecting, analyzing, and reporting that data and for helping teachers to better evaluate the effectiveness of their lessons and determine areas of strength and need.

In effect, this chapter brings full circle the concept of the GAME plan for lesson planning. As mentioned before, instruction and assessment are intertwined and together comprise the actions you take in helping your students reach their learning goals. Assessments also provide you opportunities to monitor and evaluate student learning and your own instructional choices. Table 7.1 uses the GAME plan to summarize some

Table 7.1 Data-Based Decision-Making GAME Plan

Set Learning Goals
- What content standards must I cover?
- What prerequisite skills and knowledge do my students possess?
- What skills and knowledge do they need to gain?
- How will my students demonstrate new skills and knowledge?
- Do my students have the required technology skills to use the tools and resources I've selected?

Take Action
- What activities best support the cognitive level of my students?
- What learning preferences do my students have?
- What tools and resources should I use to engage my students in learning the content standards?
- How can I ensure optimal motivation for learning?

Monitoring
- Are my students making adequate progress?
- What misunderstandings do they have?
- Are the activities helping students master their learning goals?
- Are the tools and resources promoting student learning?
- What changes to the learning activities should I make?
- Which students need enrichment materials or activities?
- Which students require supplemental materials or activities?

Evaluating and Extending
- Did my students reach their learning goals?
- Did my students reach their academic potential?
- Were there any unexpected levels of student performance?
- Did the activities support or interfere with student learning?
- Did the tools and resources support or interfere with student learning?
- What changes should I make to my approach before I use these activities and tools again?

of the questions you should consider at each step in your lesson planning and delivery. These questions can also help you determine appropriate technologies to use during instruction and assessment. As you reflect on the questions in Table 7.1, the answer to these questions will always include "It depends on what my students need." So, before you can answer these questions, you will need to collect, analyze, and reflect on the appropriate data.

Chapter Summary

This chapter has emphasized the critical role of assessment and monitoring student data in developing authentic learning experiences. Assessment is more than assigning grades; it serves a crucial role in monitoring and evaluating the academic progress of your students. Assessments should be woven throughout instruction to serve many purposes and can take many forms. Just as you will vary your instruction and select multiple methods for presenting your instruction, you will draw upon multiple assessment formats and tools to support them. Assessment data can also help you determine the effectiveness of your own instructional choices including the selection of technology-based resources. As a teacher it is important to know whether *how* you teach, with or without digital technology, is effective in helping students learn the intended content.

In the next chapter, we turn our attention to facilitating the effective use of technology systems through the physical arrangement of technology resources and their safe and healthy use. We'll also discuss hardware and software maintenance techniques, including techniques to identify and solve common hardware and software problems.

Web Resources and Activities

Visit the Education CourseMate website to

- explore different technologies to support assessments, such as online quiz generators, personal response systems, and other assessment tools;
- review examples of digital portfolios used for assessment and consider how you might incorporate some of these models for student assessment;
- review resources to help you create rubrics for use in your classroom; and
- explore digital gradebooks, learning management systems, and student information systems.

YOUR PORTFOLIO

To begin to demonstrate competency in ISTE NETS-T Standard 2.d, return to the lesson activities you began in earlier chapters and add your assessment strategies.

1. Develop assessments and scoring guidelines based on the lesson plan, using technology as appropriate.
2. Make sure your assessments are clearly connected to the content and technology standards addressed by your lesson as well as the activities contained within the lesson.

References

Andrade, H. G. (2005). Teaching with rubrics: The good, the bad, and the ugly. *College Teaching, 53*(1), 27–30.

Assessment Reform Group. (1999). *Assessment for learning: Beyond the black box.* Cambridge, UK: University of Cambridge School of Education.

Bennett, R. E. (1998). *Reinventing assessment: Speculations on the future of large-scale educational testing.* Princeton, NJ: Educational Testing Service (ETS).

Brookhart, S. M. (1999). The art and science of classroom assessment: The missing part of pedagogy. *ASHE-ERIC Higher Education Report, 27*(1). Washington, DC: The George Washington University, Graduate School of Education and Human Development.

Butler, D. H., & Winne, P. H. (1995). Feedback and self-regulated learning: A theoretical synthesis. *Review of Educational Research, 65*(3), 245–281.

Chun, M. (2010). Taking teaching to (performance) task: Linking pedagogical and assessment practices. *Change, 42*(2), 22–29.

Heritage, M. (2010). *Formative assessment. Making it happen in the classroom.* Thousand Oaks, CA: Corwin.

McCain, T. (2005). *Teaching for tomorrow. Teaching content and problem-solving skills.* Thousand Oaks, CA: Corwin.

Pub. L. No. 107-110. (No Child Left Behind Act of 2001).

Shepard, L. A. (2000). *The role of classroom assessment in teaching and learning. CSE Technical Report 517.* Los Angeles: Center for the Study of Evaluation, Standards, and Student Testing (CRESST).

Svinicki, M. D. (2004). Authentic assessment: Testing in reality. *New Directions for Teaching and Learning, 2004*(100), 23–39.

Wiggins, G. (1998). *Educative assessment: Designing assessments to inform and improve student performance.* San Francisco: Jossey-Bass.

Wiggins, G., & McTighe, J. (2006). *Understanding by design. Expanded 2nd edition.* Alexandria, VA: Association for Supervision and Curriculum Development.

8

Demonstrating Fluent Use of Technology

OUTCOMES

In this chapter, you will learn to

- Model and facilitate **safe and healthy use** of technology tools; and
- Maintain **hardware and software systems**, including troubleshooting routine problems as they arise.

ISTE Standards Addressed in Chapter 8

NETS-T 3. Model Digital-Age Work and Learning

Teachers exhibit knowledge, skills, and work processes representative of an innovative professional in a global and digital society. Teachers:

a. demonstrate fluency in technology systems and the transfer of current knowledge to new technologies and situations.

Standard 3.a requires you to "demonstrate fluency in technology systems and the transfer of current knowledge to new technologies and situations." Let's explore what that means. A *system* is a set of interrelated parts that work toward a common purpose. For example, a school system is a set of interrelated parts (e.g., facilities, administrators, teachers) that have a common purpose: educating students. At their most basic, systems have inputs, perform processes, and produce outputs. A school system accepts students as "inputs," engages in certain processes to educate them, and, hopefully, "outputs" students as more knowledgeable and productive members of society. Systems use resources, such as the teachers and funds, to complete their processes. But they also operate under certain

system
a set of interrelated parts that work toward a common purpose

191

constraints. For example, the work of a school system can be constrained by limited funding or limited numbers of qualified teachers. Managing resources is a key part of keeping a system running smoothly. Systems also receive feedback from the environment as to how well they are working. They periodically encounter problems that, if not addressed, will cause the entire system to bog down or fall apart. Knowing how to maintain a system and troubleshoot problems is critical to ensuring that the system continues to achieve its goals.

Different technologies, including computers, typically operate as a system. Just like a school system, technology systems have inputs, perform processes, and produce outputs. They use resources and react to feedback from the environment, requiring routine maintenance and sometimes repair. While your cell phone, a calculator, and other educational technologies can also be considered systems, let's consider the example of a computer system. A computer system can have many purposes, but its basic purpose is to manipulate digital data. The goal you have for that data determines your purpose for using the computer system. For example, you may use the computer to develop a lesson plan, create a short video clip to use in class, or communicate with a parent via e-mail. You typically input data by using a keyboard and mouse or any number of other input devices, such as a trackball or stylus on a touch screen. Sometimes you'll input data from other systems such as scanners, cameras, and memory devices. The computer will process the data you've put in, whether creating your lesson plan document, formatting the video clip so you can present it in class, or generating that message you want to send to the parent. And when you've completed your input, you can output the data in your desired format, perhaps by printing your lesson plan, projecting the video to a screen or whiteboard, or sending that e-mail message.

As you're using the computer system, it's important that you provide it with the appropriate resources and that you monitor feedback from the environment for it to operate successfully. In the above examples, some of the resources you'll need are toner and paper for printing the document, enough memory to manipulate large video files, and a connection to the Internet to send e-mail. Feedback from the environment you are working in might include messages from your lesson plan program that remind you to indicate relevant standards and appropriate assessments, memory errors when editing your video file, or aural and visual confirmation that your e-mail has been sent successfully.

So when you demonstrate fluency in technology systems, you are simply demonstrating the ability to use a technology system to meet a goal, manage the system's resources, maintain operations, and troubleshoot problems when they occur. Throughout this book, we have focused on planning and management strategies that support students during their technology-based learning experiences. In this chapter, we will discuss how you can facilitate effective use of technology systems through the physical arrangement of technology resources and their safe and healthy use. (Note: in this chapter we talk about the safe use of technology in terms of *physical* safety; in Chapter 10 we talk about *ethical and legal* safety or how students access and use the content available through technology.) We'll also discuss hardware and software maintenance, including techniques to identify and solve common hardware and software problems.

Safe and Healthy Use of Technology Systems in Your Classroom

When the computer revolution started in schools, large cumbersome machines—ironically referred to as "personal computers" or "microcomputers"—were often relegated to the realm of computer labs where they could exist on desks or tables designed to accommodate them with ready access to electricity and, eventually, the Internet. But as the revolution continued, a new development came about. Computers became more common in classrooms.

It seems logical that these powerful resources would be located as close as possible to where learning occurred, but this posed several problems. When boxes of computers started showing up, literally overnight, in classrooms across the nation, teachers had to find space for them—and decide how to use them. The rise in use of educational technology forced many school districts to insert bulky hardware, such as desktop computers, into spaces that were not designed for them. In the past, classrooms typically were designed as rectangular spaces with the teaching area focused on chalkboards across one wall. Although there were educational initiatives such as "open classrooms" with movable partitions, pods, and mobile or cyclical learning stations, most classrooms were built to support the most prevalent form of instruction, the lecture. Desks in rows were common, and in many schools, the number of desks in each classroom got larger as student to-teacher ratios increased. Electrical outlets were scarce, and classroom phones were almost nonexistent. It's a good thing those days are over.

But are they? School construction is an expensive endeavor, and many districts must still make do with older buildings not designed to support digital technologies (see Figure 8.1). The following tips will help you protect both your students and technology resources:

- Older desktop computers that still populate many labs and classrooms can require more than 400 watts of electrical power, so be aware of the load on your electrical circuits. If you don't have enough electrical outlets for the number of computers in your room, new outlets should be installed by a licensed electrician rather than continually adding cords and adapters that pose a safety threat to your equipment and your students. If necessary for short-term use, extension cords should be of sufficient capacity to support the technologies you attach to them, but they can be a tripping hazard so work with your principal for a long-term solution.
- Dust is the enemy of the computer, so if you still have a chalkboard in your room, ask to have it covered with an inexpensive laminate that allows you to

Figure 8.1
Many classrooms were not designed to support digital technologies. In this classroom, note the exposed cables and cords, as well as the student working at a table not intended for computer use.

use dry-erase markers and enables it to double as a projection screen. Additional measures that can prevent dust from infiltrating the technology in your room include the use of air filters on your classroom circulation system (usually installed by maintenance personnel), dust covers for equipment, and use of a hand-washing routine.

- As for liquids, you should try to avoid the combination of keyboards or laptops and coffee, soft drinks, water—any liquids, basically. The two don't mix well, and even just a tiny spill on a keyboard or laptop can make it inoperable. Many schools have strict "no liquid" policies in computer labs and around digital technologies in classrooms.
- Air circulation is also important. Computers, even laptops and other mobile devices, and their peripherals can generate a good deal of heat and require adequate ventilation. Unfortunately, the heat generated by computers, and especially older CRT (cathode ray tube) monitors, will also affect the need for air conditioning. Flat-screen displays and laptops generate less heat and use less electricity, with laptops using the least amount of energy and creating the least amount of ambient heat in a room.

Fortunately, newer schools can be designed with more current technologies in mind, and state-of-the-art hardware continues to get smaller, lighter, and more portable and powerful. Wireless technologies have enabled Internet access to classrooms that would have been prohibitively expensive to connect by physical cables. Even computers in different buildings can be connected to the Internet quickly and relatively inexpensively with wireless technologies. A cart full of wireless laptops or tablets can provide every student in your classroom with a computing device with no wires necessary for power or an Internet connection (see Figure 8.2).

Managing Use of Technology in Your Classroom

As a teacher, you will encounter a wide variety of classroom technology resources throughout your career. Although the U.S. Department of Education (Gray, Thomas & Lewis, 2010) reported that on average, there is one instructional computer with

Figure 8.2
Wireless laptops or tablets can be shared among several classrooms and moved from one room to the next using carts.

Internet access available to every 1.7 students across the nation, some schools have more than that; others have fewer. Schools will vary in the type and number of computers and other digital technologies available. They will also differ in how they make those resources available to teachers. You may find yourself in a school with all the technology resources you desire. But it's also possible that you'll find yourself in a school where technology is scarce and outdated. Sometimes, students have better resources at home than at school; other times, the only access students have is at school.

For many years, schools tried to keep personal communications technologies out of the schools. Cell phones were banned, and personal computing devices were frowned upon. But not now; more and more schools are embracing a "bring your own device" (BYOD) program where students are encouraged to bring their own laptops, smartphones, netbooks, tablets, and other mobile computing devices to class (see *Tech Tools and Tips—Learning from BYOD Initiatives* in this chapter).

This shift is made possible by two major trends:

1. The prevalence of Internet-based applications means that identical software no longer needs to be loaded on all computers.
2. Cloud-based storage means that students can access files anywhere they have an Internet connection.

With BYOD programs, students are provided with access to the school's wireless network using their own devices. This means that the use of these devices can be monitored through a school's network security features, such as filtering of inappropriate content. But BYOD programs are not without potential problems. Problematic student behavior such as cheating, plagiarizing, access to inappropriate websites, cyberbullying, student safety and privacy, and a range of other ethical problems (see Chapter 10) are of potential concern. At a minimum, districts that encourage students to bring their own devices into the classroom must expand their acceptable use policies to encompass these issues, and you need to be diligent in monitoring their use in the classroom, as with any technology.

Regardless of the shape and size of your classroom, or the type of technology you have available, there are some factors you should consider when you decide when and where to use technology in order to protect these expensive resources and reduce the possibility of student injury. Keep in mind that computer monitors and other digital devices can be distracting to students working elsewhere in the room. It may be tempting to create a cubicle with bookshelves and other furniture; however, make sure you can monitor your students' technology use. Large monitors can hide students' faces and work. Many teachers find it best to line up computers against a wall so that the monitors are facing into the room. Other students' chairs can be arranged in such a way that their backs are to the computers or other digital devices. This arrangement would allow you to supervise what is on the students' monitors with ease. Even though you may have an acceptable use policy in place (see Chapter 10), it's important to monitor student activity while using technology resources to make sure they are focused on the learning task, as well as to ensure they are using appropriate applications and web resources. A classroom full of laptops or tablet computers can make monitoring a little more difficult than five desktop computers across one wall, but by circulating around the room, you still should be able to monitor appropriate use.

Also consider the movement of students within the classroom. You and your students should have enough room to circulate throughout the room without encountering obstacles such as loose cords, cables, raised floor receptacles, and temporary power supplies, such as power poles that provide access to electricity in the middle of the room. Make sure that wires and cables are out of the way of foot traffic and don't present a hazard to either the technology or the students. Provide adequate table space for the students' materials. If students will work in groups, make sure there is enough space for several chairs.

TECH TOOLS & TIPS

Monitoring Student Devices

Whether working in a classroom or lab, using computers with easily visible monitors or small hand-held devices, it will probably be easier to solicit students' cooperation if you get them involved and help them understand your expectations. Be proactive in your strategies and include your students, whenever possible, to let them know steps you might have to take to monitor their technology use. Consider incorporating some of the following tips:

1 Design classroom rules together. Ask your students to list appropriate uses of technology, no matter what kind of device they're using. Work with them to determine classrooms rules, discussing and perhaps providing input on consequences.

2 Sponsor a technology "petting zoo." If your school is planning a BYOD (bring your own device) initiative in which the students will use several different kinds of devices, spend some time with technology experts exploring many different types of devices you are likely to come across in your classroom. Put the devices through their paces by replicating common activities in your instruction and determine how students will, and possibly should not, use them. Don't forget that some of the expert users will be your own students, so determine how they might be involved.

3 It may be theirs, but it's your classroom. Allowing students to use a personal device is a privilege, not a right. Students and parents need to understand that personal devices are only to be used for schoolwork on campus. Students and parents should understand the consequences of inappropriate use, which may range from simply turning the device off to withdrawing permission to use the device any longer in school.

4 Use the technology. Students should know that their technology use is likely to be tracked, definitely if they're accessing the school network, and that you may be required to access their device to ensure they're using it correctly. Let them—and their parents—know that you may be required to access Internet histories in browsers, read texting threads, and view recent applications. Check with your principal or technology specialist to determine what you are allowed to access on student devices to be sure you are following stated guidelines.

5 Management software isn't just for labs. Some computer labs include management software that allows you to control all of the student computers in the room. You may be able to display all or just a select number of student monitors, project them on a screen, or even lock down computers. This type of software can be installed on other computers, as well, not just in a lab, so if you have access to it in your school, learn the functionality so you can not only promote appropriate use but also incorporate some of this functionality into your instruction.

© Cengage Learning 2014

Technology-Related Health Practices

As you arrange the computers in your classroom, take care to make the arrangement as ergonomically comfortable as possible in order to reduce the physical strain that extensive computer use may cause. **Ergonomics** refers to the study and development of furniture, tools, and systems that promote productivity in a safe and healthy way. You may be familiar with desks designed for computer use that have lowered trays for keyboards, padded supports for wrists, and mouse support trays. These are designed to reduce the strain on our bodies when we use the equipment. Ergonomics relates specifically to designing work and learning environments that support the individual.

Computer equipment should be placed on ergonomically correct furniture. You should keep in mind that students come in all shapes and sizes, so what is ergonomically appropriate for one may not be appropriate for all. Chairs can be ergonomically designed to support computer work. Adjustable chairs are optimal, but if unavailable, try to include chairs of various sizes to match the needs of your students. The National Institutes of Health (2005) offers helpful information about setting up a computer workstation following ergonomic guidelines. Use the *Tech Tools and Tips—Ergonomic Checklist* to set up workstations that minimize strain and fatigue for you and your students. Keep the checklist posted near areas where computer work occurs in your classroom.

ergonomics
the study and development of furniture, tools, and systems that promote safe and healthy use

TECH TOOLS & TIPS

Ergonomic Checklist

Monitor Placement

As you begin any computer project, take a minute to make sure

- The monitor is right in front of you about arm's length away with the top of the monitor about eye level.
- The monitor is tilted back a little (about 10 to 20 degrees).
- The screen is clean.
- The brightness and contrast settings are acceptable.
- There's no glare on the screen.

Chair Adjustment

While seated in your chair,

- Make sure that you don't stay in the same position all the time.
- Do not hunch over, but sit back at an angle of 90 degrees or greater. You should be sitting so that your ankles, knees, and hips are at 90°. Your thighs should be parallel to the floor.
- Your feet should be flat on the floor or be supported. Consider creating a footrest by incorporating phone books, crates, or other materials.
- Adjust the backrest, if available, so that it supports the natural inward curvature of your lower back. If necessary, use a slightly inflated beach ball or pillow to provide back support.
- Armrests, if available, should be placed so your shoulders relax naturally and your elbows and lower arms rest lightly on them.

Desk Height

Choose a desk where

- The working height of the desk is approximately at the height of your elbows while seated.
- The keyboard is approximately 1 to 2 inches above your thighs.
- The area underneath your desk is clean and uncluttered so you can comfortably stretch your legs.
- A document holder, if used, is placed at approximately the same height as the monitor and at the same distance from the eyes to prevent frequent eye shifts between the screen and reference materials.

Keyboard and Mouse Placement

Adjust your keyboard and mouse so that

- Your shoulders can relax and your arms can rest comfortably at your sides.
- The keyboard is close to you. The mouse is next to the keyboard at the same height.
- Your forearms are parallel to the floor. You should not have to reach up for the keyboard or mouse.
- You don't have to stretch or change the height of your hands to reach the keyboard or mouse.
- If necessary, use the built-in legs found on the bottom of most keyboards to angle the keyboard. A three-ring binder laid on its side also can make a nice keyboard stand. Place a piece of shelf liner on the notebook to help prevent the keyboard from slipping.
- A rolled hand towel or a commercially purchased wrist rest placed in front of the keyboard can provide wrist support if necessary.
- Do not rest your hand on the mouse when you are not using it. Rest your hands in your lap when not using them.

Source: National Institutes of Health, 2005.

repetitive strain injuries can occur during computer use due to the sensitive nature of the soft tissues, tendons, nerves, and muscles of the hand that are subjected to repeated motions, awkward positions, or force

tendonitis inflammation, irritation, or swelling of the tendons, that connect muscles to bone

carpal tunnel syndrome a repetitive stress injury commonly associated with keyboard use in which the median nerve of the hand becomes compressed at about the location of the wrist

Take care to monitor your own computer use as well as that of your students. Even after taking ergonomic factors into consideration, some **repetitive strain injuries**, such as tendonitis, can occur during computer use due to the sensitive nature of the soft tissues, tendons, nerves, and muscles of the hand that are subjected to repeated motions, awkward positions, or force. **Tendonitis** refers to the inflammation, irritation, or swelling of the tendons, which connect muscles to bone. Another repetitive stress injury commonly associated with keyboard use is **carpal tunnel syndrome,** in which the median nerve of the hand becomes compressed at about the location of the wrist. This can cause numbness, tingling, and pain in the thumb and the side of the hand closest to it. The easiest way to address mild cases of these injuries is to ensure that workstations are ergonomically appropriate, taking special care to make sure that the keyboard is low enough to encourage proper arm and hand placement (see Figure 8.3). Both tendonitis and carpal tunnel syndrome can be treated with braces or glove-like wrist supports that are worn for extended periods. Physical therapy may also be necessary if these injuries become severe. In extreme cases, carpal tunnel syndrome may require surgery.

Different keyboards and input devices (some discussed in Chapter 6 under assistive technology) might be preferable for some of your students, especially if your curriculum requires a good deal of keyboarding. Keyboards that alter the position of the keys to provide a more relaxed presentation matched to natural hand positions can reduce strain for some students as can keyboards with audible clicks when keys are stroked. The click signaling that the key has been activated can prevent some students from pressing down too hard while typing. Trackballs, pen styluses, touch screens, and many other input devices allow options for interfacing with the computer that do not rely on a traditional mouse.

You can also teach your students some simple stretches for the head, neck, and wrists to promote healthy computer use, especially during longer work sessions. The simple stretches presented in Table 8.1 can be done seated or standing.

Computer monitors challenge our eyes in ways that printed text does not and may lead to vision problems (see Table 8.2). Unlike most print, text on a computer screen is not presented in uniform levels of light and dark, but instead, the dots of light (called pixels) that make up the images are brightest in the middle. Unlike the static images on

Figure 8.3
Ergonomically correct workstations should be the approximate height of the elbows when seated.

Table 8.1 Neck, Shoulder, and Wrist Stretches

Side Neck Stretch
1. Tilt your head to one side, moving your ear toward your shoulder.
2. Hold for 15 seconds.
3. Relax.
4. Repeat 3 times on each side.

Diagonal Neck Stretch
1. Turn your head slightly and then look down as if looking in your pocket.
2. Hold for 15 seconds.
3. Relax.
4. Repeat 3 times on each side.

Shoulder Shrug
1. Slowly bring your shoulders up to your ears and hold for approximately 3 seconds.
2. Rotate shoulders back and down.
3. Repeat 10 times.

Wrist Stretch
1. Hold your arm straight out in front of you.
2. Pull your hand backward with the other hand—palm facing front, then pull your hand down—palm facing you.
3. Hold for 20 seconds.
4. Relax.
5. Repeat 3 times each.

Source: National Institutes of Health, 2005.

Table 8.2 Avoiding Vision Problems

To avoid vision problems when using a computer monitor:
- Adjust the lights lower than for regular classroom instruction.
- Minimize glare on your screens by avoiding direct sun or overhead lights, using a glare screen, or paint walls a darker color.
- Adjust the brightness and contrast on your screen.
- Adjust the size of text on your screen. Most text applications and web browsers allow you to change the size of text with a menu command or shortcut.
- Blink more often and stay hydrated to keep your eyes well lubricated. People often blink less when doing computer work. If your classroom is especially dry or if the heating system dries out the air, some people may require eye drops to keep their eyes lubricated.
- Take a break, and if you can, go outside into natural light.
- Do eye exercises (see Table 8.3).

Source: National Institutes of Health, 2005.

---

a page, images on a computer monitor are constantly being redrawn. (If you've ever seen a rolling screen when a monitor is not in sync, you might have noticed this.) The **resolution** (clarity of an image or letter related to the number of dots per square inch) of computer monitors is also much less than printed material—which is also why many graphics prepared for presentation on a computer monitor look very jagged or unfocused when printed. Most people read slower on a computer monitor when compared to text for this reason. Software and web designers often follow the guideline of using sans-serif fonts (fonts without the small curls of ornamentation on the extremities of

resolution
clarity of an image or letter related to the number of dots per square inch in print or pixels per square inch on a monitor

Table 8.3 Eye Exercises

Palming
1. While seated, brace elbows on the desk and close to the desk edge.
2. Let weight fall forward.
3. Cup hands over eyes.
4. Close eyes.
5. Inhale slowly through nose and hold for 4 seconds.
6. Continue deep breathing for 15–30 seconds.

Eye Movements
1. Close eyes.
2. Slowly and gently move eyes up to the ceiling, then slowly down to the floor.
3. Repeat 3 times.
4. Close eyes.
5. Slowly and gently move eyes to the left, then slowly to the right.
6. Repeat 3 times.

Focus Change
1. Hold one finger a few inches away from the eye.
2. Focus on the finger.
3. Slowly move the finger away.
4. Focus far into the distance and then back to the finger.
5. Slowly bring the finger back to within a few inches of the eye.
6. Focus on something more than 8 feet away.
7. Repeat 3 times.

Source: National Institutes of Health, 2005.

---

letters) for display on the monitor to improve visibility of text. Older monitors can be fitted with screens to reduce glare but newer flat panel screens may not need this additional equipment.

Some vision problems, such as **computer vision syndrome**, can occur due to the inability of your eyes to maintain focus on items on the screen. These problems show up in people who use a computer monitor extensively almost every day. If your students complain of constant headaches, loss of focus, blurring, or sore neck and shoulders during computer use, they may be suffering from computer vision syndrome. The treatment for this vision problem is usually a type of prescription glasses designed specifically for computer use. Reading glasses are usually not appropriate as the distance

> **computer vision syndrome**
> discomfort or other vision problems that can result from using a computer screen after a period of time

APPLY to Practice

Lessons for Promoting Safe and Healthy Use of Technology

Design a lesson activity that helps students understand the safe and healthy use of technology but that also addresses a content standard from an area in which you excel. Students can brainstorm ideas or gather information from school-related health and safety tips on the Internet. They can capture images or video that demonstrate safe and healthy use of the technology in your classroom. The result of the activity might be a poster or web page that all students can access to remind them of technology safety.

TECH TOOLS & TIPS

Ten Tips for Safe and Healthy Use of Technology in Your Classroom

1. Model and monitor appropriate technology use every day.
2. Carefully plan for time to set up and put away equipment.
3. Position computer monitors where they can be observed.
4. Keep aisles and pathways clear to avoid tripping and ease movement of carts on wheels.
5. Keep computers cool with sufficient air circulation by keeping work areas clean and uncluttered.
6. Reduce dust by covering equipment and installing air filters where possible.
7. Close laptops and carry them and tablet computers with both hands.
8. Transport heavy equipment, especially large equipment, on carts with wheels, according to the school's safety policy.
9. Put away and lock up equipment when not in use.
10. Report equipment in need of repair in a timely fashion.

© Cengage Learning 2014

from eyes to screen is usually farther than to a book held in one's hands. Glare screens and antireflective coatings can help reduce some vision problems but cannot correct computer vision syndrome. If you or your students are going to work at a monitor regularly for two or more hours, you should consider visiting an optometrist who can prescribe computer glasses, if necessary.

Many states require students to meet technology proficiency standards—just like teachers—and safe and healthy use of technology is often a part of these standards. The *Tech Tools and Tips—Ten Tips for Safe and Healthy Use of Technology in Your Classroom* above presents a list of useful safety tips. You may want to create a similar list with your students as a learning activity to orient them to technology safety as it relates to your class. You can incorporate this activity while teaching students how to use a particular piece of software or hardware or even while covering content standards.

APPLY to Practice

Technology Health and Safety Top 10 Tips

Depending on the content area and grade you teach, you may need to develop a modified list of technology tips that supports the safe and healthy use of specific technologies found in your classroom.

1. Design a top ten list for your classroom. Include the content area and grade that you teach. Some complex technologies used at higher grades, such as in a science or manufacturing lab, may require their own top ten lists—or at least a top five list. If you plan to use particular equipment that requires its own list, create a list that you can use in your classroom. Modify the list so that it is relevant and engaging to your students.
2. Review technology safety lists you may find online or from practicing teachers. Do you need additional information to complete your list? What technologies presented in this book or in your class should be included? How can you use different technologies, such as image- or video-editing software, to make this information more compelling to your students?
3. Share your lists with other students in your class. Are their items different from yours? Why? Do you want to modify your list?

For younger students, you may want to consider a "Safety Certificate" they can display or take home to share with their parents. An important aspect of teaching in the 21st century is modeling and facilitating the safe and healthy use of the powerful technologies found in most classrooms.

Maintaining Technology Resources

It would be great if all you had to do was install a piece of hardware or software and then it would operate forever without any problems. Unfortunately, that isn't how things work in the real world. Classroom technologies, like all technology, require routine maintenance. Just as your car runs best with routine tune-ups, so do digital devices. Your primary areas of responsibility will vary, depending on your school's technology configuration and procedures.

Most districts and many schools will have personnel available to set up and troubleshoot equipment. These technology specialists focus on understanding and supporting hardware, software, and networks. Many states also have state or regional service offices that provide some limited technology support to the school districts they oversee. Depending on the size of your school, you may have to share the expertise of a technology support person with other schools in your district or rely solely on remote technology support personnel.

Maintaining computer workstations over a network has become a common method for monitoring, and sometimes repairing, technology from a distance, often resulting in a savings of time and cost. In a networked environment, your district technology personnel can oversee all hardware and software installations, antivirus and antispyware maintenance, and service pack updates from a distance rather than having to visit each computer physically. These workstations on a network, sometimes termed "cloned" or "ghost," typically have identical software configurations, password-protected logins, and networked peripherals, such as printers and file servers. This timesaving method also helps network administrators provide a more secure computing environment for you and your students, but requires that you take steps to ensure that you can continue to access proprietary instructional software. In addition, it necessitates that you and your students appropriately store and back up data files from activities and assessments. A common method for maintaining the security of a network is to routinely return all of the networked computers back to their approved configurations. This sometimes means removing extra programs and old data files.

Technology support personnel are often overburdened. Although businesses strive to reach tech support ratios as low as 1:25 (one tech support person for every 25 computers), the average technician to computer ratio in the school setting is 1:956, according to a recent survey (SchoolDude.com, 2010)! Of course, schools often have other types of support personnel available such as media and technology specialists, technology directors, and, to a much lesser degree, network engineers and help desk personnel. Still, with those low numbers of support personnel, regardless of the capacity of your school or district, a knowledge of both hardware and software maintenance is necessary to keep your computer system running properly, to ensure that your system is working with the most current resources, and to ensure that resources purchased in the past will be usable in the future. It's vital that you understand your responsibilities and role in maintaining technology systems and that you be able to perform basic troubleshooting and routine maintenance tasks.

Solving Routine Problems

Anyone who works with technologies will encounter problems, and computer systems are no exception. It is not a question of *if* you will encounter problems, but simply a matter of *when*. Given that you are going to encounter hardware or software difficulties during your career, how will you deal with them? Will you attempt to address the difficulties yourself, or will you let somebody else do it for you? If you're in a position to let somebody else address all difficulties for you, most of this section will not concern you. But if you don't develop some skills in this area, you can lose valuable instructional time when small problems occur in your classroom or lab. When there are no experts handy, you'll need to take problems into your own hands, so it's important to have a troubleshooting strategy that allows you to investigate the problem and identify and implement a solution. But don't worry; there are basic troubleshooting techniques that are applicable across a wide variety of technical problems.

Our recommended troubleshooting strategy begins with what you should *not* do. Because the problems you encounter may deal with either hardware or software, you should not assume that you know which one is the source of the cause. The problem may be caused by something that is broken, or it may not be. Again, you should not make any assumptions. Also, the problem may, or may not, be something that is your fault. Once again, watch your assumptions. And, finally, the problem may be with your own computer or software, or it may be with your network. One last time, don't jump to conclusions.

A Troubleshooting Model

Now that you know what not to do, let's discuss the steps you should perform when you are troubleshooting. The model we are suggesting involves four major steps: 1) identify the problem, 2) apply a solution, 3) check the results, and 4) repeat as necessary. The steps and sub-steps are described next.

Isolate the Problem. Begin by attempting to identify the problem. When you are troubleshooting difficulties, you don't know what the problem is. Instead, you are confronted with one or more symptoms and, based on the symptoms, you hypothesize what the problem is. This step requires you to act like a detective and pay close attention to any clues your computer system provides.

Attempt to isolate the symptoms. Where do they occur? Under what circumstances? When the problem only occurs when using a single software application, you may need to update or reinstall the application. When the problem occurs when using a single file, it may indicate you don't have enough memory to work with the file, or the file itself or an element in the file, such as a graphic you inserted from a website, may be corrupted or damaged. When the problem occurs globally when using any application, don't forget to check cables and connections. How frequently do the symptoms occur? Check to see if you get the same symptoms on more than one computer—an indication it might be a network configuration problem. Can you make them disappear? If so, how? If you're having problems with a website, try using a different web browser on the same machine or even a different computer. If the symptoms no longer exist, the original browser may not be configured correctly or have the proper plug-ins installed. If the site works on your home computer but not at school, the problem may be related to your network. Look for any hints, messages, or clues.

Of course, you should recognize that many problems are common occurrences, and software and hardware developers have supports to help you solve them. Often the biggest challenge is correctly identifying the symptoms. Sometimes error messages provide suggestions as to why the malfunctions are occurring. Error messages may be numbered or contain key terms that you can look up in a manual or online reference. Manuals accompanying your hardware and software generally also contain troubleshooting sections that offer solutions for many of the symptoms you might identify, regardless of whether they include error messages or not. Don't forget to check the help files online.

Identify the Best Solution. After you have hypothesized what the problem may be, you should identify one or more possible solutions. First, try the tips available in your computer and software manuals or on the manufacturer's website. In addition, user groups and discussion forums can be a good source of information. Go to the product manufacturer's site and look for a discussion group. Using the search function, enter a short phrase that describes your problem, for example "iMovie crashes." If you're lucky, you'll find someone who has solved the problem while working with the same combination of software and hardware as you. If your search of product literature and websites doesn't provide some helpful solutions or if you can't get on the Internet with the computer in question, you may need to call a technician or the product helpline, if there is one. Be aware that some technical support helplines charge for their services if your product is no longer under warranty.

Another source for possible solutions may be right in front of you. Ask your students or colleagues. Students interested in computers may have experienced this very same problem and found ways to solve it. Tell your students the problem you're experiencing and see if you receive any good suggestions. And don't forget to thank your students if they can help you out. Model good problem-solving and collaboration skills with your students, and they'll be more likely to use these same skills later.

Apply a Solution and Check Your Results. Once you've identified possible solutions, try the best one—one at a time! If your solution works, you're done. However, if the applied solutions don't solve the problem you identified, you have incorrectly identified the problem and need to hypothesize another potential solution. However, before applying a new solution, *try to return the entire system to the way it was before you started.* That's the best way to isolate the original problem. If you just keep making changes, one on top of the other, you may compound the original problem. So it's very important to try to put your technology back to the way it was before trying another solution. Then, once that is done, remember to apply relevant solutions one at a time. After each application, check results.

Repeat, if Necessary. You'll need to repeat this process as many times as necessary until a solution is found. If no solution is found after trying all relevant solutions, seek outside assistance. Walking away and seeking support from someone else can also prevent you from inadvertently making the problem worse by bending a pin, breaking a key, or erasing important data from your computer—something many of us have done when frustrated. As noted earlier, troubleshooting handbooks, helplines, discussion forums, and websites are all useful sources of information; however, these sources of support are most effective if you have narrowed the problem significantly. Your discussions will be most productive if you can tell the support technician what you have already done to try to correct it.

There's one last common error that we may all overlook—human error. Anyone who has provided desktop support or who has monitored a computer helpline can tell you dozens of funny stories about people who were convinced their computers were not operating correctly. Very often, the error or malfunction has occurred as a result of the computer doing exactly what it was "told" to do, by the user. That's OK. We've all had our share of human errors. Use the experience to learn more about your device, possibly after taking a deep breath or trying something else for a while.

Hardware Maintenance

Many common problems can be prevented with simple regular maintenance. While some districts forbid teachers from even the simplest repairs, maintenance is a different matter. There are some maintenance tasks you and your students should complete while others will be handled strictly by your school or district technology support personnel. We've broken down the hardware maintenance issues discussed in this section into four distinct areas: routinely servicing current hardware, repairing things that break, replacing those technologies that cannot be repaired, and replacing consumables.

TECH TOOLS & TIPS

Four-Step Troubleshooting Process

1 Isolate the problem. Identify the problem that you are trying to solve as specifically as possible. Identify what happens and when it happens.
- What are the symptoms?
- Where do they occur?
- Under what circumstances do they occur?
- How frequently do they occur?
- Can you make them disappear? If so, how?

2 Identify one or more possible solutions. Examine software manuals, hardware manuals, online support sites, and software discussion forums to locate potential solutions. Talk to your colleagues or students about the problem. If necessary, call the troubleshooting hotline once you have identified your problem.

3 Apply a solution and check results.
a. Select the best solution; then make one logical change at a time.
- If it works—you're done.
- If it doesn't work, *put it back the way it was!*

b. Is there another solution for the proposed problem?

c. If yes, Return to Step 3a—Apply a single, relevant solution, and select another possible solution.

d. If no, make sure things are put back the way they were and return to Step 1. Take a closer look at the problem.

4 Repeat process if necessary. If a solution is not found after trying all relevant possibilities, seek outside assistance.

© Cengage Learning 2014

Routine Servicing

Computer hardware contains electronic and mechanical components. Electronic components have three major enemies: heat, power fluctuations, and liquids. Most computer systems have fans to exhaust the heat that builds up when electronic components operate. Dust and lint limit the effectiveness of fans by covering the components as well as blocking the exhaust vents. At a minimum you should clean the cooling fan vents on a regular basis.

The screens on computer monitors are notorious for collecting dust. How you remove the dust depends on the type of monitor you have, CRT (cathode ray tube—older technology for monitors and televisions) or LCD (liquid crystal display—common in laptops). With a CRT you can moisten a soft cloth with a small amount of diluted isopropyl alcohol, wipe the screen clean with the cloth, and then wipe the screen dry with another soft cloth. LCD screens are more sensitive and require both extra care and an extra soft cloth. Manufacturers recommend gently wiping the dust from the LCD screen without using any cleaner. If the screen is still dirty, then a small amount of diluted isopropyl alcohol or a commercial LCD cleaner can be applied to the soft cloth and then used on the screen (see Figure 8.4). Remember, all of these components are sensitive to static electricity discharges, so take precautions to reduce static charges.

Dust, dirt, and grime are perennial enemies of mechanical components as well. Depending on the component, these contaminants can come from various sources, including your own hands. Dust can be introduced into media drives when they are inserted into the computer. Dust or other contaminants sticking on a CD or DVD can easily enter the drive and affect its operation. It's a good idea to examine your storage media before inserting them in their drives and to remove any dust or grime you may find. Rather than carrying these media loose in a backpack or other bag, store them in protective containers. Of course, dirt can come from other sources. Dust and grime inevitably will accumulate on your keyboard through regular use. Compressed air can be used to remove dust and lint from the keyboard, while isopropyl alcohol

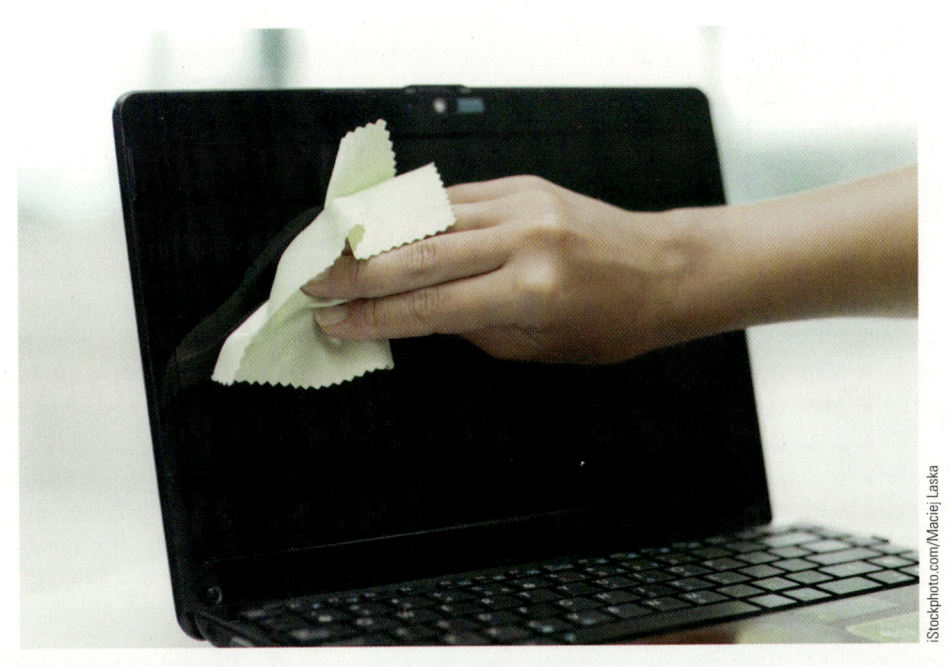

Figure 8.4
Routine maintenance of computers and related peripherals includes keeping all of the components clean.

wipes do a good job of removing grime. If you use compressed air for dust control, be aware of health and safety risks of misuse. These products should not be accessible to students.

Peripherals often include more mechanical parts than the core components of the computer system. Printers can be affected by the after-effects of paper jams and toner spills as well as wear and tear on gears and rollers. Mice with roller balls can pick up lint or other dirt that interferes with their operation, but can usually be cleaned with swabs and a little isopropyl alcohol. Periodic cleaning can reduce problems with peripherals and ensure that they're ready when you need them.

Power fluctuations also can damage or destroy electronic components. Surge protectors are available to minimize the impact of excess power. Uninterruptible power supplies (UPS) can be used to ensure a constant power supply, balancing out too much or too little power. Electricity from your local power supplier is not the only type of electricity that can damage your computer's components. As noted above, static electricity also can cause major problems, especially with chips and printed circuit boards. If you are going to do some internal work, before you work on electronic components you should discharge any static buildup by touching metal.

Repairing

In spite of your best efforts, it is likely that some hardware component will break or malfunction. When malfunctions occur there are two choices: repair or replace the component. As a practical matter, the number of components you can repair economically is quite limited. Bent pins on a connector can be straightened, but most other repairs should be looked upon as temporary, at best. In the overwhelming majority of cases, your choices are between replacing a component yourself and having someone else replace it for you. In general, just about anyone can replace pluggable components outside the computer case. These include the computer mouse and keyboard. Intermediate to advanced users can replace pluggable items within the computer case including circuit boards, memory, and hard drives. Above all, when using your school's technology, follow the school and district procedures to ensure you are operating within appropriate limits. You may need to carefully assess the problem and submit a technical support request, or troubleshoot the issue following your school's guidelines.

Replacing Consumables

A common form of technology maintenance occurs when items are replaced. Many of these items are consumable supplies such as those used by computer printers. Both ink jet and laser printers use cartridges and paper, consumable items that a typical user can replace. Another example includes the light bulbs for computer projectors. With the popularity of using teacher computer workstations that project images to a screen or whiteboard, schools quickly have become cognizant of the high cost of these consumables.

Students should be encouraged to conserve resources during their computer use. For example, they can use the preview function of the print command to determine how many pages will be printed and then print only the pages they need. They can use a small font or reduced line spacing for draft versions of word-processed documents. They can cut and paste text from the websites they use for research purposes in order to restrict the amount printed to only the necessary information (though remind them to gather the information needed to properly cite the sources). And they can use the "draft" mode to conserve ink. You may need to develop guidelines as to how much printing is allowed, always asking yourself if the file really needs to be printed or not. With blogs, digital portfolios, student information systems and learning management systems, there are plenty of ways to record and share student work that don't require printing.

Software Maintenance

Maintenance is not limited to hardware components; software also requires maintenance. In many K-12 school settings, software issues are handled at the server level by the network administrator or other technology support personnel. There may be situations, however, when you need to install or update software on your own or your school's computers, such as when existing media plug-ins on a browser must be updated before students can view content you've found on the Internet. In general, software maintenance can involve one or more of the following tasks: installing new software, reinstalling or updating current software, organizing and backing up files, and protecting software from harmful influences.

Installing New Software

The first type of software maintenance involves the acquisition and installation of totally new software. In this case you may purchase the software on storage media, such as a CD-ROM, or you may download the software from the Internet. The latter option is attractive if you need the software in a hurry and have a high-speed connection for your computer, but it's also handy to have backups of your software in case you have serious equipment failure.

Most software has become very easy to install and requires very little knowledge about the workings of the computer. You'll often be prompted during the software installation process to review terms of use and select locations on your computer for the installation of the software. Typically, the installation wizards will recommend the best options for you.

Perhaps you are familiar with downloading new software applications or upgrades to existing software from the Internet to your computer. Usually these downloads include a screen with a long list of requirements that you are supposed to agree to by selecting a button. When you select the "I agree" button, do you actually know what you're agreeing to? Do you know whether you can have multiple copies of the program? Can you share it with other teachers? Is there a limit as to how long you can use it? Whether purchased over the counter or downloaded from the Internet, you should know the uses and limits placed upon the software by its license.

All software should be considered copyright protected, and its use requires a license. When you purchase a single copy of software for your personal use, the licensing will probably restrict your use to only one computer. So, if you purchase a word-processing or gradebook program and install it on your home computer, you should check the license to see if you can also install it on a school computer. Sometimes you can; sometimes you can't. Unfortunately, there are no standards for software licensing—even for educational software—so you need to be aware of the acceptable and unacceptable uses for every software application you use.

As you will learn in Chapter 10, most acceptable use policies specify that teachers should not install software without prior authorization. Again, you should check with your technology support staff or administration to understand the procedure for installing new software on school technology. Even if you have purchased software for your own use, you may not be able to install it on a school computer without permission. And once you do, you'll still need to be careful of cloning or ghosting software that your technology support personnel may use to maintain computers on the network and that can inadvertently remove any software you have purchased and installed.

Reinstalling and Updating Current Software

Some common forms of software maintenance include reinstalling or updating software on your computer. A reinstallation may be necessary when existing software has a serious malfunction or a system crash interacts with application software. This doesn't happen often but you definitely will want to keep copies of your original software handy just in case it happens to you. A much more frequent type of software maintenance occurs when you are called upon to install updated versions of existing software. Software producers commonly issue corrections and updates for previously released versions of software. These patches usually are made available to registered users at no charge, and most are now regularly delivered over the Internet. Your computer probably checks for new updates routinely and notifies you when they're available. Producers also release "new and improved" versions of prior software and make these versions available to registered users at fees lower than those charged to new users.

File Maintenance

Another form of software maintenance deals with deleting, organizing, or archiving (backing up) individual files. Even in networked environments, it will be your responsibility to manage and organize your own files and to back them up periodically. Effective file management is also an important skill to pass on to our students.

Some software programs create and store temporary files and other data on your hard drive that should be removed periodically. If left unattended, they can occupy large amounts of storage space and slow the overall operation of your device, including smartphones and other mobile devices that access the web, use global positioning services, or push notifications. For example, temporary files are commonly generated when you visit Internet sites. You can use the options in your web browser to delete these temporary Internet files. **Cookies** are Internet files that might or might not be considered temporary (see Figure 8.5). To state it simply, these files store important information about you and your computer when you visit Internet sites. This way, the common Internet sites you visit will remember who you are and your preferences. You may or may not want to remove cookies during your routine maintenance. On mobile devices, additional data may be stored in relation to apps you've downloaded and used; you may not even realize it's there.

---

cookies
temporary computer files from websites that store information enabling sites to remember your computer and your preferences

> Cookies are small text files that are saved to your hard drive when you visit a website in order to personalize your future visits.
>
> For example, when you revisit a site and it...
>
> - greets you by name;
> - displays your last search terms; or
> - offers to sell you products that fit your tastes.
>
> ...this is because of the cookie(s) the site has saved on your computer, and accessed in order to serve you better. You may decide to delete them because they tend to build up over time and begin to compromise your computer's efficiency. If you rely on cookies for your favorite websites, however, you may not want to delete them unless you're absolutely sure which ones you are deleting.

Figure 8.5
What is a cookie?

Software programs can help you analyze the contents of your computer and other devices and determine if you have unused files or data on your computer that should be removed. You should use caution with these programs or when deleting files in general, however, as you may inadvertently remove critical files. It's good practice to review any files suggested for deletion.

On other occasions you do not want to delete files on your hard drive, but you may want to organize them to make them easier to locate. By using a combination of folders and subfolders (or directories and subdirectories) you can organize your files in a logical, efficient manner. For some mobile devices, file folders may be replaced by structures such as playlists, but the need for organization still exists. This is a good practice that can help avoid unnecessary file deletion from your computer. Often, you can get very organized by creating a relatively small number of major folders and a larger number of subfolders in which to keep your work. For example, you might want to have a folder for all your lesson plans that contains subfolders on specific topics.

Yet another type of file maintenance involves the creation and use of back-up or archive files. There are multiple reasons you may benefit from the use of archive files, but often they address one of two needs: 1) you have critical files that would need to be restored quickly in the event of a computer disaster, or 2) you have a large amount of file space devoted to files you use infrequently but which you are not prepared to delete at this time. In either case, archives can be created to contain these files. After the relevant files have been moved into the archive folders, those folders can be moved to storage media separate from your computer such as a file server, external hard drive, or cloud-based storage. This process frees up storage space on your computer and provides back-up protection in the event of computer failure. Although the possibility of a failure might seem remote, archive files serve as a form of insurance that you cannot afford to overlook. It's good practice to routinely schedule a backup of your files and those of your students. Some software can be used to do this and if your computer is connected to a school or district network, your technology staff may be using this type of software to routinely back up your files whether you realize it or not.

Safeguarding Software

The final type of file maintenance discussed here relates to protecting your software from harmful or malicious influences. These influences can take many forms, but the most common source of harm comes in the form of computer viruses. A **virus** is a computer program that executes and replicates itself and, in the process, has the

virus
a computer program that executes and replicates itself and, in the process, has the potential to cause major problems on your computer

TECH TOOLS & TIPS

When Storage Isn't There

Data storage is an area that has changed rapidly over the span of just a few years. First storage devices got smaller and less expensive, and then they disappeared altogether! Well, not exactly, but you no longer have to have a physical storage device connected to your computer, laptop, or mobile device in order to back up or organize information. Some mobile devices only share information wirelessly, so you just can't connect them to hard storage. That's been a challenge for some schools to figure out. Following are some tips from schools implementing the use of iPads (Ross, 2011).

- "Cloud computing" refers to storing data and using applications that are not physically located on a computing device. Companies like Apple, Microsoft, and others offer data storage "in the cloud" for their customers, as do sites like Dropbox, where you can store information online and share it with others through computers or mobile devices. Google Drive provides cloud-based storage and associated applications. To get to the cloud, though, many services require e-mail addresses, and schools do not universally provide e-mail addresses for students, especially young students. Before you can take advantage of some cloud-computing resources, you'll need to check with your tech staff for alternate means of connecting or the use of e-mail services designed for students, such as Gaggle.net or ePals.

- Some popular mobile devices, like Apple's iPod Touch and iPad, were designed for personal use, so management applications were not originally created to allow multiple users on a single device. This can make it difficult or time consuming to download and install apps, but schools have found some workarounds as new management tools are being created. Since these devices download apps through a recognized account tied to an e-mail address, some schools will create separate e-mail addresses for the device itself so when personnel change, they don't lose access to purchases. These devices also use playlists as directories, so some schools will create a playlist of apps for a particular grade or content area that can be synched quickly and separately, depending on which classes use the devices.

- If a wireless, mobile device doesn't allow you to connect to any external data storage, it can be especially challenging to share a classroom set of devices when students are creating or editing documents, images, videos, and other data—but have to put the device back at the end of class. Although student e-mail accounts provide one method for transferring files from the device to online storage, some learning management systems have created apps that allow students to log in to storage without the need for e-mail addresses.

potential to cause major problems on your computer. Multiple antivirus products are available to detect the presence of viruses on your computer and to offer protection against them. Most antivirus vendors have websites that offer updated versions of their products to their registered users. For these products to be effective, you have to consistently download the updates and use them to scan and repair the files on your computer. Consider requiring your students to incorporate their use routinely, such as when inserting a storage device or opening a file they've worked on outside of school. In these cases, all files should be scanned before use on school equipment.

Computers connected to the Internet are exposed to other types of intrusive programs that can track your computer activity, add unwanted codes to your computer, and perform unauthorized uploads of private user information to external parties. Firewall and antispyware programs are available to address these problems but, once again, regular updating and use of the programs are needed to ensure ongoing protection.

Among the duties of network administrators is to ensure security of the network system, in part by scanning e-mail messages for viruses, running updated virus protection software, and utilizing antispyware software. Find out how your school or district protects its technology systems and be informed of your responsibilities. Additional information about how to protect your computers against a variety of malicious influences is found in Chapter 10.

> ## THE GAME PLAN
>
> ### Technology Maintenance
>
> You will need to evaluate your role in maintaining the equipment you use in a school, as well as create a different, more extensive plan for managing your personal technology. To keep your computer operating smoothly, follow these steps to maintain your hardware and software.
>
> #### Set **G**oals
>
> Develop a routine maintenance plan for your devices. Your plan should establish a schedule that addresses the four areas of hardware maintenance and the four types of software maintenance discussed in this chapter. For example, how often do you intend to clean dust and lint from your device? How will you check for updated drivers or virus protection?
>
> #### Take **A**ction
>
> Examine software manuals, hardware manuals, online support sites, and software discussion forums to locate maintenance information. Search for protective software available from your district. Browse local retailers and online dealers to locate back-up supplies. Acquire the maintenance tools, supplies, and updates you need. Install new hardware and software according to the manufacturer's recommendations. You may even want to create a chart similar to the *Tech Tools and Tips—Maintenance Schedule* or schedule reminders for routine maintenance appointments using calendaring software.
>
> #### **M**onitor
>
> Are you cleaning and servicing all parts of your devices (hardware and software) on schedule? Have you protected your devices from power fluctuations and spilled liquids? When was the last time you updated your virus protection software? How long has it been since you checked for updates for your applications? Have any parts of your technology malfunctioned and, if so, what did you do? Have you installed any new hardware or software?
>
> #### **E**valuate and Extend
>
> Are all parts of your devices (hardware and software) functioning properly? Are you finding the software updates that you need? Do you have extra consumables on hand? Are some supply and information sources better than others?

Technical Assistance

Let's face it: when it comes to technology, none of us can be expected to know everything about every digital resource we encounter—and we don't have to. This is especially true when students use their own devices in school (see *Tech Tools and Tips—Lessons Learned from BYOD Initiatives* later in this chapter). When using digital technologies, you may have to accept the fact that you are not the most knowledgeable person in the room when it comes to the hardware and software. And that simple fact is just fine. You can adopt a confident and open attitude that allows you to accept help when offered, even from your students, as illustrated in *Stories from Practice—Keeping Up with New Technologies…and the Kids*.

Depending on their age and developmental level, your students can be a source of technical assistance (see Figure 8.6). Many children today grow up surrounded by mobile computer technologies and other digital devices in their homes. Students as young as second or third grade often know a great deal about technology. Many of us know very young children who are able to use tablet computers to access their favorite games, log on to child-specific websites on the family computer, or use cell phones and digital cameras. Take advantage of your students' expertise! It's more productive to feel confident in what you do know, and not feel threatened by what you don't know.

TECH TOOLS & TIPS

Maintenance Schedule

Be informed of your school system's policies on software and hardware maintenance. Many districts restrict general staff from running virus protection, installing hardware or making changes to the settings. Find out what your responsibilities are in performing technical computer maintenance. Sample tasks are provided below.

Please note: most cleaning chores should be completed with the power off!

Daily Tasks
- Back up all work.
- Exit all applications.
- Log off all users from the network.
- Shut down power to all computers or put into sleep/stand-by mode.
- Put mobile devices in charging stations or carts.
- Shut down power and store any peripherals.
- If used, cover computers and peripherals.

Weekly Tasks
- Move or remove files that have been downloaded to the desktop or temporary folders/directories.
- Empty trash/recycle bin.
- Organize/consolidate folders/directories.
- With the computer powered off, wipe off computers, monitors, keyboards, mice, and mouse pads with appropriate cleaner.
- Dust computers, peripherals, and work areas with lint-free cloth.
- Restock consumables (paper, toner, etc.).

Periodically (may require training or assistance)
- Clean mechanical mice (rollers and balls).
- Routinely create back-up archives.
- Use compressed air to blow dust and dirt from keyboards (do not let students do this).
- Check for wear and tear of all cables and cords.
- If possible, remove dust from inner components of workstation, especially fan blades.

Figure 8.6
Your students can share their technical knowledge with you and with each other.

TECH TOOLS & TIPS

Learning from BYOD Initiatives

Several school districts across the country have adopted laptop initiatives intended to provide greater access to technology and digital resources for students. Lately, more and more of them have embraced the concept of "bring your own device" (BYOD) or "bring your own technology" (BYOT) as an economical way to reach every child. Generally, students can bring in phones, tablets, laptops, and even some portable gaming consoles as long as they have a web browser and can access content through the Internet, so that use can follow appropriate guidelines. Having multiple types of devices in one classroom can add a bit of uncertainty into the teaching process. Teachers who have initiated BYOD projects offer the following advice for managing them in the classroom.

1 High-quality instruction that engages kids is the best classroom management strategy. Teachers agree that when kids are engaged, management issues are less of a concern.

2 Start the year with structured activities and provide more flexibility over time. Plan some activities for all students to do at the beginning of the year, such as creating goals or class rules in a whole-group setting and determining how the devices can support them. Lesson plans should contain options when it comes to technology, meaning you can differentiate learning in terms of student work products. Use a learning management system or other consistent resource for students to store work, collaborate, and obtain feedback.

3 Respect the knowledge and skills your students bring to the classroom. Teachers in many BYOD programs note that students already know how to use their devices and when students are comfortable with their technology, the burden of being the "all knowing" technology expert can be lifted.

4 Develop lessons that require technology. Students are more likely to know when and how to use their devices appropriately and effectively when they are essential to learning, as opposed to being supplemental. Develop virtual field trips, digital storytelling, geocaching, and other activities that can be supported by student devices. Try one new thing—periodically—perhaps based on what your students already know or can do.

5 Determine when tech is and isn't used. This may also be called an On/Off policy. Determine a command for when technology isn't to be used or whether students should put it down (or away). During some periods, like test time, you may even want to collect devices in a secure location.

6 You're in charge of your classroom! Make sure students understand that if you have to close or ask a student to shut down a device, only you can open the screen or tell the student to restart the device. Yes, it's the student's device, but it is a privilege, not a right, to use it in your classroom.

7 Model and promote transparency. Students should know they might be asked to display their device on the spot or with their peers. If students use their devices during class, have them send you what they've worked on or post it to your LMS at the end of class. You can use consistent forms, like KWLs, exit slips, journal entries, or other means.

8 Develop a system for students who are having problems. Create structures for collaboration by adapting non-tech activities like think-pair-share, jigsaw, and others. Some teachers require students to, "Ask three before me," to try to resolve questions quickly so that learning can get back on track.

9 Capitalize on teaching time. Set the expectation that students will come to school with fully charged devices. Determine when, where, and how students can recharge. Some will have to, so it's better to plan for the situation rather than causing a barrier.

10 Monitor, monitor, monitor! MBWA (management by walking around) is a good policy whenever technology is being used. Set up your room to best view all devices. For perpetual problem children, go back to the basics in terms of appropriate use or perhaps honor them with preferential seating close to you.

Source: © Jonathan Martin. Used with permission.

STORIES from Practice

Keeping Up with New Technologies . . . and the Kids!

It's taken me a while, but I no longer worry about asking my students for help with technology. Just the other day, I was working with my fifth-grade class on identifying the main elements of a story we were reading. We were using concept-mapping software to identify elements such as setting, mood, main characters—things like that. We did an example together in class first, but I had given my students some creative leeway when they were developing their own concept maps, you know, using different fonts, colors, and even including graphics if they wanted. A couple of the students took advantage of that opportunity and designed some really beautiful maps, so I wanted to show them to the rest of the class.

We were using laptops in the class, and instead of transferring the files I just moved each student's laptop to the projector at the front of the room. Of course, this was a day I was being observed, so there was a little added pressure. When I got the first laptop to the front of the room, I couldn't get the projector cable to connect. I tried it one way, then upside down, and was just getting really frustrated. Being observed didn't help either. So I asked the student who had designed the map, Jaime, to come up and help me connect his laptop to the projector while I told the rest of the class why I had selected his example. Of course, Jaime got it connected in just a second, and we were able to go on with the lesson immediately.

There was a time when that would have devastated me, but technology changes so quickly and you just can't know everything. Now, I tend to learn enough about a new application to get it started with my class and then the students teach me new ways to use it. Not only does this make things easier for me, it gives the students a chance to shine as well. I think that's what is meant by technology fluency—the ability to go with the flow—with confidence.

Source: Based of an unpublished interview conducted by John Ross.

Also be sure to establish your own network of volunteers to provide classroom technology support. As you will learn in the next chapter, this is a great way of establishing collaborative relationships between school and community. Parent volunteers can assist you with routine maintenance tasks such as running disk utility software, removing old files, and backing up data. Others may be able to help with more

APPLY to Practice

Develop a Plan for Tech-Savvy Volunteers

Make preliminary plans for a technology volunteer preparation program to support your class.

1. Make a list of ways volunteers can support needs specific to the grade or content area that you plan to teach. Include ways volunteers can provide help with a specific technology or technology-based activity when physically present or by employing technical skills outside of class.
2. Prepare a newsletter, flyer, web page, or set of guidelines for a potential volunteer program. Describe the expectations for participation as well as benefits you hope to achieve for your students, yourself, and the volunteers. List resources necessary to support the program as well as skills volunteers should have.
3. Share your plan with others. Are there similarities? How do their plans differ? What changes should you make to your plan? Revise your plan and record it in your portfolio.

serious problems such as computer malfunctions. Your parent network will change from year to year, so collect information about the technology skills of the parents when you gather demographic information at the beginning of the school year. A simple volunteer form can list technology-related activities for which you may need assistance. College students and other community volunteers, as well as older students in your school, may also be sources of support. Some examples of the work that volunteers can complete are:

- cleaning computer monitor screens, keyboards, and mice;
- dusting behind computers and wiring;
- supervising computer labs;
- providing technical assistance to students when working on computers; and
- providing data entry and word processing.

> **TEACHSOURCE VIDEO**
>
> Go to the Education CourseMate website and watch the video, *Teacher Perspectives: Parent Technology Volunteers.* Observe how this teacher uses parent volunteers to support the use of technology in her classroom.
>
> 1. How have you observed parents performing similar technology-support roles?
> 2. How might parents support technology use in classrooms with older students?

Chapter Summary

In this chapter, we focused on the fluent use of technology. Fluency in technology use refers to the ability to incorporate it into your classroom instruction smoothly, gracefully, and with confidence. Some people may call it seamless integration. It involves applying your current knowledge of technology systems to the new technologies you may encounter in your role as an instructional leader in your school.

In order to facilitate the fluent use of the technology resources you may find in your classroom or school, we provided guidelines for safe and healthy use. We discussed the importance of arranging computers and related tools in a way that protects both students and technology resources. We provided tips on reducing common health problems that can be associated with extensive or incorrect computer use. You learned basic maintenance and troubleshooting techniques, and we provided advice on securing technical assistance.

At the least, your responsibilities in maintaining the technology systems in your classroom will include managing and organizing your own files, and backing them up periodically. You will most likely assume the responsibility for ensuring that your technology is kept clean and reasonably dust free. Become familiar with basic troubleshooting techniques found within your equipment manuals. Check on cables, cords, and plugs. Sometimes these have a way of coming loose—and no one likes to have their requests for technical support met with the observation that equipment is simply unplugged.

In the next chapter, we turn our attention to ways that digital resources can be used to enhance communication and collaboration among students, parents, peers, and the wider community. We'll also discuss how to locate and evaluate digital resources for use in your teaching.

Web Resources and Activities

See the Education CourseMate website that accompanies this book for

- links to the National Institutes of Health guidelines for safe use.

YOUR PORTFOLIO

To demonstrate competency in ISTE NETS-T Standard 3.a, add one or more of the following items to your portfolio:

1. Create a customized list of tips for the safe and healthy use of technology tools in your classroom. Consider the grade level and content area you plan to teach and the technologies commonly associated with locating, analyzing, and evaluating relevant information. Reflect on your role and how you will model effective technology use as well as the responsibilities your students will have for learning in a 21st-century classroom.
2. Develop your own list of troubleshooting tips for common software and hardware problems you encounter.
3. Develop a plan to provide routine maintenance of technology in your classroom. If applicable, include items such as calculators, printers, handheld computers, and other technology, not just computers. Include the steps both you and your students can take and the schedule you will follow.

References

National Institutes of Health. (2005). *Ergonomics for computer workstations*. Bethesda, MD: Division of Safety, Office of Research Services. Retrieved January 24, 2012 from http://www.nih.gov/od/ors/ds/ergonomics/computer.html

Ross, J. D. (2011). *Beyond textbooks: The learning return on investment*. Richmond, VA: Virginia Department of Education. Retrieved January 24, 2012 from http://www.doe.virginia.gov/support/technology/technology_initiatives/learning_without_boundaries/beyond_textbooks/beyond_textbooks_learning_return_on_investment.pdf

SchoolDude.com. (2010). *2009 survey: The unique challenges facing the IT professional in K-12 education*. Cary, NC: Author. Retrieved January 24, 2012 from http://www.cosn.org/Portals/7/docs/SDU%202009%20Survey%20-%20v2.pdf

9

Modeling and Facilitating Use of Digital Tools

OUTCOMES

In this chapter, you will learn to

- Incorporate technology tools and strategies to **facilitate communication and collaboration** with students, parents, peers, and community members; and
- **Locate and evaluate digital resources** in response to the learning needs of your students.

ISTE Standards Addressed in Chapter 9

NETS-T 3. Model Digital-Age Work and Learning

Teachers exhibit knowledge, skills, and work processes representative of an innovative professional in a global and digital society. Teachers:

b. collaborate with students, peers, parents, and community members using digital tools and resources to support student success and innovation;

c. communicate relevant information and ideas effectively to students, parents, and peers using a variety of digital-age media and formats; and

d. model and facilitate effective use of current and emerging digital tools to locate, analyze, evaluate, and use information resources to support research and learning.

As a teacher, your scope of responsibility broadens dramatically from yourself and your immediate family to your students and their families, your school and district, and the communities in which you live and teach. You also have a responsibility to your profession, including colleagues and professional organizations that extend beyond your school and community. These responsibilities will require you to communicate and collaborate with the numerous people who have an interest in the things that go on in your classroom. In addition, your professional responsibilities will require you to model and facilitate the effective use of digital technologies within your classroom and beyond.

217

Throughout this book, we've shown you how to do just that, but two chapters (in addition to this one) are particularly applicable to ISTE standard 3. In Chapter 4, we discussed the use of digital technologies as tutors, mindtools, and support for conversations. We also provided strategies to effectively locate, analyze, evaluate, and use the information resources readily available on the web for learning and research. In Chapter 5, we discussed how to develop a classroom environment to support student learning. Throughout, we've stressed the importance of collaboration in developing the skills needed to function in an information economy.

In the first part of this chapter, we focus on ways that you, as a teacher, can use digital technologies to communicate and collaborate with the many people who will have an interest in what happens in your classroom. In the last section of this chapter, we focus on how you can facilitate effective use of digital tools through locating, analyzing, and evaluating digital resources that support student learning.

Professional Communication and Collaboration

You will find that many of the planning, instructional, assessment, record-keeping, and professional development tasks that teachers perform involve some form of communication. You'll have to communicate with your students, establish communication between home and school, and communicate with school and district administrators, staff, and other teachers. And, you'll need to communicate with others to enhance your own professional development.

But NETS-T Standard 3 goes beyond just communicating; you'll notice that standard 3.b focuses on *collaborating*—not only with your peers, but with students, parents, and community members as well. Collaboration is more than communication and more than cooperation. Collaboration requires active participation. In a truly collaborative relationship, all parties benefit; partners bring different strengths and interests to the relationship and, as a result, everyone contributes to and gains from the collaboration in some way.

Of course, open and positive communication is a critical part of successful collaborations, but there are other techniques that can enhance school, home, and community relationships as well. The following sections explore ways students, faculty, staff, parents, and the greater community can collaborate to support student success and learning through 1) communicating, 2) volunteering, and 3) providing extended learning opportunities. In the past, face-to-face meetings were the primary means of collaborating with these critical stakeholders. Today, widely available technology tools provide effective and efficient means for communicating and collaborating with everyone concerned with classroom teaching and learning.

Communicating

As a teacher, you will need to maintain open lines of communication with students, parents, colleagues, and administrators. You may need to

- communicate curricular requirements to your students;
- report and discuss student progress with students, parents, administrators, and other teachers;
- collect student contact, health, or other information from parents and guardians;
- notify parents of field trips and special events;
- generate forms that require signatures, such as permission forms and acceptable use policies;
- keep parents informed of classroom activities and schedules;
- create classroom websites;
- publish classroom newsletters; and
- interact with colleagues for professional development.

Many digital tools can be used to support communication with students, peers, parents, administrators, and the community. E-mail and mailing lists provide a quick and easy way to convey information or participate in a discussion with a group of people. Word-processing or desktop-publishing programs can be used to create newsletters and weekly letters to parents. Digital video equipment can be used to document classroom activities to share at parent-teacher meetings or classroom celebrations. Presentation software can be used to structure your classroom presentations or to present to parents and administrators. Gradebook programs, spreadsheets, and graphing software can be used to track and convey student progress to students, their parents, and administrators. Students can create podcasts, wikis, blogs, or multimedia presentations to share their learning with others in and beyond the classroom. The ideas are almost endless.

Many school districts have established procedures for communicating with parents through report cards, interim grade reports, and periodic portfolios demonstrating student work. Most districts also publish annual summative reports as brochures or special inserts in the local paper; states publicize summaries of student achievement data through online school report cards. Many schools also have procedures for contacting parents on an as-needed basis, such as through attendance records, disciplinary forms, or information from guidance and career counselors. Some schools encourage teachers to contact parents by phone on a regular basis or to distribute "good news" report cards as one way to praise student achievement. You also may want to communicate with businesses, community organizations, and other institutions that support teaching and learning. These may include other schools, museums, libraries, research facilities, and colleges and universities. These communication venues are now all supported by networked telecommunications and digital tools.

Communication should be regular and two-way, meaning that you're not just contacting parents when you have an academic or disciplinary problem to report or not just contacting community members when you want financial support for new technology or other initiatives. Consistent, periodic communication helps everyone better understand the process of schooling and can create greater understanding when you or your school wants support for a new initiative. For some general guidelines on how to better communicate with parents and the community, see Table 9.1.

> **TEACHSOURCE VIDEO**
>
> Go to the Education CourseMate website and review the video, *Teacher Perspectives: Communicating with Parents*. Consider the many ways these teachers use technology to communicate with parents
>
> 1. Are there strategies described that you plan to include in your active practice?
> 2. What other ways can technology support communication with parents from school?

Class Websites

One common way to enhance communications between home, school, and the greater community is through the use of a class website (see Figures 9.1 and 9.2). A class website can provide links to homework assignments, supplemental resources, as well as links to district-wide information, such as bus schedules and cafeteria menus. Classroom websites can make resources available to your students outside of class time, providing opportunities to explore upcoming activities and review previous materials. Students who miss class can access materials at their convenience. The website can clarify expectations for parents and publicize your work to administrators and community members.

Depending on the grade level and subject that you teach, you may want to make resources, such as the following, available to your students and their parents:

- presentation slides;
- lecture notes;
- announcements;
- class calendar and due dates;
- homework assignments;
- online practice tests;
- links to resources used in class; and
- supplemental and enrichment activities students can do at home for extra practice.

Table 9.1	Communicating with Parents and the Community

Be proactive

- Get to know parents and community members. Don't let a problem be your first contact with them. Create informal opportunities for communication to establish a friendly, cooperative atmosphere for future contacts.
- Encourage ongoing, two-way communication. Let parents and community members know that you welcome their ideas and input and will take their suggestions and concerns to heart.
- Share information about local, state, and federal education initiatives that impact your teaching.

Be informed

- Consider parents and community members as resources. Consult with them about particular problems or education issues, for example, factors that might affect a student's learning or behavior and what approaches and strategies they have found helpful.
- Gather up-to-date information about issues from respected sources—newspapers, professional journals and texts, websites, and so forth. Besides helping you design better strategies to meet your school or classroom needs, the information may also be useful to parents and community members. Parents and others often look to teachers for advice on any matter related to school.
- Consult with school and district administrators or resource personnel for information about school policies or preferred practices relevant to the issue at hand.

Be positive

- Hold high expectations for learning and behavior. Let parents know exactly what is expected of their children, what you do to teach and reinforce these skills and behaviors in the classroom, and how they can support their children's learning at home.
- Inform parents about their children's progress toward instructional and behavioral goals, and let them know about nonacademic accomplishments as well.
- Be a goodwill ambassador for your school in the community, recognizing community support and celebrating student and school success.

Be prepared

- When communicating about student concerns or needs, define and document the problem that impedes achieving educational goals. What is its source and scope? For behavioral issues, how often and in what context does the behavior occur? How does the problem or need affect the child, the school, and/or the community? What steps have been taken to address it, and with what results?
- Plan a strategy for next steps, soliciting input and support from parents and/or community members. Be ready to suggest concrete options for addressing a problem, including:
  - the goals of the intervention or project;
  - what you will do;
  - how parents or community members can help;
  - how progress toward goals will be measured and communicated; and
  - next steps based on evaluation of results.

Be respectful

- Treat people the way you want to be treated. All parents appreciate those who have their children's best interests at heart.
- Respect cultural and ethnic differences, and try to see the parents' or community's perspective. Even if you disagree with how to approach a problem, seek common ground, assuming that people are doing the best they can with the knowledge and resources at hand to do what's right for their children or community. Let them know that you respect their opinions and are committed to working with them as partners to ensure their children's—and all children's—success in your school.

Source: Adapted from *Administrator's guide to technology leadership* AEL (2000). Charleston, WV: Author.

Figure 9.1
Note how the website for Mrs. Renz's Fourth Grade Class supports communication with students, parents, and the greater teaching profession..

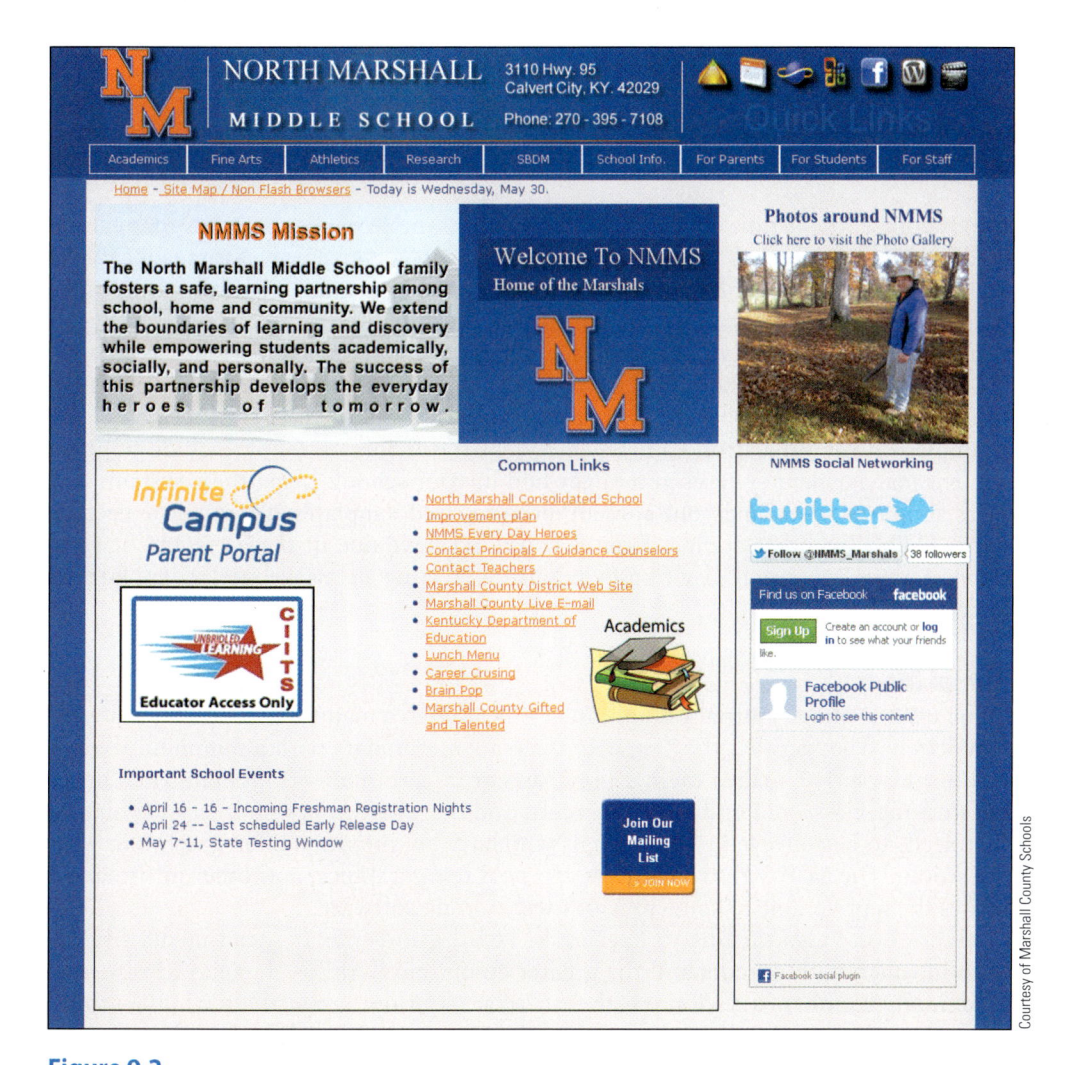

Figure 9.2
This website from North Marshall Middle School in Calvert City, KY, provides numerous ways for students, parents, and teachers to communicate with each other.

> ## THE GAME PLAN
> ### Creating Your Own Class Website
>
> **Set Goals**
> Some teachers have developed websites that are merely informative, while others have truly capitalized on some of the unique advantages of web-based delivery to support student learning. Find an example of a high-quality class website that appears to provide support for learning and allows teachers to communicate with students, parents, or others.
>
> **Take Action**
> Review some of the tools and services listed on the Education CourseMate website. Ask practicing teachers at schools you've attended or worked with about their own websites and the technologies they use to create them.
>
> **Monitor**
> What do you like about the sites you find? What might you change? What are the common features across these tools? Are there any features you'd like to add? What training or support might you need to create your own class website?
>
> **Evaluate and Extend**
> Prepare a plan or example of a class website to support learning and to communicate with students, parents, and others. Identify the features and how you'd use them. Share your findings with your peers, practicing teachers, or technology specialists to revise your ideas.

Of course, the list on page 219 is just a small sample of the materials that can be made available on a class website; it can also serve as a convenient "storage location" for your own classroom files. For example, you can create a page with links to websites that you use frequently within your instruction. You and others can have access to them anytime, anywhere you have an Internet connection.

Many school systems subscribe to content management systems, such as Campusuite or PowerSchool, which their teachers are required to use for their class websites. The examples on the Education CourseMate website for this textbook include popular content management systems you might find in your school. Using these systems can be as simple as uploading your content into prepared templates. There's little need to know HTML or other coding. Even if you don't have one of these systems at your disposal, there are several easy-to-use options for creating a class website, as you learned in Chapter 4.

Social Media

Often used as online journals, blogs can also be used in a manner similar to websites or newsletters. The fact that they are easy to create and update with a minimum level of technical expertise makes them a great way to post homework assignments, notes for students, classroom updates for parents, and the wide variety of other information that needs to be conveyed to individuals who have an interest in what goes on in your classroom. The ease with which users can post text, graphics, and other information makes them preferable to some previous web-editing software.

Schools are also turning to Facebook, Twitter, and similar social media sites to keep in touch with parents and the greater community. Although some schools and community members question whether these are appropriate media for home-school communication, other schools have found that since parents and community members are already using social media, it can be a convenient way to keep parents and community members informed.

TECH TOOLS & TIPS

Top Ten Things to Consider When Creating Websites

1. Keep each page consistent in look and feel.
2. Avoid cluttering the page with too much information, whether text or images.
3. Use consistent styles and names for navigation buttons, and keep the navigation buttons in a consistent place on every page.
4. Routinely check that the links to other websites are current, functional, and appropriate to your content.
5. Provide a guide to what is located on the site, either as an outline of pages, an introduction to each page, a site map, or a way to search the site.
6. Include links to required plug-ins for any multimedia included on your site. Popular plug-in applications include Acrobat Reader, Flash Player, QuickTime, Real Player, Shockwave Player, and Windows Media Player.
7. Include your name, contact information, the date of the website creation, and the last update, typically at the bottom of each page.
8. Include a copyright notice throughout the site and provide contact information for permission to use copyrighted material.
9. Make sure that student information does not violate students' privacy or compromise safety. Do not include student information unless parental permission has been obtained.
10. Check the usability of your site for people with disabilities, either by having someone familiar with accessible websites visit your site and provide feedback, or by using one of the free online web accessibility tools.

© Cengage Learning 2014

APPLY to Practice

Interesting Ways

Educational technology consultant and Twitter veteran, Tom Barrett, explores new and emerging technologies. He started a series of "Interesting Ways" on his blog edte.ch. From the question, "What's one interesting way to use . . .?" he and his Twitter followers have created presentations of many different and engaging ways to use a variety of technologies, including Facebook and others.

1. Search the Web for "interesting ways" teachers use Facebook, Twitter, and other communication and collaboration tools in support of their classrooms.
2. Create a list of your favorite ideas. Why do these teachers think it's a good idea to communicate in this way? What do they see as challenges?
3. Share your findings with your classmates. How do you think Facebook, Twitter, or other communication tools can enhance your home/school collaboration?

Facebook pages have their own advantages (Hartstein, 2011). For example, they can be used to:

- Share school news, announcements and happenings using the status update. The news will show up on the walls of everyone who follows the page.
- Share upcoming events using Facebook Events. Participants can respond as to whether they will be attending, and a school can easily send reminders as the event approaches.

- Showcase the school culture through photos and videos of school events and activities. However, remember that students should never be "tagged," to respect their privacy.
- Get feedback from the community. Using Facebook Questions or third-party apps, a school can solicit input on a particular topic. However, it's important to control what users are allowed to post and upload.

A Facebook page can be a great tool for keeping parents informed, but it's absolutely critical to carefully control what is posted and moderate what is being said. Individual teachers should be careful never to discuss specifics about their students in their individual profiles. "Friending" students can also prove problematic in that it may erode the boundaries between teacher and friend. Some schools and districts actually prohibit this practice.

E-mail and Text Messaging

Schools often use e-mail and text messaging for mass announcements and notifications, but it's worth thinking about how you will use these means to communicate with your students and their parents. In schools where these forms of communication are common, expectations for their use should be made clear.

Depending on your schedule, you may tell students and parents that as a general rule you will try to respond to e-mail within a certain time period, such as 24 hours or two school days. You should also have clear expectations about what type of communications will be handled through e-mail. General progress reports, reporting student success stories, or making announcements may be appropriate areas for e-mail communication. Discussing student performance, whether academic or behavioral, is best left for face-to-face meetings or sometimes a phone call.

Currently, more people own cell phones than are connected to the Internet at home, so depending on the school where you teach, texting may be a viable option for communicating with parents and families. One handy way to incorporate texting is to use a text-blasting service, in which one message is distributed to a list of people. This can be useful for distributing reminders about upcoming field trips or

THE GAME PLAN

Expectations for Electronic Communications

Set Goals
Learn more about the expectations schools have for their teachers when using electronic communications with students and parents.

Take Action
Review electronic communication policies from schools you find online as well as those who do not post this information online. Schools that do not post this information may have different expectations from those with a well-developed web presence. Review print and online teacher magazines and journals, as well, for discussions about the topic.

Monitor
What commonalities do you find across the policies? What disparities exist? Do some school districts mandate electronic communications? What are some concerns teachers express about using online communications?

Evaluate and Extend
Work with a friend or individually to develop a summary of the issues identified in communication polices that might inform the development of your own policy.

other special occasions, or when events are running overtime or must be canceled due to inclement weather. Some online communication services support this broadcast messaging, as well, and may include the option for parents to choose e-mails or texts.

If you are willing to provide your cell phone number to your students and their parents, you may want to establish time periods in which you will and will not respond to text messages or phone calls. You'll just have to monitor how often you use e-mail, text messaging, and phone calls, and how they each contribute to student success in your classroom. And of course, always be cognizant of your district's policies; some prohibit texting and other communications between students and teachers.

Volunteering

Schools have long relied on volunteers to support their activities. Room mothers, Parent Teacher Associations (PTAs), booster clubs, and work-sponsored programs are among the groups that provide much-needed moral and financial support to schools. Digital technologies provide parents and other community members with new ways to volunteer. Support groups, such as PTAs, are going digital and are organizing and mobilizing with online communication tools. They are developing websites and managing online communications, both for their members and for the schools they serve.

Parents with technical expertise can also volunteer technology services to you and your school, either after school or during class time (see Figure 9.3). Many parents who can't get to school to volunteer during the day because of work or other commitments can now help develop and support class websites; provide online homework help; coordinate functions and meetings; or help advertise events by e-mail, discussion lists, and web pages. Other parents or community members with greater flexibility in their schedules may share technology skills with students and teachers by offering training

Figure 9.3
Volunteers can support school technology use.

> **virtual field trips**
> use of audio-, video-, or webconferencing tools to tour or interact simultaneously with businesses, museums, galleries using images, animation, videos, and websites

> **telementoring**
> a process for establishing a guided mentoring relationship that incorporates information and communications technologies; also known as *eMentoring*

sessions or providing technical support advice or actual maintenance and repair. In Chapters 4, 5, and 8, we discussed the use of volunteers to help you manage your students' activities during complex, authentic learning experiences and aid in routine technology maintenance tasks; the use of volunteers also enhances collaborative school, home, and community relationships.

Parents, business and industry personnel, and other community members can also help support student learning in your classroom by providing **virtual field trips**, serving as guest speakers, or participating in **telementoring** opportunities. Career days and field trips tie into curricular areas and are common events in many schools. When students explore careers, and learn about job requirements, they come to appreciate the connection between schoolwork and potential careers—providing an authentic context to what they are studying and learning. Virtual field trips and guest speakers are the 21st century's version of these familiar events. Students can use audio-, video-, or webconferencing tools to interact with professionals (some of whom may be their parents!) synchronously or they can "tour" businesses, museums, galleries, or other sites at their convenience, using images, animations, and videos compiled on websites.

Some schools, especially senior high schools, provide service learning or mentorship opportunities where students shadow business and industry personnel to develop their skills—often career-specific skills, but social skills can also be addressed. Using various web-based technologies to support a mentoring program is referred to as **telementoring,** sometimes also called eMentoring. Business and industry professionals have the opportunity to participate in telementoring programs through local or national

TECH TOOLS & TIPS

Creating Virtual Field Trips

Develop your own virtual field trip. You might want to visit some of the virtual field trip sites on the web in order to get a better understanding of how to create your own.

1 Visit the field site yourself, armed with a digital camera and clip board.

2 Take photos of key features (for example: on a field trip to a zoo, take photos of different animals). Make notes on what you want students to notice in the photo, or information about the feature in the photo.

3 Collect any brochures that may be available at the site.

4 On your return from the site, prepare your photos and plan your virtual field trip:
- Prepare the photographs that you want to use in your virtual field trip: go through all the photos that you took, selecting the ones you want to use, and then cropping these to the size you want.
- Create a storyboard or concept map to plan out how you want to present the trip. In each storyboard box, state what photo you will include and what you want to say about the photo. You may also include questions you want to ask students as they look at and read about the photo.
- If you want to include photos from brochures that you obtained at the site, scan these using a scanner. Make sure that you include the source of the photos within your trip (state where the picture was obtained). If needed, obtain permission to use the photos.
- You can also add to your field trip by doing a search online for websites that relate to your trip. You can include links to these web pages from your virtual field trip, or you can copy images from the pages to include in your trip (secure permission if needed). As with scanned pictures, make sure that you include the source of the photos within your trip (state where the picture was obtained).

5 Put together your field trip (examples of formats: web page, PowerPoint presentation, poster display, bulletin board, or brochure).

Source: Education Department at the University of Minnesota Duluth. http://www.d.umn.edu/~hrallis/guides/Virtual/FieldTrips.html. Used with permission.

STORIES from Practice

The Home-School Connection

I've been fortunate to visit a number of different schools in several states that have been recognized for excellence both for technology use and student achievement. For these schools, technology is critical for helping students meet academic goals. I was not disappointed during my two visits to one large high school that had been acknowledged as a Blue Ribbon School from the U.S. Department of Education and an Intel Model School. The faculty and staff had embraced the power of technologies to support their work, and a range of different technologies were used both in class and to support learning once students left the building. Faculty members were adept at using interactive whiteboards in their classrooms and were able to use them in unique ways to connect with learning at home. Software that came bundled with the whiteboards allowed teachers to capture notes taken during class, still images of diagrams or figures, or even short videos that could then be posted to class websites. Both students and parents could review the web-based information. Some students used it for review while others were able to view material they may have missed while absent. Parents found it helpful for keeping up with what their children were doing in school. The material could be especially helpful in advanced classes for which parents may have little background or might need a refresher in the content.

Teachers also support homework help in other ways. One teacher added a homework hotline component to her class website. It's basically a discussion board where students posted questions about their homework. At first, the teacher related, she handled most of the questions herself, but she did so from a wireless laptop while watching television or sitting on her deck in the backyard. By the time I visited, her students had taken over the hotline, providing help to others in the class. In her class, getting the right answer was not as important as understanding how to get to the answer, and helping other students online was one way some students better understood the content. During my observation, the teacher was able to begin by reviewing the most troublesome problems as posted on the website and acknowledging some of the best ideas and strategies that were shared. The class discussion was very focused because she already knew the problems her students were having, based on a review of the hotline.

Source: John Ross.

---

programs. Usually, students receive course credit for participating in these programs and can use technology to record and report their experiences. Blogs, online portfolios, or presentation software can be used by students to demonstrate what they have learned as a benefit from this unique form of volunteering by parents and other community members.

Extended Learning

When you create opportunities for learning outside the classroom and beyond the school day for yourself, other teachers, your students, or the community, you are extending the learning potential for everyone involved.

Supplying books and other materials for students to use to perform research, develop skills, and create projects is commonplace in virtually every classroom in every school, but some schools go even further by providing laptop computers and handheld devices that students can check out in order to access instructional materials both at school and at home. Other schools loan or sell older equipment at a very low cost for home use. Older equipment can be a low-cost method for providing access to common productivity tools, such as word processors, so all students' homework can look just as good as their peers while they develop and practice technology skills.

Schools can also provide after-school access to technology by opening their computer labs, libraries, or media centers for students, parents, and other community members. In addition, they can extend learning in one area of great need in many communities—technology instruction. Although you probably grew up in a "wired" society, there are still many adults who need to develop these skills to function well in an information-based economy. During "family computing nights," parents can receive valuable technology training or access to digital resources while becoming more familiar with their children's class work and teachers. Some programs provide the opportunity for students to help train parents, grandparents, or other community members in the use of common technologies—helping to strengthen their own technology skills as well as develop a range of social skills. Training for parents can also support responsible computer use and may help allay some concerns parents have about their children using the Internet as an educational resource.

By far, the most common method for extending learning opportunities to the home is through the assigning of homework. As we enter the 21st century, many schools provide web-based material or tools to support students' work at home. You don't have to create all of your own web-based content but can instead rely on a variety of online resources to support your students' efforts to delve more deeply into content that is presented initially in class. These resources include curricular materials as well as those that offer study skills or homework help—some in real time using web-based communications tools. Putting homework information online can also help parents and agencies that support schools—such as libraries, museums, and after-school programs—in that they are better able to organize and prepare their own resources to support what you're doing in your classroom. Of course, one of the best ways to provide links to this information is through a class website, but if not available, you can compile links to helpful information in a document and send it home in print or via e-mail.

Some teachers are using commonly available software to create and post podcasts, screencasts, or short movie-like presentations of their instructional sessions for student review. **Podcasts** are generally audio recordings of lecture-type

> **podcasts**
> digital audio files downloaded from the Internet and played back on an MP3 player, iPod or computer

TECH TOOLS & TIPS

Creating Online Presentations

Here are some things to consider when creating podcasts, screencasts, or other digital presentations for your students.

1 Plan, plan, plan. Just as with developing any instruction, especially one that relies on multimedia, you need to develop an explicit plan before compiling any of the media files into your presentation. The steps presented in Chapter 2 in relation to portfolio development will serve you well here: define, design, develop, deliver. Carefully consider, then apply, each of these steps in the development of your digital media.

2 Format is everything. Whether you're using audio alone or incorporating images or video, you have to make sure they're in the correct format for your presentation. If you're unfamiliar with editing images or video, you can still create helpful audio-only podcasts of presentation notes and study guides for your students. No matter what media you include, make sure it is converted to a format that can be interpreted by the software you choose.

3 Choose your tools. Free software is available to help you create podcasts, screencasts, and other presentations on both Windows and Macintosh operating systems. Audacity is the tool of choice for audio-only podcasts on Windows, while MovieMaker can be used to incorporate video. PhotoStory is a quick and easy tool that allows you to record audio over a sequence of still images and uploads directly to YouTube. On the Macintosh, the freely available GarageBand software allows you to create audio tracks, insert images, and incorporate video. These applications often use a timeline on which you apply and arrange your media files.

4 Share your presentations. Perhaps the easiest method to post a podcast for your students is through the use of a blog. Most blogging software makes it easy to upload podcast episodes that you can then share with anyone with an Internet connection. You can upload videos or video-like presentations to many different streaming media sites or use services like SlideShare or Jing to host presentations or screencasts from your computer.

information, while **screencasts** are animated movies captured from the teacher's monitor or a whiteboard. You can create movie-like presentations from common presentation software or use an online sharing site, like SlideShare. You can even create your own channel on YouTube, TeacherTube, or other video sharing sites. Of course, many of these resources are also available from a variety of online sources, including many universities, state departments of education, and now K-12 schools that create their own iTunesU sites. Students often miss class for a variety of reasons, ranging from sports activities to extended illnesses, and podcasts, screencasts, or other online media can provide these students with access to information that may be difficult to obtain in another way. If you plan to make such materials available for students to use at home, first find out how many students have the technology needed to access them, and plan alternate options for students who lack access at home.

> **screencasts**
> animated movies captured from the teacher's monitor or a whiteboard

Benefits of Enhanced Collaboration

Through open communication, volunteering, and extended learning opportunities, parents and other community members develop a better understanding of your responsibilities as a teacher and become more familiar with the processes and procedures of your school, which may be far different from schools they attended while growing up. The collaborative partnerships that are developed can provide a variety of benefits for students, faculty and staff, parents and the community.

Through communicating with parents and other community members, you build greater understanding for your needs and the needs of your students. You can generate support for curricular and extracurricular activities, including the use of technology. Communication with your students helps them become more aware of their own progress. Communicating data from groups of students (class, school, state, or national performance data) gives your students the opportunity to monitor and evaluate their learning by comparing themselves to established norms. Students can interact with experts in a variety of career roles when parents and other community members volunteer in schools, either virtually or face-to-face. These programs also provide an opportunity for students to develop skills that allow them to communicate and interact with adults and help them develop a greater awareness of the importance of school within the local or global community.

You and your colleagues might benefit from the presence of volunteers who provide support for routine management tasks, allowing you to focus more on teaching. Of course, community and business members can volunteer funds and equipment, as well as their time or expertise. Parents and other community members benefit through the increased awareness of school programs that volunteer opportunities provide.

Extended learning opportunities provide you with extra support for learning activities beyond class time. Students can benefit from the increased opportunities for practice and reinforcement that extended learning opportunities provide. These opportunities may include increased access to resources, including technology resources, as well as access to people—you, other students, or other experts. One commonly cited benefit of extended learning opportunities is the increased access to resources, especially technology resources, that occurs when parents and other community members share school-based physical and virtual spaces, including hardware, software, and networking. You can also benefit personally from the opportunity for professional growth that communication technologies and extended learning opportunities provide. When schools extend learning opportunities to the larger community, they reinforce the important goal of "lifelong learning" for students, staff, parents, and community members.

We now turn our attention to another responsibility of teachers: selecting digital resources in support of your students' learning.

Locating and Evaluating Digital Resources

Your role in obtaining new digital resources will vary depending on the school system in which you work, and even on the specific school within that system. Many schools and districts buy computers and other technology in bulk from district- or state-approved vendors. Most of these computers are bundled with common software, such as word processors, spreadsheets, and databases, as well as communications software that allows you to access and utilize the Internet, whether through a web browser or via e-mail software. In addition, many schools provide access to instructional content through subscription services, whether an online database of journals and news articles or entire lessons and activities. You will, however, have a say in the resources that are used in your classroom.

As you learned in Chapter 4, digital resources can enhance your instruction in several ways, for example as a tutor, as a mindtool, or as a support for conversation (Wegerif, 2002). When technology is used as a *tutor,* the software explicitly teaches or provides practice with a specific body of content. When technology is used as a *mindtool,* it serves as a semantic organization tool, simulation and visualization tool, or knowledge-building tool. Mindtools can include word processors, databases, spreadsheets, multimedia or web-development software, concept-mapping software, and other tools that help students and teachers represent, manipulate, or reflect on what they know (Jonassen, 2006). As a *support for conversation,* digital resources contribute to conversations among learners, and thus facilitate group and community learning. Keep in mind that many digital resources may include components from several categories, and thus could be classified in more than one way. For example, video-editing software may contain a tutorial on techniques to maintain visual continuity as well as serve as a mindtool by providing the means to edit video footage.

Before selecting digital resources, you need to know what role you want the resources to play. In most cases, this will be defined by the learning needs of your students and curriculum. For example, you may find that some students perform better if they are able to view animations or videos of processes or systems before analyzing their component parts. Your curriculum may have complex topics that are hard for students to visualize, such as understanding the customs or social activities of past or distant cultures. Or you may want to find a safe way for students to manipulate dangerous or expensive chemicals or other substances within a limited time frame. Finally, there may be some topics that students learn more readily when they are able to work in groups and create a product such as a web page or presentation. Different combinations of technologies can meet a variety of curricular and student needs.

Examine the goals that you want your students to accomplish and if and how technology-based resources can contribute to them. Based on the tasks students should perform and the way you want technologies to enhance your instruction, you can determine the requirements for the technologies you need. What content area and grade level is of interest? Do the materials need to be suitable for a particular pedagogical approach? Do you want to use the technology as a tutor to teach new information, or will you use it to supplement information you have already presented? Or do you want to use the technology as a tool by which students demonstrate their learning? Perhaps they will use it to create a product, such as a web page or group presentation, or they can use technologies similar to those used by experts in a specific profession.

Locating Digital Resources

Once you've determined your goal, you need to take action by selecting possible technologies to meet that goal. There are many ways to identify digital resources that may meet your requirements. First, investigate the resources available to you

APPLY to Practice

Choosing Technology That Matches Your Goals

1. Identify some of the different needs you will face as a classroom teacher and determine your goals for meeting those needs. These may include goals related to instruction (e.g., develop an activity that allows my students to interact and share ideas with students from different cultural or ethnic backgrounds), goals related to your curriculum (e.g., identify resources to supplement my instruction that students and parents can access at home), or goals related to recordkeeping or resource management (e.g., create a tracking system to evaluate the effectiveness of my lessons).
2. Consider the type of software that can help you meet these goals. If the software is instructional, what type is it? How does it match your teaching style? Have you used similar software before? What additional skills are required to operate the software?
3. What hardware is necessary for running the software? Is it readily available, or does it require specialized hardware? If new hardware must be purchased, what justifications can you provide for the expense? Do you know how to operate all the hardware involved in satisfying the needs? If not, what additional skills and knowledge do you require?
4. Share your responses with colleagues. For those who selected similar goals, how did your software and hardware proposals align? What differences were there? What additional software or hardware options could you suggest for those with different goals?

---

locally. Determine what software is installed on your classroom computers and school network. Many textbooks include CD-ROMs and companion websites. Some web-based textbooks and content providers also present age- and grade-appropriate content at different reading and ability levels, so that students across a range of proficiency levels have an increased opportunity to master required content. Some content services may also provide lesson planning, gradebooks, academic games, tests and quizzes, and other student information resources so you can have "one-stop shopping" in terms of web-based materials to support your instruction. As you survey the available resources, check with the library media or technology specialists in your school and district to determine what other instructional resources are available to you. Are streaming video programs available for viewing in your class? Are videos available at the school or through interlibrary loan programs? Check to see if any software titles are maintained by the district for use in the classroom. Some schools have web-based resource centers that allow you to search, preview, and schedule instructional media well ahead of time.

Of course, the resources at hand locally are just a small sample of the resources available to you. As you well know, a massive storehouse of resources is at your disposal via the Internet. For example, museums, historical foundations, government programs, and a wide range of educational nonprofits offer interactive educational programming on their websites. WebQuests (see Chapter 4) are a popular way to organize web-based resources for teaching and learning, and you'll find many of them online. As mentioned earlier, podcasts, screencasts, and other digital presentations have become popular in education and may be used to support student learning in your classroom. Instructional videos are available from TeacherTube, Teaching Channel, and other streaming media services. And numerous free or low-cost applications, or "apps," are available for mobile technologies.

A unique category of software is **open-source software**, free software that allows users to access and modify the underlying code. Anyone can download this kind of software and contribute to its ongoing development. This means that there is a

open-source software free software that also allows users to access and modify the underlying code in order to contribute to its continued development

TECH TOOLS & TIPS

Using Streaming Media Sites

Several popular streaming media sites provide movies or movie-like content for students of all ages and in all content areas. Discovery Education builds on the wealth of high-quality video assets from its parent company, and BrainPop is a popular source of animated films with spin-offs for younger students (BrainPop Jr.) and for Spanish speakers (en Español). These may also include video-based podcasts that may or may not be organized into iTunesU sites, which many state departments, colleges, and other education organizations now sponsor. But for many teachers, the place they turn to first are the many free video sites available online that are not so professional. These include one of the web's first popular video sites, YouTube, as well as education-specific spinoffs, such as TeacherTube, SchoolTube, Teaching Channel and YouTube for Schools. These sites not only provide a wealth of content information from across the globe from amateur and professional videographers alike, but you and your students can create and post videos yourself. The following are a few tips for using streaming media in your classroom, no matter where you find it:

1. Shorter can be better. Videos can be engaging and can capture student attention, but eventually even video can dull the senses. Divide your video viewing into short segments of 3 to 10 minutes in length, depending on the age and attention span of your students. Alternate video viewing with other activities.

2. Guide the viewing. Videos supplement instruction, but you're still the teacher! Use the video to support the learning and do what it does best—demonstrate action. Tell the students what to look for and monitor what they're learning. You can do this by posing questions before a video, giving students a viewing guide, and asking probing questions.

3. Give the students control. Because many excellent short video clips are available on almost any topic imaginable, guide students to appropriate clips and let them determine when to start, pause, and rewind and review in order to reach specific learning goals. Linking these media to class websites allows students to access them at home and maybe even address the perennial parent question, "What did you do in school today?"

4. You don't always have to stream it. Some services allow you to download the media to your computer or a file server for use in your class. There are also some applications that will allow you to download videos from "Tube" sites (just be sure to follow appropriate use guidelines). Downloading the video for class time viewing reduces the strain on your school's bandwidth and can still make the source accessible if there are network traffic issues. Some districts block these sites, which is another reason to avoid concurrent streaming.

5. Post your own videos. Several sites, including YouTube, allow anyone—a district, school, or you!—to post videos, but some also allow you to create your own channel or playlist. Doing this allows you to tag helpful videos you find as well as to upload and organize your own videos. This way you can give your students one place to go to find the media you want them to see, and you can also limit who has access to the videos you and your students create and post online. Some video editing applications also upload directly to YouTube.

© Cengage Learning 2014

---

community of users who have taken an interest in the use and development of the software. Some open-source software is maintained to standards that rival commercial alternatives. Of course, you also can just use the software in your classroom and don't have to worry about becoming a developer, but you can benefit from user discussions, online communities, and subsequent improvements to the software.

The underlying philosophy of this type of software is that a community of users will be generated that uses and supports the software and that will give back to other users—all free of charge. Some of the users will create or improve functionality and then make the revised software available to anyone who wishes to use it. There are open-source versions of a wide range of applications, including operating systems, word processors, spreadsheets, databases, and many other types (see Figure 9.4). There is even open-source curricular content, such as that found on Curriki.org and FreeReading.net. You may have taken an online course using an open-source course management system such as Moodle or Sakai or posted comments on the open-source phpBB discussion board.

Modeling and Facilitating Use of Digital Tools 233

TECH TOOLS & TIPS

Using Podcasts in Your Classroom

Podcasts are digital audio files that can be downloaded from the Internet and played back on an MP3 player or computer. Although made popular by Apple's MP3 player, the iPod, the "pod" part of podcast simply refers to "play on demand," meaning that you or your students can play it whenever and wherever you want. Free software that can play podcast files is available for most computers, and many different brands of portable media players are now available. Podcasts were originally audio-only files, but newer formats allow the inclusion of images in slide-show fashion or even video, sometimes referred to as "vodcasts."

Here are some things to consider when using podcasts in your classroom:

1 The player. If you're going to use podcasts to supplement your instruction, consider the hardware that will be used and the necessary peripherals. Since they are media files, computers will have to be media-ready and will need sound cards, speakers, or headphones. Consider whether you want to play the podcasts for your whole class at one time, or have students access them on their own in a lab or other multi-computer setting. You can also make them available for students to use at home, but find out how many students have the technology needed to access them, and plan alternative options for students who do not have access at home.

2 The software. The most common software used to play podcasts on a computer is Apple's iTunes. iTunes is free and available for both Mac and Windows operating systems but is only one option. Additional software is available to play podcasts, and a quick Internet search can find several choices. No matter which application you use, you may need to collaborate with your school technology staff to make sure that an appropriate player for podcasts is installed on your computers, as not all media players are able to play podcast files.

3 The podcast episodes. Podcasts are available from a range of providers, whether specifically targeted at schools or not. The iTunes store categorizes podcast episodes and series so you can quickly find education-related podcasts. Another feature is iTunesU, which is a clearinghouse of podcasts from colleges, universities, public radio, and other education-related sources. Most of these series and episodes on iTunes and iTunesU are free.

4 Subscription service. Many podcasts available through iTunes or other services add new episodes on a routine basis. You can subscribe to them, and they automatically upload to your player when a new episode is available. Even if you don't plan to have routine updates to your podcasts, your students can benefit from this technology in the form of study guides, lecture notes, or student presentations.

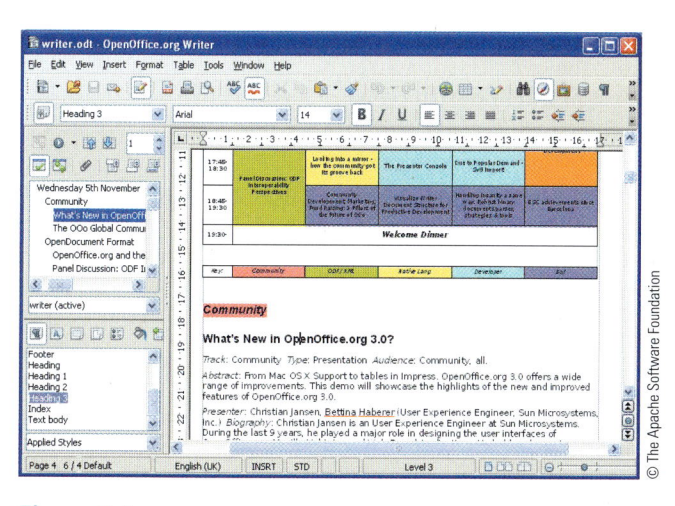

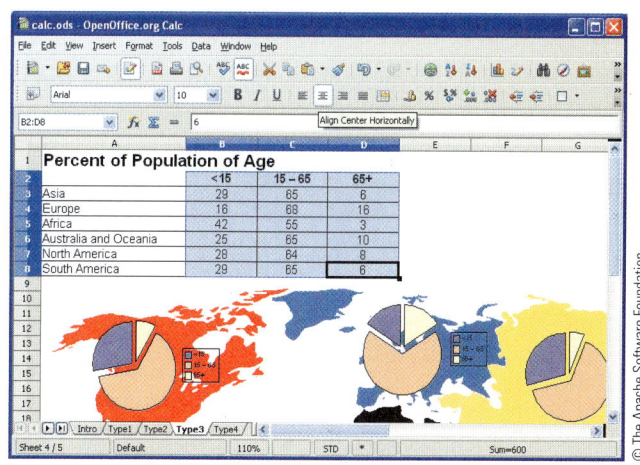

© Cengage Learning 2014

Figure 9.4
Open-source software includes common productivity applications that parallel commercial versions, such as word-processing, spreadsheet, and drawing applications from OpenOffice shown here.

TECH TOOLS & TIPS

Open-Source Software

Many open-source applications can be found for use in an educational setting, from operating systems and common word-processing tools to course management software, and even open-source content resources. Some examples include:

- Linux is a computer operating system, like Windows or Macintosh OSX, which has been available since the early 1990s.
- If you're familiar with the Microsoft Office Suite, you may find OpenOffice to be very similar. It runs on multiple operating systems, is compatible with other productivity software, and contains similar applications, such as a word processor, drawing tools, a spreadsheet, database, and presentation software.
- Amaya, from the World Wide Web Consortium (W3C), Nvu, and Mozilla's SeaMonkey are open-source web design applications you can use to create web pages. Besides HTML code, some open-source web editors support cascading style sheets (CSS), XML, and other programming languages and codes.
- Teachers in many content areas use concept-mapping tools to support their instruction, and can find open-source versions online, such as FreeMind or CMap.
- If you have taken a class online, you may have encountered the Moodle course management system. Users can post assignments, complete quizzes, and communicate with others in their class.
- FreeReading.net is an example of an open-source content resource, in this case, one that supports early literacy instruction.

The open-source movement continues to grow, and more digital applications become available or existing ones are improved, but many schools have yet to jump on the open-source bandwagon. The primary caveat when using open-source software is that it does not come with the type of support that can be included in purchased software. Although there is a community of users, and sometimes that community has discussion forums or other online help, there is no tech support person you can easily contact to ask questions when you run into problems. Many school and district leaders may resist moving away from familiar "brand name" applications to something that is less well understood, but as the number of open-source applications and curricular materials increases, it is likely that more districts will begin to explore the use of open-source materials in their schools.

For more information about open-source software, including a more detailed definition and the development of standards to support open-source applications, visit the nonprofit Open-Source Initiative online (www.opensource.org).

© Cengage Learning 2014

---

shareware
software downloaded from the Internet available for free preview for a limited time, after which purchase is required

freeware
software that has no cost

spyware
software that records usage patterns or collects information unknowingly from the user's computer

Two other common categories of software are **shareware** and **freeware**. Shareware often allows you to preview the software for a limited time and then requires purchase, but usually at a minimal cost. Freeware has no cost. For example, Google Apps for Education provides web-based word processing, web-development, spreadsheet, and presentation programs. However, some of these programs require individual registrations or limit the number of copies that may be distributed. Just as with commercial software, you should know the limitations of the licensing agreement of freeware and shareware. Unfortunately, some freeware also contains malicious **spyware**, discussed under security issues in Chapter 10. As a general rule, be careful what you download and make sure you follow the guidelines for acceptable use.

When selecting resources from the Internet, you may want to go to an online lesson plan website and note the hardware and software titles that appear most frequently in lessons related to your grade and subject. If you're interested in a particular technology, locate a teachers' discussion forum and search the archives to see if it has been discussed. If not, and the group or message board lends itself to such discussions, ask for the recommendations of others. In addition, don't forget to ask your colleagues. What digital resources do they use, and what benefits have they experienced? Are there any limitations that they've found?

> ## THE GAME PLAN
>
> ### Exploring Open-Source Software and Freeware
>
> **Set Goals**
> Examine some of the free software applications available to educators. For example, Google Apps for Education provides web-based word processing, spreadsheet, and presentation programs.
>
> **Take Action**
> Explore the applications, and compare them with similar applications with which you are familiar.
>
> **Monitor**
> What are the advantages and limitations of the free applications?
>
> **Evaluate and Extend**
> Do the free applications meet your needs? Would you want to use them in your classroom? Share your findings with your peers.

Evaluating Resources

Numerous products may catch your interest, but in order to determine what is worth purchasing, you should either evaluate the resource yourself, find out if others recommend the title, or both. To evaluate educational software, websites, and other digital resources, begin by determining exactly what criteria you will use. Some school districts have developed **software evaluation rubrics** for their teachers to use. Often, teachers develop or locate their own forms. Based on your needs and requirements, locate or develop a standard form on which to record comments and compare features across multiple programs. A wide variety of forms are available on the web and elsewhere, so you should have no trouble locating one to use or adapt to your needs. In general, you'll want to evaluate items such as the following:

- *Content.* Is the content valid? Does it teach what it says it teaches? Is it up to date? What topics and subtopics are covered? Is the vocabulary appropriate for the intended audience?
- *Free of bias and stereotypes.* These may not be intentional, but commercially prepared instructional materials, as well as content on the Internet, may include gender, racial/ethnic, or other biases or may reinforce stereotypes, as discussed in more detail in Chapter 11, that can disengage some of your students. As you review new technologies, consider questions such as the following: Does it avoid stereotypes and attitudes related to age? Does it avoid racism? Is it inclusive and appropriate for both female and male students? Does it promote recognition and acceptance of diverse cultures, languages, and religions? Is there any objectionable content, bias, or stereotyping present? Is it accessible by students with a wide range of physical capabilities? Does it avoid discrimination of any type? Does the learning resource promote tolerance and diversity?
- *Goals and standards.* When evaluating digital resources, always relate them to your required learning standards and curriculum goals. What standards or curriculum goals are addressed? Some software companies even take the extra step of matching the skills the software teaches to specific curriculum standards and learning objectives.

---

software evaluation rubrics
forms that provide criteria on which to evaluate educational software, websites, and other digital resources

- *Intended audience.* For what grade level or ability level is it most appropriate? Is it appropriate for a range of ability levels? Can you set the academic level at which your students work? Does the program adjust the level as your students progress?
- *Instructional approach.* Is the instructional approach compatible with your teaching style? Is it grounded in a well-established learning theory? Are resource guides or supporting lesson plans available? Does the publisher provide tips for integrating the program/product into the curriculum? What about student groupings or computer arrangements? Is the technology strictly lab-based, or can you incorporate it into your classroom?
- *Product quality and ease of use.* Can you and your students benefit from the new technologies fairly quickly, or are extensive training and practice required—for either you or your students? Is it durable? Are there any parts that will be easy to break or lose? Can students with small hands use it easily? For computer-based applications, consider the appropriateness of the screen design, use of graphics, animations, sound and other media elements, and the feedback provided. Are the appearance, language, text style, and graphic content appropriate for the intended audience? Is the interface logical and the software easy to use?
- *Documentation.* Is program documentation online, available as a PDF file, or as a user manual? Does it provide information on installation and use of the program? Does it provide tips on overcoming common problems? Is the documentation well written, logically organized, and easy to use?
- *User support.* How is technical support provided? Is there a "help" option available? Does the documentation, software, or supporting website contain a tutorial to teach users how to operate the program? Does the software or website include a demonstration of the program features? Is there a website that provides technical support? Is phone support available, or can you request assistance through e-mail or a website?
- *Teacher support.* Are there lesson plans? Background information? Are the objectives and prerequisite skills listed? Are there suggestions for student groupings or allocating time to the computer task? What about activities or worksheets for students to complete before or after their computer work?
- *Equipment needs and compatibility.* What are the system and memory requirements? Will the resource be compatible with your classroom machines? Platform compatibility issues used to be a bigger concern than they are now; however, some software may still be specific to only one platform. If your school installs software on a school or district-wide network, make sure the resources are compatible with the network server. Some software may also require peripherals such as scanners or cameras, and if this equipment is already available in your school, you may have to consider whether the new solution will operate on your existing peripherals or require new equipment (see Figure 9.5).
- *Cost.* How much does it cost for a single copy? A lab pack? Are site licenses available? If so, how much do they cost?

Read Reviews

It's also useful to read reviews of the potential technology resources in order to narrow the pool of programs that you actually evaluate. Both software and hardware reviews are readily available in magazines or journals, and on the Internet. Professional organizations and magazines routinely publish these reviews. Book and software distributors, such as Amazon.com, often include reviews by users on their websites. As you're reading, remember that reviews represent a subjective judgment, so make sure you identify who reviewed the technology and what criteria they used to evaluate it. Reviews can be conducted by a wide variety of people—university faculty, teachers, students, parents, independent reviewers, and so forth. No matter how well you attempt to identify the criteria on which the digital resources will be evaluated, judgments ultimately are based on an individual's past experiences,

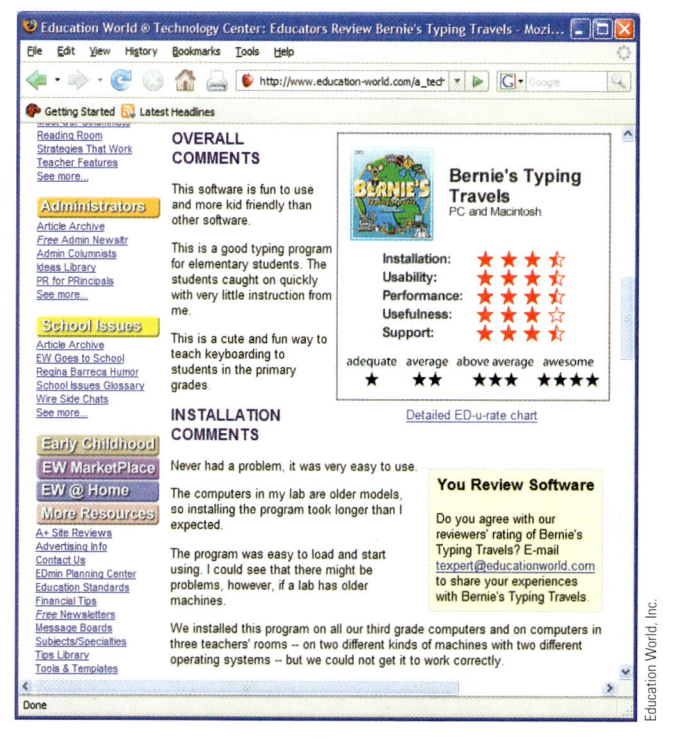

Figure 9.5
Technology reviews *by* teachers *for* teachers can provide valuable insights on software you are considering.

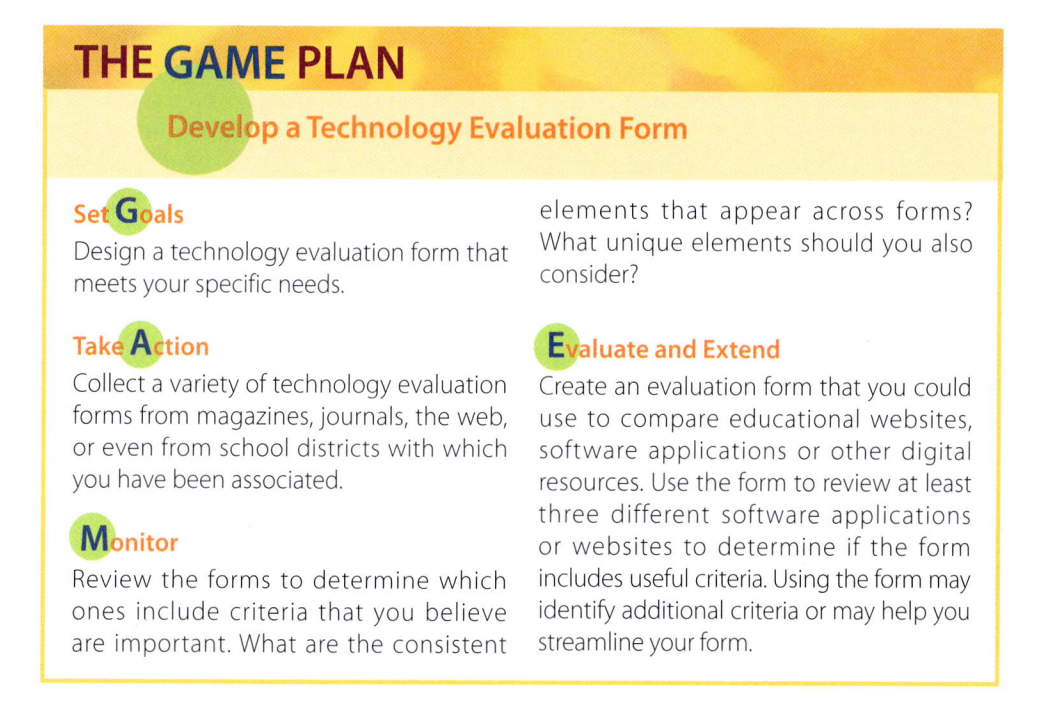

THE GAME PLAN

Develop a Technology Evaluation Form

Set Goals
Design a technology evaluation form that meets your specific needs.

Take Action
Collect a variety of technology evaluation forms from magazines, journals, the web, or even from school districts with which you have been associated.

Monitor
Review the forms to determine which ones include criteria that you believe are important. What are the consistent elements that appear across forms? What unique elements should you also consider?

Evaluate and Extend
Create an evaluation form that you could use to compare educational websites, software applications or other digital resources. Use the form to review at least three different software applications or websites to determine if the form includes useful criteria. Using the form may identify additional criteria or may help you streamline your form.

beliefs, and biases. Try to determine how well the reviewer's needs and situation match your own goals and teaching situation. A reviewer in a large, urban district who used software in a lab setting may not have the same experience as someone in a smaller school with five computers in the classroom. Also try to determine whether the reviewer actually used the software in an instructional setting, or whether they simply reviewed it based on a set of criteria. Keep in mind that just because it is recommended by someone somewhere, it may not be appropriate for your needs.

TECH TOOLS & TIPS

Selecting Apps for Mobile Devices

It's all about the apps. Finding the right app can be a daunting task, because so many are available, and more are being developed all the time. Just remember, anyone can create an app and put it on the web for download. There's no teaching or content qualification and no instructional design experience required. Some organizations and groups are starting to rate apps for education, but even some of these are still based on limited personal experience and opinion. If you're trying to find the right app, consider the following:

1 Has it been reviewed by an organization or person you trust? Reviews should go beyond personal use and should describe how it was used in the curriculum and by what kind of students.

2 Is the app from a trusted provider? Many providers are developing apps that interface with or replicate the functionality of their software that are already used to support students.

3 Does the app support evidence-based practices? You are developing effective teaching strategies to use with your students. Consider whether the app can support those strategies. While you'd like to be able to find out from the app developer what practices it supports, you may have to determine this on your own through trial and practice.

4 You're not alone. There are user groups, organizations, bloggers, conference organizers, and others who are using and promoting handheld devices and their apps. Join them. Become a part and learn from them. And if you have access to one of these devices, add your voice. You may not need to publish your own reviews, but you can collaborate with others in your school or district; contribute to blogs and other shared conversation spaces; or present at faculty meetings, conferences, or other sessions that allow you to interact with others using these new technologies.

© Cengage Learning 2014

You may want to consider using only nationally recognized sources of software reviews to narrow your pool.

As you collect information from websites, product descriptions, reviews, and recommendations, you may want to keep records of how the various products compare on criteria of interest. Read the relevant reviews in a systematic fashion and create a form, database, or spreadsheet to compile your results (see Figure 9.6). You'll want to collect information on the name, publisher or distributor, grade level, type of software, content area, and cost.

Also make note of any ideas you have about where the digital resources fit within your curriculum and lesson plans. In order to determine if a particular program—whether it's a tutorial on the Vietnam War or a web-based exploration of acids and bases—is appropriate for your classroom, you need to look at your instructional goal or objectives and the capabilities of the digital resource. Would it be used to gain attention and establish a context, to provide the primary instruction in the content, to provide practice and feedback, as remediation, or enrichment? As you begin to identify a small list of products for local review, think about where each product fits in your instruction.

It could take a substantial chunk of time if every teacher in a school were to individually review all the software titles and hardware products of potential interest, so you might want to work with other teachers in your school or grade level to share the workload. Develop a plan to disseminate the reviews to other teachers and administrators. Use the review sheet you created in this chapter or one developed by a school or district. Attempt to identify potential classroom applications of the software or other digital resources and make sure they align with the areas of need. Perhaps you could work with a school or district to develop and maintain a database to provide a centralized source of technology reviews conducted by local teachers.

Try It Out

Although others can make recommendations, the best way to determine which resources will enhance your lessons is to try them yourself. In order to evaluate new

Relevant Information from Software Reviews

Title: _____

Publisher/distributor: _____

System requirements: [   ]

Grade level: ☐ K ☐ 1 ☐ 2 ☐ 3 ☐ 4 ☐ 5 ☐ 6 ☐ 7 ☐ 8 ☐ 9 ☐ 10 ☐ 11 ☐ 12 ☐ other . . .

Type of software: ☐ Productivity ☐ Csurriculum Support ☐ Tutorial ☐ Mindtool ☐ Communication

Content area: ☐ Language Arts ☐ Math ☐ Social Studies ☐ Physical Education ☐ Music

Instructional goals: [   ]

Strengths noted in review: _____

Limitations noted in review: _____

Overall rating: _____

Cost: _____

Figure 9.6
You can make note of relevant information from your own software reviews in a database, spreadsheet, or other application.

digital resources, you need to gain access to a copy of the product for review purposes and preview the product using your criteria.

Secure a Review Copy

After you have located digital resources of potential interest, you need to access a copy of the product in order to conduct your own evaluation. Local resources and websites should be reviewed to determine if they meet your instructional needs. As you know, it's

APPLY to Practice

Find Reviews and Recommendations

1. Survey the wide variety of technology reviews that are available in print and on the web. It may be helpful to narrow your search down to a topic of interest. If necessary, you can start at the textbook's Education CourseMate website for a list of websites that provide reviews of technology.
2. Of the resources you found, which provide the most useful information? Why? What characteristics about these resources were helpful? How much trust can you place in the reviews you've found? Which of these have the credibility and longevity that support that decision?
3. Compare the resources you found with colleagues or classmates. Create a master list and keep it in your portfolio so you can return to it once you are charged with finding new technology for your classroom or school.

much easier to publish and distribute a website than other types of software, so be especially careful to explore the entire site before using it with your students (see Chapter 4 for more information about reviewing websites). Since links become outdated quickly, you should probably conduct an additional review of the links just prior to your class time.

Many times, you can download a trial version of commercial software from the publishers' website. Some software vendors will allow free previews of an entire program. Other vendors will provide a free demonstration program containing a subset of a larger program. Often trial versions are limited in some way. For example, you may be unable to save your work, the product may include a "watermark" indicating that it was created with a trial version of the software, or the version may expire after 30 days.

Universities, regional educational centers, and some district offices may maintain different hardware and software for teachers to review. You may also be able to borrow a product from another teacher for preview purposes or contact the vendor to find out if a school or district near you has purchased the product. As a general rule, if there is no way to preview the product, avoid it.

Preview the Technology

After you have conducted your own evaluation, you will want to try it with your students if you're going to use the product for instruction. Students are by far the most capable judges of the effectiveness of any digital resource. You'll need to determine whether it holds their interest and is easy to use, but most importantly, you'll need to determine if your students learn from it. It can be hard to look past the production values of the product to clearly see the effects on student learning.

If the resource is available on the web or locally in adequate numbers, you can try it with your entire class. Based on your review, you can begin to create a list of digital resources and web links to support your classroom instruction. Keep records of the results of the evaluation to use as a basis for purchase or use. Many educators keep a running list of items they'd like to purchase so they have it readily assessable when the opportunity to acquire software or hardware occurs.

Your school or district will usually have a policy or procedure for requesting and purchasing technology. You'll want to be familiar with the procedures for requesting new hardware and software purchases in your school or district and be sure you know how to voice your needs. As a nonprofit institution, your school or district may be able to obtain hardware and software at a lower cost than you can as an individual. This price might also be reduced further when items are acquired as part of a site license that allows hardware to be purchased as a class set or software to be installed on multiple computers. You'll have to check your school or district's policy for purchasing new technology for instruction before buying and installing any software. As you will learn in Chapter 10, most acceptable use policies specify that teachers should not install software without prior authorization.

Chapter Summary

In this chapter, you considered ways to use technology tools to enhance communications and collaboration within and beyond your classroom. You learned that regular, ongoing communication is one way to enhance collaborative relationships among schools, homes, and the community. Other ways to enhance relationships include volunteering and extended learning opportunities. Although you may expect to spend most of your time working with your students, other stakeholders, such as parents and community members, can offer a great deal of expertise and help to you and your students. Networked digital technologies have helped to create virtual "classrooms without walls" that have the potential to connect your classroom with others in your school, district, or community, as well as across the globe.

Digital technologies can enhance your classroom instruction in numerous ways. You can add realism to a lecture on the circulatory system with a video clip of a beating heart. Students can create their own personal history web pages that include digital pictures, videos, and interviews of relatives and friends. However, effective use of these technologies depends, in part, on the careful selection of technology resources. In this chapter, you learned how to identify your software requirements, locate resources that meet your requirements, narrow your choices through reading recommendations and reviews, and evaluate resources to determine if they are suitable for your use.

In the next chapter, we focus on modeling and facilitating the legal and ethical use of digital resources and technology tools.

Web Resources and Activities

See the Education CourseMate website for

- a list of common tools and services that schools and teachers can use to create websites, including free web services;
- virtual field trip sites that you can use to plan for or create your own virtual field trip activity;
- a list of websites that publish reviews of technology; and
- a checklist you can use to evaluate software.

YOUR PORTFOLIO

To demonstrate competency in ISTE NETS-T 3.b, c, and d, prepare the following items for your portfolio. Incorporate artifacts you have created from activities in this chapter.

1. Describe how you plan to use digital tools to communicate and collaborate with students, parents, community members, and other teachers. Include a
   a. description of one or two technology-based collaborative tools you could use to support student learning in and beyond the classroom
   b. description of methods for communicating and collaborating with parents, community members, or other teachers, either through a class webpage, e-mail, or other communications tools
   c. description of a technology volunteer preparation program to support your class

2. If you have not already done so, use the techniques in this chapter to locate, analyze, and evaluate the digital resources needed for the lesson that you began planning in Chapter 3. Or select another learning goal and identify the digital resources needed. Include the following steps:
   a. Identify your goals and requirements for technology use. Why do you want to include technologies? Are there technological or instructional requirements that constrain the type of resources selected?
   b. Locate resources that might meet your needs, including freeware, shareware, and open-source software.
   c. Read reviews and recommendations for hardware and software that would meet your students' learning or assessment needs. Based on the reviews, which resources would you select?

3. Locate a software title or website and review it using a software evaluation form of your choice.

References

AEL. (2000). *Administrator's guide to technology leadership*. Charleston, WV: Author.

Hartstein, D. (2011, April 26). How schools can use Facebook to build an online community. Retrieved February 8, 2012 from http://mashable.com/2011/04/26/facebook-for-schools/

Jonassen, D. J. (2006). *Modeling with technology: Mindtools for conceptual change* (3rd ed.). Upper Saddle River, NJ: Merrill/Prentice Hall.

Morgan-Rallis, H. (2006). Virtual field trips. *Helen's How-to Guidelines*. Retrieved May 2, 2012 from http://www.d.umn.edu/~hrallis/guides/VirtualFieldTrips.html

Wegerif, R. (2002). *Literature review in thinking skills, technology, and learning*. Future Lab Series, No. 2. Retrieved April 24, 2012, from http://archive.futurelab.org.uk/resources/documents/lit_reviews/Thinking_Skills_Review.pdf

10

Legal and Ethical Use

OUTCOMES

In this chapter, you will learn to

- Determine and model **acceptable uses of digital resources**;
- Follow practices that support appropriate **copyright guidelines** and use of **intellectual property**;
- Develop practices to encourage **academic integrity** such as detecting plagiarism, avoiding cheating, protecting confidential data, and protecting passwords; and
- Create learning environments that promote the **responsible use of technology resources**.

ISTE Standards Addressed in Chapter 10

NETS-T 4. Promote and Model Digital Citizenship and Responsibility

Teachers understand local and global societal issues and responsibilities in an evolving digital culture and exhibit legal and ethical behavior in their professional practices. Teachers:

a. advocate, model, and teach safe, legal, and ethical use of digital information and technology including respect for copyright, intellectual property, and the appropriate documentation of sources; and

c. promote and model digital etiquette and responsible social interactions related to the use of technology and information.

Digital tools generate digital concerns. The ease with which digital tools can be used to find, create, manipulate, and share information can be a boon to teaching and learning. However, these same tools can be used to quickly and easily copy other people's work, capture inappropriate or unwanted images, or spread sensitive information across the classroom, school, or globe. Consider the *Stories from Practice—Torn from the Headlines*. The scenarios are based on actual experiences from educators and others across the nation and are designed to emphasize the relevance of this ISTE NETS-T Standard 4 for all teachers.

STORIES from Practice

Torn from the Headlines

When Private Isn't Private

What we say and do in private stays private, right? Some teachers have found that using what they thought was a private social outlet can cause an uproar (CBS, 2011). Returning from her European vacation, one young English teacher did what most people do—posted pictures to her online profile. But when asked about her Facebook profile by her principal, her confusion grew to dismay. Pictures of the teacher innocuously holding glasses of alcohol were seen and reported by parents. She was confronted with two options: resign or be suspended. The story begs several questions. Are there different standards for our online lives? Or just for teachers? As a legal adult this teacher could go into a local restaurant and order a glass of wine. What's the difference between that and posting a picture online—in what was supposed to be a private space?

The Lessons We Learn

Graduation is a time of joy, a time to celebrate, and a time for speeches from top students. The same was true for this salutatorian in a Nevada high school who graduated with a 4.54 grade point average. Unfortunately, they weren't grades he earned. While a college freshman, this former "honor" student was charged with conspiracy, theft, and computer intrusion for using a stolen password to hack into the online grading system for his high school during his senior year (McMillan, 2011). For two semesters he had hacked into the grading system and adjusted his grades, and the grades of 12 others in return for payment. Now what he refers to as, "The greatest achievement of my young life" in his speech on YouTube, he notes, "I changed for the better, taking initiative, and completing assigned work. Well, sort of." Well, not really.

The President and the Pop Star

What do a pop star and the First Family of the United States have in common? Both are fighting against cyberbullying, and using new media to do so. Motivated after the suicide of a 14-year-old Buffalo, NY, student, popular performer Lady Gaga has been advocating for raised awareness of the often traumatic consequences of cyberbullying and pushing for national legislation. The singer advocates against cyberbullying through performances and appearances, and by using her popular Twitter feed (James, 2011). Known for being tech savvy, President Barack Obama and first lady Michelle Obama turned to another popular social outlet, Facebook, to introduce the White House Conference on Bully Protection and launch a series of anti-bullying websites, including stopbullying.gov and special Facebook pages on the topic.

Acceptable Use of Digital Resources

The modern school is filled with many different technologies. You're still likely to find overhead projectors, videocassette players, and other analog technologies in addition to fax machines, printers, copiers, scanners, interactive whiteboards, cameras, and an array of computing devices including desktops, laptops, tablets, and other mobile devices. These resources are intended to provide a rich experience for students and to help prepare them to use the technologies they'll need as they matriculate to higher levels of education or the workforce. While powerful digital technologies are now available in most schools and classrooms, some of the burden of using them appropriately will fall to you.

For many schools, **acceptable use policies (AUPs)** are the first line of defense in preventing irresponsible, illegal, and unethical use of a school or district's technology resources. An AUP is a document that clearly outlines what is and is not acceptable behavior for students as well as faculty and staff, and usually includes the consequences of unacceptable behaviors. After reviewing AUPs from schools and districts across the country, it's apparent that educators agree the primary purpose of school technology is to support teaching and learning. Many districts also emphasize that the use of the school or district's technology resources is a privilege, not a right, and that there are rules for expected behavior when using them. Individuals who abuse the policies set forth in an AUP often lose access privileges or, at best, are given restricted access to the resources.

---

acceptable use policies (AUPs)
a document that clearly outlines what is and is not acceptable behavior when using technology, in general, and the Internet, specifically, as well as the consequences of unacceptable behaviors

AUPs are often created by a committee, which may be composed of school board personnel, central-office and building-level administrators, media and technology specialists, parents and other community members, students, and—of course—teachers. At some point you may get to help define "acceptable use" in your school or district. AUPs have been in schools for years, even prior to the integration of computers or Internet use in classrooms, and so cover the use of all the tools and resources available for teaching and learning. As these tools have evolved, AUPs have had to change along with them. In just a few short years, schools have had to consider how their policies should reflect technologies such as e-mail, school-based web pages, instant messaging, peer-to-peer file sharing, cell phones, laptops, mobile devices, camera phones, and social networking and other Web 2.0 resources.

The tone of policies may range from informal letters to complex documents that read like a legal contract. It's common to have both students and their parents read and sign a district's AUP—which may be part of the student handbook—before students are given access to the school's technology resources. As a teacher, you will most likely be required to read and sign an AUP as well, whether the same as, or modified from, those for your students. As a teacher, it's important that you not only understand the expectations of your school or district's AUP but that you model expected behaviors described in the policy. Some schools or districts may discuss the AUP at parents' nights or technology open houses. This can be especially helpful in areas where parents may be concerned about their children's uses of the Internet and possible access to inappropriate material. Although the topics may vary from district to district, AUPs often include sections on copyright, issues of academic integrity, and Internet use. See Table 10.1 for common examples of both acceptable and unacceptable use.

Acceptable use usually governs what happens on school grounds, when using school resources, or at school activities, but as seen in the *Stories from Practice—Torn from the Headlines*, some students and teachers may be expected to hold to a higher level of acceptable use outside of school. As a matter of general practice, you should *never* consider your e-mail, text messages, "tweets," or even social profile to be private

Table 10.1 Examples of Acceptable and Unacceptable Uses of School Technology

Examples of Acceptable Use	Examples of Unacceptable Use
• Abiding by the policies and procedures of other networks that are accessed	• Altering software by deleting files, downloading programs, or copying or installing unauthorized files or programs
• Being polite and using appropriate language	• Assuming the identity or using the passwords or materials of another
• Deleting unwanted messages or old data from computers and servers	• Conducting commercial activities, advertising products, or taking part in political lobbying
• Enforcing appropriate use and reporting misuse or security issues	• Downloading text, graphics, or software, or engaging in behaviors that may be considered obscene, abusive, libelous, indecent, vulgar, profane, or lewd
• Respecting copyright and licensing agreements and citing material	• Gaining access to any pay-for-view site
• Running antivirus software on downloaded files, attachments, peripherals, or disks	• Giving out your own or others' private information, such as address, phone number, or passwords
• Signing correspondence	• Harassing an individual using the Internet
• Using online time efficiently	• Plagiarizing
• Using the Internet ethically and legally	• Transmitting material that violates any U.S. or state regulation, such as copyrighted, threatening, or obscene material, or material protected by trade secret
	• Vandalizing equipment, digital files, or wilfully spreading computer viruses

© Cengage Learning 2014

THE GAME PLAN
Acceptable Use Policies

Set Goals
Learn more about AUPs. Schools and districts list a wide range of acceptable and unacceptable uses for technology.

Take Action
Find examples of AUPs from schools across your region or the nation. You can use print-based AUPs from schools you are associated with or search the Internet for a broader perspective.

Monitor
Are you finding the examples you need? Have you considered asking for AUPs from friends, colleagues, or former teachers? What other terms might schools use to describe an AUP?

Evaluate and Extend
List commonalities and differences. What types of uses surprise you, as either acceptable or not? What types of uses do you think should be added to your master list? How do you think the lists will change over time? What new challenges are schools facing? You may want to compile your own table of acceptable and unacceptable uses as well as an additional list of items you find that seem to be unique to a particular school.

---

or confidential. Messages can be intercepted, whether intentionally or not. Seemingly "private" e-mails can be accessed by or sent to others; even "deleted" e-mail could still be on your hard drive or the service provider's mail server. Images and quotes on your social profile or that you text to friends can be reposted elsewhere. E-mail and other digital communications made on school computers are usually considered the property of the school or district. Schools or districts that provide communication or social networking services usually emphasize this point to everyone who uses the system including students, parents, and staff members. Some schools don't provide e-mail accounts to students at all, or only provide activity-based e-mail class accounts for a limited duration, such as a grading period or the length of a school-based project. Several services allow teachers to set up anonymous e-mail addresses for student use during class-specific activities only, but check with your district and follow guidelines in the AUP before using one in your classroom.

Copyright and Intellectual Property

Information technologies and the ease with which information can be created, duplicated, and shared have had significant impact on copyright law—the law that governs the right to use information. Electronic communications and files are considered a fixed medium (that is, a form of material expression), so items such as e-mail, discussion posts, text messages, web pages, and digital photos are all considered copyrighted material from the moment they are created. If the material does not explicitly state that it is in the **public domain** (i.e., creative works or information that are not "owned" by an individual but considered part of the common culture), you may be violating copyright law when you use it—even if you are using it for an educational purpose.

Although the *Copyright Law of 1976* (Pub. L. No. 94-553, see Table 10.2) is the most current copyright law, this law precedes the widespread adoption of personal computers in education, so subsequent legislation continues to have an impact on copyright regulations. Copyright law has evolved over time to adjust to the challenges of new technologies and the way we share information. This section describes

public domain
creative works or information that are not "owned" by an individual but considered part of the common culture

| Table 10.2 | **Copyright Law of 1976** |

The *Copyright Law of 1976* (Pub. L. No. 94-553):
- to reproduce the copyrighted work in copies or phonograph records
- to prepare derivative works based on the copyrighted work
- to distribute copies or phonograph records of the copyrighted work to the public by sale or other transfer of ownership, or by rental, lease, or lending
- to perform the copyrighted work publicly (in the case of literary, musical, dramatic, and choreographic works, pantomimes, and motion pictures and other audiovisual works)
- to display the copyrighted work publicly (in the case of literary, musical, dramatic, and choreographic works, pantomimes, and pictorial, graphic, or sculptural works, including the individual images of a motion picture or other audiovisual work)
- to perform the copyrighted work publicly by means of a digital audio transmission (in the case of sound recordings)

© Cengage Learning 2014

issues related to copyright, especially as they relate to the use of digital technologies and content for teaching and learning. However, due to the constant testing and interpretation of copyright law in the courts and the subsequent evolution of the law, it cannot be considered a definitive authority. It is best to keep track of changes in copyright and state and local interpretations of the law. You can visit the website of the U.S. Copyright Office at the Library of Congress and many other sites from colleges and universities, school districts, and other policy-related organizations for more information. Library and media specialists are often good sources of information about copyright in schools.

In response to the impact of information technology on copyrighted materials, the *Digital Millennium Copyright Act (DMCA)* was passed in 1998 (Pub. L. No. 105-304). The DMCA was a reaction to growing electronic commerce that heightened the penalties for copyright infringement on the Internet, but also impacted education. In particular, the DMCA placed strict restrictions on materials that could be used online for instruction. For example, as a teacher in a brick-and-mortar classroom, you could show a video or images or play sound recordings to the students present, but if you taught the same class at a distance, the DMCA severely restricted the amounts of digital media you could use. In fact, you probably couldn't use the same videos, images, and recordings in their entirety that you used with your face-to-face students.

With the number of distance learning opportunities growing quickly at all levels, copyright law was impacted again by the passage of the *Technology, Education, and Copyright Harmonization Act of 2002* (Pub. L. No. 107-273), commonly called the TEACH Act. This revision to copyright law clarified what uses of copyright-protected materials were permissible when used for distance education and also outlined required actions on the part of a school in order to be compliant.

The TEACH Act is limited to certain organizations including some educational institutions. However, to be eligible, the educational institution must be a nonprofit organization and be accredited. Public schools are normally nonprofit and accredited; however, some charter schools, virtual schools, and institutions of higher education are not, and therefore they are not eligible to use digital resources as governed by the TEACH Act (see Table 10.3 for an overview of the TEACH Act). The TEACH Act also requires that your district or school develop a policy that is distributed to all faculty, staff, students, and parents for the acceptable use of copyrighted materials. This policy, which may be part of an AUP, dictates how copyright materials will be identified to all who use them. Your district or school should also take steps to ensure that copyright-protected materials, especially digital materials, particularly used online, are accessible to the appropriate students *only* during the duration of the course and that they are not stored or distributed afterwards.

Table 10.3 The TEACH Act	
Your institution must:	**As a teacher, you must ensure copyright-protected material is:**
• Be a nonprofit organization • Be accredited • Have a copyright compliance policy • Provide notice on copyright-protected materials • Prevent copyright-protected material from being transmitted or stored beyond the period of instruction	• Directly related to, and an integral part of, instruction • Available only to registered students • Available during a time limited to instructional needs • Used in digital format, if available • Nondramatic in nature or a limited portion of a dramatic work

© Cengage Learning 2014

Your specific obligations as an educator using digital materials under the TEACH Act are to make sure the copyright-protected digital materials are an integral part of your instruction and are used under your supervision. That does not mean that you must be online at all times while your students are watching a streaming video or downloading a document used in your class. You should, however, have the ability to post and remove copyright-protected digital materials in a timely fashion related to their instructional use. You and your school or district must make sure these materials are available only to students who are enrolled in the class that requires the materials for instructional activities. This prevents you from posting copyright-protected materials directly to a school website that can be accessed by students or others outside of your class. However, using a learning management system that requires usernames and passwords is likely to be acceptable use.

When considering all of these stipulations, it is important to note that the materials you use must be legally obtained copies, and if they exist in digital format, you must purchase or obtain them in digital format. For example, you can't digitize your copy of an old VHS tape if it is available in a digital format. You also may use only 1) resources that are performances of nondramatic literary or musical works, 2) limited portions of other works, and 3) the same amount you would normally display in your face-to-face instruction. For example, while your school may have a license to show the entire taped production of "Romeo and Juliet" or the musical "West Side Story" in a classroom setting, you may not broadcast these in distance learning settings because they are both considered dramatic works.

Fair Use

So what *can* you and your students use in your classroom? It's important to understand whether material falls under the limitations of fair use, is in the public domain, or requires licensing, permission, or payment for use.

Fair use refers to the part of U.S. copyright law that allows limited use of copyrighted material without requiring permission from the copyright holder. Fair use guidelines have been established that allow for the limited use of some materials in educational settings. The following four criteria help us determine whether material falls within fair use:

1. the purpose and character of the use, including whether such use is of a commercial nature or is for nonprofit educational purposes;
2. the nature of the copyrighted work;
3. the amount and substantiality of the portion used in relation to the copyrighted work as a whole; and
4. the effect of the use upon the potential market for, or value of, the copyrighted work.

fair use
the portion of the U. S. copyright law that allows limited use of copyrighted material without requiring permission from the use of the copyright holder

When considering whether to use material you have found for instruction—whether you have reused a graphic, copied text, or downloaded an MP3 file—reflect upon these guidelines. If your purpose for using the material is transformative in some way—if it creates something new such as a critique or commentary, satire, or parody—your purpose may honor the first guideline for fair use. If it is a strict copy, it is probably not fair use under this guideline. For example, if you have created an audio collage of several different actors reciting lines from Shakespeare in an effort to illustrate characteristic features such as alliteration, cadence, or language use, you have transformed the work. Simply playing a movie back in its entirety requires you to honor the copyright restrictions of the work. That doesn't mean you can't use it; you just have to know when and how you can.

The material may meet the second guideline if the nature of the work is published and is factual rather than fictional. For example, the use of factual information (mathematical formulas, definition of DNA) that might be found or corroborated across several sources is more likely to be considered fair use than excerpting sections of journals, websites, poems, or other works of fiction and creative nonfiction that might be found on the web. Works that are out of print are also likely to be considered fair use (Harper, 2007).

The acceptable portion of the work you are using in relation to the whole is difficult to judge. There is no set number of words, lines, pages, measures or notes from musical works, or portions or number of graphics, web pages, or lines of code that can be used to measure fair use. While not a strict rule, several guidelines for educators suggest you follow a "10% rule," perhaps because of the prevalence of this amount repeated in copyright guidelines from the U.S. Copyright Office (2009). To stay within the guidelines for amount of work, do not use more than

- 10 percent or three minutes of a video, whichever is less;
- 10 percent or 1,000 words of text, whichever is less;
- 10 percent or 30 seconds of a musical work;
- 5 images from an artist or photographer;
- 10 percent or 15 images from a collection, whichever is less; or
- 2 copies of a multimedia project.

When using materials in your classroom for instruction, you are unlikely to have an effect on the potential market; however, educators should be careful about the term of use of the material. If you use a small portion of a digital work for only one semester or lesson, you are probably not affecting the potential market. But if you use the same material for more than two years, or you make more than two copies of a multimedia program, you should obtain permission for use from the copyright holder or follow guidelines for the appropriate purchase and licensing of the material. In summary, the use of copyrighted works for educational purposes is more likely to be considered fair use than their use for profit, but you should seek to understand the copyright restrictions common to any material you use regularly. Again, one of the best resources in your school will likely be your school librarian or media specialist.

Public Domain

Materials that have entered the public domain may be freely used and distributed. These materials include those for which the copyright has expired or work created by or funded by the U.S. government, and that includes a lot of information for teachers and students. Some authors also enter their work into the public domain upon creation. Determining when a copyright has expired has gotten more difficult with the passing of the *Digital Millennium Copyright Act of 1998* (Pub. L. No. 105-304). Generally, all works published in the United States prior to 1923 are now in the public domain. Since the passing of the DMCA, most works published since 1977 will remain in copyright for the life of the author plus 70 years. There are some exceptions, and you may want to check with your media specialist or the copyright holder if you believe a work may be in the public domain.

Teachers also should be careful with modern interpretations of materials that were originally published prior to 1923. For example, Walt Whitman's "Leaves of Grass" is in the public domain, but the jazz interpretations of the poems by pianist Fred Hersch are not. William Shakespeare's works, such as "Romeo and Juliet" are in the public domain, but many of the film versions are not.

Creative Commons Licensing

Perhaps because it takes a long time for legislation to evolve but technology changes constantly, there is a growing movement intended to help make material easier to use while still respecting the intent of copyright and one's intellectual property rights. Creative Commons licensing has evolved to provide guidelines for the sharing and using of intellectual property in an information-based society. Content creators who incorporate Creative Commons licensing when developing intellectual property can designate how you can use their work. They can allow or limit your use to copy, edit, remix, build upon, or distribute all or parts of their work.

Now, when you and your students are searching the Internet for content—whether text, images, music, or more—you want to keep your eyes open for the icons representing Creative Commons licensing (see Figure 10.1). The licenses generally tell you whether you should credit (attribute) the property owner, whether you can use it for commercial or non-commercial settings, and whether you can make derivatives of the original work. There is also a "share alike" licensing component that requires you to license any works you create based on the original with the same creative commons licensing. For more information about the licenses you and your students might encounter, visit the Creative Commons online (creativecommons.org).

> **Creative Commons licensing**
> guidelines whereby content creators allow or limit your use to copy, edit, remix, build upon, or distribute all or parts of their work

Icon	Creative Commons License
CC BY	**Attribution (CC BY)** This most flexible license allows you to use, remix, and distribute the work with attribution only.
CC BY ND	**Attribution – No Derivative (CC BY-ND)** As long as you don't make changes, you can use it or distribute the work.
CC BY NC SA	**Attribution – Noncommercial – Share Alike (CC BY-NC-SA)** You can use, remix, and distribute the work in non-commercial uses as long as your work bears the same license.
CC BY SA	**Attribution – Share Alike (CC BY-SA)** You can use, remix, and distribute the work under any setting as long as your work bears the same license.
CC BY NC	**Attribution – Noncommercial (CC BY-NC)** Any non-commercial uses or derivatives do not need to bear the same license.
CC BY NC ND	**Attribution – Noncommercial – No Derivatives (CC BY-NC-ND)** This most restrictive license allows you to download and share works with no changes an in non-commercial settings only.

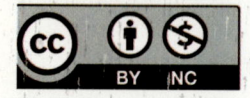

Courtesy of Creative Commons

Figure 10.1
Creative Commons licenses provide guidelines for how you can use, credit, and resuse material.

APPLY to Practice

Copyright Issues

Keeping up with copyright issues as they relate to technology can be difficult because of technology's rapid pace of change. Laws normally evolve over time in reaction to new social and technological developments, but it can take a while for the legal system to catch up. Laws also change when they are challenged in the court system. It's important that you establish strategies you can use to monitor the changes in copyright law and how these will impact the resources you can access and use in your teaching.

1. Identify web-based resources you can use to monitor copyright legislation. Several web-based government and non-profit resources exist that can respond to changes quicker than print. List these resources, the issues they follow, and links to them in your professional portfolio.
2. Share your findings with others in your class. Review the resources they have found and determine which should be added to your own list.

Academic Integrity

Just as you can benefit from the ease with which academic materials and resources may be found, searched, copied, and repurposed, so can your students. Without guidance and training, some of your students may find it all too easy to find and reuse copyright-protected material, regardless of their intentions. The use of other people's identities, such as the use of another student's, or even a teacher's password to access sensitive data, also may be alluring to some students and can have disastrous results. These issues are often addressed through AUPs or honor codes, but there are some proactive steps you can take to avoid problems in your classroom.

Plagiarism

Plagiarism is not a new problem, but digital tools have made this possibility easier. With extensive resources available on the Internet—both legitimate and otherwise—and through other digital resources such as encyclopedias, newspapers, journals, and curriculum subscriptions, a student can quickly gather and use the work of others and compile it in a digital document. Many students who know how to copy and paste on a personal computer may feel pressured to do so inappropriately when faced with the pressure of meeting an approaching deadline or getting a good grade.

The first line of protection against the inappropriate use of other people's work is to help students understand how to correctly use and cite source material. This can start in early grades. Some elementary schools have even developed policies that emphasize the importance of properly citing information students have received from other students, their parents, or from media resources such as television programs or websites. Obviously, as students get older and begin to create documents, graphics, and multimedia projects that draw on source materials, they need to understand how to appropriately cite those materials. They too, must understand individual rights and realize that even though they can find text, an image, or sound file on the Internet and quickly incorporate it into a document or movie, it is still protected under copyright law. Each writing style guide has different ways of correctly citing Internet resources. The proper way to cite information retrieved from the U.S. Copyright Offices is illustrated in Table 10.4, based on the format required by three popular style guides.

Another proactive step to prevent plagiarism is to design activities in ways that avoid the need for heavy reliance on material that can easily be appropriated from

Table 10.4 Citing Internet Resources

Citing resources can be confusing. There are multiple style guides with different procedures for correctly citing resources, and these methods can and do change over time with the release of new guidelines. The following is one example presented in three popular style guides, but because styles change, you and your students should consult the authority for the most recent guidelines.

APA Style
U. S. Copyright Office. (2009). *Reproduction of copyrighted works by educators and librarians*. Retrieved from www.copyright.gov/circs/circ21.pdf

Chicago Style
U. S. Copyright Office, *Reproduction of Copyrighted Works by Educators and Librarians*. Library of Congress. Accessed January 5, 2012. http://www.copyright.gov/circs/circ21.pdf

MLA Style
U. S. Copyright Office. *Reproduction of Copyrighted Works by Educators and Librarians*. Nov. 2009. Web. 5 Jan. 2012. <http://www.copyright.gov/circs/circ21.pdf>

© Cengage Learning 2014

other sources. Instead of assigning papers or compositions that simply require students to gather and report information, ask your students to use that information to support reflection, analysis, and evaluation. Have them use it to address open-ended problems that may have no one correct answer. Authentic instruction, which encourages more open-ended problems, becomes more important, and perhaps relevant, in the digital classroom where so much information is available with the click of a button.

Writing activities can be supported by technologies that can limit access to outside source materials and encourage deeper analysis on the part of students through debate or discussion. Threaded discussions, messaging tools, and online journals are but a few tools that can help students communicate original thoughts rather than simply finding and inserting facts, figures, and the ideas of others. Many forms of digital communication and some digital documents also can be tracked and time stamped to identify ownership and usage patterns.

Developing skills related to finding, analyzing, synthesizing, and reporting information—whether in traditional formats such as a research or term paper or in a multimedia presentation that combines text, images, audio, and video elements—is a common requirement in the academic careers of most students. Despite your good example and guidance, sometimes you may believe that a student has used the works of others inappropriately. There are some techniques you can use to investigate the actual source of the material. Keeping samples of work from students that are generated both inside and outside of class, such as through a digital portfolio, is a good practice for determining the legitimacy of a student's work. This type of student data allows you to quickly compare new works with the consistency of growth demonstrated across time, and any inconsistent use of language or rapid advancement in technique can be identified and verified with the student. Any type of strange formatting, such as changes in font, size, color, or unusual characters, logos, or other marks may indicate material that has been copied.

If you feel that a student's text-based work may contain the work of others, you can also use software applications or online resources to verify questionable passages. Schools and districts can quickly set up their own digital warehouse of student papers on which to search or may rely on commercial services that offer these services for a fee. Sometimes a simple search engine can provide the results of true authorship, and many search engines can look for documents in a variety of formats, including HTML and portable document format (PDF). Images may be more challenging, but chances are if your student did a simple Internet search you are likely to come across the same images in a similar search, and some search engines support image searches.

Generally, you can copy the passage or some key words you think may be the work of someone else and paste it into one of the search services or software applications. You can also search some of the many online paper services, sometimes called "paper mills," to look for matching titles or phrases from questionable documents. Another proactive strategy is to not only inform students that this type of service will be used, but require students to submit their own work to the service for scrutiny. This valuable lesson may help them realize just how well they are—or are *not*—doing at avoiding dishonest practices.

Cheating

With pressures to succeed academically from parents, peers, teachers, and society in general, many students may feel compelled to achieve success through dishonest means. As long as there have been tests and homework, there has been cheating, but the digital tools available to students, whether for academic purposes or not, have provided some unique methods for sharing answers and materials. Whereas students might once have passed notes in class on folded scraps of paper, they now have the capacity to store questions and formulas on calculators, send text messages to friends across the room or school, or use a camera phone or other mobile device to take a picture of a test and send it to their friends in a later class. While all of these possibilities exist, several simple strategies can help prevent both high- and low-tech cheating.

Simple observation can prevent a variety of cheating methods (see Figure 10.2). Standing and moving about the room during assessments will limit some of the more obvious methods, such as using a camera phone, PDA, or text messenger. Lab or classroom management software can be used to monitor student activity and block some functionality on student machines. Randomly assigning equipment to classes on test days can prevent some students from storing and sharing information with later classes. Some teachers also do a "cell phone check" on test days and have students store their phones and other digital devices at the teacher's desk or in the front of the room.

Much like preventing plagiarism, perhaps the best method for preventing cheating is to design assessments that encourage higher-order and critical thinking. Assessments that rely on low-level multiple-choice and identification questions are the easiest forms of assessment for students to compromise. Requiring students to

Figure 10.2
Observation is an effective way to prevent cheating during assessments, whether your students are taking a test using a computer or through other means.

> **THE GAME PLAN**
>
> **Combating Cheating**
>
> **Set Goals**
> Explore resources available to teachers to help combat cheating or plagiarism.
>
> **Take Action**
> If you have not already done so, visit some of the online resources available to teachers for identifying the authenticity of student work. One of the simplest methods for doing this is to copy and paste sentences or phrases from a student's work or relevant keywords into a search engine. You may be surprised to find the same quotes across numerous websites, whether from student papers or not.
>
> **Monitor**
> Can you find examples of the phrases or sentences you have selected? What additional resources have you found to help combat cheating and plagiarism? What strategies do they suggest? How well does your search support finding images?
>
> **Evaluate and Extend**
> Determine which resources or strategies provided you with the most helpful information.

analyze, synthesize, and evaluate information that incorporates relevant facts and data and requiring students to reflect on and interpret their own understandings will help limit sharing of answers—regardless of the technology available.

Protecting Confidential Data

Most school personnel are familiar with and have plans for the safeguarding of print-based student information. Paper-based lesson plan books, grades, health records, discipline referrals, and other sources of student information are routinely stored in vaults or other secure facilities—sometimes fire-safe vaults. These records can be important to students long after they've left the school system for such important tasks as obtaining additional schooling, employment, citizenship, or even verifying one's age for retirement purposes. Schools have long taken steps to keep this information secure. In fact, they are required to do so by law.

The *Family Educational Rights and Privacy Act* (FERPA, Pub. L. No. 93-380) requires student records to be kept confidential and places strict guidelines on who can have access to those records. Generally, schools must have written permission from the parent or eligible student in order to release any information from a student's education record. However certain agencies, such as other schools, the courts, accrediting agencies, and some officials working in services related to health, safety, and justice systems, may have access to student records without that permission.

As districts and entire states move to large-scale networked services for record keeping, you may have little opportunity to select the hardware and software that will keep these records secure in a digital environment. However, issues concerning your own and student data will arise and you should understand how you and others access that information, whether from your classroom, office, or home, and how it is kept secure.

There are some records, usually those that fall under the label of "directory information," that can be distributed under certain conditions—even on a web page. See Table 10.5 for a list of common directory information. **Directory information** is information that is contained in an education record that generally would not be considered harmful, or an invasion of privacy, if disclosed. Schools may disclose directory information without consent. However, schools must tell parents and eligible

directory information
information contained in an education record that generally would not be considered harmful, or an invasion of privacy, if disclosed

Table 10.5   Directory Information

Directory information includes, but is not limited to, a student's
- name;
- address;
- telephone listing;
- date and place of birth;
- major field of study;
- participation in officially recognized activities and sports;
- weight and height of members of athletic teams;
- dates of attendance;
- degrees and awards received; and
- the most recent, previous educational agency or institution attended.

© Cengage Learning 2014

students about directory information and allow them a reasonable amount of time to opt out of having directory information made public.

Just because an item is considered directory information, it does not give you unlimited permission to distribute or post it. Most schools will not post students' names or contact information to public venues, including print and digital news publications. Parents also have the right to restrict the posting or distribution of any information about their children, even in yearbooks, school programs, and newsletters. If your school or district chooses to seek this permission through the use of signed consent forms, whether from a student handbook, AUP, or media consent form, you should check with your school administration to verify that all students in your class or organization have indeed granted consent to have pictures or information displayed in class, print, or online.

TECH TOOLS & TIPS

Legal Issues Surrounding the Use of Images of Students and Student Work

Images of students or examples of their work can enhance a portfolio or class website; however, it is vital that you understand the legal restrictions on use. The same cautions apply to adults as well as children. While students constitute a special protected class, if you wish to include images of adults, play it smart and seek written consent, respect confidentiality, and be cautious. Remember that images published on the Internet can be viewed by a worldwide audience or distributed easily. Even when the materials will have more limited distribution, the following practices are critical when including student information or images.

1 Consent. You may not use photos or videos of others, especially minors, without consent. Specific information regarding the format of use, potential viewing audiences, distribution method, general content and purpose of images must be provided and written consent received prior to production. It is imperative that parental/guardian notification be explicit with written and dated permission obtained. Some schools seek this permission in their AUP or student handbook.

2 Identification. Standard practice is to refer to students by first name only. You can also refer to a group of students to avoid identifying individuals, such as "Students in my class..." or "Geography students at our school..." Adult names may be used in full as needed, but only with their written consent.

3 Student Work. You should secure parental/guardian permission for including student work in your portfolio. Individuals should not be identifiable. You can maintain confidentiality of identities on student work by using only first names or deleting or blocking out identifiers including city, school, and specific names.

4 Confidentiality. If your portfolio, blog, or website includes reflections about a student, never refer to that student by name. Use a pseudonym or general term and do not link sensitive reflections about a student to his/her photo or other identifying information.

© Cengage Learning 2014

Password Security

The modern school is full of passwords, identification cards, and other means to verify identity. Teachers and students alike may have identification cards with pictures and magnetic strips, as well as accounts with passwords for e-mail, access to student information systems, and favorite websites and online resources. Some schools may even use biometric devices, such as those that scan fingerprints, to identify students getting on buses, receiving school meals, or logging on to a school computer (see Figure 10.3). Keeping track of the way you access sensitive data and making sure that you keep it safe is both ethically and legally pertinent.

In terms of personal information, digital tools have made it easy to have access to an overwhelming amount of information. Often that information is secure and requires you to complete a profile so the system can verify, to some degree, that you really should be allowed to access the information it houses. The number of passwords you collect can be staggering and confusing. It's tempting to use one or two passwords over and over and to neglect changing them, but this can lead to consequences far beyond simple theft of a test document or grade tampering.

There are several steps you can take when required to maintain a large number of user names and corresponding passwords (see Table 10.6). One important step is to change your passwords frequently, at least every several months. Some network administrators may require users to change their passwords periodically. This can prevent those people who observe you logging in to your school network or e-mail system every day from exploring the possibility of using your account information, whether for malicious intent or just curiosity.

A common strategy is to use a mnemonic device, such as an acronym created from the first letter of each word in a sentence, to create your password. Generally, passwords should be at least eight characters long and use both upper- and lower-case characters as well as numbers and special characters. Consider the following:

1. Begin with the sentence, "My sister Alena likes to skate on ice."
2. Select the first letter of each word, which automatically includes uppercase and lower case letters: MsAltsoi
3. Replace some of the letters with numbers or characters that can either represent the letters or may even sound like the word they stand for. For example: MsA12sk@

Figure 10.3
Biometric devices, such as this iris-recognition technology, help to clearly identify students and staff.

Table 10.6	Tips for Creating Passwords
Do	**Don't**
• Use 8 or more characters • Mix upper and lower case, numbers, and special characters • Change your passwords often	• Use names, dates, or familiar numbers • Use any real word in any language, either forward or backward • Use a pattern of consecutive letters, numbers, or keys on your keyboard • Write them down or share them with anyone • Enter your password into a website at the request of an e-mail, regardless of who the message may appear to be from

© Cengage Learning 2014

There are software programs, some of them shareware, that can help you create passwords and store them in an encrypted format so that others cannot figure them out. If you forget a password, many websites have hint options or links to request a reminder. The system administrator may be able to reset your password or, if necessary, create a new account with a new password.

Promoting Responsible Use of Technology Resources

If you are familiar with using computers for schoolwork, communicating with friends or family, or entertainment, then probably you are also aware that some people may take actions that result in harm to others or to technology resources. The results of these actions can be annoying at the very least, but in the extreme they may lead to costly disruption of service or destruction of technology, as well as individual harm. While there are laws designed to discourage people from harming others or computers and networks, you need to make sure that you and your students become responsible users of technology, especially the Internet. Harm can result through the use of malicious software that affects vast numbers of computers and users directly or via the action of an individual against another individual or group. The software and practices described next in this chapter will continue to evolve, so it is important that you and your students learn what actions you can take to protect yourselves as well as your technology resources.

Internet Safety

Proponents of classroom Internet use view the seemingly unlimited amount of information and the ease of communicating with people all over the world as benefits. But these same characteristics may dissuade some teachers from using Internet resources for instruction due to the possibility of students coming in contact with undesirable content or individuals. Although many schools have harnessed the Internet to support instruction, students may need guidance in practicing safe, acceptable, and responsible use.

Several federal laws have significant impact on schools and how you, as a teacher, might use the Internet in your classroom. The *Electronic Communications Privacy Act* (ECPA, Pub. L. No. 99-558) was enacted in 1986 and addresses security and confidentiality issues of electronically disseminated communications. In 1998, Congress passed the *Children's Online Privacy Protection Act* (COPPA, Pub. L. No. 105-277) to help safeguard children as they use the Internet. As a result, websites that target children under age 13 must follow specific guidelines regarding the collection of personal information. Not only must they limit the kinds of information they collect, but they also must post notice about that

> **TEACHSOURCE VIDEO**
>
> Even very young students now access the Internet for learning activities. Go to the Education CourseMate website and review the video, *Teacher Perspectives: Internet Safety*, and then consider the following:
>
> 1. How could you adopt or adapt the "Internet Safety Day" model? What modifications could be made for older students?
> 2. What topics do you feel are most important for sessions such as these described in the video? What activities would you include?

information and how it is used. If your school or district website collects or stores student information from children under 13, it too must comply with COPPA.

Websites you use in class should have clearly posted privacy policies; if they solicit information from individuals, they must follow the COPPA guidelines. Furthermore, parents or guardians must provide consent for a child to enter personal information on a website. This permission may be required to be in writing—not digital format—but lobbying and action in courts will continue to test this provision of the law as software and information publishers want to capitalize on the web's ease of distribution.

The *Children's Internet Protection Act* (CIPA, Pub. L. No. 106-554) amended the earlier Communications Act of 1934 and requires schools and libraries receiving funds from the Universal Service Fund, commonly called the E-rate, to incorporate technology-based solutions to block access to material defined as obscene, pornographic, or harmful to minors. The act, passed by Congress in December 2000, is sometimes called the "Filtering Mandate." Although CIPA does not require that schools actually track how children or adults use the Internet, schools and libraries that receive E-rate funding have to certify to the Federal Communications Commission that they have complied with CIPA in two ways: 1) by installing a technology-based solution to block material deemed objectionable as outlined in the act, and 2) by adopting policies to monitor Internet use by students. These policies should address

- access by minors to inappropriate matter on the Internet;
- the safety and security of minors when using electronic mail, chat rooms, and other forms of direct electronic communications;
- unauthorized access, including activities that might be considered "hacking," and other unlawful activities by minors online;
- unauthorized disclosure, use, and dissemination of personal information regarding minors; and
- restricting minors' access to materials harmful to them.

Malicious Software

It wasn't so very long ago that most people considered e-mail to be a novelty. However, e-mail is so prevalent today that even students in kindergarten report having e-mail accounts. If you've had an e-mail account (or accounts) for any length of time, you've already learned the value and ease of sending and receiving messages, pictures, and other information anywhere across the globe. The boom in text messaging using phones or other devices has also increased the ease with which you can communicate

APPLY to Practice

Monitoring Legislation

Locate resources that allow you to identify and track legislative actions that relate to the use of educational technology in all the areas discussed throughout this chapter. These may be websites, journals, trade publications, discussion lists, or other services. Include these resources in your professional portfolio. A few examples are the U.S. Copyright Office, the American Library Association (ALA), the Consortium for School Networking (CoSN), the Library of Congress, and many universities and colleges.

with your friends, family, and others. Certainly, messaging technologies will continue to evolve, and few barriers may remain to prevent you from communicating with anyone at any time. Unfortunately, just as you can receive junk mail through the postal service, you have probably also received unwanted messages through e-mail. Unwanted messages can also come across cell phones, instant- or text-messaging devices, and blogs.

The term **spam** refers to unwanted messages across many of these technologies. The term became popular with the increased use of e-mail but may also be associated with other technologies, including text and instant-messaging devices, discussion boards, and blogs, among others. Spam can be more than annoying; it can lead to substantial losses to you as an individual as well as to organizations. Unlike junk mail delivered through the postal service, digital spam places most of the cost burden on you, the receiver. Some costs are minor, such as having to take time to delete unwanted messages from your e-mail inbox, but others can be more substantial to you personally, such as when you have to pay to receive an unwanted text message. Multiplied across the hundreds of thousands, if not millions, of recipients of a single spam message, the costs become substantial.

Spam can also include language or pictures that are unsuitable for your students and objectionable to you. These unwanted messages may also be a front for further spamming attacks. Messages that ask recipients to click on a web link to "unsubscribe," check the status of an account, or claim a prize may actually validate that your e-mail address is active and then store it or sell it to others for further spamming attacks. More malevolent intent can ask for sensitive personal information, including credit card numbers or passwords, in order to steal your identity, access bank accounts, or even to attempt face-to-face contact. **Phishing** refers to this type of spam, which may also be called **carding** or **spoofing**. Unfortunately, these messages may seem legitimate and may look like they've come from well-known and trusted sources (eBay, PayPal, and Best Buy are some well-known targets of phishing scams). They not only trick children but can be very convincing to adults.

You and your students should be wary of any e-mail that asks for sensitive information. If you feel you need to respond to these messages, you should reply by phone to institutions purporting to have sent you the phishing attempt—not by the means by which it was sent. Some institutions require you to provide answers to questions that only you know as a means of verifying your identity. Pretending to be another person or representing a business is illegal, so phishing attempts can also be reported to the authorities.

Spam can also contain malicious software, sometimes referred to as **malware**, which can cause significant harm to one or more computers as well as a computer network. You may already be aware of computer viruses or similar malware and may have been the recipient of one (or more!). The term virus (also discussed in Chapter 8) is often used to represent a wide range of malicious software types, but is usually most accurately associated with a software program that—once introduced into a computer—can attach itself to another program, replicate itself, and cause damage to software or data on the computer. A virus, and other malware, such as worms and Trojan horses, must be *introduced* to a computer by some action you or another person commits; therefore, they can often be prevented through appropriate use. Malware can be introduced to a computer by opening an attachment to a message or by sharing an infected document or file over a network or through a portable storage medium (e.g., disk, CD, or thumb drive).

You may also unknowingly install software on your computer that can be equally annoying and dangerous but may not be illegal. These include **spyware** that may record your usage patterns or may even collect sensitive information you transmit using your computer, and **adware** that incorporates the presentation of advertisements as a condition for operating the software. Adware and spyware are different from viruses

---

spam
unwanted messages through e-mail, cell phones, instant- or text-messaging devices, and blogs

phishing
a type of spam used to steal personal information, identity, and bank account numbers, or even to attempt face-to-face contact; also known as *carding* or *spoofing*

malware
malicious software that can cause significant harm to one or more computers as well as a computer network

spyware
software that records usage patterns or collects information unknowingly from the user's computer

adware
software that incorporates the presentation of advertisements as a condition for operating it

and other malware in several ways. Both are usually created by teams of software developers who see the applications as a legitimate method of collecting information from you to inform marketing and product development decisions. Also, you usually have to actively install some type of software, software that may seem very helpful or useful, in order for the spyware or adware to also be installed. While it may be obvious that you are installing adware, you often don't know that you may also be installing spyware in addition to the software you originally desired. Both adware and spyware can collect and transmit information back to the company that provided the software. This activity is often described in the Terms of Use for adware, but since you usually don't know you're installing spyware, it doesn't have Terms of Use.

The first line of defense against malware is often technological. Hardware and/or software that can prevent unwanted persons, messages, or software from entering a network or computer is called a **firewall**. Firewalls can be installed on a school or district (or larger) network server in order to help protect the entire network, or can be installed on a single computer as a personal firewall. You probably do—or should—have firewall software on your own computer right now. Commercial **virus-protection software** is also commonly used to scan files introduced to a computer or for periodic scanning of all files on a computer. Some virus-protection software can also repair infected files and delete malware from your computer. These software programs, as well as spyware blocker software, pop-up blocker software, and security software associated with your operating system should be updated periodically, which is often automated.

In addition to the use of hardware and software, you and your students should take actions to help prevent infecting your computers with malicious software. Be cautious of opening messages with misspelled words or irregular use of uppercase letters or symbols. You may be required to report suspicious messages to your network administrator, sometimes forwarding the message to the administrator with the routing of the message visible (most e-mail applications allow you to view "all headers" or "full headers" to see this information). Scan all attachments and don't open any documents that end with the .exe suffix unless you know where they came from. Students can be taught to help protect school technologies, and some teachers do this through targeted lessons, posters or guidelines, and consistent incorporation of safe practices in lessons and activities.

> **firewall**
> hardware and/or software that prevents unwanted persons, messages, or software from entering a network or computer

> **virus-protection software**
> software that scans computer files to identify and repair files infected by viruses and delete malware

THE GAME PLAN

Protecting Technology Resources

Set Goals
Learn more about malicious software and strategies to protect your technology resources.

Take Action
Find web resources that describe current viruses, worms, and other malware and how to protect your computer from them. Visit the websites for virus protection and personal firewall software vendors as well as sites for Apple Computers and Microsoft to find recommendations for protecting computers that run those operating systems.

Monitor
Review the software installed on the computer(s) you often use. Determine if they are at risk based on what you have found. Do you need additional information? Are there technology experts who can help answer questions about keeping your own computer safe?

Evaluate and Extend
Share your experiences with others. If you used or installed virus-protection or personal firewall software, what were your experiences? Did others have similar experiences?

Threatening or Unlawful Online Interactions

In your classroom or on the school grounds, it's often easy to spot students acting inappropriately. Students who threaten or bully others face-to-face can be identified and reprimanded, if necessary. But when bullying occurs through the use of social-networking tools such as Facebook, blogs, texting, and other means, it can be difficult to prevent or respond to since your school may have little or no authority in the matter. In fact, you may not be aware it is happening. The use of technologies to harass, defame, or intentionally harm another student or group of students is referred to as **cyberbullying**. The consequences of cyberbullying can be dramatic and extremely traumatic to the children involved and can result in emotional stress, withdrawal from school, relocation, and even suicide. Identifying actual cyberbullying can be challenging, but in research reported by the Cyberbullying Research Center (Hinduja & Patchin, 2011), approximately 20 percent of 11- to 18-year-old students from a random sample reported being the victim of cyberbullying at some point. Mean or hurtful comments and rumors online were the most common forms of cyberbullying reported by students in the study. About the same amount admitted to cyberbullying others, while 10 percent said they had been on both sides.

> **cyberbullying**
> using information and communications technologies to harass, defame, or intentionally harm another student or group of students

Some common methods of cyberbullying include:

- *Messaging.* Students can send anonymous messages via e-mail, text messaging, instant messaging, posting on other students' online journals (blogs), or social-networking sites, through chat rooms, or any other messaging method. The messages can be derogatory, hurtful, violent, or slanderous, and may contain offensive pictures or graphics.
- *Creating a website.* Students often create websites for school projects and can easily create a website that is hateful to another student or group of students. These websites can include lists such as "Who's Hot" and "Who's Not," similar to the popular yet often malicious "slam books" of classrooms from a bygone era. Cyberbullying websites can also contain highly objectionable language and hurtful statements.
- *Pictures, videos, and other recordings.* Camera phones have made it extremely easy to take pictures of students without their knowledge, such as when changing in a locker room. In addition, digital photos can be readily altered in offensive ways. Videos, pictures, and even audio files can be posted on websites or sent as part of messages.
- *Impersonation.* Students can impersonate another on websites, e-mail, during online games, or by stealing another student's password. The intent is often to get other students in trouble for acts they have not committed, perhaps by having their rights or access to games or web resources suspended. Students can also impersonate people by pretending to be a friend to the target student in order to win their confidence and ultimately deceive or belittle them.

Unfortunately, there may be little you or other school officials can do in some cases of cyberbullying, although the courts are testing many cases across the country. Much of what is posted on the Internet is protected by free speech and unless the cyberbully makes a threat of violence or actually commits a crime, there is little that authorities can do. Some of the speech posted on a website may be considered libel, but it is often expensive and time-consuming to prosecute. Cyberbullying often emanates from home or student devices and may not be related to school activities.

Schools may not be able to stop cyberbullying unless rules against it are written into the school or district's AUP, or the actions are covered under state law. A provision in an AUP may include the right to discipline students for their actions off campus that are intended to have an effect on a student or that adversely affect the safety and well-being of students while in school. Regardless, the best strategy to prevent and negate the effects of cyberbullying may be educating teachers, students, and parents. Many of the issues covered in this chapter, such as protecting passwords and appropriate e-mail use, are important for students to understand and follow. Students should also be aware that their actions are easily traced through digital media. Obtaining a domain to post a web page requires a credit card and the name of the owner of that domain is freely available through the domain's WHOIS database. Parents should also be informed of ways to promote responsible technology use and monitor how and what students are doing when it relates to online or mobile technologies. Some schools hold parent nights or cyber-safety classes for families. Students should also feel comfortable reporting to their parents and perhaps to school officials that they are victims of cyberbullying; some schools have developed hot lines or support services for students who may need to talk to someone or report potential cyberbullying.

At the point that inappropriate online actions involve adults, the behavior becomes more serious and can lead to **cyberstalking** or engaging with a predator. Sometimes, students participate in online activities that they may not realize are threatening. There are numerous gaming, social, and fan websites that students can visit in which they may unwittingly provide sensitive information to others. Children who visit and participate in a website devoted to playing games—even simple games, such as checkers or chess—may actually be communicating with adults who are collecting information from them, such as their interests and hobbies. Building trust with someone who seems to like the same things you do may inadvertently lead to providing contact information. The same is true of chat rooms or social networking sites, such as Facebook, in which students may provide a good deal of personal information that allows them to be easily identified, all within a context in which they believed they were acting naturally and appropriately.

Educating children about strategies for protecting sensitive information is critical. Students should realize that blogs, chat rooms, and other interactive communication vehicles can be monitored by just about anyone. Even something as harmless as creating a screen name can provide more information than necessary. For example, the screen names, "luv2cheer," "ftblhero42," and "suzeindc" all provide information of interest to online predators. The first is probably a screen name for a cheerleader, while the second is probably a football player who wears jersey number 42. The final screen name gives a location, Washington, DC, where one might find "Suze" or "Susie." These names, when combined with topics covered during a chat session, can provide a detailed profile of a child.

Some children may also create their own web pages that provide ample information about their ages, genders, and locations. Just by describing their hobbies or where they go to school ("I'm on the Middleboro swim team"), they may inadvertently be filling out their profiles. Posting a phone number, whether online or when using other messaging tools, can immediately pinpoint a child's home location. Entering a phone number in some search engines not only results in a complete address but may actually include a detailed map of how to get there!

Many schools do not authorize the use of chat software on school computers. But as chat rooms, blogs, instant-messaging, text-messaging, webconferencing, cell phones, and other technologies become more prevalent, some educators feel it is important to include technologies that are interesting and commonplace in order to engage students in learning. Regardless of which technologies you use in your classroom, those selected should be based on sound pedagogical principles and provide a strong fit for mastering the required content. When using communication software, such as chat or blogging software, it is best to take a few precautionary steps and inform the students what you are doing. While chat and discussion threads often scroll across a window quickly, software is available to record transcripts of conversations. Be aware of common chat room abbreviations and discuss them with your students and the difference between academic and social discourse. Involve your students in developing ground rules for participation, and they are more likely to behave appropriately and focus on the learning.

> **cyberstalking**
> using electronic means to stalk someone

Using Technology to Support Responsible Internet Use

Based on the requirements of CIPA and growing concerns among educators and parents alike, nearly 100 percent of all public schools reported using blocking or filtering software since 2005 (Wells & Lewis, 2006); most schools have turned to one or more

TECH TOOLS & TIPS

Ten Tips for E-mail Use

Where schools once taught etiquette for writing letters and using the telephone, they now emphasize Internet etiquette, or netiquette, for short. There aren't any universal standards, but the following netiquette tips may help you, your staff, and students ease into proper online behavior.

1 Be yourself. Don't pretend to be someone else or use someone else's password. Protect your own password and log off public machines.

2 Say hello. Include a salutation and acknowledge the person you're writing to.

3 Describe your message. Use short, descriptive titles for subject headings and restate the question or issue in a response. Quoting only pertinent material in a reply can save time and may be useful to your audience.

4 Be polite. Short messages may be seen as brusque, and UPPERCASE letters may be considered shouting. Although you may intend to be ironic or humorous, your text-based messages may lead to misunderstanding.

5 Is it important? Work out problems face-to-face, not through e-mail. Avoiding issues by sending e-mail merely delays resolution.

6 It's not that funny. Unsolicited forwards of the newest jokes often are not appreciated and can tie up someone's time and slow down server response. Spamming, or sending unsolicited mail to large groups, is seriously frowned upon, and some service providers may actually revoke your Internet service.

7 Make sure you mean it. Proofread messages for spelling, content, and meaning. Digital messages don't always remain private and can be sent quickly to hundreds, if not thousands, of people. Some e-mail has even been used as evidence in court!

8 To attach or not to attach? Large text or graphics files that require proprietary software can be time-consuming to download and may actually annoy the recipient. Software like Adobe Acrobat may work best for formatting large attachments, and files may be reduced in size by *stuffing* or *zipping* them.

9 Say goodbye. End with a signature and, if possible, make it a *brief* signature. Contact information can be useful in a signature, but unnecessary quotes, pictures, or HTML formatting may not be appreciated.

10 Clean up after yourself. On public machines, delete message files and quit the mail application to prevent others from using your password or account.

Source: Adapted from: AEL. (2000). *Principal connections: A guide to technology leadership* [CD-ROM]. Charleston, WV: Author.

technologies to help keep students safer as they use the Internet for learning. No one strategy can solve all unacceptable use problems, and you should not rely solely on technological tools. Training for parents, teachers, and students will help reduce the number and severity of problems you encounter.

Trusted Digital Resources

One method of supporting safe use of the Internet is to use known and trusted digital resources. You can direct your students to acceptable and valid material on the Internet, whether they are web-based references to which your school or district subscribes or are proven free resources.

Subscription content and curriculum services can also be valid resources and help support student inquiry in a safe environment. More than electronic encyclopedias, subscription services include content in a variety of web-based formats, and many support dynamic content generation by teachers and students as they connect schools to others around the world. Some textbook publishers offer web-based versions of their books as well as activities and materials that are only available online.

Many long-standing print or media companies with a proven track record in education, such as National Geographic, PBS (Public Broadcasting Service), and Discovery Education, have repurposed artifacts from their vast print and video archives for web delivery and generated all new forms of content just for school use.

Many of these organizations now consider web distribution so important that they develop materials and tools that capitalize on its unique attributes. Schools that use free resources must weigh the possibility that they may contain advertisements and consider how they want to limit students from leaving the assigned environment for expanded web surfing.

Social Bookmarking and Organizational Sites

While students are often taught how to search for information online, the reality is that searching the Internet can still be time-consuming and ineffective. Despite the best intentions of teachers, many students still use poor search techniques, such as taking the first found item from a search. Part of the problem may be the overwhelming number of items found in the usual Internet research, and those numbers are just going to keep getting larger as new information is put online. Other issues that make Internet research complicated include the natural tendency for most students to follow interesting links and get off-task, or to open so many windows that it's difficult to keep track of important information. Add to that the concern for students to stay on appropriate sites and avoid inappropriate material.

You can make student online research more effective and productive by identifying relevant and worthwhile resources first and organizing them for students to use. One way to do that is to create a classroom list of bookmarks, but a more flexible method is to use social bookmarking or other sites that allow you to group and organize URLs so you and your students can find them. You may already be familiar with the process of bookmarking your favorites on your computer, but what happens if you're not at your computer? Social bookmarking allows you to bookmark and tag information you find online from any computer and then share those bookmarks with others. The site Delicious was an early popular social bookmarking service, but others, like Diigo, are now available. Some offer additional features, like being able to annotate information on web pages, so you can point your students to the most pertinent information—a great scaffold for those who need it. In addition to social bookmarking, other types of organizers, like iCyte, LiveBinders, and Symbaloo, use different types of interfaces that ultimately serve the same purpose of trying to organize information you find on the web.

Filtering Software

Filtering software is one of the easiest technology-based solutions to help schools comply with CIPA. While you may not be personally responsible for installing or maintaining filtering software on your school computers, you should know whether your school or district uses filtering software, your obligations for that use, options for reporting inappropriate sites, as well as for unblocking desirable websites that have been blocked.

Designed to help prevent students from coming into contact with inappropriate material when using the Internet, **filtering software** remains a contentious issue for many. Advocates for free speech or those who oppose censorship argue against the limitations these tools place on access to information; however, the increasing amounts of information available on the Internet and the unlimited topics covered have led many schools to use filtering software. The growth rate of information is so quick that filtering software offers one strategy to providing a supportive environment for teaching and learning. Filtering software is also less time consuming than evaluating or previewing all the individual sites with which you or your students may come into contact during the school year and over subsequent years.

Unfortunately, filtering software is not always 100 percent effective. Keywords used to ban sites can be derived subjectively, and most filtering services do not publish their lists. This is to protect their proprietary information but also to

> **filtering software**
> software designed to help prevent students from coming into contact with inappropriate material when using the Internet

prevent individuals from subverting their tools by bypassing known sites that are filtered. Filters can also block desirable content, and they may not take into account the varying ages, levels of maturity, and individual needs of users—although filtering software designed specifically for students of different ages does exist. It can be difficult, however, for a district that uses filtering software across the network to allow access to material that may be deemed appropriate to students in one grade and not another. Schools that use filtering software without knowing which sites are being blocked and why may unintentionally censor materials that are constitutionally protected. Some filtering software providers allow schools to customize their installation of the software by adding or removing sites to the general list as well as providing the ability to allow teachers to identify inappropriate sites if encountered accidentally. This often takes place through a website or via e-mail, and the inappropriate site can often be removed from access within 24 hours, sometimes more quickly. You should become familiar with the process for reporting sites that should be considered for filtering, as well as those that might be inappropriately blocked.

Proxy Servers

Proxy servers are software applications that perform several functions, including filtering and storing Internet content. A proxy server can download and save frequently visited websites in a storage area called a cache. This can result in improved network performance because users can view already-downloaded websites without a long wait. A proxy server also acts as a low-level firewall and provides limited protection against network intrusions such as viruses or denial of service attacks. For many districts, filtering software installed on a proxy server is an effective way to protect the network and its users at one point of service that can be easily monitored, upgraded, or repaired, if necessary. Consider, instead, how difficult it would be to combat a network attack in even a small district with a few hundred computers if these tools were located on individual computers. The costs associated with labor alone would be enormous and could effectively shut down instructional computer use for days.

Some proxy servers have features that provide greater management of Internet use on your network by requiring verification of identity or prohibiting unacceptable use. For example, proxy servers may be used to eliminate the use of chat rooms, if desired. They can also prevent the use of software that might overload your network, such as peer-to-peer file-sharing programs that reached their zenith of popularity and notoriety with the music-sharing program Napster.

> **proxy servers**
> software applications that perform several functions, including filtering and storing Internet content

APPLY to Practice

Web Filters

1. Most public schools use some type of filter to block access to certain Internet sites. What are your beliefs about the appropriateness of web filtering? Under what circumstances, if any, would you support the use of web filters?
2. Search the web to locate descriptions of filtering software. Examine a few of the web filter sites such as Cyber Patrol and Net Nanny and determine what type of content is filtered or blocked and why. Try to determine how that information is blocked and how these practices are monitored and kept current.
3. Does the information you found influence your beliefs about the use of filtering software? Discuss your views with your peers. If there are differing opinions, what evidence can you or your peers provide to support your positions?

Summary of Using Technology to Support Responsible Internet Use

Students are taught to be responsible on the playground, in the cafeteria, and in classrooms, and with the growing reliance on the use of the Internet for many aspects of education, work, and entertainment, many teachers feel it is their obligation to give students the opportunity to learn responsible online behaviors on the Internet. You can do the same by using some of the many established Internet Safety curricula or developing your own short lessons on the appropriate and inappropriate uses of different digital resources. These lessons may include searching the web for instructional materials, sending e-mail, and participating in web-based discussions such as chat rooms and blogs. Some schools involve parents in training sessions at the beginning of the school year or provide technology nights or make presentations at parent organization meetings (such as the PTA or PTO). Parents who know how their children will use the Internet for learning and have the opportunity to practice using the same tools and resources will feel more comfortable with those uses and can support similar appropriate uses at home.

Organize your classroom so that students are guided to use Internet resources—actually, all resources—appropriately. As we mentioned in Chapter 8, place computers where the monitors can be observed easily. Limit online time and incorporate study aids, work sheets, and activities like WebQuests that are structured to encourage students to stick closely to learning goals. You and your students can also build a class launch page, social bookmarks, or other organizing sites that quickly point students toward appropriate resources and promote productive use of limited Internet time. Students can also work in groups at the computer to discourage inappropriate use.

Before beginning an Internet-based project, it's helpful to demonstrate successful search strategies and review responsible use practices. Your school may also use academic search engines or restricted content services. Make sure your students incorporate appropriate citation strategies for both digital and print materials to avoid plagiarism and copyright infringement and know the consequences of illegal use of digital materials. As students practice and follow ethical and legal technology practices in your classes, they will be more prepared to harness these tools for continued productivity and growth in the future.

APPLY *to Practice*

Responsible Use of the Internet

Create a plan for safe use of the Internet in your classroom.

1. Find examples from the news media in which teachers or students inadvertently took actions that would not have been considered safe use of the Internet. What were the outcomes? How could they have been avoided?
2. Consider your preferred plan of action for safe Internet practices for your students. Will you rely on a technology solution? Teachable moments? A combination? How is your solution based on your own experiences in using Internet resources? What reasons do you have for selecting your solution?
3. Have you ever experienced or been placed in a situation that made you feel unsafe when using the Internet? If so, what did you do? How could you use this experience to help your students make appropriate decisions and take actions to remain safe? Would your answer differ if you were working with third graders versus seventh graders versus seniors in high school?
4. Share your plan with someone in the class and discuss differing perspectives and strategies.

Chapter Summary

Schools in the digital age may face some challenges in terms of ethical, legal, and responsible use of resources; however, this chapter provides strategies you can use to model and promote acceptable use in your classroom. Most districts and schools already have acceptable use policies that you and your students are expected to follow. As technologies and the information they access change over time, you or other teachers you work with may be tapped to help your school adjust its acceptable use policies. You'll certainly be able to model acceptable use in your own classroom for your students.

Also changing are the ways we access and incorporate information and intellectual property that others may have created. While copyright legislation continues to evolve, new copyright practices, such as Creative Commons licensing, have emerged to help teachers, students, and others leverage the power of Internet technologies and the variety of media and information to which they provide access. There are many places on the web you can go to find text, images, songs, movies, and more that you and your students can use. Paired with strategies to support academic integrity, you should realize there are numerous ways you and your students can use digital information in your classroom ethically and legally.

The final section of this chapter provides technical options and strategies you can incorporate in your classroom to promote responsible use of technology. Many teachers capitalize on the growing number of content and curricular resources now available and use a combination of approaches to support and promote responsible use of technology resources. The efforts you take in your classroom can have far reaching implications as your students continue to grow and use new digital technology in and outside of school.

In the next chapter, we continue our discussion of digital citizenship. We discuss ways to "address the diverse needs of all learners by using learner-centered strategies and providing access to appropriate digital tools and resources" (NETS-T 4.b) and "develop and model cultural understanding and global awareness by engaging with colleagues and students of other cultures using digital-age communication and collaboration tools" (NETS-T 4.d).

Web Resources and Activities

Review resources that promote responsible, legal, and ethical use of technology and intellectual property on the Education CourseMate website, including

- the U.S. Copyright Office at the Library of Congress and the Creative Commons;
- links to filtering solutions and academic search engines;
- curriculum and content to support instruction related to Internet safety;
- social bookmarking and organizational sites; and
- organizations that can help you identify and track legislative actions that relate to the use of educational technology.

YOUR PORTFOLIO

To demonstrate competency in ISTE NETS-T Standard 4.a and 4.c, add the following items to your portfolio:

1. Develop a philosophy statement that discusses your commitment to responsible, legal, and ethical use of digital technologies. Provide explicit reasons why it is important for teachers and students to consider these issues in teaching and learning, perhaps drawing from headlines you've explored or experiences you've had in your own education. Include specific strategies that you will include in your instruction to advocate, model, and teach responsible, legal and ethical use.
2. Identify one aspect of responsible, legal, and ethical use that you believe will be important for your students to learn. Develop a lesson that you can use to teach these principles to students at your chosen grade level.

References

AEL. (2000). *Principal connections: A guide to technology leadership* [CD-ROM]. Charleston, WV: Author.

CBS News. (February 6, 2011). Did the Internet kill privacy? *CBS Interactive Inc.* Retrieved February 1, 2012, from http://www.cbsnews.com/stories/2011/02/06/sunday/main7323148.shtml

Harper, G. K. (2007). The copyright crash course. Austin, TX: University of Texas Libraries. Retrieved February 1, 2012, from http://copyright.lib.utexas.edu

Hinduja, S., & Patchin, J. W. (2011). Cyberbullying: Identification, prevention, and response. Cyberbullying Research Center. Retrieved February 1, 2012, from http://cyberbullying.us/

James, S. D. (2011). Gay Buffalo teen commits suicide on eve of national bullying summit. *ABC Good Morning America.* Retrieved February 1, 2012, from http://abcnews.go.com/Health/gay-buffalo-teen-commits-suicide-eve-national-bullying/story?id=14571861#.Twbn-Er1zgH

McMillan, R. (March 4, 2011). Top student charged with fixing grades for cash. *PCWorld.* Retrieved February 1, 2012, from http://www.pcworld.com/businesscenter/article/221442/top_student_charged_with_fixing_grades_for_cash.html

Pub. L. No. 93-380. (Family Educational Rights and Privacy Act—FERPA).

Pub. L. No. 94-553. (Copyright Act of 1976).

Pub. L. No. 99-558. (Electronic Communications Privacy Act of 1986).

Pub. L. No. 105-277, 112 Stat. 2681, Title XIII. (Children's Online Privacy Protection Act of 1998—COPPA).

Pub. L. No. 105-304, 112 Stat. 2860. (Digital Millennium Copyright Act of 1998).

Pub. L. No. 106-554, Title XVII. (Children's Internet Protection Act of 2000—CIPA).

Pub. L. No. 107-273, Sec. 13301. Educational Use Copyright Exemption (Technology, Education, and Copyright Harmonization Act of 2002—TEACH).

U. S. Copyright Office. (2009). *Reproduction of copyrighted works by educators and librarians.* (Circular 21). Retrieved February 1, 2012, from www.copyright.gov/circs/circ21.pdf

Wells, J., & Lewis, L. (2006). *Internet access in U.S. public schools and classrooms: 1994–2005* (NCES 2007-020). U.S. Department of Education. Washington, DC: National Center for Education Statistics.

Diversity and Cultural Understanding

OUTCOMES

In this chapter, you will learn to

- Support the diverse needs of students by employing **learner-centered strategies**;
- Plan and manage classroom activities to ensure all students have **equitable access** to technology resources; and
- Identify strategies you can incorporate in a culturally responsive classroom to promote **cultural understanding and global awareness**.

iste.nets

ISTE Standards Addressed in Chapter 11

NETS-T 4. Promote and Model Digital Citizenship and Responsibility

Teachers understand local and global societal issues and responsibilities in an evolving digital culture and exhibit legal and ethical behavior in their professional practices. Teachers:
b. address the diverse needs of all learners by using learner-centered strategies and providing access to appropriate digital tools and resources; and
d. develop and model cultural understanding and global awareness by engaging with colleagues and students of other cultures using digital-age communication and collaboration tools.

In Chapter 10, we began our discussion of digital citizenship with a focus on legal and ethical behaviors and strategies for responsible use of technologies. In this chapter, we focus on digital citizenship in a different way. Here we encourage you to look beyond your personal experiences to develop and model cultural understanding and global awareness in a way that addresses the diverse needs of all learners.

One effect of new technologies in all areas of our lives is the increasing globalization of our world. Using digital technologies, you're able to communicate with friends across the globe through participation in online role-playing games, discussion forums about your favorite hobbies, or through social-networking sites. Teachers and students, too, are connecting across the globe through the use of technologies such as electronic pen pals, video- and webconferencing, or virtual field trips. These opportunities to communicate and collaborate with individuals of different cultures create a need for greater cross-cultural understanding.

The changing cultural landscape of schools within America will also impact your classroom. If trends in census data continue, by 2020 the percentage of minority students—students described as nonwhite—in public elementary and secondary schools will be greater than white students, with Hispanic students composing the largest minority group. Further, the percentage of elementary and secondary students in American public schools who speak a language other than English at home rose from 9 percent in 1979 to 21 percent in 2008, with Spanish being the most common home language for these students (U.S. Department of Education, 2010).

The **culturally responsive teacher** is one who understands and capitalizes on the unique cultural attributes and experiences of students to promote student achievement (Gay, 2010; Villegas & Lucas, 2007). Culturally responsive teachers exhibit six key behaviors. They:

1. are socially conscious, meaning that one's understanding is influenced by one's culture;
2. view students' diverse backgrounds as assets rather than liabilities;
3. feel personally responsible for helping schools be more responsive to all students;
4. understand how learners construct knowledge;
5. know about the lives of their students; and
6. design instruction that builds upon students' prior knowledge and experiences and stretches them beyond the familiar.

In these ways, culturally responsive pedagogy is very much in line with the transformative stage of technology integration as described by ISTE (2008) and thus complements other concepts addressed throughout this book. Similar to differentiated instruction and universal design for learning (Chapter 6), and authentic instruction (Chapter 3), culturally responsive pedagogy suggests you know and understand the learning styles, preferences, and abilities of your students in order to provide successful learning experiences. Additionally, culturally responsive teachers employ ongoing and culturally aware assessments using a variety of formats, addressed in Chapter 7, to monitor student learning and evaluate instruction. In this chapter, we will build on the knowledge you've gained throughout this book by focusing on the need to address cultural and socioeconomic diversity and by describing methods for developing social consciousness, learning about the lives of your students, and helping schools become more responsive to all students.

> **culturally responsive teacher** understands and capitalizes on the unique cultural attributes and experiences of students to promote student achievement

Learner-Centered Strategies

ISTE NETS-T Standard 4.b indicates that you will "address the diverse needs of all learners by using learner-centered strategies." This standard implies that learner-centered strategies, by definition, enable you to consider and meet the diverse needs of your students. This should sound familiar. We spent a good portion of Chapter 3 describing the key components of learner-centered instruction under the overarching concept of authentic instruction. That is, the components of authentic instruction (autonomous, active, holistic, authentic, and challenging) are those that allow you to create a learner-centered classroom that better attends to your students' diverse interests, capitalizes on their diverse talents and interests, and addresses their diverse needs for knowledge and skills. Meeting the needs of learners was further supported through the concept of differentiating instruction and using digital technologies to structure and support learning based on the principles of universal design for learning. Culturally responsive instructional methods tend to be holistic and often require students to develop and employ diverse knowledge and skills—personal, moral, social, political, cultural, and academic—within a single activity (Gay, 2010). In this section we briefly discuss how specific components of a learner-centered environment can be structured to support the diverse social, cognitive, and metacognitive needs of learners.

Supporting the Social Needs of Students: Creating a Collaborative Environment

A number of educators have described the importance of creating a classroom environment that is conducive to collaborative inquiry (see Figure 11.1). If we want students to express their own opinions on controversial issues, or to feel comfortable challenging others' points of view, they need to feel assured that they will not be criticized or reprimanded for doing so. Barell (2007) referred to this as an "invitational environment" while Kolodner and her colleagues (2003) described it as a "culture of collaboration." Regardless of the label used, it is important that the underlying values of trust, open communication, and risk-taking be fostered and practiced. When students come to us from disadvantaged or impoverished backgrounds, immersion in safe, interactive learning environments is a powerful way to engage their thinking and motivate their learning. Learner-centered approaches necessitate that we attend not only to learners' *cognitive* needs, but also to their *emotional* and *social* needs.

So what does an invitational environment look like? What are its key characteristics? According to Barell (2007) the following elements are essential:

- *Teacher modeling.* Think aloud through problematic situations, share both successful and unsuccessful experiences, and model the kinds of behaviors and dispositions we want students to gain (e.g., curiosity, persistence, open-mindedness).
- *Questioning.* Use questions that challenge students to go beyond simply finding answers in a book, from a person, or on the Internet. Model and encourage students to use critical questioning strategies.

Figure 11.1
A collaborative learning environment addresses not only cognitive needs, but emotional and social needs as well.

- *Quality responding.* Respond to students' statements, questions, and expressions of feelings in ways that communicate sincere interest in knowing more about their thoughts and feelings.
- *Peer interactions and discussion.* Encourage genuine discussion in which students respond positively to each other, question each other, and openly consider multiple points of view in order to arrive at a conclusion; promote the idea that all members of the community share responsibility for learning.
- *Reflective journals.* Use both structured and unstructured journal writing to enable students to share their thoughts and feelings about what they have learned, how they have learned it, and how well they have participated in the problem-solving process. Reflection allows students to abstract from their experiences what they have felt, thought, and learned.

Some of these ideas are probably fairly familiar to you and it's likely that you will be comfortable using or promoting their use in your classroom. However, it's also important to recognize that many of these strategies are skills that develop over a period of time and will not be as easy to implement as you wish. The important thing to remember is to give yourself time and permission to go slowly, expecting your skills to gradually increase over the first few years of your teaching career. Regardless of your initial expertise, students will take their cues from you in terms of how you facilitate a learning environment that is welcoming to all.

Supporting the Cognitive Needs of Students: Promoting Content Learning

Just as creating a culture of collaboration can help you attend to your students' diverse social needs, creating a culture of thinking can help you attend to their diverse cognitive (intellectual) and metacognitive (reflective) needs. We need to remember that one of the primary reasons we use authentic instruction is to promote students' deep understanding of subject-matter content through the process of *doing*. Despite the fact that content learning is one of the key reasons for using an approach that incorporates authentic instruction, it is relatively easy for both teachers and students to lose sight of this goal and to focus, instead, on simply completing the many interesting activities in which they are engaged. The research conducted by Newmann et al. (2001) in the Chicago Public Schools illustrated that even for students in highly disadvantaged schools, their ability to "master the basics," as measured by standardized tests, improved when teachers assigned work that demanded both complex thinking and detailed communication about issues that were important in their lives.

Ritchhart, Church, and Morrison (2011) suggest that you step back and do a quick analysis of the activities in your classroom and those required for deeper understanding of a content or skill area. They suggest you consider 1) what students spend most of the time doing during a class, 2) what professionals (scientists, writers, artists, and others) do when engaged with that content, and 3) what you remember doing in order to develop new understandings in that content area. If your student actions match the other two settings, your instruction is likely to support deeper understanding, encourage thinking, and require students to *do* the subject. Generally, when professionals do their work, especially at an expert stage, they are using many different types of thinking to look at problems and make decisions based on subject-matter knowledge. It's not just repeating facts and figures. In order to encourage this deeper level of cognition among your students, Ritchhart et al. (2011, pp. 11, 13) encourage activities that promote different kinds of thinking, such as:

1. observing closely and describing what's there;
2. building explanations and interpretations;
3. reasoning with evidence;

4. making connections;
5. considering different viewpoints and perspectives;
6. capturing the heart and forming conclusions;
7. wondering and asking questions; and
8. uncovering complexity and going below the surface of things.

When using a learner-centered approach, teachers need to be prepared to deal with students' misconceptions and/or inability to make the links between the interesting activities they are completing and the content they are supposed to be learning. One way to address this is to use more direct means for helping students make these connections. The developers of WISE (Web-based Inquiry Science Environments) use the term "making thinking visible" to refer to strategies that enable students to reveal what and how they are thinking within a specific content domain (Linn, Clark, & Slotta, 2003). For example, as part of the WISE approach, students post online responses at various stages in their inquiry, which are saved and can be accessed at a later date by either the student or the teacher. Following this, prompts are used to help students connect their ideas to project topics, such as, "How do we use all of this information to solve the problem?" (Linn et al., p. 528). By directly asking students to connect ideas, we help them understand and integrate them into a more coherent whole.

A second way to aid with concept integration is to directly reinforce the learning goals. That is, we can't assume that students are aware of the learning goals they are supposed to be achieving. Kolodner and her colleagues (2003) help make this more obvious through the use of "rules of thumb," which are student-generated rules used to explain their observations during project work. Rules of thumb are posted in the classroom and are continually tested through additional student-designed experiments. And so, based on students' findings and new observations, they are continually under revision. The teacher guides students' ongoing discussions and challenges students to support their theories with evidence, but refrains from correcting assumptions until students have had the opportunity to test their rules. However, at some point, later in the process, the teacher may need to present the rule through a just-in-time lesson or mini-lecture. As you might guess, lectures aren't common in authentic learning environments, but this doesn't mean they are never used. In fact, sometimes a lecture is the best way to help students understand the content being addressed in an authentic learning activity.

To guard against students becoming more concerned about completing tasks than learning content, it is important to continually help students make links between claims and evidence, questions and information, project design and learning goals. The use of scientific reasoning should be established as part of the classroom culture. This may even be described as encouraging curiosity or wonder. Even in disciplines other than science, a culture of "expert" reasoning is important, and can help students become logical thinkers. Posting reminders around the classroom ("Support your claim!" "Present your evidence!") can keep everyone focused on this expectation. Finally, once it is clear what and how students are thinking, it is important to address their misconceptions or biases. Many educators recommend that you begin these activities by asking students to articulate their own beliefs about a phenomenon, which you can capture in a concept map or graphic organizer, or by other digital means. Often, students' initial, naive thinking can play a central role within the inquiry process, especially when teachers can capitalize on the value of failure and refinement.

The strategies described above can support the intellectual, or cognitive, engagement of all students in the authentic learning activities used in your classroom. Thus, regardless of where students enter the process in terms of background knowledge or skills, they have the opportunity to construct deeper understandings through participation in meaningful activities in the learning environment.

STORIES from Practice

Promoting Thinking and Reasoning Skills

Pete Anderson, a high school math teacher in Henrico County Public Schools in Virginia, likes to help students understand that mathematical concepts and language are found everywhere and that the critical thinking and reflection skills they can develop holistically can be applied in their math studies. To do this, he has embraced the notion of problem-based learning and kicks off the year by exploring different types of thinking by incorporating popular "whodunit" mysteries.

Using stories such as Agatha Christie's *Murder on the Orient Express,* Anderson doles out chapters over a period of a month, that students read at home. During class, he focuses his instruction on collaboration and logic problems—setting up student groups that he switches often to expose the students to others. Some of the problems are very open-ended, drawing from college textbooks such as *Crossing the River with Dogs,* which provides an introduction to structured skills that students can use to solve complex problems. The students can really struggle with these problems, especially the more advanced students because, "They're ready to take notes and do homework, but they're afraid to be wrong." The ultimate result, he hopes, is that students realize that logic and reasoning are embedded in many real-life situations, and their study of math can relate.

He tempers the open-ended problems with instruction on problem-solving strategies. He notes that his pacing guide has logic problems interspersed throughout the year, but he's chosen to place them at the beginning of instruction in order to hone student problem-solving skills so they can relate them better to the concepts of math. "It's all about reasoning," he says. He puts a lot of basic information online using podcasts and other forms, so that during class students show *how* they have solved problems and justify their reasoning. Multiple students will share their work, and Anderson focuses on the cognition—forcing students to think about what does and doesn't work and why. In this way, he truly serves as a facilitator of knowledge construction as he supports the cognitive needs of his students; students take the lead in terms of sharing and talking about their thinking. "It's also saved a lot of time," according to Anderson. "I've saved half the class time by having them do the basic work at home," he reports, so he has more time to focus on cognition and problem solving and how it relates to math.

What about those murder mysteries? At the end of the first month of school, he and the kids act out the solution, sometimes with the help of others, like the school media specialist. The Orient Express comes alive through chairs and simple sets on the auditorium stage including still images of characters from the movie. Some of the students read parts with Anderson, of course, playing famed Inspector Hercule Poirot. As he emphasizes, "In the end, it's all about reasoning. It's not just important to know whodunit, but how to figure that out."

Source: From personal interview with Peter Anderson, conducted by author. Used with permission of Peter Anderson.

Supporting the Metacognitive Needs of Students: Promoting Reflection

metacognition
the ability to think about our own thinking

An important kind of thinking, first mentioned in Chapter 2, is **metacognition**; that is, the ability to think about our own thinking. Research has shown that reflection, as a form of metacognition, is a vital component of authentic learning approaches. Reflective thinking helps students make connections among their learning goals, the processes they use to achieve those goals, and the content they are learning. It also helps them to better understand processes and explanations so that they can apply them beyond the immediate problem they are solving. That's why the monitoring stage of the GAME plan is so important. It forces students to think about what they're learning and how it applies to the current situation as well as other issues and problems.

In this way, reflection serves as the other half of the activity-construction process, enabling students to make sense of the tasks they have completed. However, when asked to reflect on what they have learned from such activities, students have a tendency to focus on the task, experiment, or the project rather than on conceptual understanding of the key concepts or principles. One way to counteract this is to provide *ongoing* opportunities for students to articulate what they're learning, whether in their small groups or as a whole class. For example, in your role as a facilitator you can ask probing questions, challenge a particular perspective or argument, or offer an alternative hypothesis, thus forcing students to interpret the information they have gathered. By alternating hands-on, investigative work with interpretive or reflective work, students can share what they have learned and benefit from the perspectives of others. Finally, the use of frequent checkpoints and record-keeping devices (e.g., group folders or file directories, digital journals or portfolios, goal charts) can keep students focused on their learning goals and provide opportunities for reinforcement or redirection. These techniques can also serve motivational purposes as they allow students to take note of the progress they are making.

While reflection is not a foreign notion to students, teachers need to explicitly promote, guide, and support it among their students by explicitly incorporating strategies and activities that facilitate reflection. Consider how this book has provided guidance to you on reaching levels of critical self-reflection. Reflection doesn't become a habit unless it is used continually. It's important to leave time in the school day for your students to engage in these types of reflective activities and to guide and support students' efforts until they become comfortable with the process. Luckily, adding reflective thinking activities to the learning environment is a relatively simple thing to do, as you've seen throughout this book. The strategies for enhancing it are found in some of our most conventional classroom activities—discussions, prompts, and modeling. And, by incorporating these types of strategies, we can greatly increase students' learning.

Another primary goal of authentic instruction is to help students develop the skills needed to regulate their own learning, and metacognition is an important aspect of this process. Authentic instruction encourages teachers to offer opportunities for students to practice self-directed learning strategies where they set their own goals, monitor their progress, and determine next steps toward goal achievement. Although it is unlikely that students will possess these skills initially, early efforts can be supported with specific scaffolds, such as the use of the GAME plan framework. For example, students can determine daily goals, rate their progress at the end of the day, and then set new goals for the next day. Using problem logs, students can reflect on the strategies used to accomplish specific goals and then rate the effectiveness of those strategies, based on how well the goals were met. While the intent of these activities is

TEACHSOURCE VIDEO

Go to the Education CourseMate website for this text and watch the video *Digital Storytelling in the High School Classroom*.

1. How do the activities in the classroom videos support principles of learner-centered instruction described in this chapter?
2. How do they support
    a. the social needs of students?
    b. the cognitive needs of students?
    c. the metacognitive needs of students?

APPLY *to Practice*

Supporting the Diverse Needs of Students

1. Describe a learning environment that stands out in your memory. It may be one that you remember fondly because of the way it nurtured your own unique learning needs or it may be one that was challenging to you.
2. In your description, describe the degree to which the diverse social, cognitive, and metacognitive needs of students were addressed. Your description may include a variety of methods or structures that do or do not support the following components:
    a. creating a collaborative environment to support the social needs of students;
    b. promoting content learning to support the cognitive needs of students; and
    c. promoting reflection to support the metacognitive needs of students.
3. Knowing what you now know, how could that learning environment have been altered to better support the diverse needs of students? If some structures or practices were successful, how could those be applied to other learning environments? What technologies supported, or could have supported, the needs of the students in the classroom?
4. Share your responses and reflect on how you can incorporate these strategies in your lesson and unit plans.

to help students develop important lifelong learning habits, they also provide teachers with valuable insights into students' specific learning needs. Ultimately, giving students ownership in their learning leads to significant benefits for both teachers and students. By helping learners appreciate their accomplishments and understand the processes that enabled those accomplishments (including the strategies that enabled them to overcome obstacles), learners gain important metacognitive skills.

Equitable Access

ISTE NETS-T Standard 4.b also indicates that you will "address the diverse needs of all learners by . . . providing equitable access to appropriate digital tools and resources." But what do we mean by providing access? Early discussions about technology access centered on the lack of hardware and networking for some schools and families. This disparity even took on its own unique label as educational and political leaders across the nation vowed to decrease the **digital divide** among the nation's students. Today, educators recognize that this divide encompasses more than access to a computer or an Internet connection and are better informed about the ways the digital divide might manifest itself in schools. Wiburg and Butler (2003) suggested four components of access that should be considered when tackling the digital divide dilemma:

1. access to up-to-date hardware, software, and connectivity;
2. access to meaningful, high-quality, and culturally responsive content and the opportunity to contribute to that content;
3. access to educators who know how to use digital tools and resources; and
4. access to systems sustained by leaders with vision and support for change via technology.

In your role as a classroom teacher, you can directly influence the first three of these components. The final component will become more important to you as you gain experience and serve in positions of leadership, whether as a teacher-leader, administrator, or otherwise. You are one of the most important factors in providing access to teaching resources in a way that is sensitive to the cultural and individual needs of your students.

> **digital divide**
> the disparity between families and students who have access to digital tools and resources and those who do not

Access to Up-to-Date Hardware, Software, and Connectivity

As technology became more prevalent in America's schools, especially during the push to provide Internet access in every school and at least one "modern multimedia computer" for every five students, the disparity between the technology "haves" and "have-nots" became increasingly evident (U.S. Department of Commerce, 1999). One of the first responses of schools attempting to address the digital divide was to purchase a substantial amount of hardware in order to achieve a student-computer ratio of 5 to 1. Since then, schools have been able to purchase and install enough computers to actually exceed this goal. The U.S. Department of Education (Gray, Thomas & Lewis, 2010) reported that in 2009 a computer was available either in the classroom or could be brought into the classroom at a ratio of 1.7 students per computer. Unfortunately, even with this much technology available, only 40 percent of responding teachers reported using computers in the classroom "often" for instruction, and that number dropped to 29 percent when the computers were located somewhere else in the school. Almost 30 percent of teachers reported never or rarely using computers for instruction, even though they are available.

According to the U.S. Department of Education (Wells & Lewis, 2006), in 2005 virtually 100 percent of all schools across the nation reported some type of Internet connection in their schools. In 2009, 95 percent of available computers had Internet access (Gray, Thomas, & Lewis, 2010). In terms of overcoming the digital divide, it is also important to consider the *type* of Internet access that is available to schools. An increasing amount of content and media demands high bandwidth, but not all schools can take advantage of these resources, especially if they have slower connections. The percentage of schools reporting some type of **broadband** connection reached 97 percent by 2005, but that's still not likely to meet the instructional demand. In 2010, nearly 80 percent of respondents to a survey of E-rate users noted that their broadband connections do not meet their current needs (Federal Communications Commission, 2010). That means we still have work to do in some schools so their teachers and students can take advantage of the growing amount of multimedia content available online.

Across several demographic populations, however, schools have been a significant factor in increasing students' access to computers and the Internet for those who do not have access at home (see Figure 11.2). While access to computers in schools is high, as described earlier, the U.S. Census Bureau (2009) noted that Black and Hispanic children still have significantly lower home access to computers and the Internet when compared to Caucasians, Asian Americans, and Pacific Islanders. The total percentage of households reporting no Internet use at home is 31.3, but those numbers jump to 45.5 percent of Black households and 47.2 percent of Hispanic households. Current levels of computer use at school are similar for children from all reported racial groups; however, some differences occur in Internet use when comparing students across racial groups, with the lowest usage levels being reported for use of the Internet at school by Hispanic students (31 percent).

As a group, girls are thought to approach technology differently from boys, and many prefer different types of activities (Cooper, 2006). Games that promote competition and require eye-hand coordination or that may employ a war-game type setting may not appeal to girls as much as boys. Girls may actually learn less during games with these features. In general, technology-supported activities for girls are more successful when they rely on collaboration and are presented within a relevant context.

Students' attitudes toward technology can be influenced by societal factors, such as friends, the media, and what they do in the classroom. Since young girls entering school report enjoying computers and since just as many girls use technology as boys, both at home and at school, it's not their ability that is lacking. Rather, it is only a perception that develops over time that they are not as capable, and this perception can be influenced by software, games, and applications that include negative gender stereotypes (Cooper, 2006). The learning environment you create in your classroom and the way female teachers model technology can help combat this perception.

When designing group activities, make sure all students have equal opportunities to perform all types of roles, and counter any tendencies to allow anyone to monopolize the use of technological equipment. Continually alter the ways you pair or group students and make sure all students have opportunities to work with students of other genders, ethnic groups, and abilities. Above all, ensure that all students, whatever their backgrounds or abilities, have appropriate opportunities to use all of the technology resources available in your classroom. It's important to realize that equitable access to technology does not necessarily mean equal time spent using technology. Each student may require different types of software and hardware for different amounts of time to master curricular requirements. Students with writing needs may need more time to work

broadband
high-capacity telecommunications that allow users to access Internet-based information at significantly higher speeds than dial-up connections

Figure 11.2
The nation's schools have helped students from all backgrounds achieve greater access to technology.

STORIES from Practice

Bring Your Own Digital Devices (BYOD): The Next Wave in 1:1 Laptop Learning in Our Schools?

Our school, St. Gregory, is in its second year as a 1:1 laptop school, and it has been a very important and valuable advance for our students' ability to research, to stay connected, to organize their calendars and school works, to communicate with teachers and peers, to publish some of their student work, to blog, to use digital video both as consumers and creators of knowledge, and much more.

We took what I believe, two years ago, was a somewhat unusual approach to becoming a 1:1 school, but one which I think will become increasingly common, so much so that perhaps in a few years it will be the new normal. We knew that many of our students already had laptops they were using, at home and sometimes at school, and we decided to build upon that foundation, structuring our program, which invites students to bring their own device (BYOD), and supplementing it with a school-provided netbook to those who chose not to (or were unable to) provide their own. I think this was the right bridge, but we may move to a format soon where all students are expected to provide their own, and we give a stipend of some sort to support those who need it.

We did this hybrid BYOD approach partly for the financial savings, partly because it seemed redundant to ask so many students who have their own already to buy a school device, but also because we saw a new format emerging, using the resources of the cloud in an OS neutral way to tap in the rich resources of the web and empower our students as creative and critical, digitally fluent, web users. This was not about using educational software pre-installed on the school-provided laptops; it was about supporting and expecting them to be networked Web 2.0 users.

Source: Blog post by Jonathan Martin available at http://21k12blog.net/2011/10/04/byod-bring-your-own-digital-devices-the-next-wave-in-11-laptop-learning-in-our-schools. © Jonathan Martin. Used with permission.

---

with software that supports the writing process than those who perform more strongly in this area. Gifted-and-talented students who are developing complex projects using multimedia authoring or presentation software may need additional time for editing and programming. Use a variety of technologies that will engage students of different abilities, backgrounds, and learning preferences and allow them to demonstrate their knowledge appropriately. Don't isolate any one student for technology use as a reward *or* punishment. There is no one formula for determining equitable access. Keep in mind that the driving force behind all of your instructional decisions should be the learning needs of each student.

Although a 1:1 computing model and high-speed network access are considered by many to be the essential components of 21st century teaching and learning, economic conditions often make it difficult for school systems to meet this goal. School districts hope that **BYOD** (Bring Your Own Device, see Chapter 8) policies can increase equitable access for all students. With parents and PTA organizations providing a significant number of students with technology access, district-owned equipment can be made available to students who do not have their own devices.

Access to Meaningful, High-Quality, and Culturally Responsive Content

Providing greater access to computers and the Internet was an important goal, yet the fervor to get schools connected to the Internet and to put five computers in every classroom often outpaced the ability of content developers to create, package, and deliver high-quality content. You have probably noticed that when you turn to the Internet for information, the number of hits returned from a simple web search can be overwhelming. And often, much of the content turns out to be pretty useless, or at least not relevant to what you really needed. And it's not just computers, any longer, that we use to access content.

One increasing trend in and outside of schools is the proliferation of mobile technologies, including smartphones and tablet computers, that are able to access Internet content, provide content, and support communication. Many schools are incorporating these devices in ways that support teaching and learning. As reported in 2010, approximately 75 percent of all teens own a mobile phone (Lenhart, Ling, Campbell & Purcell, 2010). Students who do not own a computer at home are more likely to access the Internet through a mobile phone, although cost can be a factor preventing Internet access for some teens. Because of their popularity, some schools are developing lessons that incorporate mobile phones or the information they can access, sometimes through initiatives in which students bring their own devices to school. (see *Tech Tools and Tips—Learning from BYOD Initiatives* in Chapter 8 and the *Stories from Practice—Bring Your Own Digital Devices (BYOD)* in this chapter.)

More powerful phones, often called smartphones, and tablet computers, like the popular Apple iPod Touch and iPad, provide many additional resources and applications including cameras, calendars, calculators, GPS, timers, and a wide array of applications that make them extremely powerful resources to support learning. Textbook companies and other providers are developing content that is specifically designed to capitalize on the power of these small devices (Ross, 2011). While some see tablets as an answer to providing greater access to digital resources, there are still some characteristics that must be overcome. The price point for these devices can still be as much as that of a comparable laptop, or more than a small netbook computer, and many think some activities are better completed on a computer rather than a tablet. Typing long passages or doing extensive editing on a touchscreen can be cumbersome. These devices weren't developed for an educational setting, so finding high-quality content for these devices can be a challenge. These negatives haven't stopped the frenzy with which educators have turned to tablets, however, and mobile devices will play an ever larger role in providing greater access to technology and digital content as these devices mature and become more commonplace.

Providing high-quality content is a challenge, especially as you reach out to meet the needs of all of your students, including those who are not part of the dominant culture. In general, English is the predominant language on the Internet, and many pages are written at an advanced level that can confuse, disengage, or frustrate students who have limited English proficiency. In many areas and some states, English is not the most common language spoken, and students who are immersed in a program for English language learners may not have the proficiency required to sort through much of the information they find on the Internet. When using digital content, online or packaged on a CD, DVD, or other resource, you must consider the language abilities of your students.

In addition, many students do not find examples of computer software or Internet content to which they can relate. Girls in particular may have difficulty finding strong role models in terms of characters or software content, although there are several popular titles in which girl characters are prominent (see Figure 11.3). Although computer games are notorious for promoting negative female stereotypes, girls also find it difficult to find positive role models in more traditional instructional materials, including textbooks. Print, as well as software or Internet resources, should portray girls, women, students with disabilities, and people from a wide range of ethnic backgrounds, in a positive light.

Make sure the teams that evaluate and approve instructional materials for your school have a clear policy that encourages them to review for bias. Consider political, religious, and cultural contexts. Also examine the materials for potentially controversial topics and significant omissions. Take care to ensure that they do not reinforce stereotypes and, instead, provide strong role models for students of both genders and all ethnic backgrounds. Consider using an evaluation form or creating your own that includes categories that encourage evaluators to consider biases against girls or boys,

Figure 11.3
Use instructional resources with a range of role models to relate to all of your students.
Source: © 2008 Viacom International Inc. All rights reserved. Nickelodeon, Dora the Explorer and all related titles, logos, and characters are trademarks of Viacom International Inc. Courtesy of "Nickelodeon."

STORIES from Practice

Evaluating Software

When I first used this software I just thought about the political issues involved in the simulation, which is based on a mayor running for re-election in a city with a growing immigrant population. The mayor is male, a point I did not even think about until I started my thesis. He does have females on his team of advisors. However, the problems with the simulation go deeper.

The main issue in the mayor's re-election campaign is what to do about the immigrants moving into the city. The first time I used this program, I felt it was a great activity. The second year I used it, I became aware that the choices being made by my students were portraying the immigrants in a negative light. If a group of students made decisions favorable for the immigrants, the mayor either lost the election or much of his support.

It dawned on me that biases were built into the program. Did the designer discuss the possibilities of this program with educators? In fairness to the company, I must point out that an evaluation card is enclosed with the program when it is purchased. The first time I used the program, I gave it glowing reviews! I said that it was a great learning experience for my students because they really got involved in it. I honestly did not think of all the gender and cultural issues that came with the simulation.

I still use the program today, but now I use it in a different way. I encourage students to discuss the biases that are portrayed in the software. We talk about immigration problems, but we also discuss how immigrants contribute positively to the diversity that we should be celebrating.

Source: Carolyn Sue Gardiner, St. Timothy School, Columbus, Ohio (Gardiner, 2002, p. 46).

> # THE GAME PLAN
>
> ## Gender-Equitable Resources
>
> ### Set Goals
> Find resources that encourage technology use for either boys or girls or both.
>
> ### Take Action
> Search for print and digital resources that provide strategies to encourage boys or girls to use technology for learning, that help you differentiate instruction for learning preferences associated with both genders, or that support initiatives that encourage participation in STEM-related (science, technology, engineering, and mathematics) career paths.
>
> ### Monitor
> Determine whether the material you collected is free from bias and represents valid positions. If you are finding more material for one gender over the other, what strategies might you use to obtain equal representation?
>
> ### Evaluate and Extend
> Share the resources you have found with classmates, especially with members of the opposite gender to review appropriate materials. Store the best materials or link URLs from important websites to your portfolio along with rationales for why you believe the materials are appropriate.

students from different racial or ethnic backgrounds, and students with different abilities. This isn't to say that you should never use software that contains subtle biases, but if you do, make sure you use it as an opportunity to explicitly teach students to be aware of such biases (see *Stories from Practice—Evaluating Software* on page 280).

Access to Tech-Knowledgeable Teachers

This entire book is designed to help you to become a more tech-savvy teacher, so you're on the right path to overcoming this particular contributor to the digital divide. Needless to say, teachers who lack knowledge of how to use technology are inadequately prepared to provide their students with meaningful access to technologies that may be readily available in a school. Fortunately, many states have adopted technology standards for teachers that are the same or similar to the ISTE NETS-T standards that are the focus of this book. Other states require teachers to demonstrate at least limited proficiency with a variety of technologies, such as word processors, e-mail, and the Internet.

But one of the most influential factors for how you use technology and provide access to your students will be your own beliefs about your role as a teacher and the role of technology in your teaching. If you've proceeded through the chapters in this book in sequential order, you now know about numerous technology-supported teaching strategies you can employ to engage all students, meet individual learning preferences, and achieve meaningful learning outcomes. But you can't stop here—you need to take steps to provide your future students with access to a tech-knowledgeable teacher throughout your entire teaching career. Chapter 12 explores ways that you can continue to learn about and experiment with new technologies in order to overcome this particular factor in the digital divide.

Appropriate Use of Technology in Early Childhood Education

Key to being a tech-knowledgeable teacher is knowing when and how technology use is appropriate and when it is not. This is especially true for early childhood educators. When is it appropriate to introduce digital technologies to young children? Should they be allowed to interact with digital books? Watch DVDs of changing geometric shapes for relaxation? Skype with family members?

In January of 2012, the National Association for the Education of Young Children (NAEYC) and Fred Rogers Center for Early Learning and Children's Media at Saint Vincent College issued a joint position statement on *Technology and Interactive Media as Tools in Early Childhood Programs Serving Children from Birth through Age 8*. Based on a careful review of extensive research, these groups concluded that "technology and interactive media are tools that can promote effective learning and development when they are used intentionally by early childhood educators, within the framework of developmentally appropriate practice" (NAEYC and Fred Rogers Center, 2012, p. 5). Recognizing that technology is a prevalent part of living in our current world, access to technology within the context of early childhood education programs may be particularly valuable for students who lack access at home. Through the appropriate use of technology, students learn "technology handling" skills, just as they learned "book handling skills" in the past.

They offered the following set of recommendations (NAEYC & Fred Rogers Center, 2012, p. 11):

1. Select, use, integrate, and evaluate technology and interactive media tools in intentional and developmentally appropriate ways, giving careful attention to the appropriateness and the quality of the content, the child's experience, and the opportunities for co-engagement.

2. Provide a balance of activities in programs for young children, recognizing that technology and interactive media can be valuable tools when used intentionally with children to extend and support active, hands-on, creative, and authentic engagement with those around them and with their world.

3. Prohibit the passive use of television, videos, DVDs, and other non-interactive technologies and media in early childhood programs for children younger than 2, and discourage passive and non-interactive uses with children ages 2 through 5.

4. Limit any use of technology and interactive media in programs for children younger than 2 to those that appropriately support responsive interactions between caregivers and children and that strengthen adult-child relationships.

5. Carefully consider the screen time recommendations from public health organizations for children from birth through age 5 when determining appropriate limits on technology and media use in early childhood settings. Screen time estimates should include time spent in front of a screen at the early childhood program and, with input from parents and families, at home and elsewhere.

6. Provide leadership in ensuring equitable access to technology and interactive media experiences for the children in their care and for parents and families.

You'll notice that these ideas are consistent with the themes that run throughout this book. Just as early childhood educators may use blocks, crayons, or puppets, digital technologies provide additional tools that can be used to support the individual learning needs of their students. When used strategically, technology can help differentiate instruction in developmentally appropriate ways (see Chapter 6). Technology can be used to support dual language learners by providing access to stories, games, and other activities in the language spoken in the home as well as the dominant language of the classroom (see culturally responsive teaching in this chapter). Technology can strengthen the crucial home-school connection through enhancing communication with parents, documenting progress with photographs and digital portfolios, and sharing classroom events through video or audio recordings (see Chapter 9). Above all, the appropriate integration of technology relies on a firm knowledge of the developmental needs of young children and supporting pedagogical strategies, coupled with the careful review and selection of technology resources (see Chapter 8).

For more information, see: http://www.naeyc.org/content/technology-and-young-children

Promoting Cultural Understanding and Global Awareness

The ISTE NETS-T Standard 4.d indicates that teachers "develop and model cultural understanding and global awareness by engaging with colleagues and students of other cultures using digital-age communication and collaboration tools." Throughout this book you have considered strategies and tools to support collaboration with your colleagues, your students, and their families. Today, digital tools enable you to communicate and collaborate with individuals from around the world as easily as you can communicate with the students in your classroom and the teacher next door. But cultural understanding requires more than simply using tools such as these to communicate and collaborate with those from other cultures. As a culturally responsive teacher, you should take steps to better understand your own cultural background, the culture of the community within which your school is situated, the culture within the school, as well as the culture of your peers.

If you and your students or colleagues come from different cultures, with different backgrounds, different communication styles, and different experiences with technology, the result can be disconnect and conflict. All parties can feel frustrated, isolated, and inclined to erect barriers. You can combat this outcome, however, through awareness of these possibilities and using concrete strategies to determine the cultural and linguistic preferences of the students in your class and avoiding reactions based on stereotypical assumptions. Stereotypes quickly break down when teachers consider the perspectives and needs of each individual.

There are several things you can do to become a culturally responsive teacher who teaches from a perspective of cultural understanding—some of which you can do now and some of which you can do while you are teaching.

Understanding Your Culture and the Culture of Others

To get started, several experts in culturally responsive pedagogy agree that one of the first steps you can take is to conduct an evaluation of your own cultural experiences and that of others (Montgomery, 2001; Richards, Brown, & Forde, 2006). This requires self-reflection to identify the different cultural groups you belong to, whether racial, social, language- or gender-based, or other, and how your experiences in these groups have shaped and continue to shape your life. You should also consider the connection between school and society and how you have been impacted as a member of different education-related settings and roles, whether as a student, teacher, parent, or otherwise.

Culture is a complex, intangible concept, yet it shapes how we see the world. Adding to the complexity is the fact that you may associate with different cultures or subcultures, regardless of your background or your physical characteristics. Furthermore, the reasons you associate with a culture may be different from others. It is not simply your race that helps create your cultural identification. You may identify with a particular ethnic group, but your cultural identity is often a broader characterization than your ethnic identity (LAB, 2002), as members of different ethnic groups may all identify with the same culture. A shared history is important, but even that does not complete your cultural picture. The region in which you (and your close relatives) live or have lived, your educational background, income, gender, and even physical characteristics can help shape your cultural identity, which, in turn, influences the way you behave, the choices you make, your pursuits, and your aspirations—especially in relation to education. The ability of diverse people to identify with the same culture helps to underscore the danger of prescribing blanket beliefs to individuals based on their appearance, background, or locale.

Anthropologists recognize numerous characteristics around which cultures differ. And although different cultures may have different ways of expressing these things, all cultures hold beliefs and exhibit resulting patterns of behaviors in each of these areas

Table 11.1	Exploring Culture

The following features of culture were extracted from an activity in *Building Bridges: A Peace Corps Classroom Guide to Cross-Cultural Understanding* (Peace Corps, 2002, p. 11). For each feature of culture, think of one example common to people in the country where you were born and compare that with others you know from travel, friendships, or discussions with your classmates.

- Styles of dress
- Ways of greeting people
- Beliefs about hospitality
- Importance of time
- Paintings
- Values
- Literature
- Beliefs about child raising (children and teens)
- Attitudes about personal space/privacy
- Beliefs about the responsibilities of children and teens
- Gestures to show you understand what has been told to you
- Holiday customs
- Music
- Dancing
- Celebrations
- Concept of fairness
- Foods
- Greetings
- Facial expressions and hand gestures
- Concept of self
- Work ethic
- Religious beliefs
- Religious rituals
- Concept of beauty
- Rules of polite behavior
- Attitude toward age
- The role of family
- General worldview

Source: Building Bridges: A Peace Corps Classroom Guide to Cross-Cultural Understanding (Peace Corps, 2002, p. 11).

(Peace Corps, 2002). Review Table 11.1 for additional features of culture. As you read through the following paragraphs, consider your own cultural heritage and how some of those characteristics are evidenced.

Culture is manifest in a wide variety of behaviors and beliefs, some visible and some not. Outward manifestations of culture include styles of dress, greetings, facial expressions and hand gestures. Cultures may have unique music, celebrations, rituals, dances, and art. They may have special eating habits, preferred foods, and housing preferences. Other aspects of culture may be less visible. Cultures may have different views on fairness, personal property, friendship, aging, hospitality, and modesty. They may differ in such areas as work ethics, how they value time, the concept of self, ideas about leadership, concepts of beauty, and attitudes toward personal space and privacy. The roles and responsibilities of various family members may differ across cultures. They may have different religious beliefs, values, and understandings of the natural world. There may be different rules for polite behavior, social etiquette, and hospitality. All of these cultural beliefs and practices interact in unique ways and influence an individual's general worldview.

Although these may be interesting areas for exploring similarities and differences in culture among individuals, certain aspects of people's cultural identity affect cross-cultural communications in ways that are important to establishing collaborative relationships. Different cultures have formal and informal rules that govern speaking, listening, and turn-taking behaviors (LAB, 2002). Some communication patterns that can be manifested differently across cultures include:

- *Conventions for storytelling.* Some cultures rely on personal anecdotes and experiences in storytelling that may not have a clear beginning, middle, or end while others follow strict rules that establish a main topic and then structure the story around it. Consider the influence in the dominant American school culture of the highly structured "five-paragraph essay."
- *Directness in communicating.* Communications in some cultures are indirect and may actually seem ambiguous in comparison to the directness of communication expected in many American classrooms. Indirect communication may relate to topics that are suggested but not spoken as well as conversations with close relatives or friends of individuals rather than the individuals themselves in order to communicate sensitive topics or elicit behavior through indirect influence.
- *When to listen and when to speak.* In the dominant American culture, an eloquent speaker with a firm command of language skills is praised as being intelligent and competent, and individuals are encouraged to "speak one's mind," while in other cultures listening and speaking selectively is valued.
- *When and how children should speak.* Some cultures encourage children to speak from a personal perspective in order to understand and explore their world, while others use language with children to socialize them to expected norms, as in "speak only when spoken to" or "children should be seen and not heard."
- *Speaking to an adult or elder.* Questioning an adult in some cultures can be praised as indicating a "free thinker" or honing one's intellectual skills to be a critical thinker, while in other cultures it is believed to be a sign of poor upbringing and lack of respect.

Schools have their own rules governing communication, patterns of task engagement, and organizing ideas (Gay, 2010). While not true of all schools, the nature of discourse in many schools is often **didactic**, with a single speaker dominating and all others listening. In this type of classroom, the teacher often governs communication and decides who will talk when, and the type of responses desired. Classrooms where students are taught to be direct, precise, and to follow conventions of didactic communication are referred to as **topic-centered**. This structured learning environment can be problematic to those familiar with a **topic-chaining** style of engagement and organization. A topic-chaining environment is one that has a strong social context in which time is taken to set the stage for an academic task that is followed through with cyclical and multipart conversations. Conversations and activities can be intense and emotional with emphasis on personal investment. In contrast to didactic communication, a **communal** style of communication may be employed in which listening is participatory and listeners provide prompts, feedback, and commentary to the speaker. In topic-centered classrooms, students who prefer communal communication styles may appear rude or disruptive and teachers may take steps to silence them, negatively affecting their natural preferences for talking, thinking, and academic engagement. In topic-chaining classrooms, students who prefer the structure of didactic communications may appear to lack motivation, be disengaged, uncooperative, or even resistant to an academic task, especially if it involves collaboration with others.

Cultures can also be described as individualistic or collectivist. An **individualist** perspective promotes the autonomy of the individual and measures success by individual accomplishments. On the other end of the continuum, **collectivist** perspectives situate the individual within a larger community and measure the success of the individual

---

didactic
a type of conversation or instruction in which a single speaker dominates while others quietly listen

topic-centered
classrooms where students are taught to be direct, precise, and to follow conventions of didactic communication

topic-chaining
a learning environment or method of instruction that focuses on strong social context with cyclical and multi-part conversations

communal
a style of communication in which listening is participatory, and listeners provide prompts, feedback, and commentary

individualist
a perspective that promotes the autonomy of the individual and measures success by individual accomplishments

collectivist
a perspective that promotes situating the individual within a larger community and measures the success of the individual as a factor of the whole

Table 11.2 Individualist/Collectivist Continuum		
Key Questions	**Individualist Perspective**	**Collectivist Perspective**
Why should students achieve their potential?	For the sake of self-fulfillment	In order to contribute to the social whole
What type of work ethic is encouraged?	Students should work independently and get their own work done. Giving help to others may be considered cheating.	Students should be helpful and cooperate with peers, giving assistance when needed. Helping is not considered cheating.
How should praise and feedback be used?	Students should be praised frequently. The positive should be emphasized whenever possible.	Students should not be singled out for praise in front of peers. Positive feedback should be stated in terms of the student's ability to help family or community.
What is the role of the school?	Students should attain intellectual skills in school.	Students should learn appropriate social behaviors and skills as well as intellectual skills.
What is the role of the student in education?	Students should engage in discussion and argument in order to learn to think critically.	Students should be quiet and respectful in class because they will learn more this way.
What is the value of property?	Property belongs to individuals, and others must ask to borrow or share it.	Most property is communal and not considered the domain of an individual.
How should students behave?	Teachers manage behavior indirectly or emphasize student self-control.	Teachers have primary authority for managing behavior, but also expect peers to guide each other's behavior.
What is the role of the parent in education?	Parents are integrally involved with student academic progress.	Parents believe that it is the teacher's role to provide academic instruction to students.

Source: Adapted from *The Diversity Kit: An Introductory Resource for Social Change in Education,* Table 1, p. 25, Copyright 2002 The Education Alliance at Brown University.

as a factor of the whole. People can fall anywhere along the continuum—not just the extremes—and may not exhibit consistent perspectives across all attributes.

Review Table 11.2, the Individualist/Collectivist Continuum adapted from *The Diversity Kit* (LAB, 2002, p. 25), to determine how different people may view common factors related to education and academic success. Consider the perspective you have based on your own identification and whether you know individuals who might exhibit some characteristics of the opposite perspective. Share your perspective with others and note similarities and differences. A word of caution is in order. Keep in mind that not all persons from any one area, culture, or group will exhibit the same perspective for each factor and that these generalizations are not meant to be definitive descriptions of any one culture.

To complete a self-evaluation of your own cultural preferences, it is important to share and learn from others to better understand the complex interactions that help people develop different perspectives. What one culture may view as strange may be considered normal in another. Recognizing areas in which people differ is an important step in understanding and appreciating cultural preferences within your school and community. There are no hard and fast rules that can help you determine what instructional strategies and resources will work best for all students who identify with any one culture. It is helpful to know, however, that different people (teachers, administrators, students, and parents) approach many common characteristics of education and society from opposing perspectives.

Working with Students to Develop Cultural Understanding

Although you can conduct a self-assessment of your own experiences right now, once you're in a classroom you'll need to better understand your students' cultures and how those can promote positive learning experiences. Students can create short presentations or movies of

> ## APPLY *to Practice*
> ### Individualist/Collectivist Continuum
>
> 1. Rate yourself along the dimensions of the Individualist/Collectivist Continuum as either Highly Individualist, Somewhat Individualist, In Between, Somewhat Collectivist, Highly Collectivist. To what do you attribute your responses? Share your responses with your class.
> 2. As a variation, collect the responses from an entire class and create a class profile. You can use a variety of technologies to do this, which can then be posted to a class website or discussion area. What trends do you notice? Do responses from different individuals with similar ratings correspond? What about for those with opposing ratings? Knowing these trends, how does this influence how you would interact with others in the class? What about if you had to teach this class?

their personal and family histories to share with the class. Students can use digital storytelling techniques to tell others about their cultural heritages. Information from family trees, interviews with parents and other family members, and even scanning and incorporating family photos or memorabilia into presentations can help students engage in the process of self-reflection and inform you about who they are. Classroom discussions can be supported with the use of concept-mapping software, and responses to surveys can be aggregated and presented using data-visualization software. Be aware that the process of reflection and sharing can be challenging if not done within an environment of trust and understanding. The goal is to understand what attributes others bring to the educational settings and how prior knowledge and experiences can be leveraged for positive educational outcomes. These types of activities can help both you and your students understand the similarities and differences among the prior knowledge and experiences you all bring to the classroom.

Teaching lessons that directly address issues of culture is another way to help students develop respect for diversity. Projects that connect classrooms or even individual students from different schools across the country or the globe are a popular method for introducing students to new and different cultures. For example, Ann Murray, a kindergarten teacher at Calgary French and International School, uses her Twitter account to connect her students with kindergarten students in France, New York, Indonesia, and the Philippines. She reported that it made their world so "much bigger." "All of a sudden the students were interested in maps and where places are in the world" (Black, 2011). The ePals website also supports global communication and collaboration among teachers and learners in 200 countries and territories through utilizing chat rooms and providing sample project ideas. International E-mail Classroom Connections (IECC) is another organization dedicated to helping teachers arrange intercultural e-mail connections among their students.

Building community among diverse learners is an essential element of culturally responsive teaching (Gay, 2010). Cooperative groups require students to develop skills that support collaboration such as listening, speaking, expressing one's own thoughts and ideas, as well as respecting and understanding others' perspectives, and reaching consensus. Lab management software with shared workspaces and messaging software can be used within the classroom setting, and shared communications such as a threaded discussion or wiki can be used to support group work beyond the school walls.

Once personal connections have been made, students can use Google Earth with its maps, topography, and embedded images and videos to see where others live. They can conduct research online and conduct online "interviews" with students from other cultures. As we've explained throughout this book, learners are most receptive to information that has relevance to their lives. For this reason, establishing a personal connection among students from different cultures can be a powerful means of increasing cross-cultural understanding.

> ## APPLY to Practice
>
> ### Increasing Global Understanding
>
> 1. Find a lesson plan or activity for increasing global understanding that might be appropriate for the grade level and topic you plan to teach.
> 2. Identify the technologies, websites, and software you might use to support this lesson. If no technologies are described in the lesson, modify the lesson plan to include appropriate technological support. Justify the technologies you've selected and how you will use them.
> 3. Consider how you will assess student learning from the activity. How will you evaluate the effectiveness of the lesson and the effectiveness of the technologies you selected?

Respecting Cultural Diversity in the Classroom

You should also be aware that culture affects how people react to technology (see Figure 11.4). In some communities that rely strongly on an oral tradition that involves sharing and reflection, disseminating information via mass media—including television and the Internet—can be perceived negatively (Wiburg, 2003). Further, the cultural assumptions implied by a technology and one's cultural response to technology may conflict. Some technologies, such as tutorials or drill-and-practice software, encourage the development of autonomy in the learner that may conflict with students who come from a culture of collaborative communication. In contrast, technologies designed to support group activities may conflict with students of more individualistic preferences. These cultural differences hold true in virtual settings, too, where students may require a great deal of autonomy and self-motivation in order to read materials, view course lectures or media elements, and complete assignments on time, versus being communal and collaborative and being required to participate in group activities

Figure 11.4
Consider the effect of culture on student perceptions and reactions to technology.

Table 11.3 Culturally Responsive Instructional Strategies

In order to address the learning needs of an increasingly diverse student population in the nation's classrooms, NCCREST (Richards, Brown, & Forde, 2006) describes three components of culturally responsive pedagogy: 1) institutional, 2) personal, and 3) instructional. Consider the following ten strategies you can use in support of culturally responsive instruction:

1. Acknowledge students' differences as well as their commonalities.
2. Validate students' cultural identities in classroom practices and instructional materials.
3. Educate students about the diversity of the world around them.
4. Promote equity and mutual respect among students.
5. Use valid measures to assess students' ability and achievement.
6. Foster a positive interrelationship among students, their families, the community, and school.
7. Motivate students to become active participants in their learning.
8. Encourage students to think critically.
9. Challenge students to strive for excellence as defined by their potential.
10. Assist students in becoming socially and politically conscious.

Source: NCCREST (Richards, Brown, & Forde, 2006).

through online discussion forums or other group settings. As we mentioned earlier in this chapter, content evaluation should involve consideration of the cultural preferences of your students and their communities.

The atmosphere of your classroom is influenced by its physical attributes as well as the interactions you and your students have with each other. Classroom decorations, bulletin boards, and even the arrangement of furniture should promote positive and purposeful academic engagement. Images used should represent people of different ages, genders, places, social classes, and ethnicities that relate to and extend the curriculum (Gay, 2010). Culturally responsive teachers are aware of the strengths and weaknesses of curricula and curricular materials, including cultural biases and distortions that can occur in books, periodicals, videos, software applications, and information on the Internet.

This section has introduced you to ways to develop cultural understanding and global awareness in order to become a culturally responsive teacher who is able to meet the learning needs of students from various backgrounds. It is not enough to intersperse different cultural elements and artifacts into the curriculum, such as exploring the achievements of a famous person of color, noting the existence of holidays in different cultures, or bringing in food from various countries. Instead, the instructional strategies you use to reach students from various backgrounds and experiences is what will ultimately constitute culturally responsive pedagogy.

Review Table 11.3 Culturally Responsive Instructional Strategies and consider how these instructional strategies, in addition to those presented throughout this section, could be implemented in your classroom. Reflect on technologies you already know that can support these strategies, and consider others mentioned in this section that you would like to know more about.

Chapter Summary

In this chapter, we discussed the complex issues related to equitable access to technology and developing cultural understanding to support the learning needs of your students. Special attention was paid to explicitly defining and describing a learner-centered classroom and strategies you can use to support one. The issue of equity goes beyond simple access to technology and includes actual patterns of use. Although you directly influence equitable access within your classroom, learning continues outside of the school; disparate access at home can become significant as you incorporate instructional technology into your teaching. You are encouraged to be an advocate for equitable access to technology resources in order to better prepare your students to meet the growing technological demands of society.

Access to hardware, software, and connectivity means more than simply having the technology available for your use—it's how you use the technology that's important. You are one of the biggest factors in providing access to learning resources in a way that's sensitive to the individual and cultural needs of your students. Above all, ensure that all students, whatever their backgrounds or abilities, have equitable opportunities to use all the technology resources available in an interactive classroom. Establish an atmosphere that respects students and provides ample opportunities for students to build on and extend their knowledge and skills. Based on the unique needs of your students, using culturally responsive pedagogies can help you leverage available technologies to meet their learning needs and match their learning preferences.

There is no one formula for determining equitable access, appropriately responding to students' cultural needs, or creating a learner-centered environment. Keep in mind that the driving force behind all of your instructional decisions should be the learning needs of each student. All students will be required to use technology as they matriculate through school and into their careers; you are one of the most important factors in promoting academic success for your students.

In the next chapter, we turn our attention to ways you can improve your professional practice through participating in local and global learning communities. We then discuss ways you can exhibit leadership and contribute to the professional development of others. And finally, we discuss the use of published educational research to inform your classroom practice and introduce you to action research as a method of systematically reflecting on both published research and your own professional practice in order to "contribute to the effectiveness, vitality, and self-renewal of the teaching profession and of your school and community" (NETS-T 5.d).

Web Resources and Activities

See the Education CourseMate website that accompanies this book for

- a list of resources to build cross-cultural awareness and promote connections among students of different cultures.

YOUR PORTFOLIO

To demonstrate competency in ISTE NETS-T standards 4.b and d, add the following items to your portfolio:

1. A philosophy statement that discusses your commitment to, and implementation strategies for, addressing cultural diversity and equity issues related to technology use. Provide explicit reasons why it is important for teachers and students to consider these issues in teaching and learning. Include specific strategies that address the following:
    a. creating a collaborative environment that supports the cognitive, social, and emotional needs of students;
    b. promoting reflective thinking to support student metacognition; and
    c. ensuring that all students, whatever their backgrounds or abilities, have appropriate opportunities to use all of the technology resources available in your classroom.

2. A reflection on your own cultural experiences. You can do this through identifying the different cultural groups you belong to and reflecting on how these experiences have shaped and continue to shape your life. You should also consider how these cultural influences impact your perception of, and reaction to, technology, specifically as it is related to using technology to support teaching and learning. You may also want to consider the connection between school and society and how you have been influenced as a member of different educational settings.

References

Barell, J. (2007). *Problem-based learning: An inquiry approach* (2nd ed.). Thousand Oaks, CA: Corwin.

Black, D. (2011, September 14). How a kindergarten class uses Twitter to learn about the world. *Toronto Star*. Retrieved January 20, 2012 from http://www.thestar.com/news/article/1052956

Cooper, J. (2006). The digital divide: The special case of gender. *Journal of Computer Assisted Learning, 22*(5), 320–334.

Federal Communications Commission. (2010). *2010 E-rate program and broadband usage survey: Report*. Washington, DC: Federal Communications Commission Wireline Competition Bureau.

Gardiner, C. S. (2002). The search for bias-free educational software. *ENC Focus, 7* (4), 45–46.

Gay, G. (2010). *Culturally responsive teaching: Theory, research, and practice* (2nd ed.). New York: Teachers College.

Gray, L., Thomas, N., & Lewis, L. (2010). *Teachers' Use of Educational Technology in U.S. Public Schools: 2009* (NCES 2010-040). Washington, DC: National Center for Education Statistics, Institute of Education Sciences, U.S. Department of Education.

International Society for Technology in Education (ISTE). (2008). *Refreshed ISTE NETS for teachers rubrics*. Eugene, OR: author.

Kolodner, J. L., Camp, P. J., Crismond, D., Fasse, J. G., Holbrook, J., Puntambekar, S., & Ryan, M. (2003). Problem-based learning meets case-based reasoning in the middle school science classroom: Putting learning by design into practice. *Journal of the Learning Sciences, 12*, 495–547.

LAB. (2002). *The Diversity Kit. An introductory resource for social change in education*. Providence, RI: LAB at Brown University.

Lenhart, A., Ling, R., Campbell, S., & Purcell, K. (2010). *Teens and mobile phones*. Washington, DC: Pew Internet & American Life Project. Retrieved on June 27, 2012 from http://pewinternet.org/Reports/2010/Teens-and-Mobile-Phones.aspx

Linn, M. C, Clark, D., & Slotta, J. D. (2003). WISE design for knowledge integration. *Science Education, 87*(4), 517–538.

Martin, J. (2011, October 4). BYOD, bring your own digital devices: The next wave in 1:1 laptop learning in our schools? [Web log comment]. Retrieved May 2, 2012 from http://21k12blog.net/2011/10/04/byod-bring-your-own-digital-devices-the-next-wave-in-11-laptop-learning-in-our-schools/

National Association for the Education of Young Children & Fred Rogers Center for Early Learning and Children's Media at Saint Vincent College. (2012). *Technology and interactive media as tools in early childhood programs serving children from birth through age 8*. Retrieved May 2, 2012 from http://www.naeyc.org/content/technology-and-young-children

Montgomery, W. (2001). Creating culturally responsive, inclusive classrooms. *Teaching Exceptional Children, 33*(4), 4–9.

Newmann, F. M., Bryk, A. S., & Nagaoka, J. K. (2001). *Authentic intellectual work and standardized tests: Conflict or coexistence!* Chicago, IL: Consortium on Chicago School Research.

Peace Corps. (2002). *Building bridges: A Peace Corps classroom guide to cross-cultural understanding*. Washington, DC: Author. Retrieved December 15, 2011 from http://www.peacecorps.gov/wws/publications/bridges/

Richards, H. V., Brown, A. F., & Forde. T. B. (2006). *Addressing diversity in schools: Culturally responsive pedagogy*. Tempe, AZ: National Center for Culturally Responsive Educational Systems (NCCREST).

Ritchhart, R., Church, M., & Morrison, K. (2011). *Making thinking visible: How to promote engagement, understanding, and independence for all learners*. San Francisco, CA: Jossey-Bass.

Ross, J. D. (2011). *Beyond textbooks: The learning return on investment*. Richmond, VA: Virginia Department of Education. Retrieved January 24, 2012 from http://www.doe.virginia.gov/support/technology/technology_initiatives/learning_without_boundaries/beyond_textbooks/index.shtml

U.S. Census Bureau. (2009). *Computer and Internet use*. Washington, DC: Author. Retrieved on January 5, 2012 from http://www.census.gov/hhes/computer/index.html

U.S. Department of Commerce. (1999). *Falling through the Net: Defining the digital divide*. Washington, DC: Author.

U.S. Department of Education. (2010). *The condition of education 2010* (NCES 2010-028). Washington, DC: National Center for Education Statistics, Institute of Education Sciences, U.S. Department of Education.

Villegas, A. M., & Lucas, T. (2007). The culturally responsive teacher. *Educational Leadership, 64*(6), 28–33.

Wiburg, K. M. (2003). Factors of the divide. In O. Solomon, N. J. Allen, & P. Resta (Eds.), *Toward digital equity: Bridging the divide in education* (pp. 25–40). Boston, MA: Allyn and Bacon.

Wiburg, K. M., & Butler, J. F. (2003). Creating educational access. In O. Solomon, N. J. Allen, & P. Resta (Eds.), *Toward digital equity: Bridging the divide in education* (pp. 1–13). Boston, MA: Allyn and Bacon.

Professional Growth and Leadership

OUTCOMES

In this chapter, you will learn to

- **Participate in local and global learning communities** to enhance your own technology leadership skills and the skills of others; and
- **Reflect on published research and your own practice** to make effective use of digital tools and resources in support of student learning.

iste·nets

ISTE Standards Addressed in Chapter 12

NETS-T 5. Engage in Professional Growth and Leadership

Teachers continuously improve their professional practice, model lifelong learning, and exhibit leadership in their schools and professional communities by promoting and demonstrating the effective use of digital tools and resources. Teachers:

a. participate in local and global learning communities to explore creative applications of technology to improve student learning;
b. exhibit leadership by demonstrating a vision of technology infusion, participating in shared decision making and community building, and developing the leadership and technology skills of others;
c. evaluate and reflect on current research and professional practice on a regular basis to make effective use of existing and emerging digital tools and resources in support of student learning; and
d. contribute to the effectiveness, vitality, and self-renewal of the teaching profession and of their schools and communities.

You may be reading this book as part of a formal class or on your own. You may already be teaching, or teaching may be several years in your future. But either way, once you begin to teach, you become part of a professional **community of practice** (CoP) (Lave & Wenger, 1991). As with all CoPs, the teaching profession consists of members at various points in their professional journeys. Some teachers will be newcomers to the professional community; others will be veterans. Some teachers will be in the early phases of their careers; others will be close to retirement. One characteristic of a CoP is that all participants are changed through their interactions within the community. For example, experienced teachers have much to share with newcomers, but can learn from them as well. Similarly, as a newcomer, you may have knowledge of digital technologies that you can share with more established teachers, yet there is a great deal you can learn from them.

> **community of practice**
> a group "of people who share a concern or a passion for something they do and learn how to do it better as they interact regularly" (Wenger, 2006)

Due to the increased complexity of the educational landscape, there is a growing emphasis in the nation's schools on developing teacher leaders, promoting shared leadership and decision-making, and creating communities of practice. Today, no one—administrator or teacher—is expected to possess all the expertise and bear all of the responsibility necessary for managing learning (Elmore, 2000). As part of the first generation of teachers to enter the teaching profession already comfortable with computers and other digital technologies, you have the responsibility to actively contribute to, and participate in, leadership efforts at your schools, including technology leadership efforts.

We begin the chapter with a discussion of how you can participate in local and global learning communities, exhibit leadership, and facilitate the development of the leadership and technology skills of others. In the subsequent section, we discuss the use of published educational research to inform your classroom practice and introduce action research as a method of systematically reflecting on both the published research and your own professional practice in order to "contribute to the effectiveness, vitality, and self-renewal of the teaching profession and of your school and community" (NETS-T 5.d).

Participating in Local and Global Learning Communities

In Chapter 1, we introduced the notion that teachers progress through stages of technology integration as they become more familiar with technologies that support teaching and learning. Seminal research, which led to the development of one of the first technology integration stage theories, was conducted by researchers associated with the Apple Classrooms of Tomorrow (ACOT) project (Dwyer, Ringstaff, & Sandholtz, 1991). More recently, ISTE, in conjunction with the publication of the new NETS-T has adopted the idea of teachers progressing through stages of technology integration (2008b). Accompanying the ISTE NETS-T is a four-stage rubric that profiles teachers' behaviors and proficiencies for each standard and substandard in four stages: 1) beginning, 2) developing, 3) proficient, and 4) transformative.

Reflect back on the four stages of technology integration that ISTE associates with the new NETS-T, introduced in Chapter 1. Review the indicators for each standard and estimate where you might fall within the four stages: beginning, developing, proficient, or transformative (see pp. 19–21). At what stage do you see yourself now? Since you're likely in the preparation stage of your career, you're probably in one of the first two stages. That's perfectly acceptable. But no matter what stage you may be in, you have the opportunity to "continuously improve [your] professional practice, model lifelong learning, and exhibit leadership . . . by promoting and demonstrating the effective use of digital tools and resources" (NETS-T 5).

This entire book has been preparing you to function at the more advanced levels of technology integration—to exhibit leadership by demonstrating a vision of technology integration that allows you to be one of those dynamic teachers who functions on a day-to-day basis in the transformative phase. However, implementing that vision will require you to continually update your skills and reflect on your progress—in other words, to remain a self-directed learner throughout your teaching career. As noted throughout this book, technologies will come and go, but your learning skills will be with you forever. You and your peers have the opportunity to be leaders in the world's technology integration efforts, which requires that you help other teachers become technology leaders as well. In this section, we focus on techniques that will help you continuously improve your professional practice, model lifelong learning, and exhibit leadership in your school and professional community by promoting and demonstrating the effective use of digital tools and resources.

STORIES from Practice

Get Your PLN On

There was a time where teaching could be a fairly isolated occupation. Sure, there were colleagues next door and down the hall, but for many teachers once the bell rang they shut the door and got to work. The only time they met other teachers was in the teacher's lounge or around a lunch table. Conferences are a good way to meet people, but it used to be so hard to keep those professional relationships going. That's not the case any longer. Many different types of technologies are available to help you create and maintain your own professional learning network, or PLN as it is often called. Anita Harris is an instructional technology specialist in Virginia and not only has she built and maintained a PLN composed of educators from across the country—and beyond—but she also helps others learn how to do that. She offered advice for developing and maintaining your own PLN, especially with the many helpful digital technologies available now.

Anita recommends that you start by creating some type of PLN in your school with your peers first. She says she'll meet with teachers, perhaps in that teachers' lounge or around the lunch table, and she listens to what they're talking about. When a need comes up, or maybe someone mentions they'd like to attend a conference, she challenges them to go. She wants them to get out of the building, meet new people, and learn new ideas they can bring back. And while she's a big proponent of attending conferences and becoming active in state and national organizations like ISTE, she also suggests they think locally, as regional or state conferences are more likely to be within school budgets.

She also encourages teachers to find and develop resources for themselves and their teams. To do this, you need to connect, and Anita is very well connected. She recommends you seek out other teachers in your own or nearby districts first. Visit websites from other schools. Search for others who teach in your content area or grade level. And then perhaps you'll turn to one of her favorite resources, Twitter. Anita is so well known for using Twitter to meet people, for following up after meeting them, and to disseminate her own work that she was recognized as one of the top 20 education influencers to follow on Twitter in 2012. And she found out only when someone tweeted her.

To get started, Anita recommends you find people you like, have heard, or have read about and follow them on Twitter. If you don't already use the micro-blogging service, you'll need to get the hang of using the hashtags to find resources and the people you want to follow. There are also apps like Tweetdeck that can pull together and organize your Twitter feeds and feeds from other services so that they're easy to review; they may be grouped together or perhaps displayed like a morning newspaper, as the app Zite does, but on your phone or other mobile device. And don't be shy about tweeting back the good things you're finding or using other services like a social bookmarking service to log helpful resources.

Anita recommends you start with one thing and see how it works for you, but keep building that PLN. Starting locally is helpful because teachers in your state are addressing the same standards and dealing with some of the same issues. But don't be afraid to expand your network. Ask your media or technology specialist whom they follow and what tools they use. She also encourages educators to set up "Share Fair" sessions at the school, district, or state level where educators get together and share best practices and resources. And at the end of the day, Anita says, just go out and talk with other teachers. "That's where the learning occurs," she says. "I learn more at conferences by having conversations, networking, and making connections." So get the conversation started and "Get your PLN On!"

Source: John Ross.

Local Support for Technology Integration

When you enter the teaching profession you inevitably join a local learning community. When you arrive at a new school, pay attention to the leaders in technology integration. These fellow teachers can be a tremendous source of support and assistance as you work to integrate technology into your classroom. Look for teachers who have become expert troubleshooters when problems arise with software, hardware, or the network. Or find those teachers who have participated in professional development in curriculum-based technologies that you would like to know more about. New teachers are often paired with a mentor teacher. Find out how your mentor teacher

Figure 12.1
Collaborating with technology specialists or other teachers who use technology is a great way to build skills and community.

can support your technology needs, even if it is simply through social networking and introducing you to others with similar interests (see Figure 12.1).

If your school or district employs technology specialists, find out what sort of assistance they can provide. Are the specialists available to help you plan lessons that integrate technology? Are they willing/able to co-teach a lesson with you? Specialists of this type are becoming more common in schools and are often referred to as technology integration specialists, or technology integration teachers. These technology specialists usually have a teaching background and may still teach some classes. They can help you understand the technology tools in your school, as well as assist you in developing teaching strategies, identifying technologies that support your lesson plan goals, and sometimes even team-teaching a lesson with you.

Virtual Learning Communities

Another powerful way to learn is through interpersonal communications whether face-to-face, by phone, or online. Through communicating with others, you can seek answers to your questions, as well as serve as a mentor to less experienced teachers. The stories teachers tell about their classroom experiences can inspire you and provide you with a wealth of ideas, such as the *Stories from Practice—Get Your PLN On*. You use social networking tools to communicate with your distant friends and to establish friendships with individuals whom you've never met based on common interests, and this same network can assist you with lifelong learning opportunities. For example, if you're the only teacher within 200 miles who teaches Japanese, don't worry—there are other Japanese teachers you can chat with online. E-mail, social networking tools, message boards, discussion groups, and chat rooms all provide opportunities to share ideas with colleagues, any time of the day or night.

As you look for learning communities beyond your school, don't forget to investigate the wide range of listservs, blogs, webinars, and podcasts that may be of interest to teachers. Some websites even provide discussion areas especially dedicated to first-year

Professional Growth and Leadership 297

APPLY to Practice

Participating in Online Learning Communities

1. Explore the instructional options available to you. Locate online classes and workshops that you could take to meet your career goals.
2. Locate and review several teacher sites online. Some sites are listed on the textbook's companion website, and many state departments of education also provide lists for teachers in their states.
3. What do you notice about these sites? What are the common and unique characteristics of each? List your two favorite sites and describe why you selected them.
4. Share your favorites with your classmates. Visit the sites recommended by two of your classmates. How do they differ from your favorites?

TECH TOOLS & TIPS

How to Look Your Best on a Webcam

It's very easy to look *bad* on a webcam. Often, you're looking down into the webcam, the overhead lights create unflattering shadows, and the color of the monitor background casts an unnatural glow on your face.

It's helpful to understand how most inexpensive video cameras, such as webcams, work. In order to determine what color should be what, the camera looks for white within the scene. If no white is there, the camera often attempts to make some other light color "white." So when sitting in front of a light-colored wall, the automatic white balance in the camera may want to adjust the color balance to make the wall white, causing unnatural color shifts in your skin tones. For example when sitting in front of a yellow wall, you might become a truly creepy shade of blue!

Fortunately, a few simple steps can improve the quality of the image immensely (see Figure 12.2)!

1 Place the webcam at eye level. If you're using a laptop with a built-in webcam, you'll need to raise the entire laptop. Place it on books or another raised surface.

2 Change the background of your monitor to a neutral color and turn it down to a low light level. This will prevent the monitor color from reflecting off your face.

3 Reduce shadows. Place a white sheet of paper on your desk or keyboard to reflect the light from overhead upward to soften the shadows that are formed when the light source comes from above.

4 Pay attention to your background. A solid medium to dark toned wall works well. Avoid pastel colored backgrounds for the reasons described above. A bookshelf filled with books also makes an attractive background. Experiment with different backgrounds until you find one that is flattering.

5 Solid-colored clothing is usually most flattering on camera. In fact, you may want to wear a white shirt to provide the camera with a spot of white to use to adjust its white balance.

That's it! Take a look at the difference these tips can make!

(a)   (b)

Courtesy of Liesl Combs

Figure 12.2
As you will notice in the image on the left, it's easy to look bad on a webcam. As illustrated in the image on the right, following a few simple rules can greatly improve a webcam image. Images courtesy Liesl M. Combs.

teachers. Many sites require users to "join" in order to fully participate in the discussions. Although a few sites might require a fee, many of them are free. In most cases, it's very easy to join a listserv by simply sending a message to a listserv address. Likewise, it's easy to subscribe to podcasts and group updates using commonly available software, such as Apple's iTunes. There are also many blogs, Nings, wikis, and other websites created by and for educators that you can visit at your leisure. However, make sure you don't subscribe to too many things! It can take huge amounts of time just to delete messages or backlogs of podcasts that accumulate, and much more time to review them. Some educational websites and news services, such as eSchoolNews, also provide a review of popular blogs so you can find the information you want a little more easily. You may want to use online tools to participate in a telementoring program or to collaborate with other teachers to generate curricula and instructional activities, as well as simply share ideas. And of course, online communications aren't limited to just the printed word, as web tools and services such as Skype offer the option to conduct audio- and videoconferences. All of these tools can help you connect with others to collaborate and share ideas.

Conferences and Other Formal Learning Opportunities

Attending conferences is a good strategy for increasing your knowledge of new technologies as well as providing opportunities for you to share your own experiences as a technology leader. State conferences may be smaller than national conferences and often the presenters are teachers who have to meet the same instructional requirements as you do. Smaller conferences also support a sense of collegiality that allows you to continue conversations by phone, text, social networking tools, or e-mail after they are over. There are also a number of larger national conferences that occur annually. Besides presentations by nationally recognized education and technology experts, these conferences often have special exhibit areas that allow you to explore new hardware and software. Perhaps most interesting is the impressive array of vendors who attend these conferences, with showroom floors containing row upon row of people ready to show you how their products can be used in the classroom (see Figure 12.3).

Figure 12.3
Attending professional conferences can be invigorating, but it's best to have a plan.

Web-based conferences, webcasts, and webinars offer another option for learning about new technologies from experts and colleagues. Textbook publishers, software developers, hardware vendors, colleges, universities, and professional organizations all sponsor web-based training opportunities. Typically, one or more experts will present on a specific topic using webconferencing software. Participants have an opportunity to ask questions and discuss the topic with both the presenter and other participants. Many times, web conferences include a visual presentation and audio capabilities as well as text-based chat capabilities, and if you can't attend, they're often archived so you can watch them later, at your convenience.

Colleges, universities, professional organizations, and your own school district also offer training courses in topics of interest to teachers. More and more of these educational opportunities are available online. Some courses include synchronous components where all class members log on at the same time to participate in Internet chats or meetings where students engage in group discussions or share an electronic workspace. Other instruction is available for self-study. For example, software developers, school districts, and other organizations often offer self-paced tutorials on popular software.

Exhibit Leadership

All during your career, we encourage you to participate in formal and informal opportunities to enhance your skills in technology integration for meaningful learning. But as you move into professional practice, you have the responsibility to do more than simply keep your skills up to date. Becoming a leader means more than just attending or participating in events, like the virtual communities, conferences, and professional learning opportunities just described. As you become a leader, you play a more significant role in those events, perhaps presenting at conferences about technology projects in your school, or leading discussions or events in a virtual community. This does take some time, but as your career progresses you lead by sharing your expertise and experiences in face-to-face and online settings.

The action steps outlined in Table 12.1 provide suggestions to help you and your peers exhibit leadership by embracing a vision of technology integration, participating in a community of learners in which members share ideas and collaborate to make decisions together, and nurturing the development of technology leadership skills—both yours and others. You will notice there are plenty of opportunities for you to exhibit leadership as you move through ISTE's four stages in technology integration and in doing so, learn from, and contribute to, the learning of others.

> **TEACHSOURCE VIDEO**
> Go to the Education CourseMate website for this text and watch the video, *Teacher Perspectives: Keeping Up with Technology.*
> 1. Identify the strategies these teachers use to learn about new technologies.
> 2. How might you use these in your active practice?

APPLY *to Practice*

Action Steps

1. List the steps that you plan to take in the next two years to achieve your goals for developing your skills in technology integration within the classroom. Why do you think those steps would be especially useful for you? What else do you need to know to take those steps?
2. Discuss your steps with a group of peers. Find at least one person who is in the same phase as you are. How are your action plans similar? Different?

Table 12.1 Action Steps Toward Becoming a Technology Integration Leader

Phases	Action Steps
Beginning	
Embrace vision	• Participate in training on common productivity tools and communications software to support your teaching and learning, such as using word-processing software to create lesson plans and student activities; using software to record and report student progress; and using e-mail, a class website, or other communications tools to connect with students, parents, and other teachers.
	• Use the Internet, journals, and trade magazines to find lesson activities, research, and technology reviews related to the grade(s) or content area(s) that you teach.
	• Carve out time in your life to develop your technology skills. Dedicate a block of time, such as one afternoon each week, after school, to explore issues related to technology integration.
Build community	• Work with other teachers in your school to explore technologies you believe would be appropriate for classroom use.
	• Communicate with more advanced technology users, perhaps asking them to observe your classroom, in order to get mentoring and just-in-time support when you need it.
	• Seek help or input from others who are more technologically proficient when creating lesson plans or activities.
Develop leadership	• Share your experiences with others, in person or via online communications, who are also learning to integrate technology.
Developing	
Embrace vision	• Participate in training on applicable software beyond basic productivity tools. Possibilities include spreadsheets, databases, Web 2.0 tools, graphics or multimedia-authoring software, and educational apps for mobile devices. Scanners, probeware, handheld computers, tablet computers, digital cameras, and media players are among the hardware options to be explored.
	• Incorporate a wider range of curriculum-based software and electronic reference materials such as CD-ROMs, online encyclopedias, or content-subscription services in support of your instruction.
	• Monitor your classroom instruction in relation to the effectiveness of your technology integration efforts. Investigate and reflect on alternate pedagogies made possible by available technologies.
Build community	• Collaborate with other teachers in your school, both in your own and other disciplines, to explore technologies and develop technology-based lesson activities.
	• Observe teachers who incorporate technology into their teaching, and follow up with conversations focused on ways to adopt or adapt the activities with your own students.
	• Share your lesson plans with a critical friend—another teacher, a lead teacher, or a technology integration specialist—and consider ways to modify activities to increase the possibility of success, engage students, and promote a more learner-centered environment.
Develop leadership	• Discuss and share your experiences in formal collaborative settings, whether during joint planning sessions or other staff meetings.
	• Document your lessons and activities on a class web page or digital portfolio.

(continued)

Table 12.1 Action Steps Toward Becoming a Technology Integration Leader

Proficient

Embrace vision
- Attend technology training for new and emerging technologies that support areas of need for improving student learning in your classroom. Help develop and deliver technology training to other faculty and staff in your school.
- Use a variety of technology-based resources to present and modify content that supports your instruction and meets the diverse needs of your learners.
- Incorporate and evaluate a variety of technology-based methods and materials to identify those that best match the content-based skills and knowledge required of the content area(s) you teach.

Build community
- Collaborate with others by joining professional learning communities online and teacher newsgroups. Share ideas about how to use technology in your classroom to increase the effectiveness and appeal of content-based lessons.
- Participate in virtual observations of teachers and students in diverse settings. Reflect on your own and others' practices; engage in meaningful conversations using discussion boards, e-mail, or videoconferencing tools.
- Participate on technology integration planning committees.
- Co-teach or co-plan lessons with colleagues who are interested in developing their technology skills.
- Sign up to be a coach for others in your school, district, or state.
- Develop a cadre of student helpers who can provide support to developing teachers.

Develop leadership
- Demonstrate lesson activities or share lessons learned from technology-based activities with other teachers in your school at staff or faculty meetings.
- Share your successes with other teachers through print and electronic publications such as school newsletters, listservs, or a school website. Maintain and share your digital portfolio.

Transformative

Embrace vision
- Attend and provide technology trainings for new and emerging technologies in support of teaching and learning needs in your school.
- Help to identify training needs in your school or district and help develop and deliver technology training in-person and online to faculty and staff in your school, district, or beyond.
- Differentiate your instruction and the technologies you use to optimize student learning in your classroom.
- Participate in long-range projects to monitor and evaluate the effectiveness of existing and potential technologies in support of teaching and learning, such as participating in an action-research project focused on your own teaching or that of a group of colleagues.

Build community
- Use technology to develop or nurture professional collaborative efforts with teachers within and beyond your school and district to explore new and emerging technologies and generate solutions to problems or challenges in teaching and learning faced by members of the community.
- Participate in routine observations of classroom technology integration practices, both having teachers observe your practice and observing the practices of others.
- Meet in person or use technology to support regularly scheduled discussions about current and promising technologies and technology-based activities.
- Continue routine joint planning sessions with other teachers in your grade or content area or with technology integration specialists and routinely evaluate the effectiveness of lessons in order to identify best practices that can be shared across your school or district.
- Observe and participate in team teaching or coaching with new teachers developing their technology skills.

Develop leadership
- Communicate with teachers who are working through earlier phases in order to provide mentoring and just-in-time support.
- Attend and make presentations at professional conferences.
- Write about and publish your experiences both in print publications and on the web.
- Help others to document their lessons and activities by creating a class web page or digital portfolio.
- Become a mentor for other teachers. In addition to direct involvement with teachers in your building, offer support throughout the district and beyond.

© Cengage Learning 2014

Reflecting on Published Research and Your Own Practice

As you explore new and meaningful ways to use digital resources for teaching and learning, you will undoubtedly engage in reflection on both published research and your own practice. In Chapter 2, you learned that effective professionals continually reflect on their practice in order to monitor and evaluate their actions. In this section, we'll expand on these ideas and briefly discuss how current research can inform your practice. Finally, we'll discuss how both of these ideas—reflection on your own practice and reflection on current research—can be combined into a form of inquiry called **action research**.

Reflecting on Practice

As you will recall from Chapter 2, reflection should occur both "in-action," in order to monitor your behaviors as you go along, and "on-action," in order to improve your future performance. One way to reflect *on action* is to review the performance data of the entire class to determine the effectiveness of your instruction and the technology choices you made. If the majority of a class performs poorly on an assessment or assignment, your instruction may need some revision. Begin by reviewing your lesson plan. Did you include the standard in your instruction? Did you address it often or well enough? Compare your lesson plans with your actual practice. Did you carry out the lesson as you intended? Did external events, such as field trips, early release due to inclement weather, or other events prevent students from completing all of the learning activities? Reviewing your instruction in this way may uncover discrepancies between what is commonly referred to as the "written" curriculum—what you intended to teach—and the "enacted" curriculum—what you actually taught.

Also examine the technologies you used to support your instruction and assessment. Were the technologies appropriate for the content? Did the technologies support the skill or knowledge level required by the standard? For example, if a math assessment requires students to calculate the area of an irregularly sided object, then be sure to incorporate technologies that allow students to practice and perform the calculations rather than those that perform those calculations for the students. When using technology, be sure that it doesn't act as a barrier to students who do not have the required skills. For example, students with inefficient Internet search strategies may not be able to complete a web activity in which they are given unlimited access to resources on the Internet. In this case, preselecting a few online resources or using an academic search engine may support these students and allow them to focus on the content rather than the underlying technology skills.

You should also compare student performances on external assessments with their performances on your classroom assessments. Are their performances consistent? What trends in your classroom assessments indicate a need to adjust your instruction? Students with high scores on external assessments but habitually low classroom performance, may have unique learning preferences not being addressed, or may not feel challenged with past or current curricula. In terms of your analysis, these two sources of data—classroom and external assessments—may not be available from the same source and may take some manipulation on your part, using spreadsheets or other software, to make a fair comparison.

You also have the opportunity to monitor the effectiveness of your instruction and technology choices *in action* by observing your students during activities and assessments. Note where students are having difficulties, either with the content or with the materials and resources you selected, by making annotations in your lesson plan or gradebook. As we mentioned in Chapter 2, recording your lessons using video- or audio-recording methods can help you determine how effective your lesson activities are, whether you unintentionally favor any students in terms of questioning or task assignment, as well as provide an accurate record of the pace, quality, and appropriateness of your teaching.

Teachers are routinely observed, and observation instruments are readily available that can help you develop your teaching skills prior to formal observations. By establishing a schedule for recording yourself periodically throughout the year, you not only provide yourself with the opportunity to practice different pedagogical techniques under less pressure than a formal observation, but can record and demonstrate your professional growth. It may seem daunting at first to videotape yourself, but the information you receive will pay off multifold as you learn to hone your craft.

Once you feel comfortable recording your lessons, you may also want to consider receiving feedback from your peers, such as other teachers and administrators in your school. While it's not always feasible to be absent from your own class, sharing videotaped lessons is a practical method for building your skills and opening a professional dialog with your colleagues.

Sharing what you have discovered with your colleagues is a critical step in improving your instructional effectiveness (see Figure 12.4). By posting and sharing lesson plans on a secure server, and linking them to data from student performances, over time you and the other teachers in your content area and grade level can develop "best practice" lessons that have the greatest impact. Technology can help conduct analyses and generate reports as well as provide a means to continue a dialog outside of common planning times and staff meetings. Other content experts in your school who are given access to these lesson plans and reports, such as special education teachers, can indicate common accommodations or pedagogies effective with students with different learning needs and preferences. Technology specialists and resource teachers may provide options for different technologies that also can support these lessons. These same lessons and reports can be shared in full staff meetings where lesson exemplars are presented, either through live demonstrations or from videotapes, and then discussed.

Despite the benefits to be gained by observing and reflecting on your own and other's classroom practices, the education world has become more reliant on research to inform practice. It's important that you become an informed consumer of research so that you can identify and implement strategies and technologies that hold the greatest potential to improve your practice. You'll learn how to be an informed consumer of technology research in the next few sections.

Figure 12.4
Collaborating with colleagues is an effective method for reviewing the effectiveness of your instruction.

Reflecting on Current Research

There are hundreds, if not thousands, of journal, magazine, and web-based articles that have described some aspect of technology use in education. But how do you know what will work in your classroom? In this section, we provide guidance on how you can use research to determine the answers to questions that are important to you, such as, "Does this software match the learning needs of my students?" "How does a particular technology tool support my teaching style?" "What are the best methods for helping my students master my curriculum?" But first we'll begin by reviewing some of the work of educational researchers that have come before you.

Types of Educational Research

Literature about the educational uses of technologies can be grouped into four main categories: opinion articles, descriptive studies, evaluation studies, and formal research studies (ISTE, 2002). The vast majority of articles that you will find can be classified as **opinion articles**. These include theoretical propositions, curricular ideas, suggestions for using technology in the classroom, articles promoting the wonders of the latest and greatest software, and many similar types of papers. The opinions have more credibility if they are based on the results of well-documented research or evaluation studies. They also have more credibility if they represent the consensus of many people, as is the case with the ISTE standards. But until these opinions are tested, they are just opinions. The opinions may be from very important people or experts in the field, yet they are opinions all the same. Still, opinion articles may provide you with many ideas that you can test in your classroom using the action research methods we describe later in this chapter.

Another common category of articles is **descriptive studies**. Descriptive studies describe the state of something. They can describe what happened to one individual or in one classroom, such as how a teacher's classroom management strategies changed to incorporate iPods. They can also describe the results of large-scale surveys, such as those administered by educational organizations, such as Project Tomorrow, the Software and Information Industry Association (SIIA), and the Consortium for School Networking (CoSN). News organizations also provide descriptive reports, such as the annual "Technology Counts" by Education Week that "grades" states for their technology efforts. Most qualitative research reports fall into this category because they focus on a rich description of a specific situation.

There are also formal **evaluation studies**. Evaluation studies are used to determine the effects of an intervention—a product or teaching method. Evaluation reports are a popular method for technology vendors to promote their products and services. Evaluation studies may be well documented and may use a variety of qualitative and quantitative methods to determine the effects of the intervention. However, they do not attempt to test a specific hypothesis and do not need to have a control group.

Formal **experimental research**, on the other hand, does test hypotheses and uses control groups to determine the effects of an intervention. The results of these studies should be documented well enough for you to determine the extent to which they generalize to other settings. An experimental study should have a control group that is as identical as possible to the experimental group, except for the fact that the experimental group receives the intervention or treatment. Randomly assigning participants to different groups makes the experimental design even stronger, but is not always possible. Sometimes, though, when randomization is not possible, the different groups can be matched in terms of important characteristics, or statistical tests can be run to help make sure the makeup of the groups had little or no impact on the outcome of the research. Studies in which randomization is not possible are often referred to as **quasi-experimental research**. Statistical techniques are used to determine the extent to which any observed differences between the experimental and control groups may be due to chance alone.

There is a great deal of pressure to conduct "scientifically" controlled studies to determine whether educational interventions "work," by randomizing students into

---

opinion articles
articles that present the views of one or many people but that have not been tested through research or evaluation studies

descriptive studies
research studies that describe the state of something, often based on surveys or qualitative research methods

evaluation studies
studies that attempt to determine the effects of an intervention; however, they do not attempt to test a specific hypothesis and do not need a control group

experimental research
a method of investigating hypotheses about the effects of an intervention by comparing a control group, which receives no intervention, to an experimental group, which is as identical as possible to the control group except that the experimental group receives the intervention

quasi-experimental research
experimental research in which random assignment to groups is not possible, so statistical techniques are used to determine the extent to which any observed differences between the experimental and control groups may be due to chance alone

classes, controlling teacher content and presentation, and so forth. The No Child Left Behind Act of 2001 (Pub. L. No. 107-110) calls for the use of "scientifically based research" as the foundation for educational programs. In general, scientifically based research is defined (Eisenhart & Towne, 2003) as research that

- consists of an experimental or quasi-experimental design;
- uses empirical methods of data collection that are based on measurements or observations;
- uses measurement instruments or observational methods that provide reliable and valid data across multiple measurements and observations;
- involves rigorous statistical analyses to test hypotheses;
- provides a clear description of the research methods, instruments, and data used in order to allow for replication by other researchers; and
- has been subjected to peer review by experts who are not associated with the study.

Challenges to Technology Research

Despite the increased emphasis on using research in education, you need to know that the issue is much more complex than it might seem on the surface. Federal funding for research and development related to technology in educational settings is scarce, and most federal funding for technology continues to decrease or even be cut altogether. Opponents to continued funding for technology argue that despite all the monies spent on technology, software, networking, professional development, and developing resources, there has been little measurable impact on student achievement—and for many, student achievement is measured by standardized testing. They are no doubt correct. Why would putting computers in classrooms or connecting to the Internet, in and of themselves, increase test scores?

For the most part, classic research has shown that the technology itself doesn't really make much of a difference; instead, it's the way that the technology is used that matters (Clark, 1983). In other words, it doesn't matter, in terms of grades, whether students read their biology textbook online or from a book. There's nothing inherent about the technology that makes it unique from another resource. What does matter is the design of the instruction that is delivered to the students and what they do with the information once it has been received. In our example, the design of the text itself matters. The use of titles, summaries, overviews, and clearly labeled pictures can facilitate learners' comprehension of the textbook's content (Kozma, 1991). And it also matters what they do with the information once they have read it. For example, students who have the opportunity to participate in study groups reviewing what they have read, create outlines or concept maps illustrating their understanding of the content, or relate the content to real-world problems or phenomena are better able to understand the content than those who simply read the book. These ideas are consistent with the focus of this book: it's not *what* computer hardware, software, or other digital technology you use that matters, it's *how* you use it.

Granted, different technologies have different attributes, and these specific attributes may matter. In our textbook example, an online textbook may have hyperlinks that allow you to click on a new word the first time it is introduced in the text and then jump to additional information about the topic. The ability to access related knowledge at the point of need may make a difference, but that does not mean that students could not have accessed additional information when using a traditional textbook, for example, by using a dictionary or searching the Internet. However, the computer's ability to provide immediate feedback through a variety of relevant materials and resources, which then can be quickly incorporated into student products, such as student-generated notes or a portfolio, might increase the likelihood that students will use those supporting resources, deepen their understanding, and increase their motivation for extending their learning.

Obviously it's what teachers and students DO with the computers, connections, and so forth that can make a difference. And even if good things happen when you do the right things with the right technology, those "good things" may not be measured by standardized achievement tests. Moreover, it could be argued that even if technologies never make a difference in test scores, it still would make sense to use them, in appropriate ways, for teaching and learning so that students grow up using the technologies that they will use in their future jobs and life outside of school.

Research on the Impact of Technology

That being said, many groups have reviewed the existing literature related to technology use in an attempt to draw conclusions applicable to educational practice.

One group that has attempted to summarize the research on learning with technology is the Center for Applied Research in Education and Technology (CARET). CARET was created through a partnership between the ISTE and Educational Support Systems, with support from the Bill and Melinda Gates Foundation (ISTE, 2005a). CARET summarized past and current research findings related to the effects of technology on student learning as follows (ISTE, 2005b). Technology improves student academic performance when

- the application directly supports the curriculum objectives being assessed;
- the application provides opportunities for student collaboration;
- the application adjusts for student ability and prior experience, and provides feedback to the student and teacher about student performance or progress with the application;
- the application is integrated into the typical instructional day;
- the application provides opportunities for students to design and implement projects that extend the curricular content being assessed by a particular standardized test; and
- the application is used in environments where teachers, the school community, and school and district administrators support the use of technology.

Technology can enable the development of higher-order thinking skills when

- students are taught to apply the process of problem solving and are then allowed opportunities to apply technology in development of solutions;
- students work in collaborative groups while using computers to solve problems; and
- students use technology presentation and communication tools to present, publish, and share results of projects.

Technology improves motivation, attitudes, and interest when

- students use computer applications that adjust problems and tasks to maximize students' experiences of success;
- students use technology applications to produce, demonstrate, and share their work with peers, teachers, and parents; and
- students use challenging, game-like programs and technology applications designed to develop basic skills and knowledge.

Technology helps prepare students for the workforce when

- students learn to use and apply applications that are used in the world of work such as word processors, spreadsheets, computer-aided drawing, website development programs, and the Internet; and
- students are provided information regarding the use and benefit of technology and telecommunications for the workplace.

Technology is most effective for low-performing, at-risk, or students with special needs when

- students utilize instructional programs that continuously assess individual performance by adjusting the task difficulty to their ability and experience levels;
- students utilize technology applications selected to address their unique needs, strengths, and weaknesses;

- students utilize programs that are appropriate to their own language experiences;
- students utilize technology applications guided by diagnostic educational assessments to determine which programs are aligned with their documented academic needs; and
- students receive immediate feedback and progress monitoring through use of carefully chosen technology applications.

Similar to the CARET project, Apple Computer Company (2002, p. 4) summarized the research findings related to the use of technology to raise student achievement:

- students, especially those with few advantages in life, learn basic skills—reading, writing, and arithmetic—better and faster if they have a chance to practice those skills using technology;
- technology engages students and, as a result, they spend more time on basic learning tasks than students who use a more traditional approach;
- technology offers educators a way to individualize curriculum and customize it to the needs of individual students so all children can achieve their potential;
- students who have the opportunity to use technology to acquire and organize information show a higher level of comprehension and a greater likelihood of using what they learn later in their lives;
- by giving students access to a broader range of resources and technologies, students can use a variety of communication media to express their ideas more clearly and powerfully;
- technology can decrease absenteeism, lower dropout rates, and motivate more students to continue on to college; and
- students who regularly use technology take more pride in their work, have greater confidence in their abilities, and develop higher levels of self-esteem.

Consumers of Research

While these findings have been culled from many years of research, they still represent only a starting point for thinking about how to use technology in your classroom. It's important that you don't think of these as definitive answers but rather as guidelines that can and should be adjusted when applied in your classroom with your unique group of students.

Although these results are undoubtedly valid, there is a danger in thinking that the results of one or two studies are the absolute truth. To further complicate matters, many studies have conflicting findings. It's important for you to know that research exists, but it is even more important that you know how to be a good consumer of research.

As you examine the research for practical applications that you can use, consider the degree to which the conditions in the study are similar to, or different from, your classroom. When reading a research study, ask yourself the following questions (Bitter & Pierson, 2005):

- Who are the students? What is the age and grade level of the students? How are they like my students?
- What technology is being used? What sort of computers, peripherals, and digital devices are they using? What software applications are being used? How?
- When do they use the technology? Is access limited or not? How often and how frequently do they have access to the technology?
- Where do students have access to technology? Is it available at home and school?
- Why is technology being used? What is the intended purpose? Is it being used to supplement or replace other instruction? What are the instructional goals? How well do those goals match my own?
- How are students and teachers using technology? Are electronic information sources used to supplement direct instructional methods or as a resource within constructivist learning environments? Is it used individually, in small groups, or in large group settings? (p. 93)

As you examine the research findings, think about the extent to which the findings apply to your situation. If the research was conducted with a different group of students, different content, or different equipment than you have, it doesn't mean that the results would *not* apply to your classroom. But it also doesn't mean they necessarily do. Look to the research to give you ideas of what *may* be applicable in your classroom, then conduct your own classroom research to determine whether these principles work for you or not.

Teacher as Researcher

One of the best ways to determine what works for your students is to engage in **action research** within your own classroom. Perhaps you have read about the use of blogs for daily journal writing in high school literature classrooms, yet you teach fifth grade. Still, the idea sounds interesting. According to the article you read, students generated more and better stories when they wrote for an audience. Although you teach fifth grade, you still wonder how that would work with your students. Using action research methods, you can investigate whether these techniques work for your students and your curriculum. Action research is also called *teacher research* or *teacher inquiry*. No matter which term you use, it refers to the process of systematically collecting data to investigate some issue in your classroom. Action research doesn't just help you—it allows you to "contribute to the effectiveness, vitality, and self-renewal of the teaching profession" and of your school and community, as required by NETS-T Standard 5.d.

Action research can be conducted individually, in collaboration with a small group of peers, or as part of a school-wide endeavor. At one end of the continuum is the teacher who investigates the results of an intervention in his or her own classroom (see Figure 12.5). Other times, teachers in several classrooms work together, often as a grade level or department. And finally, there is school-wide action research. We will focus on the individual teacher-as-researcher, although the methods we discuss can easily be applied to action-research projects that involve additional researchers.

> **action research**
> the process of systematically collecting data to investigate some issue in your classroom to determine whether specific techniques work for your students and curriculum; also known as *teacher research* or *teacher inquiry*

Figure 12.5
New and emerging technologies, such as interactive whiteboards, and how they support learning in your classroom make a great subject for action research.

If you are interested in learning more about action research, you can find some excellent resources about the topic on the Education CourseMate website for this textbook.

Currently, action research is closely aligned with the reflective-practitioner movement within the teaching profession. When conducting action research, you reflect on your own classroom practice in order to identify an area in need of improvement. Although the intervention could be designed to address a problem, it can also be designed to investigate something that you're curious about, or to pursue an opportunity. Perhaps, for example, you want to investigate whether students would benefit from online help sessions before their exams. Just as professional athletes are always working to improve their performances, teachers, as professionals, also should be looking for opportunities to improve their skills and performances. Action research should be part of your own professional development; as such, it is one way to continue learning so you can remain a dynamic and responsive teacher. There are several action research models, and each divides the process into a slightly different number of steps, but the process is essentially the same for each model (see, for example, Dana & Yendol-Hoppey, 2009; Mertler, 2005; Stringer, 2007). In essence, you identify an area that you want to investigate, you collect data, and you analyze and reflect on the data in order to determine your next step. This process also aligns well with the idea of data-based decision-making, described in Chapter 7, which has become popular within education. For simplicity, we will continue to use the GAME plan acronym to organize the steps in the action-research process.

Steps in the Action-Research Process

Action research is a logical extension of the GAME plan that you have been using for your own self-directed learning throughout this book (see Table 12.2). When you use the GAME plan to increase your own knowledge, you identify an area of interest and then take action by seeking information to help you meet your learning goals. As you gather information, you monitor your learning progress to determine if the information you are finding is leading you toward obtaining your learning goals. After you have completed the process, you evaluate your learning progress and processes. You look back and consider whether you attained your learning goals, whether your strategies were effective, or whether you need to modify either your goals or your strategies.

Table 12.2 GAME Plan for Self-Directed Learning and Action Research

Steps	Self-Directed Learning	Action Research
Goals	• What do I want to know or be able to do? • What do I already know about the topic? • How will I know if I have been successful?	• What do I want to know? • What is already known about the topic? • How will I know if I have been successful?
Action	• What information do I need to meet my goal? • How can I find the information I need? • What resources are needed? • What learning strategy will I use?	• What will I investigate? • What evidence or data do I need to collect? • Where will I find, or how will I collect, that data? • What research strategy will I use?
Monitor	• Am I finding the information I need? • What patterns are emerging from the information sources? • Do I need to modify my action plan?	• How is it working? • What patterns are emerging from the data? • Do I need additional data?
Evaluate and Extend	• Have I met my learning goals? If not, should I modify my goals or my learning strategies? • What will I do differently in the future?	• How did the intervention work? • What will I do differently in the future, based on my research results? • What might I recommend to others?

© Cengage Learning 2014

When you engage in action research, you take this process one step further. You identify an area of interest. You collect information or data that help you meet your learning goals. You examine the information you find in light of your learning goals and situation. You evaluate whether this information is sufficient to allow you to meet your learning goals. But then you cycle back through the process, seeking greater insight.

Establish Goals

As in all forms of self-directed learning, the first step in the action-research process is to determine the focus, or goals, of the investigation. You may want to investigate ways to improve a situation in your classroom. Perhaps your school has received a donation of 25 iPods and you wonder how they could be used to enhance your students' learning. Table 12.3 lists several questions that can help you identify an area of investigation.

Often, the focus is stated in the form of a question such as "How can iPods be used to enhance my students' learning?" but it can also be stated as a goal statement such as "The purpose of this project is to investigate how iPods can enhance my students' learning." As you identify the goal of your investigation, make sure your focus is narrow enough to be manageable, yet open-ended enough so that it *cannot* be answered with a simple yes or no. Notice that our focus is on *how* iPods could enhance learning, not simply *do* iPods enhance learning. Stating your goal in this way opens up the possibility of identifying more areas of potential interest. You want to allow for a range of insights to emerge. In addition, you want your goal to have practical implications for your classroom, in order to be worthy of your time. It should yield potential benefits, to you, your students, and others. And most importantly, you want it to be something that will sustain your interest.

As usual at this stage, you should determine what is known about your area of interest in order to develop a plan to close the gap between what you know and what you want to know. Although some authors suggest that you develop your plan of action based on your own intuition and knowledge, we prefer to build on the knowledge of other researchers, all the while keeping in mind that we, as teachers, are often most knowledgeable about *our* situations. We look to the ideas and research of others as simply a way of expanding our repertoire of possibilities.

Typically, when conducting research, you examine the research literature to see what others know that might be applicable to your situation or interest. If, for example, you were interested in how iPods could be used for student learning, a first step would be to investigate how others have used iPods in the classroom. Opinion pieces and descriptive studies, as well as evaluation and formal research studies, can provide ideas worthy of further investigation. As you conduct your investigation, clearly identify what you hope to learn from your research. In other words, how will you know you have been successful? Based on the existing information that you find, develop a plan of action for your classroom.

Table 12.3 Starting Points for an Action-Research Project

1. I would like to improve . . .
2. I am perplexed by . . .
3. Some people are unhappy about . . .
4. I'm really curious about . . .
5. I want to learn more about . . .
6. An idea I would like to try out in my class is . . .
7. Something I think would really make a difference is . . .
8. Something I would like to do to change is . . .
9. Right now, some areas I'm particularly interested in are . . .

Source: Madison Metropolitan School District (2001b). Classroom Action Research Facilitators. Used by permission.

STORIES from Practice

Reflecting on My Classroom Practice

Not long ago our district implemented a new approach to professional development that emphasized teacher research as one of its primary goals. They asked for volunteers to pilot this approach in their classrooms. Because I had already been thinking about some of the things I wanted to improve in my classroom, I decided to sign up.

I have 27 students in my 4th grade classroom, 16 boys and 11 girls. There's a pretty good balance of ability levels, from high to low, although there are more high-ability boys than girls. My students are very active and very social. They ask a lot of questions about everything, but they are not very good listeners.

One of my biggest concerns is my students' inability to work well in small groups. They argue and bicker and have a hard time staying focused. I also have a hard time judging the progress they are making when working in small groups. Some students seem to take charge and put forth full effort, while others seem to just let their classmates do the bulk of the work. How do I know that they are actually processing the information and learning?

When I started to think about how to focus this concern into a question that could guide my classroom inquiry, I wasn't sure how to get started. I wanted to know how I could better monitor the success of my students, but I wasn't sure what to try. After reading some of the literature about self-directed learning and student self-monitoring, I finally came up with a question that I felt I could investigate in my room.

One of the articles I read mentioned that when students set goals, they are motivated to meet those goals. It also mentioned that when students are allowed to reflect on the progress they are making, their motivation and performance increase. So, I decided to give this a try in my classroom. I made up a little survey to measure the students' motivation for the next group project we were going to do about early pioneers, and gave it to them before we started. Then all the students kept a log in which they wrote down what they already knew about pioneers, what they wanted to know, and how they intended to learn what they wanted to know (kind of like a personal KWHL chart). These served as the students' long-range goals.

Then, everyday the students set daily goals that were very specific. At the beginning and end of each class period, I asked the students to check their goals for the day. This really seemed to help focus them on their tasks for the day.

Although the project is not over yet, I have already collected and analyzed lots of data—the motivation surveys (which I'll give again when it's over), the students' logs of their daily goals, as well as their notes about what they accomplished each day. And I should be able to tell if they actually learned more than my previous classes by looking at their test scores and comparing those to the scores from my other classes.

I'm pretty excited about the teacher-researcher approach. It makes so much sense to take a more systematic look at how this new strategy (goal setting) impacts learning before deciding whether it's worth using. If it does, I'll use it again, probably in additional subjects. If it doesn't, then I plan to go back to the literature to get more ideas. Teacher research really helps me feel as though I am in control of my students' learning—and that's a pretty good feeling!

Source: Based on interviews conducted by Peggy Ertmer with teachers in Lawrence Township, Indiana.

Take Action

Once you have identified your area of interest and what is known about the topic, you can develop a plan of action for your classroom, using the following questions:

What will you investigate? Will you implement a new strategy? If so, what steps will you take? Or will you focus your study on existing practices? The identification of the intervention itself will probably be the easiest step for you. It is no different from planning any other teaching method.

What evidence, or data, do you want to collect? Perhaps you want to introduce your students to iPods and ask them to help you brainstorm how they could use them for learning. How would you collect data at this step? Perhaps you could have them work in groups to brainstorm solutions and record those ideas on a flip chart. This flip chart would be your data. You could give them each an iPod for a month and have them keep a journal of all the ways they find to use the iPod for learning. You could collect the journals to determine what the students identified. After the iPods were returned, you could examine the number and type of files on each iPod. You could keep your own journal of observations as to how students use them in class. Let's say the iPods also had microphones attached so that students could record classroom lessons or discussions whenever they wanted. You could determine whether the iPods actually included lectures, identify how many, and ask students to self-report how they actually used the iPods at the end of the month-long period. Consider exactly what type of data you need to answer your research question.

As you identify the types of data you need, be aware you can include both quantitative and qualitative data. **Quantitative data** is information that can covert to numbers such as test scores or self-report ratings on opinion scales. **Qualitative data**, on the other hand, typically convert to words and are usually reported in the form of an interpretive narrative. Some forms of data can be used as both quantitative and qualitative data. For example, you may examine journal entries to count the number of times students mention that they used their iPods to listen to a lecture, and also examine their entries to identify trends in iPod use. For example, music, recorded lectures, books on tape, and data backup may emerge as patterns that can be used to organize the students' patterns of use.

What research strategy will I use? As you plan your data collection, you need to take into consideration the means through which the data will be analyzed in order to ensure that you have collected the necessary information. Quantitative data are usually analyzed statistically, while qualitative data are analyzed to identify themes that emerge. In general, you should always plan to collect data from two or more sources as this increases your ability to interpret your results accurately. Consider how you will ensure that you have multiple perspectives represented in the data you collect. See Table 12.4 for a list of possible data collection methods.

As in your teaching, you'll need to plan what you will do when. One question you may have is when to stop collecting data and go to the next step. In general, you will stop collecting data when you are no longer learning anything new. There is no way to know this for certain in advance, so just make your best guess and realize that you may modify your plan as you progress through the study.

> **quantitative data**
> information that converts to numbers, such as test scores or self-report ratings on opinion scales

> **qualitative data**
> information that converts to words, typically in the form of an interpretive narrative

Monitor

When you monitor your learning, you ask, "How is this working?" When you monitor an intervention during an action-research project, you ask the same question. And you answer that question through ongoing data analysis.

Table 12.4 Ideas for Data Collection

You should collect multiple sources of data, but select the most appropriate data for the question being investigated. Data you can collect include:

1. **interviews** with other teachers, your students, or their parents on the issue you are researching;
2. **diaries, journals, or anecdotal notes** that you or your students create to record actions, thoughts, and reflections;
3. **memos, minutes from meetings, or notes from the field** if you are engaging in a collaborative project;
4. **audio, videotapes, or photographs** from your own teaching or of student interactions and performances that document behaviors over time;
5. **questionnaires or surveys** about attitudes, opinions, or learning or other preferences from those directly involved with your issue, whether other teachers, your students, or their parents;
6. **checklists** of skills, knowledge, behaviors, procedures, or resources;
7. **student records**, such as test results, past grades, attendance, behavior and discipline, and any record of interventions or enrichment activities that students have participated in; and
8. **samples of student work**, such as papers, projects, web-based communications, portfolios, formal or informal assessments, or recordings of oral reports, presentations, or performances.

Source: Based on Ferrance, E. (2000). *Action Research.* Providence, RI: LAB at Brown University.

Quantitative data are analyzed statistically. You can summarize the means, averages, and percentiles. If you've been trained in statistical methods, you may want to use statistical tests, such as *t-tests* and others, to determine the probability that the differences between students' pretest scores and posttest scores can be attributed, at least in part, to the intervention you're studying. Spreadsheet programs can help you organize your data and perform statistical calculations.

There are as many ways to analyze qualitative data as quantitative data, but in general, you will read through the data (remember that qualitative data are usually recorded in words) and look for patterns or themes to emerge. Once you have a sense of what the patterns are, you can code your data by identifying instances of these patterns in one form of data (e.g., students' journals) and then look for instances of the same pattern in a different form of data (e.g., observation or interview data). Do the same or different patterns emerge? The data analysis process is iterative. It's useful to keep logs or journals of your findings. You may want to organize your data in tables or draw flowcharts or graphs. As you read through the data, try to summarize what you are learning. Table 12.5 provides additional tips for analyzing qualitative data.

Table 12.5 Tips for Analyzing Qualitative Data

When you conduct qualitative research, you collect and analyze your data simultaneously. These processes inform each other. For example, as you analyze your first set of interview data, you realize what new questions you need to ask in your next round of interviews. As you learn more from your data during the analysis process, you generate new ideas for the next round of data collection.

1. **Review** everything you have collected. Make notes as you go.
2. **Look for themes,** patterns, big ideas. Key words and phrases can trigger themes. Determine these themes by scanning the data, not by basing them on your preconceived ideas of what the categories will be.
3. **Narrow the themes** down to something manageable (three to five of the most compelling and interesting).
4. **Revisit** your data and **code** or label information according to the themes in order to organize your ideas. Make sure that you are organizing your data based on what you are actually learning from the data, not on the assumptions you bring with you to your analysis. Some ideas may fit into more than one theme. Create subgroups under each theme.
5. **Write continuously.** Jot down what you are seeing, what questions are emerging, and what you are learning. Keep notes on those new ideas that are unanticipated. Do not be afraid to let the data influence what you are learning as you go deeper with your analysis. Think about creating visual images: a grid, an idea map, a chart, or visual metaphors are all possibilities to help make sense of the data.
6. **Review** your information after it is coded/labeled to see if there is a frequency of certain items and/or powerful, interesting, unusual comments or behaviors which are of particular interest to you. Look for those unique ideas that you had not considered that may influence your thinking. Pay attention to incidents that give you new insights.
7. **Identify the main points** that appear most frequently and are the most powerful. Don't censor the data, even if you don't like what you are learning. Include data that doesn't necessarily reflect change or growth. All of this is part of the learning experience and can still inform our practice.
8. **Write up your major points.** You can write them up by theme, chronologically, or the different modes you used for collecting information. Share your findings with a colleague. Do new questions emerge from this discussion? Jot down ideas for actions you will take as a result of what you are learning.
9. **Provide evidence.** Draw the information together to include some of the evidence that supports each of your themes. The reader should be able to draw conclusions based on the evidence you have presented.

Source: Madison Metropolitan School District (2001a). Classroom Action Research Facilitators. Used by permission.

> **triangulate**
> the process of using multiple, independent data sources to increase the credibility and validity of research findings

Throughout the data analysis process, attempt to **triangulate** your data by looking for similar *and* different evidence in other data sources. When you triangulate qualitative data, you look to see if the same themes emerge from two or more data sources. In our example, you'd want to examine the actual files on the iPods to see if they clustered into the same categories as those reflected in the journal entries. You could also analyze the actual files quantitatively by counting the number of files of each type. Finally, you can triangulate findings across quantitative and qualitative data sources, as when you examine the similarity between findings obtained from students' ratings on an attitude survey (a quantitative source) and comments made during a class discussion regarding the perceived learning value of using iPods (a qualitative source).

Think about what you can learn from the patterns that emerge. How is your intervention working? What effects can you identify?

Evaluate and Extend

Once you have analyzed your data, it's time to reflect on your learning and plan for further action. How did it work? What will you do differently in the future, based on your research? What might you recommend to others?

A key component of action research is sharing what you learned with others. You may want to discuss your findings with your peers in a grade level meeting or make a formal presentation to the Parent Teacher Association. You may want to share your ideas in an online discussion forum. And if you choose to, you could even present your results at conferences in your area, post your lesson plans on a website, or publish your ideas in a newsletter. There are multiple ways to contribute to the body of knowledge about teaching and learning that enable others to benefit from your research.

In addition to sharing your knowledge with others, you should reflect on your own learning and make a plan for future action based on your findings. Are there other things you'd like to investigate? Do you plan to make a permanent change in your teaching strategies based on the results of your study? Consider what you will do differently in the future based on your research findings. For example, you could use the results of your research on classroom uses of iPods to create a proposal requesting an additional donation of more iPods for your classroom. By engaging in action research, you can become a contributor to, as well as a consumer of, research on the use of technology in the classroom.

Technology Support for Action Research

As you can imagine, computer technologies provide wonderful tools to assist in action research. You can use the Internet and other databases to locate existing literature in order to find out what others have to say about your topic of interest. You may want to collect data using portfolios, audio or video recordings, discussions, interviews, journals, videotapes, surveys, questionnaires, student work samples, and observations, as well as test scores. As you analyze your data, you may want to use qualitative or quantitative data-analysis software, spreadsheets, databases, or graphing software. And if you choose to present your findings in team meetings, faculty meetings, newsletters,

APPLY *to Practice*

Develop an Action Research Plan

1. Choose a topic or question that you would like to investigate through action research.
2. Search for literature on that topic to determine what is known about your area of interest.
3. Develop a plan to collect data to investigate your area of interest. Will you introduce an intervention or collect data on an existing phenomenon? Make sure you plan to collect data from several sources to better illuminate the issue.

Table 12.6	Sample Uses of Technology During Action Research
Steps in the Action-Research Process	**Ideas for Technology Use**
Goal setting	Subscribe to eZines, Twitter feeds, blogs, or journals, or conduct searches to determine what the literature says about the topic. Watch videos on a teaching website. Keep a journal of ideas.
Take action	Develop surveys. Keep journals. Record video or audio of classroom events. Scan documents. Organize data collected.
Monitor	Create data tables. Calculate averages and percentiles. Create graphs. Use analysis software to code and look for themes. Create concept maps or flowcharts of trends and themes.
Evaluate and extend	Write up results for a newsletter or publication using word-processing software. Share findings in an online forum. Contribute a lesson plan to a teacher website. Create presentation slides. Add notes to lesson plans on things to do differently when taught again. Organize related materials in folders. Make back-up copies of lesson plans.

© Cengage Learning 2014

publications, conference presentations or during in-service training, word-processing and presentation software will be especially useful. As Table 12.6 illustrates, technology can be a valuable part of the entire process. In fact, we can't imagine teaching, or conducting research that will inform our teaching, without technology. Can you?

Chapter Summary

In this chapter, we focused on ways that you could engage in professional growth and leadership as you continue your professional education and move into professional practice. We began with a description of various local and global learning communities that can contribute to your continued professional growth and development. In order to prepare you to be a leader in technology integration, we discussed ways in which you could gain the skills needed to make your vision of technology integration a reality, participate in a community of practice to enhance your technology skill development, and contribute to the technology skill development of others.

You also learned to reflect on your professional practice and the research literature in order to "make effective use of existing and emerging digital tools and resources in support of student learning" (NETS-T 5.c). We discussed the nature of the research literature that addresses technology use in the classroom, but warned you not to take what you read as the absolute truth. Instead, look to determine your own classroom "truths," knowing that what works in your situation may or may not work in another because of all the varied factors that make teaching so interesting and unpredictable. Existing research studies, evaluation studies, descriptive papers, and opinion pieces provide a rich storehouse of information that you can use to gather ideas that may work for you.

In the final section of this chapter, you learned to use action research to reflect on both the current literature and your own professional practice. Action research is conducted to investigate the potential value of instructional enhancements or possible solutions to instructional problems in your classroom. Often, this involves introducing an intervention and collecting data to observe the effects of that intervention. Interventions are resources, activities, or instructional methods that may involve small changes in an individual teacher's classroom or be designed to improve the entire school environment in some way. Since the action-research process can be thought of as a form of self-directed learning, we used the GAME plan to describe the steps in the process. We encouraged you to use action research to "contribute to the effectiveness, vitality, and self-renewal of the teaching profession," your school and your community (NETS-T 5.d). Fortunately, you can, and should, use the results of research—your research—to inform your educational practice.

Web Resources and Activities

See the Education CourseMate website for this book for a list of

- online learning communities for teachers; and
- resources related to action research.

YOUR PORTFOLIO

To begin to demonstrate competency in ISTE NETS-T Standard 5, add the following items to your portfolio:

1. Create a comprehensive vision statement that summarizes your plans and hopes for technology integration in your classroom. Justify your vision statement using findings from the research on using technology to support student learning.
2. Develop a plan for lifelong learning and self-renewal. Identify several specific ways in which you plan to continue learning about creative applications of technology to improve student learning. Discuss how you will use this knowledge to contribute to your teaching effectiveness and the vitality of your school and community.

References

Apple Computer, Inc. (2002). *The impact of technology on student achievement: A summary of research findings on technology's impact in the classroom.* Retrieved June 24, 2006 from http:// www.apple.com/education/research/

Bitter, G. G., & Pierson, M. E. (2005). *Using technology in the classroom* (6th ed.). New York: Allyn & Bacon.

Clark, R. (1983). Reconsidering research on learning from media. *Review of Educational Research, 53,* 445–459.

Dana, N. F., & Yendol-Hoppey, D. (2009). *The reflective educator's guide to classroom research.* Thousand Oaks, CA: Corwin Press.

Dwyer, D. C., Ringstaff, C., & Sandholtz, J. H. (1991). Changes in teachers' beliefs and practices in technology-rich classrooms. *Educational Leadership, 48*(8), 45–52.

Eisenhart, M., & Towne, L. (2003). Contestation and change on national policy on "scientifically based" education research. *Educational Researcher, 32*(7), 31–38.

Elmore, R. F. (2000). *Building a structure for school leadership.* New York: The Albert Shanker Institute.

Ferrance, E. (2000). *Action research.* Providence, RI: LAB at Brown University.

International Society for Technology in Education. (2002). CARET, Topic: Definition of study types. Retrieved February 4, 2012 from http://caret.iste.org/RatingStudy.html

International Society for Technology in Education. (2005a). Center for Applied Research in Education and Technology (CARET). Retrieved February 4, 2012 from http://caret.iste.org

International Society for Technology in Education. (2005b). CARET, Topic: Student learning. Retrieved February 4, 2012 from http://caret.iste.org/index.cfm?fuseaction=questions&topicID=1

International Society for Technology in Education. (ISTE). (2008a). *National educational technology standards for teachers.* Eugene, OR: Author.

International Society for Technology in Education. (2008b). *Refreshed ISTE NETS for Teachers Rubrics.* Eugene, OR: Author.

Kozma, R. B. (1991). Learning with media. *Review of Educational Research, 61*(2), 179–221.

Lave, J., & Wenger, E. (1991). *Situated learning: Legitimate peripheral participation.* Cambridge: Cambridge University Press.

Madison Metropolitan School District. (2001a). Classroom action research: A process for analyzing your data. Retrieved February 4, 2012 from http://oldweb.madison.k12.wi.us/sod/car/caranalyzeprocess.html

Madison Metropolitan School District. (2001b). Classroom action research: Starting points. Retrieved February 4, 2012 from http://oldweb.madison.k12.wi.us/sod/car/carstartingpoints.html

Mertler, C. A. (2005). *Action research: Teachers as researchers in the classroom.* Thousand Oaks, CA: Sage.

Pub. L. No. 107-110. (No Child Left Behind Act of 2001).

Stringer, E. (2007). *Action research in education* (2nd ed.). Upper Saddle River, NJ: Prentice Hall.

Wenger, E. (2006). Communities of practice: A brief introduction. Retrieved May 2, 2012 from http://www.ewenger.com/theory/

Supplement

Technology Integration and Lesson Planning in the Content Areas

The majority of this book provides general guidance on integrating digital technologies into your classroom. However, in this supplement, guest authors provide specific examples and guidance for integrating technology into content-specific areas. Having been classroom teachers in the past and now continuing to work with classroom teachers, we understand your need to focus on the content standards required by your district or state. This supplement provides content-specific guidance that applies to teachers charged with addressing the curricula related to working with English language learners, language arts, foreign language, math, science, social studies, health/physical education, visual arts, and music.

There is little doubt that national and state content area standards have shaped the way teachers currently address their curricula, design their learning environments, and gauge the academic success of their students. The Common Core movement will continue to impact classroom practice and accountability measures for years to come. Many states also have adopted technology standards that are adapted from ISTE's NETS for Students (NETS-S), as discussed in Chapter 1 (see Table 1.5 on p. 16). These standards can work with content standards to help provide engaging, authentic learning in your classroom.

In the following sections, guest authors address means of using technology to create authentic learning experiences to meet content area and technology standards. In accordance with the NETS-S, each author identifies ways that you can use technology to facilitate creativity and innovation; communication and collaboration; research and information fluency; critical thinking, problem-solving and decision-making; digital citizenship; and technology operations and concepts. Whether you read only one or many of the content-specific sections, you'll notice how they build upon the ideas presented in the first part of this book.

In keeping with the spirit of this textbook, in this supplement you will also find lesson plan examples using the GAME plan template. These lesson plans provide specific examples of how you can design learning experiences that meet both content area and technology standards.

317

Technology in the English Language Arts Classroom

English Language Arts

Sheila Carter-Tod, Ph.D. and Shelli B. Fowler, Ph.D.

Traditionally, concepts of literacy associated with language arts classrooms have focused on texts as written artifact. Contemporary students, however, are coming to language arts classrooms as "digital natives," as popular gaming researcher Marc Prensky (2001) touts, having been completely immersed and surrounded by technology and digital media for their entire lives. We now teach in language arts classrooms with students whose expectations are that we're familiar with and comfortable teaching technological and visual literacies in addition to teaching traditional reading and writing skills. For this reason, it's important to develop some understanding and guidelines for thinking about why, when, and how to integrate technology into your language arts classroom (see Table S.1 for some ideas).

With greater access to new technologies for teaching and learning, you may be encouraged to promote student generation of new media texts. Selfe (2004, p. 43) defines new media texts as those "created primarily in digital environments, composed in multiple media (e.g., film, video, audio, among others), and designed for presentation and exchange in digital venues." He further notes that because new media texts can incorporate both text and visual elements and can be interactive, they can require the author and participant to use multiple literacies related to seeing, listening, and manipulating, not just reading and writing. Cope and Kalantzis (2000, p. 5) concur that new media texts require us, teachers and students, to embrace a broader definition and

THE GAME PLAN

Content Standards

Set Goals

Learn more about the *Standards for English Language Arts* published jointly by the International Reading Association (IRA) and the National Council of Teachers of English (NCTE) or the language arts standards for a state where you plan to seek a teaching position. Consider a variety of ways to integrate technology while addressing the English language arts standards.

Take Action

Explore the national standards published by the IRA and NCTE or the state standards as listed on the department of education website in the state where you plan to seek a position. Plan ways that you could meet those standards using technology in the English language arts classroom.

Monitor

Did you find the information you needed? Do you need to contact the department of education for more information about where to find the English language arts standards?

Evaluate and Extend

Discuss the plan you developed for meeting the English language arts standards using technology with others and compare your ideas. Note the strengths and weaknesses of the various examples and incorporate the best ideas into your plan.

English Language Arts

pedagogy of multiliteracy, one in which "Meaning is made in ways that are increasingly multimodal—in which written-linguistic modes of meaning are part and parcel of visual, audio, and special patterns of meaning."

The language of the *Standards for English Language Arts* (IRA & NCTE, 1996) includes several examples of student activities that are designed to develop and nurture creativity, such as evaluate, synthesize, and apply language and communication skills in a variety of settings; create original works in both print and non-print form; and act as professionals in a variety of literacy communities.

Students in the language arts classroom can use a variety of technology-supported tools to create original works in both print and non-print form. For print, you might logically think of the use of word processors, journaling, and note-taking software to support activities in your language arts classroom, but many of these applications also offer supports to scaffold students as they create original works—whether these student products remain in their print-based form or are incorporated into projects using other media. Tools such as spelling and grammar check, embedding notes, and tracking changes can guide student learning and support self-monitoring during creation. Many of these tools can also help students bridge between print and other forms of literacy through the ease of embedding and linking information in a variety of formats, such as images, media objects, and hyperlinks.

Table S.1 Ideas for Addressing NETS-S in the English Language Arts Classroom

Creativity and Innovation
Students use presentation or multimedia-authoring software to create a multimodal story map based on a story from their classroom reading series that best captures their understanding of the book's characters, setting, problems faced by the characters, and resolutions. Before creating projects, students should engage in classroom work and discussion that helps them to explore the connections between characters and plot in an attempt to identify trends, patterns, and literary conventions like foreshadowing, foils, etc.

Communication and Collaboration
Students create websites, brochures, or news stories or other informational texts for a topic of study. They connect with other students in the school or district that are reading the same materials, by exchanging e-mail, or participating in online discussions to help gauge different opinions and reactions to the reading. These opinions, reactions, and feedback, are incorporated into a class product that reviews the materials they are reading.

Research and Information Fluency
Students conduct Internet research by collaborating with the school librarian or media specialist, or with teachers from other content areas with the purpose of learning to use the Internet as a source of information. Students follow basic safety rules of the Internet, use keywords and other search strategies to find information, and use search engines and online databases to better understand the types of data each source best provides.

Critical Thinking, Problem-Solving and Decision-Making
Students design and develop a class website that supports a research project or other writing project. The writing task should engage students in an analysis of a complex, real-world issue, such as global warming; U.S. port security; causes for, and human health risks of, increased mercury content levels in tuna. Students are asked to justify the reasons for the resources and tools they include in the project.

Digital Citizenship
Based on the popular *Flat Stanley* series of books and the Flat Stanley Project website, students create digital versions of themselves using digital photos and send them to relatives and friends in distant places as an attachment to an e-mail. The recipients respond to a couple of questions about where they live, what they do, and how they use technology in their daily lives. The recipients include a picture of themselves or their location, then forward the message to other friends and relatives, copying the student each time so they can track progress of their virtual trip through a class website or blog.

Technology Operations and Concepts
Students create individual entries for class biographies using word-processing software. Computer skills such as learning to enter, edit, and format text; inserting and editing images and graphics; and opening, saving, and exiting files can be covered within the context of addressing language arts concepts related to writing as a process.

While text predominates on the Internet, tools that allow users to view, create, edit, and distribute information across the Internet as images, sounds, animations, and videos are becoming accessible to many students, especially through the increasing use of mobile devices that capture and share images, video, and other forms of information. These powerful tools make it easier for students to explore their creativity and express themselves to a range of audiences in ways that were, at one time, difficult (see Figure S.1). Now students can post their feelings and thoughts on the Internet using easy blogging or wiki software. They can take and edit digital images and videos and post these online to communicate with others. As a language arts teacher, these are also tools that you and your students can use to promote creative thinking, align your language arts instruction with student learning preferences, and give students an opportunity to express their language arts skills in a variety of ways. It's important to note that language arts teachers have long addressed creativity in available print and non-print forms, and the national language arts standards address topics such as visual language, technological and information resources, and print and non-print texts.

The greater access to digital tools similar to, or the same as, those used by professionals helps students of varied levels of language proficiency create projects that can look just like those created by their peers—which can motivate struggling students. These tools often contain wizards, widgets, examples, or help features, and may link to user groups and forums that allow students to explore the capabilities of the applications and to stretch their creative potential. Using digital tools, such as page layout, video-editing, web-authoring, and other multimedia software, students can create print and non-print projects that demonstrate levels of proficiency that rival those of professionals. Students with varied learning preferences may find different multimedia authoring

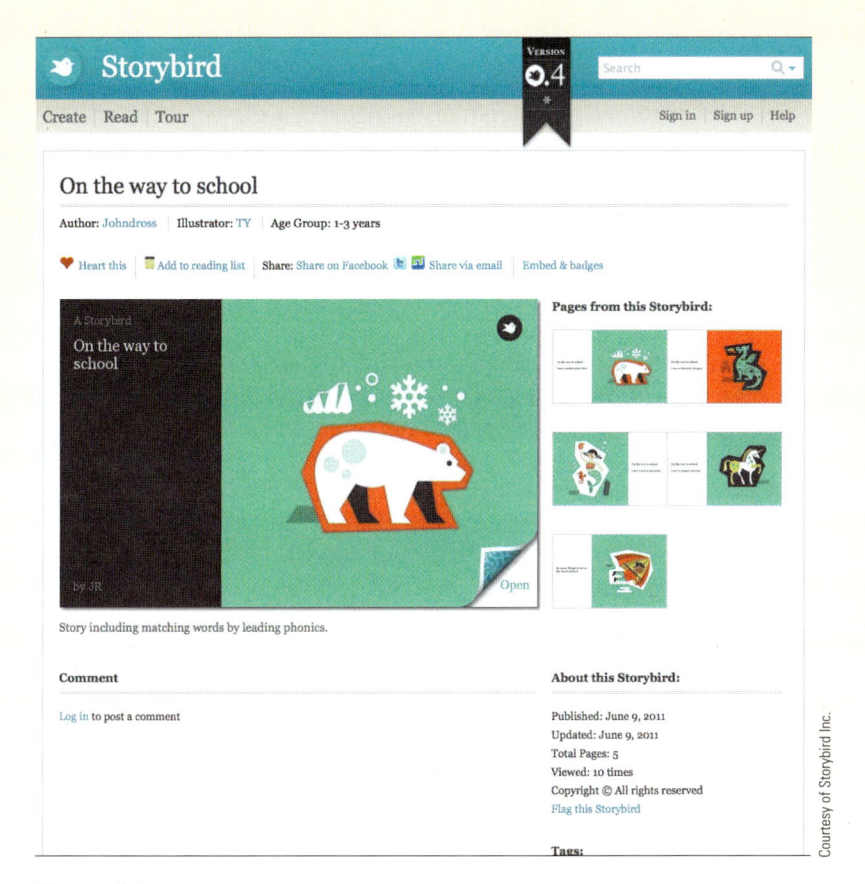

Figure S.1
Even very young students can create digital stories and build language arts skills with simple online tools.

English Language Arts

Figure S.2
A wide range of digital tools are available to help students develop language arts skills.
Source: This comic strip was generated at http://www.MakeBeliefsComix.com. Used by permission of author and site creator Bill Zimmerman.

tools more closely linked to their learning preferences, and these tools may serve as a springboard for creativity in skills related to language arts. Finding a tool matched to a student's preference for learning and expression can help some students focus on the learning at hand and create products that are professional in appearance (see Figure S.2).

Technology tools—especially communications tools—also allow students to act as professionals do in a variety of literacy communities. A wider range of literacy communities are accessible to students now than was the case just a few years ago. Students not only can access books by their favorite authors, but can often find websites, blogs, and podcasts about their favorite books and media and by authors whose work they enjoy. Crafting exemplary websites, presentations, videos, and other multimedia also requires students to develop and demonstrate a range of print and non-print literacies. As they develop these skills they can see they are truly a part of a range of literacy communities both in school and beyond that will require them to draw upon an understanding of print and non-print texts, of themselves, and of the cultures of the United States and the world.

References

Cope, B., & Kalantzis, M. (Eds.). (2000). *Multiliteracies: Literacy learning and the design of social futures*. London: Routledge.

International Reading Association and National Council of Teachers of English (IRA & NCTE). (1996). *Standards for the English language arts*. United States: Author.

Prensky, M. (2001). Digital natives, digital immigrants. *On the Horizon, 9*(5), 1–6.

Selfe, C. L. (2004). Students who teach us: A case study of a new media text designer. In A. E. Wysocki, J. Johnson-Eilola, C. L. Selfe, & G. Sire (Eds.). *Writing new media: Theory and applications for expanding the teaching of composition* (pp. 43–66). Logan: Utah University Press.

Lesson Plans for English Language Arts

Elementary English Language Arts

English Language Arts

TECHNOLOGY INTEGRATION FOR MEANINGFUL CLASSROOM USE

Daily Lesson GAME Plan

Lesson Title: What's the Solution?

Related Lessons: Before, during, and after reading comprehension strategies

Grade Level: Elementary

Unit: Elements of a story

GOALS

Content Standards:

3. Students apply a wide range of strategies to comprehend, interpret, evaluate, and appreciate texts. They draw on their prior experiences, their interactions with other readers and writers, their knowledge of word meaning and of other texts, their word-identification strategies, and their understanding of textual features (e.g., sound-letter correspondence, sentence structure, context, graphics).
6. Students apply knowledge of language structure, language conventions (e.g., spelling and punctuation), media techniques, figurative language, and genre to create, critique, and discuss print and non-print texts.
8. Students use a variety of technological and information resources (e.g., libraries, databases, computer networks, video) to gather and synthesize information and to create and communicate knowledge.
12. Students use spoken, written, and visual language to accomplish their own purposes (e.g., for learning, enjoyment, persuasion, and the exchange of information).

ISTE NETS-S

- [X] Creativity and innovation
- [X] Communication and collaboration
- [ ] Research and information fluency
- [X] Critical thinking, problem solving, and decision-making
- [ ] Digital citizenship
- [X] Technology operations and concepts

Instructional Objective(s):

Students write alternate endings to stories begun by others. They must analyze and identify the main characteristics of a story, including the story's characters, setting, and problems faced by the characters, and then propose a solution or resolution. Older students may be able to also identify more complex literary conventions like foreshadowing, foils, and other characteristics of writing.

ACTION

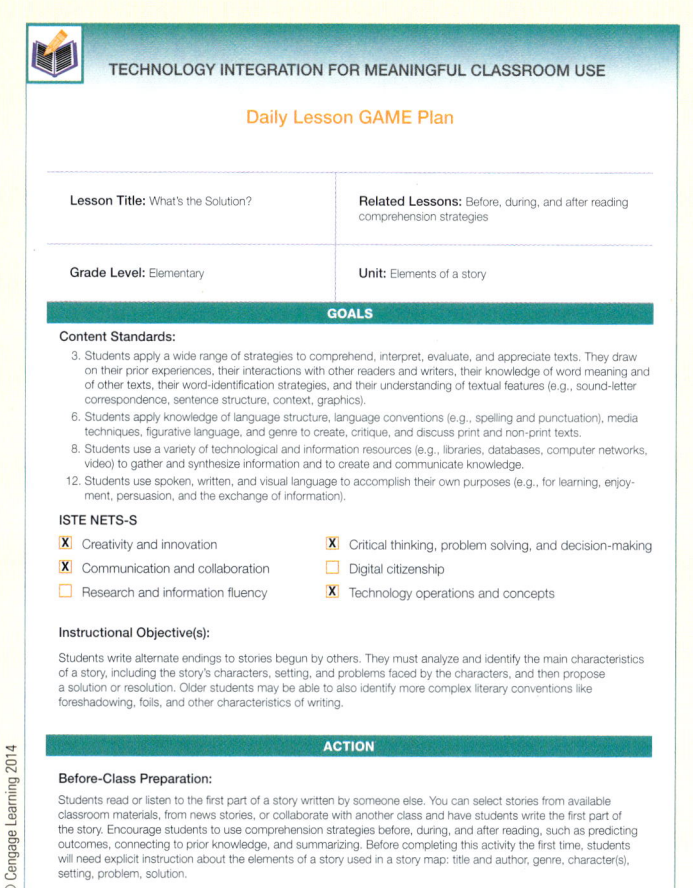

Before-Class Preparation:

Students read or listen to the first part of a story written by someone else. You can select stories from available classroom materials, from news stories, or collaborate with another class and have students write the first part of the story. Encourage students to use comprehension strategies before, during, and after reading, such as predicting outcomes, connecting to prior knowledge, and summarizing. Before completing this activity the first time, students will need explicit instruction about the elements of a story used in a story map: title and author, genre, character(s), setting, problem, solution.

During Class

Time	Instructional Activities	Materials and Resources
5–10 minutes	In whole-class instructional setting, begin the activity with comprehension questions commonly asked after reading. Review the essential elements of the story and elicit detailed responses from students. You can capture responses from the class on a concept map or other organizer or you can provide handouts for students, such as the "Five W Star" that helps students identify who, what, why, when, and where of a story. Ensure students understand the elements of a story: title and author, genre, character, setting, problem, and resolution.	Whiteboard or computer with projector Five W Star Handout Optional: Concept-mapping software
10–15 minutes	In small groups, pairs, or with individuals, students read or listen to the beginning of their assigned/selected stories. They identify the essential elements of the story, perhaps completing the "Five W Star" or similar handout. Another option is to record responses in a graphic organizer or concept-mapping software, such as Kidspiration.	Story beginnings in print or recorded format Five W Star Handout Graphic organizer or concept-mapping software
20–30 minutes	Students use concept-mapping software, such as Kidspiration, to brainstorm ideas for the resolution of their stories. The ideas are used as writing prompts that students expand upon to complete their first draft of their ending in word-processing software.	Concept-mapping software Word-processing software
10–15 minutes	Students share their story endings with the resolution of the problem with others in the class for feedback. Students can provide oral or written feedback depending on time and ability of students.	
30–40 minutes	Students revise their story endings for a final draft then record the entire story using audio editing software, such as Audacity or GarageBand. Many mobile devices also support audio recording. If time allows, students can add sound effects, loops, or royalty-free music that can be found in some editing programs, like GarageBand, or retrieved from online sources.	Word-processing software Audio-editing software Sound effects or royalty-free music
	Students can post their stories on a class website or blog to share with parents or other students. Be sure to either read or play the stories for each student or group in class and review all of the elements of the stories.	

Notes: The beginning of the story can come from just about anywhere. Students, whether in this class or another, can write them or they can be taken from a variety of fiction and non-fiction sources. This lesson is based on a video on the textbook's Education CourseMate website.

MONITOR

Ongoing Assessment(s): This activity adapts well to pairs or small groups where students can provide ongoing support and feedback to each other. As you monitor students writing, use probing questions or encourage collaboration for students who encounter difficulties. Graded artifacts can include the handout or graphic organizer, if used, the draft and final written stories, and the final recording. Student collaboration can also be monitored using a checklist.

Accommodations and Extensions: Depending on the age and readiness level of the students, this activity can be conducted in small- or whole-group instruction. The activity can also be used for an intervention lesson for struggling readers or those with limited language proficiency. Using small groups and allowing students to record responses first before writing can also help those with limited English. Students who need enrichment may be able to incorporate relevant sounds and background music.

This lesson does not need to be completed in a single day but can occur across two or more days depending on access to resources and ability level of the students.

Back-up Plan: The activity can be completed with paper-and-pencil, if necessary. It can also be completed as a whole-group activity for younger students.

EVALUATE AND EXTEND

Lesson Reflections and Notes: The "Five W Star" handout and graphic organizers can be used or referred to throughout the year for multiple stories. Depending on the ability level of students, available time, and resources, this makes a great activity for collaboration with another classroom, whether in the same school or not. Consider connecting the classrooms, either virtually or in person, after the project.

A full-size version of this lesson plan appears on the CourseMate website at www.cengagebrain.com.

High School Language Arts

TECHNOLOGY INTEGRATION FOR MEANINGFUL CLASSROOM USE

Daily Lesson GAME Plan

Lesson Title: Putting Beliefs into Words and Stories: A Personal Essay for "This I Believe"	**Related Lessons:** Persuasive Essay, Journalistic/Informative Essay
Grade Level: High School	**Unit:** Essay writing

GOALS

Content Standards:
1. Students read a wide range of print and non-print texts to build an understanding of texts, of themselves, and of the cultures of the United States and the world; to acquire new information; to respond to the needs and demands of society and the workplace; and for personal fulfillment. Among these texts are fiction and nonfiction, classic and contemporary works.
3. Students apply a wide range of strategies to comprehend, interpret, evaluate, and appreciate texts. They draw on their prior experiences, their interactions with other readers and writers, their knowledge of word meaning and of other texts, their word identification strategies, and their understanding of textual features (e.g., sound-letter correspondence, sentence structure, context, graphics).
5. Students employ a wide range of strategies as they write and use different writing process elements appropriately to communicate with different audiences for a variety of purposes.
8. Students use a variety of technological and information resources (e.g., libraries, databases, computer networks, video) to gather and synthesize information and to create and communicate knowledge.

ISTE NETS-S
- [X] Creativity and innovation
- [X] Communication and collaboration
- [ ] Research and information fluency
- [X] Critical thinking, problem solving, and decision-making
- [X] Digital citizenship
- [X] Technology operations and concepts

Instructional Objective(s):
Students analyze and compose with a clear sense of audience and purpose by identifying, analyzing, and practicing the following genres: personal essay, memoir, and narrative. Students describe the choices a writer makes related to these forms.

ACTION

Before-Class Preparation:
Review the This I Believe website from National Public Radio (http://thisibelieve.org/). This lesson requires students to write a personal essay that they turn into a digital story. Another good resource for powerful personal stories in a variety of languages is the Center for Digital Storytelling (http://www.storycenter.org).

During Class

Time	Instructional Activities	Materials and Resources
15–20 minutes	In a whole-class setting, introduce students to the This I Believe or the Center for Digital Storytelling website, its history, purposes, and other features relevant to the lesson. This can be accomplished in a computer lab or using a single-teacher workstation to project information for the class.	Computer with whiteboard or projector This I Believe or Center for Digital Storytelling website
20–30 minutes	Using examples from the website, discuss the differences between a personal essay, which is focused on a belief or insight about life that is significant to the writer, and the two other forms of personal writing: the personal narrative and the memoir.	This I Believe or Center for Digital Storytelling website
30–45 minutes	Individually or in pairs or small groups, have students create documents that list the similar and different characteristics of each genre using at least one example of each genre from the website. They can do this in a table or an expanded Venn diagram, and it can be recorded in a student portfolio or writer's notebook. Students should identify the author's main purpose and supporting details that contribute to that purpose from each example.	Word-processing software Drawing or concept-mapping software (optional)
1 or 2 class periods and/or homework	Individually, students compose a personal essay that is to become the script for their digital story from one of the following prompts or one you provide: • All of us are works in progress with a long way to go before we reach our full potential. In what skill or area are you still working to make progress? • Our society uses the word "hero" in many different ways. How do you define a hero, and who is a hero in your life? For homework, have students identify personal artifacts (pictures, awards, hobby materials, etc.) that support or contribute to their personal essays.	Word-processing software
50 minutes	Students create storyboards for their essays, incorporating descriptions of personal artifacts—either ones they've already found or ones they need to find.	Word-processing, concept-mapping, or presentation software
1 to 3 class periods	Digitize images either by scanning or taking digital pictures. Some students may also want to create digital images to support their essays. Record narration using the script. Depending on the availability of equipment (scanners, cameras, microphones, software, etc.), groups of students may work through these steps simultaneously. Compile digital files into story and export as a movie.	Scanners, digital cameras, phones or mobile devices with cameras Image-editing or drawing software, such as Fotobabble, Sumo Paint, or PowerPoint Audio-editing software, such as GarageBand or Audacity MovieMaker, PhotoStory, or iMovie
1 class period	Students share their digital stories with the rest of the class and post them to a class website or personal journal or blog. When sharing, students should explicitly describe how their essays match the characteristics of personal essays identified earlier and the significance of the topics they selected and the relationship of the imagery.	

Notes: Story files can be posted to a class web page or blog, or placed on workstations or laptops around a room gallery style. If you have an account for a video-sharing site, such as YouTube or TeacherTube, you may want to post or link the videos to your channel. The essays and the artifacts used to create them are appropriate for student portfolios or sharing with parents, and may support college application preparation. Personal essays are often included in college applications, so this activity can help college-bound students organize their thoughts and actually prepare for some applications. A similar activity can be viewed on the textbook's Education CourseMate website in the video *Digital Storytelling in the High School Classroom*.

MONITOR

Ongoing Assessment(s): Students will generate comparison charts of the three types of genres that can be assessed and stored in a student portfolio, writer's notebook, or other record. Use your standard grading and feedback processes to evaluate the personal essays. The essays can be evaluated both in terms of how well students understand and produce the concepts of the personal essay and in terms of key concepts of grammar and correctness that may have been covered in class. Digital stories can be scored using a rubric with input from students based on characteristics of personal essays they have identified from the website.

Accommodations and Extensions: Help students focus on the content and learning goals by identifying examples of each type of essay on the website in advance, perhaps even creating a bookmarked list or adding appropriate pages to a social bookmarking page. Students who have difficulty beginning or organizing a written composition may benefit from the use of concept-mapping software that converts the map to a text-based outline.

While the focus of this lesson is a personal essay, the process is malleable and can be used for other purposes. For example, students can be presented with several examples of personal essays, in print or multimedia, and can respond to them as to how they are similar or different from their own lives and experiences.

Back-up Plan: Identify several print-based examples of each genre from the textbook or other resources if Internet access is limited.

EVALUATE AND EXTEND

Lesson Reflections and Notes: The writing of the personal essay can extend over several class periods. Depending on your preferred methods, essays may go through several drafts as well as class workshop(s). Provide individual feedback and guidance as well as in-class opportunities for students to share, comment on, and revise their essays.

A full-size version of this lesson plan appears on the CourseMate website at www.cengagebrain.com.

Technology in the ELL Classroom

Jill Robbins, Ph.D.

English Language Learner

The number of students entering the nation's classrooms who do not speak English continues to increase. These students may be referred to by a range of labels, such as Limited English Proficient (LEP) students, Culturally and Linguistically Diverse (CLD) students, English Speakers of Other Languages (ESOL), or—the term used in this book—English Language Learners (ELLs). The number of students who spoke a language other than English at home rose to 11.2 million in 2009 (U.S. Department of Education, 2011). As the number of ELLs increases in the nation's classrooms, it's likely you'll be responsible for helping these students obtain a high-quality education, regardless of the grade level or content area you teach.

English language learners come into our classrooms with a range of backgrounds and experiences: they may never have been in an English-speaking environment before, their previous schooling may have been inadequate or nonexistent, and they may have extremely limited literacy in their language of origin. These students are often from families with low incomes and lower levels of formal education (August & Hakuta, 1997), so many may not have been in an educational situation where technology is frequently used, and they may not have access to a computer at home. But as noted throughout this textbook, technology opens up a world of possibilities for these learners by providing scaffolds for their learning, enhancing their abilities to communicate in English, and providing access to resources that can empower them to achieve greater academic success (see Table S.2 for some ideas).

THE GAME PLAN

Content Standards

Set Goals
Research the *Pre-K-12 English Language Proficiency Standards* developed by the Teachers of English to Speakers of Other Languages (TESOL) or the TESOL or ELL standards for a state where you plan to seek a teaching position. Consider a variety of ways to integrate technology while addressing the TESOL or ELL standards.

Take Action
Explore the national standards published by the TESOL or the ELL state standards as listed on the department of education website in the state where you plan to seek a position. Plan ways that you could meet those standards using technology in the ELL classroom.

Monitor
Did you find the information you needed? Do you need to contact the department of education for more information about where to find the ELL standards?

Evaluate and Extend
Discuss the plan you developed for meeting the TESOL or ELL standards using technology with others and compare your ideas. Note the strengths and weaknesses of the various examples and incorporate the best ideas into your plan.

English Language Learner

Learning in the content areas is highly driven by language and the 2006 TESOL standards acknowledge the central role language plays in accessing and meeting the standards of all content areas. It is not sufficient for students to be able to converse in English for them to be able to access content and be successful in their learning pursuits. There is a difference between the language used for social communications and that used for academic purposes, what one researcher describes as basic interpersonal communications skills (BICS) versus cognitive academic language proficiency (CALP) (Cummins as cited in Reed & Railsback, 2003). So although your students may be able to use some English to welcome you, talk with other students in the cafeteria, and respond to simple requests, they may not be ready to master the academic language required to understand even the most rudimentary concepts related to mathematics (hypotenuse, tangent, parallel), science (mesosphere, cumulus, precipitation), social studies (democracy, amendment, citizenship), or even technology (Internet, wiki, blog)!

It's important to understand that no single approach will fit the needs of all ELLs. Just as you are encouraged to differentiate instruction and create learning experiences that support the needs of other students, you and your school should consider the needs of your specific ELLs before selecting a program, activities, or resources.

English language learners, especially, are empowered when given the knowledge of how to use technology to support active learning, a component of authentic learning

Table S.2 — Ideas for Addressing NETS-S in the ELL Classroom

Creativity and Innovation

Students brainstorm using an interactive whiteboard (or shared online whiteboards with students at distant locations) to activate background knowledge on topics in a social studies classroom. Students can collaborate to review websites that provide content knowledge, using online translators if necessary, or can create graphical organizers of images that relate to shelter, food, and clothing of different cultures being studied.

Communication and Collaboration

Students use computers or mobile devices to create digital stories that tell their personal histories or family stories. They include audio files of interviews with parents or family members (in English or their home language) or relevant songs. Pictures and other family memorabilia can be scanned or photographed for inclusion. The digital stories can include narration by the students in English and their home languages and can be shared with their classes or posted on a class website.

Research and Information Fluency

Students carry out research and prepare information summaries by paraphrasing or restating what they read. When students identify digital images that will become part of their projects, they request permission from copyright owners or follow Creative Commons licensing guidelines (discussed on p. 250) to use the images.

Critical Thinking, Problem Solving, and Decision-Making

Students research water use in their own homes and across their regions through Internet resources and e-mails with experts and authorities. They propose conservation measures that can be undertaken by peers and families by creating web pages or posters created by desktop-publishing or drawing software that can be printed and posted around the school.

Digital Citizenship

Students brainstorm issues for a debate on school-related controversies using online collaborative tools. Following research conducted—including visiting social-networking sites and reviewing privacy and confidentiality policies—students collaborate to create a proposition statement for their debate and model the use of these communications tools either with chat or Twitter, or posting to a wiki, social-networking, or video-sharing site.

Technology Operations and Concepts

Students acquire English-language keyboarding skills and basic operations (open, save, edit, copy, paste, etc.) and use them in the course of writing assignments within the four content areas. ELLs can transfer knowledge of systems they used in their home countries by applying them to similar systems in the English-language environment; for example, students with experience using game consoles can transfer knowledge of menus and programs to navigating operating systems and common software applications.

(see Chapter 3). The ease of creating and editing documents in word-processing software, with its correction features, dictionaries, thesauruses, and other features, provides plenty of scaffolding for ELLs to engage in active learning experiences that support articulation of their own thoughts and ideas. These tools, along with common productivity tools like presentation and web-editing software, improve the quality and quantity of their written work, and open-source productivity applications such as OpenOffice or Google Docs can be used at no cost to the student for personal computers.

Students can use word-processing, journaling, blogging or other software to enhance their abilities to communicate in English by creating either a learning log or a dialogue journal (Vialpando et al., 2005). When using a learning log, students write about what they are learning in their classrooms—an activity that promotes metacognition as well as language acquisition. They can pose questions or use the logs to explore areas of confusion. Digital learning logs allow students to integrate images, hyperlinks, and other resources to support their learning. The dialogue journal takes the learning log activity further, because when teachers respond to their students in written dialogue, they model proper language use and promote language growth. You may want to provide a prompt for the students or have the students generate the focus of their entries on their own. Technology used for dialogue journals should be secure in order to protect the students' confidentiality, and shared online documents such as Live Journal or Google Docs can be password protected and allow for ease of sharing between students and teachers in different locations.

Hypertext links in curricular materials are particularly beneficial to ELLs. They can provide instant explanations of unknown words, and they contain search features that let the student expand on any concept with images, video, and additional text. Common to web-based resources, hyperlinks can also be embedded in word-processing documents, presentations, and PDF files, or in digital texts viewed on touchscreen devices. These tools can also be accessed by a variety of text-to-speech tools, some freely available with computer operating systems. The scaffolding opportunities provided by multimedia tools in the classroom and delivered via courseware give ELLs easy access to models of correct language use and can promote fluency and comprehension.

English language learners should be encouraged to explore the use of recording equipment to improve interpersonal communication skills. Skits, monologues, or role plays can be recorded using digital video or audio recorders, including those in mobile devices or computers, and viewed as an aid to self-assessment and a way to increase awareness of how the student is seen by others. Devices used to record and play back teacher instructions or a conversation can assist ELLs with the transition to mainstream classes. Students can listen repeatedly to the instructions and clarify unknown phrases by questioning a more proficient speaker.

Technology can also support language and content mastery through the incorporation of graphic organizers or concept maps. When using these commonly available tools, you select key vocabulary or concepts and images that support them (see Figure S.3). Some concept-mapping applications include clip art files that contain many images or allow you to import images—including digital images students take. During the activity, students demonstrate their understanding of the vocabulary or concepts in a variety of ways, such as pointing to the images or text, dragging them to their correct labels, or creating the labels themselves. You can encourage deeper understandings and promote comprehension by having students organize the items in a semantic web that shows the relationship among them.

Technology opens a path to discovery and increased knowledge and proficiency for English language learners. Previous constraints such as linguistic ability, economic resources, and physical borders are diminished when ELLs are given the tools with which to explore the world digitally and to create their own environments for learning. Moreover, knowledge of how to apply technology to solving problems, communicating, and expressing themselves creatively empowers ELLs to achieve success in the wider academic arena, thus setting the stage for higher education and better career opportunities.

> English Language Learner

English Language Learner

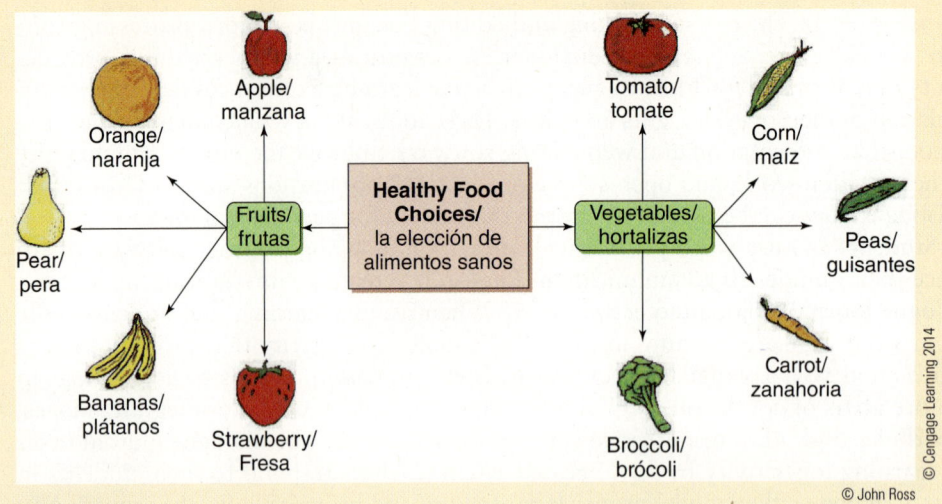

Figure S.3
Concept-mapping software provides a range of activities for representing vocabulary and promoting comprehension.

References

August, D., & Hakuta, K. (1997). *Improving schooling for language-minority children: A research agenda.* Washington, DC: National Academy of Sciences.

Reed, B., & Railsback, J. (2003). *Strategies and resources for mainstream teachers of English language learners.* Portland, OR: Northwest Regional Educational Laboratory.

U. S. Department of Education. (2011). *The condition of education 2011* (NCES 2011-033). Washington, DC: National Center for Education Statistics.

Teachers of English to Speakers of Other Languages (TESOL). (2006). *Pre-K-12 English language proficiency standards.* United States: Author.

Vialpando, J., Yedlin, J., Linse, C, Harrington, M., & Cannon, G. (2005). *Educating English language learners: Implementing instructional practices.* Providence, RI: National Council of La Raza and The Education Alliance at Brown University.

Lesson Plans for English Language Learners

Elementary English Language Learners

English Language Learner

TECHNOLOGY INTEGRATION FOR MEANINGFUL CLASSROOM USE

Daily Lesson GAME Plan

Lesson Title: My Roots and My New Home

Related Lessons: Self-introduction, Family Descriptions, Places in the World

Grade Level: Elementary

Unit: Living in the Global Village

GOALS

Content Standards:
- English language learners communicate for social, intercultural, and instructional purposes within the school setting.
- English language learners communicate information, ideas, and concepts necessary for academic success in the area of social studies.

ISTE NETS-S
- ☐ Creativity and innovation
- ☒ Communication and collaboration
- ☒ Research and information fluency
- ☒ Critical thinking, problem solving, and decision-making
- ☒ Digital citizenship
- ☒ Technology operations and concepts

Instructional Objective(s):
Students learn how to gather information about their country of origin and their current place of residence on the Internet and present it, using presentation software. Using the WebQuest method, the teacher provides a structured framework for web searching and a template for the presentation product.

ACTION

Before-Class Preparation:
Find or develop a WebQuest page with the assignment instructions and links to resources students can use for finding information about countries and cities. Include sources for images, such as National Geographic or government or tourism websites for known countries of origin for your students. Arrange for lab time or a mobile cart if computers or mobile devices are not available in the classroom.
Create a planning worksheet using word-processing software and a template in presentation software for the final product that students will create, including these slides:
  a. Title slide
  b. Slide showing the name of home country and space for an image; spaces for data on size, population, political system, etc.
  c. Slide with information on the student's journey to the current place of residence
  d. Slide showing the name of current home/residence and space for image; spaces for data on size, population, political system, etc.
  e. Changes student has observed in lifestyle, foods, or education with spaces for images
  f. Summary slide with space for image and reference list including original location of images and data used in the presentation

Create the checklist of skills used for self-evaluation.

Internet Resources:
Internet 4 Classrooms' Guide to Using WebQuests: http://www.internet4classrooms.com/on-line_quest.htm
WebQuest.org: http://webquest.org/
Zunal.com: http://zunal.com/
National Geographic videos: http://video.nationalgeographic.com/video/places/
National Geographic Music Videos from around the world: http://video.nationalgeographic.com/video/music/

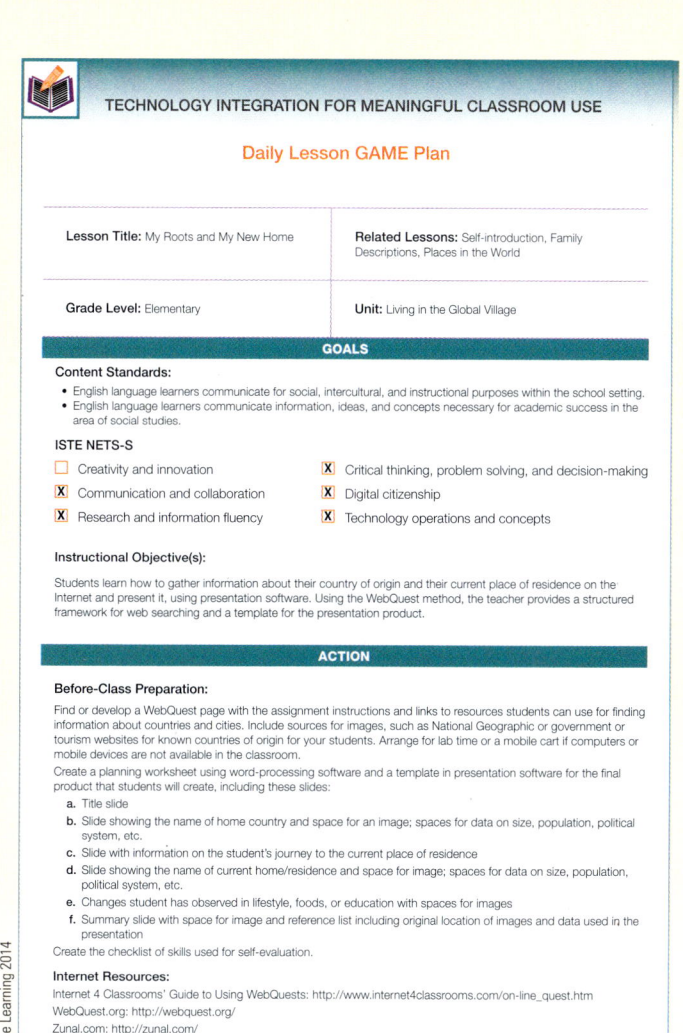

During Class

Time	Instructional Activities	Materials and Resources
30 minutes	Introduce the assignment with a model of the final product showing your home state or city or different location, compared to your current place of residence. Explain your own goal in making this presentation and how you met the problems you encountered, such as "I wanted to show how different my home is from where I'm teaching now. I thought I could do that with pictures of the countryside around my house, but I couldn't find any good ones. Instead, I decided to show pictures of the kinds of things I did as a child; like skating on a open lake, and contrast that with what I do for exercise now, working out in a gym." Walk students through the presentation and point out places you made a decision or dealt with a formatting or language problem. Model the strategies you used for problem solving when discussing these: "I wasn't sure what the population was of my hometown, and I couldn't find it in the atlas. So I decided to look on the city's website. It had all the numbers I needed." Point out where the information was found for each slide. Make links to original information active in the presentation if the computer used for display has Internet access. Introduce the WebQuest page. You may have to show students how to click on the links to get to a source for data on countries, and then how to search within the resource. Ask students to suggest a country to search for data on, and follow the WebQuest instructions for the data needed about each location. Explain that the location of each piece of information should be saved for the reference list at the end of the project. Show how to modify the template for inclusion of audio or video files (e.g., use the Insert menu in PowerPoint) and how to add more pages if needed.	Computer with Internet access and projector or interactive whiteboard Sample presentation based on template WebQuest page
5 minutes	Instruct students to use the strategy of Planning for a few minutes before beginning their research. Provide a worksheet where students can outline the points they want to include in the presentation. Next, ask students to choose a resource where they will start to look for the information.	Planning worksheet
40 minutes	Let students open the WebQuest page and begin searching for the content about their hometown and current place of residence. Make sure all have successfully downloaded and saved the template for the presentation. Allow students time to complete their research outside of class if necessary.	Computers with Internet access Presentation software
60 minutes	When students have their presentations ready, give them time to show and explain their presentation individually. If you have the equipment, videotape the students so they can watch themselves later and complete a self-evaluation of their presentation.	Presentation software Computer with large monitor or projector and screen
10–20 minutes	Ask students to reflect on what they have learned from this project. Guide this with a checklist of skills they developed such as web research, information and media manipulation, and oral presentation skills. Students should indicate their level of confidence with the skills as well as those they need to practice more.	Checklist of skills addressed

Notes: Students from the same country can collaborate on a presentation and share information they gather from the online resources. Information about the current place of residence can be shared among all class members. Students can also bring in pictures or other materials from home.

MONITOR

Ongoing Assessment(s): Monitor student proficiency with navigating the WebQuest and other websites and conducting searches. Review the planning worksheet or have students conduct a peer review of worksheets. Review student presentations in progress to make sure they are using the template properly. Check on comprehension of the assignment and when projects are complete, ask students to run automatic spelling and grammar checks before giving their presentations. Students can record commonly misspelled words for later review.

Accommodations and Extensions: This activity can be conducted in pairs or small groups, if necessary, dividing the research tasks among students. Students with poor keyboarding skills can dictate the captions they want for images they include in the presentation and have the teacher or another student type in the text. Some students with poor keyboarding skills may be able to record audio.

Back-up Plan: In the event that the network is down, prepare a folder with images of the countries represented by the students that they can access on the local computer drives. Have CD-ROM or print versions of an atlas or encyclopedia available for researching places and locating basic demographic information. Artifacts from home can be used to support presentations.

EVALUATE AND EXTEND

Lesson Reflections and Notes: Students can work in peer groups or pairs for feedback on their planning document. Collect the self-evaluation forms from each student. Summarize student comments about the lesson in your own reflection.

A full-size version of this lesson plan appears on the CourseMate website at **www.cengagebrain.com**.

Middle Grades English Language Learners

TECHNOLOGY INTEGRATION FOR MEANINGFUL CLASSROOM USE

Daily Lesson GAME Plan

Lesson Title: Radio Free ESOL

Related Lessons: Writers' Roundtable, In the Movies, Good Eats

Grade Level: Middle grades

Unit: Your Culture, Our Culture

GOALS

Content Standards:
- English language learners communicate for social, intercultural, and instructional purposes within the school setting.
- English language learners communicate information, ideas, and concepts necessary for academic success in the area of language arts.

ISTE NETS-S
- ☐ Creativity and innovation
- ☒ Communication and collaboration
- ☒ Research and information fluency
- ☒ Critical thinking, problem solving, and decision-making
- ☒ Digital citizenship
- ☒ Technology operations and concepts

Instructional Objective(s):
Students create a short radio or television advertisement for their favorite singer, actor, sports star or other favorite personality. The advertisements are aimed at convincing other students to listen to the singer, watch the actor, or otherwise provide some information about the personality's background. The ads can be posted to a class website or blog as podcasts or other media formats, or can be uploaded to a media-sharing site, like a classroom channel on YouTube or TeacherTube.

ACTION

Before-Class Preparation:
Obtain headsets for each workstation, laptop, or mobile device. Check to make sure they all function with the computer and that the computer has been properly set up for the type of microphone used. Set up a page for the class to share their ads, or use a podcast or video-hosting service, such as LoudBlog.com, YouTube, or TeacherTube. The devices will need an audio-editing application, such as Audacity or GarageBand, or access to a web-based audio editor, such as Audio Expert. Students creating videos can use MovieMaker, PhotoStory, or GarageBand or iMovie. Different apps are available for audio and video editing on mobile devices, as well, with some free apps providing sufficient functionality to complete the project.

During Class

Time	Instructional Activities	Materials and Resources
20 minutes	Introduce the assignment by demonstrating an advertisement you've made about your own favorite singer, actor, or other personality. Demonstrate the software you used to create it. Model planning for your research on the personality, such as "I want to tell you about James Taylor. I think he's from North Carolina, but I'm not sure." Explain how you found information on your personality and downloaded or linked to a sample of his or her work.	Computer with Internet access and speakers projecting on interactive whiteboard or screen. Podcasting or audio-editing software, or video-editing software
40 minutes	Instruct students to plan who they will research by making an outline of what they already know about the singer on a worksheet. Students can also use PowerPoint or concept-mapping software to organize their research. Include spaces for the personality's name, hometown, the languages they speak and/or perform in, and significant accomplishments or other notable information. In each advertisement, students will include information about the personality's background, state why they admire the personality, and tell something notable about the person, such as a favorite song or performance. They should include images or sound clips from the personality. This is a good opportunity to discuss fair use and copyright of music and images with your students, especially if posting these advertisements to a website. Generally, 30 seconds or less of a song or movie will fall under fair use.	Electronic or paper worksheet. Optional: PowerPoint or concept-mapping software
60 minutes	Allow students time to record and upload their files. Give students a chance to sit at the computers and listen to their classmates' advertisements. Have students self-evaluate by answering questions such as, "What did you learn by making the advertisement? Which of your classmates made the best case for promoting their personality? What did they say that made you interested in their personality?"	Computers with microphones and headphones. Audio- or video-editing software

Notes: Students can convey much information about their home cultures by their choices of music, movies, television, and sports heroes. This lesson may open up a discussion in the class about the cultures from which the students came and could be expanded into lessons focusing on other aspects of these cultures.

MONITOR

Ongoing Assessment(s): Be sure students select a technology with which they can be successful by determining their proficiency through an informal survey or questioning session. Review and approve the planning worksheet before any recording is made. Monitor the students' recordings to make sure they are including the information required and that they follow appropriate fair use guidelines of copyright-protected information.

Accommodations and Extensions: Students with limited technology or language background can create an image-based advertisement using word-processing or presentation software or any of a variety of image-editing apps, like FotoBabble, or online sites, such as Glogster.

Back-up Plan: For students who do not have a favorite personality, collect samples of some popular performers or athletes relevant to their age group for students to choose from.

EVALUATE AND EXTEND

Lesson Reflections and Notes: Review student outlines. If time is limited, have students share their outlines with a partner. Students can share their justifications with others to improve their advertisement outline. Compile student responses to self-evaluation activity to modify or refine the activity.

A full-size version of this lesson plan appears on the CourseMate website at **www.cengagebrain.com**.

Technology in the Foreign Language Classroom

Greg Kessler, Ph.D.

Human communication has always been interlinked with technology. Early tools for writing allowed messages to be archived and transported. The printing press contributed to an exponential increase in literacy and altered the distribution of language and information. More recently, the Internet, computers, and commonly available mobile technologies have dramatically altered linguistic interaction (see Table S.3 for some ideas).

Language instruction is typically divided into five or six skill categories: writing, reading, listening, speaking, grammar, and (often) culture. The *Standards for Foreign Language Learning* (American Council on the Teaching of Foreign Languages, 1999) organize these skills across the five areas of: communication, cultures, connections, comparisons, and communities. Although there may be a temptation to limit the use of technology to the receptive skills of listening and reading, language teachers today can use technology to address all of the language skills and the categories addressed by the national standards effectively. In fact, it seems that the integration of technology may be improving students' oral performances in unexpected ways, particularly in comparison to the traditional language classroom in which a majority of instruction (and expectation) is based upon written and grammatical evaluation. Recognizing the standards that guide foreign language learning will help you to better meet the needs of your students, regardless of the technologies you use in your classroom.

THE GAME PLAN

Content Standards

Set Goals
Learn more about the *Standards for Foreign Language Learning*, published by the American Council on the Teaching of Foreign Languages, or the foreign language standards for a state where you plan to seek a teaching position. Consider a variety of ways to integrate technology while addressing the foreign language standards.

Take Action
Explore the national standards published by the American Council on the Teaching of Foreign Languages or the state standards as listed on the department of education website in the state where you plan to seek a position. Plan ways that you could meet those standards using technology in the foreign language classroom.

Monitor
Did you find the information you needed? Do you need to contact the department of education for more information about where to find the foreign language standards?

Evaluate and Extend
Discuss the plan you developed for meeting the foreign language standards using technology with others, and compare your ideas. Note the strengths and weaknesses of the various examples and incorporate the best ideas into your plan.

Foreign Language

Technology increasingly provides opportunities for people to interact with one another in varied and flexible ways. Since language learning is fundamentally tied to interaction and communication, these technologies always have something new to offer. Students can collaborate across networks, geographies, language backgrounds, political affiliations, and any other barriers that keep humans from communicating with one another. Students who work collaboratively in a task-based language-learning environment are likely to benefit from the language negotiation with peers and construction of knowledge that such tasks require.

Web-based collaborative writing tools and environments such as blogs, discussion forums, wikis, shared whiteboards, and webconferencing tools allow students to collaborate as they construct knowledge and refine language skills. Phones, tablet computers, and other mobile devices extend these opportunities for collaboration through a variety of media formats. Through collaboration, students are exposed to more of the target language and encouraged to produce more language. They are also likely to engage in extensive negotiation of meaning, which has been determined to be effective in their overall language learning (Long, 1996). Through this kind of social interaction and negotiation of meaning, they are also likely to develop a better sense of social presence and self-reflection upon the purpose of their language learning.

The term computer-assisted language learning, or CALL, has long been used to describe the use of computer-based technologies to support language learning, perhaps most familiarly through the use of language labs. But as the concept of what is defined as a computer changes to include a range of powerful mobile and handheld devices, the nature of CALL has expanded, as have the experiences you can provide to students in your language classroom.

CALL has been steadily moving toward more collaborative and authentic activities that empower learners and guide them toward the goal of becoming autonomous

Table S.3 Ideas for Addressing NETS-S in the Foreign Language Classroom

Creativity and Innovation
Students create original works in the languages they are studying, such as biographies, historical guides, and short works of fiction using word-processing, web-authoring, and digital audio and video tools that can be accessed by a computer, MP3 player, or other digital technology.

Communication and Collaboration
Students use computer-mediated communication tools, such as e-mail, chat, or collaborative tools to develop written fluency or incorporate video- and webconferencing tools to communicate verbally with other students, their teacher, and others with greater language proficiency.

Research and Information Fluency
Students use government websites from foreign countries and mapping software to plan a (hypothetical or real) visit to a country in which the language they are learning is spoken.

Critical Thinking, Problem Solving, and Decision-Making
Students use Internet resources, currency calculators, and word-processing or document-layout software, to research and create a brochure for visitors to a country in which the language they are learning is spoken.

Digital Citizenship
Students use the Internet and other digital materials to explore and better understand cultural and human issues in countries where the language they are studying is spoken, comparing, for example, variations in dialect, pronunciation, and language use in Spanish-speaking countries, such as Spain, Central and South American countries, Puerto Rico, Cuba, and communities within the United States.

Technology Operations and Concepts
Students use word-processing, image-editing, and recording software to write in different languages, record native speakers, speak in a language of study, conduct peer reviews, and to create documents that include cultural artifacts, such as digital images of landmarks, persons in native dress, interviews of native speakers, and reflections.

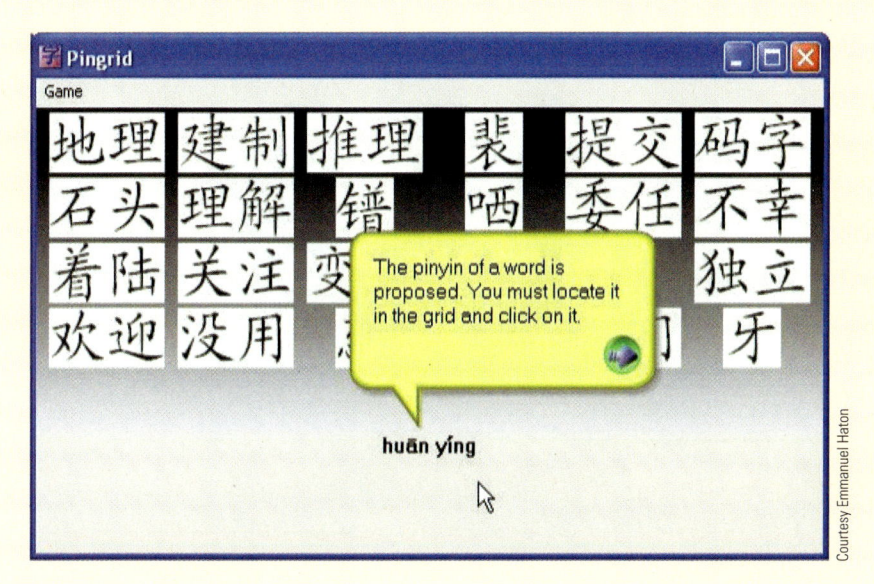

Figure S.4
A variety of tutorial software applications are available for the foreign language classroom.

language users. Providing students with the opportunity to not only participate in, but also to play a role in, designing their own instructional materials can be motivational (Kessler & Plakans, 2001). Engaging in simulated, or even real-world tasks, through web-based communication allows students to take responsibility for their own work and make better-informed decisions. Encouraging students to take more responsibility for their learning helps guide them toward successful autonomy (Little, 1999).

Tutorial CALL involves activities in which a student interacts primarily with a digital device serving as a type of tutor (see Figure S.4). This type of CALL is typically associated with grammar instruction but can also serve as effective instruction in pronunciation, writing, reading, and listening at various levels. Using the computer as a tutor can provide students with extensive exposure to accurate forms of language as well as the opportunity to gain beneficial automated feedback.

The Internet provides access to a wealth of authentic linguistic content for any target language. Education, government, and commercial sites all offer authentic language content that can provide students with the extensive exposure that will help them to critically explore a target language. Similarly, authentic cultural content can help your students develop a better understanding of the target language and culture. Obtaining information about a target language and/or culture via the Internet has greatly enhanced language learning.

Another development in Internet-based, self-access study is the online learning lab. The ability to record and play digital audio over the Internet is revolutionizing language learning. Traditional language labs have moved online, allowing students to do self-study tasks from home, a library, or another convenient location (see Figure S.5). Effective integration includes identifying useful authentic audio and video materials and providing an instructional context in which these materials can be explored by students. Such context may include follow-up discussion that reviews the material or considers alternative perspectives, outcomes, or related scenarios.

Language teachers who are familiar with the variety of digital audio and video recording, editing, and playing software and procedures for using them will be well-positioned to integrate these extremely useful materials into their classes. Teachers may also utilize these technologies to make their own recordings for students. Such recordings can integrate photos and narration into a video or animation demonstrating the target language and culture. It may also involve video that is shot on location in the target culture, thus exposing students to material they would otherwise not be able to

Figure S.5
Using online learning labs provides access to speakers of languages from across the globe.

access. Teachers may also choose to use these technologies for student projects. Students can create their own video projects that focus on a topic of interest, reflecting the target language and culture. These kinds of projects can be most effective when collaboratively performed by teams of students. This allows them to reflect upon the ongoing development of the project and critically assess their work.

Teachers can use communication tools, such as text-based e-mail and chat or videoconferencing over the web, to connect their language students with native speakers or classes of students studying their native language. For example, a high school Spanish class in Ohio can interact and even collaborate on projects with a high school English class in Chile, or anywhere else on the globe. Communication may take place in one or both languages (depending on the language proficiency of the students and the purpose of the interaction), and final projects may also be monolingual or bilingual. Students may share insights into actual language use in their countries or regions as well as cultural aspects that might otherwise be overlooked by other sources.

As has been illustrated in this section, you can choose from a range of technology tools that support CALL. However, it is important to note that although each of these forms of CALL may appear to some to take place solely between the student and the technology, there is a vital role for you—the teacher. You must make important decisions determining which content is most appropriate at all points in instruction. You must also determine the appropriateness of materials for students' levels and ages and how well the materials support the learning goals you have designed for your students.

References

American Council on the Teaching of Foreign Languages. (1999). *Standards for foreign language learning: Preparing for the 21st century.* Alexandria, VA: Author.

Kessler, G., & Plakans, L. (2001). Incorporating ESOL learners' feedback and usability testing in instructor-developed CALL materials. *TESOL Journal, 10*(1), 15–20.

Long, M. (1996). The role of the linguistic environment in second language acquisition. In W. C. Ritchie & T. K. Bhatia (Eds.), *Handbook of language acquisition. Vol. 2: Second language acquisition* (pp. 413–468). New York: Academic Press.

Lesson Plans for Foreign Language

Middle Grades Foreign Language

Foreign Language

TECHNOLOGY INTEGRATION FOR MEANINGFUL CLASSROOM USE

Daily Lesson GAME Plan

Lesson Title: Famous Person Digital Collage
Related Lessons: WebQuest
Grade Level: Middle grades
Unit: Culture

GOALS

Content Standards:
- Standard 2.1: Students demonstrate an understanding of the relationship between the practices and perspectives of the culture studied
- Standard 2.2: Students demonstrate an understanding of the relationship between the products and perspectives of the culture studied

ISTE NETS-S

- [X] Creativity and innovation
- [X] Critical thinking, problem solving, and decision-making
- [X] Communication and collaboration
- [X] Digital citizenship
- [X] Research and information fluency
- [X] Technology operations and concepts

Instructional Objective(s):

Students create digital collages of famous persons representative of a country/culture in which their target language is widely spoken. Students justify the individual(s) and the artifacts they select.

ACTION

Before-Class Preparation:

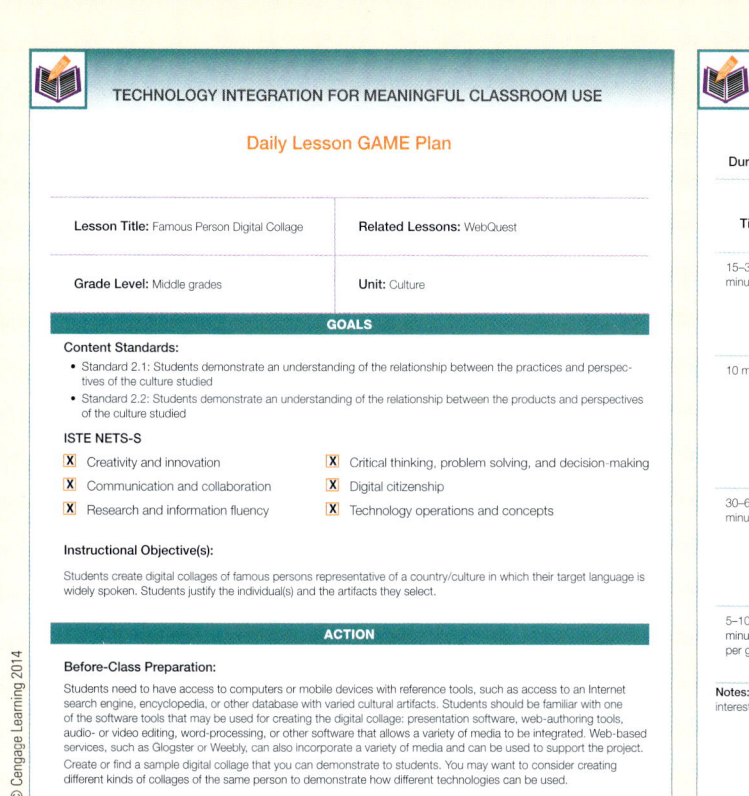

Students need to have access to computers or mobile devices with reference tools, such as access to an Internet search engine, encyclopedia, or other database with varied cultural artifacts. Students should be familiar with one of the software tools that may be used for creating the digital collage: presentation software, web-authoring tools, audio- or video editing, word-processing, or other software that allows a variety of media to be integrated. Web-based services, such as Glogster or Weebly, can also incorporate a variety of media and can be used to support the project. Create or find a sample digital collage that you can demonstrate to students. You may want to consider creating different kinds of collages of the same person to demonstrate how different technologies can be used.

During Class

Time	Instructional Activities	Materials and Resources
15–30 minutes	Orient students to the project and activate prior knowledge by raising their awareness of famous people in their own culture: artists, entertainers, politicians, historical figures, and others. Students search using digital research tools (search engines, encyclopedias, databases) to identify famous people in the target culture(s).	Computers or mobile devices with Internet access
10 minutes	Students pair or group (small group to whole class) to share the famous people they have identified and determine which may be worthy of further investigation. Students must identify persons from a range of backgrounds (the arts, politics, science, athletics, etc.), time periods, and both genders. Students should justify the reasons for their selection. Students can use consensus-building strategies or may want to rank potential people using survey or polling software.	Checklist created by students identifying important characteristics of each person and justifications for inclusion
30–60 minutes	Students work in pairs or small groups to collect information and various digital artifacts related to the famous person they have chosen. Students should collect at least three pertinent artifacts and explain why these are representative of the person they are studying. They construct their projects using multimedia-authoring software (see Before-Class Preparation for options). All sources should be appropriately documented.	Computers or mobile devices with Internet access; Multimedia-authoring software
5–10 minutes per group	Groups present famous person collages to the class and post them on a class website or link to online collages.	Computer or mobile device with Internet access projected on whiteboard or screen

Notes: Students may be grouped in a variety of ways, but it may be best to group them according to their particular interest in the persons identified.

MONITOR

Ongoing Assessment(s): Monitor student decision-making during the brainstorming session. Students' lists of persons and justifications can be collected. Monitor students as they progress through the task to ensure they identify appropriate artifacts and work within time constraints. The synthesis of information as well as target language skills can be evaluated during the presentation of the final product.

Accommodations and Extensions: Consider using a social bookmarking or organizing tool, such as Diigo or LiveBinders, to help facilitate Internet research and focus student work on the learning outcomes. Using pairs or small groups allows students to provide mutual technical support. Some students may require a template, such as a five-slide presentation with title, three slides for pertinent facts, and a reference slide.

Back-up Plan: Students use magazines, musical recordings, and other traditional cultural artifacts to construct their famous person cultural collages in paper or for incorporation in a digital format later by scanning or photographing artifacts.

EVALUATE AND EXTEND

Lesson Reflections and Notes: A checklist or rubric can be used to evaluate the final product. Over time, students can build an online "museum" or database of collages that can be shared with subsequent classes.

A full-size version of this lesson plan appears on the CourseMate website at www.cengagebrain.com.

High School Foreign Language

Foreign Language

TECHNOLOGY INTEGRATION FOR MEANINGFUL CLASSROOM USE

Daily Lesson GAME Plan

Lesson Title: Cultural Documentary

Related Lessons: WebQuest, Famous Cultural Artifacts, Famous Persons

Grade Level: High School

Unit: Cultural Awareness

GOALS

Content Standards:
- Standard 1.1: Students engage in conversations, provide and obtain information, express feelings and emotions, and exchange opinions
- Standard 1.3: Students present information, concepts, and ideas on a variety of topics to an audience of listeners or readers
- Standard 2.1: Students demonstrate an understanding of the relationship between the practices and perspectives of the culture studied
- Standard 2.2: Students demonstrate an understanding of the relationship between the products and perspectives of the culture studied
- Standard 4.2: Students demonstrate understanding of the concept of culture through comparisons of the cultures studied and their own
- Standard 5.1: Students use the language both within and beyond the school setting

ISTE NETS-S

[X] Creativity and innovation
[X] Critical thinking, problem solving, and decision-making
[X] Communication and collaboration
[X] Digital citizenship
[X] Research and information fluency
[X] Technology operations and concepts

Instructional Objective(s):

Students use the target language to collaboratively design, develop, and present a short documentary about a country in which the language they are studying is spoken. The focus on the documentary includes basic demographic and cultural information but should also highlight significant contributions or artifacts that are unique to the country. The audience for the documentary is other students and should be designed to be engaging to their peers. The final project can use presentation software, or can be a podcast combining still images and audio, or a video. Throughout this production they are strongly encouraged to use the target language in their small groups.

ACTION

Before-Class Preparation:

Preferably, students should have some skill using digital audio- or video-editing software. Students uncomfortable with digital video can use a digital camera, scanner, or obtain images from digital reference resources. Students should also have a thorough understanding of the effective use of search engines and other resources and how to cite materials appropriately.

Determine student groupings and assign or have groups select a country or region and read introductory information to prepare for the project. To mimic the documentary production, grouping could be based on video product roles, such as director, researchers, writers, videographers, and the like; however, all students should be engaged in activities that allow them to master the content objectives. Students might benefit by having a list of important types of information to include in their documentary. Find or create an example to demonstrate this information.

Find or create a rubric to evaluate the project, preferably incorporating input from the students. The rubric should focus on the content objectives but include some measure of the quality of the media production and may include measures of collaboration or planning.

During Class

Time	Instructional Activities	Materials and Resources
20–30 minutes	Share your sample documentary to help orient students to the project. Students share information they've collected from prior reading and research with their group. Each is evaluated based upon the supporting documentation presented with it and the merit that it offers to the final product. Students must reach consensus on the items to be included and their justification for inclusion. This portion of the activity continues until all artifacts are assessed or there is a group consensus that enough critical resources have been identified to produce a storyboard and script.	Computer with speakers and projector; Student lists and notes for storyboard
20–30 minutes	Students create a storyboard for their documentary using presentation, concept-mapping, or word-processing software. Each segment of the storyboard should contain text or graphics that describe the visual and aural components of the documentary. As they negotiate the timeline, they are encouraged to communicate in the target language.	Software for storyboarding
10 minutes per group	Storyboards are shared with the teacher to determine appropriate topics and length.	Storyboard
1–2 hours	Students compose a draft script for their documentaries, with one or two students composing each segment of the storyboard and identifying potential artifacts. Students should conduct peer reviews of their script segments with their group using the rubric, and sharing drafts with the teacher.	Presentation or word-processing software
1–2 hours	Students create or find media elements for their documentaries based on their storyboards and scripts, perhaps taking digital pictures, creating digital images, or finding and editing images and video.	Computers or devices with Internet access or other digital reference tools; Digital cameras, video cameras, or mobile devices with cameras; Scanner
30–60 minutes	Students record themselves narrating their scripts, giving each student an opportunity to speak. Narration can be recorded in segments.	Audio- or video-editing software
1–2 hours	Students use audio- or video-editing software to construct their documentaries by putting all of their media elements artifacts into the timeline and adding any transitions, effects, or other information.	Audio- or video-editing software
15–20 minutes per group	Students present their rough draft documentaries to at least one other student group and the teacher, sharing the storyboard, script, and other notes and information created during the project. Suggestions for elaboration, enhancement, or other improvements are made using the rubric as a guide for formative evaluation.	Computers with speakers; Copies of Rubrics
1–2 hours	Students refine their projects.	
10–20 minutes per group	Students present their documentaries to the entire class in the target language. Completed documentaries are posted on a class website or uploaded to a video-sharing site, such as YouTube or TeacherTube.	Computer with speakers and projector

Notes: Students are grouped according to the country or culture they will be exploring. Groups are no smaller than two individuals and no larger than five. Each group must have access to at least one computer or mobile device, with one per student preferred. Groups may benefit from access to a digital video camera or a mobile device with a camera or video camera, but this is also not necessary as videos can be made from still images, preexisting video, animations, text, sound files, and many other authentic products of the target culture that students can locate.

MONITOR

Ongoing Assessment(s): Students' use of the target language should be assessed throughout the process of identifying resources, gathering resources, synthesizing information, eliminating redundant or ineffective information, and presenting. A formal assessment of language abilities can be made during presentation of the project as well as in response to the student-generated language within the project itself.

Student-written language can be assessed through the review of the storyboard, script, and final project.

Accommodations and Extensions: Depending on the skill and knowledge of the students, documentaries may be limited to five minutes and no more than three topics. Some students may need an outline or template from which to create their storyboards or scripts. Giving students parameters, such as identifying at least one critical economic, social, and political issue to be explored in the documentary and lengths for each topic can help organize and focus students. Remind students that the audience is their peers and encourage them to create products relevant and engaging to other students their age.

Back-up Plan: If video editing is beyond the reach of all students, some students can create digital presentations with images and text.

EVALUATE AND EXTEND

Lesson Reflections and Notes: While student engagement can be high during multimedia projects, efforts should be made to continually emphasize the content and purpose of the activity. Focus is on language use and developing an understanding of culture. Students can meet these purposes through a range of different types of technology use, from very minimal to extensive.

A full-size version of this lesson plan appears on the CourseMate website at www.cengagebrain.com.

Technology in the Mathematics Classroom

Gilbert J. Cuevas, Ph.D.

Common technologies now found in schools have tremendous potential to support instruction in the mathematics classroom. For example, spreadsheets, graphing calculators, and a variety of free online manipulatives can help students visualize information, data, or math concepts quickly and easily, improving their understanding of mathematics content and facilitating the learning of mathematics (see Table S.4 for some additional examples). Integrating technology into classroom learning experiences requires analyzing and determining tools and strategies that will best help students master curriculum standards. You can use technology in your mathematics classroom to perform calculations; collect, analyze, and represent numeric information; create or use models and simulations; and scaffold learners to higher levels of abstraction and problem solving (Alagic, 2003).

In effective mathematics teaching, worthwhile mathematical tasks are used to introduce important mathematical ideas and to engage and challenge students intellectually. Well-designed tasks invite students to think mathematically, formulate and communicate new ideas, justify procedures, and defend the reasonableness of their answers. These activities require students to make decisions or judgments based on facts, information, logic, and/or rationalization. They require learners to justify all decisions and reasoning based on the mathematical ideas and skills being learned.

THE GAME PLAN

Content Standards

Set Goals
Learn more about the *Principles and Standards for School Mathematics,* developed by the National Council of Teachers of Mathematics (NCTM), or the mathematics standards for a state where you plan to seek a teaching position. Consider a variety of ways to integrate technology while addressing the mathematics standards.

Take Action
Explore the national standards published by the National Council of Teachers of Mathematics (NCTM) or the state standards as listed on the department of education website in the state where you plan to seek a position. Plan ways that you could meet those standards using technology in the mathematics classroom.

Monitor
Did you find the information you needed? Do you need to contact the department of education for more information about where to find the mathematics standards?

Evaluate and Extend
Discuss the plan you developed for meeting the mathematics standards using technology with others and compare your ideas. Note the strengths and weaknesses of the various examples and incorporate the best ideas into your plan.

manipulatives for every grade level and a wide range of mathematical concepts and activities.

Spatial visualization and reasoning activities conducted online or with geometry or modeling software give students opportunities to develop geometric concepts and skills as well as creative approaches to the solutions of the given problems. These lessons also provide opportunities for students to reflect and reinforce creative thinking through discussions. For example, students may be asked to compare the differences between front-right-top representations and isometric drawings, or to describe when the two different types of drawings might be most useful.

Depending on your access to, and familiarity with, common software, you can use a range of technologies to support mathematical problem solving, both in your math classroom and in other content areas. Students can create timelines in history that are developed to scale. Students can import digital images, such as pictures of the Parthenon, into math software to explore architectural and mathematical principles. And student work can be presented in class or beyond by incorporating math models, graphs, tables, and a variety of other technology-generated artifacts into reports, presentations, or class web pages.

Technology can support the development and practice of creative and critical thinking skills by helping teachers and students represent complex mathematical concepts and understanding. Complexity is relative to the developmental level of the students with whom you work. Addition and subtraction can be complex concepts to young students so you might use an online manipulative such as a "broken calculator" to demonstrate multiple methods for combining numbers and functions to generate the same result. Older students may demonstrate their understanding of mathematical concepts and make their knowledge more transparent by using graphing, data visualization, modeling, or other applications.

Technology can also help you address areas of mathematics where students have difficulty. For example, many students have difficulty connecting multiple representations of the same concept, such as connecting the verbal, graphical, numeric, and algebraic representations of mathematical functions. The use of graphic-based manipulatives that demonstrate the connection between data in a table to graphs and curves of best fit can be effective in helping students make these connections (Alagic, 2003).

Ultimately, it is important that you select technology tools that provide representations that allow your students to make the connections between their current knowledge and the new content and skills they are required to master. Tools that are too complex or that present information in a way in which the students have no background experience can actually negate the benefits of using multiple representations. There are also many forms of technology available for use in the classroom besides computers, such as calculators, probeware, and handheld devices and other tools that professionals use to support math in the workplace. They are reshaping the types of problem-solving tasks students can pursue. Settings for problems can be more realistic and address worthwhile mathematical content. These include not only computational tools, but also a range of applications in the arts, science, and history that allow for the use of mathematics in these settings.

References

Alagic, M. (2003). Technology in the mathematics classroom: Conceptual orientation. *Journal of Computers in Mathematics and Science Teaching, 22*(4), 381–399.

Clements, D. H. (2000). From exercises and tasks to problems and projects: Unique contributions of computers to innovative mathematics education. *Journal of Mathematical Behavior, 19*(1), 9–47.

National Council of Teachers of Mathematics (NCTM). (2000). *Principles and standards for school mathematics.* Reston, VA: Author.

Technology in the Mathematics Classroom

Gilbert J. Cuevas, Ph.D.

Common technologies now found in schools have tremendous potential to support instruction in the mathematics classroom. For example, spreadsheets, graphing calculators, and a variety of free online manipulatives can help students visualize information, data, or math concepts quickly and easily, improving their understanding of mathematics content and facilitating the learning of mathematics (see Table S.4 for some additional examples). Integrating technology into classroom learning experiences requires analyzing and determining tools and strategies that will best help students master curriculum standards. You can use technology in your mathematics classroom to perform calculations; collect, analyze, and represent numeric information; create or use models and simulations; and scaffold learners to higher levels of abstraction and problem solving (Alagic, 2003).

In effective mathematics teaching, worthwhile mathematical tasks are used to introduce important mathematical ideas and to engage and challenge students intellectually. Well-designed tasks invite students to think mathematically, formulate and communicate new ideas, justify procedures, and defend the reasonableness of their answers. These activities require students to make decisions or judgments based on facts, information, logic, and/or rationalization. They require learners to justify all decisions and reasoning based on the mathematical ideas and skills being learned.

THE GAME PLAN

Content Standards

Set Goals
Learn more about the *Principles and Standards for School Mathematics*, developed by the National Council of Teachers of Mathematics (NCTM), or the mathematics standards for a state where you plan to seek a teaching position. Consider a variety of ways to integrate technology while addressing the mathematics standards.

Take Action
Explore the national standards published by the National Council of Teachers of Mathematics (NCTM) or the state standards as listed on the department of education website in the state where you plan to seek a position. Plan ways that you could meet those standards using technology in the mathematics classroom.

Monitor
Did you find the information you needed? Do you need to contact the department of education for more information about where to find the mathematics standards?

Evaluate and Extend
Discuss the plan you developed for meeting the mathematics standards using technology with others and compare your ideas. Note the strengths and weaknesses of the various examples and incorporate the best ideas into your plan.

Mathematics

Keep in mind these three important ideas when planning to integrate technology in mathematics teaching (NCTM, 2000): First, *technology enhances mathematics learning*. With the technology resources available, students can examine examples or representational forms of selected concepts. Second, *teachers need to select appropriate technology uses to enhance their students' learning opportunities*. We need to remember that the use of technology does not guarantee instructional success; as with any teaching resource or tool, it depends on how well it is used. And third, *technology influences what mathematics is taught*. With technology, students can explore mathematical topics that otherwise would be either too cumbersome or impossible to address.

Clements (2000) identified three implications concerning the integration of technology in mathematics learning. First, you should decide how to combine computer- and paper-based lesson activities. Paper-based lessons are appropriate for many situations in math, especially those where the foundational skills may be important for students to develop or when technology exists but requires a level of proficiency beyond that of the students. Sometimes it is also appropriate to do some early planning or brainstorming on paper before moving into a computer-based setting.

Second, technology tools should be viewed as mathematical tools. There are some activities for which technology provides support that could not otherwise be accomplished—or it would be too difficult or time-consuming to accomplish (see Figure S.6). Spreadsheets and data visualization tools can allow even elementary students to quickly collect, manipulate, and represent data visually.

Finally, teachers need to view technologies as devices for developing student mathematical thinking. For example, one of the components of algebraic thinking deals with the representation and analysis of mathematical situations. This can play out when students are introduced to the idea of equations and the processes involved in their solution. Many web-based resources, such as the NCTM's Illuminations website, contain activities that can be used to help students develop mathematical thinking. Numerous websites offer a range of guided or self-paced lessons organized by grade

Table S.4 Ideas for Addressing NETS-S in the Mathematics Classroom

Creativity and Innovation
Students apply their math skills to replicate math-based activities from industry and business settings, such as designing scale models using computer-aided design (CAD) or geometry software, developing budgets and forecasting trends with spreadsheets, and using real-world data to track and project environmental influences on trade and commerce.

Communication and Collaboration
Students collaborate with their teacher and other students through the use of a class web page or learning management system that includes discussion software. Students ask questions of their teacher and other students and help their classmates better understand math concepts they are studying or help each other with homework problems.

Research and Information Fluency
Students turn to the Internet to find reliable sources for math-related information and tools, including problems and data sets from the real world. Students create a web page or set of bookmarks for the class for commonly visited and helpful math websites.

Critical Thinking, Problem Solving, and Decision-Making
Students use data trackers such as handhelds, probes, or mobile devices to collect data that can be represented in multiple ways and manipulated to better understand math concepts, using data visualization, graphing, or modeling software.

Digital Citizenship
Students understand that technology can be used to better understand the world around them, such as exploring digital images to understand math concepts or collecting data from their school or community that they can manipulate and use to answer real-world questions.

Technology Operations and Concepts
Students choose and use appropriate math-specific hardware and software, such as spreadsheets and databases, data trackers, calculators, and simulation software to solve problems and develop an understanding of math concepts.

Technology in the Mathematics Classroom   **339**

Mathematics

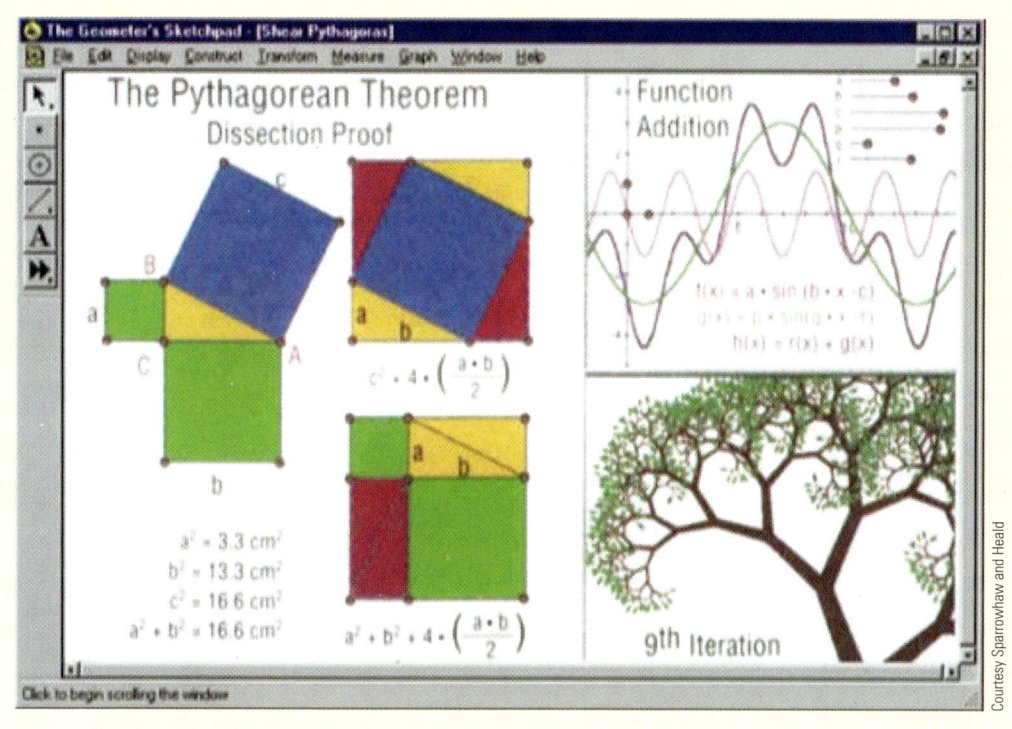

Figure S.6
Many software tools provide a range of scaffolding supports for the mathematics classroom.

band and standard and can easily be searched to find relevant activities for use in your mathematics instruction.

Web-based manipulatives and simulations also are available that allow students to input and manipulate data and view the consequences of their actions in math-specific ways. You can easily find online balances, function graphers, and 2-D and 3-D modeling software. Utah State University maintains the National Library of Virtual Manipulatives (see Figure S.7) to help you identify online

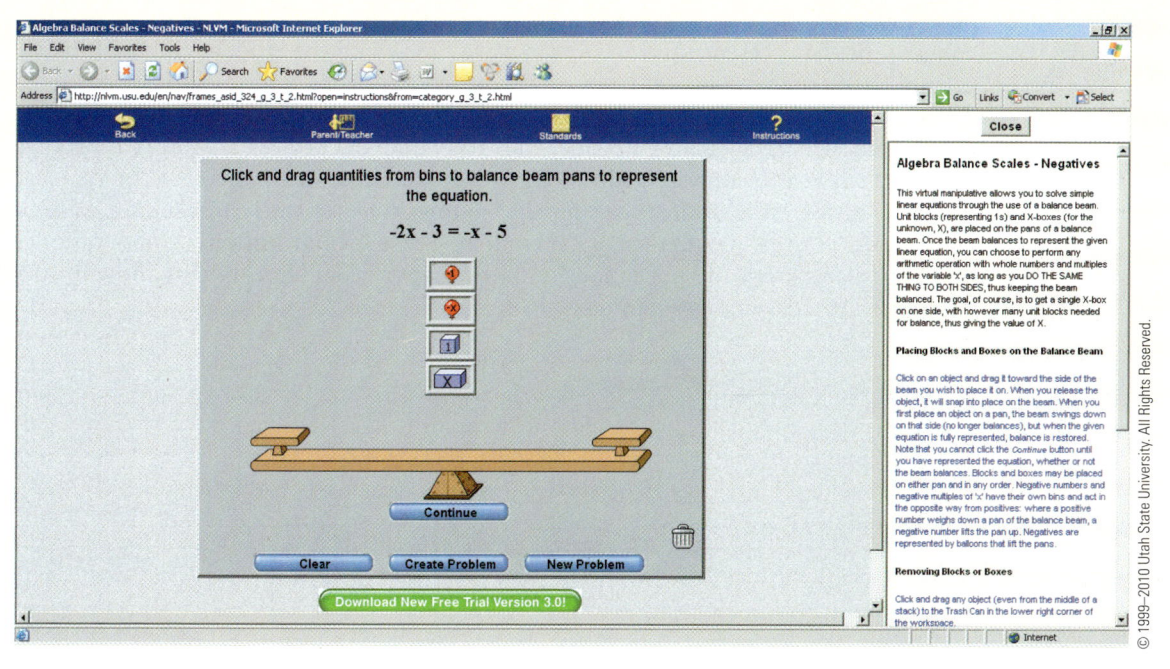

Figure S.7
Many manipulatives and simulations, like this balance from the National Library of Virtual Manipulatives, are available online.

manipulatives for every grade level and a wide range of mathematical concepts and activities.

Spatial visualization and reasoning activities conducted online or with geometry or modeling software give students opportunities to develop geometric concepts and skills as well as creative approaches to the solutions of the given problems. These lessons also provide opportunities for students to reflect and reinforce creative thinking through discussions. For example, students may be asked to compare the differences between front-right-top representations and isometric drawings, or to describe when the two different types of drawings might be most useful.

Depending on your access to, and familiarity with, common software, you can use a range of technologies to support mathematical problem solving, both in your math classroom and in other content areas. Students can create timelines in history that are developed to scale. Students can import digital images, such as pictures of the Parthenon, into math software to explore architectural and mathematical principles. And student work can be presented in class or beyond by incorporating math models, graphs, tables, and a variety of other technology-generated artifacts into reports, presentations, or class web pages.

Technology can support the development and practice of creative and critical thinking skills by helping teachers and students represent complex mathematical concepts and understanding. Complexity is relative to the developmental level of the students with whom you work. Addition and subtraction can be complex concepts to young students so you might use an online manipulative such as a "broken calculator" to demonstrate multiple methods for combining numbers and functions to generate the same result. Older students may demonstrate their understanding of mathematical concepts and make their knowledge more transparent by using graphing, data visualization, modeling, or other applications.

Technology can also help you address areas of mathematics where students have difficulty. For example, many students have difficulty connecting multiple representations of the same concept, such as connecting the verbal, graphical, numeric, and algebraic representations of mathematical functions. The use of graphic-based manipulatives that demonstrate the connection between data in a table to graphs and curves of best fit can be effective in helping students make these connections (Alagic, 2003).

Ultimately, it is important that you select technology tools that provide representations that allow your students to make the connections between their current knowledge and the new content and skills they are required to master. Tools that are too complex or that present information in a way in which the students have no background experience can actually negate the benefits of using multiple representations. There are also many forms of technology available for use in the classroom besides computers, such as calculators, probeware, and handheld devices and other tools that professionals use to support math in the workplace. They are reshaping the types of problem-solving tasks students can pursue. Settings for problems can be more realistic and address worthwhile mathematical content. These include not only computational tools, but also a range of applications in the arts, science, and history that allow for the use of mathematics in these settings.

References

Alagic, M. (2003). Technology in the mathematics classroom: Conceptual orientation. *Journal of Computers in Mathematics and Science Teaching, 22*(4), 381–399.

Clements, D. H. (2000). From exercises and tasks to problems and projects: Unique contributions of computers to innovative mathematics education. *Journal of Mathematical Behavior, 19*(1), 9–47.

National Council of Teachers of Mathematics (NCTM). (2000). *Principles and standards for school mathematics.* Reston, VA: Author.

Lesson Plans for Mathematics

Elementary Mathematics

Mathematics

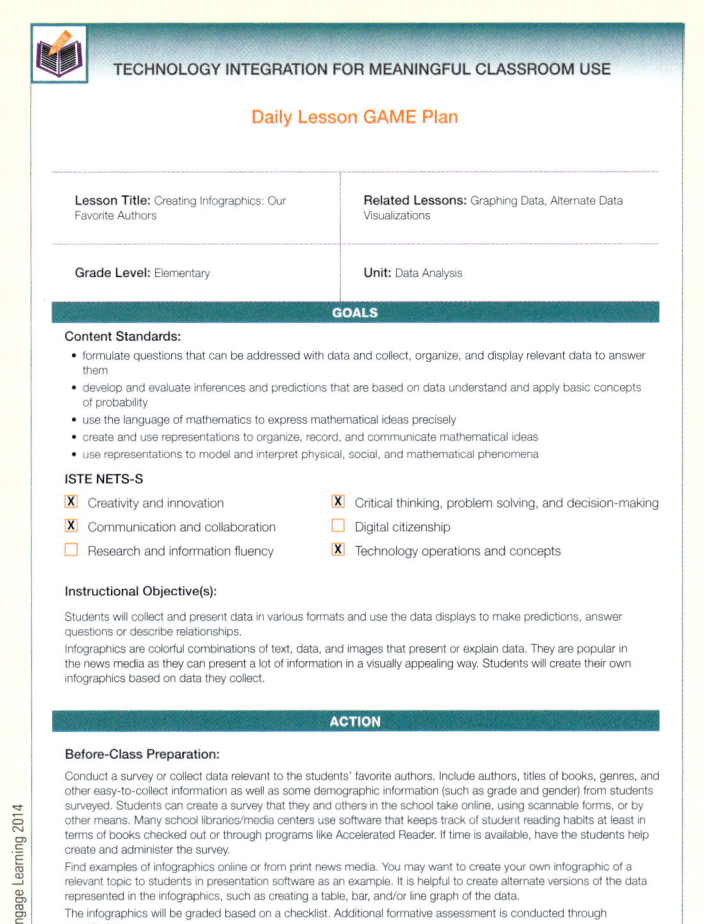

TECHNOLOGY INTEGRATION FOR MEANINGFUL CLASSROOM USE

Daily Lesson GAME Plan

Lesson Title: Creating Infographics: Our Favorite Authors

Related Lessons: Graphing Data, Alternate Data Visualizations

Grade Level: Elementary

Unit: Data Analysis

GOALS

Content Standards:
- formulate questions that can be addressed with data and collect, organize, and display relevant data to answer them
- develop and evaluate inferences and predictions that are based on data understand and apply basic concepts of probability
- use the language of mathematics to express mathematical ideas precisely
- create and use representations to organize, record, and communicate mathematical ideas
- use representations to model and interpret physical, social, and mathematical phenomena

ISTE NETS-S

- [X] Creativity and innovation
- [X] Communication and collaboration
- [ ] Research and information fluency
- [X] Critical thinking, problem solving, and decision-making
- [ ] Digital citizenship
- [X] Technology operations and concepts

Instructional Objective(s):

Students will collect and present data in various formats and use the data displays to make predictions, answer questions or describe relationships.

Infographics are colorful combinations of text, data, and images that present or explain data. They are popular in the news media as they can present a lot of information in a visually appealing way. Students will create their own infographics based on data they collect.

ACTION

Before-Class Preparation:

Conduct a survey or collect data relevant to the students' favorite authors. Include authors, titles of books, genres, and other easy-to-collect information as well as some demographic information (such as grade and gender) from students surveyed. Students can create a survey that they and others in the school take online, using scannable forms, or by other means. Many school libraries/media centers use software that keeps track of student reading habits at least in terms of books checked out or through programs like Accelerated Reader. If time is available, have the students help create and administer the survey.

Find examples of infographics online or from print news media. You may want to create your own infographic of a relevant topic to students in presentation software as an example. It is helpful to create alternate versions of the data represented in the infographics, such as creating a table, bar, and/or line graph of the data.

The infographics will be graded based on a checklist. Additional formative assessment is conducted through questioning.

During Class

Time	Instructional Activities	Materials and Resources
10–15 minutes	Share examples of infographics found online or in the news media. Explore the different types of information they present and the types of decisions or predictions they can support. Show the data in different formats, such as a line or bar graph versus the (usually) more visually appealing infographic that is likely to contain interesting pictures or icons, colors, and fonts.	Infographic and alternate data representations
15–20 minutes	Share data from the survey collected about the students' favorite authors in a table. If using data from library records, you may be able to show changes in popularity of items over time. Students should also have or know their own responses to the survey questions. (If you don't collect this at the time of the survey, they can fill it out at the beginning of the lesson before sharing the results.) Use the graphing features of the spreadsheet software to organize the data in different ways, showing the most popular books by gender or grade, or other combinations. Ask questions that encourage students to analyze the data and make predictions, such as • Do boys and girls like some of the same books/authors? • Do fourth graders like the same genres as fifth graders? • Are there any books that are popular across multiple grades or groups of students?	Survey data Spreadsheet software
20–30 minutes	Demonstrate how a data chart can be inserted in a presentation slide. The students will select one chart from the survey data, such as popular books by grade, gender, or genre, and compare it to their own responses by creating an infographic on a slide. Students can insert the summary table and then select colors, fonts, and insert images or shapes to support their comparison. Each slide should contain at least • A summary chart, such as a bar chart • A heading describing the main information presented on the slide • A description of how their own choices compare (using the notes section of the slide, if necessary)	Survey data Spreadsheet and presentation software Clip art, images, icons, or access to digital libraries of images
20–30 minutes	Students share their infographics with the class. The slides can be combined as a single presentation or even printed on a color printer and displayed. During the presentation, check student understanding by asking probing questions about the comparisons and whether additional comparisons or projections can be made.	Computer with projector or interactive whiteboard Student presentations

Notes: Many elementary students are exposed to spreadsheet software by graphing candy, toys, or other objects that have little relevance to students' lives. While this lesson uses favorite authors because data should be easy to collect from school librarians/media specialists, many different questions will work. Preferred questions are relevant to the students and can be used to make reasonable reflections or projections. A related video example using weather predictions in a second grade classroom is available on the textbook's companion website.

MONITOR

Ongoing Assessment(s): Check for understanding when reviewing the data in whole-class instruction through questioning. Have students make different projections and share their own data for comparison. Students can come to the front of the room to point out important information, or wireless responders can be used to check for student understanding in the whole-class setting. A checklist is used to grade the student final products, which are judged primarily on math content.

Accommodations and Extensions: Students with limited technology proficiency may benefit from a template and limited parameters they can change, such as selecting images from an image bank or limiting the color/font choices. You can also create several common summary graphs ahead of time that students can select from and insert into their own slides. More advanced students can take digital pictures of themselves or books, scan book covers, or search for related images online to include in presentations (their own or others). Some students may be able to compare their results to lists they find online.

Back-up Plan: The activity can be completed on paper with art supplies and pictures from old magazines.

EVALUATE AND EXTEND

Lesson Reflections and Notes: Consider additional topics that might be used to address the same math concepts. Students may also bring in infographics they find outside of class to share.

A full-size version of this lesson plan appears on the CourseMate website at www.cengagebrain.com.

Mathematics — Middle Grades Mathematics

TECHNOLOGY INTEGRATION FOR MEANINGFUL CLASSROOM USE

Daily Lesson GAME Plan

Lesson Title: At Home in Your Future
Related Lessons: Compound Interest, Saving for Your Future
Grade Level: Middle Grades
Unit: Everyday Math

GOALS

Content Standards:
- compute fluently and make reasonable estimates
- use mathematical models to represent and understand quantitative relationships
- analyze change in various contexts
- formulate questions that can be addressed with data and collect, organize, and display relevant data to answer them
- develop and evaluate inferences and predictions that are based on data
- recognize and apply mathematics in contexts outside of mathematics

ISTE NETS-S
- ☐ Creativity and innovation
- ☒ Communication and collaboration
- ☒ Research and information fluency
- ☒ Critical thinking, problem solving, and decision-making
- ☒ Digital citizenship
- ☒ Technology operations and concepts

Instructional Objective(s):
Students compare housing costs in a location they choose and project an annual income necessary for purchasing or renting and maintaining the housing.

ACTION

Before-Class Preparation:
Bookmark U.S. Census Bureau web pages, real estate websites (e.g., Realtor.com), or search engines (e.g., Yahoo! Real Estate). Download pertinent reports, such as the most current *Income, Poverty, and Health Insurance Coverage in the United States*. It is helpful to set the purchasing options in advance, and some students may require a spreadsheet template for some of the activities.

During Class

Time	Instructional Activities	Materials and Resources
15–20 minutes	Students are asked to pick a time in their future, such as 10–15 years from now, and make a few predictions or projections about what their life might be like, especially as it relates to housing needs. Where do they plan to live? Will they have a family, and if so, how big might it be? What type of employment do they expect to have? What level of education does that require? Students write a brief scenario (one paragraph) or fill out a checklist on a worksheet of these and similar items. Using this information, students identify the type of housing they might need in a location that they can research and compare. For example, a student who plans to be married with two children might select a house with three bedrooms and two bathrooms. If necessary, have students consider the number of bedrooms and bathrooms at their home as a point of comparison.	Paper or electronic worksheet; Word-processing software
15–20 minutes	Students conduct research on real estate websites or real estate search engines. Students should identify at least five different houses to compare, and should record data such as cost, square footage, number of bedrooms and bathrooms, and any other desired information. A spreadsheet is optimal, but this activity can be completed with a calculator and a print-based handout with a table or graphic organizer to help organize the data. Students should include the sources for their information. While some websites can calculate some of this information, students should be able to show all of their own calculations. Using this information, students should determine the average housing price for their five choices.	Computer or mobile device with Internet access; Spreadsheet software or calculator
30 minutes	Students should then determine possible options for purchasing housing at the average price they have identified based on the length of the mortgage, lending rates, and down payments. They can either research information such as mortgage rates online or you can provide them with specific data for possible scenarios. For example, students can calculate total expenditures and monthly payments when purchasing the home over 15- or 30-year mortgages at rates of 5, 7, or 9 percent with down payments of 0-, 10-, and 30 percent of the purchase price. If using a spreadsheet, graph the results of the different scenarios for comparison.	Spreadsheet software or calculator
15–20 minutes	Students should calculate an approximate income necessary for purchasing and maintaining the home for the different scenarios using a budget and the commonly recommended figure of 30 percent of their income for housing.	Spreadsheet software or calculator
20–30 minutes	Students then use data from the U.S. Census Bureau, such as the Annual Social and Economic (ASEC) Supplement from the Current Population Survey to determine mean earnings for different levels of educational attainment. They may also find the most current report on *Income, Poverty, and Health Insurance Coverage in the United States* helpful, as it provides data on factors that influence income, such as gender, type of household, age bracket, region, and metropolitan status.	Computer with Internet access
30 minutes to develop report; 1 or 2 class periods for report out and discussion	Students prepare a report or presentation with their findings and the impact the data may have on different scenarios. They should report on the type of housing they've chosen and its cost, the amount of their projected down payment, and the type of mortgages they have selected, as well as reasons for the selection. They should report the annual income they have projected with a 30 percent housing budget. The data and different scenarios will provide ample opportunities for individual and whole-class discussion. For example, students may want to consider how location impacts housing price for similar size houses. They may want to explore differences in reported incomes, such as men versus women, and how these impact decisions they've made. Certainly, they should report on the level of education they project needing—based on given income data—to purchase their housing selection and how this aligns with their career plans.	Word-processing or presentation software; Graphs and data tables exported from spreadsheet software

Notes: This activity can also be completed in pairs or small groups.

MONITOR

Ongoing Assessment(s): Student work is assessed at different stages of the project. Students must accurately create the spreadsheet (or other documentation), calculations, and graphs. Depending on reporting preferences (individual written report vs. class presentation), a checklist or rubric can be used to assess the final report.

Accommodations and Extensions: The complexity of the lesson can be reduced or increased to match students at different grade or technology proficiency levels. The full lesson is complex and suitable to students who work well independently, require challenging enrichment activities, and are proficient with the technology.
Standardizing options (such as identifying one housing type of three bedrooms and two bathrooms) and limiting the number of parameters to investigate (such as one mortgage rate over 30 years) will reduce the complexity of the lesson and allow students to focus on the math concepts. Students just becoming familiar with spreadsheet software can simply conduct the research on five housing choices, record their data, and calculate the average price, then a classroom composite graph can be made. Student groups can also be randomly assigned to different scenarios so that the class can explore a range of options at the conclusion of the lesson.

Back-up Plan: Data tables and reports from the U.S. Census Bureau can be downloaded beforehand and stored in a project folder or printed out. Real estate prices can also be obtained from newspapers or paper-based real estate guides obtained from real estate agencies or many retail locations.

EVALUATE AND EXTEND

Lesson Reflections and Notes: Emphasis should be placed on using math skills to make informed decisions. While students may enjoy the real estate research, they should be encouraged to consider the complete activity and how their decisions at each stage are related.

A full-size version of this lesson plan appears on the CourseMate website at **www.cengagebrain.com**.

Technology in the Science Classroom

Brian Giza, Ph.D. and Judy Reinhartz, Ph.D.

Science teachers are constantly in search of innovative ways to engage their students. In science, the emphasis on hands-on learning often causes teachers to overlook the use of technology in the inquiry process. However, technology can serve many important purposes that supplement inquiry in the science classroom. For example, technology can give learners access to locations that are unobtainable otherwise and insight into science processes. Technologies such as digital video, photography, simulations, and a growing number of online digital resources or mobile apps can transport the viewer to Arctic regions, to other planetary surfaces, to the highest mountains or the depths of the ocean, or into previously unexplored microscopic worlds. When students are given nearly immediate access to rain forests, or the cornfields of the Midwest, the hustle and bustle of a city, the beauty of star-forming regions, or other exotic locations, the challenge is not just to show the learner these previously unfamiliar locations, but to help them ask and answer questions about them. Technology can mediate an understanding of our place in our world and the cosmos, bringing the universe alive with sound and images for all to experience and enjoy (see Table S.5 for some additional ideas).

As you have learned throughout this book, effective technology use requires more than knowledge of technology. Teachers need to prepare lessons and use technology tools in ways that promote a deep understanding of science and allow students to generalize their knowledge to unique situations. Each student should be prepared to

THE GAME PLAN

Content Standards

Set Goals
Learn more about the *National Science Education Standards* developed by the National Committee on Science Education Standards and Assessment or the science standards for a state where you plan to seek a teaching position. Consider a variety of ways to integrate technology while addressing the science standards.

Take Action
Explore the national standards published by the National Committee on Science Education Standards and Assessment or the state standards as listed on the department of education website in the state where you plan to seek a position.

Plan ways that you could meet those standards using technology in the science classroom.

Monitor
Did you find the information you needed? Do you need to contact the department of education for more information about where to find the science standards?

Evaluate and Extend
Discuss the plan you developed for meeting the science standards using technology with others and compare your ideas. Note the strengths and weaknesses of the various examples and incorporate the best ideas into your plan.

Science

ask and find solutions to questions, not just memorize facts. The National Science Education Standards (National Academy of Sciences, 1996) were developed in light of a vision for change—a change in emphasis from instruction that relies on lower levels of cognition that focus on factual recall to one that is based on inquiry within the context of other disciplines that relate science to personal, social, and historical perspectives.

Technology is a *tool* that can be used to perform a *task* using sound instructional *strategies*. Teachers who have mastered effective pedagogical techniques can apply these strategies to new technology tools. For example, requiring students to note their observations of a lab experiment is an important strategy for the task of assessing student learning—whether the tools being used are more traditional, an online form accessed by a mobile device, or an audio recording a student makes for a multimedia-based report.

Modern science education strategies often include access to a range of web-based resources and—increasingly—apps for mobile devices. Such approaches send students on a quest for science information in a real-world context, and with collaborative tools, students have the ability to find, discuss, evaluate and share their findings with others in their classroom and beyond (Alexander, 2006). The goal of finding information is as old as education itself—what has changed is where students go to get this information. Fifty

Table S.5 Ideas for Addressing NETS-S in the Science Classroom

Creativity and Innovation

Students gather real-world weather data that they then analyze and present visually using spreadsheets, graphic organizers, or other modeling tools to make predictions or suggest trends for the upcoming year in various locations. They compare data collected from a website with data they have collected locally to compare and contrast trends using charts, graphics, and text and post their final projects to a class website.

Communication and Collaboration

Students conduct experiments using simulation software or visit distant locations such as a desert, arctic region, or rainforest, using simulations or by participating in a virtual field trip. Students test hypotheses and use the simulation software to determine outcomes based on the manipulation of variables, such as limiting natural resources such as light, heat, or water. Working in teams, students communicate their results in digital formats that include their own voices narrating the results of their explorations. They make their report available for download as a podcast, video, or other format for viewing on portable devices, social spaces, or local computers.

Research and Information Fluency

Students use peripherals such as light gates or probeware to collect real-time data during experiments that can be graphed using graphing calculators—either handheld or software-based emulations—to solve problems or answer questions related to energy and motion.

Critical Thinking, Problem Solving, and Decision Making

Students use a variety of online and real-world data they collect related to a local or regional concern, such as the rise of blue-green algae in a nearby lake or increased levels of toxins in the local environment. They conduct research, interview experts, propose solutions, and build virtual or physical models that they then present to relevant authorities outside of the classroom, whether in person or with webconferencing tools.

Digital Citizenship

Students explore their roles in a digital world by working on year-long group and individual projects that monitor and submit data online to projects such as the Monarch watch, bird surveys, air and water resource monitoring, and so forth. Emphasis should also include safe and appropriate use of technological resources and the legal use of copyright-protected materials.

Technology Operations and Concepts

Students build a solubility tester using simple (and common) electrical components (9 volt battery, LED, capacitor, wires). They use their instruments in laboratory activities to explore water pollution via various common effluents (salt, alcohols, oils). They use a spreadsheet application to organize and analyze their data.

years ago, students reached for encyclopedias and other print materials; today they go online, gather information from experts, and simulate or emulate common scientific research and reporting processes all within the comfort of their classroom or home.

Science classrooms are also an appropriate venue for WebQuests (discussed in Chapter 4), whether you make them or find them for use in your classroom. You can also have students build them as part of an inquiry lesson. Both forms of WebQuests are useful, with the teacher-created version being most useful when a teacher has limited time, and desires to keep the learners on task. Still, when students construct their own WebQuests and build them from prior knowledge, they integrate what they learn in a meaningful way. The knowledge that they acquire stays with them longer and is more generalizable to new contexts.

Today's science classrooms also often have access to a range of digital tools, whether designed specifically for science or not. Digital cameras and videocameras, data collection probes, and digital microscopes all serve as forms of data collection and analysis tools. For example, when these tools are used for observing and acquiring data, they are simply gathering data that can be stored and analyzed later. When a digital camera is used to observe metamorphosis by taking a sequence of images over time (see Figure S.8), it has much in common with a pH probe—both are being used to acquire incremental data during a science laboratory exercise.

A motion detector is another tool that can be applied in useful and often creative ways (see Figure S.9). Motion detectors provide the user with a few common features, such as the ability to measure motion and record the data about that motion in a computer software interface. Simple (and common) exercises such as matching the shape of a curve in a graph (which is done by moving toward or away from the detector at appropriate speeds and accelerations) can be enhanced by a challenge such as "motion detector etch-a-sketch" in which the curves generated by student motions are imported into an animation program and superimposed to generate an image. Student teams must try to match an agreed-upon drawing, instilling a deeper understanding of motion, acceleration, and graphical representations of physical phenomena.

Science educators also should consider the number of ways in which spreadsheets can be used as many professionals in the science fields often use these commonly available tools to analyze and evaluate data. Spreadsheets organize and calculate

Figure S.8
Webcam images of a butterfly emerging from a chrysalis.

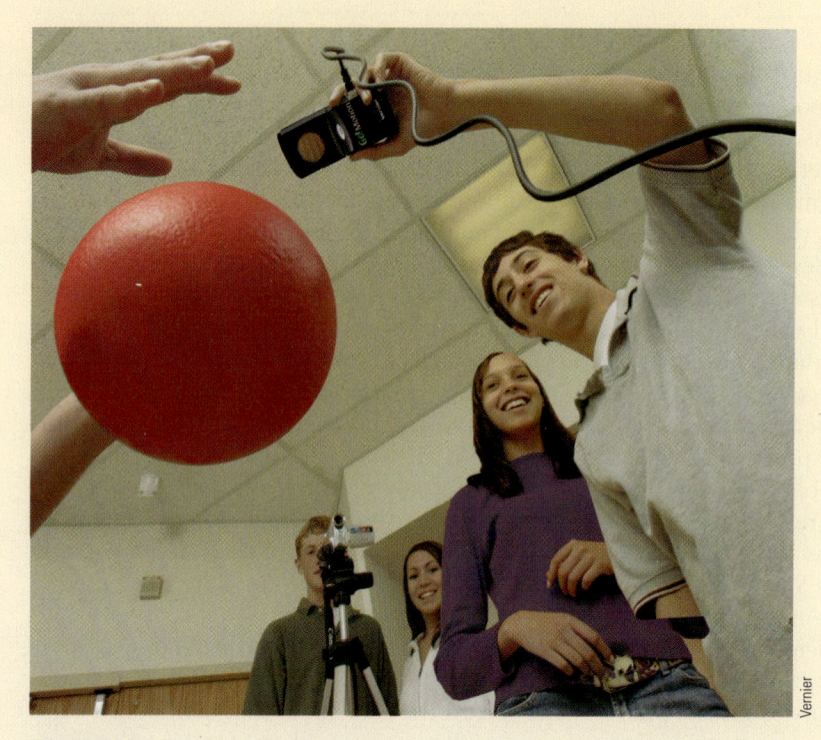

Figure S.9
Motion detectors allow students to record data.

information to solve "what if" scenarios and are perfect for inquiry science. Spreadsheets are useful in activities as diverse as classic science-fair experiments in which lighting or fertilizer conditions are plotted against plant growth, or for making sophisticated ballistics predictions about paths and distances of objects thrown by catapults. Modern spreadsheets, including several free, open-source versions, allow the user to conduct t-tests or more sophisticated statistical functions and have many of the features needed in today's science classrooms.

Technology is applied science, and when technology is used in the teaching of science it can be of great benefit, such as when it brings science to a learner's cultural context. For example, your students may be required to study sound. Recording sound is not difficult today, with portable recording built into many personal devices (phones, mobile devices, or digital audio recorders). It's also easy to import sound from recording devices into computers or to use laptops or other computers with built-in or external microphones. There are a number of software programs that can be used to analyze sound, including free applications that can be downloaded or used online.

The future of technology in science education is bright. As the number of high-quality online resources and apps for mobile devices continues to grow and provide ever-increasing instructional opportunities, it becomes easier for science teachers to inspire critical thinking and contextualize learning in ways that are powerful supports to science-learning experiences. Web-based collaborative tools support cooperative learning among science students and facilitate collaboration among teachers as well. The knack for using technology tools successfully in science classrooms is to focus on the content to be taught, the science inquiry processes, and how these are supported by available technologies. For technology use to expand into science classrooms at all levels, it is essential that you are aware of the specific digital tools and resources that are available and how to implement them.

References

Alexander, B. (2006). Web 2.0: A new wave of innovation for teaching and learning? *Educause Review, 41*(2), 33–44.

National Academy of Sciences. (1996). *National science education standards*. Washington, DC: National Academies Press.

Lesson Plans for Science
Elementary Science

TECHNOLOGY INTEGRATION FOR MEANINGFUL CLASSROOM USE

Daily Lesson GAME Plan

Lesson Title: Scientist for a Day	**Related Lessons:** Life Cycle of Organisms
Grade Level: Elementary	**Unit:** Organisms

GOALS

Content Standards:
Science as Inquiry
- Abilities necessary to do scientific inquiries
- Understandings about scientific inquiry

Life Science
- The characteristics of organisms
- Organisms and environments

ISTE NETS-S
- ☐ Creativity and innovation
- ☒ Communication and collaboration
- ☐ Research and information fluency
- ☒ Critical thinking, problem solving, and decision-making
- ☐ Digital citizenship
- ☒ Technology operations and concepts

Instructional Objective(s):
Students assume the role of various scientists, geologists, zoologists, and botanists, to observe, record, and describe the inhabitants, both living and non-living, in a designated plot of ground.

ACTION

Before-Class Preparation:
Prior to the lesson, take time to walk around outside the school. Identify several areas where the students can observe and that will elicit a variety of responses from them. Although each group of students selects the plot of ground where they carry out their observations, guide them to those areas containing a variety of organisms and non-living things. Prepare the instructions for the Outdoor Observation.
- Step 1: Decide which person is to serve as the geologist, the botanist, the zoologist, and the sampler/data recorder.
- Step 2: Stay within the area designated by the teacher.
- Step 3: The sampler/recorder tosses a hula hoop into the air. Wherever the hoop lands, that is the area that your group is to observe.
- Step 4: The geologist observes the rocks and soils of the area. The botanist observes the plant life in the area, and the zoologist observes the animal life within the area. The sampler/data recorder records the data. Be sure to count the number of organisms or rocks within your area.

Create a blog, website, or page on a learning management system for students to enter a description of the activity and their findings. Alternately, students can create their lab report using word-processing or journaling software. Create a checklist for each job and the graph. Find or create a rubric for the lab report.

Internet Resources
Living versus Non-living Things Quiz: http://www.saburchill.com/questions/lanlt001.html

During Class

Time	Instructional Activities	Materials and Resources
20 minutes	Lead a class discussion by beginning with the following: "Today we will learn how to observe like a scientist. We will also learn about three different types of scientists: the botanists, the zoologists, and the geologists. Some of you will take on the role of a specific type of scientist, while others will record data." Then provide background on each role. Have students write a short summary describing the jobs of the botanist, the zoologist, and the geologist, finding information and examples of each online, if time permits.	Word-processing or journaling software
20 minutes	Ask students to distinguish between living organisms and non-living things. There are some very general rules to follow when trying to decide if something is living or non-living. Listed here are the six rules used by scientists: • Living organisms are made of cells. • Living organisms obtain and use energy. • Living organisms grow and develop. • Living organisms reproduce. • Living organisms respond to their environment. • Living organisms adapt to their environment. Ask students, "Which scientist(s) study living organisms? Which scientist(s) study non-living things?" Students complete an online quiz distinguishing living organisms from non-living things.	Computers or mobile devices with Internet access Living versus Non-living Things Quiz (or similar website)
15 minutes	Review the instructions for the Outdoor Observation. Each person has a specific job during the time of observation. After the group discussion, divide the students into groups of four. Assign or allow students to select a job: the botanist, the zoologist, the geologist, and the sampler/data recorder. Accompany the class outside and direct the groups to four different areas near the school.	Student lab notebook Checklist Optional: mobile device
30 minutes	The random sampler/data recorder tosses the hula hoop into the air. When the hoop lands, the space within the hoop designates the plot of ground the group is to observe. The geologist observes the rocks and soils of the area. The botanist observes the plant life in the area, and the zoologist observes the animal life in the area. The students count the number of organisms and rocks within the area. The sampler/data recorder records the data. Mobile devices can be used to record data or even to take pictures or recordings to support the final product. The data will be used to create a graph. Each scientist writes his/her observations in a lab notebook. The sampler/data recorder records the number of living organisms and non-living things found within the observed plot. When the observation period is complete, the students return to the classroom. Group members compare their findings and record the information in their lab notebook.	Hula hoop Student lab notebook Optional: mobile device
20 minutes	Demonstrate the process of data reporting by creating a bar graph with spreadsheet software using the following sample data: *Rocks* — 10, *Grass* — 33, *Ants* — 15. Direct students to title their graphs and label the axes. The X-axis should be labeled *Observed Living Organisms and Non-living Things* and the Y-axis should be labeled *Number of Living Organisms and Non-living Things*. Discuss the proper method for creating the scale with the students. If a rubric is utilized to assess the graph, inform the students of the grading system.	Computer with spreadsheet software Rubric
45 minutes	Student groups create a lab report using word-processing or journaling software or they may create an entry on a classroom blog describing the activity and their findings. Students are to choose one other group's findings and write about the differences in the data from that group as compared to the data from their group. Students are to speculate why these differences could have occurred.	Computer with Internet access Rubric

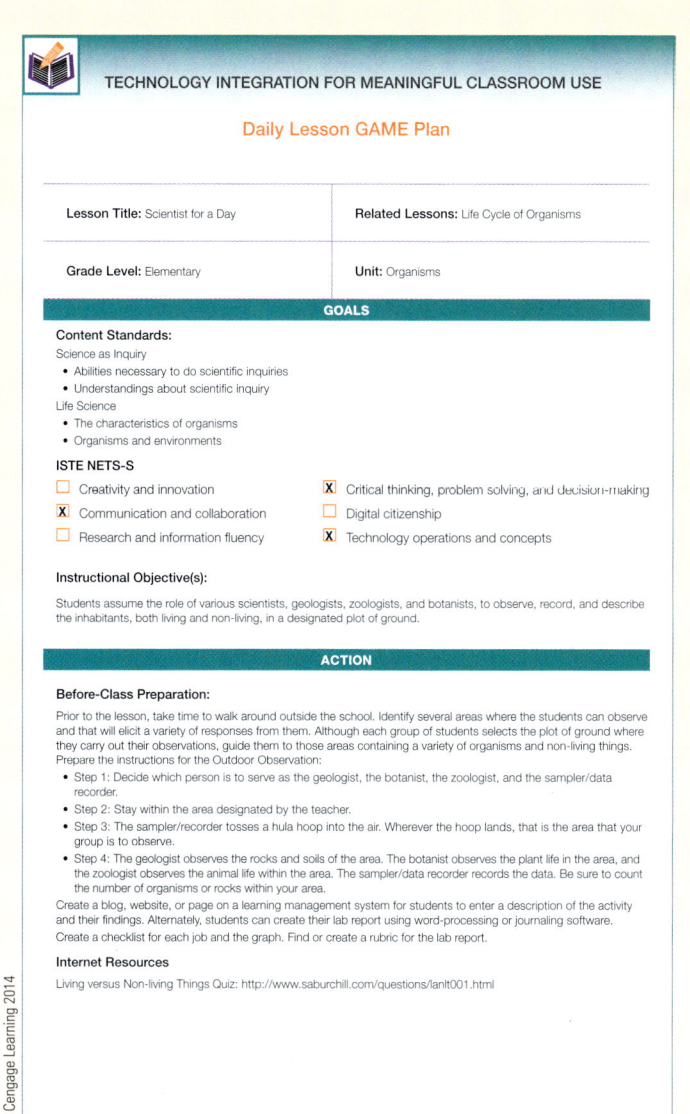

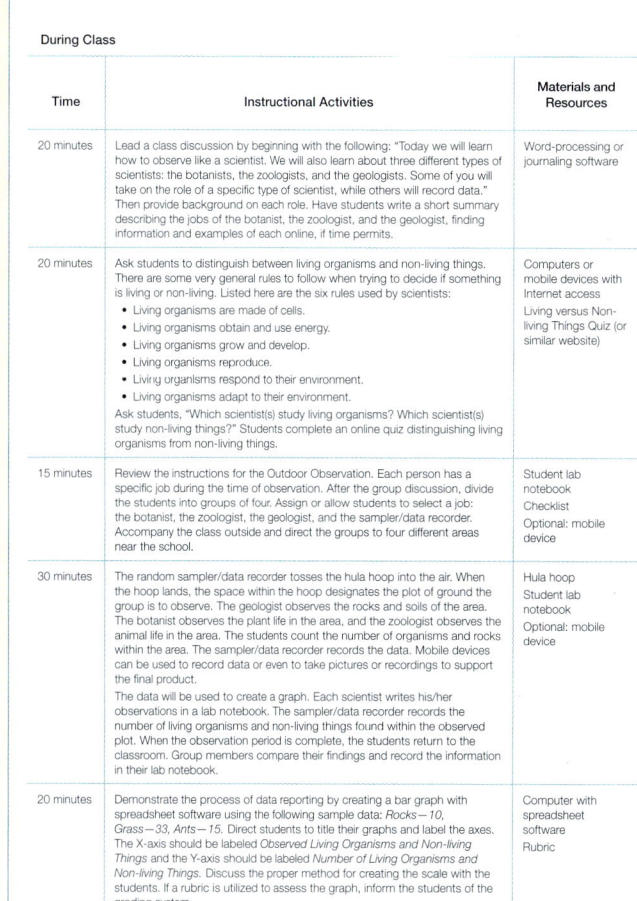

Notes: Groups should be composed of four students: one biologist, one zoologist, one geologist, one sampler/data recorder. The jobs of the sampler and data recorder can be performed by the same student. Once outside, demonstrate the proper procedure for selecting the plot of ground, by gently tossing the hula hoop.

MONITOR

Ongoing Assessment(s): Students should be monitored to ensure they are focusing on their observations and data collection. Students should use the teacher-generated rubric throughout the activity to guide their work and identify components of the graph.

Accommodations and Extensions: Provide guidance to groups having difficulty distinguishing between living organisms and non-living things found within their plots of ground.

If some students need assistance in constructing their graphs, consider placing them with a partner within the group to complete the task. Digital cameras or mobile devices with cameras can be used to create a virtual catalog of the living organisms and non-living things found in their plots of ground. Using the Internet and field guides, have groups identify the scientific names of the living organisms observed.

Back-up Plan: Students can tour the school, categorizing living organisms and non-living things and collecting data needed to complete the activity. Predetermined categories may be necessary to limit the amount of data collected. Graphing can be conducted in a whole-class setting using an overhead projector and completed using graph paper.

EVALUATE AND EXTEND

Lesson Reflections and Notes: Completed activity is graded using a checklist for the job summary and graph, and a rubric for the lab notebook and blog entries.

A full-size version of this lesson plan appears on the CourseMate website at www.cengagebrain.com.

Middle Grades Science

Science

TECHNOLOGY INTEGRATION FOR MEANINGFUL CLASSROOM USE

Daily Lesson GAME Plan

Lesson Title: Can the Trash!	Related Lessons: Waste
Grade Level: Middle grades	Unit: Reduce, Reuse, Recycle

GOALS

Content Standards:
Science as Inquiry
- Abilities necessary to do scientific inquiry
- Understandings about scientific inquiry

Science in Personal and Social Perspectives
- Populations, resources, and environments
- Natural hazards
- Risks and benefits
- Science and technology in society

ISTE NETS-S
- [X] Creativity and innovation
- [X] Communication and collaboration
- [ ] Research and information fluency
- [X] Critical thinking, problem solving, and decision-making
- [X] Digital citizenship
- [ ] Technology operations and concepts

Instructional Objective(s):
Students will receive a general overview of the world's environmental dilemmas, thereby understanding the global implications of their actions.

ACTION

Before-Class Preparation:
Ask parent volunteers or other teachers to collect their waste paper in a separate bag for a period of three days. Please be specific and inform them that no food or food containers, such as pizza boxes, are to be placed in this bag. Include only paper products such as construction paper, copy paper, newsprint, empty tubes, or boxes/cartons.

Internet Resources
The Personal Environmental Impact Calculator http://ans.engr.wisc.edu/eic/RecyclingForm.html
Carbon Footprint Calculator http://www.carbonfootprint.com/calculator.aspx

Additional Resources
You'll need a copy of the poem "Sara Cynthia Sylvia Stout Would Not Take the Garbage Out" from *Where the Sidewalk Ends* by Shel Silverstein.
Other possible readings: *The Garbage Can* by Linda Ann Nickerson and *Thank you, Mr. Garbage Man* by Erin Elizabeth Kelly-Moen

During Class

Time	Instructional Activities	Materials and Resources
15–30 minutes	Read the poem by Shel Silverstein, "Sarah Cynthia Sylvia Stout Would Not Take the Garbage Out." Lead the students in a discussion concerning the implications of the poem, the mounting garbage, and the concept of garbage disposal. Introduce the idea of the world's garbage and its size and volume. Communicate to the students that our world is in danger from pollution of the air, water, and land, overwhelming the delicate balance of nature of the planet. Many species of plants and animals face extinction at an alarming rate. Until all of the people of the world are educated and informed, this destruction will continue. Because they, the students, are the leaders of tomorrow, it is their task to become responsible users and protectors of the environment.	Poem by Shel Silverstein, "Sara Cynthia Sylvia Stout Would Not Take the Garbage Out"
20 minutes	Have students determine • how their purchasing and disposal methods affect their personal environmental impact • their carbon footprint	Computer with Internet access Websites, such as Environmental calculator websites
10 minutes	Demonstrate the process of categorization using a small bag of waste paper and separate plastic bags. Observe safe practices by wearing plastic gloves and washing your hands after the process is complete. Mass one of the categorized bags with a spring scale or large digital balance, demonstrating the use of the measuring instrument.	Bags of garbage collected over a period of three days Plastic gloves Spring scale or large digital balance
5 minutes	Demonstrate how to calculate the weekly volume (volume of waste paper/3 days × 7 days), the monthly volume (weekly volume × 4 weeks), and the yearly volume (weekly volume × 52 weeks).	Whiteboard
20 minutes	Working in pairs, students sort and categorize the waste paper collected over the three-day period. Have students use separate plastic bags for specific categories, such as newsprint, construction paper, and copier paper. Make sure the students wear plastic gloves while they are involved in the sorting process. Caution them to wash their hands after the waste paper is categorized. Students collect data by massing the separate bags using a spring scale or large digital balance. Have students create a bar graph to display their data. The X-axis should be labeled with the categories and the Y-axis should be the volume. If a rubric is utilized for assessing the bar graph, share the expectations with the students at this time.	Bags of garbage collected over a period of three days Spring scale or large digital balance Plastic gloves for each student Computers or mobile devices or student lab notebook Spreadsheet software Rubric
15–30 minutes	Students calculate the weekly, monthly, and yearly volumes of each type of material. Students will write a two-paragraph summary, based on their calculations, as to the possible effects on the environment of the amount of waste paper accumulated in a year.	Calculators or calculator software Word-processing software
30 minutes	Utilizing their findings, have students create a public service announcement that highlights reasons to recycle. Their PSA should specifically incorporate information they've collected. If a rubric is utilized for assessing the announcement, share the expectations with the student. The focus should be on science content standards, not media creation.	Image-editing or other graphic software; or word-processing or page-layout software; or website like Glogster

---

Notes: The public service announcement can be expanded to a video-based project, depending on available time and proficiency of the students.

MONITOR

Ongoing Assessment(s): Use a checklist to ensure active student participation in the investigation. Periodically check the data students are collecting online or in their lab notebook. Students use a teacher-generated rubric to identify components of the graph and public service announcement.

Accommodations and Extensions: Some students will need assistance in constructing their graph or writing their summaries. Students can collect relevant newspaper and magazine articles and share them with the class. Consider connecting with one or more classrooms in another state or country to compare recycling procedures and volume of garbage collected and recycled. Schedule a class trip to a recycling center. Have students use recycled paper when appropriate.

Back-up Plan: Have students design signs for each classroom in the building to remind them to turn off the lights and water when not in use. Identify specific strategies for using technologies more effectively. Enlist other classes and start a recycling program at the school.

EVALUATE AND EXTEND

Lesson Reflections and Notes: Grade the activity using a rubric for each completed component. Incorporate student suggestions for new categories of trash separation into the lesson.

A full-size version of this lesson plan appears on the CourseMate website at www.cengagebrain.com.

Technology in the Social Studies Classroom

David Hicks, Ph.D. and Melissa Lisanti, MA, NBCT

The teaching of social studies has been observed by generations of students and researchers as clinging to a very specific pattern of teaching: the teacher talks and students listen, read, and answer questions in textbooks. Students are then expected to memorize facts and details that, for the most part are "removed from their intrinsically human character" (Goodlad, 1984, p. 212). What is often lost or forgotten in such teaching is the recognition that "the primary purpose of the social studies is to help young people develop the ability to make informed and reasoned decisions for the public good as citizens of a culturally diverse, democratic society in an interdependent world" (NCSS, 2010, p. 3). This definition of social studies was adopted by the National Council for the Social Studies in 1992 and remains important today. Wise practice within the social studies classroom should include preparing students to actively engage in inquiry, perspective taking, and meaning making in order to develop the habits of mind that are important for the rights and responsibilities of 21st-century citizenship. (See Table S.6. for some ideas)

A growing number of social studies educators contend that the social studies classroom should be the ideal space to prepare young citizens to critically explore their world (the past and present) through the use of digital technologies in the standards-based classroom. That is, having access to current knowledge resources, digital archives, and experts—with a great number of these available via the Internet—can only benefit a teaching field that 1) advocates teaching and learning social studies from a constructivist perspective, 2) stresses the importance of teaching students to develop

THE GAME PLAN

Content Standards

Set Goals
Learn more about the *National Standards for Social Studies* from the National Council for the Social Studies or the social studies standards for a state where you plan to seek a teaching position. Consider a variety of ways to integrate technology while addressing the social studies standards.

Take Action
Explore the national standards published by the National Council for the Social Studies or the state standards as listed on the department of education website in the state where you plan to seek a position. Plan ways that you could meet those standards using technology in the social studies classroom.

Monitor
Did you find the information you needed? Do you need to contact the department of education for more information about where to find the social studies standards?

Evaluate and Extend
Discuss the plan you developed for meeting the social studies standards using technology with others and compare your ideas. Note the strengths and weaknesses of the various examples and incorporate the best ideas into your plan.

Social Studies

the knowledge, skills, and dispositions to ask questions and gather data as part of the process of inquiring into past and present issues, and 3) recognizes the importance of establishing clear standards and performance expectations for students.

The ability to access authentic social studies materials and engage in authentic inquiry is vital if students are to make real-world connections within the social studies classroom. The development of digital historical libraries and archives is changing the way teachers and students can access learning materials. Today, students can access books, maps, primary sources, newspapers, fact books, visual materials, and many other forms of information through CDs, DVDs, and online library collections and archives. Many of these archives continue to digitize their collections, and teachers and students can search and locate key historical resources.

Although a growing number of students and teachers may be acquainted with such tools as word processors, presentation tools, and web browsers, the idea of using these tools as a way to support student-centered teaching and learning is still very new for many students and teachers. The use of digital repositories as an inquiry tool becomes problematic if students are not prepared to conduct searches of the Internet and databases and, more importantly, to evaluate the trustworthiness of these resources. Preparing students to engage in inquiry requires that they be taught how to be discerning and critical users of information resources such as the Internet.

Another powerful model that teachers use to engage their students in inquiry-based social studies lessons is a WebQuest (as described in Chapter 4). It's one example of how web-based resources can be utilized to support structured, inquiry-orientated lessons, whether your students search the entire web or work within a limited set of web

Table 5.6 Ideas for Addressing NETS-S in the Social Studies Classroom

Creativity and Innovation
Widely available video-editing software, including the capacity of smartphones and other mobile technologies to capture video, allows students to craft their own digital documentaries on any of the NCSS standards or to demonstrate their understanding of important historical or current events or perspectives. Students can incorporate a range of software to develop multimedia timelines that incorporate media elements.

Communication and Collaboration
E-mail, discussion, and collaboration software including blogs, wikis, and other Web 2.0 tools have dramatically widened access to other communities around the world. Communication tools allow students multiple opportunities to engage in dialog on all of the NCSS standards with each other, with teachers, or other experts.

Research and Information Fluency
Digital archives, such as the National Archives and the Library of Congress, have made primary source materials available in vast quantities. WebQuests or virtual field trips are available from many public and private organizations, or can be created by a teacher or groups of teachers.

Critical Thinking, Problem Solving, and Decision-Making
Online resources, apps, and other software that engage students in "doing history" are abundant. Sites such as the History Inquiry Project and Historical Scene Investigation engage students in the complex decision-making processes utilized by historians. Simulation and role-playing software also promote the development of student decision-making skills.

Digital Citizenship
Social studies students must develop historical inquiry skills that support their verification of resources, especially resources found on the Internet. Social studies students can investigate, track, and debate the issues and ever-changing laws relating to the use of new and emerging technologies, including mobile technologies, social networking, and gaming.

Technology Operations and Concepts
Students can use widely available word-processing and presentation software to engage in all stages of the writing process across all social studies standards. They can access basic information on the Internet and from other digital resources on a variety of topics, store them centrally through cloud-based storage and apps, and come together as a team to develop presentations that can be shared in class and beyond.

resources that may be housed on a school server, organized through a class web page or series of favorite bookmarks, or even commercial content services including those from textbook and other content providers.

As digital technologies continue to evolve, a whole new level of authentic inquiry and activity is developing within the social studies classroom. For example, Google Earth is a stand-alone geographic search tool that brings together maps, satellite imagery, and layers of geographic information, to allow users to conduct local, national, and international searches. Users appear to "fly" around the earth to explore people, places, and environments—even different time periods. Students can use satellite images of their own communities before flying to identify, explore, and compare data from other countries and cultures. You, too, can add layers and embed links to instructional activities or even other resources in Google Earth, such as linking to streaming videos, pictures, or other websites that help provide greater context and depth of knowledge about the people and places students explore during their map inquiries.

Technology gives social studies teachers the potential to provide their students with unprecedented access to people, ideas, and events, as suggested in Figure S.10. Bringing the world into the classroom through online media including newspapers and news networks supports the teaching of current events and provides multiple perspectives on peoples and cultures from around the world. You and your students can contact students from down the block or around the world. The Newseum's Today's Front Pages allow students to compare and contrast news stories and the reporting of significant events from around the world.

A variety of digital tools are available to create local and global connections with other students, teachers, and content experts. Whether you're joining an established community, such as International Education and Resource Network (iEARN), ePals classroom exchange, or Global SchoolNet, or drawing upon local experts such as professionals from museums, libraries, or other community members, digital communication tools can help broaden your students' experiences. Such projects create opportunities for students to explore and revise their conceptions of people, places, and environments over time and space (see Figure S.11).

The integrated nature of social studies continues to offer numerous opportunities for teachers to help diverse learners explore their own interests and questions and complete social studies projects. Social studies is ultimately the study of people, places, and events throughout the ages; it is a subject that explores existential issues of life and death over time and space.

There are a number of digitally supported instructional projects that specifically model the "doing" of history and allow students to practice and explore creative thinking and problem solving in ways that would not be possible in the everyday social studies classroom. These resources provide models of historical inquiry that you can incorporate into your social studies classroom. Students can investigate evidence you compile through a combination of print and digital

Figure S.10

Students can develop inquiry skills in a social studies context at websites such as the Historical Scene Investigation.

Source: College of William and Mary School of Education. http://web.wm.edu/hsi/cases/elvis/elvis_student.html/College of William and Mary

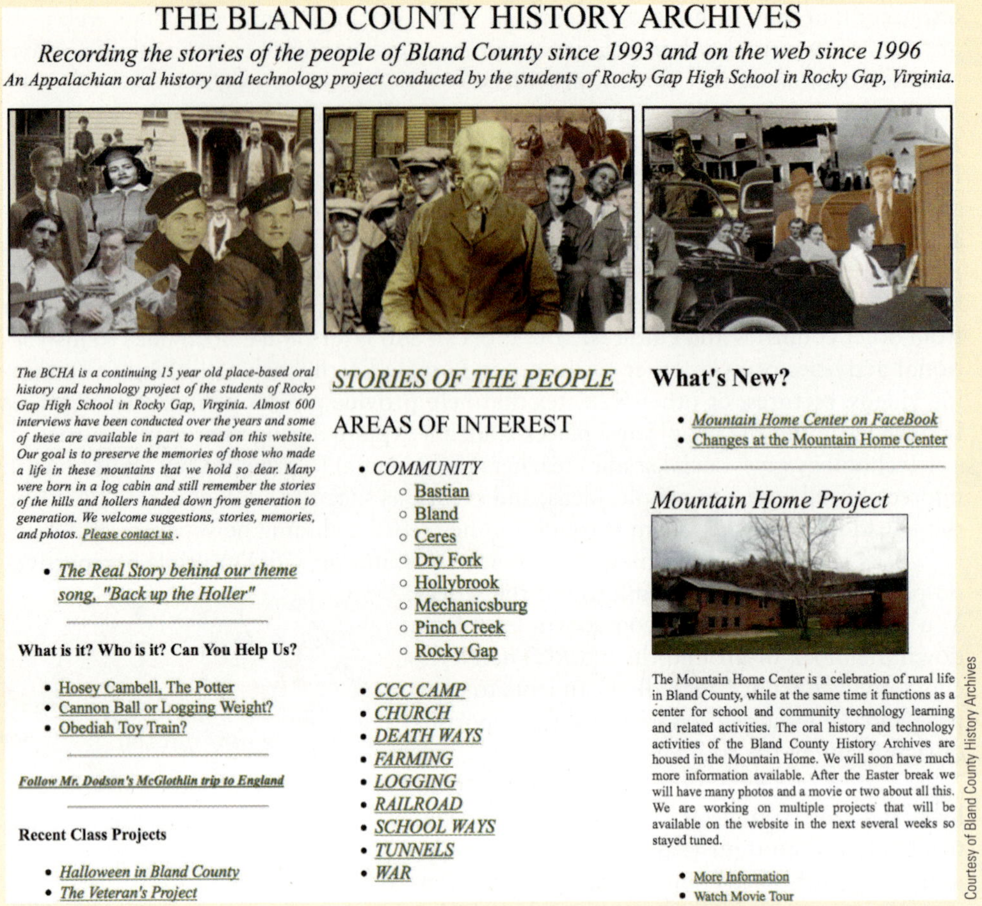

Figure S.11
Students at Rocky Gap High School built and maintain the Bland County History Archives.

resources. Your students can search for clues using a range of tools including Internet databases and other web resources, digital cameras and video cameras, as well as handheld or laptop computers. Students can compile their data using productivity tools, such as word processors, note-taking software, databases, and spreadsheets. They can present the data they have collected and support their positions with presentation, web, or multimedia-authoring software—including pictures and video elements they have collected and edited.

This section has emphasized the potential power of technology to augment and enrich standards-based social studies curriculum. Social studies instruction designed around student inquiry and meaning making will seek to harness the potential of technology: 1) access to volumes of information and historical sources, 2) outlets for creativity and production, and 3) tools for research and analysis, among others. By successfully integrating technology as a tool for social studies inquiry, providing scaffolds for understanding issues of ethics, and preparing students to navigate in a complex digital age, social studies teachers can equip students with knowledge and skills to depend on far beyond their school years.

References

Goodlad, J. (1984). *A place called school.* New York: McGraw-Hill.

National Council for the Social Studies (NCSS). (2010). *National curriculum standards for social studies: A framework for teaching, learning, and assessment.* Washington, DC: Author.

Lesson Plans for Social Studies

Elementary Social Studies

TECHNOLOGY INTEGRATION FOR MEANINGFUL CLASSROOM USE

Daily Lesson GAME Plan

Lesson Title: State Facts: "I'm going on a trip..."

Related Lessons: American History Sites and Symbols

Grade Level: Elementary

Unit: American Sites and Symbols

GOALS

Content Standards:
- Culture
- People, places, and environment

ISTE NETS-S
- ☐ Creativity and innovation
- ☒ Communication and collaboration
- ☒ Research and information fluency
- ☐ Critical thinking, problem solving, and decision-making
- ☒ Digital citizenship
- ☒ Technology operations and concepts

Instructional Objective(s):
- Students will identify key American state and national sites and symbols
- Students will provide relevant supporting information (in the form of questions) of the information they identify and answer questions posed by other students.

Determine the scope of the assignment in terms of items the students must know for relevant content standards. Based on the grade level, students can focus solely on states or expand to capitols, state symbols, or popular sites and landmarks.

ACTION

Before-Class Preparation:
Determine how students will be grouped and how many groups are necessary. Determine how many states each student will conduct research on. All students will conduct similar tasks and collect similar types of information for the states they are assigned, but grouping allows students to apply different strengths and collaborate. Create a sample state slide or two and the checklist for grading.

Internet Resources
Homework Spot state capitals: http://www.homeworkspot.com/ask/statecapitals.htm (links to actual websites for state capitals)
FactMonster 50 states: http://www.factmonster.com/states.html
Compfight (http://compfight.com/) or Wikimedia Commons (http://commons.wikimedia.org/wiki/Main_Page)

During Class

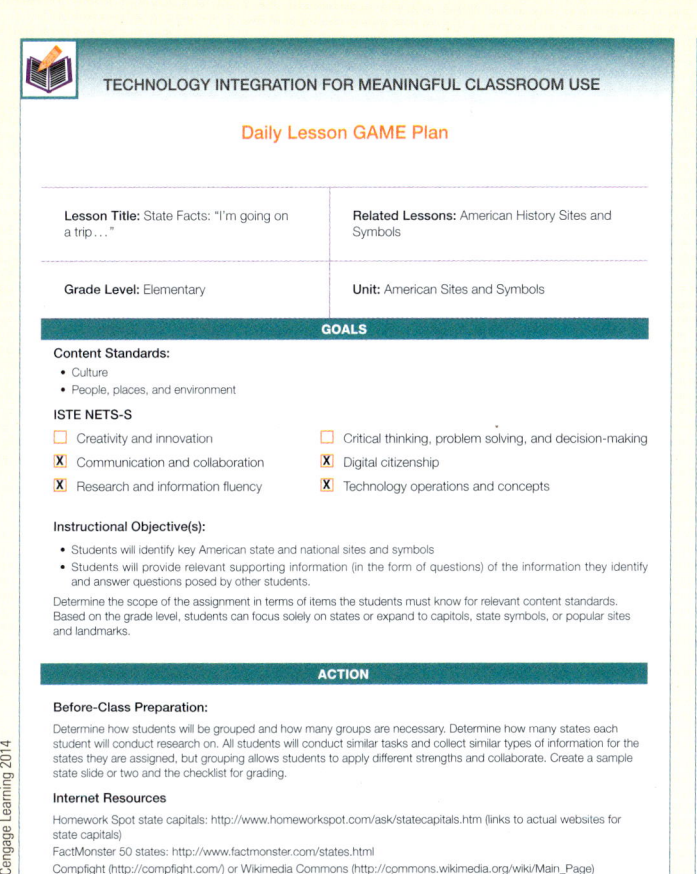

Time	Instructional Activities	Materials and Resources
5 minutes	Start the class by reciting the opening of the popular child's game, "I'm going on a trip and I'm going to bring..." to see if students have played the game before. Tell students that for their hypothetical trip, they don't have to bring rhyming items or items that begin with the same letter (some common variations) but instead are going to learn some important facts about different states that will help them determine what to pack when visiting these places. Group students as desired and assign the requisite number of states to each group. Share your state facts presentation. This may be a slide or two using presentation software. A podcast is another option.	State facts presentation Computer with projector
30 minutes	Students conduct Internet research to find the important facts and information required by relevant content standards. Students can search a variety of educational websites that provide state-specific information or visit websites from state organizations. Students collect information and relevant images for the required information and document their sources. The website Compfight allows students to search the photo-sharing site Flickr and limit their search to images under appropriate Creative Commons licensing. Wikimedia Commons has images and other relevant media also tagged with Creative Commons licenses. Students compile their information into your preferred format and must justify their selections. Presentation software works well for this activity, putting facts and images in the slide and references in the notes section. Each student can create a slide (or slides) for his or her assigned state(s), and all of the slides can be compiled into one file and shared with each student or placed on a class website.	Computers or mobile devices with Internet access Presentation or word-processing software
10–15 minutes	A slide show is created by the teacher from the individual images that have been uploaded and shown to the class. Students reflect on individual images.	Combined presentation Computer with projector

Notes: This lesson can be adapted to help students learn states, capitals, state symbols, sites and monuments, or other pertinent information about the states assigned based on relevant content standards.

MONITOR

Ongoing Assessment(s): Monitor students as they work in their groups. While all students should conduct research and create their own slides, they can rely on group members for technical, design, or other support. By working in groups, individual student choices can be assessed formatively and changed for their final slide(s) based on input from the group. Final projects are assessed based on a checklist of required elements.

The compiled presentation with slides from the whole class can be used in and outside of class to help students study the important state facts it identifies. The whole class can "take a trip" as review using the presentation, or parts of it.

Accommodations and Extensions: Consider using predetermined and bookmarked sites to help younger students find valid and appropriate information more easily. Some students may benefit from a presentation template. Depending on the skills of the students, the project can be completed using Google Earth, where students can "visit" states virtually and view pictures and movies linked to maps. Some photo-sharing sites, like Flickr, allow tags on photos, which you or your students can search or create.

As an extension, consider actually planning a trip and determine distances, travel options, and itineraries. Students can use mapping software, such as Google Maps, to suggest routes with different parameters, such as the shortest, most scenic, or a route that includes the largest number of historic sites.

This lesson has myriad opportunities for variation and accommodation, including study of different countries or even places in the solar system. Instead of creating presentations, students can create podcasts of their state information. It can, but does not have to, include images they've found and their own narration. Presentation slides can also be printed out (yes, on paper) and posted on a wall in the classroom in a rough approximation of the United States.

The ultimate accommodation would be to connect with schools in other locations and share relevant information about your own state and learn about theirs. You can connect via webconferencing through Skype in Education, ePals, or other classroom connections, or you can search the Internet for classrooms in schools in other states that might want to share via e-mail or other ways.

Back-up Plan: Important state information is, of course, available in reference books and textbooks, and students can find images in magazines.

EVALUATE AND EXTEND

Lesson Reflections and Notes: This can be a foundational lesson for review and further study of relevant state information throughout the year. Sharing the full presentation with students and their parents digitally allows them to review the information in and out of class.

A full-size version of this lesson plan appears on the CourseMate website at www.cengagebrain.com.

High School Social Studies

TECHNOLOGY INTEGRATION FOR MEANINGFUL CLASSROOM USE

Daily Lesson GAME Plan

Lesson Title: What if? Alternate Endings to the Civil War

Related Lessons: Major Events in the Civil War, Places Made Famous by the Civil War

Grade Level: High School

Unit: American Civil War

GOALS

Content Standards:
- Time, continuity, and change
- Individuals, groups, and institutions

ISTE NETS-S
- [X] Creativity and innovation
- [X] Communication and collaboration
- [X] Research and information fluency
- [X] Critical thinking, problem solving, and decision-making
- [X] Digital citizenship
- [ ] Technology operations and concepts

Instructional Objective(s):

The purpose of this lesson is to engage students more deeply in their study of conflict and to identify critical moments in history and how they shaped subsequent events. Students explore "what if" scenarios and suggest alternate endings or outcomes. This lesson uses the Civil War, specifically, but can be adapted to other conflicts throughout history. It serves as a culminating project after a unit of study on the Civil War.

ACTION

Before-Class Preparation:

Identify or create the rubric to assess the final project. The rubric should emphasize content objectives but also include some evaluation of effective communication through media. Due to the complexity of the project, it will save time to use a teacher-created or previously created rubric rather than having students create the rubric. Create handouts and identify exemplars from the Internet, DVDs, or other video resources to introduce the project.

During Class

Time	Instructional Activities	Materials and Resources
15–20 minutes	Open the class with several "what if" statements, such as: • What if Robert E. Lee had not been a Virginian? • What if John Wilkes Booth had not shot Abraham Lincoln? • What if the armies of the South had not lost at Gettysburg? All of these situations are important turning points in the Civil War. Abraham Lincoln asked Robert E. Lee, a man whom many describe as one the brightest military strategists of his time, to lead the Union army, but General Lee declined in order to lead the army associated with his home state. With many opportunities for mistakes and miscommunication, it's not unreasonable to think that John Wilkes Booth might not have been successful. And early on, the battle of Gettysburg looked like it was in the hands of the South, except for a few crucial missteps. What if these things had not happened? How might that have impacted the outcome of the war? If at all? There are many critical players and events that can be used for these scenarios. The students' assignment is to create some kind of digital product—a digital story, short video documentary, presentation, or other—investigating at least one "what if" scenario and to determine why it is plausible, the characters involved, and how it might have impacted the outcomes of the war. If available, show brief clips from a previous class or those found on the Internet, DVDs, or other video resources. Review the rubric and, if available, discuss how the examples do or do not meet the criteria.	Teacher presentation Rubric
30–45 minutes	Students can work on the project alone, in pairs, or in small groups. After deciding grouping, students select (or possibly suggest) a "what if" scenario. They collect information for their project from their studies or from new research related to: • Characters: Who are the main players in the scenario? What were their roles? How did they influence the situation? • The Events: What events led up to the defining moment for the "what if" scenario? Why were they important? • The Outcomes: What were the actual outcomes? How did they play out for the characters, the country, and how did it influence the rest of the war and the period following? • Potential Outcomes: What would have been different had the scenario not played out as it did? How would it have impacted the characters and the country? What might be different today if the event had not occurred?	Classroom materials from previous study (including textbooks, websites, and other resources) Computer with Internet access Rubric
45–60 minutes	Students create a storyboard and script for their project, using word-processing, concept-mapping, or presentation software. The storyboard should address each of the main components of the project and identify potential text, images, or links to supporting information. If working in groups, students should both contribute to the writing process and reach consensus on material to be included in the movie, such as the images, music, or sound effects they want to use.	Word-processing, concept-mapping, or presentation software
1–2 hours	Students use their preferred software, whether video-editing or presentation software, to create their final product. Each student should record part of the narration and contribute images to support the narration. Students are encouraged to add sound effects, music, and effects and transitions to their projects, but emphasis should be placed on creating accurate, high-quality content. Student projects can be uploaded to a class website or a class channel on a video-sharing site.	Computers with word-processing, concept-mapping, presentation, or video-editing software Microphones Headphones Rubric
1 class period	During the class premiere, have each student group introduce their own film. Take time to celebrate and congratulate each pair after their movie is shown. Students should be given viewing guides for each product, and discussions following each should focus on the plausibility of each groups' suggested outcomes.	Computer with speakers and projector

Notes: This lesson is based on an idea from Michael Hasley, Secondary Social Studies Specialist for Henrico County Public Schools in Virginia.

MONITOR

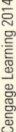

Ongoing Assessment(s): Several artifacts are created that should be monitored, such as student research notes, storyboard, and script.

Accommodations and Extensions: Some students will benefit from additional examples or even a template for their project so they can focus on the content and not the technology. Student groupings can be used as an accommodation, either organizing students by ability level so those with greater proficiency have the opportunity to face challenges, or by varied levels of proficiency, giving students different roles within a group. Despite the grouping decisions, all students should be given an opportunity conduct research, suggest outcomes, identify supporting media, and write and record some narration.

Back-up Plan: Students with limited technology proficiency or limited access can present their research findings as an oral report which can be videotaped so it can be shared online.

EVALUATE AND EXTEND

Lesson Reflections and Notes: The final movie is assessed using a rubric introduced at the beginning of the lesson. Students will be evaluated based on the accuracy of the content, describing the characters and events leading up to the scenario and the plausibility of the suggested outcomes.

A full-size version of this lesson plan appears on the CourseMate website at www.cengagebrain.com.

Technology in the Health and Physical Education Classroom

Craig P. Tacla, Ph.D., James A. Krouscas, Ph.D., and Kerry Redican, Ph.D.

Like many people, you may have decided to teach health and physical education because you are good at sports, enjoy competition, or value leading a healthy and physically active lifestyle. Teaching in this area can be enjoyable and rewarding, but you may require some guidance when working with students who don't have your same level of interest and motivation. The national standards for health (AAHE, 1995) and physical education (NASPE, 2004) clearly identify goals and objectives associated with each grade level and provide specific assessment ideas to assist teachers with the task of illustrating how their program will meet these suggested guidelines.

The health and physical education standards rarely mention technology or its use in the classroom specifically; however, teachers in this field have long used a variety of technologies to help support their teaching and promote student learning. Although the underlying goal of health and physical education has remained relatively constant

THE GAME PLAN

Content Standards

Set Goals
Learn more about the *National Standards for Health Education*, published by the American Association for Health Education (AAHE), or the *National Standards for Physical Education*, published by the National Association of Sport and Physical Education (NASPE), or the health and physical education standards for a state where you plan to seek a teaching position. Consider a variety of ways to integrate technology while addressing the health and physical education standards.

Take Action
Explore the national standards published by the AAHE and NASPE or the state standards as listed on the department of education website in the state where you plan to seek a position. Plan ways that you could meet those standards using technology to teach health and physical education.

Monitor
Did you find the information you needed? Do you need to contact the department of education for more information about where to find the health and physical education standards?

Evaluate and Extend
Discuss the plan you developed for meeting the health and physical education standards using technology with others and compare your ideas. Note the strengths and weaknesses of the various examples and incorporate the best ideas into your plan.

Health & Physical Education

over time—that of helping young people become physically fit while developing the skills and knowledge that allow them to establish and maintain a healthy lifestyle—the tools and resources available to teachers and students have evolved and expanded, just as in other disciplines (see Table S.7 for some ideas). In addition to software, online resources, data tools, and presentation software that can be found in all types of classrooms, health and physical education teachers also have access to a range of technology tools designed specifically for health and fitness, including pedometers, heart rate monitors, and digital fitness equipment.

If young people are to reap the rewards of a physically active lifestyle, they must abandon a sedentary lifestyle and embrace physical activity and movement. Technology can make a difference in getting young people (and adults) to make healthier choices, especially in the area of physical activity. Using technology can motivate students, and many technology resources are available to support better understanding of the critical components of health and physical education and how these can be made relevant to individuals. Therefore, this section describes how technology can be used by teachers to support authentic learning designed to increase physical activity among students and meet health and physical education standards.

For many health and physical education teachers, a good place to start in creating authentic instruction is the development and implementation of personal health and fitness plans. These plans can be developed for students at many grade levels and can be administered in health or physical education classrooms. The goal is to help students develop a plan that is relevant to them while addressing the major components of your curriculum, whether that be the development of motor skills, promoting physical activity, or practicing health-enhancing behaviors and reducing health risks.

A variety of technologies are available to help students develop and monitor a health or fitness plan. In order to implement this organizing activity in your health or

Table S.7 Ideas for Addressing NETS-S in the Health and Physical Education Classroom

Creativity and Innovation

Students use word-processing and presentation software to report on a personal health or fitness activity, such as recording dietary, exercise, sleep, and work patterns over a specified period. Students can use spreadsheets to track and graph lifestyle changes, such as the progress they have made using a physical fitness regimen or tracking healthy weight management.

Communication and Collaboration

Students communicate with health and fitness professionals on topics of interest, such as routinely reviewing web pages and blogs of college or professional athletes or athletic programs, investigating health issues through frequently asked questions on local and national web resources, or using an Ask an Expert feature.

Research and Information Fluency

Students use Internet resources, instructional software, or an app for a mobile device to develop a healthy personal nutrition program and monitor their daily habits, or they create a physical fitness routine to meet desired goals and record their physical activity in an app, log, or website.

Critical Thinking, Problem Solving, and Decision-Making

Students use digital video to capture and analyze their own as well as team performances in physical activities. For example, students participating in golf or tennis can analyze their swings, while students participating in team performances can evaluate the effectiveness of tactics and strategies during team play.

Digital Citizenship

Students use technology to develop, monitor, and support a healthy and fit lifestyle, including researching the principles of fitness or activities and sports of interest, monitoring their own nutritional habits, or using exercise equipment to reach personal health and fitness goals.

Technology Operations and Concepts

Students use a range of technology tools designed to support sport and fitness, including heart monitors, pedometers, stethoscopes, and electronic blood-pressure devices, in addition to instructional software.

physical education classroom, your students will 1) gather information to create personal health or fitness goals, 2) develop and implement a plan with strategies for meeting personal goals, and 3) monitor or evaluate the success of their plans.

Perhaps the most helpful information-gathering tool is the Internet. Never before has such a wealth of health and fitness information been freely available from reliable sources. Colleges and universities, government organizations, and well-known health and fitness organizations provide web-based information in a full range of health and fitness areas that your students can tap into to guide the development of their personal plans.

Once students have gathered general information about health and fitness, they'll need some personal information in order to design and implement relevant, realistic goals. They can utilize one or more health assessment technologies just for this purpose. Health assessment technologies primarily come in two forms: electronic assessment devices and assessment screening software. Weight management is an issue with which many children and young adults grapple. Online or app-based calorie calculators, body-mass-index calculators, and exercise calculators can help your students form goals for appropriate weight management using their own data. Pedometers can be used to help students set realistic fitness goals that are based on their current fitness levels. Individualized fitness or activity goal setting is made possible because many pedometers not only count steps but are now able to convert steps into distance and caloric expenditure. Others have the capability to record activity time. The increased functionality requires students to input personalized information such as weight and/or length of step, but these recent advances in pedometers open a variety of instructional opportunities never before realized by physical educators.

There are also many affordable, noninvasive forms of assessment technology available for use in the K-12 classroom. Some of these include sphygmomanometers (blood-pressure cuffs), thermometers, bioelectrical impedance devices, and breathalyzers. These devices are relatively inexpensive, and one device can be used by multiple students if the learning activity is carefully developed and implemented. It must be noted that the intention is not to diagnose but to help students learn how to gather important physiological information to determine personal health and physical statistics (see Figure S.12). So, the real focus here is the process, not the outcome.

Figure S.12
Elementary school pupils undertake a physical sports task and log the results into a laptop computer.

Health & Physical Education

With the acquisition of digital cameras, digital video-editing software, and mobile devices, teachers are beginning to utilize digital video as a way to engage their students in alternative forms of reflective assignments and self-evaluation projects (Fiorentino, 2004). Some of the reported benefits of using video include the ability to review performance immediately, zoom in or focus on skills or critical sections of the body during performance, vary camera angles to address individual or group performance, and simply play the video over and over (Trinigy & Annesi, 1996). Video can be used to help introduce new skills, from discrete practice drills to their strategic application in games or team events, as well as to assess student performance. Video can be especially helpful to demonstrate activities or skills that take place in unusual settings, such as aquatic activities or those that occur outside (Anderson, Mikat, & Martinez, 2001).

As an alternative to digital video, digital photography is another way for many schools to gain some of the benefits described above (see Figure S.13). Still photos of small groups of students can be included in journals, assessment activities, or rubrics, or used as the impetus for discussion. Teachers can create digital libraries or playbooks that contain both still images and scanned or electronically created diagrams that highlight critical features of a play in a team sport. A good recommendation is to take pictures of small groups rather than individuals. Individuals within the group can still assess their own performance, but the images of the other students in the photograph provide additional opportunities for reflection and comparison.

This section has presented a small sample of the various forms of technology you can use in your teaching. The technologies presented here have focused primarily on use in the physical education classroom, but many of the activities and related applications mentioned can be utilized in health programs as well. In order to accomplish the goal of preparing competent, proficient, and active adults, consider using the technological tools available to support health and physical education and continue to monitor and evaluate future technologies that hold the potential to enhance student and teacher performance.

Figure S.13
Students can take digital photographs of themselves and classmates to record performances of many different skills.

References

American Association for Health Education (AAHE). (1995). *National health education standards: Achieving health literacy.* New York: Joint Committee on National Health Standards.

Anderson, M., Mikat, R. P., & Martinez, R. (2001). Digital video production in physical education and athletics. *Journal of Physical Education, Recreation, and Dance, 72*(6), 19–21.

Fiorentino, L. H. (2004). Digital video assignments: Focusing a new lens on teacher preparation programs. *Journal of Physical Education, Recreation, and Dance, 75*(5), 47–54.

National Association for Sport and Physical Education (NASPE). (2004). *Moving into the future: National standards for physical education* (2nd ed.). Reston, VA: Author.

Trinigy, J., & Annesi, J. (1996). Coaching with video. *Strategies, 9*(3), 23–25.

Lesson Plans for Health/Physical Education

Elementary Health/Physical Education

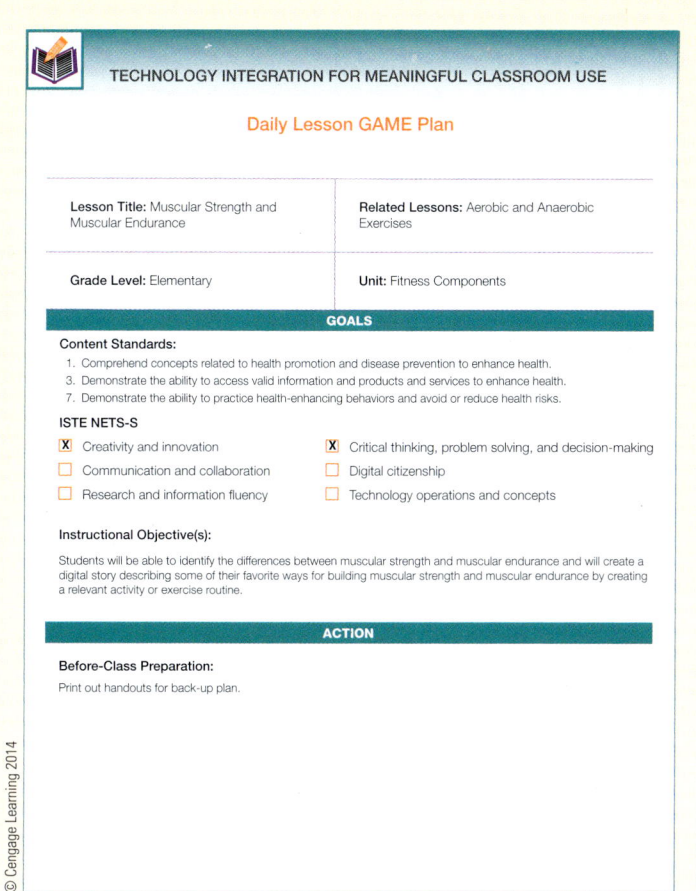

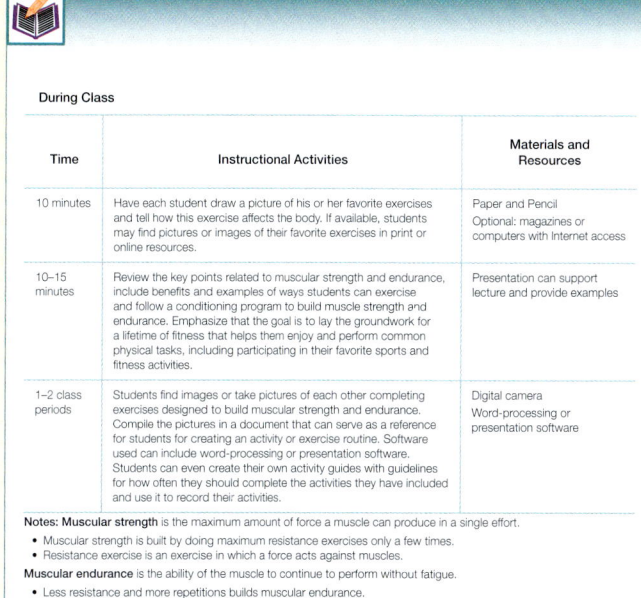

Health & Physical Education

TECHNOLOGY INTEGRATION FOR MEANINGFUL CLASSROOM USE

Daily Lesson GAME Plan

Lesson Title: Muscular Strength and Muscular Endurance

Related Lessons: Aerobic and Anaerobic Exercises

Grade Level: Elementary

Unit: Fitness Components

GOALS

Content Standards:
1. Comprehend concepts related to health promotion and disease prevention to enhance health.
3. Demonstrate the ability to access valid information and products and services to enhance health.
7. Demonstrate the ability to practice health-enhancing behaviors and avoid or reduce health risks.

ISTE NETS-S
- [X] Creativity and innovation
- [X] Critical thinking, problem solving, and decision-making
- [ ] Communication and collaboration
- [ ] Digital citizenship
- [ ] Research and information fluency
- [ ] Technology operations and concepts

Instructional Objective(s):
Students will be able to identify the differences between muscular strength and muscular endurance and will create a digital story describing some of their favorite ways for building muscular strength and muscular endurance by creating a relevant activity or exercise routine.

ACTION

Before-Class Preparation:
Print out handouts for back-up plan.

During Class

Time	Instructional Activities	Materials and Resources
10 minutes	Have each student draw a picture of his or her favorite exercises and tell how this exercise affects the body. If available, students may find pictures or images of their favorite exercises in print or online resources.	Paper and Pencil. Optional: magazines or computers with Internet access
10–15 minutes	Review the key points related to muscular strength and endurance, include benefits and examples of ways students can exercise and follow a conditioning program to build muscle strength and endurance. Emphasize that the goal is to lay the groundwork for a lifetime of fitness that helps them enjoy and perform common physical tasks, including participating in their favorite sports and fitness activities.	Presentation can support lecture and provide examples
1–2 class periods	Students find images or take pictures of each other completing exercises designed to build muscular strength and endurance. Compile the pictures in a document that can serve as a reference for students for creating an activity or exercise routine. Software used can include word-processing or presentation software. Students can even create their own activity guides with guidelines for how often they should complete the activities they have included and use it to record their activities.	Digital camera. Word-processing or presentation software

Notes: **Muscular strength** is the maximum amount of force a muscle can produce in a single effort.
- Muscular strength is built by doing maximum resistance exercises only a few times.
- Resistance exercise is an exercise in which a force acts against muscles.

Muscular endurance is the ability of the muscle to continue to perform without fatigue.
- Less resistance and more repetitions builds muscular endurance.

Benefits:
- Helps a person perform everyday tasks, such as carrying schoolbooks, climbing stairs, and lifting objects.
- Helps maintain correct posture.
- Reduces the risk of low back pain.
- Reduces the risk of being injured.
- Helps a person enjoy physical activities without tiring.
- Improves body composition by increasing muscle mass and decreasing fat tissue.
- Improves self-image because muscles are firm and the body is toned.
- Keeps bone dense and strong.
- Make the surface of joints less susceptible to injury.

Muscular strength and muscular endurance are built through a conditioning program that may use weights but can also include exercises such as sit-ups, push-ups, etc. Muscular strength and endurance are kept through a continuous program, such as training two to three days a week.

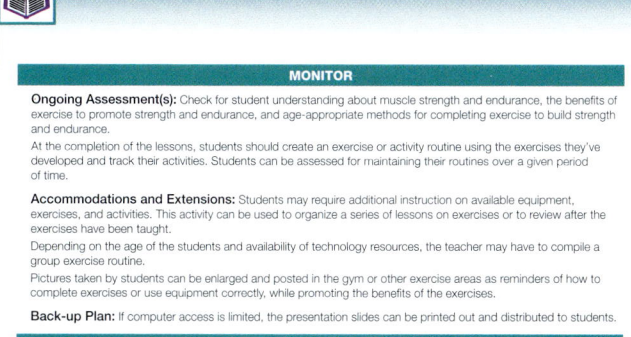

MONITOR

Ongoing Assessment(s): Check for student understanding about muscle strength and endurance, the benefits of exercise to promote strength and endurance, and age-appropriate methods for completing exercise to build strength and endurance.

At the completion of the lessons, students should create an exercise or activity routine using the exercises they've developed and track their activities. Students can be assessed for maintaining their routines over a given period of time.

Accommodations and Extensions: Students may require additional instruction on available equipment, exercises, and activities. This activity can be used to organize a series of lessons on exercises or to review after the exercises have been taught.

Depending on the age of the students and availability of technology resources, the teacher may have to compile a group exercise routine.

Pictures taken by students can be enlarged and posted in the gym or other exercise areas as reminders of how to complete exercises or use equipment correctly, while promoting the benefits of the exercises.

Back-up Plan: If computer access is limited, the presentation slides can be printed out and distributed to students.

EVALUATE AND EXTEND

Lesson Reflections and Notes: Seek permission from parents to take pictures of students, especially if used for posters or other public display.

A full-size version of this lesson plan appears on the CourseMate website at www.cengagebrain.com.

Middle Grades Health/Physical Education

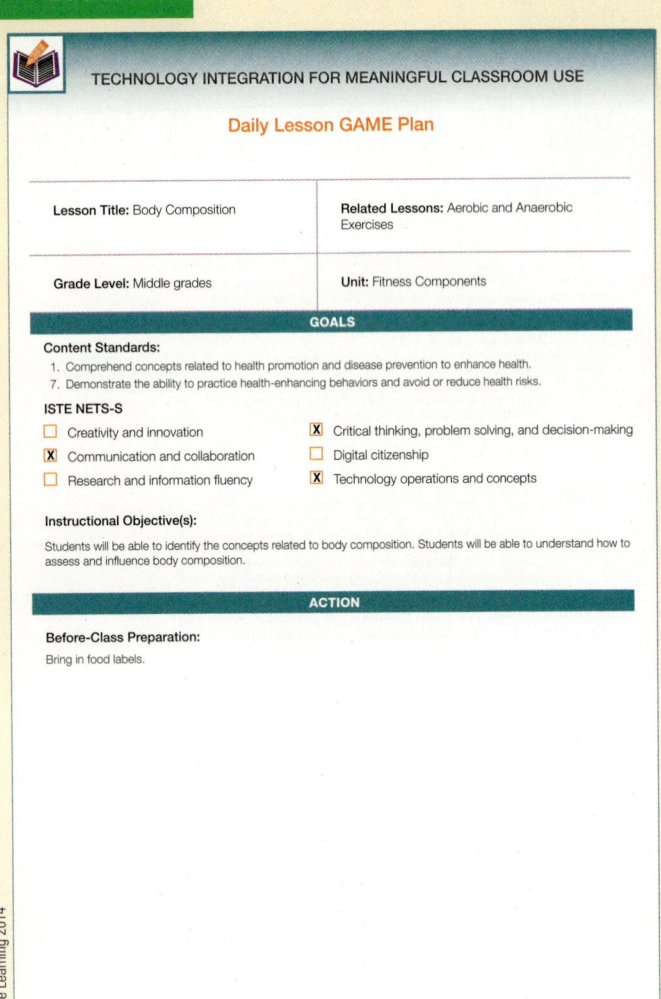

Health & Physical Education

TECHNOLOGY INTEGRATION FOR MEANINGFUL CLASSROOM USE

Daily Lesson GAME Plan

Lesson Title: Body Composition
Related Lessons: Aerobic and Anaerobic Exercises

Grade Level: Middle grades
Unit: Fitness Components

GOALS

Content Standards:
1. Comprehend concepts related to health promotion and disease prevention to enhance health.
7. Demonstrate the ability to practice health-enhancing behaviors and avoid or reduce health risks.

ISTE NETS-S
- [ ] Creativity and innovation
- [X] Critical thinking, problem solving, and decision-making
- [X] Communication and collaboration
- [ ] Digital citizenship
- [ ] Research and information fluency
- [X] Technology operations and concepts

Instructional Objective(s):
Students will be able to identify the concepts related to body composition. Students will be able to understand how to assess and influence body composition.

ACTION

Before-Class Preparation:
Bring in food labels.

During Class

Time	Instructional Activities	Materials and Resources
5–10 minutes	Capture students' questions, concerns, assumptions, or stereotypes related to being overweight or obese using a KWHL chart or concept-mapping software. Collect and quickly review responses with students at the end of allotted time.	K or concept-mapping software
10 minutes	Define and discuss components of body composition (e.g., muscle, bone, fat, and other tissue that make up the body). Discuss diseases related to being overweight or obese (e.g., cardiovascular disease, type 1 or type 2 diabetes, etc.). Discuss current statistics related to rate of obesity and adolescent obesity. Address specific questions, concerns, assumptions, or stereotypes identified by students during introductory activity.	Presentation software can support lecture and provide images of diseases
10 minutes	Discuss healthy eating behaviors as a component to disease prevention. Emphasize the connection to appropriate fuel sources for the human body and the importance of leading a physically active lifestyle.	Presentation can support lecture and provide images of muscle, bone, and fat
15 minutes	Hand out and discuss the components of food labels (e.g., serving size, calories, total fat, saturated fat, etc.).	Option: Have students find food labels or food manufacturers' websites online
1–2 class periods	Students will bring in labels from the foods they eat. Compile these food labels and have students input data into online calorie calculators and exercise calculators. Students can use presentation software to discuss how their bodies use the various types of food as fuel and how many calories are expended during the various moderate to vigorous activities they enjoy.	Presentation software Calorie calculator website Exercise calculator website or software

Notes: **Body Composition** describes the percentages of fat, bone, and muscle in human bodies.
Diseases Related to Being Overweight or Obese
Cardiovascular Disease: According to the American Heart Association, buildup of plaque on the arteries (atherosclerosis), partly as a result of high cholesterol and high fat diet, is a leading cause for cardiovascular diseases.
Type 2 Diabetes Mellitus: It is the most common form of diabetes, in which either the body does not produce enough insulin or the cells ignore the insulin. Insulin is necessary for the body to be able to use glucose for energy.
Components of Food Labels
Serving size of a food product is a confusing term, as it is found both on the Food Pyramid and on Nutrition Labels and has two related but different meanings. Make sure to explain both definitions to your students.
Calorie is a unit of food energy. In nutrition terms, the word calorie is used instead of the more precise scientific term kilocalorie which represents the amount of energy required to raise the temperature of a liter of water one degree centigrade at sea level.
Total fat is the number of fat grams contained in one serving of the food. Fat is an important nutrient that your body uses for growth and development, but you don't want to eat too much. The different kinds of fat, such as saturated, unsaturated, and trans fat, are listed separately on the label.
Cholesterol and sodium numbers tell you how much cholesterol and sodium (salt) are in a single serving of the food. Too much cholesterol can lead to heart disease. You call it salt, but the label calls it sodium; either way too much can lead to high blood pressure, and uncontrolled high blood pressure can lead to stroke, heart attack, heart failure, or kidney failure.
Total carbohydrate tells you how many carbohydrate grams are in one serving of food. Carbohydrates are your body's primary source of energy. This total is broken down into grams of sugar and grams of dietary fiber.
Protein tells you how much protein you get from a single serving of the food. Your body needs protein to build and repair essential parts of the body, such as muscles, blood, and organs.
Vitamins and minerals lists the amounts of vitamins and minerals in a serving of food. Two especially important and commonly listed vitamins are vitamins A and C. Each amount is given as a percent daily value. Other vitamins may be listed on some labels as well. Also listed are important minerals that are in a serving of the food. Again, each amount is given as a percent of daily value.

MONITOR

Ongoing Assessment(s): Check for student understanding about components of body composition and the dangers associated with being overweight or obese. At the completion of the lessons, students should be able to determine how various food sources affect their bodies and the importance of leading a healthy, active lifestyle.

Accommodations and Extensions: Students may require additional instruction on components of health-related fitness. Depending on the age of the students and availability of technological resources, the teacher may have to compile supplementary instructional materials.

Back-up Plan: Students can conduct the activity with paper and pencil and calculators, but more time should be allotted.

EVALUATE AND EXTEND

Lesson Reflections and Notes: In order to address the topic of body composition with middle school students, a positive learning environment must be established. Students must respect the feelings of others when discussing such a personal subject.

A full-size version of this lesson plan appears on the CourseMate website at www.cengagebrain.com.

Technology in the Visual-Arts Classroom

Tammy McGraw, Ed.D, and Nancy Lampert, Ed.D.

Technology's impact on the visual arts and art education is not a recent phenomenon. Throughout history, technology has shaped the tools, techniques, and media of creative expression and visual representation. The debate surrounding 17th-century Dutch master Johannes Vermeer's alleged use of the camera obscura, an early optical device that projected an image onto a screen, is not unlike current debates about digitally enhancing photographs. Each new technology challenges people to reconsider long-held beliefs about art and the production of art. As an art educator, you and your students will be challenged constantly with new technologies, so it's important to analyze each new technology carefully and embrace the ones that can enhance student learning, improve instructional practice, or support meaningful student assessment. Technology will continue to change rapidly; however, just like Vermeer's alleged use of the camera obscura, technology always will play a part—occasionally controversial—in the world of art. The goal of art educators is to help students understand the different technologies that can maximize the learning experience and produce high-quality art. (See Table S.8. for some ideas)

Six national content standards for the visual arts are applied across grades K-12, specifying what students should know and be able to do in the visual arts (National Art Education Association, 1994). Related achievement standards denote students' expected understandings and proficiencies at the completion of grades 4, 8, and 12.

THE GAME PLAN

Content Standards

Set Goals
Learn more about the *National Visual Arts Standards* published by the National Art Education Association or the visual arts standards for a state where you plan to seek a teaching position. Consider a variety of ways to integrate technology while addressing the visual arts standards.

Take Action
Explore the national standards published by the National Art Education Association or the state standards as listed on the department of education website in the state where you plan to seek a position. Plan ways that you could meet those standards using technology in the visual arts classroom.

Monitor
Did you find the information you needed? Do you need to contact the department of education for more information about where to find the visual arts standards?

Evaluate and Extend
Discuss the plan you developed for meeting the visual arts standards using technology with others and compare your ideas. Note the strengths and weaknesses of the various examples and incorporate the best ideas into your plan.

Visual Arts

Significantly, these standards focus only on student-learning *outcomes*. They do not provide a roadmap for achieving these results or limit the technologies that can be used; instead, they challenge educators to explore current and emerging technologies that can expand visual-arts learning and creative expression.

Our society seems to be inundated with image-based information. This elevates the importance of visual literacy as a fundamental part of a child's education and calls for heightened critical awareness of visual culture through production. Much of the visual media today is technological—the Internet, television, music videos, videogames, and so forth. Consequently, K-12 art students often are interested in producing their own artwork, videos, websites, and animations. Production experience increases students' ability to view, understand, analyze, and interpret the pervasive visual media that surrounds them.

Technology has tremendous potential to expand what constitutes fundamental skills and basic techniques in an art classroom. Technical execution becomes less of a barrier when students can use vector-based applications, such as Adobe Illustrator, to generate a perfect circle, produce a gradient without effort, or convert any scanned image into an editable and scalable vector path. Drawing software empowers students

Table S.8 Ideas for Addressing NETS-S in the Visual-Arts Classroom

Creativity and Innovation
A student researches the life and work of Marc Chagall for a video essay project. She taps a variety of disks and the web to obtain images depicting Chagall, his work, and life in the 20th century. Since Chagall was born in Russia, she downloads music by 20th-century Russian composer Sergei Prokofiev from an online music site. She narrates the three-minute video, describing Chagall's life, his work, and how his work compares to her own art. Now feeling that she really understands Chagall and his art, she returns to his painting, the *Green Violinist*, and uses a 2-D animation program to bring the violinist to life—dancing to a tune that she composed in GarageBand and posts her animated short online.

Communication and Collaboration
Art students create a class website that features student artwork, commentary, and a local arts calendar. The site has downloadable print publications, such as the school newsletter produced with desktop-publishing software. Three times a year, students invite a visual-arts professional to participate in a live chat so students can learn more about various careers in the visual arts.

Research and Information Fluency
Elementary art students create a mural at the entrance of their new school, but there is much debate about what should be painted. Their teacher works with the students to design a simple survey they will administer to other students and staff. The students use a spreadsheet application to collect and analyze the data, creating charts for a school-wide presentation.

Critical Thinking, Problem Solving, and Decision-Making
A local parent-teacher organization sponsors an animation workshop for sixth-grade students. The workshop is conducted by an organization that works with students to produce animated public-service announcements. The students choose tobacco use and prevention as a topic. They consult various sources, including the local chapter of the American Cancer Society, for information. Using a variety of traditional and digital tools and media, each team creates a 30-second animated public-service announcement.

Digital Citizenship
A group of middle-school art students develop a website on contemporary art and identify several virtual museum collections they incorporate. They search for information on copyright and fair use to determine if they can link directly to a Bruce Nauman work at the Art Institute of Chicago. The museum does not permit framing, but its policy on linking is unclear. After searching the web for typical agreements on linking, they e-mail the Art Institute's webmaster, requesting permission to link to the image.

Technology Operations and Concepts
An art student takes a photograph of a landscape with a digital camera and uploads the image to a desktop computer system. Using image-editing software, he manipulates the image to create a surrealistic landscape. He saves and uploads the image to his web-based portfolio. He prints a finished copy for display in the school and e-mails it to his home computer.

to create perspective drawings with greater complexity and accuracy than they might be able to accomplish manually. With paint programs, K-12 students can study color theory without mixing paint; create color wheels and charts showing primary, secondary, and tertiary colors; and overlay semitransparent digital colors to simulate color mixing. Animation software can help students create paths and transitions; similarly, page-layout applications can assist them with placing page elements consistently. Although technology eliminates some barriers related to technical execution, it does not replace knowledge, talent, and contextual understanding.

Before digital technology, art teachers were limited to whatever photographic slides, posters, and images in books they could locate. Now, they and their students can search the Internet for countless images to be viewed on display devices varying from computer monitors to data projectors. For example, imagine a discussion about the aesthetics of whether functional forms, such as vessels, should be considered art, craft, or both. The students instantly can search a wealth of digital images of vessels—from ancient and contemporary cultures all over the world—to aid their discussion.

Image-manipulation programs support new forms of visual exploration. They include the ability to add and delete individual layers of information (e.g., graphic elements, text, background images, etc.) without starting from scratch and can encourage learners to experiment with multiple options before committing to a course of action. This promotes creativity, flexibility, and a willingness to try various solutions. The history palette in these programs enables learners to review each action carefully and undo those actions at a precise point in the development of their work. These programs also help students study and manipulate lighting effects far beyond what art classes had been able to do with natural light and spotlighting. Scanning software, when used in conjunction with image-manipulation programs, lets students create digital compositions of original images without altering them, broadening the range of materials students have to work with.

Advances in video production present unique opportunities for learners to exercise autonomy over their own learning (see Figure S.14). Affordable digital video cameras and even some mobile devices are capable of producing video of a sufficient quality. Inexpensive and easy-to-use video-editing programs enable learners to import video

Figure S.14
Digital video is within the grasp of many art students.

Visual Arts

clips and still images, edit them, insert titles, create transitions and special effects, and export them for distribution in a variety of formats, including DVD or the web.

New technologies have had a tremendous impact on the social factors that influence visual-arts learning. Networked technologies have changed learners' social interactions, interpersonal relations, and communication practices. These technologies can support many of the authentic instructional methods addressed in Chapter 3, such as supporting the work of collaborative workgroups, helping students explore the driving question in a problem-based learning activity, or supporting inquiry and discovery. The Internet provides unlimited opportunities for finding exemplars from artists and museums across the globe and communicating with other artists and students of art.

Perhaps the web's most profound impact upon learning is the capability of displaying and sharing artwork on a worldwide stage. Desktop-publishing software and web-publishing software, including blogs and other services with easy-to-use interfaces, have simplified the production and distribution of classroom products while greatly expanding students' communication and design capabilities. Students of every age can maintain online portfolios at little or no cost. The web can also facilitate sharing of artwork created with traditional media.

Photo management tools, such as Flickr and Picasa, are becoming increasingly sophisticated in how they enable users to organize and share images and offer a good model for supporting communities of learners drawn from more popular social-networking sites, like Facebook. These sites go beyond merely sharing photos on the Internet by employing tools that can support online communities. For example, users attach comments or tags to describe their photos, as do others who view those photos. The resulting metadata make it much easier to find and share the images with family and friends, as well as others who possess similar interests.

The benefits of certain tools for the visual-arts classroom—such as graphics tablets (see Figure S.15), large flat-panel displays, digital cameras, and color printers—are apparent because they support the highly visual nature of art activities, but pervasive technologies such as cell phones and other mobile devices also hold creative potential. Cell phones and tablet computers that can capture and display digital images are becoming standard gear for many young people. New media offer extraordinary opportunities for personal expression and learning.

Perhaps most significantly, these brief examples have underscored the importance of evaluating the potential of each new technology for enhancing student learning, improving instructional practice, and supporting meaningful student assessment within the visual-arts classroom.

Figure S.15
Students in the visual arts classroom can benefit from a variety of technologies, such as graphics tablets with a stylus, slide scanners, and large displays.

Reference

National Art Education Association. (1994). *The national visual arts standards*. Reston, VA: Author.

Lesson Plans for Visual Arts
Middle Grades Visual Arts

TECHNOLOGY INTEGRATION FOR MEANINGFUL CLASSROOM USE

Daily Lesson GAME Plan

Lesson Title: Ad Campaign

Related Lessons: Elements of Design

Grade Level: Middle grades

Unit: Major Artists

GOALS

Content Standards:
1. Understand and apply media, techniques, and processes
2. Know art structures (elements and principles) and art functions
3. Choose and evaluate ideas, subjects, and symbols
5. Reflect upon and assess art

ISTE NETS-S
- [X] Creativity and innovation
- [X] Communication and collaboration
- [X] Research and information fluency
- [X] Critical thinking, problem solving, and decision-making
- [X] Digital citizenship
- [X] Technology operations and concepts

Instructional Objective(s):
Students research artists to determine information about their lives, artistic output, characteristics of style, and influences and then create an ad campaign to promote their artists. Students select one piece of work by the artist to focus their research. Students create a logo and one-page ad campaign with the intention of "marketing" the artwork and artist to other students.

ACTION

Before-Class Preparation:
If time permits prior to class, create a "sample" marketing advertisement for an artist and artwork of your choosing. Otherwise, make a selection and use it to focus your opening discussion.

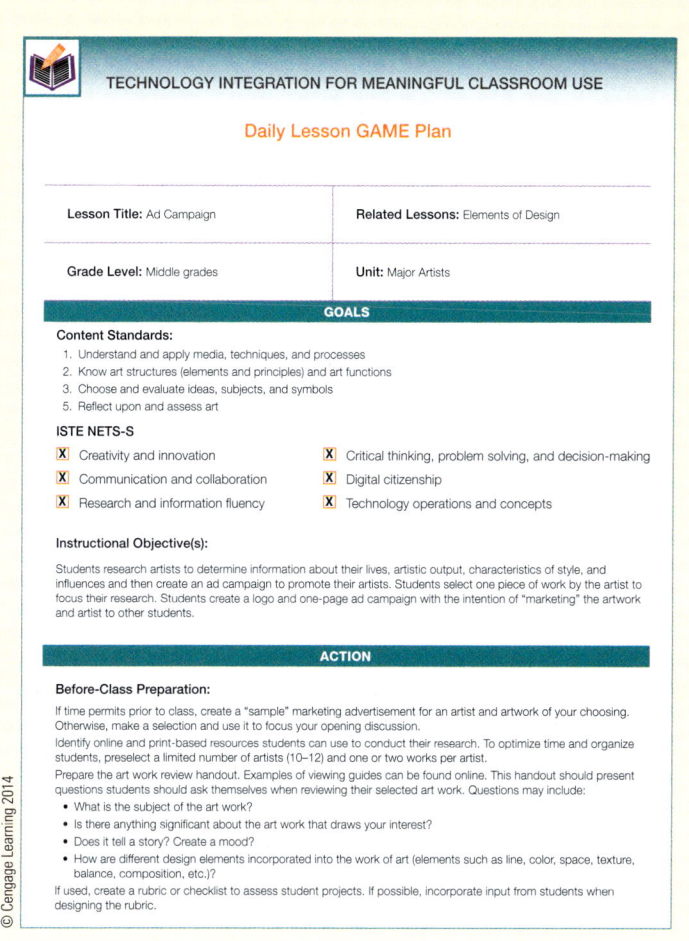

Identify online and print-based resources students can use to conduct their research. To optimize time and organize students, preselect a limited number of artists (10–12) and one or two works per artist.

Prepare the art work review handout. Examples of viewing guides can be found online. This handout should present questions students should ask themselves when reviewing their selected art work. Questions may include:
- What is the subject of the art work?
- Is there anything significant about the art work that draws your interest?
- Does it tell a story? Create a mood?
- How are different design elements incorporated into the work of art (elements such as line, color, space, texture, balance, composition, etc.)?

If used, create a rubric or checklist to assess student projects. If possible, incorporate input from students when designing the rubric.

During Class

Time	Instructional Activities	Materials and Resources
15–20 minutes	Using your sample advertisement or selected art work, conduct a mock "marketing presentation" as if your students were prospective design clients. Using your handout as a guide, discuss design elements with your students and how these may represent or relate to the artist and work of art you are presenting. Determine elements of the art work that most appeal to the students in the class.	Sample marketing presentation or work of art Museum websites
1–2 class periods	In pairs, students select (or are assigned) an artist and art work to research. Students collect and record research about the artist using journaling, word-processing, or other software, citing all resources. From their research, they compile lists of 7–10 pertinent facts about the artist and the art work. Students also review their artwork using the art work review handout. Responses are recorded and stored with their research notes	Museum or art-related websites Journaling or word-processing software Art work review handout
1–2 class periods	Students create a logo and one-page "marketing presentation" to share with the class. Presentations should be digitized but do not have to use only digital materials, perhaps creating 3-D displays that can be photographed with a digital camera.	Drawing or image-editing software. Word-processing or presentation software can also be used. Other art supplies Optional: Scanner or digital camera
1 class period	Students present their designs to the rest of the class and can post them on a class website or blog. They should describe how their designs best match the lists of facts they found in their research as well as how they relate to their artwork selections. Students should include their lists of facts and references. Students in the class should provide feedback on the "marketing campaign."	Student projects

Notes: Student projects are digitized to include in portfolios or on class websites.

MONITOR

Ongoing Assessment(s): Monitor student research to ensure students are finding appropriate information. Collect and review their final fact list and references, and completed artwork review handouts. The final products are best assessed through the use of a rubric.

Accommodations and Extensions: Students with requisite background knowledge on art and artists may be allowed to select their own subjects and artwork. Others may need explicit instruction and fewer choices.

Back-up Plan: Technology facilitates this lesson but print materials and nondigital art materials can be used to complete the lesson.

EVALUATE AND EXTEND

Lesson Reflections and Notes: In some classes, students may be able to provide feedback by completing rubrics for completed projects. In others, this type of feedback may best be handled through a teacher-led group discussion.

A full-size version of this lesson plan appears on the CourseMate website at www.cengagebrain.com.

High School Visual Arts

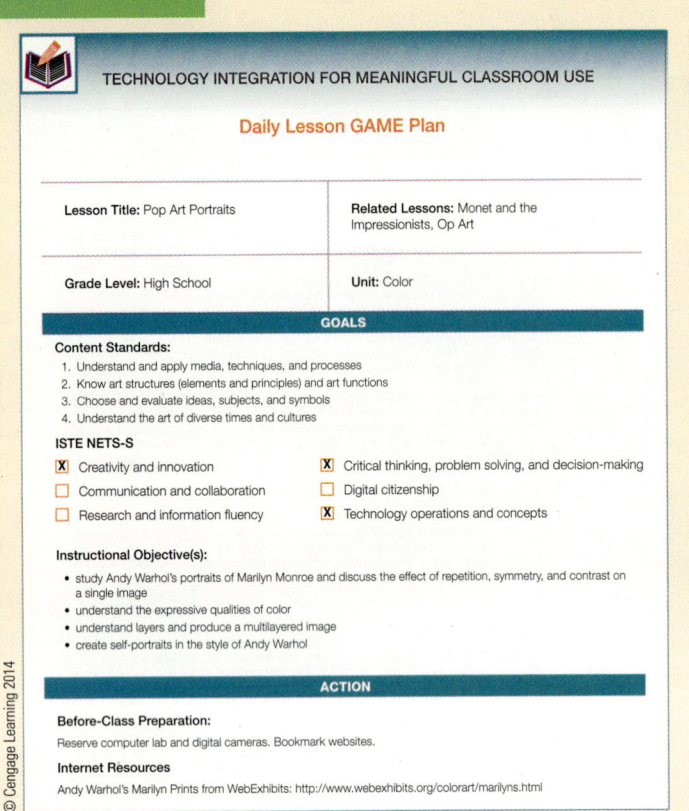

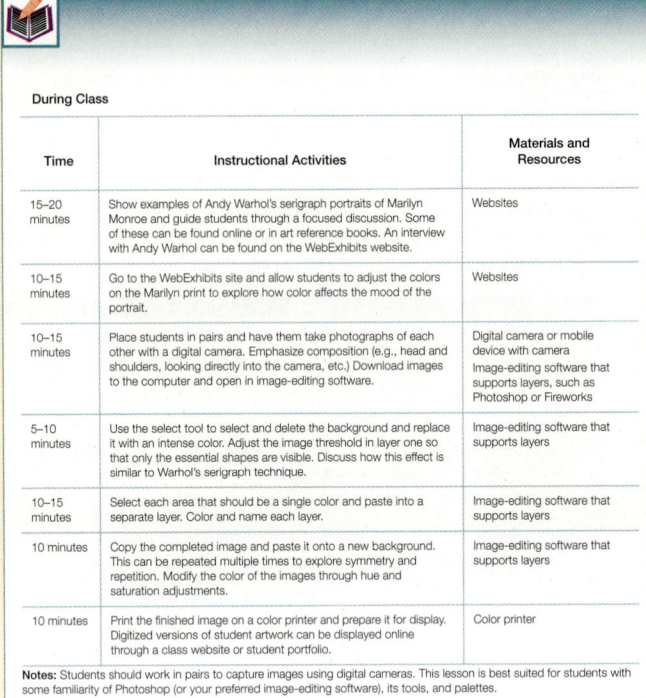

TECHNOLOGY INTEGRATION FOR MEANINGFUL CLASSROOM USE

Daily Lesson GAME Plan

Lesson Title: Pop Art Portraits

Related Lessons: Monet and the Impressionists, Op Art

Grade Level: High School

Unit: Color

GOALS

Content Standards:
1. Understand and apply media, techniques, and processes
2. Know art structures (elements and principles) and art functions
3. Choose and evaluate ideas, subjects, and symbols
4. Understand the art of diverse times and cultures

ISTE NETS-S

- [X] Creativity and innovation
- [ ] Communication and collaboration
- [ ] Research and information fluency
- [X] Critical thinking, problem solving, and decision-making
- [ ] Digital citizenship
- [X] Technology operations and concepts

Instructional Objective(s):
- study Andy Warhol's portraits of Marilyn Monroe and discuss the effect of repetition, symmetry, and contrast on a single image
- understand the expressive qualities of color
- understand layers and produce a multilayered image
- create self-portraits in the style of Andy Warhol

ACTION

Before-Class Preparation:
Reserve computer lab and digital cameras. Bookmark websites.

Internet Resources
Andy Warhol's Marilyn Prints from WebExhibits: http://www.webexhibits.org/colorart/marilyns.html

During Class

Time	Instructional Activities	Materials and Resources
15–20 minutes	Show examples of Andy Warhol's serigraph portraits of Marilyn Monroe and guide students through a focused discussion. Some of these can be found online or in art reference books. An interview with Andy Warhol can be found on the WebExhibits website.	Websites
10–15 minutes	Go to the WebExhibits site and allow students to adjust the colors on the Marilyn print to explore how color affects the mood of the portrait.	Websites
10–15 minutes	Place students in pairs and have them take photographs of each other with a digital camera. Emphasize composition (e.g., head and shoulders, looking directly into the camera, etc.) Download images to the computer and open in image-editing software.	Digital camera or mobile device with camera; Image-editing software that supports layers, such as Photoshop or Fireworks
5–10 minutes	Use the select tool to select and delete the background and replace it with an intense color. Adjust the image threshold in layer one so that only the essential shapes are visible. Discuss how this effect is similar to Warhol's serigraph technique.	Image-editing software that supports layers
10–15 minutes	Select each area that should be a single color and paste into a separate layer. Color and name each layer.	Image-editing software that supports layers
10 minutes	Copy the completed image and paste it onto a new background. This can be repeated multiple times to explore symmetry and repetition. Modify the color of the images through hue and saturation adjustments.	Image-editing software that supports layers
10 minutes	Print the finished image on a color printer and prepare it for display. Digitized versions of student artwork can be displayed online through a class website or student portfolio.	Color printer

Notes: Students should work in pairs to capture images using digital cameras. This lesson is best suited for students with some familiarity of Photoshop (or your preferred image-editing software), its tools, and palettes.

MONITOR

Ongoing Assessment(s): Check to see that students are working in layers and can use the tools to manipulate the images as required (e.g., threshold, hue, and saturation) to create the desired mood/effect.

Accommodations and Extensions: Students with limited proficiency may benefit from using effects built into some image-capture programs, such as the "Pop Art" effect in Photo Booth, or by using pop art apps for mobile devices.
Have students consider how they might use similar tools and techniques to create a portrait in the style of pop artist, Roy Lichtenstein. What processes would be similar? What would be different?

Back-up Plan: If the technology fails, students can use traditional art supplies to plan the color scheme for their portraits.

EVALUATE AND EXTEND

Lesson Reflections and Notes: Final evaluation should include an evaluation of the effective and accurate use of the software. Students should justify final color choices and may present other combinations they tried but discarded. You can conduct a discussion with the class on the characteristics of portraits that make good settings for this treatment.

A full-size version of this lesson plan appears on the CourseMate website at www.cengagebrain.com.

Technology in the Music Classroom

John D. Ross, Ph.D.

Music

Many helpful music-specific technologies that support student and professional musicians are also available for use in music classrooms (see Table S.9 for some ideas). Essential tools for all musicians, such as metronomes and tuners, went digital decades ago. Students interested in music theory and history have at their disposal a range of information resources on disks and online. These resources have the benefit of providing students with examples of music from cultures and locations from around the world that were previously very limited, exposing students to many new genres and styles. Software is also available for learning to read, compose, and arrange music, as well as developing sight-singing and ear-training skills. Even the world of marching bands took a digital step forward with the development of software for drill design that includes animation and three-dimensional views of patterns of motion. And finally, a multitude of digital instruments are used not only in classrooms, but also on stages across the world by students and professionals alike.

The national content standards for music (MENC, 1994) are global statements describing music skills that students at all grades should be able to do, generally related to: 1) performing by singing or on instruments; 2) writing, composing, and improvising music; and 3) analyzing and evaluating music, especially in relation to history, culture, and other disciplines. They should be addressed in both general and specialized music classrooms for students at appropriate age-, grade-, and ability levels and all are

THE GAME PLAN

Content Standards

Set Goals
Learn more about the *National Content Standards for Music* developed by the Consortium of National Arts Education Associations or the music standards for a state where you plan to seek a teaching position. Consider a variety of ways to integrate technology while addressing the music standards.

Take Action
Explore the national standards published by the Consortium of National Arts Education Associations or the state standards as listed on the department of education website in the state where you plan to seek a position. Plan ways that you could meet those standards using technology in the music classroom.

Monitor
Did you find the information you needed? Do you need to contact the department of education for more information about where to find the music standards?

Evaluate and Extend
Discuss the plan you developed for meeting the music standards using technology with others and compare your ideas. Note the strengths and weaknesses of the various examples and incorporate the best ideas into your plan.

Music

well supported by a range of digital technology and content resources you can incorporate into your music instruction.

You can help your students attain the skills required for musical performance if you provide them with methods and supports that will enable them to continue to learn and grow musically when you're not around. In other words, you can help them learn to practice, and there are a variety of technologies available to do just that (see Figure S.16).

For many years, music textbooks and method books have been paired with recordings that serve as models for music students. Once provided on vinyl records and cassette tapes, recordings of master performers are now available on digital disks, as digital audio files, and on the Internet. Students can hear performance techniques for most instruments and styles as well as music from various cultures, from African drumming to Appalachian fiddle techniques.

There are also helpful lessons, tutorials, and demonstrations online ranging from student to seasoned professional performances. You can find these from publishers as well as amateurs and other educators who post performances on audio- or video-sharing sites. You and your students can create your own digital recordings that can support practice at home and in class, such as accompaniments used in elementary music classes or standard warm-up exercises for vocalists.

Instrumentalists and vocalists can incorporate interactive practice software, which captures and displays a student's performance, both visually and aurally, and can contain a number of tutorials and exercises to address common skills. More advanced versions of practice software can track and notate problems with student performance, as well as record the student performance with or without the accompaniment that can be stored, e-mailed, or saved in a variety of formats for later review.

Table S.9 Ideas for Addressing NETS-S in the Music Classroom

Creativity and Innovation
Students listen to and observe performances by professionals in live and recorded venues and analyze these performances to guide their own musical growth and make decisions that impact their own performances. They use digital recording devices to support their own performing and composition or improvisation and monitor their musical growth.

Communication and Collaboration
Students post recordings of their performances online or send them to others to demonstrate proficiency or seek constructive feedback. Students use notation or sequencing software as well as recording and broadcast media to collaborate with other musicians and communicate musical thought and expression.

Research and Information Fluency
Students use online and other digital resources to learn about musical styles from different genres, cultures, and time periods. Students use digital recordings found on disks or online along with musical notation to expand their learning and to compare the role of music in different cultures as well as analyze and evaluate differences in interpretation by performers.

Critical Thinking, Problem Solving, and Decision-Making
Students use practice software and recording devices to monitor their progress and make informed decisions about strategies for continued improvement. Students use professional notation or sequencing software for composing and arranging music as well as musical instruments and recording technologies used by professionals.

Digital Citizenship
Students demonstrate appropriate care and use of digital instruments and equipment, such as sound systems, including microphones, audio and video recorders, and computers. Students demonstrate their understanding of copyright and fair use, licensing, and royalties when selecting music to perform in different settings or when including music in presentations.

Technology Operations and Concepts
Students demonstrate common basic skills related to technology, such as opening and saving files, cutting, pasting, and other basic operations when using music productivity tools related to notation, composition, and arranging. Students use common audio and video recording devices as well as MIDI instruments inherent to the study and performance of music.

Recording performance is a well-established use of technology that allows students to demonstrate musical proficiency and growth. Students can record practice sessions or sections of required music for assessment purposes. Having students record performances outside of class saves instructional time and allows you to review and provide highly specific feedback to each student, even recording your comments on a separate track so the students can hear both their performances and your comments at the same time. Recordings of ensembles, whether in class or during actual performances, can also be used as a pedagogical tool when students critique their own performances and provide strategies for improving them.

Students who learn and perform music undoubtedly need to be able to read and write the standard systems of notation. Popular music notation programs, such as Cakewalk, Finale, and Sibelius, are powerful tools used by music professionals around the world as well as being available to, and used by, music students. Simpler notation programs are also available for younger students, and some music notation software, often with limited functionality, is available as freeware or shareware that you can download from the Internet.

The content standards in the early grades often link music with more holistic conceptions of musical notation and may encourage students to draw, dance, or otherwise describe elements of music, such as fast versus slow tempos, or high versus low pitches. More advanced students can benefit from the variety of sight-singing and ear-training software that is available (see Figure S.17). These applications often combine visual and aural presentation of exercises and drills. Unlike a static recording, students can now not only listen to but can "perform" these exercises for the computer, either by tapping keys or actually singing back to the computer using a microphone, and receive feedback on their performance. Some programs include increasing levels of difficulty and tracking and reporting of student performance.

The long-established digital protocol MIDI (Musical Instrument Digital Interface) takes both composition and performance to a new level, especially through the use of sequencers and sequencing software. With sequencing software, a desktop computer can become a recording studio, and with the ease of creating websites and sharing digital recordings, performers of all ages are writing and publishing their music to share with anyone who will listen. Your students can have access to a range of sequencing software from those used by professionals to scaled-down versions designed for young musicians. Free programs like Audacity and GarageBand can also be used as sequencing tools and can incorporate additional digital media such as pictures or video.

Students demonstrate much of their understanding of musical concepts and skills through performance; however, the music content standards also require music students to develop skills for understanding different musical styles and genres. In order to demonstrate their knowledge, students can use a variety of multimedia software that allows both visual and aural presentation of musical examples and related artifacts. Students can present these materials to the music class or, if you work with teachers from another discipline, they may provide this information in a history, social studies, or language arts class to enrich their understanding of a particular culture or writing form.

Musical performances, lessons, and other artifacts can be found from both well-known and (often very good) unknown musicians and music educators from across the globe, performing or presenting music from virtually every time period, genre, and style. A quick trip around the web can unearth a variety of these resources, such as Arts-Edge from the Kennedy Center with complete lesson plans in music, dance, theatre, and the visual arts for every grade as well as connections to interdisciplinary units. Several orchestras and other professional music organizations have educational websites with a wide range of music games, audio and video

Figure S.16
Technology supports practicing, student engagement, and motivation.

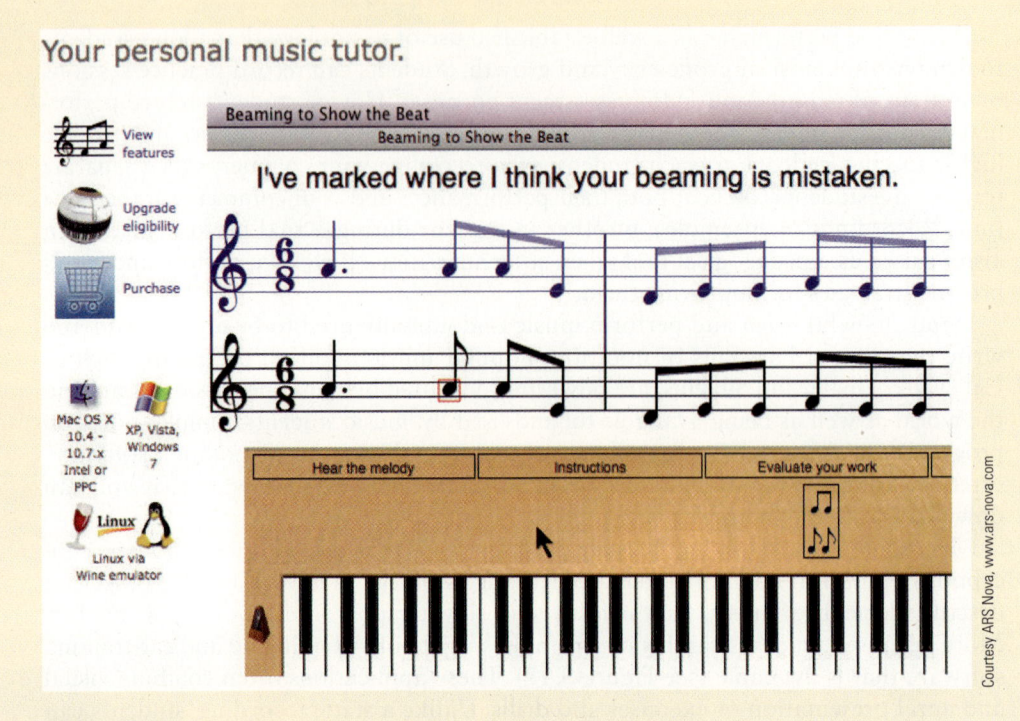

Figure S.17
Sight-singing and ear-training software helps students develop critical musical skills.

recordings, and informational activities related to composers, performers, instruments, and many other music-related topics.

Digital tools are available to support the national music content standards at every grade and proficiency level. Professional quality tools are readily available for schools so your students can address the real-world issues faced by professional musicians. They are also often available to students once they've left your music classroom, so they can continue to nurture their musical interests and develop their musical skills. Truly, with the range of technology available to support almost every aspect of music teaching and learning, you are more likely to be faced with considering *which* technology to choose in your classroom rather than whether technology is available.

Reference

Music Educators National Conference (MENC). (1994). *National standards for arts education*. Reston, VA: Author.

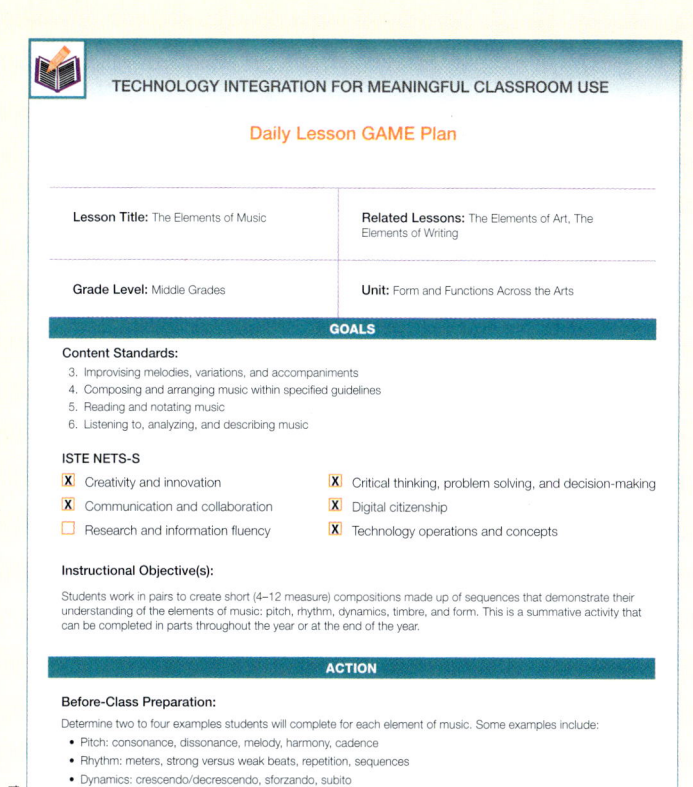

Lesson Plans for Music
Middle Grades Music

TECHNOLOGY INTEGRATION FOR MEANINGFUL CLASSROOM USE

Daily Lesson GAME Plan

Lesson Title: The Elements of Music

Related Lessons: The Elements of Art, The Elements of Writing

Grade Level: Middle Grades

Unit: Form and Functions Across the Arts

GOALS

Content Standards:
3. Improvising melodies, variations, and accompaniments
4. Composing and arranging music within specified guidelines
5. Reading and notating music
6. Listening to, analyzing, and describing music

ISTE NETS-S
- [X] Creativity and innovation
- [X] Communication and collaboration
- [ ] Research and information fluency
- [X] Critical thinking, problem solving, and decision-making
- [X] Digital citizenship
- [X] Technology operations and concepts

Instructional Objective(s):
Students work in pairs to create short (4–12 measure) compositions made up of sequences that demonstrate their understanding of the elements of music: pitch, rhythm, dynamics, timbre, and form. This is a summative activity that can be completed in parts throughout the year or at the end of the year.

ACTION

Before-Class Preparation:
Determine two to four examples students will complete for each element of music. Some examples include:
- Pitch: consonance, dissonance, melody, harmony, cadence
- Rhythm: meters, strong versus weak beats, repetition, sequences
- Dynamics: crescendo/decrescendo, sforzando, subito
- Timbre: strike, bow, male versus female voices, percussive sounds, sounds from nature, man-made sounds
- Form: binary, ternary, 12-bar blues

Develop a checklist for the activity. Identify examples from past literature, the textbook, and recordings, or create your own examples. Determine whether the activity will be completed in parts throughout the year or as a summative activity at the end of the year.

Set up workstations to include sequencing/notation software, digital recordings/loops, headphones, and microphones. Some editing applications, like GarageBand, have libraries of loops and sounds. Internet resources, such as the Podsafe Network, can also be used for source recordings.

During Class

Time	Instructional Activities	Materials and Resources
Throughout the year	Students explore the elements of music in general music, music appreciation, or specialized music courses. The elements are related to songs they sing, recordings they hear, or repertoire they perform.	Recordings, Literature, method, or textbooks
20–30 minutes	Review and use explicit examples to demonstrate the characteristics of an element (or the elements) of music. The discussion can require students to compare examples or ask students to recall or perform examples they have encountered earlier.	Recordings, Literature, method, or textbooks
10–15 minutes	Review the checklist and requirements for the activity. For example, students may be required to select two examples of an element from a longer list. If so, try to ensure each example is selected at least once. Discussion of the appropriate use of copyrighted material should be included.	Checklist
30–60 minutes	Provide direct instruction on using the available sequencing/notation software and peripherals. The amount of time spent on this segment depends on the students' familiarity and experience with the sequencing/notation software. If necessary, students will need to be shown how to: • find musical or sound sequences • record musical or sound sequences • import sequences into the software • edit, copy, and paste sequences or parts of sequences • save their work to an appropriate storage medium	Computer or mobile device that supports sequencing/notation software, Headphones, Microphone, Optional: Internet access
20–30 minutes per example	Students compose their examples for the elements of music. Emphasize that students are to focus on illustrating the element of music rather than composing long or complex examples. Students should record their justifications for why their composition is a good example either as text in a document or as a verbal testimony they record.	Computer or mobile device that supports sequencing/notation software, Headphones, Microphone, Word-processing software, Optional: Internet access
45–60 minutes per element	Students present their examples to the class and justify why their compositions are representative of the characteristic. Students can also describe any problems they faced or creative decisions they made in creating their compositions. Students should compare compositions from other students in the class that illustrate the same characteristic. Consider posting student work to a class website or blog to share with family members and other classes.	Computer or mobile device that supports sequencing/notation software, Speakers, Screen or whiteboard for whole-class display

Notes: While this activity is suitable for individuals, pairs may be used if technical support is an issue. Larger groupings are not recommended.

MONITOR

Ongoing Assessment(s): Students should be closely monitored to ensure they are focusing on creating a representative example of the element rather than lengthy compositions. A timer can be employed to help students monitor time spent. Peer review can be used to ensure the examples are easily understood.

Accommodations and Extensions: Student choice can be supported by allowing students to select two examples per element from a longer list. If access to devices is limited, determine a method for rotation that may include students working on different lesson activities offline.

The use of recordings for this activity provides an opportunity to discuss digital citizenship and the fair use of music that may be copyrighted or within the public domain.

Students can export their compositions as sound files and embed them in word-processing or presentation software or posted online, in which they can record their justifications for why their compositions are representative. These documents can be saved in student digital portfolios.

Back-up Plan: Students can identify examples from the textbook, method book, or repertoire and can perform them in whole or small groups. Students can also improvise examples based on those found in their literature.

EVALUATE AND EXTEND

Lesson Reflections and Notes: The activity can be evaluated by a checklist, perhaps with scores indicating levels of quality of the elements included.

A full-size version of this lesson plan appears on the CourseMate website at www.cengagebrain.com.

High School Music

TECHNOLOGY INTEGRATION FOR MEANINGFUL CLASSROOM USE

Daily Lesson GAME Plan

Lesson Title: Practice Guides
Related Lessons: Listening Guides
Grade Level: High School
Unit:

GOALS

Content Standards:
2. Performing on instruments, alone and with others, a varied repertoire of music
5. Reading and notating music
6. Listening to, analyzing, and describing music
7. Evaluating music and music performances
8. Understanding relationships among music, the other arts, and disciplines outside the arts
9. Understanding music in relation to history and culture

ISTE NETS-S

- [X] Creativity and innovation
- [X] Communication and collaboration
- [X] Research and information fluency
- [X] Critical thinking, problem solving, and decision-making
- [X] Digital citizenship
- [X] Technology operations and concepts

Instructional Objective(s):

Students conduct web research to develop practice guides for solo and ensemble literature to share with their peers. Each practice guide should contain information about the composer, the time period and style in which the composition was written and how those influenced the composition, and at least three challenging passages with suggestions or exercises for improving their performances. These passages may involve expression, articulation, fingering/bowing, ornamentation, phrasing, or other elements of music (e.g., pitch, rhythm, dynamics, form, and timbre) unique to the composition. This activity can be completed over a six-to-nine week period concurrently with other instruction.

ACTION

Before-Class Preparation:

Develop a checklist of required criteria for each practice guide and determine a timeline for completion. The timeline can be determined with the students and based on preparing for upcoming performances. Find or create examples of completed practice guides. If necessary, create a template for the web page or wiki entry. Designate equipment (i.e., digital recorders, digital instruments, computer workstations, etc.) for recording or notating examples used in the practice guides.

During Class

Time	Instructional Activities	Materials and Resources
30-45 minutes	Share and discuss checklist of required criteria and the examples of completed practice guides. Provide or determine the timeline collaboratively so students understand their weekly requirements. Timeline should include time for the presentation of drafts and revisions.	Checklist Timeline Practice guide examples
Weekly	Review drafts of the practice guides. Class time should be allotted to allow students to conduct research as well as to scan, record, or create examples in notation software.	Word-processing or web-authoring software Internet research Scanner Digital recording equipment Notation software
Final week	Students post revised information on a class web page or wiki. Allow time for students to review each other's work, especially those who perform in the same medium. Students can present their practice guides to the class, actually performing passages they have included in their practice guides.	Website, blog, or wiki

Notes: Some of the content of this project can be completed outside of class time as homework (in support of home practice), but weekly class time should be provided for research and technology use as well as to monitor student progress. Students who study with and incorporate suggestions from private teachers should attribute that information.

MONITOR

Ongoing Assessment(s): Weekly progress checks should be conducted in relation to the predetermined timeline.

Accommodations and Extensions: Some students may need help determining appropriate passages to include in their practice guides. Suggestions for mastering these passages can come from method books, études, or other material used in class. Students with limited web skills can create their practice guides using word-processing software. Students requiring help with recording, creating graphics, or using notation software can work with others.

The lesson should include discussions about the appropriate and fair use of copyrighted material in support of digital citizenship.

Elements of the practice guide may be related to content objectives in social studies, history, language arts, and foreign language classes. Some compositions and passages may also have connections to science or math content standards.

This lesson model can also be used in general music or music appreciation classes to create listening guides for music from any genre. Listening guides could include information about the performers as well as any pertinent social or historical information. Instead of providing practice suggestions for challenging passages, students can support the development of critical listening skills by describing important or unique treatment of different elements of music (e.g., pitch, rhythm, dynamic, form, and timbre).

Back-up Plan: Students can conduct historical research using reference books from the library and can keep written notes in their practice folders. Manuscript paper may be necessary. This project can also be completed with word-processing or presentation software if a class website is not available.

EVALUATE AND EXTEND

Lesson Reflections and Notes: Completed projects will be graded using a checklist or rubric.

The practice guides are best presented on a website in which they are cataloged and searchable, either using a database-driven site or wiki. Over time, different students may add to or revise the practice guides. Revisions should reflect appropriate attribution to previous authors.

A full-size version of this lesson plan appears on the CourseMate website at www.cengagebrain.com.

Glossary

acceptable use policies (AUP) a document that clearly outlines what is and is not acceptable behavior when using technology, in general, and the Internet, specifically, as well as the consequences of unacceptable behaviors

accessibility features features built into hardware and software that provide greater access to the technology, especially for people with disabilities

action research the process of systematically collecting data to investigate some issue in your classroom to determine whether specific techniques work for your students and curriculum; also known as *teacher research* or *teacher inquiry*

adware software that incorporates the presentation of advertisements as a condition for operating it

affective networks neural networks that relate to feelings and emotions, and which influence motivation for and engagement with a particular goal, method, medium, or assessment

analytic rubric a type of assessment rubric in which component categories are broken down

articulation the ability to describe what one has done, explain what resulted and why

assessment portfolios a collection of artifacts used to assess student learning; an authentic representation of student learning

assistive technology (AT) any item, piece of equipment, or product system used to increase, maintain, or improve functional capabilities of individuals with disabilities

augmentative and alternative communication (AAC) devices hardware and software that allow students with disabilities to communicate through pictures, words, and symbols

authentic assessment assessment in which students are required to demonstrate understanding of concepts and perform skills within real-world contexts

authentic instruction real-world issues and authentic problems, which facilitate and inspire student learning and creativity

authentic intellectual work an approach to teaching in which students work within real-world contexts by engaging in tasks that have value beyond school

blended learning learning activities in which part of the instruction is provided online and other aspects are provided in the classroom

blog online journaling and threaded discussion tool for use on the web; abbreviation for *weblog*

broadband high-capacity telecommunications that allow users to access Internet-based information at significantly higher speeds than dial-up connections

carpal tunnel syndrome a repetitive stress injury commonly associated with keyboard use in which the median nerve of the hand becomes compressed at about the location of the wrist

cognitive feedback provides an explanation of why an answer is correct or incorrect to help students develop a better understanding of the goals for performance, how their current understanding or skill levels compare to those goals, and how they might improve their performances

collaborative a characteristic of authentic instruction; working in groups in which responsibility for learning is shared with others

collaborative database a special type of database that supports a shared process of knowledge building

collectivist a perspective that promotes situating the individual within a larger community and measures the success of the individual as a factor of the whole

communal a style of communication in which listening is participatory, and listeners provide prompts, feedback, and commentary

communication tools numerous technologies used to communicate synchronously or asynchronously, such as phones, e-mail, texting, and others

community of practice a group "of people who share a concern or a passion for something they do and learn how to do it better as they interact regularly" (Wenger, 2006, see page 316)

compliance with regard to standards, refers to *who* must meet the standards and what *authority* mandates them

computer literate refers to a person who has an understanding of computer history, computer architecture and terminology, basic software applications, and programming

computer vision syndrome discomfort or other vision problems that can result from using a computer screen after a period of time

concept map a graphical tool for organizing and representing knowledge

consequences in the context of standards, refers to the results of meeting or not meeting standards, including remedial instruction and changes in pay schedules

cookies temporary computer files from websites that store information enabling sites to remember your computer and your preferences

Creative Commons licensing guidelines whereby content creators allow or limit your use to copy, edit, remix, build upon, or distribute all or parts of their work

criteria with regards to standards, refers to what is expected, such as the content one is expected to teach

critical reflection trying to understand different perspectives and using that understanding to set goals for future behavior or learning

culturally responsive teacher understands and capitalizes on the unique cultural attributes and experiences of students to promote student achievement

cyberbullying using information and communications technologies to harass, defame, or intentionally harm another student or group of students

cyberstalking using electronic means to stalk someone

databases a type of software that organizes information

data projector presentation device that connects to a computer and projects a computer desktop image onto a blank wall, screen, or whiteboard

descriptive studies research studies that describe the state of something, often based on surveys or qualitative research methods

didactic type of conversation or instruction in which a single speaker dominates while others quietly listen

differentiated instruction (DI) purposefully designing instruction to accommodate the known needs of one's students and providing them with different content, strategies, and means of demonstrating the desired learning goals

differentiation providing flexibility during teaching in terms of content, process, and product, based on the needs of your students

digital divide the disparity between families and students who have access to digital tools and resources and those who do not

directed instruction comprises instructional methods that present learners with the content to be learned, followed by multiple opportunities to practice or apply the content so as to ensure mastery of the information

directory information information contained in an education record that generally would not be considered harmful, or an invasion of privacy, if disclosed

employment portfolios a presentation of artifacts demonstrating competencies in relation to a desired position or profession

ergonomics the study and development of furniture, tools, and systems that promote safe and healthy use

evaluation studies studies that attempt to determine the effects of an intervention; however, they do not attempt to test a specific hypothesis and do not need a control group

exemplars models of acceptable performance

experimental research a method of investigating hypotheses about the effects of an intervention by comparing a control group, which receives no intervention, to an experimental group, which is as identical as possible to the control group except that the experimental group receives the intervention

fair use the portion of the U.S. copyright law that allows limited use of copyrighted material without requiring permission from the use of the copyright holder

filtering software software designed to help prevent students from coming into contact with inappropriate material when using the Internet

firewall hardware and/or software that prevents unwanted persons, messages, or software from entering a network or computer

formative assessments assessment used during instruction to monitor student progress toward mastering learning goals

freeware software that has no cost

higher-order thinking creative thinking; "complex thinking that requires effort and produces valued outcomes" (Wegerif, 2002, see Chapter 3)

holistic rubric a type of assessment rubric in which descriptors touch on each area of instruction/learning without breaking the areas down into separate rating scales per category

hypermedia hypertext with media elements (e.g., images, sounds, videos, animations, or others)

hypertext a non sequential, or non-linear, method for organizing and displaying text

individualist a perspective that promotes the autonomy of the individual and measures success by individual accomplishments

individualized education program (IEP) an individualized plan for a student with disabilities that describes the measures teachers must take to accommodate the learning needs of the student

information and communications technology (ICT) an umbrella term that refers to all technology that supports the manipulation and communication of information

information literacy ability to recognize when information is needed and to locate, evaluate, and use the needed information effectively

integrate to combine two or more parts to make a whole

intelligent tutoring system (ITS) a type of educational software that tracks student responses, makes inferences about strengths and weaknesses and then tailors feedback and subsequent instruction to improve performance; also known as *integrated learning software (ILS)* and *computer-adapted instruction (CAI)*

learning profile a description of a student's abilities, interests, learning preferences, and other relevant information that can impact learning

lexiles a scale that matches the difficulty of reading material to student ability

links in a concept map, the connections or relationships between concepts

malware malicious software that can cause significant harm to one or more computers as well as a computer network

metacognition the ability to think about our own thinking

metacognitive learners learners who "think about their thinking" and apply strategies to regulate and oversee their learning

microworld a type of simulation software that allows learners to manipulate, explore, and experiment with specific phenomena in an exploratory learning environment

mindtool the use of technology as an organizational tool, simulation and visualization tool, or knowledge-building tool

multimedia tools instructional tools that contain information in multiple formats, including text, sounds, images, animation, or movies

new learning experiences instructional experiences that are created by integrating our understanding of how people learn with the relevant technological tools that can support teaching and learning

nodes concepts, as represented in a concept map

objectives statements that describe what the learner will be able to do following the instruction

open-source software free software that also allows users to access and modify the underlying code in order to contribute to its continued development

opinion articles articles that present the views of one or many people but that have not been tested through research or evaluation studies

outcome feedback whether or not a response is correct

performance task a type of performance-based assessment that requires students to "do" the subject in question, often through open-ended problems in an authentic context

phishing a type of spam used to steal personal information, identity, and bank account numbers, or even to attempt face-to-face contact; also known as *carding* or *spoofing*

podcasts digital audio files downloaded from the Internet and played back on an MP3 player, iPod or computer

productivity applications computer programs such as databases, spreadsheets, word-processing and presentation software that allow users to create products more efficiently than is possible without the software, thus, increasing productivity

professional development portfolio a personal tool for individual learning that provides a place for collecting and reflecting on artifacts documenting professional growth over time

proxy servers software applications that perform several functions, including filtering and storing Internet content

public domain creative works or information that are not "owned" by an individual but considered part of the common culture

qualitative data information that converts to words, typically in the form of an interpretive narrative

quantitative data information that converts to numbers, such as test scores or self-report ratings on opinion scales

quasi-experimental research experimental research in which random assignment to groups is not possible, so statistical techniques are used to determine the extent to which any observed differences between the experimental and control groups may be due to chance alone

real contexts learning environments that allow students to solve actual, complex problems

recognition networks neural networks in the brain that help to identify sensory data, such as objects, facts, and patterns

reflection learner's ability to think over the process of learning and to describe what she/he has done and what she/he needs to do to achieve meaningful learning

render process of constructing a single, complete movie file from a collection of clips, stills, transitions, and/or audio input

repetitive strain injuries can occur during computer use due to the sensitive nature of the soft tissues, tendons, nerves, and muscles of the hand that are subjected to repeated motions, awkward positions, or force

resolution clarity of an image or letter related to the number of dots per square inch in print or pixels per square inch on a monitor

resource guide lists of the materials and digital resources that are applicable to the lesson

response-to-intervention (RTI) framework that uses diagnostic and progress-monitoring assessments to help group students for instructional interventions of varied intensity and types

rubrics helps students understand what is expected in a final product, usually describing varied levels of performance

scaffolds external supports for learning or solving problems

screencasts animated movies captured from the teacher's monitor or a whiteboard

self-directed learning (SDL) any increase in knowledge, skills, accomplishment, or personal development that an individual selects and brings about by his/her own efforts using any methods in any circumstance at any time; ability to set personal learning goals, take action to meet those goals, and evaluate the effectiveness of the learning processes and learning outcomes

shareware software downloaded from the Internet available for free preview for a limited time, after which purchase is required

simulation a simplified version of phenomena, environments, or processes that allow students to interact with, or manipulate, variables and observe the effects of those manipulations

software evaluation rubrics forms that provide criteria on which to evaluate educational software, websites, and other digital resources

spam unwanted messages through e-mail, cell phones, instant- or text-messaging devices, and blogs

spyware software that records usage patterns or collects information unknowingly from the user's computer

strategic networks neural networks that control processes for planning, executing, and monitoring your actions

summative assessments assessments used to evaluate learning after presenting a lesson, unit, or course

support for conversation when technology is used in such a way that it contributes to conversations among learners, and thus facilitates group and community learning

system a set of interrelated parts that work toward a common purpose

technical guidelines step-by-step instructions for using technology

technologically literate having a general, working understanding of current technologies

technology-based tutorial a complete lesson on a specific topic offered via technology, including presentation of information, practice exercises, and feedback

technology integration making technologies an integral part of the teaching and learning process that impacts resources, teacher and student roles, and instructional activities

telementoring a process for establishing a guided mentoring relationship that incorporates information and communications technologies; also known as *eMentoring*

tendonitis inflammation, irritation, or swelling of the tendons, that connect muscles to bone

topic-centered classrooms where students are taught to be direct, precise, and to follow conventions of didactic communication

topic-chaining a learning environment or method of instruction that focuses on strong social context with cyclical and multi-part conversations

transfer ability to use knowledge or skills in new situations

triangulate the process of using multiple, independent data sources to increase the credibility and validity of research findings

tutor the use of software to explicitly teach or provide practice with a specific body of content

typosquatting the practice of creating a website with a URL just slightly different from a legitimate source

universal design for learning (UDL) an approach to instruction in which teachers remove barriers to learning by providing flexibility in materials, methods, and assessments

virtual field trips use of audio-, video-, or webconferencing tools to tour or interact simultaneously with businesses, museums, galleries using images, animation, videos, and websites

virus a computer program that executes and replicates itself and, in the process, has the potential to cause major problems on your computer

virus-protection software software that scans computer files to identify and repair files infected by viruses and delete malware

visualization tools tools that allow learners to picture, or represent, how various phenomena operate within different domains

WebQuest an organized format for presenting lessons that utilize web-based resources

wiki a page or collection of web pages designed to allow users to create, edit, and link web content quickly

word cloud a visualization tool that can be used to analyze text by changing the size of each word in the cloud based on the number of times it appears in a given passage

word-prediction software software that suggest words based on common usage patterns, arrangement of letters, or rules of grammar

word-processing applications software that allows users to create, edit, and revise written documents

Index

Italic page numbers indicate material in figures or tables.

A

academic integrity. *see* ethical issues
acceptable use policies (AUPs), 208, 244–246, *245*, *246*, 261
accessibility features, 153, 155–156
action plan, *29*, 30, 32–33, 48–49, 300–301. *see also* GAME plan
action research
    data collection (qualitative/quantitative), 312–314, *312*, *313*
    evaluate and extend, 314
    GAME plan for, *309*
    goals, establishing, 310
    monitoring and analyzing data, 312–313, *313*
    starting points for, *310*
    steps in the process of, 309–310
    taking action, 311–312
    teacher as researcher in, 308–309
    technology support for, 314–315, *315*
active learning, 59–61, *61*, 69, 149
Adobe Acrobat, *263*
Adobe Connect, 99
Adobe Illustrator, 362
Adobe Reader, 154–155
adware, 259–260
affective networks, 145, 147
air circulation and computers, 194
Alien Rescue, 67–68
Alphasmart, *158*
ALTEC at the University of Kansas, 179, 183
Amaya, *234*
Amazon.com, 236
American Association for Health Education (AAHE), 355, *355*
American Council on the Teaching of Foreign Languages, *331*
American Memory Project, Library of Congress, 65, 97
analytic rubrics, 181–182, *181*
animations, 93
antivirus software, 209–210
APA style for citing Internet resources, 104, *252*
Apple
    iChat, 99, 102
    iGrab, 125
    iMovie, 97, 98
    iPad/iTunes release, *10*
    iPads, 159, 210, 279
    iPod Touch, 210, 279
    iPods, 111, 159, *233*, 310, 311–312, 314
    iTunes, *10*, *233*
    iTunesU, 228, 232, *233*
    Keynote, 93, 98
    microcomputers (Apple II), *4*, *5*, *10*
    VoiceOver, 155–156
    Zoom, 155–156
Apple Classrooms of Tomorrow (ACOT) project, 294
Apple Computer Company research, 307
apps, for mobile devices, 238, *295*
archives, 209
ARPANET (Advanced Research Project Agency Network), 7
art class. *see* Visual-Arts classrooms
articulation, 61
Arts-Edge, Kennedy Center, 369
Asian American students, 277
assessment portfolios, 39–40, 41, 45
assessments
    authentic, 170–171, 174–178
    concept mapping and, 175, *176*
    forced-choice formats, 168–170, 178–179
    formative, 49–50, 165–167, 175
    GAME plan for, 169, 178, *188*
    and learning goals, 164–165, 167
    open-ended response formats, 170, 179
    performance-based, *172–173*, 174
    portfolios and work samples, *176*
    project-based, 171, 173–174, *180*
    reflecting on practice and, 302
    scoring. *see* scoring practices
    simulations and games, 176, *177*
    standards and, 163–164, 167
    summative, 167
    technology-assisted, 186, 188–189, *188*
    universal design for learning (UDL) and, 149–150
assistive technologies (AT)
    computer accessibility features, 153, 156
    GAME plan, 160
    Individualized Education Program (IEP) and, 152, 159, 160
    legal precedents for, 151–152
    low- to high-tech continuum, 153, *154*
    mobile devices, 159
    mouse/keyboard adaptations, 157–159
    software, 153–156
Assistive Technology Act, 152
Atlantis Remixed, *94*
Audacity, 228, 369
augmentative and alternative communication (AAC) devices, 156
AUPs. *see* acceptable use policies (AUPs)

377

authentic assessments, 170–171, 174–178
authentic instruction. *see also* learner-centered education
   active learning, 59–61, *61*, 69, 149
   challenging activities, 64–66, *66*, 69
   collaborative work groups, 66–67
   complex activities, 63–64, *69*
   content standards and, 73–79. *see also* content standards
   creative thinking types, 56–57
   and the digital classroom, 252
   and directed instruction, 71–73, *72*
   holistic activities, 61–63, *62*, 69
   learner autonomy, 58–59, 69, 275
   scaffolds in, *59*, 60, 67–68, *68*
   technology support for, 68–70, *69*, *70*, 77, 79
authentic intellectual work, 63–64, *65*

B
back-up files, creating, 209
bandwidth, 276–277
basic interpersonal skills (BICS), 326
BASIC language, 4, 6
Berners-Lee, Tim, *5*, *10*
Best Buy, 259
biases/stereotypes, 235, 279, 281
BigKeys, 157, *158*
Bill and Melinda Gates Foundation, 306
biometric devices, *256*, 256
Black students, 277
Bland County History Archives, *352*
blended learning, 8, 120–121. *see also* technology-enriched learning
blogs
   and assessments, 170
   classroom, *22*
   as communication tool, 102, *104*, *122*, *124*
   communication via, 222
   GAME plan for classroom, 104–105
   as ICT tool, 9
   portfolio development and, 40
Bloom's Taxonomy, 74, *75*
bodily-kinesthetic intelligence, *141*
bookmarking resource sites, 264
brain function, and neural networks, 145–147
BrainPop, 232
broadband, 277
bubbl.us, 93
Building Bridges: A Peace Corps Classroom Guide to Cross-Cultural Understanding (Peace Corps), 284
bullying, online. *see* cyberbullying
BYOD (bring your own device) programs, 195, 196, 213, 239–240, 278, *278*

C
Cailliau, Robert, *5*, *10*
Cakewalk, 369
Calgary French and International School, 287
CALL (computer assisted language learning), 332–333, *334*
Campusuite, 222
Camtasia, 125
carding, 259

Carnegie Learning, 85
carpal tunnel syndrome, 198
Carter-Tod, Sheila, 319–322
Caucasian students, 277
Center for Applied Research in Education and Technology (CARET), 306–307
Center for Applied Special Technologies (CAST), 143–144
challenging activities, 64–66, *66*, 69
chat rooms, *122*, *124*, 262
cheating, 253–254, *253*, *254*
checklists, scoring with, 179–180, *179*
Chicago style for citing Internet resources, *252*
Children's Internet Protection Act (CIPA), 258, 262
Children's Online Privacy Protection Act (COPPA), 257–258
citing source material, 251–252, *252*
class websites, 219, *221*, 222, 223
classroom. *see also specific subject classrooms*
   blogs, 22, 104, 222. *see also* blogs
   configuration, and technology use, 193–194, *195*
   ergonomics, 196, *197*, 198
   flipped classroom. *see* blended learning; technology-enriched learning
   podcast use in, *233*
cloned workstations, 202, 208
cloud computing, 210
CMap, *234*
cognitive academic language proficiency (CALP), 326
cognitive feedback, 167
cognitive needs of students, 272–273
cognitive skills, 74–76, *75*
collaboration
   benefits of, 229
   communication and, 218–219. *see also* communication
   parent volunteering, 214, 225–227
   in specific classrooms. *see* NETS-S (National Education Technology Standards for Students)
   telementoring, 226–227
collaborative database, 90–91, *91*
collaborative learning. *see also* technology-enriched learning environment
collaborative work groups
   assigning roles in, 110, 113, *113*
   addressing content standards in, 66–67, 76
   and computer use, 110, *112*
   differentiated instruction (DI) and, 140
   equal opportunities in, 277
   individual responsibility in, 115–116
   rubric for group process, *116*
   social needs support and, 271–272
collectivist communication perspective, 285–286, *286*
Committee on Science Education Standards and Assessment, *343*
Common Core State Standards, 14
common recommendations form national curricular reports, *55*
communal style of communication, 285
communication. *see also* class websites; e-mail; professional growth
   aids (assistive devices), 155–156
   and collaboration, 218, 229

collectivist/individual, 285–286, *286*
content standards and, 321–322
cross-cultural patterns of, 285
didactic, 285
GAME plan for electronic communication, 224
with parents and the community, 218–219, *220*, *221*, 229
social media, 222–224
support for, *122*, *124*
technology development, 2–4. *see also* information and communications technology (ICT)
text-messaging/e-mail, 224–225
via blogs, 222
communication technology. *see* blogs; conversation support; websites
Communications Act of 1934, 258
community of practice (CoP), 293–294
complex activities, 63–64, *69*
compliance with standards, 17
computer vision syndrome, 200–201
computer-adapted instruction (CAI), 86
computers. *see also* assistive technologies; digital learning tools; mindtools; software
 accessibility features, 153, 156
 accessibility of, in schools, 194–195, 276–278
 as collaborative learning tool, 110, *111*
 as communication device and resource tool, 5, 7–8
 in education timeline, 5–6, *10*
 file storage/management, 127
 firewalls, 260
 hardware maintenance, 203–207
 health and safety issues, 192–202
 history of use, 4–10
 independent use of, 116
 language, 4, *5*, 6–7, *6*
 as learning and social tool, 5–6, 8–9
 for lesson preparation, 127
 literacy, 4
 maintenance. *see* technology maintenance
 and malicious software, 258–260
 monitors, 200–201, 205
 as object of study, 4–5, *5*
 positioning of, 156–157
 as programming tool, *5*, 6–7
 skills, learning, 227–229
 software maintenance, 207–210
 technical guidelines for students, 123, *125*
 viruses, 209–210, 259–260
 in whole-group learning, 111–112
concept maps
 for assisting ELLs, 327
 authentic assessment and, 175, *175*, *176*
 for ELLs, *328*
 as mindtools, 89, 92–93, *92*
 software for, *234*
conferences, 298–299, *298*
conferencing tools, 102, *103*–104. *see also* webconferencing
confidentiality, 40
confidentiality, and ethics, 254–255, *255*
consequences for noncompliance, 17
Consortium for School Networking (CoSN), 304

Consortium of National Arts Education Association, *367*
consumable supplies, replacing, 207
content, in portfolio design, 42–44, *42*
content standards. *see also* curriculum; *specific subject classrooms*
 analytic rubrics and, 181, *181*
 and creative thinking, 73–79
 and cultural responsiveness, 278–281
 and differentiated instruction, 139–140
 GAME plan for identifying, 74
 lesson planning and technology integration, 317. *see also* lesson planning
 for music (MENC), 367–368
 national, *13*
 science, 73–74, *73*
 and software evaluation rubrics, 235–236
 technology support for student mastery of, 76–79, *77*
 and universal design for learning, 148
continued learning, 27–28, 29, 32. *see also* professional growth
convergent thinking, 56
conversation support
 blogs. *see* blogs
 collaborative learning tool, technology as, 99, 101–102
 technology as, 98–99, 230
 webconferencing, 99, 102, *103*
 wikis. *see* wikis
cookies, 208–209, *209*
copyright, 246–249, *247*, *248*, 251
copyright issues, and software, 208
Copyright Law of 1976, 246, *247*
Council of Chief State School Officers, 14
Creative Commons licensing, 250, *250*
creative thinking
 content standards and, 73–79
 and database building, 90
 digital learning tools for, 94
 and NETS-T standards, 53–54
 technology use in support of, 84
 technology-based tutorials for, 89
 types of, 55–57
 via authentic instruction. *see* authentic instruction
 webconferencing and, 102
creativity, in specific classrooms. *see* NETS-S (National Education Technology Standards for Students)
criteria, standards as, 17
critical reflection, 37–38, 45, 275
critical thinking and creativity, 53, 54, 56
cross-cultural awareness, 283–286, *284*
CRT (cathode ray tube) monitors, 205
Cuevas, Gilbert J., 337–340
cultural awareness, 283–286, *284*
cultural diversity. *see also* English Language Learners (ELLs)
 computer access and, 277
 racial steretypes in rubrics, 279
 respecting in the classroom, 288–289
 in schools, 269–270
cultural understanding, 286–287

Culturally and Linguistically Diverse (CLD), 325
culturally responsive pedagogy
   access to meaningful content, 278–281, *280*
   collectivist perspective, 285–286, *286*
   cultural awareness, 283–286, *284*
   GAME plan for gender-equitable resources, *281*
   individualist perspective, 285–286, *286*
   instructional strategies, *289*
   learner-centered strategies, 270–276
   respecting cultural diversity, 288–289
   working with students to develop cultural understanding, 286–287
culturally responsive teacher, 270
curriculum. *see also* content standards; *specific subjects*
   learner-centered curriculum, 11–12
   learning goals, and UDL, 148
   national standards, 13
   open-source software for, 232
   recommendations, from national curricular reports, *55*
   technology aids in, 230
   written and enacted, 302
Curriki.org, 232
cyberbullying, *244*, 261–262
Cyberbullying Research Center, 261
cyberstalking, 262

D

data collection and analysis, 312–314, *312*, *313*
data projector, 112
data-based decision-making, 186, 188–189, *188*
databases, 89–91, *91*, *124*
decision-making, in specific classrooms. *see* NETS-S (National Education Technology Standards for Students)
deductive thinking, 57
Delicious, 264
delivery, of portfolios, 46
descriptive studies, 304
didactic communication, 285
differentiated instruction (DI). *see also* universal design for learning (UDL)
   ideas for technology use in, *142*
   learning profiles, 140
   and multiple intelligences theory, 140, *141*
   overview of, 138–140
   response-to-intervention (RTI) framework, 150
   technology and, 141–142
differentiation, 138
digital citizenship, *326*
   in specific classrooms. *see* NETS-S (National Education Technology Standards for Students)
digital divide, 276, 281, *282*
digital gradebooks, 183–186, *184*
digital learning tools
   databases and concept-maps, 89–93
   educational games, 86
   in English language arts, 321–322, *321–322*
   mindtools. *see* mindtools
   for music classrooms, 368–369
   technology-based tutorials, 85–88, *88*, 89

   WebQuest, 86–87, *88*
   website creation, 94–95
Digital Millenium Copyright Act of 1998 (DMCA), 247, 249
digital resources
   acceptable use of, 208, 244–246, *245*, *246*, 261
   evaluating, 235–240
   GAME plan for technology evaluation, *237*
   locating, 230–232, 233, 234–235
   previewing, 239–240
   ratios, student-computer, 276, 278
   reviews of, 236–239, *237*
   software evaluation rubrics, 235–236
   trusted, 263–264
digital standards. *see* technology standards
digital storytelling, 96–98, *321*, *321–322*
digital technology, 3, 5
Diigo, 125, 264
directed instruction, 71–73, *72*
directory information, 254–255, *255*
disabilities, assistive technologies for students with. *see* assistive technologies (AT)
Discovery Education, 85, 232, 263
display adjustment settings, 156
divergent thinking, 56
diverse learners. *see also* assistive technologies (AT); differentiated instruction (DI); learner-centered education; universal design for learning (UDL)
   equitable access to technology, 276–282
   learner-centered education for, 270–276
Dodge, Bernie, 87
downloads, of new software, 207–208
drill-and-practice games, 86
drill-and-practice software, 71, *122*, *124*
DropBox, 127, 210
dust, and technology devices, 193–194, 205–206

E

early childhood education, and technology use, *282*
Education City, 85
Education Week, 304
educational games, 86, 176
educational research. *see also* action research
   challenges to technology research, 305–306
   consumers of research, 307–308
   impact of technology, research on, 306–307
   teacher as researcher, 308–309
   types of, 304–305
Educational Resources Information Clearinghouse (ERIC), 106
Educational Support Systems, 306
electrical outlets, 193
Electronic Communications Privacy Act of 1986 (ECPA), 257
Elementary and Secondary Education Act, 151
e-mail
   communication via, 224–225
   as conferencing tool, 102
   and cyberbullying, 261
   malicious software and, 258–260
   privacy issues, 246
   ten tips for use of, *263*

eMentoring, 226–227
employment portfolios, 39–41, 45
engagement, multiple means of, 144, 147
English language arts classrooms
    digital learning tools, 321–322, 321–322
    GAME plan for content standards, 319
    lesson plan for, 323–324
    new media texts, creating, 319–320
    standards in, 320, 320
    and word clouds, 126
English Language Learners (ELLs)
    academic learning and content, 326
    and equitable access, 279
    GAME plan for content standards, 325
    learning logs and dialogue journals, 327
    lesson plan for, 329–330
    NETS-S for, 326
    and technology integration, 325–328, 328
English Speakers of Other Languages (ESOL), 325
Envisioning Machine, 101
ePals, 102, 112, 287, 351
equitable access
    to meaningful culturally responsive content, 278–281, 280
    to tech-knowledgeable teachers, 281, 282
    to up-to-date hardware, software, and connectivity, 276–278
E-rate, 258, 277
ergonomics, 196, 197, 198
eSchoolNews, 298
essay tests, computer scoring, 179
Essential Elements of Instruction (Hunter), 72
ethical issues. *see also* legal issues
    acceptable use policies, 208, 244–246, 245, 246, 261
    cheating, 253–254, 253, 254
    confidentiality protection, 254–255, 255
    plagiarism, 251–253
ethnicity, 283
evaluation. *see also* assessments
    of digital resources, 235–240, 237
    in GAME plan, 29, 31, 47, 50
    of instructional effectiveness, 50
    of online resource information, 105–107
    of professional growth, 35–38
    of software, 280
    of technology-enriched learning, 129–130
evaluation studies, 304
exemplars for technology-enriched learning, 126–127
exercises, 198, 199
exit cards, 166
experimental research, 304
expression, multiple means of, 144, 147
extended learning, 227–229
eye health, 199, 200–201, 200

F
Facebook, 9, 102, 222–224, 262, 364
fair use guidelines, 248–249
Family Education Rights and Privacy Act (FERPA), 254
Federal Communications Commission (FCC), 258, 277
feedback, and assessments, 167, 183

field trips, 226. *see also* virtual field trips
file maintenance, 208–209
file storage, 127, 210
Filtering Mandate (CIPA), 258
filtering software, 264–265
Finale, 369
firewalls, 260
Flat Stanley Project, 320
Flickr, 9, 364
flipped classroom. *see* blended learning; technology-enriched learning; specific classroom subjects
flowcharts, 96
forced-choice assessment formats, 168, 178–179
Foreign Language classrooms
    and CALL (computer assisted language learning) activities, 332–333
    GAME plan for content standards, 331
    lesson plans for, 335–336
    NETS-S in, 332
    and technology integration, 331–334
    tutorial software for, 333, 333
formal research, 304–305
formative assessments, 49–50, 165–167, 175
Fowler, Shelli B., 319–322
Frames of Mind (Gardner), 141
Fred Rogers Center for Early Learning and Children's Media at Saint Vincent College, 282
freereading.net, 232, 234
freeware, 234, 235
funding issues, 305
Furzier, Wally, 7

G
GAME plan
    acceptable use policies, 246
    assistive technologies (AT), 160
    authentic instruction, 178
    cheating, combating, 254
    classroom website creation, 222
    content standards, 319
    content standards, identifying, 74
    electronic communication, expectations for, 224
    English language arts classrooms, 319
    English Language Learners (ELLs) classrooms, 325
    forced-choice assessment, 169
    Foreign Language classrooms, 331
    gender-equitable resources, 281
    Health and Physical Education classrooms, 355
    lesson planning and content standards, 317
    lesson planning, and data collection, 188
    Mathematics classrooms, 337
    monitoring professional growth, 35–38
    Music classrooms, 367
    overview of, 28–29
    portfolio examples, 46
    Science classrooms, 343
    for self-directed learning and action research, 309
    self-directed learning (SDL), 30–32
    Social Studies classrooms, 349
    software learning, 35, 36

GAME plan (*Continued*)
  steps in, 29
  for student learning, 47–50, *47*
  technology evaluation, *237*
  technology maintenance, 211
  technology protection, *260*
  technology-enriched learning, 131, *135–136*
  tutorials, technology-based, 89
  Visual-Arts classrooms, *361*
games
  and authentic assessment, 176
  in authentic instruction, 64
  as educational tools, 86
  gender preferences, 277
GarageBand, 98, 228, 369
Gardner, Howard, 113, 140, *141*, 149
gender-equitable resources, 277, 279, *281*
geocaching. *see* GPS (global positioning system)
ghost workstations, 202, 208
Giza, Brian, 343–346
global awareness, 283–286, *287*
global communication, 334
Global SchoolNet, 102, 351
goals. *see also* GAME plan
  for action research, *309*, 310, *310*
  for blog posting, 104
  choosing technology for learning, 230–231
  GAME plan, setting in, *29*, 30, 32–33, 35, 47–48, *47*
  universal design for learning (UDL), 148
Google Apps for Education, 234, *235*
Google Docs, 100, 127, 327
Google Drive, 210
Google Earth, 118, 287, *351*
Google Sites, 94
Google+, 9
GPS (global positioning system), *23*, 30–31, *31*
Grab (Apple), 125
gradebooks, 183–186
grades. *see* scoring practices
grading. *see* scoring practices
graphic organizers, 91–92
groups. *see* collaborative work groups
guidelines. *see also* rubrics
  culturally responsive instructional strategies, 289
  for fair use of materials, 248–249
  password creation, *257*
  for technology-enriched learning, 123, *124*, 125–127, *125*, 306–308
  universal design for learning (UDL), *144*

H

hardware
  assistive technologies (AT), 153–154, 156–157
  maintenance, 204–207
Health and Physical Education classrooms
  GAME plan for content standards, *355*
  lesson plans for, *359–360*
  NETS-S in, *356*
  technology integration in, 355–358

Hicks, David, 349–352
higher-order thinking, 56, 74, 76, 89, 170. *see also* creative thinking
Hispanic students, 277
history
  of computer technology in education, 4–10
  of information and communications technology, 2–4
holistic activities, 61–63, *62*, 69
holistic rubrics, 182, *182*
homework online, 228
HTML (Hypertext Markup Language), 40
Hunter, Madeline, 72
HyperCard, 5, 7, *10*
hyperlinked environments, 156
hypermedia, 5, 7, 94–95, *95*
hypertext, 5, 7, *10*, 94, 327

I

IBM, 4, 5, *10*
iChat, 99, 102
iCyte, 264
iGrab, 125
iMovie, 97, 98
impersonation, cyberbullying and, 261
individualist communication perspective, 285–286, *286*
Individualized Education Program (IEP), 152, 159, 160
individualized learning, 149, 150, *150*
Individuals with Disabilities Education Act (IDEA), 142, 145, 151–152
inductive thinking, 56, *70*
InfoKeys BAT Keyboard, 157
information and communications technology (ICT)
  computer development and, 7–8
  development of computers and, 2–4, *5–6*
  literacy, 11
information literacy, 8
innovation, in creative thinking, 56
inquiry/discovery method, *70*
inquiry/discovery-based learning, 350–351, *351*
Inspiration software, 92, *93*
instant messaging, *122*, 124
instruction. *see* authentic instruction; differentiated instruction (DI); universal design for learning (UDL)
integrated learning software (ILS), 86
intellectual property, 250. *see also* ethical issues; legal issues
intelligence. *see* multiple intelligences theory
intelligent tutoring system (ITS), 85–86
Intellikeys, *158*
IntelliMetric, 179
Interactive Physics, 94
interactive white boards. *see* whiteboards
International Education and Resource Network (iEARN), 351
International E-mail Classroom Connections (IECC), 287
International Reading Association (IRA), 92
Internet. *see also* computers; digital learning tools; digital resources; online resources
  accessibility in schools, 195

action plans for self-directed learning, 35
bandwidth, 276–277
cookies, 208–209, *209*
and cyberbullying/stalking, *244*, 261–262
development of, *5*, 7–8
equitable access to technology, 276–278
online education, *5*, 8–9
proxy servers, 265
as resource in technology integration, *22*, *23*
safe and responsible use of, 257–267
social networking tools, 9
streaming media sites, 232
viruses, 259–260
interpersonal intelligence, *141*
intrapersonal intelligence, *141*
invitational environment, 271
iPads, 159, 210, 279
iPod Touch, 210, 279
iPods, 111, 159, *233*, 310, 311–312, 314
ISTE. *see also* NETS-S (National Education Technology Standards for Students); NETS-T (National Education Technology Standards for Teachers)
   continuum of technology integration, 22–23, *24*
   and Educational Support Systems research, 306–307
   student technology profiles, 33, 35
   technology standards, *14–15*
item banks, 168
iTunes, *10*, 233
iTunesU, 228, 232, *233*

J
Jing, 125, 228
Journey North, 102, *103*
junk e-mail, 259

K
Kessler, Greg, 331–334
keyboard adaptations, 157, *158*
keyboards, 197, *198*
Keynote, 93, 98
Kidlink, 102, *103*
Kidspiration, 93
knowledge construction (authentic intellectual work), 63–64, *65*
Knowledge Forum, 90
knowledge-building tools, 90
Krouscas, James A., 355–358
KWHL chart, 48, *48*

L
lab management software, 128–129
Lady Gaga, *244*
Lampert, Nancy, 361–364
LAN (local area network), *5*
laptop initiatives, 213, 278, *278*
laptop program (in learner-centered classroom), 19
LCD (liquid crystal display) monitors, 205
leadership
   community of practice (CoP) and, 293–294
   exhibiting, 299
   in technology integration, action steps for, *300–301*
learner autonomy, 58–59, *69*, 275
learner-centered classrooms, 11–12, 18–19
learner-centered education. *see also* authentic instruction
   collaborating, and social needs of students, 271–272
   content learning, and cognitive needs, 272–273
   metacognitive needs, and reflection skills, 274–276
learning by design. *see also* authentic instruction
learning communities
   local, 295–296
   and stages of technology integration (beginning, embracing, proficient, transformative), 300–301
   virtual, 296, 297, 298
learning log, 327
learning profiles, 140
legal issues. *see also* ethical issues
   confidentiality protection, 254–255
   copyright law, 246–249, *247*, *248*
   Creative Commons licensing, 250, *250*
   fair use, 248–249
   and Internet safety, 257–258
   and malicious software, 259
   public domain and copyright, 249–250
   threatening or unlawful online interactions, 261–262
   use of student images and work, 255
lesson planning
   and computer lab availability, 116–117, 127
   and curriculum, 131–132
   GAME plan for, 188–189, *188*
   GAME plan for daily lessons, *135–136*
   technology-enriched learning and, 121–123, *130*, 132, 317. *see also specific subject classrooms*
   video recorded, for self-evaluation, 38
   and virtual field trips, 62
   WebQuest, 86–87, *88*
lesson plans
   for English language arts, *323–324*
   for English Language Learners (ELLs), *329–330*
   Foreign Language, *335–336*
   for Health and Physical Education, *359–360*
   for Mathematics, *341–342*
   for Music, *370–371*
   for Science, *347–348*
   for Social Studies, *353–354*
   for Visual Arts, *365–366*
lexiles, 65–66
Library of Congress, American Memory Project, 65, 97
Library of Congress, U.S. Copyright Office, 247, 249, 251
Limited English Proficient (LEP), 325
linguistic intelligence, *141*
links, 175
Linux, *234*
Lisanti, Melissa, 349–352
Lisp, 6–7
listservs, 102, 298
Live Journal, 327
LiveBinders, 264
locally sourced digital resources, 230–231

logical-mathematical intelligence, *141*
Logo, *5*, 6–7, *6*, *10*

M
Macintosh computers, *4*, *5*, *7*, *10*
maintenance
    file, 208–209
    GAME plan for, *199*
    of hardware, 204–207
    schedule, 212
    of software, 207–210
making thinking visible, 273
malicious software, 258–260
malware, 259–260
Mathematics classrooms
    GAME plan for content standards, *337*
    lesson plans for, *341–342*
    NETS-S in, *338*
    and phases of technology integration, *23*
    technology integration for, 337–340
    and virtual manipulatives, 339–340, *339*
McGraw, Tammy, 361–364
mentoring, 295, 296
metacognition, 274
metacognitive learning strategies, 28, 274–276
microcomputers, 4, *5*
Microsoft
    Office Suite, *234*
    PowerPoint, 98, 99
    Windows 95 OS (release of), *5*, *10*
microworlds, 93–94, *94*
MIDI (Musical Instrument Digital Interface), 369
mindtools
    databases, 89–91, *91*, *122*, *124*
    digital storytelling, 96–98
    hypertext and hypermedia, 94–95, *327*
    microworlds, 93–94, *94*
    simulations and animations, 93–94, *93*, *122*, *124*, *176*, *177*
    technology and, 230
    visualization tools and concept maps, 91–93, *92*, *175*, *175*, *176*, *327*, *328*
MLA style for citing Internet resources, 104, *252*
mnemonic devices, for password security, 256
mobile devices
    and assistive technology, 159
    BYOD programs and, 195, 196, 213, 239–240, 278, *278*
    and meaningful content, 279
    monitoring student use, 195, 196
    selecting apps for, *238*
modeling, teacher, 271
models for blended learning, 120
monitoring
    in GAME plan, *29*, 30–31, 274
    group work learning, 115–116
    Internet security, 258
    professional growth, 35–38
    self-directed learning, student progress in, 49–50
    student cheating, 253
    student devices, 195, 196
    UDL and student learning, 149–150

monitors, computer, 197, 200–201, 205
Moodle, 232, *234*
Mosaic, *5*, *10*
motion detectors in science classrooms, 345, *346*
mouse, ergonomics and, 197
mouse adaptations, 157, *158*, 159
MouseKeys, 156
MovieMaker, 97, 98, 228
movies. *see* digital storytelling; videos
MP3 players, *233*. *see also* iPods
multi-content areas, 62, 98
multimedia
    boom, *5*, *10*
    portfolio development tools/software, 40, 43, 44–45, *45*
    problem-based learning (PBL) program, 67–68
    products, designing, 94
    project, rubric for assessment, *181*, *182*
    tools for assistive technology, 156
    websites, creating, 95
multiple intelligences theory, 113, 115, 140, *141*, 149
multiple means of representation, expression, and engagement, *144*, *145*, *147*
Music classrooms
    GAME plan for content standards, *367*
    lesson plans for, *370–371*
    NETS-S in, 368–369, *368*
    technology integration in, 367–370
musical intelligence, *141*
My-T-Soft, 157

N
Napster, 265
narration, recording for digital story, 97
Narrator (Windows), 156
National Art Education Association, 361–362, *361*
National Association for the Education of Young Children (NAEYC), 282
National Association of Sport and Physical Education (NASPE), 355, *355*
National Board Certification, 38
National Board for Professional Teaching Standards (NBPTS), 38
national content standards, 13
National Council for the Social Studies (NCSS), 349
National Council of Teachers of Mathematics (NCTM), 337
national curricular reports, recommendations from, 55
National Education Association, 9
National Education Technology Plan, 11–12, *11*, *12*
National Educational Technology Standards for Teachers (NETS-T). *see* NETS-T (National Education Technology Standards for Teachers)
National Geographic Society, 263
National Governor's Association Center for Best Practices, 13–14
National Institute of Health (NIH), 196, 197, 199–200
National Instructional Materials Accessibility Standards (NIMAS), 143, 145
National Library of Virtual Manipulatives (Utah State University), 339–340, *339*

naturalist intelligence, *141*
nature of instruction, *23*
NCCREST, *289*
neck stretches, *199*
NETS-S (National Education Technology Standards for Students), *16*. see also content standards
    in ELLs classrooms, *326*
    in English language arts classrooms, *320*
    in Foreign Language classrooms, *332*
    in Health and Physical Education classrooms, *356*
    in Mathematics classrooms, *338*
    in Music classrooms, 368–369, *368*
    in Science classrooms, *344*
    and self-directed learning, 33, 35
    in Social Studies classrooms, *350*
    in Visual Arts classrooms, 366
    standards, 14. see also standards
NETS-T (National Education Technology Standards for Teachers). see also content standards; standards
    and assessments, 163, 164, 167
    contribution to the teaching profession, 294, 308–309
    and creative thinking, 54
    cultural understanding and global awareness, 283–286
    engage in professional growth and leadership, 293
    facilitate and inspire student learning and creativity, 53, 83
    introduction to, 12, *14–15*
    learning experiences, 137
    model digital-age work and learning, 191, 217
    promote and model digital citizenship and responsibility, 243, 269
    providing equitable access, 276–282
    and self-directed learning, 27, 33, 35
    and technology enriched learning environments, 109
networked technologies, 186, 202, 210, 364
neural networks and learning, 145–147
new learning experiences, 18–19
new media texts, 319–320
Newseum's Today's Front Pages, 351
newsgroups, 102
NIH. see National Institute of Health (NIH)
No Child Left Behind Act (NCLB), 186, 305
nodes in concept maps, 175
North Carolina Standard Course of Study (NCSCOS), 76
Nvu, *234*

O
Obama, Barack, 244
objectives. see goals
online education, 5, 8–9, 120, 299. see also blended learning
online presentations, 228
online report cards, *187*
online resources, 99, 101
    for assessment, 168
    authentic instruction and, 57–58, *58*
    for continued learning, 296, *297*, 298
    evaluating legitimacy of information, 105–107
    facilitating online discussions, 117
    gradebooks, 183
    guides, 125
    for health and physical education classrooms, 357
    homework posting, 228
    learning lab, 333
    self-directed learning and, 35–37
    typosquatting, 105–106
    value of information, 106–107
    webconferencing, 102, *103*
    wikis, 102
ooVoo, 102
open-ended response assessments, 170, 179
OpenOffice, 40, *233*, *234*
open-source software, 231–232, *233*, *234*, *235*
opinion articles, 304
oral communication, and assessments, 174
oral presentation checklist, 179, *180*
Oregon Trail, 93
outcome feedback, 167

P
Pacific Islander students, 277
Parent Teacher Associations (PTAs), 225
parents
    communicating with, 218–219, *220*, *221*
    e-mail and text-messaging with, 224–225
    family computing night, 228
    and responsible technology use, 255, 258, 265
    and technical assistance, 214
    as volunteers, 225–227
Partnership for 21st Century Sills, 11, *11*
password security, 256–257, *257*
PayPal, 259
PBS (Public Broadcasting Service), 263
PCs, 5, 7, *10*
PDF files, 155
Peace Corps, *284*
peer interactions, 272
performance data, 186
performance-based assessments, 172–173, 174
phishing, 259
PhotoStory, 228
phpBB discussion board, 232
Physical Education. see Health and Physical Education classrooms
Picasa, 364
Pics4Learning, 97
plagiarism, 251–253
planning. see lesson planning
podcasts, 228–229, *228*, *233*
polling and webconferencing, 99
portfolios. see also assessment portfolios; employment portfolios; professional development portfolio
    authentic assessment, 176–178
    confidentiality needs, 40
    defining purpose/audience for, 41, *42*
    delivery of, *42*, 46
    designing, 42–44, *42*, *43–44*
    development software/tools, 40–41, *43*
    GAME plan for creating, 46
    KWHL chart and, *48*
    overview and types of, 39–40

portfolios (*Continued*)
   reflective statements in, 44, 45–46, 177
   steps in developing, 41–46
   of student work, and plagiarism, 253
   and website design similarities, 94–95
positioning aids, 156–157
PowerPoint, 93, 99
PowerSchool, 222
practice, reflecting on, 302–303
pre-mechanical communication, 3
presentation
   devices, 112
   online, 228
   software, 98, 99
   and whiteboards, 115
President's Panel on Technology, 8
primary instruction, 150, *150*
problem-based learning (PBL). *see also* authentic instruction
   Alien Rescue software, 67–68
   assessments for, 173
   collaborative work groups, 66–67
   and complex activities, 63
   and learner autonomy, 59
   promoting thinking and reasoning skills (example), *274*
   supporting technology for, *70*
   and technology integration standards, 18, 19
problem-solving
   and assessments, 171
   and authentic instruction, 62–63
   online discussions, 117
   in specific classrooms. *see* NETS-S (National Education Technology Standards for Students)
   in technology maintenance, 203–204
productivity applications, 7, 155
professional development portfolio, 39–40, 41, 45
professional growth. *see also* action research; educational research
   communication and, 229
   community of practice (CoP) and, 293–294
   conferences and formal learning, 298–299, *298*
   exhibit leadership, 299
   local support for technology integration, 295–296
   mentoring and, 295, 296
   reflecting on current research, 304–308
   reflecting on practice, 302–303
   self-monitoring of, 35–38
   and stages of technology integration (beginning, embracing, proficient, transformative), 294, *300–301*
   virtual learning communities, 296, 297, *298*
professional learning network (PLN), *295*
Project Tomorrow, 304
project-based assessments, 171, 173–174, *180*
proxy servers, 265
public domain, 246, 249–250

Q

qualitative data, 312, *313*
quantitative data, 312
quasi-experimental research, 304

Quia, *169*
QuickTime Virtual Reality (QTVR), 125
quiz generator, 168, *169*
quizzes, 99

R

racial issues. *see* cultural diversity; culturally responsive pedagogy
randomization, in formal research, 304–305
ReadWriteThink, 92
real-world contexts, 62, 63–64, *64*, 77, 79
reasoning skills, 273, *274*
recognition networks, 145–146
recommendations from national curricular reports, *55*
recording
   for assisting language learning, 327, 333–334
   musical performance, 369
   narration for digital storytelling, 97
   for performance assessments, 174
   in performance-based assessments, 174
   and webconferencing, 99
Redican, Kerry, 355–358
reflective journals, 272
reflective statements, 37–38, 44, 45–46
reflective thinking
   in-action/on-action, 302–303
   and active learning, 61
   on classroom practice (reflective-practitioner), 302–303, 309, 310, *311*
   cultural awareness and, 283–286, 287
   on current research, 304–308
   on group work, 115
   metacognitive needs and, 274–276
   and student monitoring, 49
   on technology-enriched learning, 129–130
Rehabilitation Act of 1973, 152
Reinhartz, Judy, 343–346
rendering files for digital storytelling, 96, 97
repairing hardware, 206–207
RepeatKeys, 156
repetitive strain injuries, 198
report cards, *187*
representation, multiple means of, *144*, 145
research. *see* action research; educational research
resolution of monitors, 199
resource guide, 125
response-to-intervention (RTI), 150, *150*
responsible Internet use, 262–266
reviews, of digital resources, 236–237, *237*
Robbins, Jill, 325–328
role-play, and authentic instruction, *70*
Ross, John D., 367–370
Rubistar, 183
rubrics
   analytic, 181–182, *181*
   for collaborative work groups, *116*
   holistic, 182, *182*
   multimedia projects and, *181*, *182*
   software evaluation, 235–236
   software for, 183

technology-enriched learning and, 126
value of, 180–183

S

safety issues
   computers in classrooms, 192–194, *193*, *195*
   health practices related to technology, 196, *197*, 198–202, *199*
   Internet safety, 257–258
   tips for safe and healthy use of technology in your class, 201
Sakai, 232
scaffolds. *see also* tutorials
   in authentic instruction, 59, *60*, 67–68, *68*
   WebQuest, 86–87, *88*
SchoolTube, 232
Science classrooms
   content standards, 73–74, *73*
   GAME plan for content standards, *343*
   interactive physics tools, 94
   lesson plans for, *347–348*
   NETS-S in, *344*
   team-taught biology example, 84
   technology integration in, 343–346
scientific reasoning, 273
scoring practices. *see also* assessments
   checklists, 179–180, *179*
   digital gradebooks, 183–186, *184*
   online report cards, *187*
   rubrics, 180–183
   scoring keys, 178–179
screen time recommendations, *282*
screen-capturing software, 125, 128
screencasts, 228–229
scripts, for digital storytelling, 96
SeaMonkey, *234*
search engines, 252
security, online, 256–257, *257*, 262
self-assessment, 32–33, *33*, *34*, *177*, 183
self-directed learning (SDL). *see also* GAME plan; portfolios
   and action research, 309–310, *309*, *310*
   authentic instruction and, 59, 275
   blended learning, 120
   and critical reflections, 37–38
   digital storytelling and, 98
   GAME plan for, *309*
   KWHL chart for, 47, *47*
   monitoring/evaluation professional growth, 35–38
   overview of, 27–29
   reflection in, 37–38
   self-assessment, 32–33, *33*, *34*
   student support for, 47–50, *48*
self-evaluation/monitoring, 35–38, 302–303
shareware, 234
sharing, 99, 303, 314
sharing digital stories, 97
shoulder stretches, *199*
Sibelius, 369
Sim City, 93

simulations
   assessments and, 176, *177*
   in authentic instruction, *70*
   in directed instruction, 71
   as mindtool in support of learning, 93–94, *93*
Skype, 102, 298
SlideShare, 228, 229
SlowKeys, 156
smartphones, 279
SMTP (Simple Mail Transfer Protocol), 5, 7, *10*
social bookmarking sites, 264
social media, 222–224, 262, 287
social needs, 271–272
social networking tools, 9
Social Studies classrooms
   GAME plan for content standards, *349*
   lesson plans for, *353–354*
   NETS-S in, *350*
   technology integration in, 349–352
software. *see also* computers
   for assistive technologies, 154–156
   concept mapping, 93, 175
   copyright issues, 208
   databases, 89–91
   digital storytelling, 97, 98
   Envisioning Machine, 101
   for file management, 208–209
   filtering, 264–265
   GAME plan for open-source and freeware, *235*
   for graphic organizers, 92
   and lab management, 128–129
   learning new, 35, *36*
   lesson planning, 132
   maintenance, 207–210
   malicious, 258–260
   management software, 196
   new, installing/downloading, 207–208
   for online presentations, 228–229
   open-source, 231–232, *233*, *235*
   for podcast use, *233*
   portfolio development, 40–41, *43*
   problem-based learning (PBL), 67–68
   reinstalling and updating, 208
   for rubric creation, 183
   rubrics for evaluating, 235–236
   safeguarding, 209–210
   screen-capturing, 125
   student preparation, *124*
   teacher preparation guidelines, *122*
   testing, 168, *169*, 179
   virus-protection, 260
   webconferencing, 99
   and whiteboard use, 114
Software and Information Industry Association (SIIA), 304
spam, 259
spatial intelligence, *141*
special needs students. *see* diverse learners
spoofing, 259
spreadsheets, *122*, *124*, 345–346
spyware, 234, 259–260

388 Index

standards. *see also* content standards; NETS-S; NETS-T (National Education Technology Standards for Teachers); technology standards; *specific subjects*
   movement, educational goals in, 12–14
   national content, 13
   state, for technology proficiency, 281, *282*
   technology. *see* technology standards
   value of, 17–18
statistical tests, 313
stereotypes, 277, 279, 281
StickyKeys, 156
storage of files, 210
storyboards, 95, *97*, 98
storytelling, cross-cultural traits, 285
strategic learners, 47
strategic neural networks, 145, 146–147
streaming media sites, using, 232
stretches, 198, *199*
student information systems (SIS), 183, *184*
students. *see also* assessments; authentic instruction; diverse learners; technology-enriched learning environment
   BYOD (bring your own device) programs, 195, 196, 213, 278, *278*
   GAME plan for self-directed learning, 47–50, *47*
   images and work of, legal issues, 255
   KWHL chart for self-monitoring, 48
   preparation and follow-up activities guidelines for, *124*
   role in technology integration, 23
   rules of thumb, 273
   student-centered learning example? more info*, 84
   technical assistance from, 211, 214
Study Island, 85
subscription services, 263
summative assessments, 167
supplemental instruction, 150, *150*
surveys, 99, 304
SURWEB, 97
Symbaloo, 125, 264
systems, 191–192

T
tablet computers, 279
Tacla, Craig P., 355–358
TCP/IP (Transmission Control Protocol/Internet Protocol), 5, 7, 10
TEACH Act (Technology, Education, and Copyright Harmonization), 247–248, *248*
teacher modeling, 271
teacher research/inquiry. *see* action research
Teachers of English to Speakers of Other Languages (TESOL), *325*, 326
TeacherTube, 9, 229, 231, 232
Teaching Channel, 231, 232
TechMatrix, 160
technical assistance, 211, 214–215, 225–226
technical guidelines, 123, *125*
technology. *see also* assistive technologies; computers; conversation support; digital resources; online resources
   appropriate use of in early childhood education, 282
   evaluating digital resources, 235–240
   and gender preferences, 277, 279, 281
   health practices related to, 196, *197*, 198–202, *199*
   impact of technology, research on, 306–307
   and kids, 214
   literacy, 4, 6, 10–13
   locating digital resources, 230–232, *233*, 234
   managing use of, 194–195
   as mindtools. *see* mindtools
   protecting technology resources, 260
   research, current educational, 304–308
   responsible use of, 257–267
   safety issues. *see* safety issues
   scaffolds, 59, *60*, 67–68, *68*
   skills, learning, 227–229
   support for action research, 314–315, *315*
   support for authentic instruction, 68–70, *69*, *70*, 77, 79
   support for directed instruction, 71–73
   support for student mastery of content standards, 77
   use in authentic intellectual work support, 65
Technology and Interactive Media as Tools in Early Childhood Programs Serving Children from Birth through Age 8 (NAEYC), 282
technology integration. *see also* authentic instruction; *specific subject classrooms*
   and creative thinking (reflection on), 54
   instructional guidelines, *130*
   leader, becoming a, 300–301
   and learning environments, 19
   and lesson planning, 317. *see also* lesson planning
   local support for, 295–296
   nature of instruction and, 23
   phases of computer development, 4–10, *5–6*
   profiles of, 22–23
   stages of (continuum), 19–21, *22–23*, 24, 294, 300–301
   students' role, 23
   teachers' role in, 2, 10, 18, 20–21, *22–23*, 24
technology maintenance
   GAME plan for, 211
   hardware, 204–207
   problem-solving, routine, 202–203
   schedule for, *212*
   software, 207–210
   support personnel, 202
   technical assistance, 211, 214–215
   troubleshooting, 203–204
technology resumé, 33, *33*
technology standards. *see also* standards
   goals of development, 10–12
   integration of, 14–24
   student technology profiles, 33, 35
   for students (NETS-S), *16*
   for teachers (NETS-T), *14–15*
technology-based tutorials, 85–88, *88*, 89
technology-enriched learning
   blended learning, 120–121
   class management and, 128–129, *130*
   daily lesson template, *135–136*
   developing guidelines, 123, 125–127

evaluation and reflection, 129–130, *130*
file management, 127
GAME plan for, 131
group collaboration, 111–113, 115–116
independent use of computers, 116, 118
planning, 121–123, *130*
preparation for, *122*, *124*, 127–128, *130*
student preparation guidelines, *124*
student use, supporting, 120–130
teacher preparation required for software programs, *122*
value of, 118–119
technology-enriched learning environment. *see also* technology-enriched learning
Technology-Related Assistance of Individuals with Disabilities Act of 1988, 151
telementoring, 226–227
templates, 115, 127, *135–136*, 175
temporary Internet files, 208
tendonitis, 198
test scanners, 178–179
testing software, 168, *169*, 179
tests, statistical, 313
text messaging, and cyberbullying, 261
text messaging, as communication method, 224–225
text-blasting service, 224–225
The Diversity Kit (LAB), 286
think-aloud checklist, 179, *179*
Toolbook, 7
topic-centered communication, 285
topic-chaining communication style, 285
transfer, of knowledge, 61
triangulating data, 314
Trojan horses, *259*
troubleshooting
  model for technology maintenance, 203–204, *205*
  online discussions, 117
tutor, technology as, 85, *122*, *124*, 230
tutorials
  Foreign Language software, 332–333, *333*
  music skill development, 369, *370*
  technology-based, 85–88, *88*, 89
  technology-enriched learning and, *122*, *124*
Twitter, 222, 287, *295*
typosquatting, 105–106

U

unacceptable use of school technology. *see* acceptable use policies (AUPs)
Understanding by Design (Wiggins & McTighe), 171, 172, 174
universal design for learning (UDL). *see also* differentiated instruction (DI)
  CAST and, 143, 145
  digital technology and, 143, *143*, 147–148, 150–151
  goals, setting, 148
  individualized learning, 149
  monitoring and evaluation, 149–150
  multiple intelligences theory, 140, *141*, 149
  neural networks foundation, 145–147
  overview of, 138–139, 142–143

principles, guidelines and checkpoints, *144*
response-to-intervention (RTI) framework, 150, *150*
unninteruptible power supplies (UPS), 206
URLs (Uniform Resource Locators), 105, 106, 125
U. S. Census Bureau, 277
U. S. Copyright Office (Library of Congress), 247, 249, 251
U. S. Department of Commerce, 276
U. S. Department of Education, 8, 106, 151, 160, 194–195, 276
U. S. National Educational Technology Plan, *5*, 8, *8*
U. S. Office of Technology, 21
USB drives, 127
Utah State University's National Library of Virtual Manipulatives, 339–340, *339*

V

Vantage Learning, 179
Venn diagrams, 92, 175, *176*
Vermeer, Johannes, 361
video conferencing. *see* webconferencing
videos. *see also* digital storytelling
  and authentic instruction, 67
  creation of, in visual-arts classrooms, 363–364
  cyberbullying, 261
  and directed instruction, 71–72
  and holistic learning, 62, *63*
  media streaming sites, 232
  recording lessons for reflection, 38, 302–303
  sharing sites for, 228, 229
virtual field trips, 60–61, *61*, 62, 226
virtual learning communities, 296, *297*, 298, *300–301*
virtual schools, 9
viruses, 209–210, 259–260
virus-protection software, 260
vision and computer use, *199*, 200–201, *200*
Visual-Arts classrooms
  GAME plan for content standards, *361*
  image-manipulation software, 363
  lesson plans for, *365–366*
  NETS-S in, *362*
  technology integration in, 361–364
visualization tools, 91–92
VoiceOver, 156
volunteering, 225–227
volunteers, in technology support, 214

W

Web 2.0 tools, *5*, 9, 67
webcams, 99, 297, *345*
webconferencing
  in classroom presentations, 112
  as communication tool, 99, 102, *103*
  and professional growth, 299
  technology-enriched learning and, *122*, *124*
  and webcams, how to look your best, *297*
WebEx, 99
WebQuest
  as digital learning tool, 86–87, *88*, 231
  in Science classrooms, 345
  in Social Studies classrooms, 350–351

websites. *see also* online resources
   classroom, 219, *221*, 222, 223
   and cyberbullying, 261
   as form of hypermedia, 94–95, *95*
   GAME plan for creating, 222
   privacy policies of, 258
   social bookmarking and organizational sites, 264
Wegerif, R., 56, 84
White House online, *5*, *10*
whiteboards
   interactive, 111–112, 114–115, *114*
   webconferencing and, 99
Wikipedia, 9, *10*, 90–91, *91*, 106
wikis
   as collaborative learning tool, 101, 102
   individualized learning and, 149
   technology-enriched learning and, *122*, *124*
Windows 95 OS (release of), *5*, *10*
Windows Magnifier, 156
Windows Narrator, 156
Windows Snipping Tool, 125

WindowsLive, 127
wireless responders, 166, *166*
wireless technologies, 194
WISE (Web-based Inquiry Science Environments), 273
WiseMapping, 93
word cloud, *12*, 91, *100*, 126
word processing software, *96*, 155
Wordle, *12*, *100*, 126
word-prediction software, 155, *155*
work samples, 176–179
workstations, 118, 157, 202
worms, computer, 259
wrist stretches, *199*
WYSIWYG, 40

Y
YouTube, 9, 228, 229, 232
YouTube for Schools, 232

Z
Zite, *295*
Zoom (MAC), 156